History of
Modern Design

Graphics and Products since the Industrial Revolution

History of Modern Design

Graphics and Products since the Industrial Revolution

Laurence King Publishing

Published in 2003 by Laurence King Publishing Ltd
71 Great Russell Street
London WC1B 3BP
United Kingdom
Tel: + 44 20 7430 8850
Fax: + 44 20 7430 8880
email: enquiries@laurenceking.co.uk
www.laurenceking.co.uk

A catalogue record for this book is available from the British Library.

ISBN: 1 85669 348 1

Senior Editor: Samantha Gray
Design: Peter Ling and Andrew Shoolbred
Cover design: Lovegrove
Picture research: Peter Kent

Printed in China

Front cover: Arne Jacobsen, Egg chair, 1957. Courtesy of Fritz Hansen.
Back cover: Herbert Bayer, cover for *die neue linie*, 1930, The
Wolfsonian Florida International University, Herbert Bayer Archive.
Terry Jones, i-D, no. 28, magazine cover, UK, 1985, photograph by Nick
Knight. Harley Earl, Cadillac Eldorado coupe, 1953, Cadillac Museum,
Hachenburg, Germany.

Part One: J. Parry, *London Street Scene*, Courtesy Alfred Dunhill
  Museum & Archive, London
Part Two: Jules Cheret *les Girard*, Musée de la Publicité, Paris
Part Three: Henriette Reiss, *Rhythm Series*, Goldstein Gallery, University
  of Minnesota
Part Four: Marianne Straub, *Surrey*, Courtesy Warner Archive
Part Five: Ron Arad, *Big Volume 2*, Courtesy Ron Arad Associates
  Limited

Contents

Preface

The material and methodology for this book were developed over eight years of teaching a course entitled *History of Modern Design* in the College of Media Arts & Design at Drexel University, and almost twenty years of general undergraduate art history teaching experience. During these past eight years it has been rewarding to hear students reflect upon everyday objects in relation to the values and attitudes of their time, to consider the complex interplay of technological, commercial, social, and esthetic considerations that deepen our understanding of their beauty and the range of their meanings.

One of the persistent difficulties in offering this course over the years has been the issue of a textbook. History of fine art courses are far more common than those in the history of design, and there is no shortage of art-history texts to provide images and narrative to accompany general and more specialized courses relating to a variety of periods and movements. Yet despite the many colleges and universities that educate professional industrial, interior, graphic, merchandising, textile, and fashion designers, I found in my teaching that no introductory text served the needs of a course that integrated material from a broad range of specialized design fields over the past three centuries. Rather than being limited to a single area like graphic design or industrial design, the present survey covers the history of these fields in relation to one another and the common themes they share, whether technology, production, consumption, or reform.

At first I relied upon a list of reserve readings, and in time supplemented these with my own outlines for lecture notes available through the university's computing services center. Subsequently I received a grant from the university to create a website that allowed an appropriate format to be developed for the presentation of a combination of text links and images for study and student preparation. Putting these notes into book form has been for me a formidable task. The required reading, travel, and study took me far from my own original training in the art of medieval Spain, requiring substantial historical perspective to provide a context for studying the objects and a desire to follow through with combining perspectives from both consumption and production for each chapter. In the course of writing and re-writing, I tried to organize the material both chronologically and thematically. Briefly stated, the themes are:

SPECIALIZATION AND THE TECHNOLOGY OF MATERIALS AND PRODUCTION
REFORM AND THE ROLE OF STANDARDS FOR DESIGN
THE EQUALITY OF THE ARTS
DESIGN FOR MECHANIZED PRODUCTION
"GOOD" DESIGN AND POPULAR CULTURE
PLURALISM AND DESIGN

In preparing this *History of Modern Design* I have benefited from a number of previous studies, beginning with most students' (of my generation anyway) introduction to modern design history, Sir Nikolaus Pevsner's *Pioneers of Modern Design*, and including more recent titles such as Penny Sparke's *An Introduction to Design and Culture in the Twentieth Century* (1986), Adrian Forty's *Objects of Desire* (1986), and Richard Woodham's *Twentieth-Century Design* (1997). There is also the excellent series of books by a range of specialists published by Oxford University Press. These include a number of volumes devoted to period styles (*Arts and Crafts, Art Nouveau, Art Deco, Bauhaus,* for example), as well as John Heskett's excellent *Industrial Design* (1980). Also, Phillip Meggs's *History of Graphic Design* is a most informative survey of that material with a strong emphasis in the nineteenth and twentieth centuries.

As I began teaching the history of modern design, I found myself drawn to the period rooms and decorative arts galleries of museums rather than to their more crowded painting and sculpture galleries. As a result I've been pleased to observe, in my adopted city of Philadelphia, that the Philadelphia Museum of Art has redesigned its galleries to merge fine with decorative art in a way which can only aid in the appreciation of our subject. It is also encouraging to note the recent increase in art-historical journals that have devoted issues to the applied arts, and those monographs that have done much to promote interest in the history of design. It is necessary to mention a few of the latter, as they greatly aided in formulating many of the sections for the individual chapters that follow: Nancy Troy's *Modernism and the Decorative Arts in France. Art Nouveau to Le Corbusier*, the Guggenheim Museum's massive catalogue for *The Great Utopia. The Russian and Soviet Avant-garde, 1915–1932* exhibition, the American Craft Museum's catalogues for their series of exhibitions on domestic design entitled *The Ideal Home* beginning with the period from 1890–1910, and Debora Silverman's *Art Nouveau in Fin-de-Siècle France: Politics, Psychology, and Style*. Many of these books incorporate ideas drawn from a significant literature on the study of consumption, stemming less from art history than from social anthropology and the field of popular and mass culture.

Aside from those mentioned above, a number of exhibitions and their accompanying catalogues introduced me to a wide range of material that has been incorporated into this text. These include *German Graphic Design* (2001), *Godwin* (2000), and *Swedish Glass* (1997) at the Bard Graduate School in New York; *Henry Dreyfuss* at the Cooper Hewitt (1998), the traveling collection of chairs and other furniture from the Vitra Museum in Switzerland (1999–2000) at the Allentown Museum and the Cooper Hewitt; *Mackintosh* (1994) and *American Modernism* (2000) at the Metropolitan Museum of Art (1994); the *Aluminum by Design* exhibition at the Carnegie Museum in Pittsburgh and the Cooper Hewitt (2000–2001); the *Art in Rome in the Eighteenth Century* exhibition in Philadelphia (2000); *Will Price* at the small Arthur Ross Gallery in the Fine Arts Library at the University of Pennsylvania; and the extensive *Art Nouveau* exhibition at the Victoria and Albert Museum in London and the National Gallery of Art in Washington, D.C. (2000).

Recent monographs stemming from renewed interest in A. W. N. Pugin, Christopher Dresser, Russel Wright, C. R. Mackintosh and others are filling gaps in our knowledge and bringing new material to light, including the publication of primary source material and a wide range of visual material: they are among the numerous healthy signs of growing public and scholarly interest in an area with wide-ranging appeal to students, artists and designers, art historians, and collectors. Great Britain remains most active in the field of design history, through a variety of conferences, the *Journal of Design History*, the Design Research Society and its on-line publication *Design Research News* (DRN), and the number of courses offered at colleges and universities. Finally, the journal *Design Issues* not only contributes articles on the methods of designers but also frequently offers historical perspectives and reviews. It is my hope that the approach to this introductory text will be viewed as balanced and tolerant, and that the analyses will promote appreciation and suggest the synthesis of description and a framework based upon the interconnections of social, commercial, esthetic, and technological perspectives on design. In addition, as a teacher I have always enjoyed the challenge of comparing works of art from different or even successive time periods that share formal or ideological similarities. I am happy for the students in the College of Media Arts & Design who have made the study of design history part of their education and hope that what they have learned will in some way be incorporated into the contributions they are certain to make to their chosen design professions.

NOVEMBER, 2002
PHILADELPHIA, PA

Acknowledgments

This volume appears as a result of the support and encouragement of many individuals and institutions. From the outset I want to acknowledge my dissertation advisor at the University of Pittsburgh, now Professor Emeritus John Williams, who has remained a mentor, friend, and a supporter of a direction in my research that strayed far from the subject of medieval Spain that we continue to share. I also want to thank another faculty member at my alma mater, Professor David Wilkins, for actively supporting the project through his contacts at Prentice Hall when the manuscript was first submitted for review. David also taught the very first art history course I took as a freshman in 1969, encouraged me to major in the discipline, and made me feel welcome and valued as a student in the Fine Arts Department.

The teaching and administrative positions I have held at Drexel University in Philadelphia have made it possible for me to research and write this introductory volume on the history of modern design. I am grateful to my former dean, J. Michael Adams, for supporting my participation in our London Study Abroad program during the winter term 1999. I also wish to thank my current Dean, Jonathan Estrin, and former Provost, Richard Astro, for taking into account the importance of this project in assigning my teaching and administrative load during the 2000–2001 academic year, and for supporting a critical sabbatical leave during the 2002–2003 academic year.

The most substantial debt I owe for this book is to my students at Drexel University, who have listened and contributed to the trial-and-error presentation of its ideas over a period of more than eight years. The choice of material, its organization, and the framework for presenting that material have all have taken shape in the context of the classroom term-by-term over several years. Testing new approaches, introducing new examples, and revising content and assignments have been a constant challenge, and I have learned much from students' thoughtful responses, essays, and evaluations while preparing the text and illustrations. Observing the creative work of our students as a guest at critiques continues to be a great source of satisfaction, for it permits me to see that the future of design will remain in able hands and imaginative, engaging minds.

Having so many professional designers as colleagues in the College of Media Arts & Design at Drexel University is indeed a blessing, and has stimulated the progress of this book in a number of ways. I have benefited from their expertise in ways too numerous to mention, from casual conversations in hallways and offices, to attending critiques, to specific requests for specialized information. John Langdon and Mark Willie of the Media Arts Department, along with Peter Bartscherer of the Design & Imaging Studio deserve special mention for sharing their knowledge with me on issues related to graphic design and typography, and John also kindly provided several of the line drawings for typefaces and logos that appear among the illustrations. Paul Runyon and Mike Froio provided considerable photographic assistance. I want to thank the staff of the University's Hagerty Library for their help with ordering books, access to archival material, and especially with procuring a substantial amount of interlibrary loan material. It is not possible here to name them all, but their dedication and research assistance in general have been invaluable. Ed Laudenslager of Armstrong & Yoder Printing took an afternoon of his time to walk me through the company printing facilities so that I might gain a first-hand understanding of the modern process of image and text reproduction and color presses. Old friends Betty and John Reilly were living in London when I taught there during the winter 1999 and their kindness and hospitality helped to make that stay especially memorable, along with John Pearson of the Foundation for International Education who arranged so many

museum visits for our class. My brother, Dr. Richard Raizman, invited me to accompany him on two trips to Paris while I was at work on this book. I appreciated his patience during endless tours of period rooms and furnishings in one collection after another, graciously followed by relaxing meals and long walks without any particular agenda. A special thanks is due Professor Nancy Troy of the University of Southern California for commenting on an early draft of what is now the first two parts of this study in 1996, with recommendations to include more vernacular material and introduce other perspectives that I have tied to take to heart. I am also grateful to the anonymous reviewers who suggested areas for improvement and expansion to the original manuscript and the much-enlarged revision that went to press.

Laurence King Publishing Ltd. of London, England, together with Prentice-Hall in the United States, collaborated to make this project a reality. I want to thank Lee Ripley Greenfield and Mr. Laurence King for their interest and strong support. Thanks are due to the project manager, Samantha Gray, and the photography researcher, Peter Kent, for all of their work as the project took shape. Obtaining photographs and permissions for the more than 500 illustrations contained in a book of such wide-ranging material represents an enormous behind-the-scenes effort, and the layout and design also involved careful and coordination and sensitivity. I'm also grateful to Bud Therien at Prentice for his assistance as the project moved toward completion.

I want to thank my wife, Lucy, and children Becky and Josh, for their patience over a period lasting several years. Visiting buildings and examples of design in museums, collections, historic houses, even flea markets and fairs, has been a part of virtually every family excursion and vacation over the past decade, and my own itineraries and preoccupations at leisure, home, and at the university have frequently taken precedence over the wishes of my family. Now my children are too old to want to go to Disneyworld with their parents. Sorry kids.

Finally I'd like to thank my parents, Albert and Adele Raizman, for allowing me to find and pursue my own interests and inclinations as a student. Rather than offering advice or direction, they permitted me to study what I found stimulating and satisfying, and for this I'm most grateful.

PHILADELPHIA,
SPRING 2003

Introduction

What is Design?

Whether in relation to fashion, software, information, or an array of household products, the term *design* regularly enters our vocabulary to describe some of the most common aspects of our everyday experience. As used throughout this book, the definition of *design* acknowledges two primary meanings found in the *Oxford English Dictionary*. The first refers to the elements of a work of art and an awareness of the order and arrangement of those elements. In this sense the *design* of a writing table (as illustrated, for instance, in figures 1.6, 8.8, or 16.3) consists of the size and proportion of its individual parts, the textures, grains, colors, or other characteristics of the materials used, the motifs or patterns, if any, used in its decoration, and the overall contrasts or harmonies among these various elements. Thus an analysis of design may reveal the intricacies or ease of construction, address issues of use such as durability, efficiency, or convenience, consider the exploration and transformation of materials, and the relative complexity or simplicity of the arrangement of forms.

Defined in this manner *design* is common to all of the visual arts, both fine and applied, and indeed the same sorts of criteria may be analyzed with respect to a wide variety of objects, from paintings and sculptures to engravings, the front-page of a website, or an electric toaster, each based at least in part upon a range of choices or possibilities within a given medium or production technique in relation to an intended audience or viewer. Also linked to this meaning of the term are the series of foundation courses entitled *Design* that are generally required of College and university students majoring in the visual arts in the United States and abroad. Versatility is often a theme in such courses, where students analyze and manipulate basic abstract elements like shapes, colors, textures, and patterns common to a wide range of media in both fine as well as in applied art.

A second broad meaning of *design* refers to the conception for the completed form of an object, often a sketch, model, or set of instructions that is a preliminary stage in the process that leads to a finished product. In some cases artists or craftsmen execute their own designs. In other cases they experiment directly with materials and processes in the creation of prototypes that are produced or modified for production. In still other cases, for instance when we purchase a pair of *designer* jeans, we presume that this article of clothing, while the result of methods of mechanized and specialized mass production, represents in some way the distinctive creative flair of the designer. As in the first meaning, the conceptual stage in the development of a finished work is common to all of the visual arts: after all, preliminary sketches precede the completion of many kinds of objects; indeed, acknowledging this meaning of *design* within a broad range of artistic activities that involve the interaction between ideas and the manipulation of materials remains essential to an understanding of the term.

What Makes Design "Modern"

For most historians an increasing separation between *design* as conception, and the subsequent production of that design, is critical for an historical understanding of the term in its specifically modern context. In this view modern design is the result of acceleration in the division of labor and the introduction of mechanized production during the nineteenth century. A number of authors have equated these emerging circumstances with the development of an international style in the twentieth century embodying the dictum "form follows function". Other writers stress that modern design emerged as part of a capitalist economic system that placed control of expanding production in the hands of industrialists and manufacturers and that frequently determined particular approaches to design as well as new techniques of marketing and advertising in order to stimulate consumption. In the latter view the modern context for *design*, while implying a continuing relationship with the visual arts broadly defined, tends to concentrate upon mass-produced goods and printed materials included under the label of decorative art, applied art, industrial art, and graphic art rather than upon fine arts, where designing and making are more frequently performed by the same individual and are more clearly related to that individual's initiative and discretion. As a result, the study of modern design often focuses upon economic conditions that inform its practice.

Modern Design and Consumption

Of equal significance in establishing the context for a specifically "modern" design are the role played by a vastly enlarged audience for the products of design beginning in the later eighteenth century and the complex dynamics of mass consumption. Part of this complex dynamic assumes that products serve as signs for desires that often have little to do with need or the actual function of the products themselves (we buy, and discard, commodities like wristwatches, electric razors, or cellular phones for reasons that go far beyond our need to get to work and school on time or to communicate with one another – see figures 15.1, 15.8, and 16.19). Another relevant reading of consumption holds that buying (or *exchange*) is an active process, in which consumers create meaning for the designed goods they purchase rather than being manipulated by the strategies of manufacturers or advertisers. In other words, the same product may mean different things to different audiences, and the economic, social, and psychological motivations for consumption contribute to our understanding of the way design functions in society. The phenomena of sumptuary laws, enacted during the later Middle Ages and in the Renaissance in the west and in Japan, demonstrate the social meaning of consumption. These laws imposed restrictions on dress and the purchase of commodities for some members of society. Such restrictions, rarely if ever successful, represented an effort to prevent the blurring of distinctions between social classes and the perceived threat to authority that such ambiguity might bring; the relaxation of such restrictions not only encouraged commerce and competition, but also shows the relation between commodity consumption, social mobility, and individual freedom.

Design, Values, and Meaning

Thus both as arrangements of forms or as the broadly economic, social, and political considerations that bear upon the conceptions for those forms, design also is the visible expression of values and attitudes. Examples include the longing for permanence and the display of authority by the French monarchy in the later seventeenth century, the social aspirations and pretensions of the English middle class in the later eighteenth century, or the spirit of rebellion and protest among youth in the nineteen-sixties. The meanings of design also emerge from the interest of manufacturers in adapting technology to appeal to an expanding and heterogeneous market for products, the promotion of standards as part of an effort to create social cohesion for that same elastic market, or in the utopian dream of mechanized mass production as a vehicle for a collective and egalitarian social order. In these and in other cases, the products of design give tangible form to the assumptions and beliefs that inform and guide our actions as individuals and as members of a society.

As a subject for historical investigation concentrating upon describing and understanding change, the meanings of design may emerge from the study of art history, technology, politics, economics, as well as consumer behavior – that is, we may appreciate the products of design as objects of beauty and creative human endeavor, as efforts of designers to engage with new materials, methods of production, or to promote particular social ideologies, as outcomes of economic conditions within a system of capitalist free enterprise which requires and stimulates ever-expanding markets and increasing levels of consumption, as challenges to that system, and as examples of the complex motivations of the mass market. A plurality of perspectives allows us to think about the considerations of artists, engineers, designers, manufacturers, and consumers in determining the meaning of design history.

The material for this study includes vessels and other objects made from glass, ceramics, plastic, or metal, tableware, furniture, textiles in their use for curtains, carpets, upholstery, clothing, and wall coverings, patterns printed or woven for surface decoration, lighting, housings for electric appliances, machines, and equipment, automobiles and tools, books, posters, magazines, illustrations, advertisements, and digital information. This list, though hardly exhaustive, is sufficiently representative to demonstrate that design plays an integral part of each of our lives. It surrounds us in the home and office in the form of industrial equipment, products, and packaging, and bombards us with promotional images in the mass media.

Continuity and Change: A Longer View

A survey of three hundred years permits an appreciation of continuity as well as change, and the thoughtful consideration of both of these phenomena is a major theme of this book. It provides for the examination of the rich legacy of craft production, the creative use of natural materials and newer materials that have emerged as a result of industrial or digital technology, the discourse revolving around an artificial and often-contested duality between artist and artisan within the western tradition of the visual arts, the expanding market for the products of design, and the phenomenon of reform and standards as they attempt to regulate and inform that market.

Finally, the Age of Exploration, from the journeys of Columbus and other adventurers at the close of the fifteenth century to the voyages of Captain James Cook in the eighteenth century, created the basis for a cross-cultural fertilization that also forms an integral part of the history of modern design. The transformations in the craft industries that lie at the heart of Part I are, simply put, unthinkable without the economic and cultural interaction that transpired at that time between east and west. Awareness of new processes like the manufacture of porcelain and lacquer in Europe during the eighteenth century, of products like woven silk and cotton, of pastimes like tea-drinking, all profoundly affected the history of design through trade, competition, and travel, stimulating invention, marketing, and unprecedented commercial expansion on a new global scale.

One may also extend this theme further into history, for instance to the techniques of papermaking, invented in China, brought to southern Europe by Muslim civilization, and expanding in Europe with the invention of printing using moveable type in Germany in the fifteenth century.

More recently such expansion has come to include a wealth of new man-made industrial materials, processes, and information, from steel to titanium, plywood to plastic, and cotton to nylon, from wire to transistors, and from microprocessors to nanotubes. The research, development, and applications for these technologies depend upon far-reaching lines of communication stretching across geographic and linguistic barriers. Thus the history of modern design is indeed a "global" history, and it is important to recognize the interconnections between cultures both western and non-western.

The text and illustrations which follow attempt to suggest themes of resonance as well as change in the history of design from the eighteenth through the twentieth centuries. It is my hope that the selection and presentation of the material will encourage students to appreciate design and to examine the relation of both unique and everyday objects to a variety of forces and influences that give them meaning.

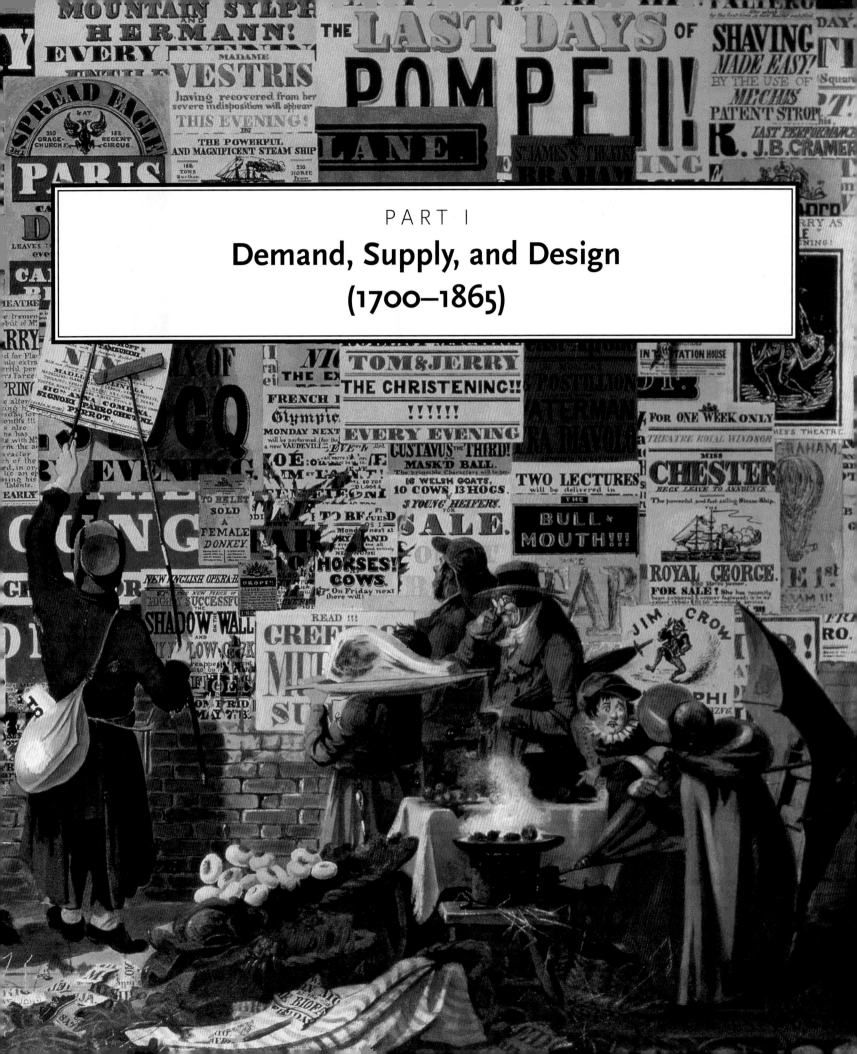

PART I

Demand, Supply, and Design
(1700–1865)

Introduction

At the beginning of the eighteenth century parallel revolutions in methods of production and patterns of consumption profoundly affected the history of manufactured products in Europe and in North America. As an elastic growth in consumer demand stretched across geographic and social boundaries, widespread changes in the organization of labor and the technology of manufacturing occurred. New materials and processes were developed, greater productivity achieved, and a confidence in the attainment of material comfort emerged, linked to the desire for social mobility and individual fulfillment. This dynamic, interdependent relation between production and consumption, involving new technologies, marketing, communications, and commercial practices, provides the basis for the study of modern design.

The early nineteenth century witnessed the expansion and acceleration of manufacturing and consumption amid continued technical advances and a political climate generally favorable to production, trade, and competition. Yet with expansion came calls for reform and regulation of the practice of design. The education of designers in government-sponsored schools, and prescriptions for the proper role of decoration in manufactured products were part of an attempt to create and promote common principles for an increasingly diverse consuming public.

Chapter 1

Demand and Production

1.1 Charles LeBrun, *Louis XIV inspecting the Gobelins Manufactory*, tapestry, manufactured at the Gobelins Tapestry Manufactory, *c.* 1663–1675. Chateau de Versailles, France.

State-owned Manufactories

In France the growing demand for luxury goods and furnishings at the court of Louis XIV (1638–1715) stimulated the development of large state-owned production facilities known as "manufactories." Such an enterprise was established just south of Paris at Gobelins in 1662, eventually employing 250 workers in the production of tapestries and other furnishings, many of them hired from smaller, independent workshops that existed earlier. At Meissen in Germany a royal manufactory for the production of a highly prized hard-paste porcelain (until this time only produced in China and imported for a luxury market) was built in 1710 under Augustus II, elector of Saxony and king of Poland (1670–1733). In 1756, a porcelain manufactory originally established in France

at Vincennes (1738) was relocated near Paris to Sèvres, whose range of wares satisfied both royal demand and the tastes of a sophisticated urban elite in the later eighteenth century. In one of a series of fourteen tapestries (*c.*1667) designed by the court painter Charles Le Brun (1619–1690), who directed many of Gobelins activities, Louis XIV is depicted visiting the Royal Manufactory at Gobelins (fig. 1.1). At the left the king is presented with a lavish array of textiles and furnishings produced at the workshops. A consciously overwhelming display, the abundance of goods is meant to reinforce visually the hierarchy of social prestige and political power. The richness of the setting, along with the sense of formal ceremony that pervades the scene, emphasizes the direct relationship between absolute monarchy and the flourishing of culture.

Although the products of Gobelins and other manufactories only served the needs of a small and wealthy clientele, economists such as Jean-Baptiste Say (1767–1832) articulated the principle that royal and aristocratic consumption meant material progress for all of society, stimulating the economy on a more general level by employing more people at all levels of production, promoting exports of such goods abroad, increasing wealth through trade and putting more money into circulation. In the mid-nineteenth century, the Empress Eugénie of France, who supposedly never wore the same gown more than once, remarked that in maintaining her wardrobe she was helping to provide the silk workers of Lyon with their livelihood!

Indeed, in much of Europe only royalty possessed sufficient wealth to realize such high levels of productivity. Large-scale facilities such as Gobelins and Sèvres required significant investment in raw materials, equipment, space, and labor, as well as the costs of oversight and administration. As the scale of operations increased, the need to achieve greater volume, efficiency, and control led to specialization. One of the best-informed guides to the practices of labor and industry at the time was the French writer Denis Diderot (1713–1784), whose *Encyclopédie*, first

published between 1751 and 1772, contains hundreds of engraved illustrations documenting the accumulated knowledge of his time. The degree of specialization in both labor and tools is remarkable in its complexity and rationalization. An engraved plate from the *Encyclopédie* (fig. 1.2) gives some indication of the size of the tapestry manufactory at Gobelins and the orderly arrangement of a large number of looms in a spacious, well-lit interior. Throughout the nineteenth century illustrated books, often printed in series, depicted the rational organization of labor into specialized tasks in large, well-managed facilities for making a wide variety of "useful manufactures." Such volumes were often published by manufacturers themselves as a form of advertising, or in small formats for children as a means of education and entertainment (story books for children were among the earliest genres for printed color illustrations).

The division of labor did *not* lead to a decline in quality or to the dry and repetitive work associated with nineteenth-century forms of mechanized mass production; in fact it inspired innovation and experiment. Translating the sketches or cartoons of court painters into tapestries was a challenge demanding great skill. It required the development of a wide array of dyes to match

1.2 Interior, Gobelins Factory, High Warp Looms, engraved plate from *Encyclopédie*, Denis Diderot, 1770.

the subtle palette of paint pigments, the attention to delicate individual details, and the preservation of the overall unity of the composition through monumental scale and the integrity of the two-dimensional picture plane. During the eighteenth century the Gobelins Tapestry Manufactory developed a palette of over ten thousand vegetable dyes for their products to approximate the varied tonalities and hues of the sketches they transformed into wall hangings on the loom. In the mid-nineteenth century the chief of this department, Michel-Eugène Chevreul (1786–1889), was among the most respected color theorists of his day. Chevreul published a book on the theory of color, and his advice was frequently sought by late nineteenth-century artists, such as Georges Seurat, interested in approximating on canvas the heightened sensations of colors in nature. Using models provided by "designers" was not a servile act of copying; rather it involved a creative transformation from one medium to another demanding great knowledge of materials, cooperation with other phases of production, and a keen interest in process.

The state-owned system of manufacture stimulated the involvement of painters and sculptors in the applied arts. Court painters such as Le Brun and later François Boucher (1703–1770) were responsible for supplying designs to the manufactories at Gobelins and Sèvres, and both artists held the position of "Director" for the activities of their large workshops. Such a practice insured unity of style and expression in all aspects of interior decoration, and corresponded to an ideal image projected by the monarchs and courts that were their primary if not exclusive patrons. Quite appropriately, the decorative arts of the period bear the name of the French kings, from the Baroque grandeur of Louis XIV, to the more intimate and sensual Rococo of Louis XV, and finally to the more restrained classicism of Louis XVI. The products and furniture from all three periods demonstrate the most refined levels of skill and craftsmanship in the carving of the chassis and mechanical parts such as drawers or doors, the more sculptural carved decoration, intricate marquetry and inset plaques, and the gilded metal fittings.

Painters or sculptors who provided models to manufactories enjoyed a more professional status than the craftsmen who produced those models. The elite audience for painting and sculpture acknowledged the fine arts as "liberal" rather than manual, and judged their value along moral and intellectual lines as well as technical ones. The artist's choice and development of a subject was expected to educate as well as to please the patron, and the training of fine artists in "academies" rather than in workshops, as well as the exhibition of their works at the biennial Parisian salons further expressed this difference. Despite the existence of such distinctions there appears to have been a healthy collaboration between artists and craftsmen in France throughout much of the eighteenth century, which contributed to the quality and reputation of luxury goods and furnishings produced for a discriminating clientele.

In working closely with weavers or other craftsmen the artist/designer balanced concerns for a convincing image or narrative with respect for the integrity of surface reinforced by borders and other areas of patterned, planar decoration. Perhaps unlike some of their revolutionary counterparts at the end of the eighteenth century, who dismissed craftsmen as servile employees dependent upon the favor of wealthy and aristocratic clients, court painters such as Boucher would hardly have been offended to see their sketches embroidered on a fire screen or on the back of an upholstered chair. These artists moved freely and seemingly without conflict between the salon and the drawing room, official and private, serious and sensual. And indeed the quality and refinement associated with the decorative arts of the pre-revolutionary period would become an inspiration for a number of later French Art Nouveau and Art Moderne designers seeking to revitalize their national heritage in the competitive economy of the late nineteenth and early twentieth centuries.

Porcelain

Porcelain from the Royal Manufactory at Sèvres ranged from extensive dinner services consisting of plates, saucers, and cups for multi-course meals, to display pieces such as candelabra and potpourri containers featuring carved decoration and more fanciful shapes as well as brilliant glazes. Upon close observation dinner plates reveal smooth surfaces, precisely patterned scalloped edges, and delicately painted borders whose floral patterns appear to float against polished, milk-white surfaces. It is generally agreed that such elaborate services, numbering to hundreds of individual pieces, were of distinctly higher quality than the Chinese export pottery specifically manufactured for European and American markets at the request of trading companies that now faced competition from the more recently established domestic manufactories. Services of export porcelain often were individualized through the inclusion of coats of arms for the families who commissioned them, or were based upon drawings or prints supplied to the Chinese manufactories. At manufactories such as Sèvres or Meissen, a closer collaboration between designers and craftsmen generally produced more symbiotic results.

Better known for their display in eighteenth-century period rooms in the major museum collections throughout Europe and the United States are the pink and turquoise, green, or even violet and yellow vases with figures, elaborately carved handles, relief decoration, framed scenes, and gilded accents. Such display pieces reveal greater specialization of labor and a resulting brilliance of effect. Among the most complex and fanciful of this type is the monumental potpourri container (fig. 1.3) in the

1.3 Potpourri container in the shape of a masted ship, soft-paste porcelain, 14 ¾ x 13 ³⁄₁₆ x 6 ½ in (374 x 335 x 145 mm), c.1761, manufactured at the Royal Porcelain Manufactory at Sèvres, France. Waddesdon Manor.

shape of a tall boat whose sweeping pyramidal "sail" is perforated to allow fragrances to escape. On either side a carved personification of a "wind" is blowing in either direction. The container dates to c.1761 and was modeled by an Italian-born goldsmith known as Jean-Claude Duplessis (c.1695–1774) who worked at Sèvres and was responsible for some of the more inventive production at the manufactory.

The Guilds

Alongside the large state-owned industries that flourished in France and elsewhere during the eighteenth century there co-existed a longstanding tradition of independent craft organizations known as guilds (in French as *corps*), many of which were incorporated as early as the thirteenth century. Guilds consisted generally of smaller workshops employing apprentices and journeymen working under the direction of a master who was trained in all aspects of a particular skill such as furniture-making, glass manufacture, or metalwork. Masters owned or rented space for manufacturing their goods on commission from a patron and might also act as merchants for the sale of goods they produced. Guilds maintained high standards of craftsmanship and, aside from the state-owned manufactories whose products they reserved the right to inspect, enjoyed a monopoly of craft production. In the later nineteenth century the founders of the Arts and Crafts movement romantically recalled, in an age of increased mechanization and mass production, the technical knowledge and high levels of skill and individual accomplishment associated with the guilds. Even in the early twentieth century, faculty at the Bauhaus in Weimar (1919) were given the title of "master" rather than professor to reflect a connection with the guild tradition, and direct experience with materials and craft production remain part of design education in most colleges and universities.

In more practical terms, guild organizations paid taxes to a monarch or prince in exchange for exclusive rights to manufacture and distribute their products in a particular region, effectively protecting them from open competition. Like state-owned or subsidized manufactories, the guild system depended for the most part upon the patronage of a privileged clientele who commissioned unique and individual works. In practice, however, this system of production and its market was undergoing a transformation in the eighteenth century. Masters increasingly became retail merchants, responsible chiefly for original designs that they provided as models for workshop production in manufactories or published to show to prospective clients.

André-Charles Boulle (1642–1732) was a master cabinet-maker who designed furniture and gilt fittings for Louis XIV and other aristocratic patrons both in France and elsewhere in Europe. In the upper and central rectangular portion of a standing cabinet dating to about 1715 and attributed to Boulle, a gold medallion depicting Louis XIV is inserted, indicating that the cabinet was intended as a gift denoting royal favor or for a royal residence (fig. 1.4). The stately architecture of the cabinet includes two half-length figures, male and female, symbolizing strength and life respectively, an iconography reflecting the type of didactic and humanistic themes associated with the fine arts.

Although a luxury work such as this cabinet was made to order, expanding demand in the eighteenth century often led to the production of basic types of furniture rather than entirely unique pieces, and during this time a typology of standard pieces such as commodes, consoles, sofas, bergères, and secretaries emerged. In response to the development of typologies, and the accompanying specialization of production, entirely new guilds were formed. The industry of furniture-making is one such example, and the growing complexities of production were illustrated in the plates of Diderot's *Encyclopédie*. In the mid-eighteenth century the making of a luxury item such as a dressing table or bureau might involve the efforts of a number of distinct crafts. A basic carved chassis might be the responsibility of the carpenter or *menusier*, while the veneers and marquetry designs were the work of an *ébéniste* or maker of a specialized kind of woodworking using a variety of rare woods and techniques of inlay. A goldsmith or porcelain manufactory supplied gilt fittings or ceramic plaques, while a separate group of craftsmen was responsible for upholstery, utilizing woven fabrics ordered from yet another manufactory, usually located in the French city of Lyon.

Specialization also resulted in the development of other varied areas of expertise. In addition to determining the size, overall form, and different types of materials, construction, and decoration of a particular table or chest of drawers, artisans also gave careful consideration to the mechanical functions of individual parts. The efficiently designed sliding table with "pop-up" mirrors combined the function of a desk with that of a vanity, as seen in an example (fig. 1.5) from the workshop of German-born master Jean-Henri Riesener (1734–1806) made for the French queen Marie Antoinette (1755–1793). Specialization also increasingly necessitated the services of the *marchand mercier*, a merchant (mercer) or furniture dealer who often acted as a liaison between customer and craftsmen. These individuals often subcontracted a commission to several

1.4 André-Charles Boulle (attributed), cabinet on stand, with medallion of Louis XIV, c. 1665–1670. Wallace Collection, London.

Many products of this manufacturing system remain among the most precious examples of eighteenth-century comfort. A good example is a secretary (fig. 1.6) dating from the late eighteenth century that combines marquetry designs from the workshop of Adam Weisweiler (1744–1820; like Riesener, a Prussian master craftsman working in Paris) and a series of Sèvres plaques used as surface decoration. This piece is remarkable less for its grandeur or elaboration than for the precision of its manufacture and the convenience of its pull-down writing surface, which takes up less space than a large desk. Such furniture was designed with spatial efficiency in mind for clients furnishing apartments in the city rather than more expansive country estates.

1.5 J-H. Riesener, secretary, ebony with black marble top, and black and gold lacquer panels, 1771. Metropolitan Museum of Art, New York.

shops or coordinated the efforts of a number of master craftsmen to create furniture for sale in the merchant's shop. In Paris many of the merchants' retail premises were located in the fashionable rue de St. Honoré, still a center for upscale retail and "designer" shops today. In the eighteenth century, commercially minded mercers attracted customers with shop signs hanging outside the door (an example is Antoine Watteau's sign for the merchant Edmé-Francois Gersaint's store Au Grand Monarque, though located at the Pont Nôtre Dame rather than on the rue St. Honoré and dating to 1720) and framed portraits of royal clients hanging on the walls. The mercer's role in coordinating the efforts of a number of guilds is a telling feature of eighteenth-century commerce. It demonstrates that the production of luxury goods involved a broad range of interrelated activities that included various kinds of "making" as well as an ability to translate the desire of a wealthy and cultured client for beauty, comfort, display, practicality, and convenience into a manufactured object that remains part of our understanding of the term design.

1.6 Adam Weisweiler, secretary, with Sèvres plaques after Boucher and Pater. Wallace Collection, London.

1.7 Jean-François de Troy, *La Lecture de Molière* (The Reading from Molière), oil on canvas, 29 ⅛ x 36 ⅝ in (737 x 934 mm), *c.* 1725.
Private Collection.

Since the furnishings of a single room of luxury furniture might cost more than the annual salary of a skilled worker, only an exclusive clientele could enjoy the beauty and comfort of such furniture. The literary pastimes of this elite clientele are the subject of Jean François de Troy's *La Lecture de Molière* (*c.*1725, fig. 1.7), a painting whose interior setting is less frequently depicted by de Troy's contemporaries Jean-Baptiste-Joseph Pater or Jean-Honoré Fragonard, artists who preferred scenes of music parties or picnics in park-like surroundings. The furniture depicted in de Troy's interior contributes more than a measure to the comfortable informality of the scene, and the participants' enjoyment of the pleasures of reading and listening.

In 1791 the revolutionary government in France abolished the monopolies enjoyed by the guilds for craft production as vestiges of monarchy and privilege. The guild system, which had overseen both the education of apprentices as well as the protection of production values, had to adjust to a succession of new official patrons, from the revolutionary government to the "Directory," "Consulate," and finally the restored monarchy. Those governments assumed responsibility for education, initiating state-sponsored schools for craft, and craftsmen were generally forced to compete amid more entrepreneurial conditions. The new circumstances created in the aftermath of the French Revolution were not always conducive to maintaining the effective and progressive collaboration and interchange between craftsmen, artists, mercers, and clients that had contributed to the quality and reputation for luxury goods both in France and abroad throughout much of the eighteenth century. Tracing the history of the decorative arts in the aftermath of the revolutionary period involves a consideration of many factors, including the introduction of steam power in production technologies, the emergence of middle-class patronage, an interest in the nature and meaning of standards in design, and new commercial strategies for expanding consumption in a more competitive economic climate. The effect of such developments will be fully explored in the next chapter.

The Printer's Art

The formation of private libraries by aristocratic and other wealthy patrons in the eighteenth century, as well as the pastime of reading aloud or privately (as illustrated in de Troy's *La Lecture de Molière*, fig. 1.7), stimulated significant changes in the craft of printing that also form a part of the history of modern design. Diderot's *Encyclopédie*, for instance, is noteworthy not only for what its engraved plates reveal about the complex organization and practice of many industries, including several of the decorative arts, but also for its ambitious scope as a publishing venture. The *Encyclopédie* grew to encompass seventeen volumes of text and hundreds of engraved illustrations released over twenty-one years, and earned a considerable profit for its publisher almost exclusively through subscription sales. Although the increased demand for printed material was hardly limited to France, the example of the Didot family of printers in Paris, spanning several generations from the eighteenth to the early-nineteenth centuries, serves to demonstrate the new concerns with typography, page design, and the overall quality of production. The portability of books and the printers' practice of publishing specimen books of their typefaces and border decorations for clients and workshop use (or for posterity in the more luxurious examples) created a good deal of communication and cross-fertilization both in Europe and across the Atlantic. The reputation of the Didot family, for instance, was recognized by the American printer and statesman Benjamin Franklin, who apprenticed his grandson to a branch of the Parisian firm in 1785.

The printer's art involved the coordination of many skills and broader interests that we would characterize today as information technology. The contributions of the Didot family, however, were hardly isolated, and should be seen in relation to Giambattista Bodoni (1740–1813) in Parma and William Caslon (1692–1766) in London, to name only two of the best-known eighteenth-century typographers. Others, such as John Baskerville (1706–1775) in Birmingham, are appreciated today not just for typography but also for related specialized aspects of the industry such as papermaking and the careful preparation of paper for the press (it had to be dampened before printing). The various processes involved in printing and papermaking are also painstakingly recorded and illustrated in the plates of Diderot's *Encyclopédie*.

Like other craft-industries at the time, each component of the printing process became increasingly specialized in the eighteenth century. Those affected included the designers of type and layout, founders or punch cutters who carved and cast the matrices for the font, and the printers who oversaw typesetting, the presses, and the preparation of paper. Punch cutting was an exacting process that involved several stages of creating a matrix from which a cast letter form was produced. This craft itself was a precise form of foundry work, and it is not surprising that the English master typographer William Caslon began his career as a decorative engraver of metal gun barrels. The printer's expertise extended as well to the spacing between letters and lines in a particular font. Thought was also given to the amount of text per page and to the balance between text and patterned decoration that was often included in the form of borders or frames for titles.

Generally, historians of typography, such as Philip Meggs, view the late eighteenth century as a period of particular interest, "an epoch of typographic genius." Examining a leather-bound volume published by the firm of Didot more than justifies this claim. The reduction of crowding between letters as well as lines, the ample borders, and the precise contours of letter forms are all the outcome of careful planning and execution, and of attention to the role of each element separately and in relation to one another. Letters of the Didot typeface, illustrated in a volume of the poetry of Virgil (fig. 1.8) published in 1798 by the firm of Pierre Didot (the set consisted of several volumes), are crisply cut and employ a distinct contrast between thick and thin strokes, a tendency that emerged

AENEIDOS

LIBER OCTAVUS.

Uᴛ belli signum Laurenti Turnus ab arce
Extulit, et rauco strepuerunt cornua cantu,
Utque acres concussit equos, utque impulit arma;
Extemplo turbati animi; simul omne tumultu
Conjurat trepido Latium, sævitque juventus
Effera. Ductores primi, Messapus, et Ufens,
Contemptorque deùm Mezentius, undique cogunt
Auxilia, et latos vastant cultoribus agros.
Mittitur et magni Venulus Diomedis ad urbem,
Qui petat auxilium, et Latio consistere Teucros,
Advectum Aenean classi, victosque Penates
Inferre, et fatis regem se dicere posci,
Edoceat, multasque viro se adjungere gentes
Dardanio, et latè Latio increbrescere nomen:
Quid struat his cœptis, quem, si fortuna sequatur,
Eventum pugnæ cupiat, manifestiùs ipsi,
Quàm Turno regi aut regi apparere Latino.
    Talia per Latium: quæ Laomedontius heros
Cuncta videns, magno curarum fluctuat æstu,
Atque animum nunc huc celerem, nunc dividit illuc,
In partesque rapit varias, perque omnia versat.
Sicut aquæ tremulum labris ubi lumen ahenis,

23

1.8 Virgil, *Bucolica, Georgica, et Aeneis*, Paris, Pierre Didot, 6 ¹/₁₆ x 3 ¹/₂ in (153 x 89 mm), 1798.

earlier in the eighteenth century. The typographer has also paid attention to uniform thickness throughout each letter of the alphabet to create consistent weight for the entire font. Uniformity was also applied to the height of each line of text (sometimes known as the x-height) and to the repetition of shapes among the bodies of individual letter forms. Careful examination and comparison with earlier eighteenth-century books also shows that faces such as Didot also increase the length of lower-case letters like "g" or "d" that reach above or below the x-height, creating the impression of wider space between lines and less crowding of the text. Pierre Didot and other typographers also devoted attention to the serifs or letter endings of their fonts. While retaining curved brackets on capital letter

forms such as the horizontal arms of the "L" or "E", such transitional elements were eliminated at the base and tops of other letters. These changes are usually attributed to the printers' desire to reduce the calligraphic character of fonts and their association with the inconsistency of handwritten letters. Considered together, the characteristics of the Didot font are usually described as "Modern," while less contrast between thick and thin strokes and shorter ascenders and descenders are referred to as "Old Face," whose characteristics may be seen in the specimen books of William Caslon (fig. 1.9), considered a master of the

Two Lines Great Primer.

Quouſque tandem abutere Catilina, p
Quouſque tandem a-butere, Catilina, pa-

Two Lines Engliſh.

Quouſque tandem abutere, Catilina, patientia noſtra? quamdiu nos e-
Quouſque tandem abutere Catilina, patientia noſtra?

Two Lines Pica.

Quouſque tandem abutere, Catilina, patientia noſtra? qu
Quouſque tandem abutere, Catilina, patientia noſtra? quam-

1.9 William Caslon, sample of Caslon typeface, Roman and Italic: *William Caslon and Son's Specimen*, London, 1793.

more traditional letter forms. Both Caslon and Didot's typography belong to the broad family of fonts known as "Roman," based upon the carved inscriptions (epigraphy) known from Roman Imperial monuments like the Pantheon and Trajan's Column.

Historians of typography have also noted that printers were interested in considering a balance between the elegance of the forms or page design and the legibility of the text. This in turn may be seen as a counterpart to transformations in other crafts where specialized expertise and experiment led to new levels of practical as well as esthetic achievement. Increasing the amount of white space on the page of printed type tends to make it more inviting to the reader—something that appears to have been taken into account by the printer in the design of the page layout. On the other hand, thin strokes may lack the strength to stand out on the page and consequently may tire the reader's eye. Creating the desired effect—the balance between delicate effect and legibility—constitutes an important part of the printer's art.

As mentioned above, a number of eighteenth-century printers published extensive specimen books showing the range of their achievement and providing models for others to follow. Among the most comprehensive is Giambattista Bodoni's *Manuale*, published in two volumes in 1818 (fig. 1.10) by his wife, five years after the printer's death. Recruited as court printer to the duke of Parma, Bodoni enjoyed the creative freedom to produce the *Tipografico* as a luxury work, with examples of dozens of typefaces in standard and italic fonts, as well as alphabets in Greek and Hebrew. The text of each page is framed by a bold, double band with very wide margins on all sides. Other contemporary printers often employed borders around their texts, but also developed a vocabulary of patterned geometric or floral patterns that complimented the visual weight of the typeface, and recalled the intricate decorative flourishes of medieval scribes who copied their texts by hand in manuscripts. Bodoni limited this practice in his *Manuale*, concentrating more upon the typeface itself and the overall design of the page.

Other innovations were meant to insure consistency in measurement and standards among the fonts developed by different printers. Drawing upon earlier initiatives to create families of type (fonts) in standardized sizes of uniform quality (in the late seventeenth century Louis XIV commissioned a mathematician to design letter forms in a

1.10 Giambattista Bodoni, specimen of Ducale in three weights, from *Manuale Tipografico*, Parma, 1818.

recognized "Royal" style based upon Roman epigraphy), François-Ambroise Didot (1730–1804), one of the sons of the founder of the printing dynasty, François (1689–1757), helped to develop a standard system of measurement in which the sizes of letters were referred to by points, seventy-two to an inch. The point system gained currency in France, was later adopted in Britain and in Germany, and is still in use today (for instance, the type sizes that we effortlessly manipulate on our computer screens are based on the same system).

Chapter 2

Entrepreneurial Efforts in Britain and Elsewhere

2.1 The Portland (Barberini) vase, black jasper ware,
10 x 7 ⅛ in (254 x 187 mm), *c.* 1790, manufactured
by Josiah Wedgwood. Wedgwood Museum.

Wedgwood, Design, and Antiquity

In eighteenth-century Britain the initiatives of a new breed of craftsman–merchant led to a number of successful enterprises in the decorative arts that both competed with continental luxury production and expanded the trade in such goods to include an upwardly mobile middle class. The inherent flexibility of the specialization of labor, combined with the ingenuity of entrepreneurs, helped to make such successes possible. Once again such efforts required not only capital investment and oversight of a number of interdependent activities involving both manufacture and marketing, but the existence of more competitive conditions often made both efforts and results more varied and dynamic.

One of the most ingenious entrepreneurs of this period was Josiah Wedgwood (1730–1795), who came from a family of potters in Staffordshire, an area known throughout Britain at the time for the production and sale of earthenware. As a trained craftsman, Wedgwood's early contribution was primarily technical. He successfully developed a process for making a cream-colored glazed earthenware that was considerably more refined than other local products, and that adopted the then-current preference in the luxury market for simple, regular shapes and a restrained approach to both relief and painted

2.2 Josiah Wedgwood, Queen's Ware with green *Water Leaf* pattern, earthenware, *c.* 1790. Wedgwood Museum.

decoration. Such decoration was supplied by a firm in the city of Liverpool, and may be seen in examples of creamware plates and serving dishes dating from 1790 (fig. 2.2). Wedgwood's experiments were the result of a worldly outlook not uncommon among merchants of the time, and his creamware competed with more costly imported porcelain wares being produced in France and Germany for an exclusive market in the urban centers of Europe. Wedgwood produced a large service of his creamware for Queen Charlotte of England, and this royal commission helped significantly to establish his firm's reputation, indeed after 1765 the design was known as Queen's Ware. Following this success he built a larger factory that he named Etruria in 1769. In the editions of his published catalogues Wedgwood praised the influential patrons whose approval meant so much to the success of his wares:

> The demand for this said *Creamcolour*, alias *Queen's Ware*, Alias *Ivory*, still increases. It is really amazing how rapidly the use of it has spread almost over the whole Globe, and how universally it is liked. How much of this general use, and estimation, is owing to the mode of is introduction—and how much to its real utility and beauty? are questions in which we may be a good deal interested for the government of our future Conduct ... For instance, if a Royal, or Noble introduction be as necessary to the sale of an Article of *Luxury*, as real Elegance and beauty, then the Manufacturer, if he consults his own interest will

bestow as much pains, and expence too, if necessary, in gaining the former of these advantages, as he would in bestowing the latter.

The demand for fine wares extended to the United States, where Thomas Jefferson purchased a creamware dinner service manufactured by Wedgwood for his estate at Monticello in Virginia, although Jefferson later acquired a Sèvres dinner service following an extended visit to France from 1784 to 1789. Wedgwood capitalized on the enlarged Etruria facility to increase production. These efforts included the division of labor, the use of molds rather than potters' wheels, and the employment of a transfer method of printing decorative borders rather than handpainting. Wedgwood's initiatives and innovations saved time and insured uniformity and high quality, maximizing consumer choice within a limited range of shapes and decorative patterns.

Subsequent technical experiments by Wedgwood led to new products based upon the mixture of clay with lapidary materials to produce basalt and jasper wares, opaque surfaces in black and blue respectively, cast in molds with figural relief decoration in white imitating frieze-like compositions. Such wares catered to the contemporary aristocratic interest in recalling the stability and enduring humanistic values of the classical past, expressed in the admiration and acquisition of Greco-Roman antiquities, the rediscovery of the ancient Roman cities of Pompeii and Herculaneum, and the popularity of visiting (often in the company of knowledgeable guides) these and other ancient sites on the Grand Tour. One of the most celebrated Roman objects of this period was the so-called Portland or Barberini vase, adapted from a cameo glass original of the 1st century BC brought to Britain from Italy by an antiquities dealer and manufactured by Wedgwood in a series of copies beginning in 1790 (fig. 2.1). Others were based upon drawings that Wedgwood commissioned from artists, including sculptor John Flaxman (1755–1826), and then were carved into relief molds for use on a variety of vases and plaques to be set into pieces of furniture or frames.

Wedgwood marketed his classically-inspired lapidary wares by successfully combining technical innovation and the most modern manufacturing methods with designs appealing to a sophisticated taste for the products of a past age. His success was also due in no small part to working closely with artists such as Flaxman. During a period of great social and economic change, Flaxman's Neoclassical imagery satisfied nostalgia for a golden age and gave reassurance of continuity with a selective view of an idealized past. In addition to his expertise and vision as an innovative craftsman in the broadest sense of the word, Wedgwood's skills extended to marketing and merchandising, involving collaboration with artists serving as designers.

In an age of material progress and commercial expansion, Wedgwood's success also underscores the significant role commodities played in communicating social status. According to a number of historians, the market for commodities becomes "elastic" when traditional class distinctions are blurred by new wealth amassed through trade, industry, and manufacturing, and by the mingling of social classes that constitutes part of the urban experience. Within this context of social ambiguity, the desire for manufactured products takes on new and complex levels of meaning.

New wealth held the promise of social mobility; and consumption was one of the signs of social status, through the emulation of fashion in dress and the acquisition of furnishings displayed in the home. Fashions and manners might as easily *reveal* wealth as provide the *pretense* of wealth, but it is the real prospect of social progress in Britain that provides the backdrop for the expanding market in the decorative arts and for experiments in production and marketing undertaken by Wedgwood and others.

Reactions to furnishings, including pottery, appear in the novels of Jane Austen (1775–1817), for instance, in *Northanger Abbey* (begun 1798 but published posthumously) when the protagonist, Catherine, comments favorably upon the elegance of her host's breakfast set. The host, General Tilney, responds that the English set compares favorably with Continental porcelain production, but is already two years old; the sight of much improved specimens in town had almost tempted him to purchase an entirely new service. As revealing as such remarks may be in ascertaining contemporary attitudes toward home furnishings, it is the effort, or perhaps better the *game* of discerning wealth and position, for the purposes of arranging marriages or favorable relationships, which lies at the heart of the novel and in which fashion and manners play a considerable part.

2.3 Robert Adam, interior, Lansdowne House, London, 1765, re-installed in Philadelphia Museum of Art.

But if emulation created demand, and if technology and rationalized labor contributed to making products available to a new market of socially conscious middle-class consumers, it was also important to pay attention to practical considerations of distribution and retailing. A shrewd businessman, Wedgwood helped to finance the construction of canals to control transport, supply, and delivery, and always looked for ways to expand the market for his wares, for instance by opening a showroom in London and publishing an illustrated catalogue from which retail merchants could select and purchase goods. Wedgwood's career is a far cry from the image of the village craftsman. His skills and interest in quality may have initially been nourished in that milieu, but they matured and prospered amid increasingly entrepreneurial conditions. In such circumstances, upwardly mobile middle-class buyers were beginning to experience and enjoy the comforts and convenience that commodities provided as well as the status they conferred, all formerly associated with a small landed aristocracy. Portraits from this period often register the pride and self-assurance of self-made individuals and their families through the possessions that surround them in their homes.

The emergence of the designer in craft production in Britain is also seen in the career of Robert Adam (1728–1792), an architect who supplied drawings of furniture and other interior furnishings to manufacturers involved in the decoration of homes for wealthy clients. Furniture designed by Adam incorporates elements of classical architecture and decoration, often formal but enlivened by gilding and brightly-colored silk fabrics. The drawing room dating to 1765 (fig. 2.3) in the Earl of Shelburne's London home, known as Lansdowne House (reflecting the earl's later title Marquis of Lansdowne), was designed by Adam to display the earl's collection of ancient Greek and Etruscan pottery. The sophistication and coordination of Adam's interior is seen in its festive color scheme of blue and pink, the careful arrangement of the earl's ancient vases, and even in the French-inspired design of the chairs. It reveals a cosmopolitan taste removed from the solid carved mahogany furniture and coarser fabrics of earlier Georgian interiors, and indicates as well a new appreciation for the decorative arts in conveying the enlightened attitudes and distinction of their owners.

Commodities and the "Fashionable"

In *Northanger Abbey*, General Tilney's apology for owning a breakfast set "already two years old" and his admission of being tempted to purchase a new one reflects a preoccupation with fashion in the late eighteenth century. The frequent introduction of new styles and the co-existence of different styles, not just in dress but in other commodities as well, are phenomena in the decorative arts during this time that challenge a generally more succes-

sive and linear view of artistic change. Indeed, while Wedgwood's own Queen's Ware and classically-inspired lapidary wares are perhaps the best-known products of his manufactory, the published catalogues of his wares reveal a wide range of styles typical of the late eighteenth and early nineteenth centuries in Britain.

The same eclecticism can be observed in the furniture of Thomas Chippendale (1718–1779), whose London workshop prospered during favorable market conditions in the mid- and late eighteenth century. Chippendale's fame rests not only on the high quality of his furniture but also on the publication of his designs beginning in 1754 in a volume known as *The Gentleman and Cabinet-Maker's Director*. Chippendale's publication was intended less as a workshop manual for craftsmen than as a catalogue for wealthy buyers looking to furnish their London houses and apartments. Moreover, its first printing was timed to coincide with the opening of parliament after a general election, when new members would be relocating to London (an early instance of advertising linked to anticipated demand). Many of the designs imitate contemporary examples of highly ornate carved furniture from France, but the plates of the *Director* also present more subdued versions of these models that are less delicately-carved and therefore less costly. In addition, Chippendale's *Director* illustrates examples of furnishings in the Gothic and other styles (figs. 2.4 and 2.5). Indeed this heterogeneity and consciousness of style was characteristic of later eighteenth-century dress and other applied arts.

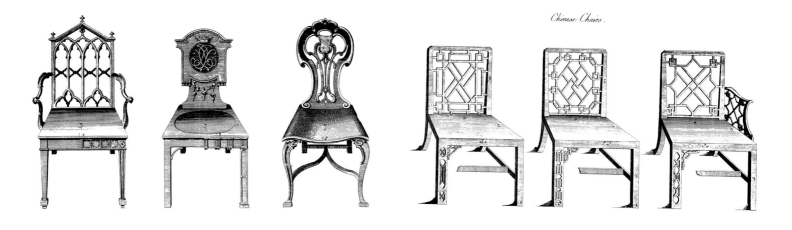

2.4 Thomas Chippendale, Gothic chairs, plate from *The Gentleman's and Cabinet-Maker's Director*, 17 1/4 x 12 1/4 in (451 x 311 mm), 1754.

2.5 Thomas Chippendale, Chinese chairs, plate from *The Gentleman's and Cabinet-Maker's Director*, 17 1/4 x 12 1/4 in (451 x 311 mm), 1754.

Scott (1771–1832), while fascination with Egypt, also popular at the same time in France, was stimulated by Napoleon's military campaigns to the region in the late eighteenth century (fig. 2.6). In this new era, royalty were not the only authorities in the creation of ideal images for imitation. Questioning tradition was an expression of identity and individuality, parallel to the growing and prized emancipation of the artist that was associated with the Romantic movement in the late eighteenth and early nineteenth centuries (and commercially exploited by manufacturers). An expanding, elastic market, by nature, reflected more diverse tastes than those of a homogenous, aristocratic patronage. Thus, in general terms, eclecticism was a result of the democratization of culture expressed through commerce and consumption.

The phenomenon of fashion laid the groundwork not only for the variety of styles in Chippendale's *Director* but also for even more curious invention. Thomas Johnson

2.6 Thomas Hope, chair in the Egyptian style, from a design by Thomas Hope, English, c. 1805. Faringdon Collection, Buscot Park, Berkshire, England.

The wider range of "fashions" that emerged in the late eighteenth century in Britain went considerably beyond the principle of emulation and its implication of a "top-down" explanation for changes in taste. Fashions drew from history (more properly historicism, the tendency to attribute values and attitudes to the past) and travel, and revealed the growing sense of individual identity—far less monolithic or authoritarian than before—with an accompanying tendency toward change. Some styles, such as the Neoclassicism of Wedgwood's basalt or jasper wares, recalled the enlightened, enduring values and stability of Greco-Roman civilization even as they were embodied in contemporary political regimes, while others appealed to heightened emotionalism associated with nature, the Middle Ages, or exotic places in the Near and Far East. For instance, the interest in goods and furnishings in the Gothic style stemmed largely from the novels of Sir Walter

2.7 Thomas Johnson, wall light, mahogany, 43½ x 30 x 16½ in (110.5 x 76.2 x 41.9 cm), 1758. Philadelphia Museum of Art.

(1714–*c*. 1778) was a British craftsman who specialized in the design of decorative frames and particularly of candelabra mounted on the wall, also known as girandoles. Although the asymmetrical composition and spiral pendants seen in many of his published designs may have been inspired by the contemporary French taste for chinoiserie (western imitation or evocation of Chinese Art), many of Johnson's works demonstrate startling originality. A carved wooden candelabrum attributed to him (fig. 2.7) represents a rustic scene complete with figures, architecture, and landscape. The freedom of invention is hardly conceivable without the existence of a public eager for novelty, even fantasy. Thus we may conclude that the accelerated pace of fashion in commodities, linked with the expression of Romantic ideals of individuality and a willingness to break with tradition, was a potent social as well as economic catalyst to both consumption and inventiveness in design. Fashion-able design and an eclectic range of products satisfied both the psychological and social aspirations of consumers and stimulated the productivity and profit of merchants, manufacturers, and artists.

Even as the dynamic of modern fashion emerged in the eighteenth century, conflicting attitudes toward the phenomenon may be observed. Novelty and change may indeed attest to heterogeneity and a democratizing tendency signifying a relaxation in social boundaries and greater freedom of expression. Yet at the same time fashion was also criticized for its emphasis upon ostentation and its conformity to values rooted in materialism—increasingly it was blamed for the decline of traditional standards. In contrast to the neutral observation on consumer attitudes in *Northanger Abbey*, Jane Austen's later novel *Mansfield Park* (1814) treats fashion with a decided cynicism. The acquisition of commodities alone never substitutes for the pleasures and sensibilities of the "good" life, and Edmund, the cousin of the novel's central character, Fanny, laments that his friend and romantic interest, Mary Crawford, has fallen victim to the lure of fashion and materialism: "It is the influence of the fashionable world altogether that I am jealous of. It is the habits of wealth that I fear."

To sum up, the Neoclassicism of Robert Adam's interiors or Josiah Wedgwood's lapidary wares represents an *official* expression of taste, reason, and republican solidarity in the decades preceding the age of political revolution and reform. At the same time, fashion and eclecticism

represent an equally significant but *popular*, and even threatening individual identity that often accompanies an expanding audience for design.

The United States

In North America the demand for commodities accompanying westward expansion in the early nineteenth century and the scarcity of labor hastened the adoption of rationalized production methods and the beginnings of mechanization. The key element, according to the author John Heskett, was the mass production of interchangeable parts in the manufacture of firearms in the early nineteenth century, a process that required precision and careful oversight in order to insure exact uniformity. At the outset the high capital costs of experiments with machine-made parts and rationalized methods of production were underwritten through government contracts to manufacturers for substantial quantities of uniform goods. The main advantages to this method were the ease of repair and replacement of parts, and the vast savings in the cost of labor, especially in the time-consuming tasks of filing and fitting parts to each product. The principle upon which this productivity was based was, once again, the division of labor; the virtues of a rational approach to production were praised by British economist Adam Smith (1723–1790), whose description of a pin factory extols the virtues of dividing tasks, and links such developments to general material progress:

> One man draws out the wire, another straightens it, a third cuts it, a fourth points it, a fifth grinds it at the top for receiving the head ... and the important business of making a pin is, in this manner, divided into about eighteen distinct operations, which in some manufactories are performed by distinct hands ... This separation too is carried furthest in those countries which enjoy the highest degree of industry and improvement; what is the work of one in a rude state of society being generally that of several in an improved one.

The American tendency to extend Smith's principles to specialized sequences of machines designed to fabricate increasingly complicated and precise, interchangeable

2.8 Navy .36 Caliber Revolver, Colt Firearm Company, manufactured in London Armoury for the British Navy, 1851.

parts may be seen in numerous examples—from the manufacture of rifles by Simeon North and later by Samuel Colt in Hartford, Connecticut in the 1840s (under contract from the American government, fig. 2.8), to the clock mechanisms made by Chauncey Jerome at around the same time, and also to the early development of the sewing machine around 1850, manufactured by Isaac M. Singer and other companies for factory rather than domestic use. The success of this approach to production, which became known as the "American System of Manufacture," should also be viewed in light of the absence of guilds or strong craft traditions, whose working methods and continued emphasis upon skill could not easily be adapted to the strict uniformity imposed by Jerome and others. Historians such as David Hounshell remind us, however, that the transition to this "American System" was slow, and that even successful companies such as Singer continued to employ workers to finish individual parts until demand forced greater attention to insuring quality with increased reliance upon the sequence of special-function machines.

In Europe the "utilitarian" approach of these early American manufacturers was often criticized as being "artless" for the lack of those outward signs of beauty, workmanship, and culture that linked products with luxury living. However, decoration was less a requirement of the production process than a marketing consideration, and the use of stenciled decorations and carved cabinets for sewing machines and wall clocks soon accompanied their introduction to the domestic market, together

with installment or hire payments to facilitate a family purchase, initiated by Singer in the 1850s.

Labor organizations, especially in Britain, often viewed mechanization as a threat to jobs and lobbied for restricted use of machines by manufacturers, and such restrictions eventually allowed American goods to compete for British markets. By the second half of the nineteenth century, design, historicism, and printed advertising had become prominent features of manufacturing in the United States, as techniques of mass production were adapted to the introduction of variety and choice in stimulating consumer demand for goods and furnishings.

The so-called American System of Manufacture is only part of the history of the decorative arts and design in the United States during the later eighteenth and early nineteenth centuries. British manufacturers, for instance, produced a variety of clothing and other goods in large quantities specifically for the American market. And colonial craftsmen and workshops, inspired by the pages of Chippendale's *Director* and other contemporary model books, produced technically accomplished carved furniture for well-to-do families in cities such as Boston and Philadelphia in the second half of the eighteenth century. In addition, Thomas Jefferson designed his own practical, even ingenious furniture, constructed by craftsmen on the premises of the estate. These were intended to increase his own productivity and efficiency, and included such items as a revolving bookstand and a table with a revolving top for his study (known as the *cabinet*).

Chapter 3

Growing Pains—Expanding Industry in the Early Nineteenth Century

3.1 Michael Thonet, chair, beechwood with wicker seat, approximately 35 in (88.5 cm) high, 1836–1840. Victoria and Albert Museum, London.

New Materials and Processes

Following the war of 1812, Britain enjoyed peaceful relations with the United States, and the Peace of Vienna, forged in the wake of Napoleon's defeat at Waterloo in 1815, inaugurated a period of reduced political hostility in Europe that encouraged trade and the growth of markets for manufactured goods. One of the most precipitous technical advances of the time was the invention of the cotton gin (patented 1794) by the American Eli Whitney. The cotton gin mechanically removed seeds from balls of raw cotton, a task that had previously been done painstakingly by hand, and greatly increased the production of raw cotton in the southern states. Whitney's invention, coupled with the introduction of steam power to the process of spinning in British factories, reduced prices and made cotton fabric (until this time usually imported from manufactories in India) available to middle-class buyers. Prices were also lowered through the use of slave labor on southern plantations. This in turn contributed to the expansion of women's fashion and the manufacture of ready-to-wear clothing, stimulated further by printed fashion plates that provided models of feminine beauty and propriety in dress.

The industry of printing also experienced substantial growth, which led to broad ramifications for a host of other related areas. Advances in printing technology, including the introduction of steam-powered cylinder presses, lithography and chromolithography, papermaking machines, and continuous-feed paper, helped to create a more informed and literate public. This was especially evident in the widespread proliferation of popular illustrated weekly broadsides and journals. A parallel development occurred in the design and printing of patterns for cotton and other fabrics. A single worker operating a rolling machine to print patterns could produce as much as 200 workers printing cloth using the older method of hand blocking. The use of engraved metal rollers permitted the possibility of more intricate and detailed patterns, including modeled forms or scenes, which might have been technically challenging or prohibitively expensive if printed by existing craft methods. Continuous printing processes were also introduced for patterned or scenic wallpapers, using longer lengths of paper and making paper wall coverings an attainable form of interior decoration for the middle class. The construction of railroads, first in Britain and then throughout Europe and the United States, also aided the expansion of commerce, as the speed and ease of transportation of raw materials and commodities was greatly increased. The railroad also contributed to the growth of personal travel and accompanying commercial activity. And European involvement in the affairs of South America, North Africa, India, and less successfully in Asia spread trade globally. Finally, the development of advertising and shopping experiences familiar to today's consumers emerged in this period (the first modern department store, the Bon Marché, would open in Paris in the 1860s). Posters, printed advertisements, lighting, and plate glass all contributed to enhance the experience of shopping. Writers and illustrators of the period document displays of goods behind large expanses of plate glass, attractive salesgirls behind counters, and the use of handbills and sandwich boards to attract shoppers.

The range of products and processes developed during the first half of the nineteenth century is overwhelming, but a sampling may suffice to suggest the breadth of man-

ufacturing activity. During this period, for instance, the process known as silver electroplating was developed by G. R. Elkington of Birmingham, England and patented by 1840. This process involved a chemical reaction created by electricity that attached a thin coating of silver to base metals such as nickel for the production of a wide variety of metal wares (today the same process is used to protect metal automobile parts with a coating of chromium). Electroplating quickly replaced the use of pewter, eclipsed a mid-eighteenth century method of plating using copper between layers of silver, and made "silverware" and silver tea services popular as symbols of comfort and leisure in many middle-class homes (fig. 3.2). A slightly later innovation in metallurgy is the discovery and first applications of aluminum, dating to around 1855. Early experimental uses of the new material included jewelry, which is not surprising since its price was comparable to that of silver or gold. Only when electrolytic processes for extracting aluminum were introduced industrially toward the end of the nineteenth century did applications expand to include casting for architecture, furniture, and other products.

Examples of the manufacturing expansion also encompass the development of new materials for furniture, including the wider use of cast iron and bentwood for chairs and benches. In 1830 German-born cabinet-maker Michael Thonet (1796–1871) used steam to bend

3.2 George Elkington, designs for electroplated silver tureens from Elkington's Catalogue, 1847.

beechwood rods into curved shapes that were then assembled to make chairs, hat stands, and supports for tables (fig. 3.1). His invention eliminated the need for carving and other costly handwork, and acquired a reputation when it came to the attention of Prince Klemens Metternich, advisor to the Austrian emperor, who commissioned a large order of furniture from Thonet for the emperor's palace at Liechtenstein.

German architect Karl Friedrich Schinkel designed chairs made of both cast and wrought iron, primarily for use in gardens and public parks. The chairs (fig. 3.3) are constructed from identical sidepieces with X-shaped supports connected by cylindrical rods at the seat and the upper back, where a filling of foliate and other decorative motifs was attached and molded to fit the concave shapes of the connecting rods. The design and construction of these early nineteenth-century examples of cast-iron

furniture are remarkably similar to benches used today in parks or commuter rail stations, where simple cast-iron supports are connected with riveted planks of painted or varnished wood.

Yet another material that was used significantly more during the first half of the nineteenth century was papier-mâché, made from wood pulp, then molded and baked to create furniture, often with elaborate finishes resembling expensive lacquer and inlay. Manufacturers experimented with more durable forms of the material that achieved popularity, particularly in Britain (fig. 3.4). Papier-mâché also became an important material in the newspaper printing industry during the nineteenth century where it was used to convert flat formes of type into curved surfaces that served as molds for making metal cylinders for newly-invented rotary presses (see page 42).

3.3 Friedrich Schinkel, outdoor chair, cast iron, 33 ¼ x 18 x 21 in (86 x 46 x 54 cm), c. 1821. Vitra Design Museum, Germany.

3.4 Chair, papier-mâché. Victoria and Albert Museum, London.

3.5 Desk, cherry, mahogany inlays, spruce, and beech, 41 ⅛ x 64 ½ x 28 in (105 x 164 x 711 mm), c. 1830, Private collection, Munich.

3.6 Square piano, composite cast iron frame, rosewood and rosewood veneered case, 88 in (223.3 cm) wide, 46 ½ in (118 cm) in length, 1851, manufactured by Nunns and Clark, New York. Metropolitan Museum of Art, New York.

Materials technology was not the only area of expansion in the design and production of furniture. Invention is also demonstrated by the style of German and Austrian furniture and decorations known as Biedermeier that emerged in the second quarter of the nineteenth century. This new style expressed values of comfort and leisure for a prosperous middle class of merchants and professionals with considerable disposable income. Designs for furniture were generally restrained both in their use of carved ornament and elaborate inlay, resulting in a style more related to Neoclassical forms (fig. 3.5). Beyond issues of style, practical considerations were of equal importance. For example, manufacturers of Biedermeier furniture made extensive use of the invention of coil-spring upholstery that was patented by an upholsterer named Georg Junigl in Vienna in 1822.

Painted views of domestic interiors from this time often include a piano, which during this period became a focal point of middle-class home entertainment. Unlike the standardized forms of grand and upright that would become common in the twentieth century, nineteenth-century pianos offered much more variety in size, shape, number of keys, and especially ornament. Legs and borders were often decorated with elaborate carving in a range of original as well as revival styles. The mid-nineteenth

century "Square" piano, manufactured in the United States by Nunns and Clark (fig. 3.6), is distinguished by heavily carved legs, music holder, and pedal stands, associated with the rich decoration and robust forms of furniture from the period of Louis XIV (see fig. 1.4). In this era of expanding middle-class consumption, the division and specialization of labor—effectively initiated in the later seventeenth and eighteenth centuries and made more efficient through new tools, processes, and techniques of production—were increasingly employed and adapted to meet and exploit the prevailing taste for a variety of eclectic period styles.

Though Biedermeier furniture is known and admired today chiefly for the quality of its craftsmanship and an emphasis on practicality and comfort, much early nineteenth-century furniture possesses a sense of grandeur both in scale and decoration that suggests an interest in public display rather than convenience or private enjoyment. In the wake of the French Revolution, Napoleon cultivated an imperial or Empire style that was clearly designed for display rather than relaxed living. The style was realized in designs by architects Charles Percier (1764–1838) and Pierre Fontaine (1762–1853), and manufactured by craftsmen who had been trained prior to the French Revolution of 1789 (fig. 3.7). The function of such

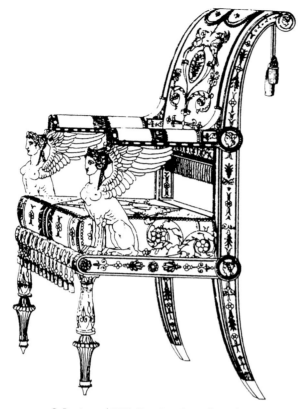

3.7 C. Percier and P.F.L. Fontaine, design for a chair, *Recueil de decorations intérieures*, 1812, Paris.

was usually not in any sense typical, since its purpose within the context of public exhibition was to attract attention—to truly be showpieces. The competitive atmosphere of the exhibitions, along with their sheer marketing potential, encouraged designers and craftsmen to demonstrate their ingenuity in solving practical challenges of storage and comfort. For example, the first roll-top desk was designed by François Puteaux's for King Louis-Philippe and included in the 1819 Paris *Exposition de produits de l'industrie* (fig. 3.8). While specialization and other technical advances in woodworking made the manufacture of such pieces possible, their production stems from the nature of the expanding commercial life in the early nineteenth century, in which neither subtlety of effect nor simple practicality appear to have been the aim. That such grandeur or grandiosity was a tendency in the furnishings of this period seems to be demonstrated by a passage from Stendhal's *Le Rouge et Le Noir* (The Red and the Black), published in 1830. Toward the end of the novel, Mathilde, a member of a privileged and well-bred aristocratic family, is pleasantly surprised by a parlor in which she's asked to wait, and contrasts its "refinement and

furniture was to project an aura of imperial dignity and majesty, with forms based upon those found in examples of Roman wall painting, ancient Greek vase painting, or in subjects from Roman history painted by such Neoclassical artists as Jacques-Louis David (1748–1825). Decorative features, such as sphinxes or the letter "N" referred directly to the emperor himself.

Following Napoleon's exile and the Peace of Vienna (1815), the French government began to organize exhibitions of national industry to re-establish (after the disruption of the revolution and its aftermath) its reputation for luxury products and to stimulate the export trade. The first two of these industrial showcases were held in 1819 and 1834 in Paris, and were a means for manufacturers to demonstrate the quality of their products and have a venue to market them to visitors from other nations. They also paved the way for the even more ambitious international exhibitions beginning with the Crystal Palace in London in 1851 (see pages 51–3). The furniture presented at the fairs was often large and imposing in both size and scale and

3.8 Louis François Puteaux, roll top desk (open), 1819. Musée Carnavalet, Paris.

3.9 Linked armchairs, apartments of Napoleon III. The Louvre, Paris.

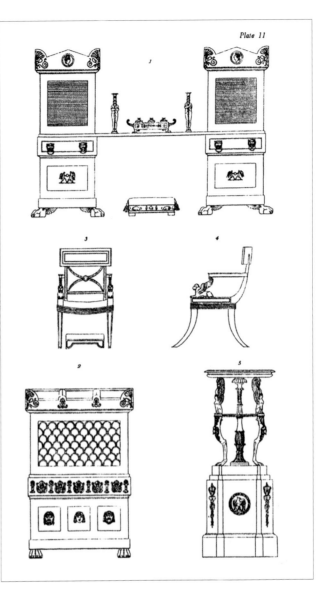

3.10 Thomas Hope, design for writing table, arm chair, and pedestal, drawing, 1807, John Morley, *Regency Design*, 1790–1840.

delicate luxury" (presumably a reference to pre-revolutionary elegance) with the "vulgar magnificence" one finds today in Paris in the "best houses." Perhaps the extreme of such magnificence is the apartments designed for Napoleon III (Emperor 1852–1870) in Paris, now installed in the Louvre. Carved, gilded, and utilizing the newer technique of "tufted" upholstery in red silk and damask throughout, the furniture and setting embody a mid-nineteenth century conception of luxury through richness and abundance of material as well as elaborate carving and construction. While frequently borrowing from the past for inspiration, some furniture in the apartments displays a remarkable originality of form, for instance, the odd combination of three connecting armchairs, apparently to facilitate conversation (fig. 3.9). Such originality became a hallmark of furniture later in the century as more modern ideas and attitudes toward the decorative arts emerged (see page 55).

As a characteristic, heaviness also appears frequently in interior furnishings in early nineteenth-century Britain. Perhaps the best-known and most original guide to the furniture of the period is that provided by architect Thomas Hope (1769–1831), whose *House Furniture and Decoration* was published in 1807. Drawing upon the same antique and Egyptian sources mined by the French architects Percier and Fontaine, Hope created designs with richly carved decoration and frequent inclusion of animal forms, such as table feet ending in claws and chair arms carved and gilded in the form of sphinxes or winged lions (fig. 3.10). Hand-colored engravings of Hope's designs were published in monthly magazines beginning around 1809. *Repository of the Arts*, published by the German emigré Rudolph Ackermann (1764–1834), is a good source for the furniture designs from this period, and one is struck by the massiveness of many of these pieces. One example from the magazine is a reclining chair (fig. 3.11) with front legs and an attached foot rest carved in the form

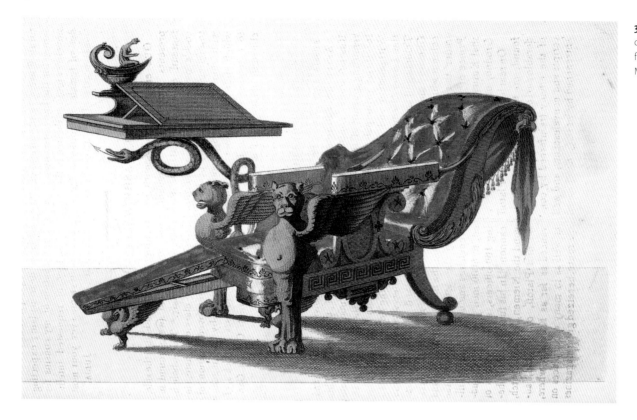

3.11 Pocock's reclining patent chair, hand-colored illustration from the *Repository of the Arts*, March, 1813.

of winged beasts, and a reading lectern, which appears to swivel, in the form of an attacking snake! While such a chair was certain to make a visitor take notice, its sheer mass and amplitude undermine the practical advantages and comfort for its user.

Beyond the Printed Page

In the eighteenth century, the printing industry had been geared primarily to the production of books for a limited readership. During the early nineteenth century, printers and typographers greatly expanded the range of their production to meet the needs of an increasingly literate public that read daily and weekly newspapers, and to compete for public attention in advertising. Larger type sizes, new fonts, and the introduction of the process of lithography to create or transfer images for illustrations exemplify the inventiveness in materials and production techniques that transpired during this time.

Printers, particularly in the commercially active center of London, developed a wide variety of new typefaces and a wide range of sizes for signs, handbills, and newspaper advertisements in an effort to grab the attention and interest of consumers or influence public opinion. Casting large letters in metal proved expensive and unwieldy, so typographers cut type in wood. By the second half of the nineteenth century, wood type was cut with the help of templates and routing machines that made grooves more quickly and precisely than hand-held knives and chisels.

If the terminology used today by historians of the printing industry seems arcane, there is good reason. Much of this specialized vocabulary has not changed since the early development of the industry. For example, new faces developed in the early nineteenth century were generally called "fat," and are characterized by very large letters with proportionally thicker heavy strokes, often contrasted with thin strokes. The contrast between thick and thin strokes recalls that of the later eighteenth-century "Modern" faces (see page 25) but on a much larger scale. Fat faces appeared early in the nineteenth century, often accompanied by simplified bracketed serifs that looked triangular and tended to make letters appear dense and rather close to one another (fig. 3.12). The term "Egyptian" is also often used to refer to fat faces. One type of "Egyptian" face uses "slab serifs," heavy letter endings that

SIX LINES PICA. Cast in Mould & Matrixes.

MILTON, Burnham. 12345790

V. FIGGINS.

3.12 Vincent Figgins, six lines pica no. 1 (fat face), cast type and matrices, 1821.

R. THORNE £126780 diminishing

3.13 Thorowgood, six lines pica Egyptian (slab serif), cast type and matrices, 1821.

R. THORNE. BRIGHTON

3.14 Thorowgood, five-line pica shaded no. 2, cast type and matrices, 1821.

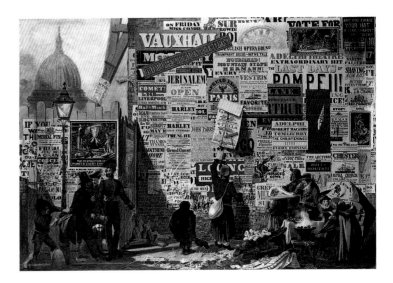

3.15 J. Parry, *London Street Scene*, watercolor, 30 x 43 in (760 x 1065 mm), 1835. Alfred Dunhill Museum and Archive, London.

anchor the letters to an insistent horizontal line and also reduce the space between them, strengthening the immediate impact of each word (fig. 3.13). Designers in the twentieth century returned to such slab serif lettering for visual impact in developing corporate logos (see figs 4.85 and 4.86, page 270). Also appearing during the same period are three-dimensional letters featuring shadows to one side, or faces that appear in the white of the paper against a border of pure black (fig. 3.14). Finally, the most varied faces are those where the fat letter forms are filled with scrolls and other patterned decoration. A number of British printers contributed to these developments. Specimen books from this period feature several of the new typefaces, though even these are quite conservative when compared with a watercolor painting by John Parry from 1835 of a wall covered with advertising posters and announcements (fig. 3.15), which reveals the commercial context that fueled these typographic developments, the ancestors of twentieth-century highway billboards and neon signs.

Curiously, another new face linked to the growing demand for advertising eliminated serifs altogether and used strokes of uniform thickness, thereby permitting the very close spacing of letters and giving a strong sense of overall density. Known at the time as a form of "Egyptian" type or sometimes as "Grotesque," these letters (fig. 3.16) were also called "sans serif." Sans serif typography was adopted almost as an article of faith in the twentieth century as an approach that was sympathetic to the modern age of mechanical production. Ironically, twentieth-century typographers felt that serifs belonged to a calligraphic tradition and that their elimination reduced the individual

WITHOUT RESERVE; HOUSEHOLD FURNITURE, PLATE, GLASS,

3.16 Vincent Figgins, two-line great primer sans-serif, 1830.

and human qualities of a printed page or poster (see page 183). In the post World War II period, many multinational corporations also favored sans serif faces as the basis for logos and identity programs, capitalizing upon the close similarity among letter forms to create a strong sense of visual unity (the "Mobil" logo is one example; see fig. 5.22).

The technology of the printing press also developed rapidly in the early nineteenth century, primarily as a result of the increased circulation of newspapers. Efforts concentrated upon speeding up the production process, first with larger and easier-to-operate presses, often made of cast iron rather than wooden parts, then with the use of steam to provide mechanical power. Steam-powered presses, first introduced by a German engineer working in London named Friedrich Koenig (1774–1833), operated on a principle derived from copper-plate printing, where the type forme moved horizontally on a bed, first under an inking roller and then under a cylindrical press. These steam-powered presses were installed in 1814 at the London newspaper offices of *The Times*. Later versions printed simultaneously on both sides of a sheet of paper. Michael Twyman, who has traced these developments and their impact, relates that circulation of *The Times* from the late eighteenth century to 1830 grew from 1,500 copies per day to 11,000. The next major development, occurring simultaneously in Britain and in the United States, was the use of continuous rolls rather than individually cut sheets of paper to further increase the speed of production. Continuous feed presses required transferring the flat type formes to a curved surface, accomplished by the use of the malleable material of papier-mâché, to make curved impressions that were then used for creating cylindrical metal formes (the process is known as stereotyping). By 1850, circulation of *The Times* had reached 38,000 copies daily.

Lithography, meaning literally "stone writing," was the name given to a planographic printing process developed in Germany by Alois Senefelder (1771–1834) in the early nineteenth century. Based on the chemical repellence of oil and water, a design was drawn with greasy ink or crayons on a flat limestone surface (the best limestone was known to come from Bavaria). The stone surface was then coated with water, which was absorbed by the stone only in those areas not covered with the crayon. An oily printing ink was next applied to the surface of the stone, which

adhered only to the drawing, being repelled by the wet part of the surface. The stone was then covered with a sheet of paper and placed beneath a press to make a printed impression.

Lithography has been called the most significant development in printing in the nineteenth century, although its progress in the early nineteenth century was hampered first by the slow progress of the technology during the Napoleonic Wars and second by the lack of machine presses to speed up printing until after 1850. Known for its versatility and the relative ease of the process in comparison with intaglio and relief methods of printing, lithography could be used for reproducing both illustrations and text, and thus became a popular medium for the design of advertising posters. Its commercial success was insured as well by the use of color inks and the development of a complicated but effective process called chromolithography.

Wallpaper and Fabric Printing

The technology of continuous printing transformed other industries in the nineteenth century, particularly the manufacture of printed wallpapers. Though printing by hand from engraved wooden blocks continued as a production method for a number of wallpaper manufacturers, the introduction of patterns engraved on metal cylinders fed continuously by rolls of paper dramatically increased production and created a much broader market by the early 1840s. Even before the advent of rotary printing and steam-powered pressing machines, wallpaper manufacturers had produced a wide range of styles. A typical selection available to clientele ranged from colored patterns to large scenic designs composed of multiple blocks, from papers that imitated textures such as marble to "flocked" papers that were produced from pulverized silk or wool attached to glue-coated designs. Also popular were patterned vignettes using delicate line and the background color of the paper to create trompe l'oeil effects, reflecting a continuing taste for chinoiserie and the imitation of Roman mural painting. The adoption of industrial technology increased the output of all types of printed wall coverings, leading to widespread invention and borrowing from a variety of sources such as wall painting, tapestry, and other woven fabrics, creating an even wider array of

3.17 Anonymous, block-printed wallpaper, c. 1840–50. Victoria and Albert Museum, London.

3.18 *The Vices and the Virtues*, central panel of *The Garden of Armide*, block-printed wallpaper, designed by Edouard Muller and produced by Desfosse, Paris, c. 1855. Musée des Arts Decoratifs, Paris.

patterns and scenes. These include elaborate imitation ironwork, patterned architectural decoration in the Gothic style (fig. 3.17), and a trompe l'oeil garden scene (fig. 3.18).

Methods for mechanically printing relief patterns in color on wallpaper were similar to methods for printing on textiles, chiefly on calico cloth. This fabric, formerly imported from India, became a middle-class commodity with the invention of the cotton gin in the United States and the industrialization of the textile industry in Britain, including the introduction of steam-powered spinning to roller rather than hand-applied printing. In Stendhal's novel *Le Rouge et Le Noir* (The Red and the Black) (1830), the author refers to the social pretensions of the "wealthy

calico printers" in the French town of Verrieres, an indication of the growth of this new industry.

In the early nineteenth century, the manufacture of machine-printed cotton was simultaneous with the introduction of more automated methods for the weaving of silk. The center of this latter development was the French city of Lyon, which had supplied the fashionable capital of Paris and other European cities with woven silk since the early eighteenth century, when the industry employed more than 20,000 silk workers. The industry was disrupted during the French Revolution, but revived after the Peace of Vienna (1815), when a new type of hand-operated loom was introduced that manipulated the weaving of silk threads through a series of cards that were punched to create patterns. Though usually named the "Jacquard" loom for one its innovators, Joseph Marie Jacquard (1752–1834), several other people were responsible for equally significant contributions to the process.

The developments in the silk and cotton industries during the first half of the nineteenth century helped to expand the market for women's clothing. Two valuable guides to this expansion are the interest of portrait painters in depicting the wardrobes of their wealthy subjects, and the more numerous and stereotypical hand-colored woodblock and engraved illustrations of contemporary dress known as fashion plates. Fashion plates appeared as a feature in monthly subscription magazines (sometimes as few as two or four at the beginning of each issue) that also included commentaries on the fashion trends and other matters relating to public appearance and behavior. Although there are examples of fashion plates in both France and England from the 1770s, publishers substantially expanded the practice of issuing colored illustrations by subscription or including them in periodicals during the early nineteenth century.

With the revival of its center for silk manufacturing in Lyon, and the restoration of its monarchy after 1815, France set the tone for fashion and for fashion plates. As the popularity of the genre increased, artists and amateurs specialized in the production of drawings that were then engraved, printed, and colored. Fashion plates were both a product of and a contribution to a more "public" social life in the early nineteenth century: there was an increasing consciousness not only of one's dress but also of being seen or noticed. As in the fashion plate (fig. 3.19) from Rudolph Ackermann's *Repository of the Arts* (1827), props such as chairs or benches provide an added context or even implied a narrative or "story" for such images. They reveal foremost a feeling for the activities associated with leisure: these often include reading, playing an instrument (after the 1840s the most popular instrument was the piano), walking in the park, attending balls, or spending time with friends and children, all presented with generalized young women in relaxed, informal poses. Until the 1820s, the preference in women's fashion was for high-waisted long dresses (known as the Empire style), enlivened by satin ribbons or velvet borders and elaborate coiffures. During the second third of the century fuller skirts and patterned cloth, both printed and woven, become more common, and pastimes illustrated in the fashion plates grew to include attendance at horse races and concerts. The popularity of these plates is evidence that dress was a means through which the habits of the wealthy were communicated to an increasing number of those who aspired to such practices, and who might use the plates to plan their own wardrobes. Through marketing, merchandising, and less costly means for the color reproduction of illustrations, the second half of the nineteenth century brought such habits into an even broader commercial realm.

3.19 Fashion plate, hand-colored engraving, from Rudolph Ackermann, *Repository of the Arts*, 9 ³⁄₈ x 5 ¹¹⁄₁₆ in (240 x 146 mm), *c.* 1827.

Chapter 4

Design, Society, and Standards

4.1 North transept portal, Chartres Cathedral, France, c. 1210–1220.

Early Design Reform

Cities were the focus of industrial and commercial activity throughout the nineteenth century, and the growth of urban populations throughout Europe presented challenges in terms of housing, sanitation, unemployment, safety, and the relationship among classes and their developing cultures. The year 1830 saw outbreaks of social unrest in Europe and working-class resistance leading to armed conflict and its suppression through stronger central authority.

A portion of the emerging class of industrialists, merchants, and professionals during the first half of the nineteenth century took an interest in the living and working conditions of factory workers and other laborers whose numbers swelled in the cities of Europe. Along with industrial wealth came a desire, even a sense of obligation, to shape the values of a more complex and diverse society, and to address issues of social and economic welfare for all. Such attitudes took a variety of forms, including the role of the arts. Reformers took an interest in the education of designers and in the cultivation of discriminating taste in the public at large. Design "reform" aimed to set standards for taste in the public interest and was part of a broad response to industrial and commercial expansion toward the middle of the nineteenth century. While reformers often employed polemic rhetoric for effect, their efforts seldom achieved the reception they intended or took account of the increasingly heterogeneous market for manufactured products. Nonetheless, their attitudes and projects had the effect of further investing the decorative arts with social and moral meanings that are a significant part of the dialogue that informs the history of modern design.

Not all observers welcomed the increase in production of and demand for goods and furnishings with the same enthusiasm as economist Adam Smith. In the early nineteenth century Britain experienced a staggering expansion of industrial manufacturing, particularly in the production of textiles, cast iron, and the construction of railway engines, rolling stock, and track, which was accompanied by an increasing demand for coal as a source of fuel. Industrialized production of commodities and related resources strained the dynamic relationship between production and consumption created by rationalized labor and increasing demand from an elastic market for manufactured commodities. The expansion of production and trade was accompanied by competition, and overproduction in a competitive market combined to make large-scale manufacturing a volatile and uncertain business, often with decidedly negative consequence for a new class of industrial workers. Thus one consequence of industrialization was the emergence of a chiefly urban laboring class tied to the long hours and increasingly monotonous routine of a factory system of production, and often living in squalid and undesirable housing.

Even as emerging urban industrial areas in Britain such as Manchester, Birmingham, and Liverpool gained a voice in parliament, and as the industrialists who were chosen to represent their interests lobbied for free trade and the further expansion of markets for their products, there was ample cause for concern about the negative human consequences of these early stages of industrialization. The demand for labor in industrial centers resulted in problems of crowding, sanitation, disease, and increasing alcoholism. Workers remained socially and politically marginalized, without electoral power and with little choice but to suffer low wages, poverty, dangerous working conditions, and long hours, the last made possible through the new technology of gas lighting that extended evening working hours. Working-class discontent led to uprisings and revolts between 1810 and 1830, followed by the beginnings of workers' organizations (trade unions) and the practice of organizing strikes to protest against low wages.

The exploitation of the working class was a theme among a number of writers, including Scottish-born Thomas Carlyle (1795–1881) who, lamenting the extreme contrast between the prosperity of the upper and middle classes and the poverty of the working class, pleaded for some sort of reform:

The condition of England ... is justly regarded as one of the most ominous, and withal one of the strangest, ever seen in this world. England is full of wealth, of multifarious produce, supply for human want in every kind; yet England is dying of inanition. With unabated bounty the land of England blooms and grows; waving with yellow harvests; thick-studded with workshops, industrial implements, with fifteen millions of workers, understood to be the strongest, the cunningest and the willingest our earth ever had; these men are here; the work they have done, the fruit they have realised is here, abundant, exuberant on ever hand of us: and behold, some baleful fiat as of Enchantment has gone forth saying, "touch it not, ye workers, ye master-workers, ye master-idlers; none of you can touch it, no man of you shall be the better for it; this is enchanted fruit!." On the poor workers such fiat fall first, in its rudest shape; but on the rich master-idlers nor any richest or highest man escape, but all are like to be brought low with it, and made "poor" enough, in the money sense or in a far fataler one.

In response to the needs and demands of an expanding working class in Britain, and fearing that unrest might lead to revolution, parliament undertook efforts to implement standardized codes for the due process of law, pursue broad-based educational opportunities, establish public museums, restrict employers' use of child labor, and reform the prison system. Just as attempts were made to regulate working conditions, so too were efforts undertaken to regulate commercial production, as seen, for instance, in the adoption of standardized widths for the laying of railroad track in England. With many privately-owned and competing companies, such shared standards insured the ease of connecting one railway line to another. Although the factory system did not dramatically affect traditional craft industries, aside from stimulating the adoption of the division of labor or steam power for running machines such as potter's wheels for more efficient and uniform production, the reform of design in manufactured domestic goods was also part of this general effort to regulate expansion and laissez-faire capitalist enterprise, and respond to the broad social changes that accompanied this growth. Reform efforts were motivated generally by the desire to reduce the fear of social unrest and to provide working people with the basis for shared values among all classes that made change and progress appear synonymous.

Whether stirred by the fiery rhetoric of Carlyle or by less radical calls to action and responsibility, many reformers, whether artists, architects, industrialists, or politicians, were motivated by a sense of social responsibility and a desire to improve the lives of working people. Such attitudes may be viewed as a genuine concern for improving the quality of life and the public interest, or as efforts to exert social control, promoting values "imposed" from above in order to prevent disruptive protest or revolution. Understanding the nature of early design reform involves reconciling these opposing views and recognizing that reform embodied complex attitudes aimed at balancing common values with an appreciation for the democratic, spontaneous impulses of an emerging popular culture.

Early design reformers in Britain directed their efforts toward creating standards and models for designers and manufacturers to follow. Many, including Matthew Digby Wyatt (1820–1877), welcomed technology in the form of new materials and processes to which guidelines might be applied, especially in relation to metals and casting; others, such as A. W. N. Pugin (1812–1852), called attention to the moral and ethical implications of design, ignoring the varied tastes and motivations of consumers. Still others, such as Sir Henry Cole (1808–1882), lobbied for schools of design, a museum devoted primarily to the decorative arts, and exhibitions to display national and international contemporary design. In all cases, however, reformers believed in the existence of fixed standards for design and the need to establish and implement them in the common culture—standards that they felt ultimately would be in the best economic, social, and moral interests of an ever-expanding consuming public. Interestingly, many reformers used the latest technology in the printing industry to publish illustrations of their designs in book form as part of an effort to familiarize an expanding middle-class readership with the practice of good design.

Reform and the Gothic Revival

One of the strongest advocates for the importance of standards or principles of design was A. W. N. (Augustus Welby Northmore) Pugin. Pugin, an architect, designer, and author who worked with Sir Charles Barry on the design and interior decoration for the Houses of Parliament, contrasted the eclecticism of contemporary English architecture and design with the stylistic unity of its medieval and specifically its Gothic past. For Pugin the consistency of the latter expressed a moral as well as esthetic harmony. Pugin's conversion to Roman Catholicism (1835) and his passion for the beauty and "truth" of the Gothic style led him to a passionate investigation and appreciation of the style. As a result he complained bitterly about the indiscriminate and superficial application of any type of decoration to a wide variety of furnishings and utilitarian goods, which he felt was motivated by greed and self-interest.

Pugin's "principles" of design were based upon his understanding of Gothic architecture. He believed that painting and sculpture were essentially embellishments of architecture and as such should be subordinated to, rather than independent from, the structure they decorate.

This rational, subordinating principle or organization is certainly not absent from other architectural styles, including examples of classically-inspired furniture discussed in chapter one (see fig. 1.4), but for Pugin the principle is best exemplified and more easily enforced with respect to the Gothic style. Looking at the early thirteenth-century north transept portal of Chartres Cathedral, for example (fig. 4.1), one can observe that the jamb statues maintain their character as columns supporting a porch, other carved figures do not project beyond their containing niches, and virtually all individual elements are part of a larger unit that is in turn related to the tripartite division of the doorway. As suggested by Margaret Belcher, within such a framework a unity is imposed upon all of the arts that might also serve as a metaphor for an ideal world in which all individuals are unified by a single faith and live in harmony with society. In addition, Pugin advised respect for the characteristics of materials and argued, for instance, that carved materials, such as wood should not look like they are molded (like bentwood), and that while it is natural for artists and artisans to transform the materials they work with, stone should always retain in some

4.2 A. W. N. Pugin, *Fleurs-de-Lis and Pomegranate* pattern, block-printed wallpaper.

measure its essential "stony" character, and should not pretend to be something else. The arbitrary use of pointed arches and quatrefoils for the base of a lamp or the back of a chaise was for Pugin a superficial appropriation of details, which revealed a lack of understanding of both the stylistic and symbolic unity of the Gothic style. Other grievances included the use of illusionistic patterns for wallpapers or carpets since it violated the structural function of the walls and floors. He registered some of his objections in a satirical drawing of "monstrosities" where the Gothic style is used to construct a collection of unidentifiable products that make use of medieval characteristics in varying degrees. Presumably he would have abhorred as well the overlapping forms of the Gothic wallpaper design (see fig. 3.17), manufactured in England between 1840 and 1850.

In 1841 Pugin enumerated his principles derived from the Gothic style in *True Principles of Pointed or Christian Architecture*, illustrated with engravings based on the author's drawings. In this book he wrote that "there

should be no features about a building which are not necessary for convenience, construction, or propriety," and "all ornament should consist of enrichment of the essential construction of the building." He also published books of illustrations intended as models for the design of furniture, metalwork, ceramic plates and tiles, and ecclesiastical garments. A number of manufacturers produced his designs, the moral as well as aesthetic dimension of which can be seen in a plate manufactured by Minton in 1849 whose border is inscribed with the admonishment "Waste Not Want Not" in bold Gothic lettering. Elaborated in many forms by other contemporary designers and authors, Pugin's "true principles" became the basis for many nineteenth-century approaches to design standards that often refer to the "harmony of beauty and utility."

As an early reformer, art criticism for Pugin was inseparable from social criticism, and a disregard for design principles as he defined them was a deviation from both beauty and moral truth. Eclecticism and lack of discrimination was a sign of decay, and ignoring the "proper" use of materials was dishonest and resulted in ugly designs. On the positive side, adherence to principles was socially as well as esthetically desirable, and in this way the decorative arts could contribute to the well-being of society, instilling common values during a time of uncertainty and change brought about by industrialization and the rise of laissez-faire capitalism. Wedded to a discriminating historicism and looking to the past to influence the future, the moral dimension of Pugin's views lent a

4.3 A. W. N. Pugin, dining room table, c. 1845. Palace of Westminster, London.

4.4 A. W. N. Pugin, Armoire, c. 1851, manufactured by Crace. Victoria and Albert Museum, London.

polemic sense of urgency to his writings. His views were based on a firm belief in the ability of the arts to influence social change, and were shared by a number of artists and collectors during the Victorian Age.

Many of Pugin's designs for patterns and interior furnishings were inspired by fourteenth- and fifteenth-century examples he had studied and recorded in England and France. Motifs such as the quatrefoil or fleur-de-lys are common, as are other plant or lobed forms that share the same simple characteristics—repetition or symmetry, crisp contours, and flat shapes. This approach can be seen in the bright "Fleur-de-Lys and Pomegranate" wallpaper pattern used for a number of conference and committee rooms at the Palace at Westminster in London (fig. 4.2).

Turning to furniture, a dining table of around 1845 (fig. 4.3) designed by Pugin uses simple curved timber beams in the shape of pointed arches to enrich the support structure, and indeed the table looks strong enough to stand on, rather than simply to sit at. Other pieces, especially the large cabinets intended for domestic interiors (many manufactured by the firm of J. B. Crace), are simple in shape and resemble in their tripartite composition the facade of a Gothic cathedral; yet they also contain elaborate and intricately carved decoration characteristic of much of Pugin's furniture (fig. 4.4). The same embellishment of surface appears as well in some of the chalices and other metal ecclesiastical objects designed by Pugin and manufactured by Hardman: such decoration is demanded neither by convenience nor construction, and reminds us that propriety is, after all, a matter of judgment. Many of Pugin's designs were commissioned by or intended for august religious or political settings and circumstances, especially parish churches and in particular the chambers of the Houses of Parliament. The interior of the House of Lords adhered to Pugin's *True Principles*, but its deeply coffered ceilings, carved paneling, gilt screens, and carved stone figures were more appropriate to *public* ceremony than to *private* comfort or ordinary use. Indeed, Pugin's principles are as noteworthy for their limited application as much as for the serious and polemic tone in which they are formulated and espoused. While he holds a well-deserved place in the history of modern design, his direct legacy is more visible in the widespread construction of Gothic Revival churches in Britain and North America in the late nineteenth and early twentieth centuries.

Henry Cole and the "Cole Group"

Beginning in the 1830s the British government took an interest in the reform of design, primarily through the establishment of schools of design devoted to the education of artists designing specifically for manufactured goods. A lengthy government report of 1835–6, prepared by The Select Committee on Arts and Manufactures under the auspices of the Board of Trade, noted that the arts in Britain had received very little encouragement and that the result was both a decline in demand abroad for British goods and an increase in foreign imports at home (a negative trade balance in contemporary economic terms). There was a belief among a number of committee members that the arts of painting and sculpture should form the basis for the education of designers in "manufactures," because the basis of academic training in the fine arts was drawing, and because the noble and didactic aims of the fine arts would elevate the general standards of public taste. The select committee also advocated specific recommendations for such standards, based upon a balance between beauty and utility and the use of decoration derived from the study of botanical forms.

Among the most prominent individuals to take up the cause of reform in the wake of the report was Sir Henry Cole, a civil servant who believed that "an alliance between fine art and manufactures would promote public taste" as well as restore Britain's competitive edge in the expanding world market for manufactured goods. Cole's attitudes were strongly influenced by the House Report of 1835–6. Under the pseudonym Felix Summerly, Cole edited a series of illustrated travel books and storybooks intended for children (known as the *Home Treasury*) that were intended to "improve" upon the quality of children's books currently available in the market. Throughout his career in public service he argued that public museums should serve the interests of the working class and be "the antidote to brutality and vice," providing models for behavior and social harmony. Turning to design, the "harmony of beauty and utility" in the decorative arts also served as a metaphor for the socially acceptable virtues of moderation and restraint, and government-sponsored design education provided practical training for artisans in expanding industries producing a wide range of domestic products. Cole furnished designs (both his own and those of his artist-friends) for tea sets and other manufactured goods, founding "Summerly Art Manufactures" in 1847 to demonstrate the successful merging of the theory and practice of design.

Richard Redgrave (1804–1888) was a painter of frequently moralizing subjects who participated in a number of Cole's initiatives, including providing illustrations for the *Home Treasury* and designs for the "Summerly Art Manufactures" venture. As a designer, Redgrave's porcelain "Well-Spring" vase of 1857 (fig. 4.5) is an example of the early design reform movement. The painted decoration of reeds, appropriate to the pitcher's function of containing liquid, is treated in a simplified linear style that grows from an abstracted crisscross pattern of roots at the base. Equally appropriate is the sense of illusion created by the overlapping reeds, since the natural transparency of glass, for which the design was intended, would allow for the tentative exploration of virtual space. Summerly's products did not always adhere to such subtlety: Redgrave's "Well-Spring" vase, designed for manufacture in glass, was later produced by the Minton Company in porcelain, where much of the subtlety of its effect is lost.

Neither Pugin nor Cole condemned the use of unskilled labor that resulted from specialization in manufacturing or the use of new technologies to increase the efficiency of production. Rather, they were interested in being practitioners of, and advocates for, common standards of taste that might inform the production of useful goods by manufacturers for an increasingly discriminating consuming public both at home and abroad. If machines or specialization (sometimes taking the form of piecework, that is, the hiring out or sub-contracting of particular parts of a product that are later assembled and sold)

4.5 Richard Redgrave, *Well-Spring* vase, porcelain with hand painting, modelled in 1847, manufactured in 1865. Victoria and Albert Museum, London.

4.6 Alfred Stevens, warm-air stove, cast bronze with printed earthenware panels by Minton 1851, manufactured by Hoole, Sheffield, England. Victoria and Albert Museum, London.

could increase efficiency and lower cost, it was only natural that such means be employed by manufacturers. While concerned with the welfare of working people, the reform efforts of Cole and his group related more to finished products than to the process by which they were manufactured: new processes were employed while preserving principles or standards inherited from the past. Unlike Pugin's insistence upon the morality and unity of the Gothic style, however, Cole and his group accepted a broader range of styles within their approach to reform. Designers might work in a variety of historic styles yet still adhere to a balanced relationship between beauty and utility, as well as be concerned with appropriate representational imagery that contradicted neither function nor the

nature of materials. The early reformers questioned neither the existence of universal standards for design nor the need to impose them for the mutual benefit of society.

Cole was actively engaged in education, and sensed that his ideas would never gain acceptance without taking into account education and public relations. He helped to sponsor a periodical entitled *Journal of Design* (1849–51) that published illustrations for designers and manufacturers to follow, and also was named director of Britain's government-run schools of design, where his ideas could be adopted through the teaching of principles and focus upon drawing as the mainstay of academic training in the fine arts. Following the Crystal Palace Exhibition of 1851, Cole realized his long-standing ambition to establish the South Kensington (later Victoria and Albert) Museum as a collection devoted to the decorative arts and the improvement of public taste. From the 1860s onward the South Kensington Museum installed gas lighting to permit working people to view the collections until ten o'clock three nights each week.

In addition to Redgrave, the sculptor Matthew Digby Wyatt was an advocate of design reform. He devoted much of his attention to the proper use of decoration in the manufacture of cast-metal objects such as coal-burning stoves and fireplaces used increasingly for household heating. He published books with illustrations of product designs based on reform principles. Wyatt's principles were incorporated by sculptor Alfred Stevens (1817–1875) in his design for a stove dating from 1851 (fig. 4.6). The stove uses cast sculptural ornament in high relief to help conduct heat, reconciling decoration and commercial considerations with utility and efficiency.

The Great Exhibition of 1851

The Exhibition of Art and Industry held in London at Hyde Park in 1851 served as a watershed for design at mid-century and confirmed emphatically the reality of a heterogeneous middle-class consumer culture in Europe that associated ordinary commodities with ideas of progress, abundance, and social transformation. Never before were the decorative and industrial arts made the focus of such widespread attention, crossing boundaries of class and presenting a kind of visual excitement that stirred the popular imagination. Supported by Prince Albert and

4.7 Animated Christmas and New Year card in the form of a cut-out showing the entrance to the Crystal Palace and, when opened, the interior of the Main Hall, colour lithograph, 4 ¹⁄₁₀ x 3 ³⁄₅ in (105 x 92 mm) open. Victoria and Albert Museum, London.

States. *The Exhibition of the Art and Industry of All Nations,* as it was called, was originally conceived as a national fair, but in the process of planning became international, attracting 14,000 producers, half of whom were from outside Britain. It was housed in a temporary structure (fig. 4.7) designed by gardener turned architect Sir Joseph Paxton (1801–1865), attracting great interest by its frank use of both cast and wrought iron, its breathtaking expanses of glass, and the complete absence of traditional building materials such as stone. Relying upon uniform prefabricated parts, the Exhibition Hall was built in the short span of six months, a necessity resulting from a lack of agreement in earlier planning and construction efforts. Though Paxton's choice of materials and method of construction had previously been used in utilitarian structures such as railway stations and greenhouses, the Crystal Palace, as it was dubbed by contemporary writers, nonetheless sounded a note of modernity, progress, and confidence in the possibilities of industrialized technology. And although the goods on display were not for sale, the sense of abundance and proximity of products to the spectator linked the exhibited objects with the promise of unlimited availability to the middle class and the fulfillment of all desires. Recently, historian Thomas Richards has placed the exhibition in the context of nineteenth-century theatrical *spectacle,* suggesting the transformation of goods as they entered a "vast space of association." Such magical, quasi-religious reactions to the Crystal Palace and its exhibition were not uncommon. Queen Victoria herself remarked that when standing inside the structure she was "filled with devotion." The Great Exhibition seemed to promise the fulfillment of universal progress, ingenuity, prosperity, and peace, merging God's own blessings and bounty with human industry and initiative for the universal benefit and enjoyment of humankind. By the early 1860s, enterprising investors and merchants had translated the magical associations of such vast spaces into a new kind of shopping experience with the advent of the department store, first in Paris with the opening of the Bon Marché in 1869, followed shortly after in the United States with Wanamakers in Philadelphia, and Macys in New York, and then in Britain with Selfridges in London. These large, multi-storied businesses competed with boutiques and other smaller, specialized retail establishments. They also introduced uniform pricing (rather than

promoted by Cole and his group of reformers, the Great Exhibition of 1851 expanded upon earlier national exhibitions of industry in France and created the framework for numerous international exhibitions in the late nineteenth and twentieth centuries both in Europe and in the United

bargaining with merchants), seasonal sales, and a large and diverse inventory of ready-made goods.

The combination of optimism, belief in progress, and materialism seen in the broad public reaction to the Crystal Palace is mirrored in the confident social aspirations of characters in contemporary fiction on both sides of the English Channel. In Honoré de Balzac's *César Birotteau* (1837) the protagonist comes to Paris as a poor provincial with no formal education or connections and rises, through hard work and prudent investment, to become a respected and successful Parisian perfume merchant. Upon being awarded the prestigious medal of the Legion of Honor for his support of the monarchy, César undertakes the expansion and decoration of his apartment with the help of an aspiring architect in order to give a ball celebrating his financial and social achievement. While subsequent investments and speculations bring disaster to César, and demonstrate the unpredictability of both fortune and friendship based upon it, self-improvement and social advancement are portrayed as realistic middle-class aspirations in this nineteenth-century novel.

Popular interest in the Great Exhibition may also be gauged from the proliferation of printed materials in the form of illustrated catalogues, color illustrations issued in series, and smaller scale ephemera in the form of sheet music, note cards, and Christmas cards celebrating the event and printed using the recently-developed process of chromolithography (see page 60).

And yet, while the Great Exhibition may have demonstrated the transformation of the commodity beyond the level of utility, the organizers themselves expressed disappointment in the results, for there was little evidence that public taste had been improved or that standards of design had been widely adopted. The cover page illustration that appeared in the issue of Cole's *Journal of Design* devoted to the exhibition aptly expresses the didactic aspirations of the organizers (fig. 4.8). An allegorical figure of Peace holding a dove stands in front of a globe and is flanked by two kneeling figures—a designer and a craftsman. To her right a well-groomed gentleman, clearly designated as the designer, holds a drawing of a chalice and is surrounded by books. These attributes—in combination with his long stylish hair and long-sleeved tunic, both of which are impediments to physical labor—associate the designer with the fine arts and their inclusion in the liberal arts. In great contrast, the craftsman kneeling opposite him, and

4.8 Cover page for the catalogue of the Great Exhibition, 1851, London, published in *The Journal of Design*.

whose hand he clasps, wears cropped hair and a worker's smock with rolled-up sleeves, and is surrounded by the tools of his trade, including an anvil, and some finished products. The scene suggests that the healthy (if subservient) collaboration between craftsman and artist contributes to global prosperity and peace.

Ralph Wornum, the Keeper of the Queen's Collection of Pictures, won a prize for his essay devoted to the goods on display at the exhibition, published in the *Crystal Palace Illustrated Catalogue*. Wornum expressed his belief, held also by the exhibition's organizers, in the harmony between beauty and utility, and criticized the use of naturalistic flowers and plants for the decoration of carpets and other floor coverings as a violation of fitness to purpose. He further lamented an overabundance of luxury furniture and other products at the expense of less costly examples of good taste directed toward the needs of average middle-class consumers. He was critical as well of the whims of fashion and argued that principles of good taste

4.9 Sideboard, illustrated for the catalogue of the Great Exhibition, London, 1851, manufactured by M. Fourdinois, Paris.

4.10 Carved wall panel, illustrated for the catalogue of the Great Exhibition, London, 1851, manufactured by M. Crutchet.

provided a reliable and permanent foundation for excellence in design. Readers today may be easily mystified by much of Wornum's analysis. For instance, two examples of wood carving illustrated in his essay (figs. 4.9 and 4.10) look similar in their overall rectangular form, two-tiered composition, and abundance of deeply-undercut relief decoration. However, Wornum lauded the former, from a sideboard exhibited by the large and well-known Parisian workshop of Fourdinois, for its use of imagery (the carving symbolized the continents of Europe, Africa, Asia, and America and foods associated with them, appropriately relating the imagery to the function of the piece for serving food); at the same time he condemned the latter carving for being overwrought. Wornum's analysis demonstrates that judging good examples of "art-manufacture," especially if such judgment analyzed furniture for its thematic or literary character, often touched upon the gray or less obvious territory of propriety. Such arguments might well have appeared *too* "elevated" for the

general public to grasp or even care about. Moreover, this kind of criticism ignores the motivations of many middle-class consumers, who looked to commodities not for emblematic meaning nor instruction, but rather for escape and fantasy.

Indeed, public reception to aspects of early design reform was sometimes critical. For his efforts to establish standards for taste through exhibitions and education, Sir Henry Cole was much in the public eye, and was frequently a target of ridicule. In the novel *Hard Times*, which appeared in serial form in 1854, Charles Dickens poked fun at government efforts to impose standards of taste. A commissioner (a thinly veiled portrait of Cole) visits a government-run school and asks the students whether they would use a carpet bearing representations of flowers. A young girl, sent to the school by a well-meaning benefactor, replies that indeed she would, because she is very fond of flowers. But the commissioner sternly asks whether in that case "she would put tables and chairs upon them and have people walking over them with heavy boots". "It wouldn't hurt them, sir—they wouldn't crush and wither if you please, sir. They would be the pictures of what was very pretty and pleasant, I would fancy." But the commissioner replies, "Ay, ay, ay. But you *mustn't* fancy" [italics added]. While the motives behind such regulations were perhaps well-intentioned in a paternalistic sense, Dickens is here defending the democratic freedom of choice as inherently more fundamental than issues of good taste, whether or not it results in excess, sentimentality, and all that we tend to refer to as "kitsch." Dickens effectively used the example of a child to connect the absence of "good taste" with innocence rather than vulgarity or dishonesty.

While critics found examples to support principles of good design and the harmony of beauty and utility, there is generally little acknowledgment of the innovative and even playful qualities found in many objects on display at the Crystal Palace. These include a "Centripetal Spring Armchair" designed in the United States by Thomas E. Warren in 1849 and manufactured by the American Chair Company of Troy, New York. The chair, complete with a rotating seat, is upholstered in velvet and is made from cast iron and wood. It also features eight bent steel strips connected under the seat to a cone-shaped piece in the center to provide a springing mechanism for the seat. The principle was adapted for use in railway carriages and on other forms of transport to absorb the shock of movement, though one can only presume that such innovations would have been criticized by reformers who would have thought the appearance of the cast iron supports far too delicate for the purpose of support (fig. 4.11).

Many of the critics of the Great Exhibition were architects and fine artists. For instance, the German architect and theorist Gottfried Semper (1803–1879), who lived for a time in London and taught at the School of Design there, was dismayed by the uneven quality at the Great Exhibition and compared it with the Tower of Babel. Richard Redgrave arrived at much the same conclusion, writing that "the absence of any fixed principle in ornamental design is most apparent in the Exhibition." Semper, however, was optimistic that the study of its best objects should form the basis of standards that took into consideration the rational use of new materials and techniques, function, and considerations of decoration. Following the opening of the Great Exhibition, Owen

Jones (1809–1874), a designer who also served as an organizer for the exhibition and was an advocate of design reform, wrote that the majority of goods on display demonstrated "novelty without beauty, beauty without intelligence, and all work without faith." One can understand his disappointment, for Jones had spent nearly two decades designing illustrations and decorations for books printed using the most recent developments in chromolithography and color wood-engraving, and had also published examples of decorative patterns based upon drawings from the fourteenth-century Moorish Alhambra palace in Granada, Spain. The plates of Jones's Alhambra volume were intended not as illustrations of a famed site for a travel book, but rather to be didactic models for designers. In spite of his reaction to the Great Exhibition, Jones continued his reform efforts, and in 1856 his *Grammar of Ornament* was published, the most extensive "dictionary" of design standards at that time. The *Grammar of Ornament* contained 100 illustrations printed in color (using the chromolithographic process, see page 60) of patterns based upon both western and non-western examples in media ranging from carpets to ceramic tiles, relief sculpture to illuminated manuscripts. Jones advocated a broad historicism based upon principles (thirty-two in all) that appear at the end of the volume. The principles are related to those established by Pugin from the

4.11 Thomas E. Warren, spring swivel chair, varnished cast iron, varnished steel, wood, velvet upholstery, 42 x 24 x 28 in (107 x 61 x 71 cm), 1849. Vitra Design Museum, Germany.

4.12 Owen Jones, Moresque ornament, from *Grammar of Ornament*, 1856, Private Collection.

study of Gothic architecture, but are applied more widely both geographically and chronologically: "Construction should be decorated. Decoration should never be purposely constructed;" "Flowers or other natural objects should not be used as ornaments, but conventional representations founded upon them sufficiently suggestive to convey the intended image to the mind, without destroying the unity of the object they are employed to decorate. Universally obeyed in the best periods of Art, equally violated when Art declines." *The Grammar of Ornament* went through numerous printings throughout the late nineteenth century, and its approach to ornament and color was adopted for the decoration of buildings during this period. By using a variety of historical examples from different cultures, the *Grammar* suggests the universality of standards

that can form a basis for all designers (fig. 4.12). In addition to advocating the use of models from other periods and cultures, Jones allowed for the possibility of constructing original patterns based upon the study of nature tempered by the rules he enumerated. The British designer Christopher Dresser (1834–1904) contributed original plates to the *Grammar* featuring ornamental shapes based upon leaf and floral motifs in a style that simplified organic forms into flattened linear contours. Dresser was a student at the London School of Design and collaborated successfully with manufacturers in creating a number of novel designs for industrial production. During his career, along with other contemporary artist- and architect-designers, Dresser attempted to extend the reformers' standards by advocating greater originality in

4.13 Charles Eastlake, example of wallpaper design from *Hints on Household Taste*, 1868.

4.14 Carpet, Messrs. Turberville Smith, London, from the catalogue of the Great Exhibition, 1851.

pattern design and greater invention in the treatment of historical styles, including Japanese design, which he became interested in during the 1860s.

Another British designer to follow Jones's example was Charles Eastlake (1836–1906), whose *Hints on Household Taste in Furniture, Upholstery, and Other Details* was published in 1868. Eastlake criticized the lack of discrimination in matters of design, but his prose focuses less upon the moral and social dimensions of design than upon principles of design as a sign of cultivated middle-class taste and a vehicle for self-improvement:

> We require no small amount of art and instruction and experience to see why direct imitation of natural objects is wrong in ornamental design. The quasi-

fidelity with which the forms of a rose, or a bunch of ribbons, or a ruined castle, can be produced on carpets, crockery and wallpapers will always possess a certain kind of charm for the uneducated eye, just as the mimicry of natural sounds in music, from the rolling of thunder to the crackling of poultry, will always delight the vulgar ear. Both are ingenious and amusing but neither lie within the legitimate province of art.

A comparison of one of Eastlake's wallpaper designs (fig. 4.13), manufactured by Jeffery & Company and appearing in *Hints*, with the printed or woven designs at the Great Exhibition (fig. 4.14) clarifies the restraint and principles of "convention" or schema underlying design reform.

4·15 James Burns, drawings printed from woodblocks,
6 x 8 in (152 x 208 mm), *Nursery Rhymes, Tales, and Jingles*, 1844.

Images for All

An entrepreneurial spirit, coupled with production technology and the gradual elimination of taxes on paper and printed materials, helped to create the circumstances for the success of illustrated weekly journals aimed at an emerging mass-market, including working people, that reached a circulation in Britain of over 200,000 copies by the middle of the nineteenth century. In this climate the role of the arts took on a certain added value. One of the earliest examples of this type of affordable illustrated journals is *The Penny Magazine* (beginning in 1832), published by Charles Knight (1791–1873), who began his career as a craftsman and printer. Knight is known for his development of an economical method for producing color images from multiple engraved wood blocks. *The Penny Magazine* contained reproductions of works of art (part of an emerging "canon" of masterpieces) whose subject matter was intended to provide examples of personal and social virtue. Knight's venture was endorsed by the Society

for the Distribution of Useful Knowledge, whose membership supported the role of the arts as a civilizing force in Victorian society. Knight's magazine was joined by other weekly journals, often called miscellanies that included examples of decorative art. While a painting's narrative might provide edifying models of behavior, the decorative arts could convey through form and decoration a balance between beauty and utility, or even individual and community, thus serving the moral as well as physical needs of society. In addition to Knight's didactic messages, the miscellanies also featured illustrations accompanying popular serialized and sensationalized fiction dealing with crime, intrigue, sex, and the occult. Illustrations and fiction that encouraged self-improvement, restraint, temperance, and social harmony co-existed with the broader commercial appeal of aberrant behavior, escapism, and political radicalism—a rich and diverse combination best characterized by the term "popular culture."

Aside from lithography, other methods of satisfying a growing demand for black-and-white as well as color illustrations for reproduction in books, magazines, advertisements, and newspapers were developed during the first half of the nineteenth century. Owing to the efforts of printer Thomas Bewick of Newcastle-upon-Tyne (1753–1828), the technique of producing woodblocks by cutting with engraving tools against rather than with the wood grain produced greater precision and tonal range in the depiction of subtle textures and three-dimensional form. Prior to the invention of the half-tone photomechanical process, wood engravers worked directly from blocks printed with photographs.

Fine detail was also achieved beginning in the 1820s using a process that created steel-engraved plates, replacing previously used copper plates. The surface of steel plates was more durable than copper—greater numbers of printings could be run on a steel plate with minimal loss of quality. Steel plates also offered more precision when printing large quantities of thin lines to suggest subtle gradations of tone in relief. The method, developed in the United States by Jacob Perkins (1766–1849), was particularly effective in the creation of plates for postage stamps and paper currency, where their complexity made counterfeiting more difficult.

English printers such as Charles Whittingham, Joseph Cundall, and Henry Shaw were knowledgeable in

4.16 H. Noel Humphreys, from *The Miracles of Our Lord*, chromolithograph in about 12 colors, 6 ½ x 4 ½ in (165 x 114 cm), 1848.

all phases of book production, and combined a respect for craft with the benefits of new techniques of mechanical reproduction. Whittingham worked in collaboration with the publisher Thomas Pickering at the Chiswick Press in a London suburb for the publication of a number of titles, adhering to the highest standards of typography, illustration, layout, and binding (though generally on cardboard rather than more expensive leather). Whittingham and other book printers rejected more modern typefaces with their stronger contrast of thick and thin strokes (more common in the nineteenth century for larger display types) and returned to more traditional faces derived from William Caslon (see pages 25–6 and fig. 1.9). Many printers took an avid interest in illustrated books for children, printed from wood engravings in both black and white as well as color. The firm of Robson, Levey & Franklyn published James Burns' *Nursery Rhymes Tales and Jingles* in 1844, using Caslon types, rustic frames sometimes hung with vines, and wood-engraved illustrations (fig. 4.15). The asymmetrical yet balanced relationship between framed text and illustration provided both consistency and variety from poem to poem, and suggested a desire to create designs that were visually appealing to young readers. Other contemporary publishers were more lavish in the use and variety of decoration and typefaces. This is most evident in the title pages of contemporary fiction that often appeared in serialized form. George Routledge (1812–1888) of London published a series of novels known as the "Railway Library," presumably meant for reading while traveling and a forerunner of paperback fiction that, along with the daily news, occupies commuters on today's suburban trains and airlines. The cost of most illustrated books was generally beyond the means of working people. But the appeal of stories told with pictures, before the widespread popularity of photography and the advent of film (and later of television) was great, and was satisfied through the less expensive illustrated broadsides and weekly journals such as *The Penny Magazine*.

Images in popular weekly journals and broadsheets were printed in black-and-white. But concurrently with these strictly tonal processes, a significant development in color printing, known as chromolithography, was taking place. Patented in the 1830s by Godefroy Engelmann (1788–1839) in France, the new technology quickly spread to England, Germany, and the United States. Chromolithography produced images in color using a series of stones, each inked with a different color and printed in succession using exact registration of the paper. The process, as perfected in England by William Savage (1770–1843), was used initially for the accurate color reproduction of paintings for expensive, high-quality illustrated books beginning in the 1840s.

A number of early books with illustrations produced by chomolithography were facsimile editions of manuscripts such as the ninth-century Hiberno-Saxon Gospel book known as the *Book of Kells*. Others were private prayer books meant to rival their older medieval counterparts, such as H. Noel Humphrey's chromolithographed plates for *The Miracles of Our Lord* published in 1848 (fig. 4.16).

In the late nineteenth century, the chromolithographic process was adopted for the color printing of popular greeting cards and souvenirs. Early examples are the souvenirs printed for the 1851 Great Exhibition in London. These prints show the cast-iron and glass structure and give a sense, in "living" color, of the festival-like atmosphere of the event (see above, fig. 4.7). The application of chromolithography to trade, business cards, and advertising (often a giveaway inside a product box) would soon follow, and be especially popular in the United States.

Popular Graphics in the United States

Illustrated weekly magazines were also popular in the United States, beginning in the 1850s with the publication of *Leslie's Weekly* and *Harper's Weekly* in New York. *Harper's Weekly* covered contemporary events and used the process of wood engraving to reproduce drawings by a number of artists who served as visual reporters, recording events based upon first-hand observations. The artist Winslow Homer (1836–1910), for instance, supported himself early in his career by documenting battles of the American Civil War for *Harper's Weekly*. Another illustrator for Harper's was Thomas Nast (1840–1902), a gifted draughtsman whose family moved to New York from Germany in 1846.

As a young man Nast traveled at Harper's expense to Europe to cover a prizefight in Britain, as well as Garibaldi's military campaigns to create the nation of modern Italy in 1860–61; he was also sent on assignment to report first-hand on some of the events of the American Civil War. But Nast was increasingly interested in shaping public opinion through illustrations aimed at a broad readership. In addition to documenting actual events, he illustrated general themes relating to the Civil War and to war in general that had tremendous popular appeal. One of numerous examples, *Christmas Furlough* (fig. 4.17) appeared in late 1863 during the second full year of the Civil War. The design consists of several separately titled and framed scenes set against a background suggestive of a winter landscape. The focus is upon a returning officer visiting his wife and family, with all of the safe, reassuring associations of a homecoming. The theme is reinforced by Nast's composition and use of light. Our attention is drawn immediately to the pyramidal unit formed by the embracing couple in the center vignette. In a smaller vignette to the left, a warm glow of light envelops sleeping children, enhancing the homespun ambiance.

Frequently carefully staged and employing compositions dependent upon the western tradition of religious and historical painting, Nast's approach to drawing often emphasized bold tonal contrast and a reduced interest in detailed description. His original drawings were translated into the medium of the engraved wood block by other artisans. Nast popularized the use of human and animal figures such as Uncle Sam, Columbia, the Republican party Elephant and the Democratic party Donkey as metaphors for collective entities or concepts, seen for instance in his 1865 reaction to the death of President Abraham Lincoln in a somber image entitled *Columbia Mourns* (fig. 4.18). Nast was responsible for introducing the familiar image of Santa Claus as a kind if slightly mischievous white-bearded man delivering gifts to children through the chimney on Christmas Eve, an image he based on the Germanic folklore he knew from his early childhood. Yet another aspect of Nast's output was political cartoons that made use of exaggeration or caricature. While Nast certainly had precursors who used caricature as a tool of political change, and may have borrowed from them, the combination of effective images and an inexpensive vehicle for circulation gave a new power to the role of illustration. Public officials feared Nast's pen and were well aware

4.17 Thomas Nast, *Christmas Furlough* from *Harper's Weekly*, December, 1863.

of his ability to influence opinion against greed and corruption. The most celebrated of his campaigns was directed against a high-ranking official of the New York City local government, William "Boss" Tweed, from 1869 to 1871. With both *Harper's Weekly* and the *New York Times* supporting the reform of city government, Tweed and his so-called "Ring" were indicted on charges of fraud, bribery, and corruption, and in time the reign of the "Ring" came to an end, in no small measure due to the role played by the popular press and Nast's cartoons. Weekly journals such as *Harper's*, and editors such as Fletcher Harper, who supported freedom of expression through the popular press, helped give significance to the emerging profession of illustration—one that continued to be a vehicle for public discourse, as well as finding new arenas for expression in advertising and in narrative images accompanying adventure stories and other children's books.

The efforts of chromolithographic printers in the United States in the field of color reproduction were even more enterprising and widespread than their European counterparts. Louis Prang (1824–1909) was a German-born printer who emigrated to Boston before 1850 and, using the painstaking methods of other experimenters in

4.18 Thomas Nast, *Columbia Mourns* from *Harper's Weekly*, April, 1865.

the field such as William Savage in Britain, produced a wide range of chromolithographic reproductions of paintings that were distributed in albums or individually. Marketed as "chromos," such prints satisfied a demand for works of art among the middle class, tied to the desire for

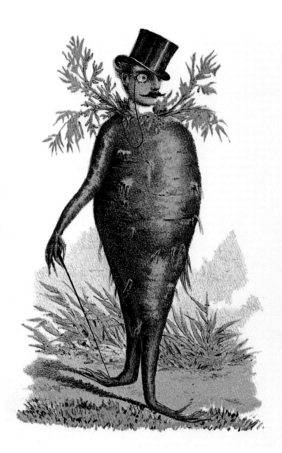

4.19 Trade card, chromolithograph, Louis Prang Publishing, Boston, Massachusetts.

4.20 Trade card, *Mrs. Winslow's Soothing Syrup*, chromolithograph, Louis Prang Publishing, Boston, Massachusetts.

social progress through education and the cultivation of taste. Prang extended his market by printing small popular color images for a variety of new purposes, including trade cards, advertising cards, and "decalcomania" that people cut out and pasted on pieces of paper to exchange notes and greetings. Beginning in the 1850s, color images on decals and cards were reproduced on large sheets that were cut and sold separately in packaged sets. Their initial success soon led to their application on product labels, eventually leading to the proliferation of advertising images that would characterize the broad public experience of the urban scene in the late nineteenth century. Examples range from bizarre anthropomorphic carrots, corncobs, and peapods (fig. 4.19) recalling the type of playful invention sometimes seen in medieval decorated

initials, to scenes of ideal families, enjoying the benefits of products designed for self-improvement. Such persuasive techniques, which became more common in the 1920s, are seen in the advertising card depicting a carefree mother and child whose happiness is connected with alleviating the annoyance of normal teething (fig. 1.57). Chromolithography was also extensively used on a large scale for advertising posters in the later nineteenth century (see pages 86–7 and figs. 5.29 and 5.30).

A Balance Sheet of Reform

Early design reformers sought to identify and apply universal standards to manufactured commodities, based upon the study of examples from history and other cultures, or upon principles derived from architecture and engineering. These efforts were political in nature, in that the reformers attempted to claim as universal a rather narrow set of criteria and felt a responsibility to educate, and hence convince manufacturers and a growing consumer public to accept such criteria. And the effort was epistemological as well, for it was grounded in a belief that laws underlie all spheres of human endeavor, from mathematics and the physical sciences to the application of ornament on household goods. Such views ignored the fact that the tastes of new manufacturers and classes of consumers might be dictated by a different set of assumptions—particularly their relation to social aspirations, and to issues of identity and individuality. The reform agenda also did not sufficiently recognize the sheer excitement and flow of imagination stemming from experiments with new processes and the promise they held for commercial expansion. It has been argued that those who lamented the spectacle of decorative variety and ostentation among the middle class were seeking to perpetuate not only traditional tastes but also a conservative social system based upon the well-meaning but exclusive preferences of a small, dominant elite. In this view the advocacy for standards in design in the mid-nineteenth century is seen as the polarization of conflicting and competing attitudes toward the nature of fashion and taste in the eighteenth century, expressed in more polemic and public terms.

And yet such exclusivity, conservatism, and elitism can hardly be reconciled with the genuine efforts to include a meaningful role for invention and application in production and materials technology, for instance, in the development of chromolithography. Nor does it fully account for the interest in and incorporation of the art of non-western cultures, or a recognition of some degree of heterogeneity and the diverse nature of a popular culture. Significantly, the standards developed by the early design reformers would show an ability to adapt to changing attitudes concerning the fine arts. Indeed, the search for standards seems in many ways a natural tendency during any great period of change, and consistently so in the history of modern design. Whether they are standards for decoration, utility, performance, or safety, a desire for regulations and commonality has continued amid the expansion of design and been part of the dialogue of the social, esthetic, and technical issues relating to it.

Conclusion

> So if one seeks to understand it [society], one must realize that it embodies at one and the same time everything that it has been, is, and will be in future; it is an accumulation over the long term of permanent features and successive inflections.

So wrote French historian Fernand Braudel concerning the social order roughly from the fifteenth to the eighteenth centuries. Braudel's words might be applied as well to the history of modern design: both what it had been and much of what it was to become are embedded in the complex interplay of changes in the technology of production and the social dynamics of consumption in the eighteenth and early nineteenth centuries.

Clearly the task of design, whether the contribution of patron, artist, mercer, or entrepreneur, was distinguished from, as well as related *to*, the work of craftsmen, and resulted from increasing complexity in the process of production and the growth of demand. Consumption effectively blurred lines between social classes, while novelty became a means for manufacturers to attract an expanding market with the promise of social distinction. In short, this phenomenon, seen increasingly with changes in production technology, is both an expression of the democratization of culture as well as the *commodification* of the Romantic cult of individualism. These elements, along with their contradictory natures, all appear in the course of the eighteenth century, and provide a useful basis for examining the full-blown expansion of the industrial revolution in the successive decades of the nineteenth century, and the calls for reform that would inevitably follow it.

Perhaps the central issue to emerge during the first half of the nineteenth century is the apparent conflict between technology, commercialization, and democratization on the one hand, all of which signify change and a state of flux, and the search for standards on the other, the need to regulate change through the application of principles that might stand beyond the whims of fashion, the desire for profits, and the innovations of industry. It is in this context that early design reform can be placed. Although the forms and function of decoration may have been the battleground for the proponents of design reform, such debates were part of a broad effort to educate, or rather to indoctrinate, an expanding, and potentially threatening public.

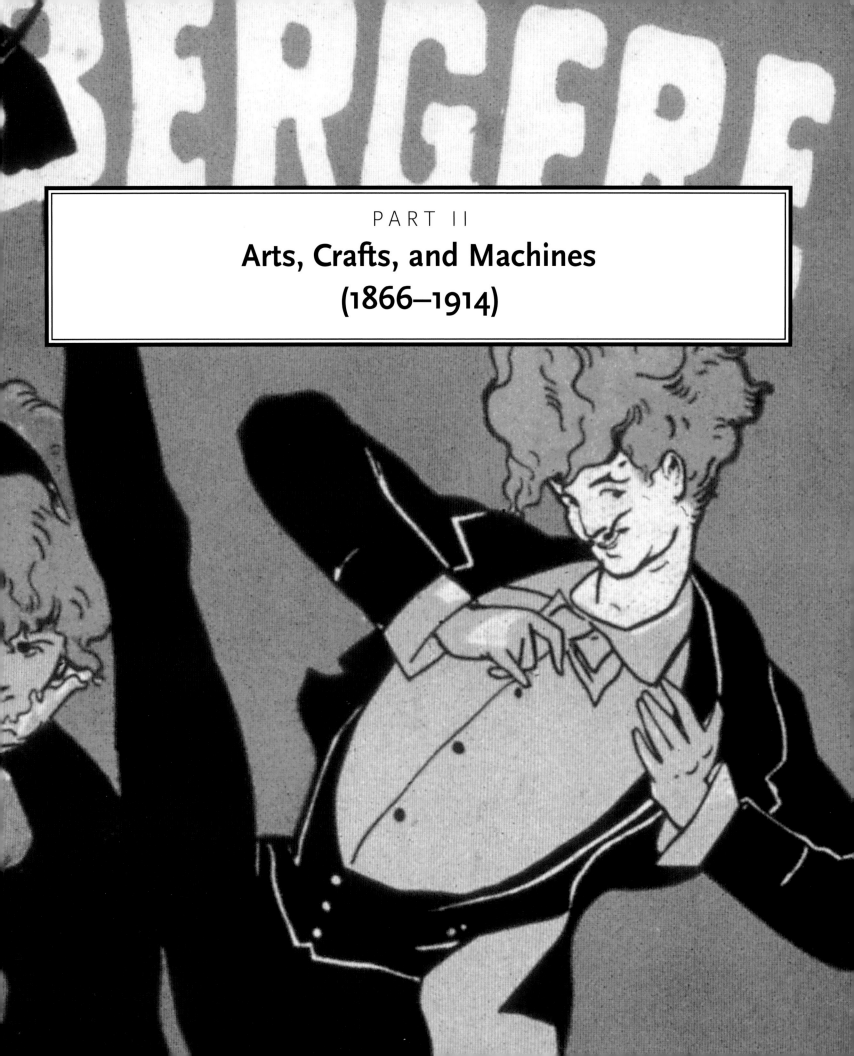

PART II
Arts, Crafts, and Machines
(1866–1914)

Introduction

In the second half of the nineteenth century the activities of the early design reform movement dovetailed with other reform initiatives both in Europe and in the United States in raising awareness of the importance of the applied arts. In Britain a number of architects and fine artists became increasingly involved in many aspects of interior design and decoration, the effect of which was to call attention to the esthetic and expressive aspects of the applied arts and to emphasize the unity and integration of all the visual arts. Such efforts usually centered upon the domestic setting and the cultivation of a private, often meditative taste. At the same time a number of younger designers sought to consider issues of manufacturability and to form organizations and publish journals to promote links to the craft industries. The activities of these individuals and associations played a part in the increasing number of well-attended international exhibitions both in Europe and in the United States, and the success of the department store beginning in the 1860s served to stimulate the manufacture and marketing of the products of design to an expanding consumer-oriented middle class. In the United States printed advertising and mail-order catalogues with illustrations in the 1880s also spurred demand for manufactured goods and furnishings and were accompanied by new initiatives in methods of rationalized and mechanized production, culminating in the moving assembly line of Henry Ford for the production of the Model T automobile in the early twentieth century.

Beginning in the later 1850s in Britain, the writings of John Ruskin and the activities of William Morris placed the issues of design and production within a new ethical framework based upon an almost religious attitude linking craft, art, and social reform. Ruskin and Morris criticized the dehumanizing aspects of mechanization and the increasing division of labor in factories, and their ideas formed the basis of workshops and crafts organizations on both sides of the Atlantic dedicated to the social benefits of handicraft. Finally, with Germany playing a primary role, design organizations, schools, and exhibitions sought to reconcile what were seen as conflicting attitudes towards uniformity, standardization, and the scientific management of production on the one hand and individuality on the other, working to establish rational and socially responsible forms for modern mass-produced goods aimed at middle-class consumers. Amid the various debates and activities, the esthetic, commercial, and social roles of the applied arts provided expanded possibilities and meanings for the activities of design in the years leading up to World War I.

Chapter 5

The Equality of the Arts

5.1 Christopher Dresser, *Leaves and Flowers from Nature, no. 8*, color lithograph, from *The Grammar of Ornament*, Owen Jones.

Design Reform and the Aesthetic Movement

An introduction to new attitudes toward the decorative arts emerging in England in the second half of the nineteenth century might begin with the career of designer Christopher Dresser, who contributed original plates to Owen Jones's *The Grammar of Ornament* featuring design motifs based upon leaf and floral forms in a style that simplified organic forms into flattened shapes defined by crisp contours (fig. 5.1). Dresser's background as a student at the London School of Design and his interest in the

collaboration of designer and manufacturer demonstrate his strong ties to design reform and education, but the originality of his designs, early interest in the craft traditions of Japan, and his views regarding the expressive meaning of pattern and decoration, all suggest a more individual orientation for the artist–designer as well as a more active role for the designer in the process of manufacture.

Rather than concern with historicism or the appropriateness of representational decorative forms in relation to use, Dresser concentrated upon the transformation of naturalistic motifs into expressive pattern and on the

for feet and brackets for handles. Dresser was inspired by examples of native metalwork he had seen during a trip to Japan in 1866–7, and his designs for metalwork were praised at the time for their originality in comparison with contemporary work featuring naturalistic relief decoration produced either by casting or other traditional craft techniques. Although the lack of decoration and elementary geometry of Dresser's work for the Dixon Company anticipates the early twentieth-century concern with product "types" designed for mechanized mass-production, Dresser's work was aimed at a discerning middle-class audience, and the great variation of shapes, materials, decoration, and surfaces suggest that his concerns were more esthetic and cultural than economical. Nevertheless, his designs for simple metal objects share characteristics with the handcrafted furniture of social reformers whose issues are discussed in greater depth below. To summarize, Dresser's oeuvre is far from limited to concerns with simplicity and utility, and includes expression, originality, *as well as* an interest in issues such as interchangeability and the reduction of handwork in the manufacturing process.

5.2 Christopher Dresser, earthenware plate with partial glazing, *c.* 1872, manufactured by Watcombe Pottery Company, England.

integration of ornament with existing methods of workshop manufacture. A decorated ceramic serving plate of 1872, manufactured by the Watcombe Pottery Company and attributed to Dresser (fig. 5.2) illustrates his approach to design. Its composition is a lively yet balanced play of triangular and circular shapes, related harmoniously to the form of the plate and abstracted from a variety of plant forms. The Watcombe plate follows Owen Jones's prescription for schematic or conventionalized natural forms to decorate flat surfaces and the design conforms to the shape of the field to be decorated. It also emphasizes invention based upon a fascination with nature and its creative transformation as decoration.

Dresser also designed numerous examples of metalwork, including tea sets, toast racks, and other serving dishes and utensils. The striking series of electroplated silver tea sets designed for the Dixon Company of Sheffield and other manufacturers beginning in 1879 (fig. 5.3) emphasize the purity of the material's smooth surface, and include the use of identical inverted cone-shaped parts

5.3 Christopher Dresser, silver-plate designs from the costing book of James Dixon and Sons Limited, *c.* 1879. Sheffield, England.

Dresser's interest in the decorative arts of Japan, and the originality of his designs and patterns are characteristic of the work of a number of artists and architects for whom the unity and equality of the arts emerged as a provocative concept pointing to directions and new possibilities for their activities. The term Aesthetic Movement was often used to refer to these activities which were labeled as such during the 1870s and 1880s and even satirized in the British periodical *Punch* and in forms of popular entertainment such as Gilbert and Sullivan's operetta *Patience* (1881). The importance of this movement to the history of modern design can hardly be underestimated, since it succeeded in shaping the attitudes of artists, manufacturers, and wealthy consumers toward the decorative arts. The Aesthetic Movement may be seen both as an outgrowth of early design reform while at the same time moving from a preoccupation with standards and paternalism toward a reconsideration of the sources of inspiration, materials, processes, and subjective meaning. Designers associated with the movement adopted a freer and more individual approach to historical styles, and greater freedom in their use of materials and decoration. They also explored the expressive dimension of the decorative arts and advocated for equality between the fine and applied arts. Their efforts were marketed through a series of international exhibitions in London (1862), Vienna (1873), Paris (1867, 1878, 1889, and 1900), Brussels (1897), Turin (1902), and in the United States (Philadelphia in 1876, Chicago in 1893), illustrated journals, and by the opening of new shops or *boutiques* specializing in contemporary crafts and interior design.

The painter James Abbott McNeill Whistler (1834–1903) is regarded as one of the leading figures of the Aesthetic Movement in Britain. As an American-born painter who studied in Paris and resided in London beginning in 1859, Whistler's involvement with interior design, seen for instance in the painted decoration and easel painting he contributed to the design of the Peacock Room in the London home of the Liverpool industrialist F. R. Leyland in 1876 (now in the Freer Gallery in Washington, D. C.), asserted his belief in the equality of the arts. The room (fig. 5.4) was designed by architect Thomas Jeckyll to house Mr. Leyland's collection of Chinese porcelain. Its shelves, hanging globe lanterns, ceiling coffers and rectangular-backed chairs are unified through a shared rectilinear vocabulary consisting primarily of rectangles and

hexagons. The severity of the décor was balanced by the collection of blue and white porcelain placed originally on the shelves. Leyland also purchased a painting by Whistler for the room. Entitled *Princess in the Land of Porcelain*, the canvas depicted a young female figure wearing a Japanese kimono and was hung above the fireplace. The artist also contributed to the elaborate design of the interior by painting delicate undulating, asymmetrical wavy lines in gold on the paneling and cabinets. He also painted peacocks on the door screens on one side of the room, added without the owner's permission. Whistler demanded remuneration for the additional work, and Leyland's refusal to pay led to a dispute between the two men. In time Leyland agreed to pay one-half of Whistler's fee, but insulted the artist further by paying him with a check written for pounds, the currency of trade, rather than guineas, the currency generally exchanged for the work of artists and professionals.

British writer and critic Oscar Wilde (1854–1900), a vocal proponent of the Aesthetic Movement, articulated the attitudes that informed the creation of such exotic and personal interior spaces as the Peacock Room. In a passage from his essay "The Artist as Critic" (1891), Wilde recognized the expressive content of abstract form in the

5.4 James McNeill Whistler, *Harmony in Blue and Gold: The Peacock Room* for the Frederic Leyland House, oil paint and metal leaf on canvas, leather and wood, 1876. Courtesy of the Freer Gallery of Art, Smithsonian Institution, Washington D.C.

decorative arts and acknowledged the possibilities of their newly elevated status:

> The art that is frankly decorative is the art to live with. It is, of all visible arts, the one art that creates in us both mood and temperament. Mere colour, unspoiled by meaning, and unallied with definite form, can speak to the soul in a thousand different ways. The harmony that resides in the delicate proportions of lines and masses becomes mirrored in the mind ... The marvels of design stir the imagination ... By its deliberate rejection of Nature as the ideal of beauty, as well as of the imitative method of the ordinary painter, decorative art not merely prepares the soul for the reception of true imaginative work, but develops in it that sense of form which is the basis of creative no less than of critical achievement.

Dresser's comments on the design for a pattern from his 1862 book *The Art of Decorative Design*, although written in a more analytical style of prose, evoke much of the same spirit as Wilde's essay on the expressive content of the applied arts:

> I have sought to embody chiefly the idea of power, energy, force, or vigour; and in order to do this I have employed such lines as we see in the bursting buds of spring, when the energy of growth is at its maximum ... I have also availed myself of those forms to be seen in certain bones of birds which are associated with the organs of flight, and which give us an impression of great strength.

The Peacock Room and other furnishings and interiors of the period demonstrate an affinity for Japanese art shared by many adherents to the Aesthetic Movement in Britain. Dresser traveled to Japan and lectured widely on the art of that country, praising both the quality and character of Japanese craft as well as the religious significance of Japanese design. After the opening of trade with Japan in 1852, artistic and commercial interest in the country was stimulated by objects brought to Britain by its first official representative Sir Rutherford Alcock, by a Japanese Court at the London International Exhibition of 1862, and by the acquisition of a collection of Japanese objects by the South Kensington Museum in the early 1870s. In 1875

collector and merchant Arthur Lazenby Liberty (1843–1917) opened a shop in London featuring Japanese craft, while the more popular interest in Japan was demonstrated by the success of another Gilbert and Sullivan operetta entitled *The Mikado* (1885). Many of these activities influenced attitudes toward design and the decorative arts in Europe and in the United States. Japan offered collectors and European artists and designers a tradition that valued the decorative arts and the creativity of the artisan. In his book *The Traditional Arts and Crafts of Japan* (1882), Dresser wrote extensively on the practice of Japanese craft, and observed the esteem accorded to skilled artisans:

> I cannot help thinking that the Japanese are right in regarding the man who can make a beautiful pot, a lovely cabinet, a charming fabric, or a perfect netsuki as a being superior to the mere buyer and seller of goods; for while the one denotes his best energies to mere money-making, the other ennobles matter by the impress of his mind, love, intelligence, and skill ...

It was, at least in part, the high regard for craft in Japan that allowed artists and artisans greater freedom in drawing, permitting them, in the famous art-historian Sir Ernst Gombrich's words, to "break the rules," for instance in the uneven spacing of motifs applied to surface decoration or in the irregular forms and textures of ceramic vessels. Designers such as E. W. Godwin (1833–1886) rarely imitated Japanese furniture directly but used the lattice forms depicted in Japanese colored woodblock prints to create an Anglo-Japanese style as in an intricately constructed buffet (fig. 5.5) made of ebonized wood and intended for the display of ceramic wares. Godwin's buffet is severely geometric, composed of a variety of rectangular solids and voids relieved only by triangular supports for shelves and legs and circular fittings of silver. Neither wood nor metal components are carved, though the materials and construction are costly and the simplicity, like that of Dresser's electroplated teapots, represents a new appreciation of esthetic purity rather than an interest in efficient production or savings in cost.

Designs produced under the Aesthetic Movement included but were not limited to original adaptations of Japanese style or pattern decoration as seen in Godwin or Dresser. As we have seen, Dresser's overriding interest was in the expressive character and practical applications

5.5 E. W. Godwin, buffet, ebonized mahogany and inset panels of embossed Japanned leather paper, 102 ¼ x 157 in (260 x 399 cm), manufactured by William Watt, *c*. 1867. Victoria and Albert Museum, London.

historicism and incorporation of original patterns, such art furniture not only proclaimed the individuality of the designer but also exhibited both a freedom and inventiveness associated with the creative activity of painters and sculptors.

Recognizing increasingly commercial circumstances in their profession, artists were eager to enter the market for decorative arts as designers and broaden the sphere of their activities. Aesthetic furniture was in most cases directed toward a wealthy clientele, and the manufacturers for these products, such as Watt, Gillow, or Collinson & Lock, were willing to produce items from artists' designs for display at international exhibitions in major European cities as well as in the United States (Philadelphia, 1876). Art furniture was marketed as well through entrepreneurs and collectors such as Liberty in London, and later Samuel Bing (1838–1905) and Julius Meier-Graefe (1867–1935) in Paris (see page 87).

Another form of marketing was the studio. Artists such as Whistler were known for the design of the interiors in their own homes and studios, at least in part to draw the attention of potential clients or patrons of their work. Another well-known painter with an interest in cultivating

of a variety of botanical forms. Godwin also drew freely from other traditions in creating original forms for a variety of interior furnishings. He collaborated, for instance, with Whistler on the interior design of the painter's apartment in London known as White House, and on a display for the furniture-maker William Watt at the 1878 International Exposition in Paris.

Other designers linked to the movement, including Charles Eastlake and Bruce Talbert (1838–81), turned to the Gothic style as advocated by Pugin or to the solid forms of the seventeenth century in what is known as the Queen Anne revival, approaches that were also in keeping with the harmony of beauty and utility adopted by the early design reformers. Eastlake's designs achieved popularity through their publication in his *Hints on Household Taste*: as mentioned in Part I, while Eastlake's standards in design were linked to reform, his concerns were more esthetic and lacked the moral or political component of zealots such as Pugin or Cole. A cabinet by Talbert (fig. 5.6), dating probably to the 1870s, is rectilinear in overall construction but allows ample opportunity for elaborate decoration in the panels, using complex techniques of marquetry. With its self-conscious adaptation of

5.6 Bruce James Talbert, cabinet, walnut with ebonized turnings, 58½ x 65½ x 20 ½ in (148.6 x 166.4 x 52.1 cm), manufactured by Gillow and Company. Art Institute of Chicago.

5.7 Walter Crane, frieze for the Arab Hall of Lord Leighton's house, 1877–79. Leighton House, London.

the importance of the decorative arts was Lord Frederic Leighton (1830–1896), who also served as President of the Royal Academy of Art and was made a peer in 1896. Leighton's house in Kensington was built from 1878 to 1880 and contains a two-storey Arab Hall combining Islamic tiles with contemporary examples of tiles designed by Walter Crane (1845–1915) and William de Morgan

(1839–1917). Both of these artists contributed to the flowering of the decorative arts in the later nineteenth century, Crane as a designer and illustrator, and de Morgan as a craftsman devoted to the art of ceramics (fig. 5.7). Leighton was also responsible for a large mural painting in one of the hallways of the Victoria and Albert Museum, an endeavor that realized Sir Henry Cole's dream for a major

5.8 Frederick, Lord Leighton, *The Industrial Arts as Applied to Peace*, cartoon for mural. Victoria and Albert Museum, London.

facility to house collections primarily devoted to the decorative arts and welcoming London's working people. The mural bears the title *The Industrial Arts as Applied to Peace* (a small sketch hangs in Leighton House). The subject is reminiscent of the didactic aims of early design reform, but this idealizing work depicts a group of Athenian maidens trying on clothing and jewelry while muscular workmen transport ceramic containers and rolled-up woven carpets that have recently arrived by boat! Peace is here defined presumably by the absence of conflict as well as by the women's enjoyment of the benefits of leisure spent adorning themselves with exquisitely crafted objects (fig. 5.8). The value of the decorative arts is seen here less in relation to standards of taste or general material progress than to the cultivation of private esthetic experience and personal luxury.

The Aesthetic Movement in the United States

In the United States numerous products of "Aesthetic" design, as well as a pavilion devoted to Japanese art, were on view at the 1876 Centennial Exhibition in Philadelphia. Five years later Oscar Wilde made a lecture tour of major American cities where he commented upon new attitudes toward the decorative arts. Institutions such as the Metropolitan Museum of Art began to add examples of contemporary furniture and other decorative objects for the home to their collections in an effort to elevate public taste, and schools and societies promoting the study and practice of the decorative arts thrived in a number of American cities. In the last quarter of the nineteenth century, American artists turned to the design and manufacture of stained glass and metalwork, achieving

5.9 John La Farge, *Peonies Blown in the Wind*, leaded opalescent glass, 75 x 45 in (190.5 x 113.7 cm), from the Marquand House, Newport, Rhode Island, *c.* 1880. Metropolitan Museum of Art, New York.

5.10 Louis Comfort Tiffany, "Waterlily" table lamp, bronze and leaded Favrille glass, 26 ½ x 18 ½ in (67 x 47 cm), 1904–15, manufactured by Tiffany Studios. Metropolitan Museum of Art, New York.

considerable success at home and exerting influence abroad. In the field of stained glass especially, Americans John La Farge (1835–1910) and Louis Comfort Tiffany (1848–1933) received numerous commissions for their work—mostly from private patrons but also occasionally from public institutions. Both men were painters and received training in Paris before turning to the decorative arts (La Farge studied and practiced law before becoming an artist). The new status of the decorative arts as well as the opportunities for commissions in relation to architecture influenced Tiffany, who wrote, "I believe there is more in it [i.e. the decorative arts] than in painting pictures." After establishing his own company for interior decoration in 1879, Tiffany became artistic director for the company founded by his father, Charles Tiffany, which

manufactured objects in silver and other metals. Both Tiffany and La Farge experimented with new materials and techniques to achieve subtle coloristic effects in their works, Tiffany introducing "favrile" glass in 1892 for bowls and vases, and La Farge developing "opalescent" glass for windows. The varied colors and surfaces of La Farge's opalescent glass enriched the iridescence of his windows, producing an effect that resembled the thick impasto of oil paint (fig. 5.9). Tiffany's windows achieve the same richness, but the designer also reached beyond unique commissions to produce a variety of vases and other objects aimed at a wider audience eager to appreciate the rich esthetic effects of a vase or lamp with cast bronze base. In an electric lamp (fig. 5.10) manufactured between 1904 and 1915, the rust and yellow colors of stalks and leaves dominate a few remaining touches of pale green suggesting an autumnal mood. This mood is echoed not only in the drooping and "tired" curves of the stalks but also on the fallen leaves and petals casually strewn on the base. The subtlety of effect in color, the close relationship between form, techniques of construction, and decoration, the lack of reference to "period" styles, as well as in the expressive unity of the whole, mark the high level of interest in the decorative arts in the United States during this time and express the aspirations of the

5.11 Glass flasks, 14 x 7 ⅛ in (36 x 19 cm), 14 x 4 ⁵⁄₁₆ in (36 x 11 cm), and 12 ⁵⁄₁₆ x 4 ⁵⁄₁₆ in (34 x 11 cm), Persian, *c.* 1885. Victoria and Albert Museum, London.

5.12 Louis Comfort Tiffany, Favrille glass vase, 13 ¾ x 3 in (35 x 8 cm), manufactured by Tiffany Studios, 1896–1900. Brooklyn Museum, New York.

movement to achieve equality among the arts. In addition to inventive experiments with techniques and materials, Tiffany was inspired by a variety of non-western traditions. For example, he was influenced by glass flasks from Persia, both in terms of their translucence and their irregular and asymmetrical shapes (figs. 5.11 and 5.12).

In 1895 Tiffany was asked to design and execute two glass domes for the new Chicago Public Library on Michigan Avenue. The commission included a dome for the large reading room to the front of the building, as well as a second large dome for a room serving as a memorial to soldiers who had died in the Civil War. The glass dome of the larger reading room rises on pendentives from white marble piers covered with mosaic tiles. The color scheme of green, gray, and white is cool, and the overall impression is bright and radiant. Tiffany seems to have been cognizant both of the role of the dome in providing the best use of natural light as well as the need to emphasize contrast and clarity through color and material. The memorial dome is more meditative: somber in color, utilizing mostly orange and brown tones, with foliate motifs filling the glass panels as well as nine sections of frosted

glass blocks set into the floor and admitting soft light from below (fig. 5.13). In both rooms Tiffany emphasized the ability of color and light to create a mood appropriate to the function of the place, a realization of Wilde's comments quoted above.

The influence of art furniture and the ideas of the Aesthetic Movement can be seen as well in the highly individual approach to architecture by Philadelphia architect Frank Furness (1839–1912), who contributed furniture designs to a number of interiors for the buildings he designed. His furniture displays a logical approach to the roles of construction and ornament, and also an eccentric combination of Gothic and Islamic features that may derive from familiarity with the plates of Owen's *The Grammar of Ornament* as well as Dresser's *The Art of Decorative Design* (fig. 5.14). Art furniture is also often associated with the New York firm of Herter and Company, which provided both period and original furnishings requiring extensive craftsmanship and expensive materials for the apartments and mansions of wealthy industrialists such as the Rockefellers and Vanderbilts in Manhattan. The firm later helped furnish summer homes

5.13 Louis Comfort Tiffany, War Memorial Room, interior with leaded glass dome and blocks of frosted glass flooring, 1895. Chicago Cultural Center (formerly Chicago Public Library).

5.14 Frank Furness, desk and chair, (desk: walnut, white pine, and poplar, 71 x 62 x 32 ½ in (180 x 157 x 81 cm); chair: walnut, ash, cypress wood, leather upholstery, 30 ¾ x 17 ⅜ x 22 ¼ in (78 x 44 x 57 cm)). Philadelphia Museum of Art.

in Newport, Rhode Island, and the Hudson River Valley. An example is a low secretary with inlaid marquetry panels from the James Goodwin House in Hartford, Connecticut, dating to 1874–78 (fig. 5.15).

Although designers such as Tiffany occasionally received important public commissions, the focus of the Aesthetic Movement, both in Europe and in the United States, was the cultivation of the domestic interior as a setting for individual and family life. Rather than the older concept of "household" where generations of parents and children lived or even worked under the same roof, the family home in the later nineteenth century provided a new sense of comfort, privacy, and self-expression, increasingly distinguished from the anonymity and

5.15 Table, rosewood with inlaid woods, 29 ¼ x 48 x 29 ¾ in (75.6 x 122 x 75.6 cm), manufactured by Herter Brothers, New York, 1874–78, for the James J. Goodwin House, Hartford, Connecticut. Wadsworth Atheneum.

uniformity of the office and factory. The impersonal associations of modern life in the metropolis might be balanced by thinking of the home as a refuge or retreat, a place for private and personal activity. The new climate of a consumer culture stimulated by store displays and illustrated advertisements reified these values in goods and furnishings (see fig. 5.20, p. 81 and fig. 3.1, p. 141).

Within this private sphere, women were encouraged to participate in an expanded range of crafts and media traditionally practiced in and associated with the home, including embroidery, woodcarving, and the decoration of pottery. Local decorative arts societies and schools housed exhibitions and offered classes aimed primarily at middle-class women, who might engage in pursuits that were becoming more appreciated as "art," while at the same time maintaining their status and respectability in society and not threatening a traditionally male-dominated workforce. Involvement in the production of household furnishings opened up a sphere of creative activity to women. But at the same time women's participation tended to reinforce a type of gender inequality suggested below by the increasing polarization of women's from men's fashions. Despite an elevated and esthetic status ascribed to the

decorative arts, women's creative activities continued to be associated with traditional domestic roles. Moreover, the women who painted pottery were rarely involved in its production or in the areas of sales or marketing. Such a separation of gender roles can be seen at the 1876 Centennial Exposition in Philadelphia, where women's decorative arts were displayed in a separate pavilion.

Pottery was one of the more prominent media for women's involvement in the Aesthetic Movement in the United States. Women took an active role in the development of art pottery, concentrated primarily in the Northeast and the Midwest. In Cincinnati, for instance, Maria Longworth (1849–1932) became aware of the Aesthetic Movement through the efforts of British designers who were commissioned to decorate a number of homes for wealthy Cincinnati families. The list included her father's estate, called Rookwood, as well as the home she lived in with her first husband, George Nichols. Longworth studied ceramics at the University of Cincinnati's School of Design, and helped to organize the Cincinnati Pottery Club. With the backing of her father, she founded the Rookwood Pottery in 1880. Examples of Rookwood ceramics received medals at the 1889

Exposition Universelle in Paris and a number of them (fig. 5.16) show the assimilation of Japanese-inspired techniques in the use of irregular forms and asymmetrical arrangements of decorative motifs; indeed, the presence of Japanese ceramic artist Kataro Shirayamadani at Rookwood beginning in 1887 had an impact on the company's production. Rookwood Pottery and the work of other local ceramicists, such as Longworth's rival Mary Louise McLaughlin (1847–1939), made Cincinnati a center for the production of esthetic ceramics, fostered as well through the publication of books and the training offered at the University of Cincinnati and private schools. Adelaide Alsop Robineau (1865–1929) was another woman artist who explored new directions in ceramics around the turn of the century. Robineau worked in

Minneapolis and later in Syracuse, New York, and became aware of esthetic tendencies in the decorative arts through international exhibitions, particularly the Columbian Exhibition in Chicago in 1893. Her Viking Ship Vase from 1905 (fig. 5.17) combines carved and molded decoration with smoother wheel-thrown shapes and attention to the irregularities of surface and overlapping glazes to suggest a wind-tossed sailboat in a seemingly unlikely medium. Robineau's work stretched the expressive possibilities of her medium in original directions more commonly associated with the art of sculpture.

Even with the professional limitations noted above, women's achievements in the decorative arts were considerable and their participation more common than in the fine arts. Despite the emphasis upon the equality of the

5.16 Earthenware vase with freesia design, painted by Harriet Elizabeth Wilcox, 1890, manufactured by Rookwood Pottery, Cincinnati.

5.17 Adelaide Robineau, Viking Ship Vase, porcelain, 1905. Everson Museum of Art, Syracuse, New York.

arts in the Aesthetic Movement, women still moved less easily into the fine arts, and even painters such as Mary Cassatt (1844–1926), who studied in Philadelphia before settling in Paris in 1874, tended to be limited both in their choice of subject matter as well as medium. For instance pastel was thought to be a more appropriate medium for women artists than oil.

Dress

Attitudes toward women in the later nineteenth century may also be gleaned from a consideration of dress and fashion. Another indication of the wider diffusion of ideas about the equality of the arts and the new, elevated status surrounding the decorative arts is the emergence of high fashion or haute couture in Paris in the second half of the nineteenth century. The profession of fashion designer is almost synonymous with Charles Frederick Worth (1825–1895), who worked in London in the textile trade before moving to Paris with his wife and securing commissions for garments from the Empress Eugénie as well as other wealthy patrons beginning in the 1850s. Worth created the ideal image for aristocratic women in the later nineteenth century—in an age when some fashionable ladies rarely, if ever, wore the same garment twice, and when weekend parties might require several changes of clothing in a single day. Worth's wider success in Parisian society was made possible through the sewing machine, which accelerated the pace of constructing elaborate and highly ornate garments by the many seamstresses he employed. Worth also introduced more comfortable surroundings for buying and selling, invented fall and spring lines for fashion to sustain and increase consumer interest, and designed his clothing in closer relation to the human body, reducing if not eliminating some of the confining undergarments that characterized nineteenth-century dress. Certainly Worth's success grew from an emerging esthetic interest in and appreciation for the varied textural and coloristic effects of garments, as seen for instance in the portraits of the French artist Jean-Auguste-Dominique Ingres (1780–1867), whose painstaking technique captured the nuances of light falling on the folds of the dress of Mme. Moitessier in a painting from 1851 (fig. 5.18). Curiously, as interest in women's fashion grew in the mid-nineteenth century, fashions for men became

5.18 J. D. Ingres, *Mme. Moitessier, seated*, oil on canvas, 47 ¼ x 42 ¼ in (120 x 107 cm), 1851. National Gallery, London.

in a sense more anonymous in the general adoption of trouser suits and a preference for black. While men and women competed for distinction in dress through the early nineteenth century, the increasing emphasis upon women's fashion in the later part of the century expresses gender discrimination: women's "preoccupation" with fashion signaled they had no need to work; indeed to do so would be to bring into question their husbands' ability to support them. Furthermore, many women were excluded from the workplace and the elaboration and complexity of much of women's fashion suggests a degree of impracticality that reinforces inactivity.

But the unique place occupied by Worth is due to his sovereignty as an artist, creating an individual and distinctive "look" for each patron, reflecting the patron's good "taste" and the designer's creativity and originality. Worth experimented with varieties of fabric for nuances of color,

5.19 Franz Xavier Winterhalter, portrait of Princess Tatyana Alexanrovna Yusupova wearing a spangled tulle dress by Charles Worth, 1858. The Hermitage Museum, Leningrad.

texture, and light, not unlike the interest of designers such as Tiffany or La Farge in the subtleties of reflection for colored leaded glass (see page 74). Such effects can be seen in the portrait of one of Worth's clients by the German portrait painter Franz Xavier Winterhalter (1805–1873), displaying the stiff folds and sparkling accents of gold thread in a garment made of silk tulle (fig. 5.19). Not surprisingly, the best-known photographic portrait of Worth depicts the designer wearing a beret, reminiscent of a famous Rembrandt self-portrait.

While the products of the Aesthetic Movement were displayed and sold in small shops, studios, and at international exhibitions for an exclusive clientele, the experience of shopping for the middle class was revolutionized in the 1860s with the emergence of department stores both in Europe and in the United States. These large stores, with their varied goods all sold under the same roof, provided a permanent setting for the "spectacle of consumption" as witnessed in international exhibitions such as the Great Exhibition and merchandized in boutiques and artists' studios. Department stores such as the Bon Marché in Paris and John Wanamaker in Philadelphia endeavored to turn shopping into a pleasurable experience and encouraged shoppers to identify consumption with the fulfillment of an idealized dream of comfort, luxury, and self-realization. They housed displays for furniture, fabrics and other home furnishings, and foods, all purchased in large quantities and sold at fixed prices (rather than by bartering between customer and vendor) with "specials" and seasonal sales to entice consumers. By the end of the century, shoppers visiting department stores such as Harrods in Knightsbridge, London (only a short walk from the Victoria and Albert Museum) were treated to bright, colorful, and spacious interiors whose architectural surfaces were covered with enamel-like patterned glazed tiles: an example is Harrods' Meat Hall, dating to 1902 (fig. 5.20). In addition to stimulating commercial activity, free concerts and recitals provided accepted, elevated forms of public entertainment.

Design Reform in France: L'Art Nouveau

Although the image of "Art Nouveau" brings to mind the swirling linear style associated with posters, furniture, and applied decoration in the 1890s in France, the term is perhaps best understood in the broader context of later nineteenth-century ideas about esthetic design and the unity of the arts as they took root on French soil.

As numerous Realist and Impressionist paintings of the period reveal, the 1860s and 1870s in Paris witnessed far-reaching changes in the character of urban life, beginning with the construction of grand boulevards, bridges, monuments, and public gardens under Napoleon III (reigned 1852–1870), continuing with the building of the Paris Opèra and the emergence of other middle-class forms of entertainment. There was significant commercial expansion of the city as well, for instance in the opening of Bon Marché and other department stores that soon followed.

the ideals of the Central Union at this time. It features a naturalistic approach to decoration rather than a relationship with past styles, and the depiction of kegs exemplifies "fitness" of decoration to purpose also recalling aspects of design reform in Britain earlier in the century. Certainly the membership of the Central Union took an interest in elevating the quality of the applied arts in France and in educating consumers and manufacturers, but increasingly the efforts of this organization moved away from an involvement in the improvement of industrial production for a broader public and toward both the restoration and renewal of the luxury crafts and the reputation they enjoyed during the eighteenth century. In fact, after 1889 the organization dropped the word "industrial" from its title, and concentrated instead upon promoting the strength of the country's artisanal heritage. Industrial production was increasingly associated with uniformity and

5.20 Meat Hall, with tiled walls, Harrod's Department Store, 1902.

Middle-class life was viewed as a "spectator sport," and the term *flâneur* was coined to describe that type of gentleman who delighted in strolling the avenues, window shopping, or meeting friends at a café. Casual slices of this life are captured in paintings such as Manet's *Corner in a Café Concert* (1878–79, fig. 5.21). International exhibitions of art and industry, modeled on the Crystal Palace, were also part of public life in the third quarter of the nineteenth century, being staged in 1867 and again in 1878 in Paris.

The department stores' need for larger quantities of furniture placed inordinate pressures upon the system of workshop production, forcing artisans to increase production while receiving the same or even lower wages, leading to a decline in quality and deterioration in working conditions. In part as a response to these circumstances, a private organization of manufacturers and skilled artisans known as the Central Union of Fine Art as Applied to Industry was created as early as 1864 to promote high standards in design based upon the harmony of beauty and utility, standards inherited from the design reform movement in Britain (see page 45). The Central Union sponsored exhibitions and even created a "library" where artisans and manufacturers might consult drawings as models for production. The silver and gilt beer service (fig. 5.22) by Fannière Frères and dating to 1865 illustrates

5.21 Edouard Manet, *Corner in a Café Concert*, oil on canvas, 39 ¼ x 30 ½ in (100 x 77.5 cm), 1878–79. National Gallery, London.

5.22 Fannière Frères, beer service, silver with gilt, pitcher 9 x 5 in (230 x 125 mm), 1865. Musée d'Orsay, Paris.

"renewal" of craft that would inspire artists and artisans and appeal to discriminating taste. Le Maison de l'Art Nouveau was criticized, however, for its lack of a more obvious stylistic coherence, and as a result Bing realized the necessity of appealing to a French audience with a more consistent and recognizable "French" style.

In this climate of strong national feeling a number of French designers emerged whose works betrayed respect for and continuity with the high levels of craftsmanship attained in eighteenth-century luxury goods and furnishings. At the same time this pride in the past merged with more modern concepts of artistic originality deriving from French Symbolism, which saw the arts as the vehicle for subjective expression leading away from the more optical style of Impressionism in the 1870s and the early interest of those painters in the urban pastimes of the middle class. Such qualities emerged, for instance, in the glass objects designed and crafted by Emile Gallé (1846–1904), who trained as a glassmaker in the city of Nancy in northeast France. Gallé experimented with color, light, and texture in the medium of glass, exploring effects beyond the traditional associations with the material. Many works are

unfavorable competition with other nations, and was viewed as a betrayal of a significant cultural legacy.

In addition to reviving appreciation for the eighteenth century, advocates for design reform in France also encouraged contemporary approaches that displayed high levels of refinement, originality, and sophistication. German-born merchant Siegfried Bing (1838–1905) was involved in the activities of the Central Union. Bing collected and sold examples of Japanese decorative arts in Paris, and helped to mount exhibitions of Japanese crafts that he admired for their refinement and the craftsmen's feeling for the nature of materials. Bing encouraged contemporary French designers to create new and original works, and visited the United States where he saw and praised the work of Louis Comfort Tiffany in stained glass.

In 1895 Bing transformed his gallery of Japanese arts into a showroom with the name Le Maison de l'Art Nouveau featuring Japanese crafts as well as contemporary objects commissioned from Tiffany, and interiors designed and furnished by Belgian artist and designer Henri van de Velde (1863–1957, see pages 96–7). Despite the eclectic and international character of Le Maison de l'Art Nouveau, Bing felt that the work was unified by its refinement and quality, demonstrating the kind of modern

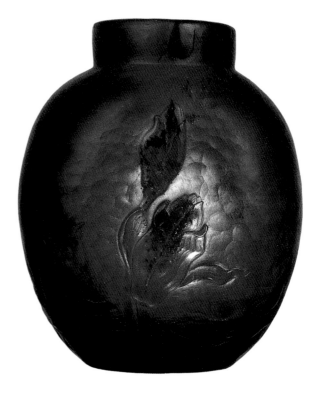

5.23 Gallé, Waterlilies vase, glass, *c.* 1901. Private collection.

highly individual, more like glass sculptures than utilitarian objects. In his "Waterlilies" vase of 1901 (fig. 5.23) the flame-like shapes of the petals and leaves are lightly etched against an unevenly textured background with translucent colors ranging from lavender to blue to indigo. The irregular convex shapes of the surface not only accentuate the subtlety of the light but also suggest the reflections of clouds in a pond. Gallé's heightened sensitivity to nature and obsessive manipulation of materials to obtain the most delicate and subtle effects are contemporary with the series of studies of the same subject by Claude Monet (1840–1926) as well as the similar explorations of translucence and iridescence in glass by Tiffany and La Farge. The feeling for growth, transformation, and juxtaposition in Gallé's works anticipates the automatic techniques of Surrealism in the 1920s, and in fact both movements were influenced by contemporary ideas about dreams and the unconscious. Gallé's work shares with Symbolist artists an interest in private, psychological experience, and the primacy of feeling and mood over purely optical experience. Gallé was inspired by Symbolist poets Charles Baudelaire (1821–1867) and Paul Verlaine (1844–1896), and phrases from their verse are sometimes inscribed directly in the glass surfaces of his objects. Such works achieve one of the aims of the later Central Union, to revitalize the arts by obliterating any boundary between them and restore the shared esteem in which French luxury products were held in an increasingly competitive international market.

Gallé also designed furniture for workshop production featuring carved forms but relying primarily upon elaborate marquetry for intricate linear and spatial effects. By employing more modern production techniques and woodworking machines, Louis Majorelle (1859–1926), who also worked in Nancy, made furniture in the Art Nouveau style available to a wider audience. His writing desk (fig. 5.24) includes gilt mounts and other fittings that recall more directly the heritage of eighteenth-century Rococo furniture. In the curving supports for the shelves atop the desktop, Majorelle conceives of decoration as something more integral rather than "added on" to construction, blurring the distinction between ornament and structure. The boundary between sculpture and furniture is virtually eliminated in the highly original works of Rupert Carabin (1862–1932), who worked in Paris after 1870. Carabin's one-of-a-kind pieces (fig. 5.25) also

5.24 Louis Majorelle, writing desk, mahogany and acacia woods, gilt and chased bronze, chased and beaten copper, 37 ⅖ x 67 x 27 ⅗ in (95 x 170 x 70 cm), 1903–5. Musée d'Orsay, Paris.

stretch the limits of comfort for sitting, making the user somewhat uneasy amid the metamorphoses of organic forms into a menacing forest in which snakes and other creatures lurk.

In addition to glass and furniture, ceramics was another area of great vitality for French decorative artists. Asymmetrical forms, irregular surface textures, and the subtle overlaying of glazes suggest experiment and intuition in the manipulation of the medium, again parallel to the contemporary interest in the treatment of surface on canvas among the Symbolist painters. Ernest

5.26 Ernest Chaplet, porcelain vase, 14 ½ x 6 ½ in (36.8 x 16.5 cm), 1893–1900. Victoria and Albert Museum, London.

5.25 Rupert Carabin, armchair, walnut, 1896. Private collection.

Chaplet (1835–1909) learned the craft of ceramics at the Sèvres manufactory, and used his skills to explore a wide range of expressive effects in the medium, including the high-temperature firing of glazes with metal oxides to produce colors of great richness and depth on smooth, regular forms (fig. 5.26). Chaplet was widely known for his intimate understanding of the ceramic process, and produced highly original and sculptural stoneware based upon the designs of Paul Gauguin (1848–1903). Other ceramic artists, such as Pierre-Adrien Dalpayrat (1844–1910) experimented with uneven or "unfinished" textures and irregular shapes, revealing a greater sense of process and the direct manipulation of materials by the artist (fig. 5.27). While this type of work does not have a stylistic similarity with the linear rhythms more commonly associated with French Art Nouveau, it nevertheless shares with other examples of the period the vision of craft as a vehicle for psychological expression through the exploration of original esthetic effects.

In 1901 the *Societé des Artistes/Decorateurs* was established in France to protect the status of the applied arts against any encroachments by industry and to reinforce

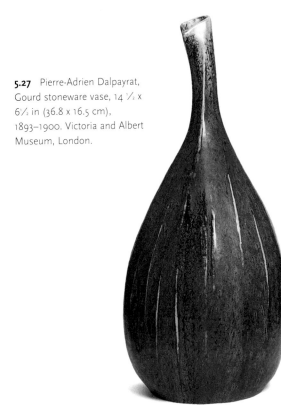

5.27 Pierre-Adrien Dalpayrat, Gourd stoneware vase, 14 ½ x 6½ in (36.8 x 16.5 cm), 1893–1900. Victoria and Albert Museum, London.

Art Nouveau in Print and in Public

Not all the products of l'Art Nouveau were private and exclusive. In the increasingly commercial conditions of metropolitan centers such as Paris, the new esthetic approach to the decorative arts formed part of a more generalized modernity that reached a broader and more heterogeneous public. At the Exposition Universelle held in Paris in 1900, l'Art Nouveau dominated the architectural constructions for the fair and full interiors featured examples of decorative art in the new style. French architect and designer Hector Guimard (1867–1942) was particularly conspicuous in externalizing elements of l'Art Nouveau. Guimard adapted the elastic plant-like tendrils and flowers associated with many products of esthetic crafts to the railings and entrances to the newly-constructed Paris underground transportation system known as the Métro, a few of which are still in use (fig. 5.28). Cast iron was used for this vast project, integrating the refinement of the pre-revolutionary past with modern industrial techniques of

the unity and equality of the arts that Art Nouveau sought to achieve. During this period the decorative arts acquired associations with originality and expression, while the fine arts were increasingly recognized for their autonomy from the imitation of nature and an appreciation for the "truth to materials" or medium. Artists freely crossed the increasingly seamless border between fine art and applied design, among them Odilon Redon (1840–1916), Pierre Bonnard (1867–1947), Maurice Denis (1870–1943), and Édouard Vuillard (1868–1940). These artists pursued associations of the word "decorative" that suggested personal and expressive possibilities in a variety of media beyond easel painting: working, for instance, in lithography, wallpaper design, and painted screens, though often for private commissions rather than more commercial manufacture. Their efforts might be included as well with those of Lucien Pissarro (1863–1944), the son of Impressionist painter Camille Pissarro (1830–1903), who pursued a career in book publishing, but left France for London where an active private press movement held the promise of an even more receptive public (see page 118).

5.28 Hector Guimard, Metro station entrance, cast iron, *c.* 1900. Paris.

5.29 Jules Cheret, *Les Girard*, poster for the Folies-Bergère, color lithograph, 21 ¼ x 17⅞ in (54 x 44.5 cm), 1877. Musée de la Publicité, Paris.

5.30 Henri de Toulouse-Lautrec, *La Goulue* (Louise Weber) at the Moulin Rouge, poster, color lithograph, 33 x 48 in (83.8 x 122 cm), 1898.

production. Guimard also used cast iron for the design of window grilles and a series of original numbers to mark the entrances to houses and buildings. In these and other ways the arts served a socially progressive role, beautifying the city, expanding production, and attracting tourism and trade.

Aspects of l'Art Nouveau were also popularized via print media, chiefly in the design of posters, made possible through the technical development of chromolithography. Posters were an effective and, most importantly, a colorful means of advertising products, stores, restaurants, and cafés, and were a ubiquitous presence in the city, enlivening walls, buildings, and kiosks. Among the most significant class of patrons for poster advertisement during this time were the providers of popular entertainment. The dance halls, circuses and cabarets located in Parisian districts such as Montmartre served as a focus for middle-class leisure, in particular that element representing freer, less structured and uninhibited public forms of self-expression. Whether as participants or spectators, the middle-class public found an

outlet for playfulness, fantasy, and sensual pleasure in the world of dance halls and cabarets.

Jules Cheret (1836–1932) was an early master of poster design, beginning his career as an apprentice to a printer and spending time in England learning the technique of chromolithography, which had been successfully developed in the printing of color images primarily for illustrated books (see page 60). Cheret approached the composition of the poster as an integration of text and image to create a unified design on a monumental scale, even when the actual size of the poster was not particularly large. In the poster advertising a group of dancers known as Les Girard from 1877 (fig. 5.29), for example, areas of bold text at top and bottom of the tall rectangular format announce the venue and particular act or time of the performance. The placement of the letters deviates from the strict horizontal format, and instead connects and interacts with the three dancers in the center, almost like a prop for their elongated limbs. The sense of movement is strengthened by pinwheel-like shapes of arms, legs, and coat tails, and by the virtual elimination of detail and background. Cheret explored the medium of chromolithography in order to achieve these effects, in particular by working directly on the stone in order to obtain the most spontaneous effects.

An expressive treatment of line, as well as compositional elements derived from Japanese woodblock prints, can also be found in the lithographic posters of painter Henri de Toulouse-Lautrec (1864–1901), which advertised the performances of popular Montmartre entertainers such as Löie Fuller and Louise Weber (known as La Goulue). The latter is featured in a poster of 1891 for the Moulin Rouge (fig. 5.30), printed in a large edition of 3000 for public display throughout Paris. In this poster the illustration is simplified by strong contours for the foreground figures of Valentine le Désossé and La Goulue herself, while the silhouetted forms of the crowd and typography maintain the planarity of the image and the unity of all elements of the composition. For his posters Toulouse-Lautrec also worked directly on the lithographic stone, and the vitality that emerges from the exaggerated gestures and bold composition suggests a mood of gaiety and abandon that is completely fitting in an advertisement for nightlife entertainment.

Although in a smaller format, the same characteristics are found in the illustrated covers for popular fiction of the time, while more subtle and sophisticated effects appear in the illustrated journals aimed at a more esthetically-minded audience. An example is the cover for the Berlin-based periodical *Pan*, designed by Joseph Sattler (1867–1931) in 1895 (fig. 5.31). The journal's founder and editor was Julius Meier-Graefe, who operated a boutique for modern decorative arts in Paris called the Maison Moderne and was a strong advocate for the unity of the arts. In the cover illustration for *Pan*, the half-length figure of the Greek god peeks out from behind the tendrils of elongated plant forms that happen to be the extensions of the letters that make up the title. Respecting the flatness of the page, Sattler was able to connect and relate the various elements of the layout. There is a similarity in this approach to the way that designers of furniture integrated decoration and construction. In Sattler's example the equality and interrelationship of the elements in the layout permitted both originality and experimentation in the medium of chromolithography.

Turning to the Chicago-born performance artist Löie Fuller, both Cheret and painter Manuel Orazio

5.31 Joseph Sattler, cover for magazine *Pan*, color lithograph, 15 ¹¹⁄₁₆ x 9 ⁵⁄₁₆ in (40 x 23.5 cm), 1895. Victoria and Albert Museum, London.

(1860–1934) designed advertising posters featuring this popular entertainer (fig. 5.32). Orazio hints at the erotic component in the dancer's performance by outlining the partially nude body beneath a sheer garment. Orazio's poster also has a stronger sense of abstract and suggestive forms: hair, flowers, drapery become swirling and cascading shapes making it difficult to distinguish representation from more purely abstract decoration. Löie Fuller's dance was also the subject of a series of fifteeen ceramic figurines designed by Agathon Leonard for the Sèvres manufactory in 1898 and displayed at the 1900 International Exhibition in Paris. In addition, Fuller's performance was captured on moving film in the early years of this new medium's development. On film there appears to be little if any suggestion of nudity. Rather we see the dancer's white scarf and circular arm movements combine to somehow transform her body into the form of a flower in bloom as if by magic. The theme of metamorphosis, seen in the transformation of letter forms into representation or hair into flames or pure decoration in other media, is here found in relation to the human figure in movement. Historians have noted a relationship between artists' esthetic fascination with this theme of transformation in nature and Darwin's theory of natural selection (first published in 1859), which revealed nature in a constant condition of flux rather than permanence, but at the same time guided by a process of selection toward perfection. The dancer's appeal certainly incorporated an abstract esthetic dimension, but also extended to other audiences, who were attracted by the excitement of novelty, fantasy, and the promise of the unexpected.

Poster design was thus in part a "popular" form of expression, an outlet for the creative energies of a number of gifted artists both in France and elsewhere in Europe and in the United States, and appealing to an audience beyond the traditional gallery or museum visitor. Eugène-Samuel Grasset (1841–1917) developed a style for the design of graphic material sometimes referred to as *cloisonné*. His approach uses strong black lines and figure-ground contrast to reinforce the planarity of the surface while the linear treatment of drapery folds or strands of wavy hair create secondary patterns resembling the cells of leaded glass or jewelry, two media in which Grasset also worked. In an advertisement for *Encre L. Marquet* (Marquet Ink) the diagonal lettering runs parallel to wavy cloud-like shapes that balance the opposing diagonal direction of a woman who sits thoughtfully, pen in hand (fig. 5.33). Grasset's figures are often less spontaneous than those of Cheret or Toulouse-Lautrec, but the female image does indeed dominate the art of the poster as part of the gay and carefree world of entertainment, or as an idealized image linked to the purchase of particular products.

Alphonse Mucha (1860–1939) came to Paris from his home in Moravia (Czechoslovakia). His posters advertising the performances of actress Sarah Bernhardt were effective in promoting the actress's career in Paris. Many of Mucha's posters employ a severely vertical format in which figures are framed by arches or other more exotic architectural motifs that suggest the stage, and which also provide a frame for lettering. In the 1895 *Gismonda* poster (fig. 5.34), the actress's costume emphasizes decorative brocade patterns that relate to the palm (referring to the play's final act in which Bernhardt is part of an Easter Day

5.32 Manuel Orazio, poster for Löie Fuller, color lithograph.

procession) and garlanded hair. The arch framing the actress's head, as well as a banner below the ground line, frame the text and link the image to the text. Despite foreshortening and shadow, the reduction of detail and simplification of modeling create monumentality and compositional unity for effective communication. Later posters are freer in the use of abstraction to suggest metamorphosis, especially in the kinds of abstract treatment of shape to suggest hair or plant forms.

In the United States, *Harper's Magazine* published cover illustrations by Eugène Grasset as well as by American designers such as Edward Penfield (1866–1925), while some of the boldest approaches to the medium can be seen in the oeuvre of Will Bradley (1868–1962). Bradley's early illustrations, influenced by Aubrey Beardsley (1872–1898), had appeared in the

5.33 Eugène Grasset, advertisement for Marquet Ink, color lithograph, 1892.

5.34 Alphonse Mucha, Sarah Bernhardt in *Gismonda*, poster, color lithograph, 84 ¼ x 30 in (215.3 x 76.2 cm), 1895.

fig. 5.36) as well as René Lalique (1860–1945). Fouquet collaborated with Alphonse Mucha on several pieces of jewelry, and Mucha was responsible for designing Fouquet's new store on the rue Royale in Paris in 1900 (fig. 5.37). The boutique opened in time for the Paris World's Fair of 1900. Patterned tile floors and friezes, plant-like pilasters and other architectural details, relief sculptures of peacocks, and wall-mounted glass cases in the shape of bubbles unify wall, ceiling, and floor into a total work of art. Mirrors serve to make the space appear larger, indulging the fantasy of the spectator and creating an imaginative setting for effectively merchandising the exotic creations for sale in the cases.

Art Nouveau was a complex phenomenon in France. While its creations were unified by an almost obsessive

British journal *The Studio*, and examples of his work were exhibited at the opening of Le Maison de l'Art Nouveau in 1895 at Siegfried Bing's invitation. In the United States Bradley was active in many areas of the expanding print media. He published illustrated books for his own private and short-lived Wayside Press in Springfield, Massachusetts, and also contributed to a magazine called the *Chap Book*, published by the American Type Founders Company (see page 124). As seen in an 1896 advertising poster for Victor Bicycles (fig. 5.35), Bradley used four colors to create a strong and coherent image. Repetition in the black silhouettes of the riders and in the elongated floral decoration constitutes another form of simplification, while the use of black ties the border with its lettering to the image. Bradley's posters and illustration also create effective figure-ground reversal—for instance, in the negative shapes created between the arm and torso of the larger female figure.

Finally, the public and commercial expression of Art Nouveau also emerges in the design of interiors and displays related to fantasy and the experience of shopping. For instance, transformations of natural forms in glass, metals, wood, and ceramics yielded effects that were combined in miniature in the production of jewelry. Abstract attenuation of plant and animal forms, subtle effects of texture and color, exquisite craftsmanship and originality all emerge in the work of Georges Fouquet (1862–1957,

5.36 George Fouquet, winged serpent corsage ornament, gold, enamel, diamonds, and pearls. Private collection, New York.

5.37 Alphonse Mucha, interior for boutique, Paris, for Georges Fouquet, jeweler, 1900. Photograph: Musée Carnavalet, Paris.

preoccupation with expressive transformations of nature, the movement was in many ways heterogeneous. Its products contained elements of private and introspective experience, of reform involving the use of industrial materials and technology, and a significant commercial profile as well, seen in the rich development of the chromolithographic poster and its connection to the commodification of leisure.

Glasgow: Charles Rennie Mackintosh

The Scottish architect Charles Rennie Mackintosh (1868–1928) devoted much energy to the dialogue between the esthetic and broader social issues relating to the visual arts. In his native Glasgow the construction and outfitting of ocean liners and locomotives dominated the local economy and demanded the widespread use of standardized methods of production for furniture and other elements of interior decoration. The Singer sewing machine company also had a factory in Glasgow, and the city's population was proud of its growth, wealth, and reputation for engineering and industry.

While recognizing the importance of prefabrication and serial production in these industries, Mackintosh

believed the role of the artist/designer was to integrate individual and local identity with modern methods of production. In his own architecture and interior design Mackintosh combined simple construction boldly stated through vertical and horizontal constructive forms, integrated with decorative elements that either played upon this geometry (as in the Library of the Glasgow School of Art, 1907–9, fig. 5.38) or betray a debt to the tense linear rhythms of Celtic art and personal interpretations of floral and vegetal forms. In many of his projects Mackintosh collaborated with his wife, Margaret MacDonald, whose drawings and designs for tapestries, embroideries, and relief panels express sensuality and a delicate linear quality that appears in ornament carved in wooden furniture or molded in cast iron and other metals. MacDonald's picture frame (fig. 5.39) is made from hammered aluminum on wood—an early such use of the material which was becoming more affordable due to cheaper methods of extraction. Moreover, aluminum was a local choice as well, since Glasgow was the center for aluminum production in Britain.

5.38 Charles Rennie Mackintosh, interior of Library, Glasgow School of Art, 1907–9.

5.39 Margaret and Frances MacDonald, picture frame, aluminum and oak, 27 ³/₁₆ x 12 ¼ in (69.2 x 32.4 cm), 1897. Carnegie Museum of Art, Pittsburgh.

The same vocabulary of an attenuated rectilinear framework forming borders for more organic floral and human forms can be seen in the murals MacDonald designed for Miss Kate Cranston's Buchanan Street Tearooms in 1896–7 (fig. 5.40). The tearooms, which afforded a number of opportunities for Mackintosh and MacDonald to create original interiors between 1895 and 1903, were a unique expression of Glasgow's modernity in design. Frequently owned and managed by women, Glasgow tearooms attempted to introduce the kind of unified esthetic character found in domestic furnishings and interiors into a more public setting. Mackintosh designed several tearooms for Miss Cranston from 1896 to 1902, where middle-class clientele might appreciate the ambience resulting from a coordinated approach to interior design.

Mackintosh's attempt to reconcile the individual with the uniform welcomed technology and new materials in the development of a modern approach to design, and identified mass production with simple undecorated forms such as wooden beams or cast-iron supports derived from architecture and an association between simplification and lower production costs. Integrating decoration into this constructional scheme meant for Mackintosh preserving the human and individual element both in architecture and in the wider context of unified decoration and design.

5.40 Charles Rennie Mackintosh, design for mural decoration, tearooms, Buchanan Street, Glasgow, pencil and water color, 14 ¼ x 29 ¼ in (36.2 x 75.6 cm), 1896–7. Hunterian Gallery, University of Glasgow.

Austria

The designs of Mackintosh, represented in illustrated journals and displayed at international exhibitions in Vienna (1900) and Turin (1902) stimulated the artistic efforts of a group of artists and architects in Vienna known as the Secession. These artists, like the Pre-Raphaelites in Britain and Les Vingt in Belgium, rebelled against the rigidity and elitism of academic standards for the fine arts and sought both freedom of expression as well as active involvement in the decorative arts. The attitudes of the Secession are revealed in the motto inscribed on their exhibition hall in Vienna: "Die Zeit ihre Kunst, Die Kunst ihre Freiheit" ("To every time its art, to every art its freedom").

Josef Hoffmann (1870–1956), an architect and leading member of the Secession, and Kolo Moser (1868–1918) created an organization to link designers, craftsmen, and manufacturers in the shared hope of improving the quality and elevating the status of the decorative arts in Austria. The organization, known as the Wiener Werkstätte (Vienna Workshops), was founded in 1903. Hoffmann was deeply impressed by the example of Ashbee's Guild of Handicraft (see below, page 115) as well as by Mackintosh, and wrote to the architect in Scotland for advice. In his response, Mackintosh encouraged the Viennese efforts, sounding a note of optimistic idealism in his plea for the role of the artist in improving the quality of everyday life through design:

> If one wants to achieve an artistic success with your programme ... every object which you pass from your hand must carry an outspoken mark of individuality, beauty and most exact execution. From the outset your aim must be that every object which you produce is made for a certain purpose and place. Later ... you can emerge boldly into the full light of the world, attack the factory-trade on its own ground, and the greatest work that can be achieved in this century, you can achieve it: namely the production of objects of use in magnificent form and at such a price that they lie within the buying range of the poorest. First those who (look down at applied art) must be overcome and taught that the modern movement is not a silly hobby-horse of a few who wish to achieve fame comfortably through eccentricity, but that the modern movement

is something living, something good, the only possible art—for all and for the highest phase of our time.

Products of the Werkstätte include a range of domestic items from clothing to glass and tableware, to wallpaper and individualized calling cards (given to servants when paying a social visit), which were almost exclusively produced on commission from wealthy private clients. Each product bore the stamp of the artist, the manufacturer, and the distinctive interlocked "W"s of the organization's logo, as an expression of individual responsibility and the spirit of collaboration. Designers varied in their approach, but all were committed to originality and an avoidance of historicism. Hoffman's designs parallel the interests of Mackintosh in incorporating repeated geometric decorative patterns as a simple form of decoration, as seen, for instance, in a chair manufactured for the exclusive Purkersdorf Sanitorium in 1905 that has a series of small circular perforations cut in its back (fig. 5.41).

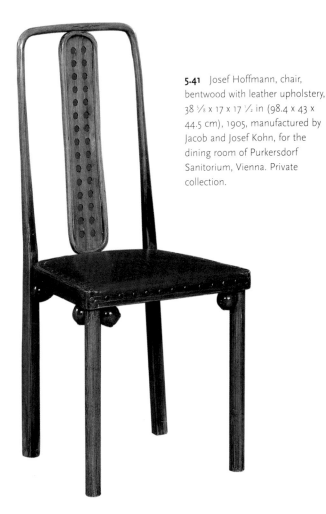

5.41 Josef Hoffmann, chair, bentwood with leather upholstery, 38 ⅛ x 17 x 17 ½ in (98.4 x 43 x 44.5 cm), 1905, manufactured by Jacob and Josef Kohn, for the dining room of Purkersdorf Sanitorium, Vienna. Private collection.

Another example is the basket that seem to be formed from simple stamped sheets of metal (fig. 5.42). The gaming chair designed by Hoffmann in 1904 for a children's playroom (fig. 5.43) is also characteristically geometric, but here design relates ingeniously to setting, where the repeated square- and diamond-shaped motifs pertain to checkers and backgammon, and where the "reversibility" or symmetry of these board games is mirrored in the chair itself, which seems (almost) capable of being turned upside down while remaining functional. Other examples of objects designed by members of the Werkstätte include a champagne glass manufactured in 1907 in the Czechoslovakia but sold in Austria by a Viennese retailer. The glass, based upon older techniques practiced in the region but treated here with great subtlety and sophistication, was designed by Otto Prutscher, and is made of clear mold-blown glass overlaid with colored glass and then cut to make the stem appear like links of chain (fig. 5.45).

Kolo Moser's designs were no less original or ingenious, and also required painstaking craftsmanship and expensive materials. Like Mackintosh, Moser preferred rectilinear shapes and forms and the dialogue between constructive and decorative elements in design. An example is a women's pull-down writing desk and armchair, manufactured by Caspar Hrazdil and dating to 1903 (fig. 5.44) that come apart like interlocking pieces of a puzzle to reveal their function. Both elements employ a shared vocabulary of patterns in inlaid wood of squares and shapes resembling schematic papyrus plants of varying sizes. In the center of the desk panel is a frieze of standing maidens holding hoops inlaid in brass. Despite a debt to motifs derived from the ancient civilizations of Egypt and Greece, the design is free from conventional approaches to historicism and original in its clever disguise of the pull-out chair as well as in Moser's apparent intention to save space.

Perhaps the best-known work associated with the Wiener Werkstätte is the decoration of a home in Brussels for the wealthy Belgian banker Adolphe Stoclet, built between 1904/5 and 1911 by Hoffmann with interior design and furnishings being carried out and executed almost exclusively by designers and artisans associated with the workshops. No expense was spared for the materials and decoration of the Stoclet House which include different varieties of rare marbles and an elaborate series of mural decorations designed for the dining room by the

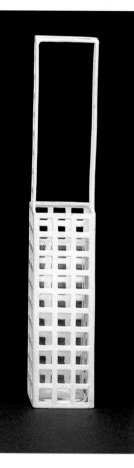

5.42 Josef Hoffmann, skyscraper basket, silver, 9 ½ x 1 ½ in (24 x 3.8 cm), 1905. Private collection.

5.43 Josef Hoffmann, gaming chair, painted wood and cane, 22 x 22 x 23 in (55.8 x 55.8 x 58.4 cm), for Knips Country Residence, Seeboden, Austria, manufactured by Rudnicker, New York. Metropolitan Museum of Art, New York.

5.44 Kolo Moser, made by Caspar Hrazdil, lady's writing desk, thuya wood, inlaid with satinwood and brass, engraved and inked, gilt-metal feet, 57 ¹¹/₁₆ x 47 x 23 ⅛ in (145.6 x 119.4 x 60.3 cm), 1903. Victoria and Albert Museum, London.

5.45 Otto Prutscher, champagne glass, mold-blown clear glass, overlaid colored glass, cut, 8 x 6 in (20.3 x 15.15 cm), c. 1907, manufactured by Meyr's Neffe, Adolfov, Czechoslovakia. Private collection.

Viennese Secession painter Gustav Klimt (1862–1918). Klimt's murals, based upon color drawings by the artist, combined a number of materials such as marble inlay, enamel, gold, and ceramic tile. The brightness of the color, precision of contours, and expanses of geometric and curvilinear pattern consistently support the flatness of the marble walls containing the inlay decoration. Figural representations such as the embracing couple (fig. 5.46) are equally removed from naturalism and perspective and their garments are filled with patterns created from the exotic materials. In the dining room of the Stoclet House the abstract language of wall decoration imposes discipline but also allows freedom for the artist's personal vision of the intensity of human love as well as nature's abundance. These themes have a particular

5.46 Gustav Klimt, *Fufillment* (or *Embrace*), tempera, watercolor, gold, silver and pencil on paper, 76 ⅛ x 47 ⅝ in (194 x 121 cm), c.1905–9. Design for the main wall of the Stoclet House dining room, Brussels.

resonance in fin de siècle Vienna, where the topic of modern society's alienation from nature and the depths of emotional response were brought to light by Sigmund Freud (1856–1939), and through whom terms such as "repression" and "drive" have become part of our ordinary vocabulary.

Belgium

Adolphe Stoclet's choice of the Wiener Werkstätte for the design of his Brussels home was not surprising, in that the Belgian banker was familiar with Vienna and spent much time abroad. Yet artists in his native Belgium also had an interest in modern attitudes toward design. One of the country's most articulate spokesmen and practitioners for the unity and revitalization of the arts was Henry van de Velde. As a painter van de Velde was affiliated with the progressive Belgian modernist movement known as Les Vingt, but began to adapt a Symbolist style featuring abstract shapes and linear rhythms derived from organic forms to the design of furniture, books, and metalcraft. In almost all of his works the decorative elements, usually characterized by taut curvilinear contours invested with spring-like energy, are integrated with structural elements such as the legs of a chair or the branches of a candelabrum (fig. 5.47). In works such as these van de Velde merged ornamental and constructive elements, fusing esthetic expression with an interest in the ease of production and its effect upon cost. Deeply concerned with the negative social consequences of industrialization and influenced by the ideas of the Arts and Crafts Movement (see page 106), van de Velde's designs exhibit a sense of decorative restraint to avoid the appearance of being exclusive or indulgent. He also turned much of his attention to lettering and other forms of graphic presentation, producing advertisements for his own domestic furnishings and a color poster for the company Tropon that manufactured concentrated egg products for cooking (fig. 5.48). In the Tropon poster van de Velde developed original lettering, and the importance of the company name is reinforced with concentric outlines that frame it and suggest in a simplified and abstract way pools of poured liquid (compare a similar abstracted design of liquid in Beardsley's *The Climax*, see below, fig. 5.75, page 117). The black title contrasts boldly with the rich orange

5.47 Henry van de Velde, candelabrum, electroplated bronze, 23 1/16 x 20 in (58.5 x 50.8 cm), 1902. Collection Musée Royaux d'Art et d'Histoire, Brussels.

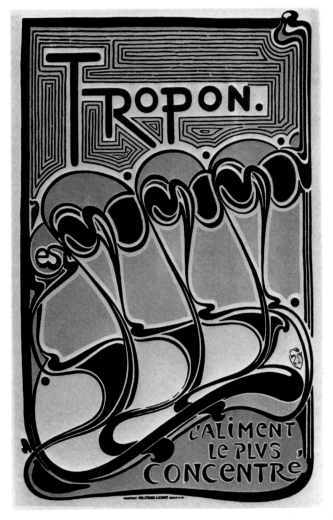

5.48 Van de Velde, poster for *Tropon* "the most nourishing food", color lithograph, 40 x 30 1/8 in (101.6 x 77 cm), 1898. Private collection.

and yellow ground colors that are reminiscent of the intense hues and shocking color harmonies in the works of Post-Impressionist painters such as Vincent van Gogh, whose work Van de Velde admired and emulated earlier in his career (see fig. 6.8, page 114). The Tropon poster also demonstrates the interest of manufacturers in promoting their products in connection with progressive ideas in the arts as a marketing strategy (see below, pages 130–131).

Van de Velde exhibited widely, contributed to publications on modern decorative arts, and was equally interested in the reform of craft education with stronger ties to the fine arts. In this latter role he was appointed in 1904 as director of a school of craft (Kunstgewerbeschule) in Weimar, Germany, a post he held until the outbreak of World War I. In 1919, following the war, the school was consolidated with Weimar's Academy of Fine Art to become the Bauhaus (see page 181).

Van de Velde's originality in advertising design is matched by other Belgian posters in which artists experimented with imaginative letter forms and the transformations of representation and decoration in relation to large flat surfaces and unmodulated color. An example is the advertisement for a brand of Belgian coffee designed by Fernand Toussaint (1873–1955, fig. 5.49). In this poster the hot steam from a cup of coffee held by a young, well-dressed female figure materializes in swirling rhythms

5.49 Fernand Toussaint, poster for Café Jacqmotte, color lithograph, 31 x 43 ⅛ in (78.7 x 110 cm). Museum für Kunst und Gewerbe, Hamburg.

Bovy's (1858–1910) dining room of *c.* 1898 (fig. 5.50) feature chairs and a chiffonier in which wood is treated as an entirely flexible material, creating a sense of movement, for instance, in the set of chairs with bending concave and convex contours for the top, back, seat, and legs.

Munich

The city of Munich in Germany had a strong heritage of public support for the arts in the nineteenth century. In addition to museums built in the first half of the century, the city sponsored construction of a large exhibition hall in 1854 inspired by London's Crystal Palace Exhibition Hall of 1851. A number of Munich-based artists felt constrained by traditional distinctions between the fine and applied arts in terms of education and the organization of exhibitions. Contemporary with debates of a similar kind in Britain and elsewhere in Europe, artists took a keen interest in design and craft production, and an international art exhibition of 1897 in Munich included two rooms devoted to the decorative arts. In 1896 the journal *Jugend* ("youth") was launched in Munich to promote contemporary arts and entertainment, and its circulation reached 200,000 copies per week around the year 1900. The journal's title became the basis for the word Jugendstil ("youth style"), a

that form the undulating letter forms of the words "Café Jacqmotte." Also, on the bottom right is a circular monogram for the coffee containing elastic forms for the letters "C" and "J" making use of figure-ground reversal. This experimental and distinctive use of letter forms appears in artists' signatures (for Van de Velde, for instance, see the Tropon poster, fig. 5.48), as well as in monograms for organizations and companies such as the interlocked "W"s of the Weiner Werkstatte or the General Electric trademark, contained within a circle and dating to *circa* 1890.

Other examples of modern design in Brussels are less restrained than those of van de Velde, and employ a vocabulary based upon forms inspired by rich natural growth. Often utilizing expensive woods and extensive carving, ensembles such as Gustave Serrurier-

5.50 Gustave Serrurier-Bovy, dining room furniture, 1897–98. Musée départemetal de l'Oise.

5.52 Ludwig von Zumbusch, cover for *Jugend*, II, vol. 40, color lithograph, 11 ²∕₅ x 8 ⁴∕₅ in (29 x 22.5 cm), 1897. Private collection.

5.51 Otto Eckmann, *Iris* woodcut cover for *Jugend*, (Munich), color lithograph, 11 ²∕₅ x 8 ⁴∕₅ in (29 x 22.5 cm), 1901. Victoria and Albert Museum, London.

reference to new ideas in art and design in Germany. A second Munich-based journal, *Simplicissimus*, was also founded in the same year. A key figure in the practice and promotion of new attitudes toward the equality of the arts was Otto Eckmann (1865–1902), who abandoned painting to pursue a career as a decorative artist. Eckmann designed woodcut illustrations for the periodicals *Jugend* (fig. 5.51) and *Pan* that depicted plants and flowers with strong outlines—gently undulating flattened shapes emphasizing an equality of figure and ground that were based upon familiarity with Japanese woodblock prints. Decorative forms that grew from this approach were developed in furniture designs, tapestry, and other media

including letter forms and typography. Painter and illustrator Ludwig von Zumbusch (1861–1927) also dramatically transformed the abstract linear qualities that characterize Eckmann's oeuvre in an early cover for *Jugend* (1897, fig. 5.52). The chromolithograph illustrates two exuberant female dancers with wave-like hair floating against a simplified seaside landscape and framed by two attenuated elm trees into whose foliage the word *"jugend"* is cut using original letter forms emphasizing related circular and spiral shapes.

Another figure who played an active role in the arts in Munich at this time was Richard Riemerschmid. His contributions are particularly noteworthy because of a later involvement in the Deutscher Werkbund, an organization formed in 1907 that inaugurated a discourse to establish a more practical and unified approach to design in Germany (see page 130). Riemerschmid was particularly versatile, participating as a designer in newly formed craft organizations in Munich and later in Dresden to produce original designs in furniture, ceramics, and metalwork. Before his involvement with the Werkbund, Riemerschmid's designs successfully combined expressive curvilinear decoration with the constructive elements of a variety of furnishings. A restrained example is a music room chair, whose curving side arms form a support for the front legs and the back, introducing an integrated element of decoration that does not interfere with the movements of a seated musician (fig. 5.53). Likewise, a curved knife handle for a set of silver cutlery is not only a graceful decorative accent but also is efficient to use, even allowing an opening for the user's pinky finger (fig. 5.54).

Jugendstil in Munich certainly constituted a collaborative renewal of art and handicraft, based in part upon the ability of artists to elevate the everyday world of products and in so doing improve the general quality of life and the urban environment. Through the formation of workshops and establishment of schools to educate designers and craftsmen, Jugendstil artists were interested in creating a "people's" art, even if the market for their products remained an exclusive one. The social relevance or benefit of Jugendstil in an increasingly industrial and materialistic age was a target of satire, even within the movement itself, as evidenced by a short verse appearing in *Simplicissimus*:

> The world will not be cured with blazing fire or knives,
> But painlessly improved—by being "stylized."

Scandinavia, Eastern Europe, and the Vernacular

Esthetic ideas helped to nurture and stimulate new developments in the decorative arts in the cities of eastern Europe and Scandinavia beginning in the 1890s. Whether drawing ideas and forms from the British Isles, the United States, or western Europe, Scandinavian and eastern European artists created an original approach to the decorative arts, often based upon an appreciation for native folk traditions. Their search for national identity was indeed a creative rather than historicist exercise, and was both

5.53 Richard Riemerschmid, music room chair, oak with leather upholstery, 30⅝ x 18⅞ x 22½ in (77.8 x 47.9 x 57.2 cm), 1899, manufactured by Werkstätten für Kunst im Handwerk, Munich. Philadelphia Museum of Art.

highly selective and eclectic. Education or training outside of their homelands, the circulation of journals, and attendance or participation at international exhibitions stimulated design activities in countries such as Denmark, Finland, Norway, Hungary, and Czechoslovakia, and added to the international scope of the unity and equality of the arts.

In Finland, the architect Gottlieb Eliel Saarinen (1873–1950) used native building materials such as granite to create a national artistic identity distinct from Russia (of which Finland was then a province) or Germany, based upon a Romantic vision of Finnish history. Cultural identity was thus linked to political independence, international recognition, and a revitalization of the Finnish economy through manufacturing and trade. Saarinen's "Koti" chair of 1896, designed for an exhibition, emphasizes simple and solid craftsmanship rather than sophisticated

5.54 Richard Riemerschmid, cutlery, silver, knife length 9 ⅜ in (23.7 cm), manufactured by Werkstätten für Kunst im Handwerk, Munich.

nineteenth-century Finnish design involved an awareness of expressive meaning in the decorative arts deriving from a feeling for nature as well as from the dignity of handicraft.

Finland was successful in sponsoring its own pavilion, separate from that of Russia, at the Worlds Fair held in Paris in 1900. The pavilion was designed primarily by Saarinen, with mural paintings by Gallén-Kallela and featuring carved cases with examples of Finnish handicraft.

Conscious of an increasingly international setting for modern design after the end of World War I, Saarinen participated in design competitions abroad, and eventually emigrated to the United States in the early 1920s, becoming director for the Cranbook Academy of Design in Bloomfield Hills, Michigan (see page 206).

5.55 Eliel Saarinen, *Koti* chair, oak and re-upholstered seat, 1896. Museum of Art and Design, Helsinki.

techniques (fig. 5.55). Such designs may be seen as a visual counterpart to widespread interest in the oral folk traditions of Karelia (a region of Finland), whose poems and songs were first published in the second half of the nineteenth century. The European-trained painter Akseli Gallén-Kallela (1865–1931) also contributed to the movement to create a Finnish art that included handicraft, designing a wool rug (fig. 5.56) that was woven using a native technique known as *ryiji*. The asymmetrical curvilinear shapes seen in this example make their appearance in contemporary Finnish stoneware as well as in other textile and wallpaper patterns. Their similarity to products of esthetic design in Belgium, France, and Britain demonstrates that a Finnish national style in the arts was less a recreation than an invention, that involved eclectic sources that were both contemporary as well as based in a nostalgia for native folk traditions. Both sources for late

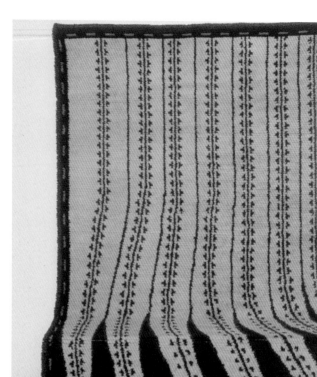

5.56 Akseli Gallén-Kalella, *ryiji* rug, *The Flame*, Finnish, wool, 120 x 67 ¼ in (304.8 x 172 cm), 1899 (woven 1884). Gallén-Kallela Museum, Espoo, Finland.

5.57 Georg Jensen, coffee and tea service, chased silver, ivory, 2–9 in (5.3–23 cm) high, 1905. Private collection.

Original and esthetic approaches to the decorative arts are also found in Denmark—for instance, in the studio established by Georg Jensen (1866–1935) in Copenhagen in 1904. Jenson's silver coffee service (fig. 5.57) dates to 1905. The lid of each bowl and pitcher is decorated with a swirling stem resembling a pod, imparting an organic quality to the ensemble through the curving ivory handles and swelling forms of the spouts.

Czechoslovakia was another eastern European country that took part in and helped to shape new approaches to the decorative arts in the later nineteenth century. The city of Prague was the focus for much design activity, directed both toward an expressive and original conception of decoration as well as an interest in integrating a range of esthetic effects involving materials and process with simple forms for furniture, glass, and ceramic wares. Glass manufactories in Bohemia in the eastern region of the country, such as Loetz in the town of Klastersky Mlyn, experimented with new processes and effects based upon exaggerated linear interpretations of natural forms inspired by the success of Tiffany. Some of these manufactories produced works for the Wiener Werkstätte (see page 98). An integration of construction and decoration is also seen in the stained glass doors and entrance with wrought metal framed panels of the Novak Building in Prague dating to 1901–4.

One of the more original Czech artists involved in the design of manufactured products was Jan Kotera (1871–1923), who worked for several companies in a variety of media. Kotera's textiles often incorporate a curvilinear decorative vocabulary freely adapted from Czech folk traditions. Yet a number of his designs exhibit a more striking integration of expressive and constructive elements in design. An example is a monumental clear glass punchbowl and lid that was exhibited in 1904 at the World's Fair in St. Louis (fig. 5.58). The precision and regularity of this bowl and its engraved decoration have a direct, almost anonymous, character, while at the same time its complex series of carefully cut surfaces produce unexpectedly brilliant reflections.

The region of Czechoslovakia known as Moravia was also the birthplace of another well-known designer and illustrator of the period, Alfons Maria, later known as Alphonse Mucha, whose posters and interiors were discussed above (see page 88). Mucha attended art schools in Vienna and in Paris, but returned to Prague later in his

5.58 Jan Kotera, crystal glass punch bowl, 1904, manufactured by Harrachow glassworks, Prague, (for St. Louis World's Fair). UPM, Prague.

5.59 Decorated plate, Zsolnay earthenware pottery, 1889. Zsolnay Museum, Pécs.

career where he worked on a large series of murals celebrating the folklore of his native country, another example of the attraction of artists at this time to ethnology.

The city of Budapest in Hungary had become one of Europe's larger urban centers by the year 1900, with a population of more than a million residents. Part of the Austrian empire, decorative artists were inspired both by vernacular craft traditions and contemporary esthetic ideas in the creation of a national Hungarian identity. The unique character of Hungarian design around the turn of the century is demonstrated by the production of the Zsolnay Pottery in the city of Pécs, in the southern part of the country. Much of the glazed stoneware produced there, beginning in 1862, incorporated decorative motifs based upon indigenous rustic folk traditions, whose flat, bright geometric patterns were collected and published by ethnologists and also used as the basis for architectural decoration in buildings designed by architect Ödön Lechner

(1845–1914). Examples of this work were inspired by native Hungarian craft traditions, for example in a plate designed by Jozsef Rippl-Ronai (1861–1927), a painter who devoted attention to the decorative arts, including pottery, weaving, and book illustration (fig. 5.59). The Zsolnay factory, employing as many as 1000 workers around the year 1900, also produced pottery with clearer associations to contemporary designs focusing upon elongated natural shapes and a wide variety of coloristic and textural experimentation (fig. 5.60).

Vernacular traditions are a rich aspect of the sources mined by decorative artists in the later nineteenth century, as revealed in the countries of eastern Europe and Scandinavia. The preceding pages provide only a sampling of the contribution of such traditions to modern design during this time. The variety of folk traditions adapted by artists is certainly connected to the theme of the unity or equality of the arts. In addition, the promotion of folk

5.60 Vase, Zsolnay earthenware pottery. Zsolnay Museum, Pécs.

recent displays and interiors from Scotland, Vienna, and Paris. As in other countries, the economic benefit of competing in the international market for manufactured products was an incentive for design, stimulating new directions in a country where the classical past was such a strong part of craft traditions.

Leonardo Bistofoli's poster for the 1902 Turin Exposition (fig. 5.61) is animated by the linear energies found in contemporary posters and illustration in Paris and other metropolitan centers. There is a hint of conservatism, however, in the traditional modeling and foreshortening of the figures, in comparison, for instance, to Ludwig von Zumbusch's cover illustration for *Jugend*, which renders a similar theme with a stronger degree of abstraction (see fig. 5.52).

Despite instances of tentative or even derivative approaches to more abstract and expressive elements in late nineteenth-century design, the creative use and combination of materials and virtuoso craftsmanship are admirable, for instance, in the chimneypiece, made of walnut, brass, and ceramic tile, manufactured by Vittorio Valabrega (1861–1952) for the international exhibition in Paris in 1900 (fig. 5.62). On the panel directly above the tile border framing the fireplace is a carved motif representing flames. At the same time the carved licks of flame resemble both the strands of hair and elongated vine scrolls that decorate other areas of the work.

traditions was a characteristic of national identity as well as economic self-sufficiency at the turn of the century. Ironically, the interest in reviving folk traditions and nostalgia for pre-industrial societies survived and was incorporated into an increasingly competitive, commercial, and international modern economy.

Italy

In Italy, unified only after 1861, artists, craftsmen, and manufacturers consciously promoted an interest in the equality of the arts and in the creation of a modern and original approach to design in the later nineteenth century. The city of Turin, in northern Italy, was the new nation's first capital and a center for design activity, hosting an important international exhibition in 1902 that included

5.61 Leonardo Bistofoli, poster for International Exposition of Modern Decorative Art in Turin, color lithograph, 43 5/16 x 56 7/8 in (110 x 144.1 cm), 1902. Museo Civico L. Bailo, Treviso.

5.63 Carlo Bugatti, "Snail Room", 1902. Photograph from the International Exposition, Turin.

5.62 Vittorio Valabrega Company, chimney piece, walnut, glazed ceramic, brass, and glass, 119 ¹¹/₁₆ x 75 x 15 ¹³/₁₆ in (304 x 190.5 x 40 cm). The Wolfsonian-Florida International University, Miami Beach, Florida: Mitchell Wolfson Collection.

In Italy there are also examples of highly original, even idiosyncratic approaches to design, best seen in the furniture of Carlo Bugatti (1856–1940). Bugatti, father of the automobile maker Ettore Bugatti (1881–1947), was trained as a painter but began creating his own furniture in the later 1880s. An ensemble, known as the "Snail Room", was featured at the International Exposition held in Turin in 1902 (fig. 5.63). Its furniture, including chairs, tables, and a massive, twisting bench, were constructed of wood transformed into elastically curved and stretched shapes, covered in vellum (sheepskin) with inlays of hammered copper. Despite the eclectic sources for the decorative vocabulary used in his furniture, Bugatti's designs are hardly derivative or historicist. Rather they exhibit a freedom from precedent and an inventiveness that informs much of the work treated so far in this chapter, namely the liberating effect of a closer relationship between fine art and craft.

Chapter 6

The Joy of Work

6.19 Vase, copper and silver, 6 ¼ x 3 ½ x 2 ½ in (17 x 8.9 x 6.3 cm),
attributed to Karl Kipps, *c.* 1910. Kurland-Zabar collection.

Ruskin, Morris, and the Arts and Crafts Movement in Britain

The loose brushwork and lack of traditional finish in some of Whistler's more suggestive paintings, such as *Nocturne in Black and Gold: The Falling Rocket*, aroused the contempt of the English writer and influential art critic John Ruskin (1819–1900). Ruskin's verbal attack (1877), in which he accused the painter of "flinging a pot of paint in the public's face", prompted Whistler to sue for libel, a case which he won but for which he received only token remuneration. The confrontation is ample evidence of the painter's strong belief in the freedom and independence of artists from both convention and public criticism. Ruskin's views of the *moral* value of the arts, both for the viewer as well as for the maker, probably precluded an appreciation of Whistler. Yet in spite of their dispute both men shared a belief in the dignity of the decorative arts and a dislike of rules and regulations that compromised an artist's integrity. Ruskin's views on these issues were widely read and highly influential in his own day, touching not only on the practice of design but also, and with equal influence, upon the relation of the arts to moral and social concerns.

Like A. W. N. Pugin, Ruskin admired the crafts of the Middle Ages and saw the decorative arts as a vehicle for enlightenment and social change. His solution, however, lay neither in historicism nor a moral "reading" of the Gothic style, nor in an indulgent "esthetic" view of the decorative arts often referred to at the time as *art for art's sake*, but rather in an elevated view of labor, which he felt was fundamentally undermined by mechanization, the division of labor, and a capitalist system that increasingly alienated workers from the products of their efforts. For Ruskin, the specialization inherent in the division of labor, and a market that stimulated cheaper and faster production, deprived people of the satisfaction of making products from start to finish as he believed they were made in the guilds during the Middle Ages:

> We have much studied and much perfected, of late, the great civilized invention of the division of labor; only we give it a false name. It is not, truly speaking, the labour that is divided; but the men: divided into mere segments of men – broken into small fragments and crumbs of life; so that all the little piece of intelligence that is left in a man is not enough to make a pin, or a nail, but exhausts itself in making the point of a pin or the head of a nail.

Ruskin's views on art and design drew in part upon his own careful descriptions and drawings of architecture and decoration; the sensitivity he developed to working methods of craftsmen formed the basis for conclusions about the nature of craft and sweeping solutions to the problems of an industrial society. In looking at carved architectural ornament from the Gothic period, Ruskin admired the dialogue between artisan and materials, the imperfections, the differences between one carved capital and another, the struggle to overcome the resistance of stone or wood with the tools at hand in the realization of an idea. The methods of the craftsman were, for Ruskin, the basis for joyful work and the equality among the arts in which craftsman and artist alike shared in the act of human labor. As a result Ruskin deplored the machine,

because machines made work *easy* or just plain *dull*, and because they made things uniform and lacking in the individuality of their handmade counterparts:

> All the stamped metals, and artificial stones, and imitation woods and bronzes, over the invention of which we hear daily exultation – all the short, and cheap, and easy ways of doing that whose difficulty is its honour – are just so many new obstacles in our already encumbered road. They will not make one of us happier or wiser – they will extend neither the pride of judgement nor the privilege of enjoyment. They will only make us shallower in our understandings, colder in our hearts, and feebler in our wits.

It probably comes as no surprise that Ruskin was no admirer of Joseph Paxton's Crystal Palace, for no cast-iron structure, regardless of its grand proportions or economy of construction, could aspire to being "art" in the sense of having been the product of joyful labor in the way Ruskin understood it.

In addition to his analysis of art and architecture, Ruskin's views also stemmed from a renewed sense of urgency regarding social reform. The only child of a wealthy wine merchant and the beneficiary of a large inheritance, Ruskin was nevertheless sensitive to the levels of poverty, unemployment, and poor working conditions in Britain and felt a sense of social conscience not uncommon among wealthy families of his day, which found outlets in political activism, philanthropy, and other private initiatives aimed at the well-being of the poor and working classes. Rather than applauding the economic expansion and material progress of his own time, he blamed industrialization and materialism for helping to create poverty, inequality, and misery, and saw meaningful work as a means to alleviate it. Indeed, his exaltation of labor was in some way a compensation for his own loss of faith, for if religion was of little comfort to humanity in the modern world, then it might perhaps be replaced by some substitute spirituality. For Ruskin that substitute was the happiness provided by *work*, and thus the products of work acquired new levels of meaning. It follows, almost of necessity, that if labor was its own reward, then the technological and material progress of the nineteenth century represented for Ruskin only a kind of empty materialism that ignored the spiritual values which should inform an ideal society:

the foundations of society were never yet shaken as they are at this day. It is not that men are ill-fed, but that they have no pleasure in the work by which they make their bread, and *therefore look to wealth as the only means of pleasure.* [Italics author's own]

Earlier in his career Ruskin had championed the cause of the British landscape painter J.M.W. Turner (*Modern Painters*, vol. 1), but he grew to question whether the uplifting qualities embodied in Turner's works would enrich the experience and add to the well-being of working people. Ruskin then focused his attention on architecture and the decorative arts because their cost as well as their utility might have a greater impact upon the workers who made and enjoyed such buildings and goods. Work was a common element in the lives of both the middle and working classes, a basis for social equality linked to mutual respect among people. And unlike Pugin or Owen Jones, it was joy rather than taste that governed Ruskin's attitudes:

[T]he right question to ask, respecting all ornament, is simply this: Was it done with enjoyment – was the carver happy while he was about it? It may be the hardest work possible, and the harder because so much pleasure was taken in it; but it must have been happy too, or it will not be living.

In other words, Ruskin advocated no particular style or set of rules for designers to follow other than that the work be a unique creation reflecting the skill, pride, and effort of the craftsman. His views share an interest in individuality with Dresser and even with Whistler and other designers who were part of the Aesthetic Movement, but Ruskin's overriding emphasis was upon the moral and spiritual benefits of craft rather than upon accommodating the technology of production or the contemplation of beauty.

While Ruskin remained primarily a writer and theorist commenting on issues concerning design and society, William Morris (1834–1896) was more interested in integrating theory with practice. Like Ruskin, Morris came from a wealthy middle-class family and benefited from an annual income, yet he also possessed a strong sense of social responsibility characteristic of the Victorian Age. As a student at Oxford preparing for a career in the clergy, he

was deeply moved by Ruskin's ideas concerning the relation between art and social reform, and also shared friendship and ideals with a group of young Romantic artists and poets who called themselves the Pre-Raphaelite Brotherhood (PRB). The group was critical of the materialism that accompanied modern industrialism and was committed to creating a closer relation between art and craft in reaction against the established policies of the Royal Academy in England and the elevated status it accorded the fine arts. It was his kinship with the PRB that led Morris to abandon his training for the ministry and pursue a career as an artist–craftsman. One can detect the echo of Ruskin in Morris's own writings, which have had a lasting effect upon designers in the later nineteenth and twentieth centuries:

yet I cannot in my own mind quite sever them [the arts of architecture, painting, and sculpture] from those so-called Decorative Arts, which I have to speak about; it is only in latter times, and under the most intricate conditions of life, that they have fallen apart from one another; I hold that, when they are so parted, it is ill for the Arts altogether; the lesser ones become trivial, mechanical, unintelligent, incapable of resisting the changes pressed upon them by fashion or dishonesty; while the greater, however they may be practiced for a while by men of great minds and wonder-working hands, unhelped by the lesser, unhelped by each other, are sure to lose their dignity as popular arts, and become nothing but dull adjuncts to unmeaning pomp, or ingenious toys for a few rich and idle men...

In addition, Morris was a poet, novelist, publisher, socialist, translator, preservationist, and public speaker, whose myriad activities were influential both in Britain as well as in Germany, Belgium, France, and the United States (in fact, Morris's writings were influential even for those, such as Frank Lloyd Wright, who freely interpreted and "modernized" his views). The spiritualization of craft, its link to social reform, and skepticism toward the widely-held view that industrialization and progress went hand in hand characterize Morris's attitudes and became the basis for a number of organizations and other initiatives that are known generally as the Arts and Crafts Movement.

Morris's interest in design emerged with the interior decoration of his home, the Red House, in Kent beginning in 1858, designed by his friend Philip Webb (1831–1915). The house eschewed the tendency toward superficial period styles as well as expensive (or expensive-looking) materials in favor of straightforward brick and a less formal, asymmetrical plan. Rather than purchase furnishings from a showroom or manufacturer, Morris and his friends took on the task themselves, leading to the formation of the firm of Morris, Marshall, Faulkner and Company (later Morris and Company) in 1861. At the outset the firm was based upon friendship and shared ideals. Morris's wife, Jane, took an interest in the embroidery workshop, and Philip Webb and Dante Gabriel Rossetti (a member of the PRB) designed furniture and stained-glass windows. For instance, among the furnishings for the home was a set of simple chairs with hand-woven rush seats that used modestly-tooled spindles for legs and backs. The chairs were based upon designs by Webb and Rossetti that derived from rustic country examples (fig. 6.1). Such furnishings established a link with craft traditions only minimally affected either by contemporary commercial

6.2 The Morris Adjustable Chair, ebonized wood with velvet "Bird" design upholstery, 39 x 24 ¼ x 31 in (99 x 63 x 79 cm), designed by Philip Webb, manufactured by Morris, Marshall, Faulkner & Co., from 1866. Victoria and Albert Museum, London.

considerations or by the use of machine tools and techniques. Not all furniture manufactured by the firm was economical or even restrained in decoration—indeed individuality, the love of nature, and the joy of craft all found expression in design, especially in ornament. Where decoration appears, as in the carved legs of the so-called "Morris Chair" (fig. 6.2), an early example of a reclining armchair designed not by Morris but by the manufacturer William Watt in 1883, it seems intended to provide an outlet for the skill and invention of the craftsman as well as the delight of the owner within the constraints of material and construction costs.

As a craftsman Morris first concentrated upon the design of windows and the painted decoration of wooden furniture, and then became primarily a designer of patterns that were used for the manufacture of ceramic tiles,

6.1 Armchair from the Sussex range, possibly designed by Philip Webb, ebonized beech with rush seat, 33 ¼ x 20 ½ x 17 in (85.6 x 52.4 x 43 cm), c. 1860, manufactured by Morris, Marshall, Faulkner & Company. Victoria and Albert Museum, London.

6.3 William Morris, *Pimpernel* design for wallpaper, block-printed, manufactured by Jeffrey & Co. for Morris & Co., 26 ¼ x 20 ¼ in (68 x 52.5 cm), 1876. Victoria and Albert Museum, London.

embroideries, wallpapers, carpets, and printed fabrics. In many cases Morris found craftsmen to execute designs, but he also practiced techniques himself, installing equipment in his residence first in London then in the suburb of Hammersmith after 1878. He also leased facilities for weaving at Merton Abbey, Surrey, where he experimented in the development of vegetable dyes for fabrics rather than commercially available anodyne dyes. For ceramics he seems to have been more than pleased with entrusting production to artist–craftsman William de Morgan, an independent potter who had worked previously for the firm, and who also produced his own designs, including tiles for the home of Lord Alfred Leighton (see page 72). Whether directly or indirectly involved in actual production, Morris advocated close collaboration between designer and craftsman and refused to use machines even

for the manufacture of wallpapers or printed fabrics: "it is not desirable to divide the labour between the artist and what is technically called the designer, and I think it desirable on the whole that the artist and designer should practically be one."

Although deeply indebted to Ruskin, Morris's own designs avoid illusionism and seem to follow the general tendency of earlier design reform and contemporary designers such as Dresser and Eastlake to view decoration in the context of architecture that is, as an embellishment to construction; it was the unity and implied collaboration in his understanding of architecture, that guided his approach. He also believed in the importance of individual expression, and advocated original designs in addition to those inspired by nostalgia for earlier periods, chiefly the European Middle Ages.

Morris's patterns may be described as a dialogue, often tense, between a love of natural beauty found in plants and flowers and the discipline needed to transform this appreciation into patterns suitable for surface decoration. An example is found in his "Pimpernel" wallpaper of 1876 (fig. 6.3). Against a dark green background lighter green flowers are symmetrically arranged and repeated, but varied in their position; each is framed by interlocking spiral vine tendrils in brown loosely entwined by thin green leaves. A secondary motif is defined by smaller and flatter green leaves with round blue morning glories placed at intervals on the stems. The naturalism is at its height with the almost windswept flowers with their undulating contours, slightly reduced for the thin leaf forms and becoming more regularized and schematic for the blue flowers, tendrils, and smaller oval leaves. The sense both of nature's luxuriant variety and the care with which the designer preserves its freshness within the constraints of pattern is remarkable in all of Morris's best work, and prevents his designs from becoming stale or dry.

The firm of Morris and Company was reasonably successful during the 1860s and 1870s, profiting from orders to design and execute stained-glass windows and other furniture for churches, as well as commissions from wealthy clients for a wide variety of furnishings for domestic interiors. These patrons could afford the labor costs of Morris's production methods and shared his vision for a society based upon meaningful and satisfying work. An example of a Morris and Company interior is "The Green Dining Room" at the South Kensington (now Victoria and

6.4 Morris and Co., "The Green Dining Room", Victoria and Albert (South Kensington) Museum, 1866. Photograph: Victoria and Albert Museum, London.

to the subjective vision of the artist, asserting his or her independence from the motivation for profit or for official recognition. One might say that the Arts and Crafts Movement was directed toward process and in ending or at least reducing the alienation between an artisan and the product of his or her labor. In theory at least, manufacturers and buyers would support such an aim as an expression of social responsibility. Artists of the Aesthetic Movement attempted to identify and give visible form to subjective experience through the decorative object or product. Receptivity to subjective, private expression generally demanded a cultivated audience, though in defying convention and taking liberties with tradition there was a certain degree of solidarity between Aesthetic artists and other marginal or rebellious elements elsewhere in society. The intersection of these margins emerges in particular in the world of entertainment, where posters advertising cabarets or book jackets for popular fiction often borrows the abstract and exaggerated forms seen also in esthetic interiors.

Morris and Socialism

Despite the success of Morris and Company, the founder became increasingly disillusioned by the inability of his efforts to effect broad social change and to reach his intended working-class audience. In the 1870s he was an outspoken critic of the British government's foreign policy in the Balkans (which he believed was motivated by economic rather than humanitarian interests), and in the 1880s he became actively involved with the Socialist movement in Britain in the hope of creating social equality and reducing the pressures for production and consumption that fueled the capitalist system:

> what I mean by Socialism is a condition of society in which there should be neither rich nor poor, neither master nor master's man, neither idle nor overworked, neither brain-sick brain workers nor heart-sick hand workers ... in which all men would be living in equality of condition, and would manage their affairs unwastefully and with the full consciousness that harm to one would mean harm to all – the realization at last of the meaning of the word COMMONWEALTH.

Albert) Museum in London, commissioned as a lunchroom for visitors (1866, fig. 6.4). The interior is coordinated through a wall-treatment of painted vine-scroll patterns in molded stucco relief, rug, stained glass, lighting, ceramic panels, painted panels with repeated figural and plant motifs, and painted furniture all provided by the firm, and all intended to convey the love of nature and the appreciation of craftsmanship. In 1875 Morris assumed sole proprietorship of the firm. In addition to maintaining facilities at his residence and leasing separate facilities for production, a storefront showroom was maintained on Oxford Street, London, where other fashionable retail establishments were located, and the firm continued to exhibit work at international exhibitions, for instance in London in 1862 and in Philadelphia in 1876.

Clearly there were shared elements in the work of the Arts and Crafts Movement and the Aesthetic Movement, and some designers, such as de Morgan, Sir Edward Burne-Jones (1833–1898), and Walter Crane, seemed to move rather comfortably between the two. But there were differences as well, at least in terms of emphasis and audience. For Morris, artists with a social conscience could best direct their efforts by being craftsmen, where their products would most serve the needs of society and provide the satisfaction of meaningful work. For the Aesthetic designer, the decorative arts were the vehicle for giving concrete form, in media other than painting or sculpture,

Another recurrent theme in his writings, echoing Ruskin, is the excessive self-interest that was created by competition:

> Manufacturers are so set on carrying out competition to its utmost, competition of cheapness, not of excellence, that they meet the bargain-hunters half way, and cheerfully furnish them with many wares at the cheap rate…

Morris was active in organized socialist activities in London, and his views echo themes of the alienation of labor, the concentration and growth of capital, and the "fetishism" of commodities found in the writings of Karl Marx (1818–1883) and Friedrich Engels (1820–1895). While Morris offered an alternative to industrial capitalism in terms of production, he could not account for or effectively resist the increasing attraction of consumption across all classes of modern society. Ironically, the success of Morris and Company depended almost entirely upon an exclusive market, thus bolstering the capitalist system he hoped to eliminate by the renewal of craft.

Morris did acknowledge a role for mechanization in the production of goods and furnishings, particularly if it reduced drudgery. But his view of the role of the machine was narrowly circumscribed and he felt its products should never deprive a craftsman of the opportunity to find pleasure in work. Nevertheless his views appear to be, not without some irony, the basis for the later equation of machine-made goods with simple designs and smooth surfaces: "The more mechanical the process, the less direct should be the imitation of natural forms." Such an approach was espoused by American architect Frank Lloyd Wright (1869–1959), whose own attitudes toward the machine are considered below (see pages 126–7).

Morris as Publisher

William Morris's last design venture was the founding of Kelmscott Press in 1890, and brought together his attitudes about art and design with his experience as an author. Morris produced an illustrated edition of Chaucer's *Canterbury Tales* as well as a short volume containing Ruskin's "Nature of Gothic" chapter from *The Stones of Venice*, which eloquently stated the his beliefs in the dignity of work. Morris's close friend Edward Burne-Jones designed woodcut illustrations for the *The Works of Geoffrey Chaucer* (fig. 6.5), while Morris himself designed a series of border patterns used on pages with illustrations, as well as the typeface and block initials of various sizes. He drew the typefaces himself, influenced by the more calligraphic example of William Caslon rather than the mechanical precision of modern fonts. The decorative richness of the illustrated pages fulfill Morris's objective to make the book itself an object of beauty, even if some historians find it less well-suited to reading, perhaps a result of the distraction of elements other than type. The Kelmscott Press was located at the artist's home in Hammersmith. The venture emerged at a time when photomechanical reproduction was transforming the character of illustration, and when steam presses were finally being introduced into the book publishing industry. Inspired by the example of the nearby Chiswick Press (see page 59) and independent efforts of printers and other craftsmen to maintain the handmade character of the printed book, Morris succeeded in restoring the vitality of the private press, even if this unified approach to the printed page generally attracted a limited and well-to-do clientele.

Toward the end of his career Morris's vision for a better society took the form of utopian writings, often published

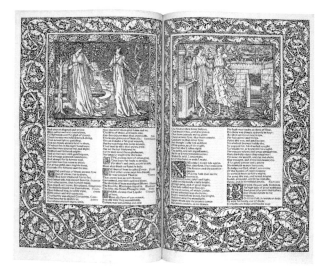

6.5 William Morris (wood-engraved illustrations after designs by Edward Burne-Jones), folio from *The Works of Geoffrey Chaucer*, printed at the Kelmscott Press, 16 ¾ x 11 ½ in (42.5 x 29.2 cm), 1896. Cheltenham Art Gallery and Museums.

in serial form in the Socialist journal *Commonweal* that he edited. The romance *News from Nowhere* (1890) takes place in England in the twenty-second century, but its setting is reminiscent of the riverside village community of Hammersmith where Morris lived after 1878:

> ...*all* work is now pleasurable; either because of the hope of gain in honour and wealth with which the work is done, which causes pleasurable excitement, even when the actual work is not pleasant; or because it has grown into a pleasurable *habit*, as in the case with what you may call mechanical work; and lastly (and most of our work is of this kind) because there is conscious sensuous pleasure in the work itself; it is done, that is, by artists...

Eventually Morris's equation of simple forms with machine production would give way to views among some of his followers that linked the machine to the working class and newer, twentieth-century utopian dreams for social equality and a more collective model for design. But for Morris the joy and dignity of craft remained the most important elements in the attainment of human happiness, and it was difficult to combine this attitude with an acceptance of mechanization and serial production except in a limited way, either from a social or an esthetic standpoint.

6.6 Arthur Haygate Mackmurdo, title page, *Wren's City Churches*, woodcut on paper, 11 ⁷⁄₁₇ x 8 ¾ in (29.2 x 22.25 cm), printed by G. Allen, Orpington, Kent, 1883. Victoria and Albert Museum, London.

The Influence of William Morris in Britain

William Morris's ideas and example found fertile ground for development in Britain, continental Europe, and the United States, but his views at times underwent considerable transformation and interpretation. Arthur Heygate Mackmurdo (1851–1942) was born in Britain in the year of the Great Exhibition. He was a friend of both Morris and Ruskin, and traveled with the latter to Italy in 1874. Like Morris, Mackmurdo was concerned with the preservation of historic buildings, and he is perhaps best remembered for the lithographically-printed title page of a book entitled *Wren's City Churches* (fig. 6.6), that he published privately in 1883 containing illustrations of churches designed by the English architect Sir Christopher Wren (1632–1723). An architect by training, Mackmurdo advocated an elevated status for craft and the abolition of the distinction between fine and applied art. He was a founding member of a group of artists known as the Century Guild, dedicated to the following goals: "to render all branches of art the sphere no longer of the tradesman but of the artist, to restore building, decoration, glass painting, potter, woodcarving and metal to their rightful place beside painting and sculpture." The flame-like shapes for the title page from *Wren's City Churches* are based upon a floral form but clearly are exaggerated to suggest a heightened sense of movement and growth, enhanced by the strong contrast between figure and ground. Banners displaying the title have the same sense of elasticity as the floral motif, and stand out only by being placed against a larger expanse of white ground. Mackmurdo used the same design for a chair also manufactured by the Century Guild in the same year (fig. 6.7). Here the asymmetrical design is not applied or added on to the chair but actually forms the

6.7 Arthur Haygate Mackmurdo, chair, mahogany with leather upholstery, 38 ¼ x 19 ½ x 18 ¹¹⁄₁₆ in (97.2 x 49.5 x 47.6 cm), 1883, manufactured by the Century Guild. Victoria and Albert Museum, London.

6.8 Vincent van Gogh, *Irises*, oil on canvas, 29 x 36 1/4 in (73.7 x 92.1 cm), 1890. Metropolitan Museum of Art, New York.

support of the backrest. The abstract, subjective treatment of naturalistic forms seen in these examples by Mackmurdo may be compared to contemporary Post-Impressionist art in France, for instance in the more subjective approach to still life of Vincent van Gogh's *Irises* from 1890 (fig. 6.8), with their sinuous contours and emphasis upon the flatness of the picture plane. In both cases the formal characteristics of the decorative arts approximate those of avant-garde painting in that the artist is guided by a conscious subjectivity that transforms a more naturalistic manner of working, suppressing illusionism in favor of surface pattern.

The Century Guild also published a journal entitled *The Hobby Horse* that disseminated ideas about craft and art, including articles by Oscar Wilde. A journal cover produced in 1886 by guild member and co-founder Selwyn Image (1849–1930) in woodcut (fig. 6.9) shows the title contained in a rectangular box placed within the rectangle of the framed page and seemingly held in place by a maze of intertwined branches, roots, and plants, all possessing a sense of strong linear movement and energy.

6.9 Selwyn Image, front cover for the *Hobby Horse*, woodcut illustration printed on paper, for the Century Guild, 1886. Private collection.

6.10 Charles Robert Ashbee, bowl and spoon, silver and chrysoprase, bowl: 3 x 10 ⅝ x 4 ¼ in (7.6 x 27.3 x 10.8 cm), 1904. Metropolitan Museum of Art, New York.

Other organizations and associations promoted the ideology and practice of Arts and Crafts. An Arts and Crafts Exhibition Society was founded in 1888 to organize shows of craft objects, and the versatile designer William Lethaby (1857–1931) established a school in London based upon a close relationship between designer and maker and the practical value underlying all art:

> a work of art is first of all a well-made thing. It may be a well-made statue or a well-made chair, or a well-made book… Most simply and generally art may be thought of as the "well-doing of what needs doing; every work of art shows that it was made by a human being for a human being

Other craft associations, both in Britain and in the United States, represent a direct connection with Morris's efforts to link handicraft to esthetic as well as social values through communities of workers living and working together in utopian harmony. Charles Ashbee (1863–1942) was another versatile designer and educator who until the early twentieth century shared Morris's belief in the artistic dimension of design as well as the great social benefit of the useful arts. After graduating from Cambridge University in 1886 Ashbee moved to Toynbee Hall, a residence for university graduates in a working-class section of London established to rebuild relationships between social classes. In 1888 Ashbee helped to found the *Guild and School of Handicraft*, based in London's East End (this section of the city was associated with high-volume piecework for the furniture

industry) and employing as many as fifty workers. His interest in the preservation of craft traditions stemmed from long experience as a designer and a belief that the applied arts provided the means for original work: "the education of the hand and eye are only fully achieved in the education of the *individuality* of the workman."

Ashbee's work respects and explores the nature of handcrafted materials, and his designs possess a striking originality in both the character of the decoration and its relation between ornament and structure, as seen in a silver bowl (fig. 6.10) of 1904. In this work the smooth surface has been worked by hand, and the symmetrical handles extend outward with an elastic and graceful curve, whose expressive effect is enhanced by contrast with the simple shape and treatment of the bowl (Ashbee's inspiration may have been examples or representations of the ancient Greek drinking cup known as the *kantharos*). After meeting Frank Lloyd Wright on a visit to the USA in 1901 and following the economic failure of the Guild and School of Handicraft in 1908 Ashbee came to accept the role of machinery in design and to admire Wright's ability to suggest a compatibility between machine production and the social responsibility of the designer (see pages 126–7). Later, Ashbee relocated his guild to a rural community in Gloucestershire, acknowledging perhaps that the ideals of the Arts and Crafts Movement were more compatible with rural rather than urban conditions.

Despite its lofty social aims and the fervor of its rhetoric, the Arts and Crafts Movement, both in regard to Morris and Company and immediate followers such as Ashbee and Mackmurdo, found a place and achieved success within a limited commercial milieu shared by the Aesthetic Movement. Ashbee's withdrawal from city to countryside demonstrates the difficulties inherent in championing craftsmanship in an increasingly industrial and commercial age. Morris may have been embarrassed by this contradiction between intentions and outcomes. The commercial success of the firm and his own celebrity as an artist–craftsman were at odds with the classless society he envisioned and the role the arts would play within it, but Morris's considerable efforts at least permitted the growth and development of his ideas in the founding of guilds and crafts organizations, as well as in education, where his idealism could also take root. Moreover, his example and writings proved to be the basis for other design initiatives where his ideas were often freely interpreted:

both Frank Lloyd Wright in the United States (see page 127) and Henry van de Velde in Belgium (see page 96) drew inspiration from Morris's example and writings.

Craft and Efficiency

One effort to reconcile craft with social reform was the embrace of simple, utilitarian furniture designs that reduced or eliminated decoration, resulting in less costly products with a shared esthetic of solid yet more impersonal forms. The rejection of the signs of costly labor might demonstrate for the buyer sympathy with the honesty and integrity of hand craftsmanship as well as the responsibility of a practical, unpretentious lifestyle. An example is Charles Voysey's chair of 1904 with simple oak construction, rush seat, and two vertical slats for the back, each carved to form a heart at their intersection (fig. 6.11). Yet as discussed by design historian Adrian Forty, simple undecorated furniture was often purchased by wealthy families for furnishing servants' quarters, reinforcing class distinctions and the associations between decoration and more sophisticated, enlightened tastes.

In architecture, the efficiency style also informed the building of garden suburbs near London in areas such as Hampstead. Such suburbs were made up of small brick houses, built to standardized plans, with ample green space, and nearby shops and services to encourage mingling among social classes. The idea of the garden suburb was admired in Germany as a model for responsible housing and formed the basis for debate over design standards in the Deutscher Werkbund, an association of designers, manufacturers, and artists formed in 1907 and discussed in greater detail below (see page 129).

Books, Illustration, and Type

Morris's Kelmscott Press was one among several publishing ventures that emerged during the last quarter of the nineteenth century. Illustrated books, art journals, and a burgeoning illustrated literature for children constituted the means by which the Aesthetic and Arts and Crafts Movements communicated their ideas to different audiences.

Publishing is a collaborative enterprise, and a number of printers, binders, and illustrators were involved in

6.11 C. F. A. Voysey, chair, oak with rush seat, 1904. Geffrye Museum, London.

Morris's Kelmscott Press. Emery Walker (1851–1933), for instance, worked as a printer at the Chiswick Press not far from Hammersmith where Morris lived and began his own press. Prior to the initiation of the Kelmscott Press, Walker had contributed to the Century Guild's *The Hobby Horse* journal whose quality and character had stimulated Morris's own venture (see page 114). After Morris's death in 1896 Walker and the bookbinder T. J. Cobden-Sanderson (1840–1922) began their own publishing company known as the Dove's Press, also in Hammersmith (in fact, directly across the alley from Kelmscott on the Thames riverside). These efforts combined interrelated concerns for the quality of paper and ink, the esthetics of calligraphy, as well as legibility in type, harmonious relation with borders, initials, and illustration, and the overall unity of the page or open double-page.

More esthetic, expressive interests in printing also emerged in Britain with the publication of a journal in 1893 entitled *The Studio*. In addition to publishing illustrations of contemporary furniture and furnishings, *The Studio* included illustrations by artists with a highly subjective approach to the representation of nature and the human form, related to contemporary Symbolist attitudes to art discussed above. For instance, the first issue of *The Studio* contained plates from Oscar Wilde's poem based upon the New Testament story of Salomé, published originally in French and designed by the young English illustrator Aubrey Beardsley (fig. 6.12). Beardsley's *The Climax*, representing Salomé's embrace of the severed head of John the Baptist, is strongly calligraphic and conforms to a two-dimensional approach to page design. The illustration also makes use of the asymmetrical superimposed wave patterns in the upper left corner familiar from Japanese decoration, a motif borrowed as well by Whistler in his painting of the built-in furniture in the Peacock room. The drawing, in addition to its relation to the themes of lust and violence, permits the artist considerable freedom and invention in the transformation of hair, plant forms, and the pool of liquid (perhaps blood) from which a thin flower grows at the bottom right of the composition.

Another prominent figure in the publication of books involving artists connected with aesthetic ideas was Charles Ricketts (1866–1931). Ricketts carefully considered the unity of page design involving typography, illustration, and decoration. He published a collaborative project between Wilde and Beardsley, an illustrated poem entitled *The Sphinx*. Much lighter in overall effect than the books of Morris's Kelmscott Press, the pages of *The Sphinx* use blocks of text, decorated initials and framed illustration to achieve balance and a strong sense of the relationship among individual elements unified by shared qualities of weight and density. Ricketts worked with different printers to publish books under the name of the Vale Press. Other titles include a large but thin volume of *De Cupidinis et Psychis Amoribus Fabula Anilis*, an erotic Latin poem translated by Charles Holme with woodcut illustrations, that appeared in 1901. Here the textured paper and ragged edges, old face typography, and varied width of columns to accommodate intimate scenes of lovers (fig. 6.13) are aspects of private and personal books meant for discriminating taste.

6.12 Aubrey Beardsley, design for *The Climax*, from Oscar Wilde's *Salome*, print, 9 x 5 in (22.9 x 12.7 cm), 1893. Private collection.

Lucien Pissarro (1863–1944), son of the French Impressionist painter Camille Pissarro, pursued a career in private press publishing in London. Together with his wife Pissarro founded the Eragny Press in Hammersmith in the early 1890s and approached all the elements of book design, including typography, with equal interest. Early books used Rickett's Vale font, while later volumes employed a font drawn by Pissarro himself and called Brook type, much admired for its legibility. Borders were printed in color and constitute a distinctive characteristic of the Eragny Press (fig. 6.14).

Aesthetic attitudes and the Arts and Crafts movement also had an impact upon the publication of illustrated books for other markets, including children. Interest in children's literature was strong among early design

6.14 Lucien Pissarro, page from *Ishtar's Descent into the Nether World*, paper, 1903. Private collection.

6.13 Charles Ricketts, *De Cupidinis et Psychis Amoribus Fabula Anilis*, 1901. Hagerty Library Archives, Drexel University, USA.

reformers such as Henry Cole who saw these books as a means of cultivating taste and instilling values of moderation (see page 50). In the later nineteenth century attitudes about children's books changed to include a more innocent, playful, in short, a more "child-like" point of view, less didactic and allowing for greater experimentation with media and expression. In departing from illusionism and naturalism, children's illustrators shared an approach to imagery related to their Aesthetic Movement counterparts. In attempting to adopt the viewpoint of a child, they entered into an imaginative state of mind that was akin to many others working in the fine and decorative arts at this time.

The embossed gold seal found on many well-known children's books today is named for a pioneer in the new approach to children's books, English illustrator Randolph Caldecott (1846–1886). Caldecott was a self-taught artist who only became a professional illustrator after moving to London from Manchester in the early 1870s. He served as a freelance illustrator for popular weekly news journals in London and several of his illustrations were reproduced in *Harper's New Monthly Magazine* published in New York. Among his best-known works are a series of books published by George Routledge with color wood-engravings by Edmund Evans. The collaboration of illustrator and engraver is a significant one, for Evans's methods of reproduction preserved the simple, abbreviated quality of Caldecott's drawing, set off against broad unmodulated areas of lightly tinted color, and was a creative rather than mechanical process that contributed to the success of Caldecott's work. Eliminating the more conventional detail and cross-hatching used in the wood-engraving process, picture-books such as *Hey Diddle Diddle* (1882, fig. 6.15) achieved wide popularity in both Britain and

Ruskin for its idyllic recreation of natural beauty in a pre-industrial era. The frequent use of blank space in her compositions reveals an affinity to the decorative tendencies of Aesthetic design, and as a woman her creative energies were channeled toward the applied arts rather than to the male-dominated fine arts at this period of time.

Greenaway's first popular success was an illustrated book published by George Routledge in 1879 entitled *Under the Window*. A frontispiece for *Marigold Garden; Pictures and Rhymes* (first published 1885, fig. 6.16) features high-waisted dresses that recall the simpler fashions of the earlier eighteenth century and a type of idealized child's face (it has been suggested that the artist derived the type from the collection of dolls she owned). Greenaway also used bands of flowers to frame the illustration and serve as a motif to suggest a landscape setting. In this case a garden twists around the playful composition of figures in various poses dancing in a circle. This

6.15 Randolph Caldecott, illustration from *Hey Diddle Diddle*, print, 1882, printed by George Routledge & Sons, London.

France. He also earned respect among noted designers such as Walter Crane and artists such as van Gogh and Gauguin, both of whom owned copies of Caldecott's relatively inexpensive picture books. The recognition, in artistic as well as popular circles, of Caldecott's illustrations, along with the emergence of exhibitions and galleries devoted to the print media, is an example of the interrelationship among the arts that animated both artists and the public during the later nineteenth century.

Contemporary with Caldecott's picture books were those of another British artist, Kate Greenaway (1846–1901). Greenaway's father was a freelance wood engraver who had worked with Evans for the publisher of the illustrated journal *Punch*, and Evans was also responsible for reproducing Greenaway's drawings for color reproduction. In addition to illustrated poetry and children's books, Greenaway also produced greeting cards for a mass public. Greenaway's career and illustrations touch upon a number of emerging attitudes toward the decorative arts in the later nineteenth century. She received training at the government-sponsored design schools established around the middle of the century to prepare designers for industry, and her work was praised by

6.16 Kate Greenaway, illustration from *Under the Window: Pictures and Rhymes for Children*, c. 1900. Frederick Warne & Co., London and New York.

component in her illustrations grew out of her own sketches from nature as well as the conventionalized approach to drawing she learned at the schools of design she attended. It has also been pointed out that the strong contours and areas of flat color found in Greenaway's as well as Caldecott's children's illustrations were derived from effects in Japanese woodblock prints that contributed so much to the contemporary Aesthetic Movement in Europe as well as in the United States.

The illustrations of Greenaway, Caldecott, as well as Walter Crane, were reproduced from the artists' original drawings rendered on wood for engraving, or in the case of Greenaway, translated onto stone for chromolithographic reproduction for greeting cards. Black and white illustrations for more timely publications such as newspapers and weekly magazines used specialized labor to more quickly translate drawings into wood, and by the 1880s photomechanical methods of reproducing images were beginning to alter these techniques. At first photographs of original drawings were printed on wood for hand-engraving, eliminating either the artist's or engraver's role in this stage of production. A more significant development was the use of acid to engrave a wood or metal block printed with a photographic image, eliminating the need for any handwork at all except in the finishing stages. Direct methods of printing involving artists and craftsmen persisted, however, in the form of book illustration, flourished in poster design, and in more editorial forms of imagery for cartoons and caricatures in newspapers and magazines.

The Arts and Crafts Movement in the United States

John Ruskin's writings were read extensively in the United States during the second half of the nineteenth century and examples of furnishings from the firm of Morris, Marshall, Faulkner and Company were on display at the Centennial Exposition of 1876 in Philadelphia. The influence of the Arts and Crafts Movement may be seen in the popularity of the Gothic style favored by Ruskin and Morris for parish churches and their interior furnishings, and also in relation to the promotion and revival of craft societies and the initiation of craft education in cities such as New York, Cincinnati, and Boston. Reaching a peak in the decades between 1890 and 1910, the Arts and Crafts

ideology also stimulated considerable interest in the relation between design and social reform, leading to the establishment of craft workshops, artisan communities, and some practical efforts to meet the challenges posed by mass production, mechanization, and advertising.

Gustav Stickley (1858–1942) is perhaps the best known of many American Arts and Crafts furniture manufacturers in the early twentieth century, in part because furniture bearing the Stickley name continues to be manufactured, and also because it has been featured recently in popular films such as *A River Runs Through It* (1993). Stickley learned furniture-making while serving as an apprentice at his uncle's chair factory in Massachusetts, and became familiar with Arts and Crafts ideology and practice through the writings of William Morris and the published designs of British architect M. H. Baillie Scott that appeared in journals on the decorative arts on both sides of the Atlantic. In 1898 Stickley visited Britain and in 1900 founded the Craftsman Workshops near Syracuse, New York, with himself as master craftsman. He published a journal called *The Craftsman* beginning in 1901 to promote both his furniture and the values of the honesty and satisfaction of handicraft stemming from the ideology of the Arts and Crafts Movement. Stickley hoped his designs would appeal "strongly to the directness and common sense of the American people" with furniture that was solid, natural in materials and construction, and avoided carved decoration and time-consuming marquetry. *The Craftsman* included plans for building your own house, essays on reformers such as Ruskin and Morris, and designs for furniture, textiles, and other crafts to encourage readers to engage in handicraft, hoping to "extend the principles established by Morris, in both the artistic and the socialistic sense," equating beauty with "simplicity, individuality, and dignity of effect."

Although he admired and promoted the virtues of hand craftsmanship, Stickley's interests were more commercial than other more ideologically-minded craftsmen, and in his factory machine tools were used to save production time in a competitive high-end market. Sometimes referred to as a "new" industrialist, Stickley adopted such efficient measures in the workshop but also included vocational education for workers, maintaining at least some affiliation with the social reform associated with the Arts and Crafts Movement. His oak sideboard from 1905–10 (fig. 6.17) is devoid of carved ornament: the plain surfaces and rectilinear shapes of the various constructive elements are relieved only by hammered copper fittings such as hinges and drawer handles. Stickley furniture shows great respect for the skill and intelligence of the craftsman in the selection and treatment of natural materials, and reveals care in the preparation of surfaces, as well as in the construction of joints and other fittings. The slats that appear in many examples of Craftsman furniture reduce the block-like heaviness of the design and serve as a modest decorative feature integrated with structural forms. Other furniture manufactured by Stickley was designed by Harvey Ellis (1852–1904) and feature taller proportions, thinner forms and inlay decoration reminiscent of Mackintosh and the Wiener Werkstätte. While some of Stickley's production methods deviated from the ideals of Ruskin and Morris, the style of his furniture embodied the virtues of clean, comfortable, natural, and modest living among an urban public seeking to give expression to the longing for social conscience, honesty, and the dignity of labor in an urban world increasingly dominated by large companies, the emergence of national brands, advertising, and the impersonality of modern industrialized society.

The success of Stickley's enterprise encouraged him to move into new and larger headquarters in New York City in 1913. By that time he had numerous showrooms and distributors for Craftsman furnishings throughout the country, and participated in Arts and Crafts exhibitions as a means of marketing his products. Despite expanding into the production of leathercraft and textiles, however, less expensive imitations and the waning of taste for the particular "Craftsman" style (his only product line) led Stickley to declare bankruptcy in 1915, and *The Craftsman* ceased publication the following year.

Self-contained craft communities were another expression of Arts and Crafts ideology in the United States. Among the most successful was the Roycrofters, founded by Elbert Hubbard (1856–1915) in 1893 and based in a suburb of Buffalo, New York. The Roycroft workshops concentrated primarily upon the printing press, publishing editions of the founder's periodical *The Philistine* and the series of small paperbound books entitled *Little Journeys*, as well as metalcraft, leather-making, and furniture resembling the Craftsman style. Some of the designers employed by Hubbard also worked independently as well as for other manufacturers, but the Roycroft

6.17 Gustav Stickley, sideboard, oak and copper, 47 ½ x 56 x 21 ¾ in (120.7 x 142.2 x 55.3 cm), 1905–10. Yale University Art Gallery.

community was based upon Hubbard's somewhat paternalistic concern with the physical, intellectual, and spiritual well-being of the workers. Like Stickley, he had visited Britain and became acquainted with the writings of Ruskin and Morris as well as the publications of Morris's Kelmscott Press. Early books of the Roycroft community were written by Hubbard but also contained verse by American poets such as Ralph Waldo Emerson (1803–1882) and Edgar Allan Poe (1809–1849). Among the most popular series were the *Little Journeys*, a series of short biographies of famous writers, teachers, and businessmen (the first volume was a biography of Williams Morris) in a small format. Hubbard used an Old Style typeface named Bookman, approximating Morris's variation of Roman typography developed for the Kelmscott Press, and included decorated title pages as well as hand-coloring for wood-engraved decorated borders and illustrations (fig. 6.18). The *Little Journeys* and other publications of the Roycroft Press attempted to reconcile the individuality and craftsmanship of the private press movement initiated by Morris with the effort to create a democratic art, if not for the masses, at least for a broader middle class. In this endeavor Hubbard was a zealous and tenacious reformer. He was able to lower costs by printing books in a small format, but his success also depended

The Roycroft Shop GREETING

THE ROYCROFTERS are a community of workers who make beautiful Books and Things—making them as good as they can. The paper on which Roycroft books are printed is the best procurable, and some of the initials are illumined. As a gift you probably cannot present anything at equal cost that would be more acceptable than a hand-illumined Roycroft book. Our work is the product of Hand & Brain in partnership. In things made by hand there are no duplicates; and further, there is a quality of sentiment attached to articles thus produced that never clings to fabrics made in vast quantities by steam. If you desire we will gladly send you " on suspicion " several volumes to choose from—a postal card from you will do it. We pay express both ways.

THE ROYCROFTERS
East Aurora
N. Y.

6.18 Elbert Hubbard, *The Roycroft Books. A Catalog and Some Comment Concerning the Shop at East Aurora, New York, and Its Workers, The Roycrofters*, 7 ½ x 5 ¹¹/₁₆ in (19 x 14.6 cm), 1902.

upon a tight control of wages and autocratic authority to dictate the terms by which welfare was to be defined on behalf of his worker community. Not all of his workers reacted well to the nature of the communal enterprise as defined exclusively by Hubbard: some of his most original and gifted designers, including Karl Kipp (1882–1954) in the metal shop and the printer Dard Hunter (1883–1966), left the community intermittently to work independently.

The motto for the Roycrofters was "head, heart, and hand," and in addition to the practice of design and craftsmanship in the workshops, the community lived together, participating in a Roycroft band and baseball team. As a young man Hubbard had been a successful salesman for the Larkin Soap Company and continued to demonstrate a flair for commercializing Roycroft products. He operated a

hotel on the premises, and after spending a weekend in an interior decorated with Roycroft furnishings, visitors could purchase souvenirs from the Roycroft shop. Many products of the Roycroft copper workshop were designed by Karl Kipp, a former banker who worked at the community from 1908 to 1911 and again beginning in 1915 following Hubbard's death. The hammered copper surfaces and modest geometric decoration of a small vase (fig. 6.19) demonstrate the simple and human quality of handcrafted goods produced at Roycroft. It is somewhat curious that Hubbard, and to a lesser extent Stickley, promoted the Arts and Crafts ideal of satisfying and rewarding work yet at the same time borrowed from the practices of rationalized and specialized labor (see page 133), industrialization, and benefited from advertising in a rapidly expanding consumer culture, for whom "product" was more important than "process." Other craft communities, such as Rose Valley near Philadelphia, founded by architect Will Price (1861–1916), maintained the Ruskinian ideal in a purer form. Price coined the

6.19 Vase, copper and silver, 6 ¾ x 3 ½ x 2 ½ in (17 x 8.9 x 6.3 cm), attributed to Karl Kipps, *c.* 1910. Kurland-Zabar collection.

6.20 Charles Sumner and Henry Mather Greene, chiffonier, black walnut, ebony, lignum vitae, semiprecious stone inlay, 62 x 37 ½ x 21 in (157.5 x 95.3 x 53.3 cm), c. 1909, designed for the Gamble House master bedroom.

phrase "the art that is life" to characterize his experiment, hoping to unite artist and artisan in utopian harmony. But few could afford the cost of Rose Valley products, and the community ceased craft production in 1906, only five years after it began.

Located in Doylestown in southeastern Pennsylvania, Henry Chapman Mercer (1856–1930) founded the Moravian Pottery and Tile Works around the turn of the century to produce molded ceramic tiles and mosaics for use primarily as architectural and mural decoration. Independently wealthy and well-respected as an anthropologist and archeologist, Mercer observed the decline and disappearance of local, pre-industrial crafts in Pennsylvania. To preserve this endangered legacy, he began collecting tools and artifacts of the area and eventually built a museum to house the objects. He built his private residence and the museum using reinforced concrete with himself as architect and hiring local laborers to help with construction. At the same time he founded a tile workshop and produced tiles using plaster molds with designs based upon historic models primarily from the Middle Ages but also from a variety of other sources. Mercer experimented with a process of two-coat glazing which varied the finish of each tile, and though hand-operated machines were used for shaping the slabs and pressing the tiles, each had an individual character from glazing and the many stages of the process which involved handicraft. Although Mercer may not have been directly acquainted with the British Arts and Crafts Movement, his life's work and writings are entirely sympathetic with Morris and Ruskin. Perhaps the consummate "do-it-yourselfer," Mercer stated that the value of the products of the Moravian Pottery and Tile Works lay beyond the beauty of the colors and designs and had more to do with the dignity and usefulness of work. Perhaps the most well-known commission of the Moravian Pottery and Tile Works was for the floors of the State Capitol Building in Harrisburg, Pennsylvania, completed between 1902 and 1907. Even if only moderately successful or long-lived, the Arts and Crafts workshops, communities, and publications in the United States demonstrate sensitivity to the impact of urbanization and industrialization and the threat these processes posed to individuality and attitudes toward the meaning of work.

The plain surfaces and slatted elements in much Craftsman furniture were featured in the products of a number of firms in the United States around the turn of the century and are sometimes known as the Mission style. For Charles Sumner (1868–1957) and Henry Mather Greene (1870–1954), architects who also designed interior furnishings for a number of exclusive clients mostly in southern California, the Mission style was combined with inlay decoration, delicate carving to embellish surfaces, and the use of mahogany, walnut, or teak which permitted alternative methods of construction than working with oak (fig. 6.20). The work of the Greene brothers shares a concern with materials, construction, and a subdued, natural esthetic with more commercially minded designers such as Stickley, but was less concerned with the democratization of the style and issues of social reform. The brothers' work also emphasizes some of the qualities of Japanese interior design, particularly interest in horizontal and vertical detailing and open, interpenetrating spaces.

6.21 Shaker ladderback chair, maple, 40¼ x 9½ x 13½ in (103.5 x 24.1 x 34.3 cm) high, *c.* 1830–70. Philadelphia Museum of Art.

Certainly parallel but not always included in the literature on the Arts and Crafts Movement in the United States are the craft activities of the Shakers, a sect who emigrated to America in the late eighteenth century, settling in self-sufficient communities with the aim of uniting life and work and guided by beliefs in simplicity and humility. Shaker furniture, like the ladder back chair (fig. 6.21), utilizes natural materials and certainly is an outgrowth of ethical conviction. Yet the Shaker concept of "meaningful" or "dignified" work lacks something of the element of individuality that not only united artist and craftsman, but also constituted joy rather than drudgery for the maker, qualities frequently mentioned by Morris and Ruskin and embodied in the various expressions of Arts and Crafts in the United States. As a result Shaker designs, while fashionable among Arts and Crafts consumers (and remaining popular among the buying public today) and even influential among other designers, have been less subject to the innovation and change inherent in a more individualistic conception of artistic activity, as well as the commercial activity and competitive setting for that activity.

Printing in the United States

For his Kelmscott Press, William Morris drew three typefaces, all based upon earlier approaches to type design that he admired for their even stroke weight and the retention of calligraphic tendencies. His efforts, in effect, gave "new life to old faces," reviving interest in the Gothic script of the Middle Ages, suggesting variations to those fonts based upon Caslon's old face specimens, and inventing original letter forms geared to new purposes such as signage as well as to books.

In the United States, two typographer–book designers based their work upon admiration for the Kelmscott fonts, and variations upon it that became widely used in more commercial settings. Both Frederic Goudy (1865–1947) and Bruce Rogers (1870–1956) were drawn to the beauty of Kelmscott books they encountered as young men and embarked upon lifelong careers in type founding and book design. Their interests included punch cutting and page design, and their careers testify to a respect for craftsmanship practiced in the broadest sense of the word as understood by Morris. The model set by Goudy and Rogers extended to a younger generation including William Dwiggins (1880–1956) and Morris Fuller Benton (1872–1948), both of whom developed influential typefaces used in modern book publishing. Dwiggins is remembered for having coined the term graphic designer to describe the varied professional activities that stemmed from craft origins in the publishing industry and included typography and page design. Each of these designers studied historical typefaces and produced modern versions suitable for text and titles. In addition to old-style faces by Caslon, Rogers produced a version of the Bodoni font for modern typesetting. Benton was employed as a punchcutter for the American Type Founders Company (ATF), where he cut the type for Goudy fonts as well as developing his own typefaces. As noted by typographic historian Alexander Lawson, small variations in these historically-inspired typefaces led to their wider use: by adjusting the height of ascenders and descenders, old-style typefaces could be more economically set without decreasing legibility. Will Bradley, whose advertising posters and illustrations were described above (see pages 89–90) was also employed by ATF, which published *The Chap-Book*.

Technology continued to affect the development of the printing industry in the later nineteenth century. Among

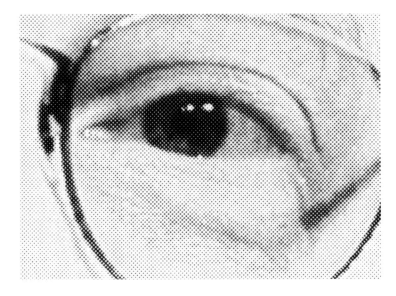

6.22 Enlarged photographic reproduction using halftone printing process.

6.23 Howard Pyle, *On the Tortugas*, wood-engraving from original illustration for "Bucaneers and Marooners of the Spanish Main." *Harper's Magazine*, August 1887.

the most significant changes was the introduction of method of automatically setting type. As in the first half of the century, it was the newspaper industry, with its high-volume circulation and daily editions, that stimulated invention, leading to the introduction of a system known as Linotype at the *New York Herald* in 1886, and quickly spreading through Europe and the United States. The inventor of the Linotype machine was Ottmar Mergenthaler (1854–1899), who emigrated to the United States from Germany. His machine released negative impressions of letter forms through the operation of a keyboard, then cast each line of type in metal for the letterpress, eliminating the need for the hand-setting of type. The need for thousands of individual letters to form the casts was met by punch-cutting machines, which emerged at the same time. As a result of this invention, the price of newspapers decreased and the number of pages printed increased, further increasing circulation and space for advertising. The Monotype machine, developed by Tolbert Lanston (1844–1913) in the 1880s and 1890s, offered an alternative to the Linotype. It produced multiple impressions of letters from a single matrix operated by a perforated tape that positioned the matrix to make molds for casting. While developed for the newspaper industry, typesetting machinery was also adopted for book printing. In both cases typographers wrestled with the challenges of maintaining consistency and legibility in adopting new and increasingly mechanized technologies.

Another technical development in printing was the mechanical reproduction of images using photographs. Translating a photographic plate into a mechanically-produced image required the use of a screen to reproduce the tonal complexity of the image in a simpler form. Known as half-tone, the process made photography the basic tool of reporting and recording events for newspapers and magazines, and at the same time threatened the jobs of professional and specialized craftsmen who had created images using the technique of wood engraving (fig. 6.22). The simplified shadows of the half-tone method of reproduction was adopted by graphic designers in the illustration of products in a larger format, for instance in the posters of Lucien Bernhard in Germany (see pages 132–3 and fig. 7.28).

Photographic reproduction was also used in the field of illustration. Yet while journalism shifted to photography as an eyewitness to faithfully record events, illustration still thrived in the realm of fiction, political and social commentary in the mass media, advertising, and in the children's book, carrying on a tradition of narrative art outside of easel painting. *Scribner's Monthly, Harper's Magazine, Century*, and other publications were among the journals that provided a sphere of activity for illustrators. Howard

Pyle (1853–1911) was one of several artists who worked at Harper Brothers under art editor Howard Parsons, providing illustrations to stories that were published serially. Early illustrations were wood-engraved from line drawings, while later examples were photographed and reproduced tonally and in four-color reproduction. Pyle brought to life stories of danger and adventure, taking readers to distant lands and places peopled by heroes and villains. Pyle lent immediacy to his scenes by often juxtaposing near and distant space and using strong contrast to heighten dramatic effect. An example is a tonal reproduction from Pyle's *Book of Pirates*, originally published in *Harper's Magazine* (August, 1887), illustrating a shipwrecked sailor on a beach against a backdrop of empty sea and sky (fig. 6.23). The appeal of Pyle's illustrations was to escape and fantasy. The gap they filled in the lives of their vast readership was soon shared with a new medium, that of the moving picture, which introduced a new set of real-life heroes and heroines in the form of actors and actresses. While photography reduced the demand for illustrators in news reporting for newspapers and weekly journals, books continued to offer a creative outlet for illustrators' activities in the late nineteenth and early twentieth centuries. A new demand for narrative also arose during the same time through advertising, although not all illustrators were comfortable with the use of illustration techniques to sell products.

Chicago and Frank Lloyd Wright

In 1896 and again in 1901 the British Arts and Crafts designer and advocate Charles Ashbee (see page 101), founder of the Guild and School of Handicraft, visited the United States, traveling extensively and reporting on contemporary design activities he observed. Ashbee, who was a firm believer in hand craftsmanship, the well-being of workers, and a close relationship between designer and artisan, was impressed by a young American architect named Frank Lloyd Wright (1869–1959). Many of Wright's early mid-western "Prairie" houses, such as the Ward Willits' house of 1900–2 (fig. 6.24) related to Arts and Crafts principles in a variety of ways, for instance, in their effort to harmonize with their surroundings through asymmetrical plans and horizontal extension, in the attention to the use of natural materials, in a restraint toward the use of ornament, and in an attempt to unify architecture with the elements of interior design and decoration.

But in a significant way Wright's ideas on architecture and design differed from those of the Arts and Crafts Movement. In a well-known lecture delivered in Chicago in 1901, Wright told his audience that the dream for a democratic architecture could only be achieved by embracing the machine, which saved time and reduced drudgery. He stated that the machine's ability to produce simple products of high quality and noble beauty had been

6.24 Frank Lloyd Wright, Ward Willits' House, 1900–2, Valley Place, Mamaroneck, New York.

6.25 Frank Lloyd Wright, dining room furniture, 1900. Susan Dana House, Springfield, Illinois.

obscured only by the greed of manufacturers and the ignorance of the public: "William Morris pleaded well for simplicity as the basis of all the art. Let us understand the significance to art of that word—SIMPLICITY—for it is vital to the art of the machine!" Indeed the invocation of William Morris recalls the British designer's own comments quoted earlier, that "the more mechanical the process, the less direct should be the imitation of natural forms," yet another instance of the wide effect and varied interpretation of his writings. Eventually Ashbee modified his own views to accept the necessity of the machine along the lines envisioned by Wright, admiring the architect's courage in confronting the challenge of mass production rather than ignoring its possible social benefits in improving the lives of a broader public.

Wright's linking of machine technology, esthetic simplicity, and a democratic art provided a moral, ideological basis for a modern "functional" style that emerged in the interwar period in Europe, and is contemporary with initiatives in Germany as well (see pages 98–100). Decoration was viewed as being dishonest and commercial if made by machine, and exclusive and socially irresponsible if made by hand: the designer should strive rather to create new and original forms designed for mass production to meet the needs of an expanding audience. Wright's approach to design using restraint in decoration and calling for the machine manufacture of simple units or components was contemporary with the theories of economists such as Thorsten Veblen (1857–1929), who criticized the purchasing habits of middle-class Americans as a form of "conspicuous consumption," linking buying not with comfort and material progress but rather with the acquisition of social position and substituting the status acquired through buying with "real" status, formerly the result of honor and respect earned on the basis of deeds. For Veblen, fashion and consumption were threats to the existing social order; for Wright, they were threats to a discriminating esthetic and the establishment of a true and natural "modern" taste, appropriate to its time and taking full advantage of new production technologies.

Wright published some of his early designs for domestic architecture in popular magazines such as E. Bok's *Ladies' Home Journal* with the title, "A small house with lots of room in it" and a suggested cost of less than $6000. But despite the simple elegance of Wright's designs in comparison with the more common preference for ornament and adaptations of period styles ranging from Gothic to Baroque, Wright's homes were almost invariably custom-built for affluent clients, and his furniture was neither mass-produced nor achieved broad appeal for consumers, who preferred more traditional expressions of comfort and beauty linked to richness of effect. Moreover, even the design published by Wright in the *Ladies' Home Journal* is misleading for a modern reader, since comparative price indices suggest that a $6000 home in 1901 would cost more than $100,000 in today's market and economy.

Another expression of Wright's preference for simple forms was the design of colored leaded glass windows, like the set of bay windows for the Susan Dana house in Springfield, Illinois (1903, fig 6.25). While their composition suggests they might have been constructed from uniform prefabricated geometric units, the production of such windows was still time-consuming, intricate, and ultimately craft-based. In other words, Wright seems to have created the converse of Morris's recommendation that machines not imitate hand-work—the windows are hand-made yet suggest how machines "should" make things. Despite the arguments presented in his writings and speeches that "the Machine is the great forerunner of democracy," Wright was hardly advocating democracy in the sense of "freedom of choice." Instead he was equating an esthetic preference based upon simplicity with technical necessity, then assuming that the result elevated the taste of the public, that is, design that the public *should* want.

6.26 Louis Sullivan, detail of Wainwright Building, 1890–91. St. Louis, Missouri.

6.27 George Washington Maher, textile, silk velvet with appliqué of silk damask, 79 x 45 ⅛ in (2.7 x 1.16 cm), *c.* 1903. The Saint Louis Art Museum

Wright's career in Chicago should not be considered in a vacuum, for the city was a major commercial metropolitan center, and his ideas took shape in an active artistic environment. After a disastrous fire of 1871 architects and artists were attracted to Chicago during an intense period of rebuilding and modernization, including the hosting of the Columbian Exposition of 1893, and the building of an elevated mass transit system. A premium on office space in the city's center led to the design of several tall buildings, constructed from steel and with an elevator. One of the most prominent architects during this period of artistic activity was Louis Sullivan (1856–1924). Sullivan was acquainted with the writings of Ruskin and the background of the Arts and Crafts Movement, and advocated an elevated view of decoration as an essential element in

architecture, based upon appreciation for nature and the spiritual energy embodied in natural forms. He devised original forms for architectural decoration, used as framed panels (often molded in terracotta or cast in iron) to balance and enliven the repetitive grid-like structure of tall buildings such as the Wainwright Building in St. Louis, Missouri, dating to 1904 (fig. 6.26). The same curvilinear patterns appear in the windows, carpets, and furniture designed by George Grant Elmslie (1871–1952) and George Washington Maher (1864–1926) for homes in the midwest around the turn of the century. Elmslie, born in Scotland, worked for Sullivan and Frank Lloyd Wright. Maher's *Thistle* textile, for the Patten home in Evanston, Illinois (1901, fig. 6.27), is one of the more exuberant examples of his work, while window designs remained more restrained and geometric.

Chapter 7

Mechanization and Industry

7.12 Singer model, a family sewing machine, 1865. National Museum of American History, the Smithsonian Institution.

Germany

While Wright's views of a reformed esthetic for the machine did not take root in American industry, in Germany similar attitudes, fueled by the belief that a more unified approach to design was in the national interest, produced more collaboration, compromise, and experiment in the direction of a practical approach to industrial production. Organizations uniting artists and manufacturers such as the Wiener Werkstätte took root in Germany, and a number of government initiatives supported design reform, including the formation of applied arts schools in Düsseldorf, Breslau, Weimar, and Berlin. Other efforts included support for German participation in international exhibitions in Paris (1900) and

St. Louis (1904), as well as the mounting of an exhibition in Munich (1908). Out of this milieu a large organization made up of artists and manufacturers was formed in 1907 to promote the interests of the German applied arts, known as the Deutscher Werkbund.

A significant figure in many of these activities was Hermann Muthesius (1861–1927), who visited Britain from 1896 to 1899 to study English architecture (published as *Das Englische Haus*), and subsequently became the Minister of Trade for the Prussian government. Like other advocates of design reform Muthesius believed in the harmony of beauty and utility, but felt that individuality should be subservient to the creation of more practical, rational forms of furniture and fittings. Through the introduction of design concepts such as modularity, interchangeability, and the use of mechanized production, consumer choice and variety could become part of the dialogue between designer and manufacturer. In this endeavor we can perhaps see an extension of the practice of scientific management (see page 133) applied to a wider range of consumer goods, presuming that a "right" method could be found if efficiency was the overriding criterion for determining final form. Although social reform played a part in the practical approach to design outlined by Muthesius and others, products were aimed at middle-class rather than working-class consumers, and German design is perhaps best seen as a compromise between artists' interest in original designs as an alternative to historicism, and manufacturers' concerns with materials, production costs, and attracting consumers. Certainly Muthesius's criticism of contemporary Scottish design as being impractical in its degree of refinement suggests the middle-ground he hoped to establish:

> Once the interior attains the status of a work of art, that is, when it is intended to embody aesthetic values, the artistic effect must obviously be heightened to the utmost. The Mackintosh group does this and no-one will reproach them on this particular point. Whether such enhancement is appropriate to our everyday rooms is another question. Mackintosh's rooms are refined to a degree which the lives of even the artistically educated are still a long way from matching. The delicacy and austerity of their artistic atmosphere would tolerate no admixture of the ordinariness which fills our lives. Even a book in an unsuitable binding would disturb the atmosphere simply by lying on the table, indeed even the man or woman of today – especially the man in his unadorned working attire – treads like a stranger in this fairy-tale world. There is for the time being no possibility of our aesthetic cultivation playing so large a part in our lives that rooms like this could be general. But they are milestones placed by a genius far ahead of us to mark the way to excellence for mankind in the future.

The willingness of a number of artists and architects to work within the constraints outlined by Muthesius, and of a number of industrialists to accept restrained contemporary designs, is a unique characteristic of German design in the decade leading up to the start of World War I,

7.1 Richard Riemerschmid, cutlery, 1911/12, for Atelier Karl Weisshaupt, Munich.

stemming at least in part from a strong sense of nationalism in the wake of German unification (1871) and a search for a common identity through design. Although criticized by the Belgian architect–designer van de Velde for its inhibition of artistic freedom and individuality, and opposed by a number of manufacturers for being undemocratic, the approach of Muthesius had many adherents among Germany's large industrialists and leading artists. Among designers, Munich-based Richard Riemerschmid (see page 100) abandoned the tense, rhythmic curves of the Jugendstil for practical designs of furniture and other household consumer goods. His set of cutlery manufactured by Atelier Karl Weisshaupt in 1912 (fig. 7.1) features straight, mildly elongated handles and plain surfaces, contrasting with the engraved decoration and more asymmetrically curved handles of the Jugendstil (fig. 5.54).

7.2 Richard Riemerschmid, kitchen ensemble, machine furniture range, pine, gray and black lacquer, iron fittings, 1905. Dresdener Werkstätte.

7.3 Peter Behrens, AEG Turbine Factory, 1908–9.

Advertised as "machine-furniture," Riemerschmid's kitchen ensemble (fig. 7.2) used geometric or slightly tapered shapes and eschewed decorative carving and moldings. Although the wood was machine-cut and included laminates, assembly and finishing required handwork and the final cost depended upon the varied quality of finishes and the materials used for metal fittings (brass or iron). In preserving these and other elements of workmanship, the products were beyond the price range of the working class and appealed to middle-class consumers for whom the designs embodied comfort, efficiency, and modernity rather than "mere" utility. Other designs by Riemerschmid, in part influenced by similar American products, were based upon the use of standardized units that could be expanded, and the ease of packing, transport, and assembly were also factors in the design.

Another designer associated with the Werkbund and design reform in Germany was the architect Peter Behrens (1868–1940). Like Riemerschmid, Behrens abandoned the Jugendstil for a more practical approach to design, seen for instance in his turbine factory for the German General Electric Company (Allgemeine Elektrizitäts Gesellschaft or AEG) of 1908–9 (fig. 7.3). The design is noteworthy for its use of the modern materials of concrete, large expanses of plate glass, exposed metal, and a vast interior space unimpeded by columns better to meet the

requirements of plant operations. While aspects of the proportions and treatment of the exterior articulation suggest a modernized classical temple front, historical references and decorative elaboration are understated, and are consistent with the steel and glass construction. From 1907 Behrens worked as a consultant for AEG to develop promotional materials and to work with product engineers to design electrical appliances for industrial and domestic use. Promoting the use of electricity for cooking and other domestic purposes aside from lighting was a concern of companies such as AEG as they sought to maximize demand for electric power (in particular other than rush hour when electric commuter trains required large amounts of power). Recognizing the advantage of standardized components in reducing labor costs, Behrens introduced variety into the line of electric tea kettles through the use of interchangeability of material, finish, and handles to promote consumer choice. He also preserved associations with handicraft in the use of a molded exterior that resembled a hand hammered surface (fig. 7.4).

Behrens' work for AEG also anticipated corporate identity programs used frequently later in the twentieth century. He ensured the use of a consistent typeface and layout for all company printed materials, and a more unified approach to product design involving considerations

132

7.4 Peter Behrens, electric tea kettle, brass, chromium-plated metal, bakelite, and cane, 8 ¼ x 6 ⅜ in (21 x 16.5 cm), c. 1908–12, manufactured by Allgemeine Elektricitäts-Gesellschaft (AEG), Berlin.

7.5 Peter Behrens, Prospectus for AEG Lighting, color lithograph and letterpress printing, 4 ¼ x 6 in (11.2 x 15.5 cm), 1912. Klingspor Museum, Offenbach.

of setting, shape, proportion, and finish that suggested, beyond the mere name, a design "personality," that is, characteristics of appearance that identified practicality and restrained decoration with honesty, responsibility, and reliability. These characteristics in turn became a recognizable ethos for the company. The hexagonal logo designed by Behrens for AEG suggests, in its analogy to a beehive, the subordination of individual elements to a unified corporate image. Moreover, Behrens himself was a well-known architect whose work for AEG helped to legitimize the company's contemporary products and add to their marketability. The Behrens logo appears in a 1912 illustration for a corporate prospectus that limits communication to a straightforward drawing of the AEG filament lightbulb above the bold Roman typeface designed by Behrens for all the company's materials (fig. 7.5). It is interesting to compare the blunt character of this illustration to a catalogue illustration for the same corporation designed in 1900 by Munich artist Otto Eckmann (fig. 7.6). In the earlier poster, elasticity characterizes an idiosyncratic typeface that merges paired letters and combines lower and uppercase forms, while the rectangular frame provides a visualization of electrical current emanating from inverted bell-like transformers above and below. The energetic line and integration of illustrative and decorative elements indicate a Jugendstil approach, while Behrens' poster eliminates all symbolic and expressive references, leaving only the bold, simplified shape of the bulb and the easily recognizable letter forms that

identify the corporation with one of its basic products. Behrens's graphic design for AEG shows an affinity to the posters of a young, self-taught Viennese artist named Lucien Bernhard (1883–1972) who was working in Munich in the first decade of the twentieth century and also had joined the Deutscher Werkbund. Bernhard produced a number of advertising posters of striking simplicity, emphasizing letter forms linked to products in the most direct and effective way. An example is the 1907 poster for Adler Typewriters (fig. 7.7), where both the typewriter and its shadow are treated as equal partners in the presentation of the image. Although the presentation

7.6 Otto Eckmann, cover for AEG catalog, Paris World Exhibition, color lithograph, 1900.

7.7 Lucian Bernhard, poster for Adler Typewriters, color lithograph, 27 ⅕ x 37 in (69 x 94 cm), 1910. Berlin.

of the typewriter is in a three-quarter view, the simplified tone and justification of the image with the border at the left virtually negate recession and create a powerful presence for the product. Critics have suggested that such a treatment of shadow is the result of the influence of photography, where the half-tone method of commercial reproduction (see page 125) reduced the tonal range of the original image.

The American System of Manufacture and Fordism

Notwithstanding the pleas of Frank Lloyd Wright or efforts in Germany to reform the esthetics of machine production, engineers and manufacturers in the United States emphasized efficiency and the expansion of the market for consumer products with continued rationalizing efforts to increase production as well as to expand merchandising, advertising, and marketing strategies. In this competitive climate there was often little room for reconciliation or accommodation between art, reform, and industry.

To reduce the cost of labor, Philadelphia-born Frederick W. Taylor (*d.* 1915) conducted experiments in the 1880s aimed at increasing productivity among workers. Taylor measured the amount of time taken by workers to perform a variety of routine tasks. In one experiment he demonstrated that a man shovelling coal would work at optimum efficiency with individual loads of twenty-two pounds, and even made drawings for the design of a shovel to best hold the load. Once determined, Taylor's recommendations were enforced in the workplace by managers and became standards for labor productivity and wages, demanding higher levels of compliance on the factory floor. Taylor's analyses are described under the heading of scientific management. His findings reinforced the connection between the division of labor and efficiency as described in the eighteenth century by Adam Smith (page 32), but applied the principle to reduce the number of movements necessary to perform a given task in order to save more time and increase productivity. Taylor's system required a degree of conformity that might have made John Ruskin shiver, but the sacrifice was part of the bargain. As described by author Robert Kanigel,

> There it was, the Faustian bargain in embryonic form: You do it my way, by my standards, at the speed I mandate, and in so doing achieve a level of output I ordain, and I'll pay you handsomely for it, beyond anything you might have imagined. All you have to do is take orders, give up your way of doing the job for mine.

Taylor's approach to uniformity in production is parallel to later governmental efforts to create uniform standards for the sizes of plumbing and electrical fittings, where issues of safety and performance might be studied, products tested, results analyzed, and "correct" measurements established for all manufacturers to insure compatibility without the confusion that might be caused by unfettered competition. Standards of this kind were implemented in the United States and later, after World War I, in Germany in an effort to control expenses in the building of low-cost housing. Standards were applied to public utilities as well as the telephone industry. The Bell Telephone Corporation had a monopoly on producing handsets, which as a result were only available in a limited number of models during the 1920s. Such efforts, pioneered in government contracts for firearms with interchangeable parts, as discussed in Part 1 (see page 32), tended to lead to uniformity outside the commercial considerations of a free enterprise system.

Industrialist Henry Ford expanded upon Taylor's scientific management. According to historian Peter Ling, rather than analyzing existing tasks Ford and his managers saved time and increased productivity by rethinking

7.8 End of the line, Ford Motor Plant, Highland Park, Illinois, *c.* 1913. From the collections of Henry Ford Museum and Greenfield Village.

7.9 Conveyers, main power house, Ford Motor Plant, River Rouge, Dearborn, Michigan, 1927. From the collections of Henry Ford Museum and Greenfield Village.

the location of parts and the sequence of operations in manufacturing, eventually developing the moving assembly line. Through the assembly line, and Ford's decision to manufacture only a single model, labor was defined primarily as a factor of time rather than skill or thought, and maximized by demanding production schedules dictated by floor managers and satirized by Charlie Chaplin in the 1936 film *Modern Times*. Ford's assembly line required an open and easily expandable interior factory space, made possible through the use of electric power to run machinery. Once up and running it marked a significant advance in quantity production. Through steel frame construction, inexpensive building materials, and the use of a modular principle to facilitate expansion, Ford's architect Albert Kahn (1869–1942) created large, simple, well-lit factory spaces to serve the needs of the moving assembly lines, first at the Highland Park plant in 1908 and later at the larger River Rouge facility (figs. 7.8 and 7.9).

Ford's production methods transformed the automobile from a luxury item requiring elements of fine, specialized craftsmanship for details of construction and assembly to a middle-class form of transportation with an elastic market through complete uniformity, standardization, and interchangeable parts for ease of repair and replacement. Between 1907 and 1916 the price of Ford's Model T (Tin Lizzie) actually went down as demand

increased. The car, available only in black, sold more than sixteen million units during this period, and remained virtually unchanged and unchallenged in the market. Only in 1927 did Ford introduce the Model A in an effort to adapt to changing economic conditions and competition. The Model T retained the basic carriage form inherited from horse-drawn transportation, and there was little "modern" about its design in terms of harmonious proportions or a sense of a unified or simplified external form. But the ability of industry to produce an automobile within the means of many through the application of technology was almost universally admired and contributed to making mechanization and mass production part of the ideology of middle- and working-class economic progress in the United States and abroad in the period between the two World Wars.

Ford's mechanized mass production demanded conformity, repetition, and strict control in the workplace, and such practices differed profoundly from the ideals of joyful and meaningful work that animated Arts and Crafts reform and various "esthetic" movements in the nineteenth and early twentieth centuries. As discussed above, the crafts workshop founded by Elbert Hubbard's Roycroft community (see page 119) was an attempt to humanize the workplace by creating a sense of cooperation among employees while incorporating more modern methods of production, provision of housing, and low wages for commercial viability. Hubbard admired the success of Ford and other industrialists whose biographies he published at Roycroft under the heading *Little Journeys to the Homes of Great Businessmen*. These and other pamphlets were purchased in great quantities by corporations hoping to inspire loyalty among their own workers. Such efforts suggest a desire to reconcile Arts and Crafts ideology to market conditions profoundly affected by mass production—to his credit, Hubbard's Roycroft remained in business throughout most of the Great Depression, only declaring bankruptcy in 1938. It is also interesting to note that both Stickley and Hubbard opposed the modern labor reform movement. Deeply influenced by William Morris's attitudes toward craft, they felt that the concept of organized labor excluded a satisfying role for the individual beyond compensation in wages. Indeed, Ford's response to the difficulties of maintaining a dependable workforce under the pressures of the assembly line in the Highland Park factory was to introduce the "Five Dollar Day" in 1914, a plan that encouraged workers to save a portion of their wages toward the purchase of their own Model T automobile.

Following World War I, the moving assembly line, machine-production of interchangeable parts, and standardization, achieved success in other American industries, most notably in the uniform mass production of appliances such as refrigerators, vacuum cleaners, and washing machines. Appliances were powered by electricity and strongly promoted by power companies hoping to increase domestic consumption of electric energy beyond its primary use for lighting in the home. The industrial-looking standardized forms of these new appliances suggested efficiency in the kitchen (also encouraged by the reorganization of the room's work space), while the use of white enamel paint connoted personal hygiene, making the ideal kitchen a combination of well-managed factory and laboratory (figs. 7.10 and 7.11). American author

7.10 Advertisement for electric appliances manufactured by Westinghouse Electric & Mfg. Company. *Good Housekeeping*, December 1923.

7.11 Modern kitchen and storage space. Photograph: *Good Housekeeping*, November 1923.

Christine Frederick studied food preparation from the standpoint of efficiency, extending as well into the design of the kitchen. Frederick's *Scientific Management in the Home* (1912) contained diagrams demonstrating the relationship between various aspects of kitchen work in order to maximize efficiency, and her efforts became the basis for domestic kitchen design in public housing developments in Frankfurt in the 1920s (see page 190).

Developments in Merchandising, Printing, and Advertising

While the unchanging Model T marked a new stage in the implementation of industrial technology in the early twentieth century, the application of Ford's mass production manufacturing to kitchen and other appliances was not an automatic formula for sustained market growth. It is clear that for certain types of manufactured products, particularly those intended for domestic rather than industrial, office, or even kitchen use, considerable energies were devoted to variation and esthetic preference, promoted heavily with new forms of advertising and merchandising.

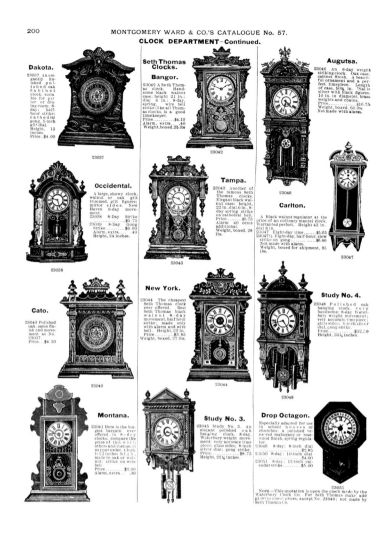

7.13 Catalogue page, clock department, Montgomery Ward catalogue, 1895.

7.12 Singer model, a family sewing machine, 1865. National Museum of American History, the Smithsonian Institution.

Indeed, the very success of the factory and office as primary locations of managed and increasingly routine work helped to create a stronger need to disassociate living space from workplace; if the factory turned men into machines and the kitchen into a "scientifically managed" space, the other rooms of the home became the refuge and antidote for the anonymity and repetitive tasks in the workplace. This distinction between home and work has been cited as the primary reason why manufacturers at first found it difficult to successfully market sewing machines for domestic use (see page 33). The standardized models manufactured by Singer in the mid-nineteenth century were too reminiscent of the factory to appeal to consumers (the earliest models could be mounted on their packing crates), and only by acquiring domestic associations through painted detailing in gold, a more tapered appearance, and a more traditionally carved table (fig. 7.12) did sewing machines successfully enter the home as a piece of furniture rather than as an industrial "tool." These observations might suggest the variety of reasons why piano manufacturers such as Steinway abandoned the elaborate treatment of wood cases for various models (see fig. 10.34). One might speculate that the buying public began to accept more easily simplified and standardized pianos, due in part to not having to overcome negative associations of "plain" pianos with the workplace, and also because manufacturers such as Steinway (founded 1853) relied upon new techniques of advertising and the personal endorsements of professional musicians to help market their products, rather than carved decoration which might be easily imitated.

Creating the perfect home, free from associations with the workplace, was most often the responsibility of women. Rather than competing for work in the "public" world, women were encouraged to cultivate a comfortable and worry-free environment for their families. While this role might allow for their direct participation in handicraft, as the primary consumers of household goods and furnishings they were increasingly targeted by advertisers.

In addition to the need to distinguish home from office or factory through design, manufacturers were able to increase sales by creating different products for particular markets. Their efforts are evident in the mail-order catalogues published by Montgomery Ward (1872) and Sears, Roebuck and Company (1891), or in a number of monthly periodicals whose circulation increased dramatically through the incorporation of paid advertisements that covered the costs of production so reducing the price to readers. Leafing through the pages of these catalogues, the reader confronts images of a seemingly limitless array of domestic products with minor variations meant to attract the interest of different groups of consumers. What they all have in common, however, is the ability to reinforce the values of family to be preserved and expressed in the home through consumption (fig. 7.13). While urban consumers found such variety in large department stores such as Macy's or Wanamaker's, mail-order catalogues catered mainly to rural populations whose range of options for consumer goods were previously limited to the local "general store."

Such tendencies toward homogeneity have continued with the increasing influence of the mass media, as well as large "discount stores," malls, and franchised stores and outlets.

Conclusion

The numerous individual, group, corporate, and larger institutional or even national design initiatives described in this chapter revolve in some way around the varied responses to industrialization and mechanized mass production during the late nineteenth and early twentieth centuries, ranging from the protests and nostalgia of John Ruskin and William Morris to the aggressive pursuit of rapid uniform production by Henry Ford. Somewhere in between these two extremes lie the various expressions of aesthetic design and reform (whether they be "art" furniture, Jugendstil, or Art Nouveau), Werkstätte, Werkbund and other associations, and large commercial ventures such as department stores and catalogue companies described above, which sought to balance the uniformity and rationalization demanded by an emerging system of industrial production with the individuality of the designer and the motivations of a growing consumer culture. Each phenomenon constitutes a particular response to the threat as well as the promise of industry, the dream of providing the many with what was once the privilege of the few, and at the same time a tendency to deprive designers of freedom of expression and to limit consumers in their freedom of choice. The issues involved are complex and even contradictory: the emphasis upon subjective expression and freedom in a number of design initiatives encouraged materialism and the symbolic associations of consumption. And as Debora Silverman and other historians have remarked, the political milieu in which design reform developed in France in the later nineteenth century was a conservative one in which the cultivation of an Art Nouveau was expected to create economic opportunity as well as to reduce middle-class fears of unrest among an industrial working class. The social, economic, and political meanings brought to bear upon design activities in the period from the mid-nineteenth century until the beginning of World War I make this period one of great vitality, originality, and tension, in which there emerges a critical dialogue between art, craft, industry, social reform, and an ever-expanding commercial culture.

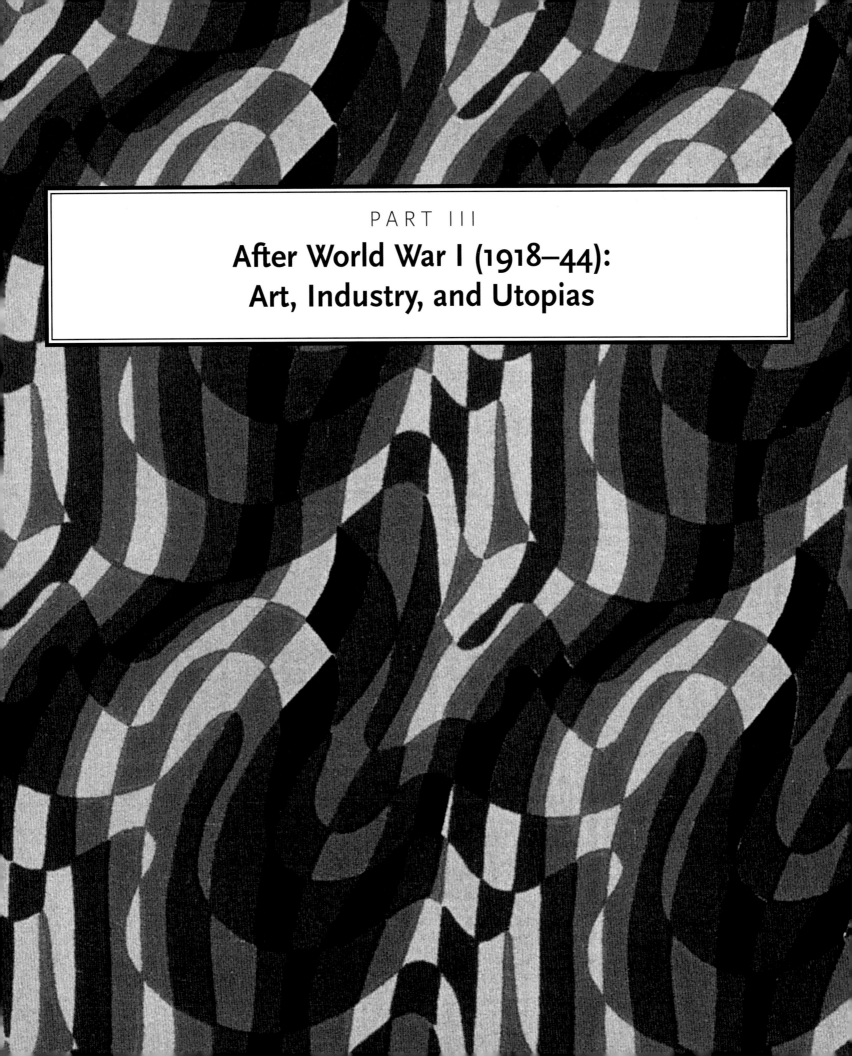

PART III
After World War I (1918–44):
Art, Industry, and Utopias

Introduction

The period under review in this chapter, roughly encompassing the years 1918 to 1944, includes three landmarks of modern design history: the long-awaited Exposition Internationale des Arts Décoratifs et Industriels Modernes in Paris (1925); the foundation of the German school for design education known as the Bauhaus (1919–33); and the emergence of the profession of industrial design in the United States, vacillating between esthetic, commercial, and social benefits of design, and culminating in the spectacle of the 1939 New York World's Fair.

There is no single theme that unites these events or landmarks of the period, yet each may be seen as a particular type of reaction to the tensions and aftermath of World War I (1914–18). The origins of the style known as Art Moderne or Art Deco may be traced to the years just before the war. But the persistence of French organizers to house an international exhibition devoted to modern decorative arts in 1925, originally planned to take place in 1915, suggests the active promotion of French pre-eminence in the design and manufacture of modern furnishings and luxury commodities. Practitioners in these fields saw themselves as artist–craftsmen, proud of the equality they shared with painters and sculptors and cognizant of an exclusive and discriminating international market for their goods.

The Bauhaus presents a complex and shifting institutional history. Its first director, architect Walter Gropius, was a veteran of World War I. The school was located in the city of Weimar, and its commitment to the renewal of craft through the active involvement of fine artists in workshop production suggests an ambivalence toward mass production and industrialization. This is partially explained by well-founded fears of the destructive rather than constructive potential of technology seen in the weapons industry, as well as by the commitment to individuality advocated by Henry van de Velde (see pages 96–7), who directed the Arts and Crafts School (Kunstgewerbeschule) in Weimar before the outbreak of conflict in August 1914. In the early 1920s criticism of the school's lack of productivity and the incompatibility of its emphasis upon the individuality of the artist–craftsman with economic recovery and revitalization led to a focus that was more practical and industrial. This revised mission at the Bauhaus was launched with the theme "Art and Technology: A New Unity." The shift was apparent in the appointment of new faculty, in the design and construction of buildings for the school's new home in Dessau in 1926, and in the more objective, scientific, and egalitarian socialist outlook of its later director Hannes Meyer. The shift at the Bauhaus was contemporary with the international efforts of artist–designers in Soviet Russia and in other European countries, who, under banners such as Constructivism (Russia), l'Esprit Nouveau (France), and de Stijl (Holland), developed a plain, machine-inspired esthetic, embraced mechanized mass production, and debated the role of collective standards as a basis for the products of design in a classless society. Such radical views were meant to replace the outmoded individualistic values that were viewed as contributing to the belligerence and

Jules Abel Faivre, *On les aura*, poster, 44 x 16 in (112 x 41 cm), France, 1916.

Alfred Leete, *Your Country Needs You*, poster, 30 x 20 in (76 x 51 cm), 1916. Britain. Imperial War Museum.

destructiveness unleashed during World War I. The experimental use of modern industrial materials for furnishings, elimination of carved or molded ornament, and use of photomechanical processes for printing are often associated with these movements, but were not limited to them or to their ideologies. Simple, undecorated forms and the expressive use of sans serif typography and page layout in printing emerged in the 1930s in more broadly commercial and mainstream contexts as well.

World War I also mobilized artists and illustrators on both sides of the conflict to build broad public support through the mass media of posters and billboards. Governments sponsored such efforts as part of their campaign to enlist recruits, sell war bonds, and create a sense of national solidarity and purpose. The effort to use mass media to shape public opinion is a theme inherited from nineteenth-century reform (see pages 114–5) and renewed during World War I. There is a remarkable similarity among such war posters. Often aimed at a male audience, the combination of idealism and monumentality is used to identify war with heroism, as seen in Jules Abel Faivre's (1867–1945) 1916 poster image of a young soldier in a plea to buy war bonds (above left). The direct appeal and imperative tone of both image and text in Alfred Leete's (1882–1933) *Your Country Needs You* poster of 1914 in Britain (above right) made for powerful rhetoric. Such images combined the contrast and simplicity found in German posters by artists such as Lucien Bernhard (see fig. 9.60, page 204) with a sense of viewer confrontation derived from the stock techniques of advertising copy writers exhorting potential customers to buy particular products. War posters blurred the boundaries between art, advertising, and patriotism, and contributed to the tremendous impact that the advertising profession assumed during the 1920s and 1930s.

The United States emerged after World War I as a world leader in the mechanized mass production of automobiles and related products such as kitchen appliances, due to the unparalleled success of Henry Ford's standardized, unchanging Model T. After the mid-1920s, however, consumption levels needed to be sustained through advertising and through design. The appearance of Art Moderne in the US was stimulated by the emigration of European designers after World War I in search of opportunity, and a renewed interest in avant-garde art among a relatively small group of American artists, collectors, museums, and merchandisers. Out of this context developed an indigenous modern expression sometimes known as the Skyscraper Style, inspired by the fast-paced rhythms of urban experience and the emergence of jazz music, and marketed through museum exhibitions, department stores, illustrated magazines, and the popular cinema.

The appearance of the professional industrial designer, beginning in the later 1920s and 1930s, was primarily a product of manufacturers' interest in stimulating consumption through an appeal to novelty and fantasy in a more competitive economic climate. This development, however, was also promoted as reform, that is, contributing to social progress, esthetic improvement, hygiene, and the application of science to everyday life, clearly expressed in the modern style known as Streamlining. The planners of the 1939 World's Fair in New York saw design as contributing on a broad scale to economic growth and improved living standards for the middle class. It was hoped that the consequent reduction of social ills would act as a bulwark against the rise of Fascism in Europe and the economic hardships of the Depression. On the eve of the United States' entry into World War II, the success of these efforts demonstrated that modern industrial design, sponsored by large corporate manufacturers, could have broad consumer appeal through largely symbolic associations between new product designs, technology, progress, and values of efficiency, health, freedom, and comfort. Purged of some of its collectivist connotations, the promotion of modern industrial design reaped even larger rewards for designers, manufacturers, and retailers in the two decades following the end of World War II.

Chapter 8

Paris and Art Moderne Before and After World War I

8.1 Manuel Orazi, poster for "La Maison Moderne", poster, 31 x 44 ½ in (79 x 113 cm), color lithograph, *c.* 1901.

By 1905 Siegfried Bing's La Maison de l'Art Nouveau showrooms had closed, following the fate of a similar design workshop venture under the direction of the German connoisseur Julius Meier-Graefe known as La Maison Moderne, which had folded during the previous year. There is no single cause for the demise of Art Nouveau. Scholars have argued that competition from antique dealers for the luxury market in furniture may have reduced the market for Art Nouveau. It is also possible that department stores marketing less expensive imitations of the style deprived the more exclusive audience for modern decorative arts of the social distinction and cultured sensibility associated with modern goods and

products. A sense of that milieu is seen in Manuel Orazi's poster for "La Maison Moderne" from *c.*1900, featuring a slender woman seated in a softly lit interior next to a display of contemporary hand-crafted glass and ceramic objects (fig. 8.1). Consciously or not, even the workshops of Gallé and Majorelle may have contributed to the diffusion of the Art Nouveau market through manufacturing less expensive products such as lamps and vases designed for serial production.

While the popularization of Art Nouveau designs may have been responsible for declining appeal among more exclusive consumers in the second decade of the twentieth century, many of the circumstances that nurtured Bing's and Meier-Graefe's showrooms remained intact, particularly the belief in the equality of the arts and the encouragement of self-expression and innovation in the decorative arts. These values continued to be supported under the auspices of the Société des Artistes Decorateurs (S.A.D.) and the annual Salon d'Automne in which fine and decorative arts were exhibited together. In addition, the publication of periodicals devoted to the design arts (*Art et Decoration*, for example) continued to provide avenues for promoting the work of modern decorative arts to a luxury market. French designers were not willing to relinquish the reputation for individuality and originality they had acquired through their association with fine art as well as the sense of continuity with their national legacy of craft excellence prior to the French Revolution. Amid these circumstances designers found new sources of inspiration, including contemporary painting and sculpture, original adaptations of late eighteenth-century Neoclassical furniture design and fashion, as well as sensational entertainments in Paris such the Ballets Russes. The new directions taken by French designers may also be seen against the background of tensions, both political and cultural, between France and Germany. In this context the new designs appear as a sophisticated response to the simpler shapes and more rational approach of German examples of furniture exhibited in Munich in 1908 and in Paris in 1910, where they generally received a favorable public and critical response.

As most students of early twentieth-century art are aware, bold, non-naturalistic color and a higher degree of abstraction distinguished the paintings of a group of artists at the 1905 Salon d'Automne who acquired the nickname "Fauves" (Wild Beasts), coined by critic Louis Vauxcelles. A similar boldness and intensity of expression characterized productions of the Ballets Russes in Paris, particularly the costumes and stage sets designed between 1909 and 1913 by Russian artists Alexandre Benois (1870–1960) and Léon Bakst (1866–1924) for productions

8.2 Léon Bakst, costume design (Odalisque) for *Schéherazade*, 1910.

8.3 Georges Lepape, Mme. Poiret wearing "harem" pants designed by Paul Poiret, 1911.

8.4 Maurice Dufrène, pair of mahogany and upholstered chairs (Salon d'Automne), 1913.

of *Cléopatre* and *Schehérazade*. These productions featured an element of eroticism associated with Near and Middle Eastern cultures expressed in vibrant colors for sets and costumes. Such a shared milieu involving fine arts, entertainment, and fashion is seen, for instance, by comparing a costume design by Léon Bakst for *Schehérazade* (1910), and a fashion drawing showing "harem" pants designed by French couturier Paul Poiret (1879–1944) from 1911, both aimed at an elite audience (figs. 8.2 and 8.3). A similar exoticism is found as well in paintings and sketches of Matisse based upon visits to Morocco in 1911–12

Furniture and Modern Art

While inspired in part by the solid forms and refined craftsmanship of French Neoclassical furniture during the late eighteenth century, there is little that is sober or subdued about the early twentieth-century reinterpretation of this tradition. Taut curves and spirals, bold color contrasts created by lacquered surfaces and mother-of-pearl or ivory inlays, prancing stags and luxurious vegetation create a sense of nature's vitality and pleasures, only slightly restrained by the discipline of symmetrical compositions and the craftsman-like integration of ornamental and constructive forms. Maurice Dufrène's (1876–1955) pair of mahogany upholstered armchairs, based upon an eighteenth-century "type" known as a bergère and exhibited at the 1913 Salon d'Automne (fig. 8.4), exemplifies the new

direction pursued by French designers in the years just before the outbreak of World War I. Dufrène began his career as a painter and worked as a furniture designer and manager at Julius Meier-Grafe's La Maison Moderne showrooms, which featured interiors in the Art Nouveau style. Dufrène's furniture reveals an appreciation for craft and workshop production, and from the second decade of the twentieth century he embraced a rational, self-contained approach to design. In the pair of armchairs, for instance, the broad contours of both the back and seat are comfortably balanced and embellished by the spiral scroll at the termination of the armrests and the seams of the upholstery to create a design remarkable for its simple harmony between structure and decoration. The expressive similarity between fine and decorative art recalls a statement in Henri Matisse's "Notes of a Painter" (1908). In this essay the artist made an analogy between painting and psychology, comparing the tranquility he hoped that his canvases would provide with the comfort of a good armchair:

> What I dream of is an art of balance, of purity and tranquility, devoid of troubling subject matter, an art which could be, for every mental worker, for the businessman as well as for the man of letters, for example, a soothing balm, a mental calmative, something akin to a good armchair which eases his physical fatigue ...

The acknowledgment that both paintings and furniture could bring relief from the work and distractions of daily life (Matisse's remarks stem from a similar statement made by French writer Charles Baudelaire, 1821–67), reinforces a shared milieu for modern artists and craftsmen in the pursuit of a common and practical goal for creative expression, namely to provide joy and a sense of well-being to their discerning public. Their frame of reference included fine art, domestic goods and furnishings, clothing, and fashionable entertainments such as the opera and Ballets Russes.

Louis Süe (1875–1968) and André Mare (1887–1932) were also painters who pursued careers in the decorative arts beginning around 1910, though unlike Dufrène their background in design did not include a direct involvement with craft and production. Their black ebony cabinet (fig. 8.5), part of an ensemble dating to 1927, is based on a simple rectangular form, relieved by tapered legs, a scalloped lower edge to the cabinet doors, and rounded edges above with floral designs lightly carved in relief. The top of the cabinet flares outward to provide a kind of "rail" for objects to be safely placed there. When closed, the cabinet doors reveal a lavishly decorated composition of flowers constructed of inlaid mother-of-pearl, balanced but not symmetrical, and brilliantly set off against the black lacquered surface of the cabinet. The ensemble includes a gilt table whose legs and relief decoration match that of the ebony cabinet. Each piece of the ensemble shares common elements but is not part of a coordinated set. As art historian Nancy Troy has observed, designers during this time seem to have consciously pursued a less "coordinated" esthetic in which variety of color, texture, and shape mirror the disjointed character and hectic pace associated with the experience of modern urban life. Critic Gustave Kahn made such connections in his review of the 1912 Salon d'Automne, also known as "La Maison Cubiste," noting the relationship

between the interiors of the exhibition and the dislocations and changing viewpoints of early Cubism.

And yet, while a Cubist "esthetic" may have played a part in the critical reception of a new approach to interior design, and the style's angular facets and overlapping planes also contributed in the 1920s to the development of an emerging esthetic of the urban experience, overt references to the decorative arts in the early Cubist paintings of Braque and Picasso consist primarily of the incorporation of cheap printed wallpaper and the borrowing of wall-painters' techniques for imitating wood grain. Such appropriations are encroachments from ordinary daily life upon the territory of high "Art," both in terms of their lower middle-class associations and the implied blurring between mechanical reproduction and the privileged realm of the painter's easel. Thus while Cubist paintings attacked the privilege associated with both fine art and luxury craft, early twentieth-century critics did not generally acknowledge this provocative crossing of boundaries. Instead, they looked at abstract and compositional elements of Cubism in relation to contemporary luxury craft such as those ensembles displayed at the 1912 Maison Cubiste. Different interpretations of Cubism make the relation between this movement and twentieth-century decorative arts complex, raising issues ranging from abstraction to the relation between the realms of exclusive and vernacular design. In a similar fashion, some of the experimental typography that emerged in literary works during these same years, treated in more detail below (see page 191), borrowed techniques from newspaper advertisements, disturbing traditional expectations for the printed pages of a book.

Like many of his contemporaries, Frenchman Jacques-Émile Ruhlmann (1879–1933) studied to be a painter but turned to design around 1910. His designs are free interpretations of French Neoclassical or "Empire" furniture, upholding the French patrimony of virtuoso craftsmanship distinguished by luxury and the most exact standards of quality. Yet, as seen in a desk from 1919 (fig. 8.6), his furniture is replete with invention and novelty, employing veneers of exotic woods such as amboyna (imported from Laos) and macassar ebony (from Indonesia), with drawer pullers of ivory attached by green silk thread accenting a greyish-green sharkskin writing surface. The desk is supported by swelling legs that project outward from the desk-top and are delicately tapered in a form known as "fuseau."

8.5 Louis Süe et André Mare, furniture ensemble (exhibited at Société des Artistes Decorateurs), 1927.

8.6 Jacques-Émile Ruhlmann, desk, designed for David-Weill residence, Paris, beech, amboyna veneer, shagreen, and ivory, 37 x 47 ½ x 29 ½ in (94 x 121 x 75 cm), c. 1919. Metropolitan Museum of Art, New York.

The new style emerging in these years was, of course, not limited to wood furniture and techniques inherited from the tradition of the great French *ébénistes* of the eighteenth century. New materials and techniques particularly challenged modern designers in many media, as in the interior furnishings of Armand Albert Rateau (1882–1937), for instance a 1922 chaise longue of patinated bronze (fig. 8.7). In Rateau's work foliate forms are simplified into spirals or arabesques, and gracefully proportioned stags frequently appear as well, their forms also simplified into crisp, athletic contours, so unlike the meandering curves of Art Nouveau. Rateau's chaise longue was commissioned for a terrace outside of the bedroom in the Paris apartment of couturier Jeanne Lanvin (1867–1946), and it is perhaps worthwhile to note that in many cases the patrons for the new style in French decorative arts were designers themselves, such as Lanvin or fellow couturier Paul Poiret. In fact, Poiret was a patron of many of the early exhibitions of the new style at the Salon d'Automne of 1911 and the "Maison Cubiste" of 1912, as well as employing the Fauve painter Raoul Dufy (1877–1953) to design textile patterns. Dufy's designs, whether woven for upholstery or block-printed for curtains or wallpaper, often include figures set amid foliage or

stage-like props that lend themselves to repetition and reinforce two-dimensional pattern. An example, from 1929, is a block-printed wallpaper design depicting paired ice skaters and their observers (fig. 8.8). The emphasis upon leisure pastimes and pattern has much in common with the formal as well as thematic character of eighteenth-century tapestry and porcelain described in Part I (see figs. 1.1 and 1.3, pages 17 and 20). A photograph of this particular pattern appeared in the society magazine *Vogue* in a regular section devoted to the arts. In a freer treatment for a mural rather than a tapestry, Dufy decorated an enormous hall for the 1937 Paris World's Fair, with hundreds of figures and motifs illustrating the theme of electricity. Dufy's approach emphasized the discovery and benefits of electricity in human terms, and might be contrasted with more abstract, geometric treatments of electricity-inspired themes in posters and other media (see fig. 10.43).

In 1911 Poiret opened Atelier Martine to produce and sell fabric designs and furnishings, employing a group of young girls from working-class neighborhoods to sketch floral patterns based upon visits to the city's botanical gardens. Poiret's own silk textile (fig. 8.9) possesses the characteristics of the atelier: here a simple pattern of pink and silvery-white radiating petal-like shapes explode against a black ground, restrained only by the discipline of the repetition of the simplified lozenge and circular shapes. As mentioned above, Poiret's own fashions made use of the bold and even discordant color combinations of the Ballets

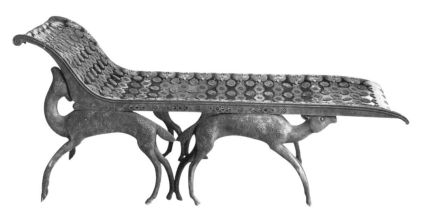

8.7 Armand-Albert Rateau, chaise longue, patinated bronze, 25 ¹⁄₁₆ x 60 ¼ x 23 ¼ in (64 x 153 x 59.5 cm), c. 1920–23. Musée des Arts Décoratifs, Paris.

8.8 Raoul Dufy, wallpaper design, 1929. Private collection.

8.9 Paul Poiret, textile, printed silk, 70 ¼ x 50 ¼ in (180 x 129 cm), manufactured by Maison Martine, *c.* 1919. Metropolitan Museum of Art, New York.

Russes after its appearance in 1910 and the staging of ballets based upon *Schéhérezade* and other themes taken from the lore of the Near and Middle East. He created the idea of "harem" pants for women (see above, fig. 8.3), and his fashion designs permitted more freedom of movement and a closer relationship between garment and body that was considered quite shocking for the time. Poiret's celebrity contributed to his commercial success, and stands within a late nineteenth-century tradition of artists' studios that were specifically designed as meeting places for potential clients (see page 71). Such notoriety, however, was short-lived for Poiret, whose reputation was damaged at the outbreak of World War I, when the popularity of his designs in Germany led to false accusations in some circles that he was an enemy sympathizer.

Glass and Metal

An examination of glass design in the period around 1910 reveals a lively interest in experimentation with a variety of techniques to permit individual and original expression in the medium. In many ways early twentieth-century French glassmakers drew inspiration from Émile Gallé, and as with other craft traditions, glass artists were often trained as painters or sculptors. Perhaps as a result of Gallé's example and reputation, early twentieth-century glass does not always make a distinct break with Art Nouveau. The enameling technique known as *pâté de verre*, produced by refiring colored ground glass in molds, resulted in translucent surfaces of varied color whose rich effects were reminiscent of the earlier style, even if the technique,

8.10 François Décorchment, bowl, *pâté de verre*, 1909. Musée des Arts Decoratifs, Paris.

8.12 René Lalique, *Oiseau de Feu (Bird of Fire)* glass lamp with bronze base, *c.* 1925. Private collection.

to be successful, required thick walls and often resulted in smoother surfaces and more regular shapes than those of Gallé. An example is a *pâté de verre* vase designed and produced by François Decorchment (1880–1971, fig. 8.10). Other French designers directed their efforts to clear glass, often with thick walls pressed into molds to accentuate relief surfaces, or sometimes trapping bubbles in a technique known as "*verre soufflé*" or "bubble glass." The increasing emphasis upon working with clear rather than colored glass is seen in the oeuvre of Maurice Marinot (1882–1960), who abandoned an early career as a painter to work with the medium of glass. After experimenting with the process of *pâté de verre*, Marinot began exploring the potentials of transparent glass. Results were thick-walled and sculptural, emphasizing, with bubbles and streaks, internal rather than applied decoration, as seen in a vase from 1924 (fig. 8.11).

Also identified with new explorations in the field of glass design in the early twentieth century was René Lalique (1860–1945), who

8.11 Maurice Marinot, bottle with stopper, blown glass with acid-etched decoration (*verre soufflé*), 10 ¼ in (27.3 cm) high, 1924. Philadelphia Museum of Art.

operated his own facility near Paris for the manufacture of limited editions of his designs. Lalique was trained as a jeweler, and earlier in his career created some of the most celebrated examples of Art Nouveau jewelry using precious metals, stones, and enamel. Before the end of the first decade of the new century he began experimenting with glass as an inexpensive material rather than precious gems, purchasing a light bulb factory in 1911 to further his knowledge of the medium. Like Marinot, Lalique explored glass primarily as a transparent rather than opaque medium, using etching with acid to achieve contrast and textured effects. Throughout his career Lalique's work was admired for its purity and brilliance, seen in the *c.* 1925 *Firebird* lamp (fig. 8.12), which took its name from a well-known production of the Ballets Russes that was staged in 1910 and again in 1926 with music by the Russian composer Igor Stravinsky (1882–1971). In this work the "ordinary," clear form of the material is rendered almost magically invisible, revealing a floating female figure whose feathered wings and plant-like tail echo the elaborate, fan-shaped shade. The reputation Lalique established before World War I continued after the Armistice in 1918. As early as 1907 he was asked by perfumier François Coty (1876–1934) to design labels for perfume bottles. The partnership grew to include the design of the glass bottles themselves, strengthening a link between art glass and the marketing of perfumes in the wake of the expansion of the industry with the introduction of synthetic perfumes in the early years of the twentieth century.

Other early twentieth-century designers were also attracted to the idea of transforming ordinary and inexpensive materials into highly original works through a reconsideration of their creative possibilities. For instance, Swiss-born Jean Dunand (1877–1942) came to Paris originally to study sculpture. His teacher, Jean Dampt (1854–1946), advocated egalitarian views toward the arts, and with his mentor's encouragement Dunand pursued and achieved critical success in the field of *dinanderie*, a term used to refer to small vases and utensils manufactured from non-precious materials such as copper and brass, using various kinds of patina for textures and colored surfaces and the technique of repoussé for introducing patterns based upon geometric and schematic floral forms. Occasionally the organic shapes of Dunand's early *dinanderie* vases recall the irregularity of Art Nouveau pottery or glass, but often his works exhibit a preference for more regular contoured, even classical shapes, and spiral decorative motifs. Such works were shown at the exhibitions sponsored by the Societé des Artistes Decorateurs and were illustrated in the publication *Art et decoration*. In 1912 Dunand began learning the technique of applying lacquer to a variety of *dinanderie* from a well-known Japanese craftsman named Seizo Sugawara who was living in Paris. Lacquer is a colored or transparent substance made from the sap of trees grown primarily in the Far East. A long process of refinement and purification is required to produce it, and its application to surfaces of wood or metal objects must be equally painstaking. Although used primarily as a protective coating to preserve and protect materials (with Dunand's assistance the French air force used lacquer to coat the surface of plywood propellers during World War I in order to prevent the dangerous deterioration of the material in wet or humid weather), Dunand became interested in lacquer's potential for surface decoration, which he developed more fully after the war. His painstaking methods produced layered surfaces of great subtlety and brilliance on a variety of

8.13 Jean Dunand, samples of decorative lacquers.

8.14 Ruhlmann, Grand Salon, Hôtel d'un Collectionneur, exposition internationale des arts decoratifs et industriels modernes, 1925, Paris, with black lacquer cabinet from the workshop of Jean Dunand.

wooden screens, metal bowls, and furniture. An idea of the variety is seen in a composite photograph revealing the range of effects that might be achieved with the medium (fig. 8.13). Dunand's obsessive dedication to craft is demonstrated in this description of the lacquering process for a wooden screen:

> ...as many as forty coats of lacquer had to be applied and, as the lacquer in drying tended to contract and could thus twist the wooden panel of a screen out of shape, another coat had to be applied on the reverse side to counteract the tension: both coats drying simultaneously ensured that the base remained true. The drying process presented complications, taking any time between three and four days, and paradoxically could only be satisfactorily accomplished in a room kept perpetually damp by means of streams of water flowing down the walls. Further complications were added in that the drying process could only take place in a darkened room and for some mysterious reason was affected by the moon's influence, the best result occurring when the moon was full. After each coat a process of careful rubbing down and smoothing to a perfect surface had to be performed before another coat of lacquer could be applied.

Other examples of the technique include the large black cabinet inlaid with a "hedgehog" in ivory designed by Polish-born painter Jean Lambert-Rucki (1888–1967), exhibited in 1925 in the Grand Salon of the Hôtel d'un Collectionneur for the Exposition Internationale des Arts Décoratifs et Industriels Modernes (fig. 8.14).

Many of the designers associated with the Art Moderne style were already active in the years 1905–15, while others emerged more fully only after World War I. Metalsmith Edgar Brandt (1880–1960), who worked with wrought iron and experimented with combinations of metals and alloys, was a counterpart to the interest of artists–craftsmen in the effects of rare veneers in wood or in the possibilities of lacquerwork. Brandt's techniques resulted from the use of new technologies, such as autogenous welding, which permitted the combination of different metals in the creation of furniture, lighting, plaques, doors, and screens. The projecting wrought-iron table with marble top from 1925 (fig. 8.15) is distinguished by the broad curves of its legs terminating in spirals.

8.15 Edgar Brandt, console, wrought iron, welded and polished, marble top and base, 32 x 60 in (81 x 152 cm) wide, *c.* 1925. Art Institute of Chicago.

These contours are reminiscent of the sweeping lines of the inlaid mother-of-pearl bouquet in the cabinet of Süe et Mare (see fig. 8.5, page 146) or the classically-inspired forms of lacquered vases by Jean Dunand (fig. 8.16). More original are the plaques and screens Brandt created for special commission, such as the Cigognes d'Alsace (fig. 8.17), a large grille in patinated wrought iron and tin. This design of 1922 was repeated, supported by a plywood surface, in a commission of 1928 for the interior wall panels of elevators in Selfridges Department Store in London (removed in 1971 to comply with new fire regulations and now relocated to the Museum of London with an additional example in the Victoria and Albert Museum). These large relief plaques rival the effects of illusionistic decoration in paint and stucco relief from a Baroque church or palace, with an arrangement of flying storks emerging from the center of an asymmetrically-placed octagonal opening from which schematically-rendered rays emanate outward and are embellished with hammered spiral forms in relief, repeated in smaller and more shallow variations

8.16 Jean Dunand, urn-shaped vase, oxidized, lacquered brass inlaid with silver, 20 in (50 cm) high, *c.* 1922. DeLorenzo Gallery, New York.

8.17 Brandt, "Les Cigognes d'Alsace," grille, patinated wrought iron and tin, 8 ft 2 ⅓ in x 6 ft 7 in x 3 ½ in (2.6 m x 2 m x 9 cm), exhibited at the Salon des Artistes Francaises, 1922.

8.18 Jean Dupas and Jean Dunand, "The Chariot of Aurora" wall decoration, lacquer and metal leaf on plastic relief, 216 x 312 x 2 in (548.6 x 792.5 x 5.1 cm), 1935. Carnegie Museum of Art, Pittsburgh.

8.19 Jean Puiforcat, five-piece tea and coffee service, silver and crystal, tallest piece 9 1/8 x 9 x 3 5/8 in (23.2 x 22.9 x 9.2 cm), 1925. Minneapolis Institute of Art.

Another metal designer to emerge after World War I was Jean Puiforcat (1897–1945), who came from a family of nineteenth-century silversmiths in Paris. His father had directed the business toward the luxury market, and also had acquired an impressive collection of antique silver objects for display in the workshop's showrooms. Throughout his career, which began in 1917 after his return from service in World War I, Puiforcat maintained an interest in both stone sculpture and silver, and was strongly influenced by the simple abstractions of the human figure by Aristide Maillol, (1861–1944). Like Maillol as well as Roumanian-born sculptor Constantin Brancusi (1876–1957), Puiforcat's designs temper naturalism with an underlying desire for permanence as expressed in a refined sense of geometry, balance, and regularity. Puiforcat also admired these qualities of rational beauty and geometric precision in the products of modern industry, particularly the design of the great luxury ocean liners, whose tapered bows appear to be the inspiration for a tea and coffee service of 1925 (fig. 8.19). A similar simplified abstraction of this basic form appears in the advertising posters of Russian-born artist A. M. Cassandre (1901–1968), seen, for instance, in an advertising poster for the luxury liner *l'Atlantique* in 1931, in which the simplified shape of the hull is inscribed within a rectangle, again emphasizing its abstract geometric character and monumentality (fig. 8.20). To further exaggerate the purity of the forms, Cassandre used a pneumatic airbrush to apply color to the lithographic stone, introducing an element of subtle tonal control beyond the capability of more direct means of drawing or painting with brushes.

Cassandre likened his task as a poster artist to that of a telegrapher who was the transmitter rather than the author of information to be communicated. Despite the impersonal tone of this self-assessment, Cassandre's designs continued a tradition of art posters with the aura of an individual style, in this case revealing an artist well-versed in the formal language of Cubism and incorporating sophisticated verbal as well as visual puns not lost on the initiated spectator. His well-known 1932 poster for Dubonnet (fig. 8.21) develops in three stages and gains strength through repetition of a seated figure enjoying the apertif. The heavily drawn outlines of the letters of the brand name and seated figure are completed in the successive, diag images. The progression suggests satisfaction (the drinker is both "filled-in" and "filled-up"), while

throughout the large plaque. The Cigognes is a unique showpiece that tests the limits of a medium usually associated with a limited vocabulary of stock motifs, textures, and patterns; in this example the inherent tensile strength of the wrought iron is maintained in the rod-like projections from the octagon containing the storks, while the varied relief of the textured spirals and the illusionism of the radiating composition itself suggest an almost cloudlike softness that takes the material beyond its usual associations.

Such displays of virtuoso technical skills found expression as well in luxury ocean liners during the 1920s and 1930s, sometimes known as "floating palaces." A well-known example, also evoking a Baroque theme, is the "Chariot of Aurora" lacquer and metal relief on plaster panel from the Grand Salon of the *SS Normandie*, designed by painter Jean Dupas (1882–1964) and executed by Jean Dunand in 1935 (fig. 8.18). The "Chariot of Aurora" is one of four panels depicting gods and goddesses in relation to the themes of travel and navigation. Sun rays emanate across clouds and schematic wave-like imbrications from a flaming disk. In this example Aurora (the dawn) rises in a chariot accompanied by nude figures who are fused with representations of winds, rain, spring flowers, and the autumn harvest.

8.20 A. M. Cassandre, poster for "L' Atlantique", 1931. © Mouron. Cassandre. All rights reserved.

8.21 A. M. Cassandre, advertisement "Dubonnet," 94 ½ x 126 in (240 x 320 cm), 1934. ©Mouron. Cassandre. All rights reserved.

the words (DUBO or *du beau*, i.e. handsome or fine; DUBON or *du bon*, i.e. good) reinforce the message. Some writers have remarked on a similarity between Cassandre's imagery for this poster and early animated filmstrips, while others invoke an affinity with Cubist abstraction. Indeed, Cassandre's symbols and letters had the ability, in a single or repeated image, to appeal with both immediacy and sophistication.

Following the end of World War I, economic reconstruction and a renewed sense of national solidarity in France helped to expand the commercial scope of Art Moderne. One element in this expansion was the growth of retail outlets for the marketing of modern design and decoration. In 1919 Süe et Mare founded the Compagnie des Arts Françaises to provide a showroom for their own products and those of their collaborators, and in the same year Ruhlmann established a storefront business as an addition to the private commissions that were virtually the sole basis of his earlier work. During the same period metal craftsman René Joubert founded a company to market the works of modern designers, called Décoration Interieure Moderne (D.I.M.), and the prominent French department stores also inaugurated special showrooms for the display of modern furnishings: Bon Marché opened Pomone in 1923 under the direction of furniture designer Paul Follot (1877–1941), and in 1921 Galleries Lafayette opened La Matrise directed by Maurice Dufrène.

The Paris Exposition of 1925

As early as 1911 the French government began to plan for yet another large international exhibition of the decorative and industrial arts to take place in Paris, but the effort was delayed due to disagreements over the criteria for exhibitors and finally to the outbreak of World War I. Following the war planning resumed, resulting in the *Exposition Internationale des Arts Décoratifs et Industriels Modernes* of 1925. Due to lingering hostilities Germany was not invited to exhibit, and the United States declined to participate, based upon an inability to comply with the criteria established by the organizers that stipulated all designs be modern and not based upon historical period styles (see page 204). Despite efforts on the part of the organizing body to encourage ensembles of furnishings that suggested real living and working spaces and visual-

ized "new modes of life," most of the exhibits focused upon products and ensembles aimed at an exclusive market, created by individual artist–designers.

The exhibition grounds featured pavilions sponsored by the major Parisian department stores and associations of industries such as perfumes and decorative glass manufacturers, a Gallery of Boutiques exhibiting the works of individual designers, as well as pavilions sponsored by invited nations including Finland and the Soviet Union. Exhibitions spaces were allotted to French design organizations, most prominently the Société des Artistes Decorateurs, as well as the more recently formed l'Esprit Nouveau, the latter featuring a model furnished apartment by the Swiss-born designer and architect Charles-Édouard Jeanneret (1887–1965), known since 1921 as Le Corbusier. A number of members of the S.A.D. also contributed ensembles individually, and after much discussion this organization was asked to design a model French embassy with reception areas and living rooms assigned to different members.

Many of the interiors and furnishings at the exhibition featured the luxurious decoration and rare materials used by designers such as Ruhlmann and Süe et Mare. Ruhlmann's Hôtel d'un Collectionneur was a separate structure consisting of a number of interiors designed both for living as well as lavish entertaining. The Hôtel's Grand Salon (see fig. 8.14, page 150) was an oval-shaped room with ceilings over 20 feet (6 meters) high and a chandelier resembling a hanging fountain created by tiers of concentric circles hung with strips of glass beading. The monumental black lacquer cabinet, produced in the workshop of Jean Dunand and discussed above, was placed opposite the fireplace. The centerpiece of the room was a grand piano in macassar ebony, whose S-curve was accentuated by Ruhlmann and echoed in its tapered legs. The piano's legs were inlaid in ivory and flared outward like the hooves of a fawn where they met the floor. Above the marble fireplace hung a large painting by Jean Dupas entitled *Les Perruches* (*The Songbirds* or *The Parakeets*, fig. 8.22), depicting a group of draped and nude women with elaborate coiffures, some clothed or partially-clothed in heavy satin or silk brocaded fabrics, and set in a landscape of lush fruit, foliage, flowers, and plump birds. Photographs of the painting in situ reveal harmonies in color between the skin tones of the nudes and the light background of the fabric wall covering as well as the grained marble of

8.22 Jean Dupas, *Les Perruches* (*The Songbirds* or *The Parakeets*), Grand Salon, Hôtel d'un Collectionneur, Exposition Internationale des Arts Decoratifs et Industriels Modernes, 1925. Private Collection.

the fireplace. Dupas' image of abundance and sensual pleasure, both in nature and through the products of fashion, is a fitting counterpart to the comfort, grandeur, and luxury of Ruhlmann's Grand Salon.

Other interiors for the exhibition were distinguished by a preference for angles rather than curves, and by the use or imitation of industrial materials such as smooth metal sheeting, expanses of plate glass, polished marble, or lacquer. Jean Dunand designed a Smoking Room (fig. 8.23) for the model French embassy constructed by members of S.A.D. The room was square with beveled corners creating an octagonal space, surmounted by a tiered ceiling resembling a stepped pyramid or ziggurat. The walls were covered with black lacquer panels and the ceiling painted silver with red accents in the corners. The same color scheme was repeated for a square table in the center of the room and four square armchairs with silver paneled sides. The geometric severity of the interior extended to the fabric patterns for cushions and pillows of the built-in sofa and abstract patterns of a wall hanging facing the doorway. Imagining the smoking room filled with a collection of diplomats in starched white collars and

black evening attire increases the esthetic effect of formal elegance Dunand may have envisioned. The relationship between architecture, decoration, and furnishings is as complex as Ruhlmann's Grand Salon, while the severity of the design suggests a source of inspiration based not upon the luxurious and sensual forms of nature but rather deriving from a heightened feeling for straight lines and flat planes. Sophisticated and restrained in both color and its variety of form and decoration, the smoking room has an air of psychological remoteness, not unlike the somewhat aloof demeanor captured in contemporary advertisements and discussed below (see page 225 and fig. 10.35).

Not all exhibits and interiors emphasized luxury living. Francis Jourdain's (1876–1958) Physical Culture Room and the adjoining Lounge designed by Pierre Chareau (1883–1950), part of the S.A.D.'s French Embassy (fig. 8.24), also employed smooth wood paneling attached to walls and ceiling to resemble riveted metal sheeting. A daybed in Chareau's Lounge was suspended from steel bars attached to the ceiling, and the square clock, rectangular divisions of screens, and simple, plaid patterns for curtains and fabrics repeated the theme of horizontal and vertical lines and planes that extended into the three-dimensional interior space. The interest in exercise demonstrated by Jourdain's Physical Culture Room for the model French embassy seems more appropriately to fulfill the hope of the organizers to offer examples of design that pointed to "new modes of life," in this case an emphasis upon health and hygiene. Such values also played a role in the design of kitchens based upon a more efficient arrangement of work and storage spaces, as well as the elimination of carved or molded decoration to reduce the accumulation of dust (requiring less cleaning in middle-class households without servants.

Even more spartan than Jourdain's and Chareau's physical culture room and adjoining lounge was a model housing unit known as the Pavillon de l'Esprit Nouveau and designed by Le Corbusier. This structure was perhaps the most radical French expression of new attitudes toward design, embracing the use of standardized pre-fabricated materials and rejecting decoration as a vestige of outmoded craft methods of production (fig. 8.25). The furnishings of the apartment included bentwood chairs, tables, modular built-in cabinets and shelving with thin dowel-like legs serving to divide the open rectangular space into living, dining, and study areas. Much of the

8.23 Jean Dunand, "Smoking Room," Ambassade Française, Exposition Internationale des Arts Decoratifs et Industriels Modernes, 1925. Paris.

8.24 Francis Jourdain and Pierre Chareau, Physical Culture Room, Ambassade Française, Exposition Internationale des Arts Decoratifs et Industriels Modernes, 1925. Paris.

8.25 Le Corbusier, interior, Pavillon de l'Esprit Nouveau, Exposition Internationale des Arts Decoratifs et Industriels Modernes, 1925. Paris.

furniture was available commercially through office-supply catalogues (although for the exhibition the pieces were custom-made to conform with the proportions of the interior). Le Corbusier referred to such furniture as "type-objects," basic, anonymous, and permanent forms resulting from a process of gradual refinement based upon utility, economy, and a feeling for the permanent sense of beauty and harmony residing in simple geometrical forms. The architect used the term "mechanical selection" to refer to the process leading to these final forms for a variety of man-made products. Described as a "machine for living in" and compared to similar descriptions of automobiles as "machines for transportation" and airplanes as "machines for flying," Le Corbusier's Pavillon de l'esprit nouveau suggested that the basis of a design for modern living was to be found in the efficiency and economy of the office rather than in the luxury and individuality of the traditional home or apartment, and relied more upon the skills of the engineer than those of the artist. Moreover, such a collective approach, developed in admiration of the accomplishments of engineering in the construction of bridges, airplanes, and other products of modern technology, was seen by Le Corbusier as essential to solve pressing social and economic problems confronting the French nation in the aftermath of World War I.

The inclusion of the Pavillon de l'Esprit Nouveau at the 1925 Paris International Exhibition suggests the coexistence of competing visions of a modern design to address the needs of modern life. Le Corbusier's spare interior and the angular decoration in Dunand's Smoking Room are examples of a broad and varied interest in the relationship between design and the machine in the interwar period. In the hands and minds of designers and theorists, the machine might serve as the vehicle of standardized mass production, as the basis for a morally grounded esthetic of utility, or equally as the inspiration for a decorative vocabulary expressive of the dynamism of the modern age. The phenomenon is so widespread and diverse during the 1920s that it merits greater attention below.

Mechanical Beauty I: Dynamism

In the years both before and after World War I a number of artist/designers were attracted less to the world of nature than to the machine-made environment as a source of inspiration for their work, a new language of form that embodied the dynamism of mechanized forms of production and transportation.

There are, for instance, numerous references in the writings of Italian poet Filipo Tommaso Marinetti (1876–1944) to the particular beauty of machinery as a symbol of speed, progress, and freedom, suggested in the following passage from his "Manifesto of Futurism," published in the French newspaper *Le Figaro* on 20 February 1909:

> We declare that the splendour of the world has been enriched by a new beauty—the beauty of speed. A racing car with its bonnet draped with exhaust-pipes like fire-breathing serpents—a roaring racing car, rattling along like a machine gun, is more beautiful than the winged victory of Samothrace.

> We will sing of the stirring of great crowds—workers, pleasure-seekers, rioters—and the confused sea of color and sounds as revolution sweeps through a modern metropolis. We will sing the midnight fervor of arsenals and shipyards blazing with electric moons; insatiable stations swallowing the smoking of the smoke; bridges flashing like knives in the sun, giant gymnasts that leap over rivers; adventurous steamers that scent the horizon; deep chested locomotives that paw the ground with their wheels, like stallions harnessed with steel tubing; the easy flight of aeroplanes, their propellers beating the wind like banners, with a sound like the applause of a mighty crowd.

Futurist artists derived their means of expressing the excitement of speed and change from the fragmentation and spatial dislocations of Cubism as well as the experiments of Jules Marey (1830–1904) and others with time-lapse or chronophotography, a technique that showed movement as a series of overlapping and abstracted linear patterns. In the medium of painting results may be seen in the frenetic rhythms of works by Gino Severini (1883–1966), Giacomo Balla (1871–1958), and others, and was the inspiration for American artist Earl Horter's (1880–1940) painting *Rhapsody in Blue* (1927), incorporated into an advertisement and illustrated below (see fig. 10.34, page 224).

8.26 Filipo Tommaso Marinetti, *At Night in Her Bed*, 1919.

and in the institutions that governed political and social life and resisted change and progress. The tone of Futurism was revolutionary.

Marinetti's' medium for spreading the gospel of Futurism to the masses was the written word, not as phonetic symbol but as expressive image. In his poetry he followed the lead of Symbolist poet Stéphane Mallarmé (1842–1898) in arranging type on the page to convey the meaning of words or sensation of sounds. Different sizes of type within the same line, and different fonts within the same word, liberated the printed page from its usual directional order and standard spacing. An example is the poem "At Night in Her Bed" from a collection entitled *Words in Liberty* dating to 1919 (fig. 8.26), describing a letter from an artillery man to his girlfriend, who lies supine at the bottom right of the page. Fragments of handwritten words are interrupted by the sounds of gunfire, as well as abstract shapes and words such as "explosion" and "simultaneity." The reader's attention shifts from place to place without clear or prescribed organization aside from a tendency for the eye to wander downward. While earlier examples of Marinetti's Futurist poetry operate within the regularizing framework of parallel vertical and horizontal spacing of letterpress typography, the calligraphic character of "At Night in Her Bed" appears to have been composed somewhat like a collage, with portions of cut-out text pasted on the page along with other cut-out shapes

Crossing the boundary from fine to applied art is hardly a surprising development in Futurism. Marinetti used the popular press as a vehicle for communicating his ideas, and addressed the reader with an aggressive, imperative tone characteristic of the techniques of persuasion in print advertising. Electricity as a source of power for light, the internal combustion engine and the airplane for travel, suggested a spirit of liberation that removed limits to human potential in any number of areas of endeavor. Such developments in turn called forth new techniques of expression in art that dematerialized form and freed the artist from convention and tradition. Marinetti hoped to move beyond the salon, the gallery, and the refuge of the bourgeois domestic interior, and reach an audience of industrial workers and youth in factories, on streets and athletic fields who experienced more directly the vitality of the urban environment. Such a public might be mobilized to tear down all that was traditional and static, both in art

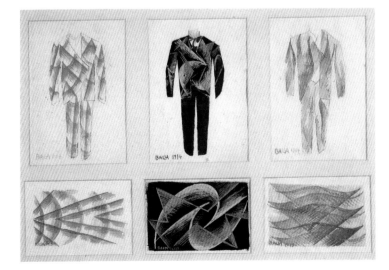

8.27 Giacomo Balla, illustration of the "anti-neutral suit," *Futurist Manifesto*, published 1914 in Volantino della Direzione del Monumenti Futuristi. Milan.

8.28 Fortunato Depero, advertisement for Campari, *c.* 1927.

8.29 Robert Delaunay, *Simultaneous Open Windows,* oil on canvas, 18 x 14 ¼ in (45.5 x 37.5 cm), 1912. Tate Gallery, London.

and handwritten words. The collage was then photographed and exposed as a negative on to a metal plate for offset printing. This technology permitted far greater freedom for typographic experiment, and emerges more prominently in the later 1920s (see page 194).

From 1912 painter Giacomo Balla took an active interest in fashion (mainly men's fashion) and published treatises on the subject beginning in 1914. Asymmetrical geometric patterns printed on or applied to clothing were meant to mirror the rhythms of urban life as seen in a vest with appliqué patterns designed by Balla made in 1915, or a drawing of the so-called "anti-neutral" suit of 1914, designed by Balla for Futurist poet Francesco Cangiullo (1884–1977) to be worn in demonstrations supporting Italy's entry into World War I (fig. 8.27). This suit, as well

as drawings of others designed by Balla, was decorated with asymmetrical circles, triangles, ellipses, cones, and spirals. According to the artist, modern clothing should avoid "faded and murky colors" and "symmetry," and strive to liberate emotion and action by being "aggressive," "agile," and "dynamic." It should also permit free movement. Balla and other Futurists appreciated the seasonal changes in the fashion world that provided continuous opportunities for creativity for designers and excitement for consumers.

While perhaps not the call to political action envisioned by Marinetti, the nervous energy generated by sharp contrasts and the rhythmic repetitions of geometric shapes associated with the Futurists made their appearance in the interwar period in advertisements, realizing in

8.30 Fernand Léger, *The City*, oil on canvas, 7 ft 7 in x 9 ft ½ in (2.3 x 2.8 m), 1919. Philadelphia Museum of Art.

the mass media the hope of communicating Futurist ideas to a popular audience. Fortunato Depero (1892–1960) promoted his services as a graphic designer through the publisher Dinamo Azari in Milan in the 1920s, and also designed advertising for the Italian distiller Campari, manufacturer of a refreshing rose-colored apertif. Depero created a series of black-and-white newspaper advertisements that made use of simplified angular shapes for typography, the cone-shaped drinking glass, and a mechanical-looking figure (fig. 8.28). The product name in this example is composed of letters in descending size, resembling a megaphone and visually corresponding to the reverberating blare of a shouting vendor.

In France, mechanolatry (the love of machines and mechanization) also emerged in painting prior to World War I in the works of Fernand Léger (1881–1955). Leger incorporated bold stencil lettering derived from nineteenth-century display typography used for signs and printed advertisements along with the smooth surfaces of industrially manufactured cylindrical forms resembling pipes, iron rods, or artillery cannon barrels in explosive canvases such as *The City* from 1919 (fig. 8.30). Until the second decade of the twentieth century, the attitude of many French artists and critics toward the machine was ambivalent (see page 237), as demonstrated by the virtual absence of the Eiffel Tower as a subject in contemporary painting for almost two decades after it was built as the showpiece for the Paris World's Fair of 1889.

The tower appears, however, as the focus of a series of works devoted to the subject by Robert Delaunay

(1885–1941) beginning around 1910. Delaunay completed many works based upon the tower, increasingly employing abstraction to convey the energy and elegance of its curving tapered shape (*Simultaneous Open Windows*, 1912, fig. 8.29), and combined the Parisian landmark with airplanes and their spinning propellers to further suggest the triumph of technology, as in his *Homage to Blériot* of 1913, commemorating the French pilot's daring solo flight across the English Channel.

A tall painted panel by Delaunay, based upon the Eiffel Tower, was included in one of the interiors for the model French embassy at the 1925 *Exposition des Arts Décoratifs et Industriels Modernes*. But a more persistent link between the fragmented and dynamic style of these works and the decorative arts was made by Delaunay's Ukrainian-born wife, Sonia Terk Delaunay (1885–1979), who pursued a form of abstraction in relation to motion and prismatic

8.31 Sonia Delaunay, *Etude pour Bal Bullier*, pastel on paper, 11 x 7 ½ in (28 x 19 cm), 1913. Private Collection.

8.32 Sonia Delaunay, sketch for interior of dining room in the Delaunay apartment, Boulevard Malesherbes, Paris, gouache on paper, 11 ⅜ x 16 in (29 x 41 cm), 1924.

color for interior design, fabrics, fashion, and other furnishings. Sonia Delaunay's sketches for dancers' costumes (fig. 8.31) emphasize movement through twisting elliptical contours that resemble the shifting curvilinear planes of the *Windows on the City* series of paintings by her husband and the dematerialization of form that characterized the particular beauty of rapid movement. Abstract patterns of related geometric shapes in primary colors were used to coordinate the interior of a dining room sketched by Sonia Delaunay in 1924 that contained furniture, carpets, and curtains (fig. 8.32). The Delaunays used the term "simultaneity" to describe the transcendence of material form that emerged in the experience of modernity, and in 1925 a Boutique Simultanée was included among the Gallery of Boutiques featured at the Paris Exhibition; the following year Sonia collaborated with her husband on the costumes and set designs for a new production of *Cléopatre*, performed by the Ballets Russes in Paris.

Mechanical Beauty II: Classicism

In addition to associations between machines and dynamism, connections between simple geometry and many modern industrial forms also emerge in the early 1920s, for instance in the refined silver tea sets and pitchers designed by Jean Puiforcat and resembling the forms of modern ocean liners (see fig. 8.19, page 153). Such parallels appear earlier in the paintings and essays of Le Corbusier and Amédée Ozenfant (1886–1966), who, from around 1918, used the name *Purism* to refer to their approach to the machine. In their writings, Le Corbusier and Ozenfant explored the relationship between pairs of polar concepts such as intuition and logic, the eye and the mind, the individual and the universal to argue for the existence of permanent standards for beauty in all forms of art, defined as harmony, proportion, and clarity. In their Purist paintings, these artists suggested similarities among mechanically mass-produced objects such as flasks and bottles, elementary geometry, and the tectonic clarity of Classical art and architecture. They claimed that all of these forms were governed by universal principles of logic and economy, determined as it were by a "law" of mechanical selection analogous to the process of natural selection proposed in Darwin's theory of evolution:

From all this [previous discussion and observations] comes a fundamental conclusion: that respect for the laws of physics and of economy has in every age created highly selected objects; that these artificial objects obey the same laws as the products of natural selection and that, consequently, there thus reigns a total harmony, bringing together the only two things that interest the human being: himself and what he makes.

Mechanical selection provided a basis for the design of both domestic architecture and machine-made consumer products, determined by underlying anonymous, inevitable, and universal principles rather than by individual expression. Ornament and decoration only detracted and obscured the perfection of this underlying process of mechanical selection. Together with Francis Jourdain in 1920, Le Corbusier published a journal entitled *L'esprit nouveau*, in which illustrations and accompanying texts linked the enduring qualities of Classicism with the marvels of modern engineering such as steamships, airplanes, and factories. The journal, subsidized by the French government, advocated collective standards and standardized industrial production rather than individual approaches to design. The tone of *l'Esprit Nouveau* was urgent, arguing for reform and solidarity in the face of pressing economic and social problems in France following World War I. This is the political context that informs Le Corbusier's model for low-cost housing at the Pavillon de l'Esprit Nouveau for the 1925 *Exposition Internationale des Arts Décoratifs et Industriels Modernes* (see fig. 8.25, page 157), note the Purist painting on the wall above the dining table at the right). Despite provocative illustrations of cylindrical grain silos, turbines, and airplanes that lent validity to the "law" of mechanical selection and the polemic, even apocalyptic tone of books such as Le Corbusier's *Towards a New Architecture* (1923), the principle was largely symbolic: aside from ship cabins, railway compartments, and examples of office furniture such as those ordered by Le Corbusier to furnish the Pavillon, neither logic nor claims of universality had much appeal beyond the drafting table and private commissions. More applicable to design were the realities of a market economy and mass consumption, whose dynamics were being explored more fully in the United States (see page 223).

After 1925 a group of designers including Le Corbusier, Jourdain, Chareau, and even Puiforcat (whose use of precious materials precluded his designs from reaching all but the very wealthy) quarreled with the S.A.D. over increasingly elitist attitudes that failed to consider the esthetic merits and broader social benefits of industrial materials and production. Indeed, Le Corbusier had admired the collaborative model of the Deutscher Werkbund and its attempts to synthesize artistic, commercial, and social concerns, while the S.A.D. appeared to promote only unique works created for the luxury market. In 1929 this group of dissenters split with the S.A.D. and formed their own design organization known as the

8.34 René Herbst, chair (chaise sandows), tubular steel and rubber straps, 32 x 18 ¼ x 17 ½ in (81.5 x 46.5 x 44.5 cm), 1927–28. Vitra Museum, Germany.

8.33 Eileen Gray, B-1027 table, tubular steel and glass, 24–40 x 20 in (61–100 x 50 cm), 1927–30. Vitra Design Museum, Germany.

Union des Artistes Modernes (U.A.M.). Examples show a desire to link furnishings with factory assembly rather than craft production, redefining the designer's role in relation to standardization and the use of interchangeable parts rather than craft manufacture. An example is the 1927 circular side table (entitled B-1027 after the name of her villa at Roquebrunne on the Mediterranean coast) constructed of steel and glass by Irish-born designer Eileen Gray (1878–1976) and resting on a horseshoe-shaped base. The connection with the machine extends to the incorporation of working parts, in this case the set screw that enables the height of the table to be adjusted (fig. 8.33). Experimentation with industrial materials such as steel also characterizes the work of U.A.M. member René Herbst (1891–1983), whose metal chair dating to

8.35 Anonymous, French terrace chair, varnished steel and wood veneer, 32 ½ x 17 x 18 ½ in (83 x 43.5 x. 47.5 cm), 1926. Vitra Design Museum, Germany.

1928 is constructed of steel tubing connected at the seat and the back by elastic strips with hooked ends resembling today's bungee cords (fig. 8.34). In eschewing traditional decoration and upholstery and embracing industrial materials, such prototypes were intended to evoke sympathy with efficiency and hygiene as modern values. Yet while the experimental use of new materials in furniture was bold and inventive, these models for industrially produced furniture with an esthetic linking plain surfaces and the absence of decoration to a less materialistic and more efficient lifestyle proved marginal, failing to interest manufacturers or connect with consumers beyond private commissions for wealthy clients. Examples of actual industrial furniture in France, used for seating in sidewalk cafés or other outdoor settings, were often utilitarian but generally lacked the mechanistic pretensions or unified geometric esthetic of U.A.M prototypes. More an equivalent in furniture of the Model T Ford, the anonymously designed French "terrace chair" (fig. 8.35), is constructed of a welded two-piece varnished steel frame, and the uneven surface created by the welding process is not disguised in any way. The seat is made of thin embossed plywood riveted to the frame (imitating leather tooling), and the design can be efficiently and conveniently stacked. It was manufactured in Lyon from around 1926. What is remarkable is that the design of such prosaic objects held interest for this and other groups of designers in the interwar period, who saw them as the basis for a more unified approach to a specifically industrial design.

Chapter 9

The "First Machine Age" in Europe

9.22 Gustav Klutsis, "Let's Return the Coal Debt to the Country!", poster, lithograph, 40 x 28 in (101.6 x 71.2 cm), 1930. Private collection.

Purism and l'Esprit Nouveau emerged in an international context that included design activities in Holland, Russia, and Germany. Through illustrated journals and exhibitions, artists, architects, and designers debated the meaning of ornament, the adoption of universal and collaborative rather than individual approaches to design, often addressed to perceived working-class needs. Projects and prototypes showed sympathy for non-objective abstract art, the marvels of engineering, and rhetoric supported the primacy of social responsibility and reform as motivations for design in relation to modern life in a more egalitarian, industrial world. Each movement, building upon views expressed earlier by Frank Lloyd Wright (see pages 126–7) and William Morris (see pages 106–13), identified machine-made products with plain geometric shapes and the modern urban environment, linked to strong utopian sentiments. As Penny Sparke noted,

> The philosophical leap from the idea of the machine to that of simple, geometrical form was made by all the Modern Movement protagonists. It was a leap of faith rather than fact but one which, nevertheless, underpinned all aspects of the machine aesthetic, both in theory and practice.

By the late 1920s many of these attitudes would produce a recognized, common expression of modern architecture equated with functionalism and the rejection of ornament known as the International Style. The equation of progress with standardized apartment blocks and minimal metal and glass furnishings designed for mechanized mass production might best be seen as a response to the needs of a monolithic mass public during times of economic hardship. The ideology behind such social engineering presumed collective rather than individual needs on one hand, and at the same time identified decoration and individual esthetic expression as unnecessary and decadent vestiges of the past. The fact that such solutions emerged internationally lent credibility to the search for unified solutions to architectural and social problems that reached into the broad realm of designed goods. One might observe that the search for common values, historically part of the spirit of reform beginning with the mid-nineteenth century, grew from a desire for unity in a time of perceived crisis. In this case the belief was that industrialization would rebuild confidence in progress that was shaken by the tragedy of World War I.

Despite a shared sense of purpose and conviction, many modern designers found it difficult to reconcile a number of often competing concerns with spiritual, esthetic, social, and commercial aspects of design, resulting in conflict and contradiction rather than the common truths often implied in idealistic manifestoes and theoretical writings. In referring to this development as the "first machine age," critic Reyner Banham noted: "emotion played a larger part than logic in the emergence of the [first-machine-age] style." Nevertheless, there was a tendency in these related movements to supplant the older paradigm of the artist–craftsman with a newer model for design, one that equated artist with engineer, experimenting with modern industrial materials and processes and concerned with ease of construction and the application of objective criteria through which collective needs were balanced with individual needs.

De Stijl

De Stijl (The Style) was the title of a journal published in Holland and founded in 1917 by the artist–designer Theo van Doesburg (1883–1931). Contributors included the Dutch painters Piet Mondrian (1872–1944) and Vilmos Huszar (1884–1960), Belgian sculptor George Vantongerloo (1886–1965), Dutch furniture-maker and later architect Gerrit Rietveld (1888–1964), and architects Robert van 't Hoff (1887–1979) and Jan Wils (1891–1972). Although De Stijl designs were not exhibited in the Dutch pavilion at the 1925 *Exposition des Arts Décoratifs et Industriels Modernes*, Mondrian lived and worked in Paris both before and after World War I and designs by van Doesburg, Rietveld, and other De Stijl designers were shown in 1923 at the Galerie de l'Effort Moderne owned by Léonce Rosenberg, where they were seen by Le Corbusier.

The term "movement" can only be used loosely in connection with De Stijl: no group exhibitions of De Stijl were ever held, and maintaining shared ideals and a spirit of collaboration among its various participants was difficult, especially in light of the strong personality of van Doesburg: indeed, for one reason or another many of the contributors to early issues of *De Stijl* severed their relationship with the journal over differences with van Doesburg during the course of its eleven-year history.

The manifesto printed in an early issue of *De Stijl* cites individualism as a cause of the conflicts that led to the outbreak of World War I, and proposed a new balance between individual and universal consciousness:

> There is an old and a new consciousness of time. The old is connected with the individual. The new is connected with the universal. The struggle of the individual against the universal is revealing itself in the world-war as well as in the art of the present day. The war is destroying the old world with its contents: individual domination in every state. The new art has brought forward what the new consciousness of time contains: a balance between the universal and the individual. (from Jaffé)

Many of the ideas expressed in the De Stijl manifesto recall an ideology of reform found in the theories of Dutch architect Henrik Berlage (1856–1934) who had used the phrase "unity in diversity" to advocate a balance between unique and standardized elements in architecture and design. Another Dutch architect, J. L. Mathieu Lauweriks (1864–1932), promoted the reconciliation of unity and variety within the framework of geometric composition. Such views were certainly shared by Deutscher Werkbund member Hermann Muthesius (see pages 129–30) who argued against the expressive approach to decoration in Art Nouveau and recommended a more sober, solid, and restrained esthetic. As noted by Philip Meggs, Lauweriks's influence as a member of the faculty at the Dusseldorf School of Arts and Crafts may be seen in the consistent and standardized layouts for promotional material developed by Peter Behrens for the AEG (see page 203, fig. 9.58).

Berlage also admired the designs of Frank Lloyd Wright (see pages 126–7). The American architect's use of flat roofs and wide overhanging eaves explored the interpenetration of interior and exterior and were well-received by *De Stijl* contributors. Dutch designers used this idea as a basis for many of their own architectural projects. They extended the principle to an analogy with the equality between figure/ground in painting and solid/void in sculpture; that is, in each of these media they noted the active role of negative space as an esthetic principle. Indeed, blurring the boundaries between fine and applied arts was a fundamental tenet of *De Stijl*, which included illustrations of painting, sculpture, typography, furniture, interior ensembles, and architecture. For van Doesburg, furniture was sculpture for the interior, and architecture a sort of walk-in painting, which placed the viewer "within painting instead of in front of it and thereby enable[d] him to participate in it." Similar ideas, in more utopian language, were expressed by Mondrian, who felt that architecture and the applied arts would more fully realize what painting had achieved in a more limited way, that is, the attainment of harmony and balance, based upon the abandonment of representation and naturalism and an asymmetrical formal balance between an elementary vocabulary of rectangles created by the intersection of black strips of uniform width. Mondrian's numerous essays on this topic employ dualities similar to the writings of Ozenfant and Jeanneret (Le Corbusier) on Purism. Paired terms such as individual/universal, conscious/unconscious, subjective/objective, mutable/immutable appear in a number of Mondrian's writings, in which he argues for "equilibration" between opposites, realized through the interplay of positive and negative space and the asymmetrical balance of rectilinear elements in walls, floors, furniture, and windows. Mondrian referred to his new conception of art as Neoplasticism or the "New Plastic," and anticipated its application to the built environment in some of his essays published in *De Stijl* and elsewhere:

the new spirit must be manifested in all the arts without exception ... As soon as one art becomes plastic expression of the abstract, the others can no longer remain plastic expressions of the natural. The two do not go together: from this comes their mutual hostility down to the present. The New Plastic abolishes this antagonism: it creates the unity of all the arts.... (From "Neo Plasticism: The General Principle of Plastic Equivalency," published in French by the Galerie de l'Effort Moderne, Paris, 1920)

Our age has reached the climax of individualism: the mature individual can now increasingly find equilibrium with the universal. When our mentality actually attains this equilibrium, it will also be clearly expressed in every aspect of outward life, just as it is expressed abstractly in the new plastic. (From "The New Plastic in Painting," published in *De Stijl*, 1917)

Mondrian also insists that there should be no distinction between art and life, that the work of art should not be separate from living, an idea articulated in an essay of 1923. Before proceeding to develop the theme that both the machine and the urban environment are demonstrations of progress from the natural to the abstract, he writes:

Indeed, the evolution of art consists in its achievement of a pure expression of harmony: art appears only outwardly, as an expression that (in time) reduces individual feeling. Thus art is both the expression and (involuntarily) the means of material evolution: the achievement of equilibrium between nature and non-nature—between what is in us and what is around us. Art will remain both expression and means of expression until (relative) equilibrium is reached. Then its task will be fulfilled and harmony will be realized in our outward surroundings and in our outward life. (From "The Realization of Neo-Plasticism in the Distant Future and in Architecture Today," published in *De Stijl*, 1922)

DE STIJL

By the beginning of 1921 Itten's negative approach had begun to cause Gropius great concern and he decided to curb Itten's influence by making a number of administrative changes. Paul Klee, who brought an intellectual and highly analytical approach to teaching, had joined the staff at the end of 1920, and Gropius now sought to persuade Wassily Kandinsky to return from Russia. Kandinsky agreed, and in the spring of 1922 he was appointed *Formmeister* in the department of mural decoration. Early the following year, when Itten resigned following a further disagreement with Gropius over the conduct of the preliminary course, Laszlo Moholy-Nagy, who was then 28, was appointed to replace him. Together Klee, Kandinsky, and Moholy-Nagy gave Bauhaus

9.1 Vilmos Huszar (attributed), lettering for early issues of *De Stijl*, 1917–18.

The De Stijl principle of balance between universal and individual and the equivalency of the universal with an elemental geometric vocabulary of forms found expression in a variety of media. The typeface (fig. 9.1) used for the title page during the first few years of publication, for instance, was designed by Vilmos Huszar, and uses a limited number of black rectangles of the same width to construct a variety of letter forms using only parallel shapes and right angles. In a related fashion, Gerrit Rietveld's armchair of 1918 (fig. 9.2), painted around 1923) was assembled from varied lengths of standard milled stock to which a rectangular plywood back and seat were added. In Rietveld's chair, joints extend beyond the point where right angles meet, accentuating the incorporation of negative space and associations with non-objective sculpture.

In 1920 Mondrian and Van Doesburg worked on a new cover for *De Stijl* that further provides a concrete illustration of "Neo-Plastic" ideas. In this simple cover, using a sans serif typeface (fig. 9.3), typographic elements are arranged as horizontal rectangular fields in a balanced, asymmetrical composition. The sizes of the typeface determines a hierarchy of information, and even the overlapping of the letters spelling "De Stijl" with the bold letters "N B" (Nieuwe Beelding/New Plastic) suggests the visual equivalency of the two elements; moreover the vertical rather than traditional horizontal placement of the words at the right of the cover reinforce their function as visual elements in a balanced composition.

Color was especially important to van Doesburg for it served to activate spaces and surfaces so that they might be better understood and experienced as abstract form, as

9.2 Gerrit Rietveld, red/blue armchair, 33 ⅞ x 26 ¾ x 26 ¾ in (86 x 68 x 68 cm), 1918 (painted 1923). Stedelijk Museum, Amsterdam.

9.3 Piet Mondrian and Theo Van Doesburg, Title for *De Stijl*, volume 4, no. 1, January 1921.

"realized" works of art. Often this transformation entailed collaboration, which signified not only the integration and unity of the arts, but also a working method that reinforced the balance of individual and group as opposed either to the hegemony of one art form over another or the egocentric model of the individual artist. Van Doesburg contributed patterns for colored brick tiles in a Dutch building known as De Vonk in Noordwijkerhout, designed by J. J. P. Oud (1890–1963) in 1918 (fig. 9.4) as a company-sponsored vacation residence for female workers. Van Doesburg also designed windows composed of colored squares for other architectural projects. At De Vonk the tile compositions above doorways or in hallway floors, although limited to these particular areas of the building, attempt to integrate color and architecture. Other examples of the "realized" work of art are photographs of the various studios used by Mondrian in Paris (fig. 9.5). In this interior, framed paintings, painted rectangles tacked to walls, and the empty easels in the room form an abstract composition reminiscent of the artist's canvases, but extending into three dimensions, serving as a model for the De Stijl interior.

Perhaps the best-known De Stijl project is the Schröder House in Utrecht, built in 1924–25 for a widow and her three children, and designed by Gerritt Rietveld

9.5 Piet Mondrian, *Studio of the Artist*, Paris, 1926. Documentation Archive, Gemeentemuseum, The Hague.

9.6 Gerrit Rietveld, Schröder House, Utrecht, 1924–25, photographed c. 1925.

(figs. 9.6 and 9.7). Mrs. Truus Schröder-Schräder contributed many suggestions to the design, such as the need to provide privacy in the otherwise open design of first floor, achieved through the experimental use of folding and sliding partitions. With its geometric areas of painted floor, painted furniture, projecting balconies with tubular steel railings, flat roof, expanses of square and rectangular glass even around the corner, rectangular "slab" construction (actually brick-faced with cement rather than

9.4 J. J. P. Oud, De Vonk residence, Noordwijkerhout, with colored tiles designed by Theo van Doesburg, 1918.

9.7 Gerrit Rietveld, Schröder House, interior, Utrecht, first floor interior, 1924–25, restored 1985–1987, photographed 1987.

standardized prefabricated units of concrete), the Schröder house fulfilled many of the esthetic principles embraced in *De Stijl*, in particular the attempt to create a "living" work of non-objective art, to extend the experience of non-objectivity to a built environment. The effort to use modern materials and standardized units of construction suggested that the design for the home might be seen as a modified or more customized version of a standardized design for working-class housing. Indeed, according to Paul Overy, Mrs. Schröder-Schräder was concerned that the furniture be simply constructed and that the decor avoid associations with luxury.

Throughout its publication *De Stijl* sought to harmonize esthetic and universal egalitarian considerations in design. The reconciliation between these goals remained difficult both in process and in result. Despite shared principles, individualistic preferences persisted and a strict functional approach to design did not emerge as an overriding law or principle. As Rietveld noted in commenting upon his furniture,

To me De Stijl represented a unit of construction which I considered of prime importance. A practical realization was not always feasible. Function was for me a thing by itself which I never overlooked, it is true, but it did not come into play until the construction and spatial exercises in De Stijl had been completed.

In 1928–9 van Doesburg was asked to participate in the design of a series of interiors known as the Café L'Aubette in the center of Strasbourg to be used for dining and public entertainments. Responsibility for the project was shared with Strasbourg native and artist Jean Arp (1887–1966) and his wife Sophie Täuber (1889–1943), who asked van Doesburg to assist. The various rooms were designed individually with little collaboration, but the connection confirms van Doesburg's increasing receptivity to more subjective and expressive tendencies of contemporary abstract art. Indeed, Arp had been associated with the radical and anti-rational Dada movement in Zurich during the war and remained interested in incorporating the element of chance into his work. Perhaps the most striking design for the project was van Doesburg's "Ciné-Dancing" intended both as a theatre for film projection as well as a cabaret (presumably akin to our own notions of multimedia performance). In this room the diagonals created by large, colored, diamond-shaped panels on the screening wall and ceiling created a dynamic tension with the rectangular and tectonic elements of the architecture in walls, windows, doorways, and balconies (fig. 9.8). When L'Aubette opened van Doesburg declared that the design was the result of "unbridled imagination," a phrase certainly at some variance with the De Stijl manifesto's insistence upon a balance of universal *and* individual consciousness. The introduction of the diagonal into van Doesburg's work, beginning around 1923, alienated Mondrian from *De Stijl*, and from 1925 he stopped contributing to the journal.

In terms of projects on a civic scale, architects such as J. J. P. Oud followed a course that increasingly moved away from the collaboration envisioned by van Doesburg and the spiritual, anti-materialistic esthetics articulated by Mondrian. Already in 1921 Oud had rejected color designs supplied by van Doesburg for the later housing blocks at Spangen (Rotterdam), and Oud's approach to low-cost housing leaned toward uniformity and an increasing emphasis upon efficiency, economic necessity, and social responsibility, precluding the incorporation of the De Stijl vision to create a "living work of art."

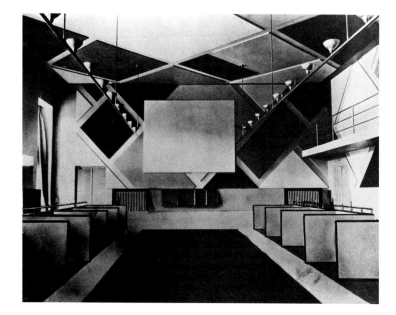

9.8 Theo van Doesburg, Cinema-Dance Hall at the Café L'Aubette, Strasbourg, 1928–29. Documentation Archive, Musées Municipaux, Strasbourg.

9.9 J. J. P. Oud, Housing Block, Weissenhof Colony, Stuttgart, 1927. Photograph: Nederlands Documentatiecentrum voor de Bouwkunst, Amsterdam.

Oud's group of housing units constructed at Weissenhof (Stuttgart) in 1927 for an international exhibition sponsored by the German Werkbund relied upon standardized elements for rectangular windows and doors set into flat expanses of plain white walls, but without the introduction of color, assymmetrical composition, or three-dimensional effects characteristic of De Stijl. Although contemporary with the Café L'Aubette interiors, Oud's Weissenhof project eschewed for the most part the integration of painting and architecture seen in the Schröder House and in other De Stijl architectural projects. It offered instead an economical and standardized solution to urban housing using modern prefabricated materials and industrial methods of production (fig. 9.9). Weissenhof continues to function as low-income housing in Stuttgart and is frequently cited among the early examples of a functional "International Style" emerging in the later 1920s (see page 223). The interiors of the Café L'Aubette, however, despite the initial enthusiasm of the artists and press, became the object of indifference and public criticism. Within a few years the interiors had been indiscriminately altered by the owners and no longer reflected the original designs. Van Doesburg's ideal of uniting art and life in the abstract environment proved a disappointment in the public arena, where it was unable to sustain public interest or to effectively present practical solutions to social problems or to shape a shared vision for the unity of modern art and a vision of contemporary life.

Constructivism

Between March and June 1925 Russian artist and designer Alexander Rodchenko (1891–1956) was in Paris installing a furnished interior based upon his design for a Soviet Workers Club as well as assisting with other Russian exhibits for the Exposition des Arts Décoratifs et Industriels Modernes (fig. 9.10). The Workers Club was essentially a rectangular reading room. It contained two long wooden tables with hinged leaves that tilted to hold newspapers and journals, and a series of chairs with rounded backs built from eight standardized components. Rodchenko also designed and built a pair of armchairs, each with a shelf to the side that could be moved and attached to form a chess table when the chairs were placed facing one another. A glass wall case contained a series of

9.10 Aleksandr Rodchenko, photograph of Soviet Workers Club, Exposition Internationale des Arts Decoratifs et Industriels Modernes, Paris, 1925.

posters that moved on rollers, and a moveable platform consisted of an elevated speaker's rostrum, folding table for the display of pamphlets and books, and folding screen for posters or film projection. The Soviet press contrasted the simplicity of Rodchenko's Workers Club with the luxury and clutter they felt characterized the majority of interiors at the Paris exhibition, no doubt intended as a criticism of Ruhlmann's Hôtel d'un Collectionneur or the model French embassy designed by members of the Société des Artistes Decorateurs. Indeed the absence of carved decoration and emphasis upon standardized, interchangeable components for furniture, as well as the use of plain industrial materials such as plywood and sliding metal doors point to the replacement of the artist–craftsman with the newer paradigm of the artist–engineer. In this regard the furniture of the Workers Club went further toward an objective approach to design, beyond the esthetic considerations of De Stijl, and similar in some respects to the anonymous "type–object" furniture of Le Corbusier's interior for the Pavillon de l'Esprit Nouveau. However, the Soviet furniture was designed and built in a workshop setting rather than commercially manufactured. Its standardized forms and uniformity were appropriate visual counterparts to the collective values of the Communist society for which they were created.

Rodchenko's Workers Club was a mature product of Constructivism, one of several evolving efforts on the part of artists who wished to participate directly in the restructuring of the Russian state following the revolutions of 1917 and the Bolshevik victory in the civil wars that ended in 1920. In 1918 the new communist Russian government established a ministry of culture known as the Peoples Commissariat of Enlightenment (Narkompros) under the direction of Anatoly Lunacharsky (1875–1933), a Communist Party official and playwright who advocated a tolerant attitude toward radical artistic ideas. Narkompos and the various institutes and schools it formed replaced their more academic and conservative pre-revolutionary predecessors, permitting progressive artists a platform for putting into practice utopian ideologies that linked non-objective abstract art to Socialist revolution. Both artists and revolutionaries shared a universal aim to liberate the masses from the tyranny of the past, and for a time they affirmed together the ability of art and design to transform the values and conditions of modern life.

The new abstract art played a significant role in the formation of Constructivism. Abstraction's most articulate spokesman in Russia both before and after the revolution was Kasimir Malevich (1878–1935) who used the term Suprematism to refer to his non-objective style of painting. Malevich defined Suprematism as the expression of feeling in art, and noted the formal similarity between the simple geometric squares and rectangles of his canvases and the forms of modern technology and industry in their transcendence of organic naturalism. In this way he forged a symbolic link between the new art and the promise of technology. Malevich's paintings manipulated abstract geometric elements to suggest states of mind, as seen in titles for his works such as *Suprematist Composition Expressing the Feeling of Movement and Restraint* or *Suprematist Composition Expressing Magnetic Attraction*. Malevich encouraged the integration of "art into life," and through his association with the art organization and school located in Vitebsk and renamed as UNOVIS (Affirmers of the New Art) in 1920 he helped to coordinate efforts to use Suprematist decorations for signs and banners and the embellishment of temporary architectural constructions such as stages and speaker platforms (fig. 9.11). The expanded agenda led UNOVIS members such as Vasily Kandinsky (1866–1944), who had pioneered an expressive abstract non-objective style in

174

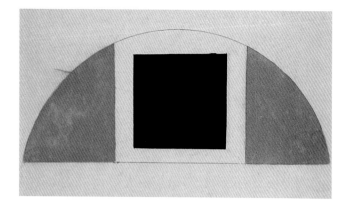

9.11 Temporary displays designed by members of UNOVIS in Vitebsk.

9.12 El Lissitsky (Lazar Markovich Lissitsky), poster, *Beat the Whites with the Red Wedge*, lithograph, 20 ⅞ x 27 ⁹⁄₁₆" (53 x 70 cm), 1919. Stedelijk Van Abbemuseum, in Eindhoven, the Netherlands.

Germany before World War I and returned to Russia after the revolution to adopt a more precise geometric vocabulary in his paintings, and to approach abstraction in a more analytical rather than intuitive way, experimenting with the psychological effects of shapes and colors. According to Christina Lodder, Kandinsky even conducted a survey of his colleagues to study their psychological responses to colors and other formal elements of design. Malevich used the term "collective creative art" to emphasize the universal rather than individual aspects of Suprematism, and encouraged UNOVIS artists to exhibit works anonymously.

A related, but more practical element in the program of UNOVIS was the recognition that non-objective art might be justified not only as a vehicle for universal spiritual expression but also for the more direct purposes of propaganda. For El Lissitsky (1890–1941, born Lazar' Markovich Lissitsky), who studied architecture in Germany and later worked with Malevich at UNOVIS, the use of abstract art as a means to a political end found expression in a number of projects. His well-known poster entitled *Beat the Whites with the Red Wedge* dates to 1919 and was designed during the civil war between Bolsheviks and Mensheviks (fig. 9.12). Here the message of Red (Bolshevik) power and domination is conveyed entirely in abstract terms through the penetration of the red wedge into the white circle. The division of the poster further pits left against right and the diagonal composition and direction gives the wedge a decided "upper" hand as well. As El Lissitsky said:

The new art is formed, not on a subjective, but on an objective basis. This, like science, can be described with precision and is by nature constructive. It unites not only pure art but all those who stand at the frontier of the new culture. The artist is companion to the scholar, the engineer, and the worker.

El Lissitsky also directed a short-lived program in architecture at UNOVIS, and later began to create his imaginative series of PROUNS (acronym signifying "for the new art"), a group of paintings and lithographs composed of abstract geometric shapes with an ambiguous suggestion of perspective and three-dimensional projection (fig. 9.13). Lissitsky referred to the PROUNS as "stations of interchange between architecture and painting," affirming the utilitarian possibilities of geometric abstraction.

While El Lissitsky's work represents a variety of possibilities for moving beyond the self-sufficiency of traditional art forms such as easel painting into the more utilitarian realms of architecture and graphic design, Vladimir Tatlin (1885–1953) was active in attempting to bridge the gap between abstract art and the masses.

Part III : After World War I (1918–44): Art, Industry, and Utopias

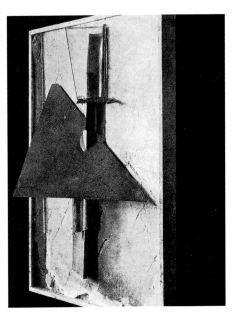

9.14 Vladimir Tatlin, *Selection of Materials: Iron, Stucco, Glass, and Asphalt*, 1914. Whereabouts unknown.

9.13 El Lissitsky, *Proun #H333*, 1923, gouache and collage with multicolored paper and airbrush on paper, 17 ½ x 17 ⅛ in (44.5 x 44 cm). Private collection, Munich.

He used ordinary industrial and mass-produced materials in the creation of abstract collages, where works of art become "objects" and are grouped together with tools and other commodities as equal elements of the everyday environment of the proletariat. Strongly influenced by examples of Cubist collage seen by Tatlin in Paris as early as 1913, but animated as well by a desire to view art in relation to Socialist revolution, works such as *Selection of Materials: Iron, Stucco, Glass, Asphalt,* dated to 1914 (fig. 9.14), utilize ordinary materials such as wood, metal, and stucco as elements in an abstract relief composition. Although hardly functional, such experiments, sometimes referred to by their supporters as "laboratory work," were intended to provide a basis for the creation of future utilitarian products that incorporated a preference for simple geometric shapes and forms, and encouraged non-objective attitudes.

In 1922 El Lissitsky began to publish an international journal of the new art entitled *Vesch/Objet/Gegenstand.* Translated simply as "Object" in English, the journal featured articles and photographs of works of fine art, decorative art, and industrial products, including projects by De Stijl artists as well as by Le Corbusier (work by El Lissitsky was featured in a 1922 issue of *De Stijl* as well). The use of half-tone photographic reproductions of illustrations rather than etchings or engraving was technologically advanced in the early 1920s, and conveys Lissitsky's interest in promoting the increased use of photographic images as a form of mass communication. The cover of one of the journal's issues from 1922 (fig. 9.15) reinforces the abstract relationships between bold sans serif typography, non-objective compositions of geometric shapes, and industrial forms, in this case a locomotive with a cowcatcher resembling Tatlin's abstract constructions and diagonally relating to the Russian word "Vesch." The vertically and diagonally-oriented letters, horizontal and vertical bars used as separation, and use of different letter sizes recall the typographical experimentation of the Futurist poet Marinetti (see fig. 8.26, page 159). But whereas Marinetti used such elements to make the page into a kind of poetic "image" to be experienced with a new sensibility characteristic of the dislocations and simultaneity of modern life, Lissitsky and other Russian Constructivists were equally interested in creating a sense of order that communicated information more objectively. Although flexible, Lissitsky's layouts make use of either an actual or implied grid to create a framework for the visual presentation of information via text, titles, illustration, spacing, and photography.

9.15 El Lissitsky, cover for *Vesch/Objet/Gegenstand*, 1922.

9.16 Vladimir Tatlin, model for the *Monument to the Third International*, painted wood, iron and glass, 20 ft (6.1 m) high, 1919/1920. Russian State Museums, St. Petersburg.

Tatlin's *Monument to the Third International* (fig. 9.16) was displayed at the Eighth Congress of the Soviets held in Moscow in 1920, where Lenin revealed his plan for the electrification of Russia. It was Tatlin's hope, however, that the structure would be built in Petrograd, straddling the Neva river and serving as the headquarters for an organization directing worldwide Communist revolution. According to Christina Lodder, Tatlin felt that the model erased the distinctions between painting, sculpture, and architecture, and combined the expressive experimentation with materials and utilitarian concerns. Made of wood but painted to look like iron, the model resembled a spiraling helix supported on one side by a thrusting diagonal tower, and containing three rotating cylindrical glass modules (rotating at yearly, monthly, and daily intervals) that

housed offices for different branches of the Third International. The emphasis upon the "working parts" of the monument and its use of iron and glass may be viewed as elements linking mechanized industry and design to the working class. These symbolic references of both materials and design were noted at the time: Lissitsky compared the strength of iron to the will of the proletariat, and glass to the clarity of its conscience; others saw the spiral form as symbolic of dynamism, energy, and change. For Tatlin, the monument was a utopian structure meant to stimulate other artists to experiment with the integration of art into life and unite the artist and the engineer.

Rodchenko was active among those artists who increasingly came to believe that it was necessary to take a more utilitarian direction in their activities, contributing directly to addressing collective social needs through design and justifying their endeavors in terms of their practical applications. His efforts were closely associated with an organization known as INKHUK (The Institute of Artistic Culture) in Moscow beginning in 1920, and with an exhibition that took place there in 1921 known as the Third Obmokhu, named for a group known as the Society of Young Artists. From these organizations a Working Group of Constructivist Artists was formed. These Constructivists viewed their efforts as being more in line with Marxist ideology that embraced a materialist view of culture (as opposed to a spiritual or esthetic view) as the most appropriate to the collective needs of a new social order. The emphasis upon production and utility among the artists at INKHUK created a tension with those who felt that the imposition of practical considerations in design represented too strict an approach compared with earlier interpretations of Constructivism that focused upon the integration of art and life. As a result of this growing conflict concerning the role of artists and the functions of works of art in the new Communist state, a number of artists left Russia for the west, including Kandinsky as well as the sculptor Naum Gabo (1890–1977).

Works exhibited at the Third Obmokhu exhibition included a series of hanging "constructions" by Rodchenko as well as sculptures on pedestals by brothers Georgy (1900–33) and Vladimir Stenberg (1899–1982). Like Tatlin's *Monument to the Third International*, Rodchenko's constructions were made of wood and painted silver to imitate metal and thus to relate to industrial materials. The Stenberg brothers' sculptures (fig. 9.17) resembled models for bridges, cranes, and other machinery for heavy industry. Although abstract and formally inventive in terms of their exploration of three-dimensional space and denial of mass, the works also were viewed as attempts to forge a closer relationship with industrial modernization and materials, and were less grandiose and utopian than Tatlin's *Monument to the Third International.*

INKHUK members became actively involved in an institution known as the Higher State Technical Workshops, established by the Communist Party in 1920 to further integrate artists with production. By this time Rodchenko had come to question the compatibility of painting and sculpture with the practical aims of

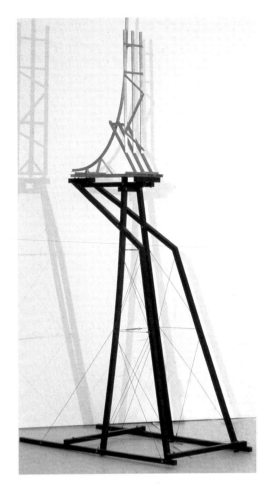

9.17 Vladimir Stenberg, *Spatial Construction KPS 42 N IV*, 1921, reconstruction 1977, aluminum, 104 x 27 ½ x 51 in (264 x 70 x 130 cm). Galerie Gmurzynska, Cologne.

Constructivism. A number of INKHUK members envisioned the demise of traditional media associated with the fine arts such as painting and sculpture. Instead they promoted the training of "artist–constructors," a new kind of versatile and non-specialist creator who might apply universal principles to the design of clothing, furniture, lighting, architecture, and other utilitarian goods manufactured by machine.

It is to this period of Constructivism that Rodchenko's model for the 1925 Soviet Workers Club at the Paris exhibition belongs. Although the furnishings of the Workers Club were fabricated and assembled in a workshop setting, the concept of the "artist–constructor" was meant to apply to the design of prototypes for mechanized industrial production in collaboration with engineers, removed

9.18 Rodchenko, poster for Russian section, Exhibition Internationale des Arts Decoratifs et Industriels Modernes, 1925, Paris.

from the direct manipulation of materials by craftsmen. The designer's role was envisioned as more akin to the methods of a draftsman than those of the fine artist. The furnishings suggest the designer's adherence to a set of criteria based upon the needs of a collective and egalitarian Socialist society, defined as the use of a minimum number of standardized parts, modern industrial materials, and adaptable, flexible construction. Together with the appeal to objectivity and anonymity, Rodchenko incorporated the precision of construction units based upon geometric rather than organic form,

preserving a modest connection between "constructive" design and the abstract compositions of the Suprematists.

While Rodchenko and other production-oriented Constructivists complained that projects such as Tatlin's *Monument of the Third International* were too utopian, their own designs in some ways were hardly more practical. The furnishings for the Workers Club were one-of-a-kind products and few if any prototypes were sold to industrial manufacturers, whose activities were hampered by a depressed economy and the lack of necessary skills and technology to produce the new designs. It is unlikely that workers were

179

9.19 Rodchenko, sketches for Dobrolet trademark, India ink and gouache on paper, 1923.

9.20 Rodchenko, cover for *Nov Lef, no. 6*, 9 x 6 in (22.5 x 15 cm), 1927

able to enjoy the kind of club Rodchenko created for the 1925 Paris exhibition. To judge from the indifferent reaction to Rodchenko's project within Vkutemas and to later attempts to replace traditional representational textile designs with decorative patterns based upon themes of industrialization, the public reception of Constructivist design was equivocal. In addition a number of younger artists and former Constructivists during the early 1920s had turned to realism. These artists embraced easel painting and an idealized naturalistic style as appropriate to an art of mass persuasion capable of winning the endorsement of the Communist Party as a tool to build support for official policy.

Without clear public or party support, Constructivist hopes to unify or at least influence industrial production and further develop the potential contributions of the "artist–constructor," the activities of "industrial design" in Russia were marginalized. Amid these circumstances Rodchenko and other Constructivists found an outlet for their activities in the production of posters, journals, and advertisements based upon the application of Constructivist principles to the mechanical reproduction of printed materials, and incorporating photographs and photomontage to accommodate the revived interest in realism. Rodchenko's poster for the Russian section of the 1925 Paris exhibition (fig. 9.18) employs bold san serif typography in two horizontal borders with crossing diago-

nals formed by larger outlined letters forming the initials "URSS" from upper left to lower right and overlapping black squares from upper right to lower left. Squared letter forms dominate but relate to other rectilinear compositional elements as well as simple color contrasts to create a bold composition. Often in Rodchenko's graphic work diagonal lines contrast with circular forms to create a dynamic effect. The effect is seen in a series of advertisements for the Russian aircraft manufacturer Dobrolet that also uses alternating colors and type aligned around the border of one of the concentric circles of the company trademark (fig. 9.19). In the advertisement shown the diagonal takes the form of a simplified propeller, while in other posters representational elements often take the form of photography and photomontage. Occasionally these images also substitute for abstract elements in the overall composition, activating the white space around them and heightening the contrast of figure and ground. An example is the cover for the journal *Novi Lef* (For the New Left) from 1927, in which the profile head of a smiling worker extends to the left and right limits of the unframed page, and the square title at the upper right corner touches the figure's hat creating a strong figure-ground equality (fig. 9.20). Through juxtaposition, overlap, and contrasts in scale photographs also acquire a sense of drama on their own or in relation to the text and the bold contrasts of the composition. This can be seen,

9.21 Rodchenko, book cover for the series *Mess Mend* by Dzhim Dollar (Marietta Shaginyan), 6 ¾ x 13 in (17 x 33 cm), 1924.

9.22 Gustav Klutsis, "The Coal Debt Shall be Repaid to the Country!", poster, lithograph, 40 x 28 in (101.6 x 71.2 cm), 1930. Private collection.

for instance, in one of a series of book covers for the *Mess Mend* novels written by Dzhim Dollar (Marietta Shaginyan). The *Mess Mend* covers (fig. 9.21) employed the same basic compositional formula amid variations, suggesting an analogy with interchangeability and efficient production. Critics have also noted similarities of the collage compositions in these and related cover designs with techniques of montage in filmmaking.

By the mid-1920s tolerance for the universal pretensions of abstract art and its Constructivist progeny during the early years of Narkompros had eroded. The hope for defining a set of official collective standards and an art that contributed to the establishment of the Communist state began to be realized. But sadly for the Constructivists, such standards were not along abstract

and non-objective lines. Soviet artists were increasingly made to comply with a policy demanding an heroic naturalism depicting working-class, athletic, or military activities and designed to provide persuasive and hopeful images to the Russian masses. An example that still owes something to the Constructivist principles of dynamic composition is Gustav Klutsis's poster entitled *The Coal Debt Shall be Repaid to the Country!*, from 1930 (fig. 9.22). In this more repressive environment, artists such as Rodchenko and Lissitsky continued to produce graphic designs using photography that still permitted a measure of experimentation in design and technology. One of the most striking examples is Lissitsky's poster for an exhibition of Russian art that took place in Zurich in 1928, with a photograph depicting a male and a female youth in

9.23 El Lissitsky, "Russian Art Exhibition", poster, intaglio, 49 ¾ x 35 ½ in (126.5 x 90.5 cm), 1928. Private collection.

three-quarter view who share an eye as they peer into the distance (fig. 9.23). This image exemplifies the kind of photographic experimentation undertaken by Russian Constructivists. It may also be seen as a metaphor for the collective ideal of social and gender equality.

The Bauhaus

The Soviet Workers Club was but one indication of the international scope of Constructivist activities: El Lissitsky's essays on modern design were published in issues of *De Stijl*, and his own journal *Vesch/Objet/Gegenstand* contained texts by van Doesburg, Mondrian, Le Corbusier, and others advocating collective standards for design, the use of new technologies, and mechanized industrial production. These ideas also found expression in a school of design located in Weimar, Germany, known as the Bauhaus.

The Bauhaus (from the German verb *bauen*—to build) opened in 1919 from the consolidation of Weimar's Academy of Fine Arts and the city's Arts and Craft School (Kunstgewerbeschule), both of which had closed during World War I. The school's first director was Walter Gropius (1883–1969), an architect who had worked in the office of Peter Behrens prior to the war. Gropius's architectural commissions included the well-known Fagus shoe-last factory at Alfeld an der Leine near Hildesheim, designed in 1911 in collaboration with Adolf Meyer (1881–1929) and often viewed as an early example of a modern, functional approach to building. In addition to architecture Gropius was active in the Deutscher Werkbund and had developed designs for railway cars and their efficiently furnished compartments. Within the Werkbund, however, he supported artistic freedom and individuality rather than the imposition of typical, standardized forms as advocated by Hermann Muthesius.

The text of the Bauhaus manifesto (1919) also shows little interest in either objective standards for design or industrial technology, and is concerned instead with ideas regarding the equality and collaboration of artist and craftsman, pointing to the medieval building as a collaborative model for integrated design activity to overcome the opposition between fine and applied art:

Architects, painters, sculptors, we must all return to crafts! For there is no such thing as "professional art." There is no essential difference between the artist and the craftsman. The artist is an exalted craftsman. By the grace of Heaven and in rare moments of inspiration which transcend the will, art may unconsciously blossom from the labor of his hand, but a foundation of handicraft is essential for every artist. It is there that the primary source of creativity lies.

Let us therefore create a new guild of craftsmen without the class-distinctions that raise an arrogant barrier between craftsman and artist! Let us together desire, conceive and create the new building of the future, which will combine everything—architecture and sculpture and painting—all in a single form which will one day rise towards the heavens from the hands of a million workers as the crystalline symbol of a new and coming faith.

The model of the medieval guild, and with it the legacy of William Morris and the Arts and Crafts Movement, emerge in this strongly utopian passage in which the products and activities of design will transform both the visible and more broadly human conditions of society. The guild model also emerges in Gropius's practice of naming the Bauhaus faculty "masters" rather than professors, and in the cover illustration of the school's manifesto, from a woodcut by early faculty appointment Lyonel Feininger, depicting a cathedral bathed in the light of three stars, symbolizing perhaps the unity of painting, sculpture, and architecture. Such ideas formed the basis of the philosophy of education at the Weimar Bauhaus, even though architecture was not among the fields of study offered at the school during its existence there.

Although Gropius inherited a small number of faculty from the Weimar Academy of Fine Arts, many of them were hostile to the revamped curriculum for the Bauhaus and lobbied successfully to maintain their independence from the new school. As a result the director was able to hire a number of new "masters" for the Bauhaus over the first few years of the school's existence. The new appointments were almost exclusively fine artists, who embraced abstraction and subjective self-expression as the basis for art, but who at the same time were committed to a less elitist role for artists in contributing to the design of useful products and in the integration of art and life. What was envisioned seems to have been a healthy collaboration between artist and craftsman in educating new designers to reinvigorate the production of useful goods culminating in the construction and interior design of buildings, informed and conditioned by the discipline and unity implied in the architectural enterprise. Such ideas were shared among the faculty appointments in 1919, which included Johannes Itten (1888–1967), Gerhard Marcks (1889–1981), and Lyonel Feininger (1871–1956), as well as the hiring of Paul Klee (1879–1940) in 1921 and Vassily Kandinsky (1866–1944) in 1922.

A key element in the curriculum of the Bauhaus was the common first semester of study (preliminary course or *Vorkurs*) before students selected one or more areas of specialization in the Bauhaus workshops (ceramics, glass painting, mural painting, furniture, metalwork, textiles). Georg Muche (1895–1987) assisted with the *Vorkurs*, and other mandatory but non-specialized courses in form and theory were taught by Klee and Kandinsky. The purpose of the *Vorkurs*, directed by Swiss-born artist and educator Johannes Itten, was to stimulate students' interest in materials, drawing techniques, and forms so that their innate creative ability might be best directed toward study in a particular workshop. Surviving examples of student work demonstrate contrasts of textures among different materials in an abstract composition, drawings from life that exaggerate a sense of rhythm in nature, and relationships among geometric shapes. Despite the freedom of choice implied by the required *Vorkurs*, women were almost always directed toward the weaving workshop, which was viewed by the faculty as appropriate for female students (only with difficulty did Marianne Brandt obtain permission to pursue her apprenticeship in the metal workshop). In fact, so strict was the gender bias that a separate *Vorkurs* was taught to the women students at the Bauhaus.

Scholars have been careful to point out that the early *Vorkurs* did not seek solely to familiarize students with the objective analysis of the elements of art as a visual language, but rather to draw connections between artistic activity and the discovery of unconscious reality. It is in this context that Itten's mysticism and use of breathing and other synaesthetic exercises are best understood, as well as the connection between Itten's teaching and Kandinsky's own *Concerning the Spiritual in Art*, published in 1911, prior to the analytical approach the artist pursued in his own work and teaching in Russia (see pages 173–4). Despite the fact that a non-specialized preliminary course had been introduced in some form earlier in the *Kunstgewerbeschule* developed by Peter Behrens at Düsseldorf and also formed part of the curriculum in design education in Russia at INKHUK, the preliminary or foundation course, however broadly defined, tends to be associated with the Bauhaus, perhaps as a result of the emigration of Bauhaus faculty and their students to the United States and Britain where the concept became institutionalized as a cornerstone of design education after World War II.

In the workshops instruction was the shared responsibility of a technical master (*Lehrmeister*) skilled in the particular area of craft, and a master of form

(*Formmeister*), in almost all cases a fine artist whose presence would contribute to the dialogue and creative effort aimed at renewing the essential unity of the arts proclaimed in the Bauhaus manifesto.

The efforts of the Bauhaus in the early Weimar years are best summarized in the construction and interior design and decoration for the Sommerfeld House in Berlin, a residence (now destroyed) commissioned privately from Gropius but involving the collaboration of the Bauhaus workshops (fig. 9.24). The client was shipping industrialist Adolf Sommerfeld, who provided a large quantity of teak wood normally used in the construction of boats; the project demonstrates the early Bauhaus emphasis upon craftsmanship and an integration between construction and original decoration.

The horizontal emphasis of the elevation and the strongly projecting eaves of the roof of the Sommerfeld

9.24 Joost Schmidt with students, carving for the staircase, Sommerfeld House, photograph, 1921–22.

house recall the Prairie houses of Frank Lloyd Wright (see pages 126–7). The doorway and staircase of the entrance area are decorated with wooden relief panels that echo and develop the angular construction of the teak paneling, exploring relations of geometric forms in two and three dimensions, as well as a variety of textures created by sanding and chiseling. These motifs, either in regular patterns or asymmetrically balanced compositions, are repeated in a series of leaded glass windows behind the staircase as well as in appliqué embroidery curtains, all products of the Bauhaus workshops. Like Wright's Prairie houses, the Sommerfeld House remains strongly based on handicraft despite the emphasis upon regular geometric form rather than organic shapes in decoration that imply carving. One might also compare the colored brick reliefs designed by van Doesburg to articulate the doors and windows of Oud's De Vonk residence of 1918 (see fig. 9.4, page 170) with the Sommerfeld reliefs and windows in terms of the integration of ornamental elements. In the De Stijl example the decoration relates more to standardized units of simple materials, requiring less of the time-consuming handwork of the early Bauhaus efforts. Moreover, decoration at the Sommerfeld House remains more subordinate to, rather than integrated with, construction, as in the more collaborative approach envisioned by van Doesburg or Mondrian and realized in 1924 in projects such as the Schröder House in Utrecht (see fig. 9.6 and 9.7, pages 170–71). There Rietveld applied color to sliding panels, furniture, and walls to create a greater degree of identity between decorative and structural elements to achieve the "living work of art" central to the aims of De Stijl.

Despite the collaborative effort on the Sommerfeld House and the limited commercial success of its weaving and ceramics workshops, the Bauhaus struggled for adequate resources from the Weimar government and battled local resistance to its unorthodox approach to instruction. In addition, the school was criticized by designers more aligned with Constructivism who felt the school's methods and products were allied too closely to craft production and the fine arts, rather than with a more unified and collective approach geared toward mechanized industrial production. As a result, claimed its detractors, the Bauhaus produced the kind of individual and indulgent esthetic activity at variance with the social aims expressed in the 1919 manifesto. One of the most vehement of such attacks appeared in *De Stijl*. The journal's editor, Theo van Doesburg, moved to Weimar in 1921 and attended an International Congress of Constructivism held there in 1922. Although van Doesburg never officially taught at the Bauhaus, he seems at one time to have been considered for a teaching position there, and was acquainted with Gropius.

The director appears to have been sensitive to criticisms of the school's shortcomings. Gropius had already been in contact with Dutch architect J. J. P. Oud (associated at one time with De Stijl and employed by the housing authority of Rotterdam) and was interested in new developments in Dutch architecture related to standardization and newer pre-fabricated materials for government-sponsored housing. In response to financial, political, and ideological pressures upon the school, Gropius began to shift the focus of the Bauhaus mission and curriculum. One of the most important changes that took place during

9.25 Joost Schmidt, Bauhaus exhibition, poster, 28 ¼ x 19 in (60.5 x 48cm) 1923. Weimar.

this time was Gropius's decision in 1923 to force the resignation of Itten and to hire Hungarian painter and Constructivist László Moholy-Nagy (1895–1946) as a replacement.

The two men had met in Berlin where Moholy-Nagy was living, having left Hungary following an unsuccessful socialist revolution. Moholy-Nagy became responsible for the *Vorkurs* and for the more industrial focus that began to inform Bauhaus education and products. He brought with him a strong commitment to mechanized mass production and new material technology in design and reduced the importance of craft specialization and traditional workshop training. To emphasize the point, in what has become part of the canonical literature of modernism, Moholy-Nagy designed a series of paintings and communicated instructions by telephone to assistants to have them produced. His efforts along these lines parallel Rodchenko's call for a new conception of the designer as the artist–constructor rather than artist–craftsman. Unconscious and spiritual associations with the creative process were de-emphasized, while creative solutions for efficient living and an appreciation of the esthetic potential of new industrial materials emerged. Moholy-Nagy placed photography on an equal footing with the fine arts and experimented with kinetic sculpture. He extolled the potential of the machine as a liberating force both in social and in creative terms: "Constructivism is not confined to the picture frame and the pedestal. It expands into industrial designs, into house, objects, forms. It is the socialism of vision—the common property of all men." In Moholy-Nagy's vision for the Bauhaus, students' familiarity with mechanical processes and industrial materials would enable them to apply their knowledge to a variety of fields rather than be limited only to specialized study of a particular material. Indeed such versatility, in a sense, compensated for the loss of individuality and less direct handling of traditional materials implied by the use of standardized components and mechanized mass production.

When the Bauhaus mounted an exhibition of its work in 1923, Gropius proclaimed the shift in orientation in a speech entitled "Art and Technology: A New Unity." The poster (fig. 9.25) for the exhibition was designed by former Bauhaus student Joost Schmidt (1893–1948) and is composed of tilted rectangular and circular shapes, creating an "X"-like axis or grid. The grid imparts hierarchical and ordered relationships to the placement of the text for the words "State Bauhaus," "Exhibition" as well as location and date. The poster also contains the new logo for the Bauhaus designed by Oskar Schlemmer (1888–1943), a simplified profile head drawn with ruler and reduced to a pictogram built upon rectangular and circular shapes.

Again the 1923 exhibition might best be summarized by a collaborative enterprise, the construction and decoration of the Haus-am-Horn, a model for low-cost housing designed by Georg Muche and Adolf Meyer, who formerly had served as assistant to Itten in the *Vorkurs* and continued to be *Formmeister* in the Bauhaus weaving workshop. The centrally planned Haus-am-Horn is designed with a large clerestory-lit living room surrounded on all sides by smaller rectangular rooms, each designed to fulfill a particular need for domestic living. The experimental design of the house was determined primarily by economic and objective functional considerations. It was constructed of prefabricated building materials (steel and concrete) and, like Le Corbusier's 1925 Pavillon de l'Esprit Nouveau, was

intended as a prototype for public housing units that could be built cheaply and in a short period of time.

Faculty and students in the Bauhaus workshops were responsible for the design and manufacture of furnishings for the interior spaces of the house. Photographs of the living room show simply constructed furniture using overlapping joints and standardized lengths of wood, all devoid of carved decoration or color, and entirely rectilinear in form (fig. 9.26), recalling chairs designed by the Dutchman Gerrit Rietveld (see fig. 9.2, page 169). Lighting was designed by Moholy-Nagy and employed tubular metal forms emphasizing lightness, geometry, and an implied relation between these esthetic characteristics and mechanical mass production of standardized parts. Textiles and carpets were also based upon abstract geometric designs and created a shared sense of geometric form, smooth, industrial surfaces, and a reduction in techniques associated with individual craftsmanship. The Haus-am-Horn kitchen (fig. 9.27) featured plain wall-

9.26 Georg Muche and Adolf Meyer for Bauhaus workshops, Haus-am-Horn, living room, 1923.

9.27 Georg Muche and Bauhaus workshops, Haus-am-Horn, kitchen, Bauhaus exhibition, 1923. Bauhaus-Archiv, Museum für Gestaltung, Berlin.

mounted cupboards and free-standing cabinets below, creating a continuous counter space that replaced the more customary use of tall individual units like those designed by Riemerschmid around 1910 (see fig. 7.2, page 131). Plain storage jars in simple shapes from the ceramics workshop also formed part of the kitchen design. Many features of the Haus-am-Horn kitchen were employed in the rational kitchen designs of the later 1920s and 1930s, associated with low-cost housing in the city of Frankfurt and stemming from studies of household efficiency that introduced a more scientific approach to design in relationship to the analysis of domestic work rather than esthetic considerations.

Renewing the Bauhaus commitment to educating a new type of designer for industry, Gropius hired a number of the school's own recent graduates as masters, replacing the former system of *Formmeister* and *Lehrmeister* in several workshops. Fine artists such as Klee and Kandinsky continued to exert an influence at the Bauhaus through required courses in form and theory, but their role in the workshops was much reduced as the connection between artist and materials was re-examined in light of the importance of technology. The "young masters" as they were called, applied standards of economy and efficiency as well as receptivity toward industrial materials and mechanical production to the design of books, lighting, furniture, textiles, and exercises for the *Vorkurs*. The new direction,

however, failed to please the Thuringian government that sponsored the school. In 1925 the Bauhaus in Weimar was closed and relocated to the industrial city of Dessau. With renewed local support Gropius designed new facilities for the Bauhaus, renamed as the Bauhaus Höchschule für Gestaltung or "Institute for Design." At Dessau new facilities included modern presses and other equipment for the printing workshop and Jacquard looms for the weaving workshops. The new focus also provided the possibility for some faculty to acquire direct industrial experience, and faculty and students began to create prototypes for industrial production. Another change was the creation of a Bauhaus department of architecture.

John Heskett has emphasized that the effect of the Bauhaus upon industrial production in Germany was limited. Nevertheless some Bauhaus designs were manufactured for a broad market, such as Marcel Breuer's tubular metal and wood chair (fig. 9.28) manufactured by Thönet beginning in 1928. Breuer's design was based upon a novel cantilevered principle of support requiring two rather than the traditional four legs for support, a result of exploring the possible applications of new materials to craft-based industries like furniture-making. Dutch Constructivist designer Mart Stam (1899–1986) also developed a similar cantilevered tubular metal chair as early as 1925, but that design was not manufactured in large quantities. In addition to Breuer's success with Thönet, lighting fixtures designed by a number of Bauhaus students were manufactured by Kortung and Mathieson, including those of Marianne Brandt (1893–1983) and Wilhelm Wagenfeld (1900–1990). Gunta Stölzl (1897–1983), who was a student in Weimar, became professor in the weaving workshop, and was sent to the city of Krefeld to study industrial fiber and dyeing technology. Stölzl maintained a middle ground between early Weimar and Dessau, never abandoning handweaving and craft as a source of individual expression, while encouraging experimentation with the use of unusual materials such as cellophane. She also focussed attention upon characteristics such as reversible fabrics and the relationship between fabrics and acoustics, design problems that were more in line with the new objective orientation toward end-use, and considerations beyond a largely symbolic relationship to mass production.

The printing workshop at the Bauhaus, with the support of Moholy-Nagy and under the direction of former

9.28 Marcel Breuer, tubular metal chair, chrome-plated steel and wood, and cane, 32 x 18 ¼ x 22 ½ in (81.3 x 46.4 x 57.2 cm), manufactured Gebrüder Thönet, 1928.

9.29 Herbert Bayer, universal alphabet, 1926.

Das Buch, welches anläßlich der ersten Ausstellung vom 15. August bis 30. September 1923 des Staatlichen Bauhauses zu Weimar nach dessen 3½jährigem Bestehen erscheint, ist in erster Linie Dokument dieser Anstalt; es reicht aber, dem Charakter der Anstalt entsprechend, weit über eine örtliche oder spezifische Angelegenheit hinaus ins allgemeine, gegenwärtige und zukünftige Gebiet künstlerischen Schaffens und künstlerischer Erziehung.
So wie das Staatliche Bauhaus das erste wirkliche Zusammenfassen der im letzten Jahrzehnt gewonnenen Einsichten in künstlerischen Entwicklungsfragen bedeutet, so nimmt das Buch spiegelnd Teil an diesen Fragen und bedeutet jedem, der sich über den Stand dieser Dinge unterrichten will, hierzu ein willkommenes Mittel. Darüber hinaus bleibt es ein geschichtliches Dokument. Denn das Bauhaus ist, obwohl zunächst einzigartig, keine insulare Erscheinung, sondern ein kräftiger Trieb, der sich voll entfaltet und auch völlig sich ausbreiten wird. Das

student Herbert Bayer (1900–1985), was successful in introducing Constructivist approaches to graphic design involving photomechanical reproduction rather than more traditional letterpress techniques. The workshop published a series of *Bauhausbücher* as well as a Bauhaus journal. In Dessau, Bayer created a series of "universal" sans serif typefaces based upon modular shapes and a limited number of letter forms and decreasing the vestiges of hand-lettering (fig. 9.29). He also eliminated capital letters, used in German for all nouns as well as at the beginning of sentences, creating regularized heights and greater possibilities for arranging text as an abstract element on the page. The printing workshop was able to introduce page layouts in which typography, photography, and heavy rules were all considered equal and complimentary design elements, serving to direct the viewer's attention and impart order to the arrangements of information. An example is Moholy-Nagy's title page for the prospectus of the Weimar Bauhaus from 1923 (fig. 9.30), printed in red and black. Here sans serif typography is used in a variety of sizes to reflect a hierarchy of information and an asymmetrical balance of horizontal and vertical elements based upon an implied grid. The same approach is seen in Bayer's catalogue of prototypes from the Bauhaus workshops from 1925. These examples also create a new sense of awareness of the white space of the page. The empty white areas in these layouts come to life as a result of contrast and the overall sense of abstract geometric design. There is a strong parallel between the prominent

9.30 László Moholy-Nagy, prospectus for Weimar Bauhaus, 10 x 10 in (25 x 25 cm) title page, 1923.

role of such "empty" white space in these layouts and the sparsely-furnished interior of the Haus-am-Horn and other experimental housing projects being planned during the same years. In these projects white walls dominated and space "materialized" in relation to standard rectangular tables, chairs, and shelves (see fig. 9.26, page 185). In this way mechanized mass production, involving standardization and uniformity, was, at least symbolically, linked to a universal and egalitarian socialist vision for the society of the future. The machine thus held, for some artists, the promise of an international and enlightened socialist brotherhood, erasing distinctions of class, and embracing a shared modern esthetic in which decoration and clutter had become outmoded, wasteful, and selfish.

In 1928 Gropius decided to resign as director of the Bauhaus, naming the Swiss-born Hannes Meyer (1889–1954), who served as professor of architecture, as his successor. Meyer was an unpopular choice at the outset, even though under his directorship the Bauhaus became more financially independent through commissions and sales of its prototypes. Meyer argued that design was synonymous with man-made things and was a product of "function x economy." His views placed design solely in the service of working-class needs based upon objective standards of economy, brought to fruition through participation of the workshops in "real" projects for housing and utilitarian products. Moreover, Meyer tended to view design at the Bauhaus as a largely deterministic process, resulting more-or-less automatically from objective considerations of climate, hygiene, economics, and engineering. His approach marginalized the value of fine art in relation to design, and forced the resignation of several faculty.

Although equally committed to technology and the social mission of the Bauhaus, Moholy-Nagy resigned quickly after Meyer's appointment as director. Moholy-Nagy held the position that modern design required an accommodation to standards and uniformity, but argued that versatility and more open-ended experimentation with new technology and materials preserved the sense of esthetics and creativity in design. In Moholy-Nagy's view versatility and experiment helped to relieve the fear of mindless and dehumanizing factory work and narrow specialization, as well as to combat a product-oriented, materialist view of design. To the end his position maintained the vision of a creative role for design and design education rather than the more pragmatic implications of collective standards in design.

In time Meyer's own position became untenable. Gropius had always attempted to avoid confrontation with government officials in the interests of the school's survival, but Meyer's politics were more revolutionary; under his directorship, political theory was taught as a classroom subject and a Communist student group was formed. After resigning in 1930 Meyer moved to Soviet Russia where he hoped his activities and principles would find more ready acceptance. His place was taken by the well-established German architect Ludwig Mies van der Rohe (1886–1969), who had served as the director for the 1927 Weissenhof exhibition of modern housing projects in Stuttgart. Mies eventually moved the school from Dessau to facilities in Berlin.

In 1933 the National Socialist (Nazi) Party came to power in Germany. This government's strong nationalist feeling cast suspicion upon the international and cosmopolitan character of the Bauhaus. The school's association with left-wing politics and radical ideas was linked to the influence of "foreigners" and conspired to bring about its demise, fourteen years after its opening in Weimar in 1919.

The importance of the Bauhaus is not the result of its limited success in developing prototypes for industrial production, but rather is due to the compelling nature of its ideal of collaboration between art, craft, and industry in the education of designers. This contribution is perhaps best exemplified in the career of Moholy-Nagy, who is remembered less for particular masterpieces of art or industrial products than his vision and embodiment of the versatile artist–engineer, able to balance individuality with universality and process with product. It is true that the emigration of Bauhaus faculty to other colleges and universities, respect for many of its products among institutions such as New York's Museum of Modern Art, and even the tendency to write the history of art and design as the history of the contributions of individuals or "stars," have all added to the continuing power of a Bauhaus "image" that may vary somewhat from the institution's reality. Nevertheless, the Bauhaus continues to exert an enormous and continuing influence upon post-secondary education, where many of its features still form the basis of art and design curricula. Despite the marginal, utopian, and even esoteric element in Bauhaus ideology (which existed as well in those related international movements with which it came into contact), and despite the realization that the school perhaps never achieved the dreams and promises of its promoters, the Bauhaus provided an environment in which designing for industry and in concert with technology became inspiring goals for a gifted and committed body of faculty and students to pursue, and the boldness of that effort remains a significant legacy.

Beyond the Bauhaus

A small number of Bauhaus faculty remained in Germany after the school's closing in 1933 and designed products for industrial manufacture. Trude Petri, who studied at the Bauhaus, designed the Urbino line of porcelain dinnerware for the Staatliche Porzellan-Manufaktur in Berlin (1930–4, fig. 9.31). The milk-white color, glass-like surfaces, and circular forms of plates and serving platters, feet, and handles all suggest the beauty of pure geometric form. The gently tapering forms for tureens and lids introduce both an organic element as well as a sense of precision and elegance also found in the contemporary tubular metal furniture of the school's last director Mies van der Rohe (fig. 9.32). Both of these examples were produced in limited quantities by prestigious manufacturers for

9.31 Trude Petri, "Urbino" dinnerware, porcelain, Staatliche Porzellan-Manufaktur, Berlin, 1931, tureen 6 x 11 ½ in (15 x 29 cm). Metropolitan Museum of Art, New York.

9.32 Ludwig Mies van der Rohe, MR armchair, chrome-plated tubular steel and painted cane, Berliner Metallgewerbe, Berlin, 1927, 31 x 20 ½ x 32 ½ in (79 x 52 x 82.5 cm). Metropolitan Museum of Art, New York.

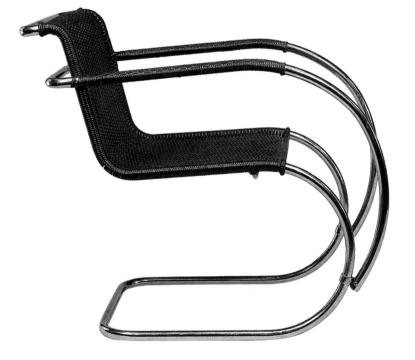

wealthy consumers by "star" designers, anticipating the international market for sophisticated functionally-inspired products and furniture after World War II, yet ideologically removed from the socialist attitudes of Moholy-Nagy or Hannes Meyer. Another German industrial designer of the period is Wilhelm Wagenfeld, who had studied and taught at the Bauhaus and went on to design the line of Kubus glassware for the Lausitzer Glasverein in 1938 (fig. 9.33). These inexpensive jars for kitchen use were made of a newly developed heat-resistant pressed glass, had interchangeable lids, and dimensions that permitted stacking for efficient storage. The absence of molded decoration in relief surely owes a debt to the modernist machine esthetic, along with a relationship to efforts promoting standardization and efficiency in the design of offices and kitchens that took place in Germany during the later 1920s.

Initiatives to develop standards in the design of the workplace and in the home applied Frederick Taylor's theory of scientific management maximizing productivity in factory work through the study of movement in the performance of a variety of tasks (see page 133) to a wider variety of tasks. Books such as American author Christine Frederick's *Scientific Management in the Home* (1915) proposed that the placement of sinks, cabinets, serving tables, ovens, refrigerators, and work surfaces should derive from the rational study of food preparation, food service, and storage, defining a new dimension of research-based design for industrial production (see page 136). The ideas of Frederick parallel the efforts of Henry Ford to rationalize the assembly of automobiles at his Highland Park plant and also were particularly relevant in Germany.

9.33 Wilhelm Wagenfeld, Kubus-Geschirr (cube-shaped dishware/storage containers), manufactured Lausitzer Glasverein, Weiswasser, Germany, c. 1938, 3 ⅛ x 7 ⅛ x 7 ⅛ in (7.9 x 18.1 x 18.1 cm). Art Institute of Chicago.

9.34 Grete Schütte-Lihotzky, *The Frankfurt Kitchen*, 1924. Germanisches Nationalmuseum, Nuremberg.

Housing shortages after World War I and a sluggish economy suggested to some that new construction should aim at efficiency and the fulfillment of minimum requirements for living, and that standards based upon such considerations should be adopted by manufacturers. And in an era when fewer families could afford servants, a rational approach to housework reduced its menial connotations and added an element of "science" and analysis to tasks and responsibilities usually assumed by women. Indeed "home economics" was once a required subject for young women in junior high schools across the United States and still persists in many curricula as an elective, along with crafts and courses in wood-shop, metal-shop, or drafting for young men. In addition to efficiency, the designs for kitchens and office furnishings considered the effect of glare and brightness in lighting as well as posture in the design of furniture, maintaining some commitment to design standards based upon considerations of human factors. One of the goals of such research was to make objective criteria the basis for a "science" rather than an "art" of design, limiting the role of subjective expression.

The applications of such practical considerations for design often required the backing of local governments, as in the city of Frankfurt in the late 1920s when Ernst May held the position of City Architect. One influential result of these activities was the Frankfurt kitchen (fig. 9.34) designed under the direction of Grete Schütte-Lihotzky (1898–2000). The Frankfurt kitchen adopted the strategies devised by Christine Frederick and featured moveable "track" lighting and continuous work surfaces with built-in storage cabinets above. The contracts for low-cost, "minimum-existence" housing enabled designs for furniture and fittings to be mass-produced inexpensively in large quantities according to standard measurements. Smooth surfaces and the absence of decoration were warranted for ease of cleaning and hygiene, while government sponsorship of the project assured manufacturers of a ready market for the products without the need for variations to attract the consumer. As noted by Heskett, the unique social, political, and economic circumstances in Frankfurt between 1925 and 1930 provided the basis for a rational and standardized approach to domestic design beyond the limits of office furniture or prototypes such as those used by Le Corbusier in the Pavillon de l'Esprit Nouveau.

A unified approach to standardization in housing and interior design may also be seen in 1927 when Mies van der Rohe served as director for an exhibition of modern housing held in Stuttgart and known as the Weissenhof

191

Siedlung. As mentioned above, the Dutch architect and early member of the De Stijl circle J. J. P. Oud designed one of the housing blocks at Weissenhof, and other blocks were designed by Mies, Le Corbusier, former Werkbund member Bruno Taut, and others. Although observers criticized the sterility of some of the interiors at Weissenhof, the association between working-class housing, prefabrication, simple furnishings, expanses of plain white walls, and the rejection of ornament was shared among all of the model apartments, and suggested the application of objective criteria as the basis for responsible modern design.

The Printing Industry and the "New Typography"

Sans serif typography and a new esthetic sensibility toward graphic design reached beyond the limited circulation of books and journals such as *De Stijl*, the *Bauhausbücher*, and *Vesch/Objet/Gegenstand* during the later 1920s and 1930s. Large commercial type foundries in Europe and the United States were interested in ways to expand their range of typefaces in the interwar period, and also had the means to promote their efforts to the printing industry. Mass-circulation lifestyle magazines such as *Vogue* (first published in 1892), incorporating photography and portraying contemporary fashion and leisure pastimes, also mined new approaches to graphic design in an effort to appear bold and distinctively "modern."

ABCDEFGHIJKLMN OPQRSTUVWXYZ? abcdefghijklm nopqrstuvwxyz! 1234567890

9.35 Morris Benton, Franklin Gothic typeface, 1903–1905.

The absence of serifs and other calligraphic features of typography, as well as the use of modular or interchangeable elements, had a symbolic appeal to the movements associated with the "First Machine Age" in the interwar period. For instance, the sans serif typefaces designed by Huszar in Holland and at the Bauhaus by Bayer (see figs. 9.1, page 169 and 9.29, page 187) embodied the principle of generating a variety of letter forms from a limited number of related units as a metaphor for standardized mechanized production. The major foundries, however, had introduced versions of sans serif faces for book printing around the turn of the century as part of a reform effort coinciding with the establishment of the Werkbund in Germany and the introduction of standards in other industries, for instance, in the sizes of pipefitting or electrical wiring, adapters, and sockets. In printing, standardization applied as well to sizes for envelopes and paper for letters, invoices, and other common business needs, including filing cabinets for offices.

Once again, terminology in the field of typography is at times confusing, as the sans serif faces were known in Europe as "Grotesk" and in the United States as "Gothic." Franklin Gothic (fig. 9.35) was produced by the American Type Founders Company and cut by Morris Benton between 1903 and 1905. Although it lacks serifs, Franklin Gothic retains Roman letter forms for the characters "a" and "g," and rounded letter forms narrow as they approach vertical stems rather than being monotone throughout. In Germany, the Berthold Foundry of Berlin introduced the closely related font known as Akzidenz Grotesk at about the same time.

Historically these Gothic or Grotesk fonts were designed for display, and developing them in the context of the printed page required control of letter forms, spacing, and weight. The commercial foundries addressed these practical concerns of legibility, precision, and meeting the varied printing needs of the market. Foundries developed large, extended "families" of fonts in a variety of weights as well as in expanded and condensed forms. Such efforts continued traditions of expert craftsmanship established in the eighteenth century, and were often the result of a number of individuals working under contract for large companies whose resources enabled them to undertake such large-scale efforts. It is not surprising that ATF, which brought out the Franklin Gothic typeface around the turn of the century, was itself a product of the

ABCDEFGHIJKLMN
OPQRSTUVWXYZ?
abcdefghijklm
nopqrstuvwxyz!
1234567890

9.36 Paul Renner, Futura typeface, 1927.

9.38 Jan Tschichold, trademark, Der Bücherkreis, Berlin, 1931, line drawing after Tschichold by John Langdon.

ABCDEFGHIJKLMN
OPQRSTUVWXYZ?
abcdefghijklm
nopqrstuvwxyz!
1234567890

9.37 Rudolf Koch, Kabel typeface, 1927.

consolidation of a number of smaller foundries joining forces to face competitive market conditions. As noted in Part II, it was this foundry that produced the journal *The Chap Book* under the direction of Will Bradley to promote its services to commercial printers (see page 90). In 1926 Munich typographer and teacher Paul Renner (1878–1956) developed the influential sans serif typeface known as Futura, including bold, light, condensed, and expanded variations demanded by the printing industry. The font was produced by the Bauer Foundry in Frankfurt. Futura is known as a *modular* sans serif because several of its letter forms share the same element, for instance, the

circular small case "o" is used for the letters "a," "b," "d," "e," "p," and "q"). The modular principle, implying interchangeability, is certainly inherent in experimental typefaces such as Huszar's capital letters for the *De Stijl* journal before 1921 (fig. 9.36 and fig. 9.1, page 169), but was applied with greater attention to legibility and the effects produced by modern automatic typesetting equipment. Other foundries followed with their own competitive versions of modular sans serifs typefaces in Germany, for instance, Rudolf Koch's Kabel for the Klingspor Foundry in 1927 (fig. 9.37). One difference between the Futura and Kabel typefaces was Koch's preservation of features of the Roman alphabet, for instance, the "a" as well as the slant used in the crossbar of the "e."

One of the strongest advocates and promoters of Constructivist principles into industrial printing during the later 1920s and early 1930s was Jan Tschichold (1902–1974). Tschichold was trained in lettering in Leipzig, Germany and acquired a mastery of calligraphy, used at that time for lettering in newspaper advertising. As a young man he visited the exhibition of products from the Weimar Bauhaus in 1923 (see fig. 9.25, page 184). Tschichold saw advantages in sans serif typography and asymmetrical page design as means toward simple and direct communication of information to the reader for a variety of printing applications including advertising. The desire to both expand the concerns of the typographer to include the composition of text and image as well as to subject this language to analysis and discipline became a mission for Tschichold. In this

9.39 Jan Tschichold, film poster, *Casanova*, for
Phoebus-Palast, Munich, 1927.

9.40 Jan Tschichold, book cover for
Constructivist Exhibition, linocut and letterpress,
35 ¼ x 50 ¼ in (90.5 x 127.7 cm), 1937.

vein one might think of him as a reformer, seeking to apply guidelines (new rather than inherited in contrast to nineteenth-century reformers) expressing shared universal values of economy, efficiency, and flexibility. The trademarks he developed from the later 1920s onward, often commissioned by publishing companies, appear somewhat conservative by present-day standards, but reveal an ability to combine letter forms and abbreviated, recognizable images into unified messages, as seen in an example for the Bücherkreis (Book Circle) of Berlin (fig. 9.38). At the time trademarks were a recognized part of advertising strategies in Germany, presenting a unified, recognizable, and coherent visual identity for product brands for a national market.

Most of Tschichold's attention, however, was directed to the varied tasks of commercial printing ranging from posters to stationery, catalogues, and books. In a manifesto published in 1925 and again in his 1927 book entitled *The New Typography*, Tschichold articulated an objective rather than individual or expressive approach to typography. This was based upon principles of clear and direct communication that demanded the use of sans serif typography, half-tone photomechanical reproduction for images, and asymmetrical layout. For posters, rectangular elements relating to the frame dominate, while the use of diagonal type and shapes, or other deviations from the strict discipline of the sans serif letters create tension and arouse interest (fig. 9.39). This poster is one of several examples produced not by the film distribution company but by the movie theater to provide visual identity. Like his Constructivist contemporaries, Tschichold attached importance to white space, making it an integral element in composition. Its prominence conveyed a feeling for economy and purity, as in a book cover illustrating the works of designers and artists associated with the Bauhaus, De Stijl, and Constructivism (fig. 9.40).

Tschichold's "New Typography" and related writings provided practical information for printers to adapt asymmetrical layout and a hierarchical ordering of elements within the structure of a geometric grid to the needs of title pages, stationery, and even invoices. The grid permitted exact measurement and insured precise relationships among parallel and perpendicular elements on the page. Elements of this approach became the basis for the so-called International Typographic Style in Switzerland after World War II as well as house styles developed for corporations working on an international scale. The "New Typography" imposed a certain degree of conformity upon the designer, but still required adjustments rather than simply the application of a formula. As a result, Tschichold's designs have an inherent sense of "rightness" in their balance and in the feeling for the relationship among the various elements of the page. The guidelines for the "New Typography" could be listed as rules or even described as laws, but they could not be programmed.

Tschichold actively promoted the use of half-tone photographs for modern printing and included examples of "typo-foto" (the use of photography as a typographic element in page layout) by Constructivist artists such as El Lissitsky and Moholy-Nagy. He wrote that photography was the "most obvious means of visual representation in our time," and, like sans serif typography, possessed objectivity and a more impersonal quality that characterized a universal approach to modern visual communication. He defined the unity that could be created by using the technique of photomontage and argued that the contrast between the solidity of sans serif and the graded tonalities of the half-tone attracted and maintained the attention of the viewer. The reproduction of photographs opened up new possibilities for the printing industry and provided the basis for much experimentation.

Tschichold, like El Lissitsky and Moholy-Nagy, was fascinated with the *process* of photography, and illustrated examples of photograms in *The New Typography*, where objects were exposed directly on light-sensitive plates in the darkroom (fig. 9.41). This technique, as well as photomontage, where photographic images were juxtaposed and related to lettering, opened up a variety of possibilities ranging from advertisements to covers for politically charged underground publications. German designer Max Burchartz (1887–1961) used photomontage to create the straightforward trade prospectus for the Bochumer company that manufactured industrial parts for machines and railway switching equipment (fig. 9.42). For Burcharz the power of the photograph was its unmediated, truthful representation of the visible world in comparison with the more interpretive techniques of drawing and illustration. Dada artist and activist John Heartfield (1891–1968) composed the image of a dying tree (fig. 9.43) as a Christmas poster, combining sprigs of pine branches on a base in the form of the swastika, symbol of the Nazi Party. Heartfield was also responsible for several covers using photomontage techniques for the Communist Party journal *AIZ* (Workers' Illustrated Newspaper). Heartfield's posters and covers were often cut-and-pasted together, then re-photographed for printing, and the resulting quality is often grainy. The power of the composed images derives from the contradiction of a familiar image with an unfamiliar,

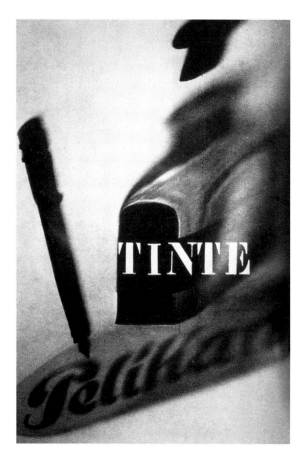

9.41 El Lissitsky, photogram as advertisement for Pelikan Ink. Private collection.

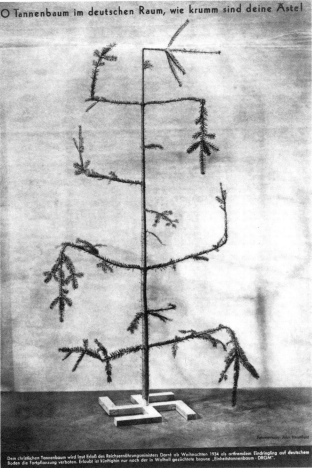

9.42 Bochumer Verin fur Bergbau und Busstahlfabrikation (Bochum Association for Mining and Cast Iron Manufacture), designed by Max Burchartz and Johannes Canis, industrial prospectus, 11 ¼ x 8 ¼ in (30 x 21 cm), 1925. Private collection.

9.43 John Heartfield, *O Tannenbaum in deutschen Raum, wie krumm sind deine Astel* (Oh German evergreen, how crooked are your branches), Christmas tree poster, 1934. Siftung Archiv der Akademie der Künste, Berlin.

even opposite meaning or association. The contrast between both visual statements is strengthened through the objective and impersonal qualities of photography. With increasing technical proficiency, the designer's manipulations of the medium become less readily apparent, and the power of juxtaposed images more provocative.

For these and other reasons the photomechanical reproduction of images using letterpress and offset printing techniques was a passion shared by individual artists, collaborative art movements, commercial companies, and governments. Whether for advertising or in the context of politics, artists, as well as governments and businessmen recognized that photography was a mass medium with great powers of persuasion. After departing the Bauhaus in 1928, Herbert Bayer worked for an advertising agency

in Berlin and was art director for the German fashion magazine *die neue linie* (his typography for the magazine used all lower case letters). Covers for this journal employed high-quality four-color printing technology. Bayer took advantage of the resources of this high-end commercial publication to utilize the techniques of montage and photomontage extensively, exploring its expressive possibilities with more varied formal means at his disposal. Results were often startling and provocative juxtapositions of scale triggered the viewer's associations with travel or to contemporary events. Aside from the monotone sans serif used for the title, text was rarely used. The cover of an issue from 1930 is a study in contrasts (fig. 9.44). Bayer conveys an image of Mediterranean travel, suggested by a bright blue ground, and simplified

9·44 Herbert Bayer, cover for *die neue linie*, 14 ¼ x 10 ½ in (36.5 x 26.7 cm), 1930. The Wolfsonian Florida International University, Herbert Bayer Archive.

9·45 "Koln, Mai bis Oktober, Weltschau am Rhein", poster, designed by Werkstatt F. H. Ehmcke, René Binder, and Max Eichheim, lithograph, 28 x 20 in (70.5 x 50 cm), 1928. The Wolfsonian Florida International University.

model of a Doric temple. The cover also includes the large head of a fashionable female figure (the heavy eyelids suggest a comparison with the early fifth-century B.C. Severe style of Greek sculpture) above the drawing of a woman standing on the steps of the temple.

The justifications of the "New Typography" were logical, and criticisms of the limitations and conservatism of centered layouts were valid. Tschichold and like-minded designers found numerous commercial outlets for their modern approach to advertising. The lithographic poster promoting a large international exhibition devoted to the graphic arts held in Cologne in 1928 betrays its debt to elements of the "New Typography," and might be compared to the Bauhaus Weimar exhibition poster by Joost Schmidt of 1923 (fig. 82 and fig. 9.25, page 184). Designed by René Binder and Max Eichheim for the Ehmcke Workshop, the poster combines rectangular shapes of different colors

intersecting at right angles and the use of monotone sans serif lettering. In addition to strong contrast and a hierarchy of information with ample white space, the designers incorporated abstract shapes for the twin towers of Cologne's Gothic cathedral and the tall tower built for the exhibition as symbols identifying the city.

Even the National Socialist Party in Germany used techniques of photomontage as a form of persuasion. A poster from 1936 superimposes the image of the plain, industrially designed "People's Radio" against a bird's eye view of a vast crowd that bleeds to the edge of the paper (fig. 9.46). The juxtaposition combined with the bold text signifies radio as a form of mass communication identified with the voice of the Führer as if every listener is present at a rally, each a part of a powerful assembly. The traditional German fraktur lettering reads "All of Germany listens to the Führer with the People's receiver." As in

9.46 *Ganz Deutschland hort den Fuhrer mit dem Volksempfanger* (All of Germany listens to the Fuhrer with the People's Receiver), designed by Leonid, lithograph, 47 x 33 ½ in (119.4 x 84.8 cm), printed by Preussischer Druckerei und Verlgs AG, Berlin, 1936. The Wolfsonian Florida International University.

9.47 *Studenten an's Werk* (Students to Work), poster, anonymous, color lithograph, 46 ½ x 32 ¼ in (117.8 x 83.2 cm), published by Deutschen GmbH, Berlin, 1937. The Wolfsonian Florida International University.

much contemporary poster art from the Soviet Union in the later 1920s and 1930s, the National Socialist government favored idealized monumental images of youthful workers and athletes to build a sense of nationalist good feeling toward the policies of the Third Reich. Both illustration and photography were used to convey a sense of duty on the part of all citizens toward the good of all, as seen, for instance, in an anonymous poster of 1937 (fig. 9.47). In this example images of young workers against a background of factories are carefully placed below two handsome youths wearing the Nazi swastika badge on their arms to create a stable pyramidal composition illustrating the phrase "Students to Work!"

Notwithstanding instances of the appropriation of techniques of the "New Typography," the National Socialist Party in Germany was suspicious of the activities of the Bauhaus and other independent artists and designers

sympathetic to Constructivism. Tschichold fell victim to these suspicions, and after being arrested in 1933 he fled to Switzerland where he continued to work as a freelance designer. Tschichold came to regret the polemic and dogmatic tone of his own early writings, recognizing that no single typeface or layout design, however rational or well-intentioned, can meet the demands for legibility for every type of text or every audience. In short, there were authoritarian, even totalitarian implications of the "New Typography" that Tschichold came to question, preferring instead to reject dogma and ideology in favor of a more flexible dialogue between designer, text, and audience. As a tool of communication, he believed that creative modern graphic design should not be determined by a set of strict principles nor imposed upon every task or user.

Outside of Holland, Germany, Switzerland, and the Soviet Union, several designers took an interest in the

9.48 Henrik Berlewi, advertisement for radio station advertising, illustrated in Damase, Jacques, *Révolution typographique depuis Stéphane Mallarmé*, Geneva.

"New Typography." Henryk Berlewi (1894–1967) established the advertising firm Reklama Mechano in Warsaw, Poland. His use of sans serif typography, asymmetrical layout, ample white space, and abstract geometric shapes for advertisement certainly are in sympathy with the guidelines of the "New Typography," while a statement from 1924 appears both as a rejection of individualism and an embrace of the dynamism of modern life: "Art must break with the practices of the perfumed, perverse, hypersensitive, hysterical, romantic, individualistic, boudoir-type art of yesterday. It must create a new language of forms, available to all and in harmony with the rhythm of life." Both tendencies appear in his advertisements encouraging companies to use radio as a form of advertising. One example suggests a radio tower and includes a variety of different weights of upper case sans serif type, arranged horizontally and diagonally (fig. 9.48).

Britain and Graphic Design: A Synthesis

In Britain, a number of artists with varied backgrounds took an interest in modern graphic visual communication. Edward Johnston (1872–1944), a master typographer and teacher who designed decorative initials for the Dove's Press established by Emery Walker and T. J. Cobden-Sanderson in Hammersmith (see page 46), created a sans serif typeface for the London Underground in 1916 that remains in use to this day (fig. 9.49). The commission for this monotone sans serif typeface for the expanding Underground system came from Frank Pick (1878–1941), who at that time held the title of Manager for Underground Electric Railways. Pick also commissioned posters to decorate Underground stations and advertise travel and the use of public transportation from a number of younger artists.

One of Johnston's students was Eric Gill (1882–1940), who developed a family of typefaces known as Gill Sans for the British Monotype Corporation in 1928. Gill Sans was used exclusively by the London and North Eastern Railway for all of their printed materials. Historians generally find the British sans serif faces less mechanical than their Continental counterparts, though they certainly rely more upon compass and straight edge than faces based more directly upon the Roman alphabet (fig. 9.50).

Both Johnston and Gill, like Tschichold, wrote numerous essays and books on the subject of typography, gener-

JOHNSTON

This broadsheet is set in Johnston type. Edward Johnston (1872-1944) was one of the followers of William Morris (1834-1896) who took a leading part in reviving an interest in good lettering after the decadence of the late-Victorian fashions. In 1916 Johnston was commissioned by Frank Pick (1878-1941) to design a special fount for the exclusive use of London's Underground and its associated companies. The resulting Johnston sans-serif type was the forerunner of many sans-serif founts both in England and abroad, including that of Eric Gill (1882-1940) who was Johnston's friend and pupil in this specialised field of design. Johnston is the standard type used for all official signs and notices throughout the London Transport system, and it is also used, where appropriate, for much of London Transport's general typographical publicity.

ABCDEFGHIJKLMNOPQRSTUVWXYZ1234567890
abcdefghijklmnopqrstuvwxyz &£.,:;'-""!?()*

9.49 Edward Johnston, "Railway" typeface, 1916. London Transport Museum.

ally intended for printers and dealing with a wide range of practical, esthetic, scholarly, and social issues related to the subject. Many were published in the journals *The Fleuron* and *Signature*. Both men explored the advantages of sans serif typography and were inventive in expanding its application, particularly in the transportation industry, where clear signage and immediate recognition of information were important considerations. At the same time they continued to produce typefaces of great sophistication and subtlety based upon Roman letter forms. Eric Gill's Perpetua for British Monotype, for instance, released in 1929 (fig. 9.51), has long ascenders and descenders, as well as a gradual narrowing of the strokes of lower case letters such as "d" or "p" toward their stems.

Stanley Morison (1889–1967) of British Monotype supervised the design of several typefaces derived from eighteenth-century precedent but adapted to the requirements of modern printing technology. His best-known face was developed for the London *Times*, and known as Times New Roman (TNR, fig. 9.52). First printed in 1932, Times New Roman has been widely praised for its legibility combined with economical considerations through the use of shortened ascenders and descenders that reduce the space between lines in the text. Gill, Johnston, and Morison each invented or supervised the invention of fonts adapted to new production technologies, emphasizing clear communication and acknowledging the varied requirements of printing in a modern industrial society. They explored the use of sans serif typography and were open-minded to its advantages, but their own training and experience prevented them from adopting it exclusively.

Tschichold reached the same conclusion, probably for the same reason: for book design, serif typefaces and symmetrical layout were the most direct and effective means of communication. Tschichold's work designing editions of books for Penguin after World War II using Times New Roman and stately framed titles (fig. 9.53) violated the principles he had articulated in *The New Typography*, whose authority he himself had come to doubt. In many ways these designers continued the tradition of great printer–typographers from the eighteenth century

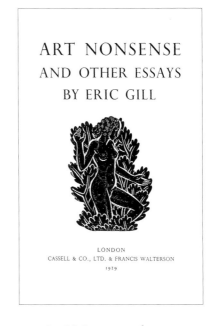

9.51 Eric Gill, Perpetua typeface, 1929.

ABCDEFGHIJKLMN OPQRSTUVWXYZ? abcdefghijklm nopqrstuvwxyz! 1234567890

9.50 Eric Gill, Gill Sans typeface, line drawing by John Langdon.

ABCDEFGHIJKLMN OPQRSTUVWXYZ? abcdefghijklm nopqrstuvwxyz! 1234567890

9.52 Stanley Morison, Times New Roman typeface, 1932, line drawing by John Langdon.

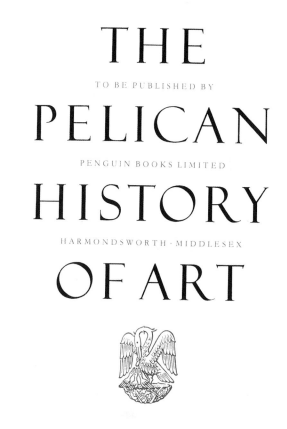

THE

TO BE PUBLISHED BY

PELICAN

PENGUIN BOOKS LIMITED

HISTORY

HARMONDSWORTH · MIDDLESEX

OF ART

9.53 Jan Tschichold, prospectus cover for *The Pelican History of Art*, 1947.

described above and revived by William Morris in the late nineteenth century. Indeed, many aspects of the industry had changed. Commercial printing had expanded, the half-tone screen permitted the mechanical reproduction of photographs, and typographers had to take into consideration the way in which mechanical typesetting was affecting the look of a printed page. The design of new type required invention, a respect for tradition, knowledge of industrial process, and a feeling for the purposes of and audience for written communication. The collaboration between these large typefounding companies and individual typographers produced typefaces and offspring of those typefaces with a currency that their inventors might not have been able to imagine, thanks to the miracles of the digital age. A deep understanding of history and the printing industry helped to make designers such as Gill and later Tschichold less radical in their professional practice than some of

their counterparts in the interwar period. But their work maintained a sense of continuity with the printer's craft, adaptation to the technical and varied commercial requirements of an expanding printing industry, and experiment with new ideas and possibilities for the printed word. In this manner their work reached a wider public and is more often incorporated into contemporary practice than consigned to reproductions in the literature of art history.

As Vice-President of the London Passenger Transport Board (established in 1933 through merger of remaining independent service companies), Frank Pick again had the opportunity to apply elements of the "New Typography" to issues of communication and identity in the public transportation industry. Through a design policy that encompassed architecture, interior design, furniture, and signage, Pick created a comprehensive and cohesive visual identity for the London Underground transportation system (fig. 9.54). For the public, the unified identity system created the impression of order, reliability, and unity among the various lines and interchanges that comprise the Underground transit. Colorful travel posters on station walls encouraged travelers to explore the attractions of urban and suburban London. For the employees, visual identity created the sense of a single entity, while in fact the newly formed London Transport Board was made up of dozens of competing private companies.

For a new map of the LTB's routes, Pick turned to an industrial draftsman named Henry Beck to reduce the confusion and uncertainty of navigating the vast interconnected routes of the public transportation system. The map (fig. 9.55) is a model of efficient communication, limiting the direction of routes to angles of 90 and 45 degrees. In this way the parallel lines not only make the system itself appear rational, but also make it easier for the traveler to locate stations and connections between routes when changes are necessary. The design, in a word, is "user-friendly," helping to break down barriers that inhibit the use of a service that might otherwise appear complicated. As a result of the map, the city itself became more manageable and accessible to the visitor. As noted by Adrian Forty, the simplicity of the London Underground map was not in every respect a virtue. The map had no uniform sense of scale to gauge distances between stops or a means of explaining the sometimes lengthy walking distances that accompany changing from

9.54 London Transport, combined bench and station sign, *c.* 1935.

9.55 H. C. Beck, Map, London Underground, chromolithograph, 6 ¼ x 9 in (157 x 226 mm), 1933. London Transport Museum.

one color-coded line to another. One result was that suburban locations often seemed far closer to the center of the city than they were. Such distortions might indeed make what looked like a simple trip from Picadilly to Hampstead or Walthamstow into more of an adventure than a tourist had bargained for. And yet aside from the deception (and perhaps the weather), the trip still remains worth the while.

This approach to design demonstrates that geometric abstraction can attain the level of an almost universal communication that functions effectively for the traveler. Such an approach became the basis for transportation symbols designed in the early 1970s for airports and may be seen as a practical legacy of the visual strategies of the "New Typography." Indeed, an Austrian sociologist named Otto Neurath (1882–1945) initiated the Isotype Movement in Vienna before moving to Holland in 1934. Neurath worked with artists to develop universal pictorial symbols to communicate statistics in a concise and direct manner intended to encourage the sharing of information on social and economic issues for the general public. Like the London Underground map, the Isotype Movement was part of the developing profession of graphic design in the interwar period.

Scandinavia

In the interwar period the countries of Scandinavia developed an approach to design that succeeded in achieving a balance among individuality and the preservation of craft materials and traditions with standardized mass production and social reform. Scandinavian design in the interwar period first emerged through the hiring of artists such as Edward Hald (1883–1980) and Simon Gate (1883–1945) by large Swedish glass manufactories such as Orrefors in the production of art glass for a mostly luxury international market. Hald had studied painting with Matisse in Paris, and examples of his work in etched crystal glass, as well as those of Gate, were displayed at the 1925 Paris Exposition Internationale des Arts Décoratifs et Industriels Modernes. Hald's designs resemble contemporary work being produced by Lalique in Paris and later by Steuben in the United States (see pages 90 and 206) and are seen in a 1920 blown glass vase depicting "Girls Playing Ball" (fig. 9.56). At the same time the Swedish organization known as the Svenska Slöjdföreningen under the direction of Gregor Paulsson, advocated the adoption of standards based upon practicality and strongly influenced by the views of Hermann Muthesius through the Deutscher Werkbund (see page 168). An effective compromise between individuality and the perpetuation of craft traditions on the one hand and standardization and modern industrial manufacturing methods and materials on the other was already becoming identified as "Scandinavian" modernism in the mid-1930s primarily through Swedish and Finnish participation in

9.56 Edward Hald, *Girls Playing Ball* vase, blown glass, engraved with underplate, 9 ¼ x 11 ⅝ in (23.5 x 29.5 cm), Orrefors Glassworks, 1920. Orrefors Museum, Sweden.

comfortably support the weight of the human body. The armchair was first designed for use throughout the Paimio Tuberculosis Sanatorium in Finland, built between 1929 and 1932. Utilizing newer industrial materials and processes, Aalto minimized and even eliminated upholstery as well as decoration. Moreover, the quantity of furnishings needed for the commission allowed Aalto to give serious consideration to the requirements for serial production, and in particular the use of laminated rather than carved woods permitted uniformity and ease of construction. Thus the designs appeared industrial as opposed to hand-crafted, while the use of organic forms and natural wood surfaces softened the geometry and austerity of comparable metal or wood furniture constructed from standardized components (see for instance Rietveld's "Red-Blue" chair of 1918, fig. 9.2, page 169). Aalto's furniture combines a commitment to industrial materials and processes, as well as a consideration of factors such as comfort and psychology that extend beyond utility and economy. In place of an esthetic of geometric purity and austerity his designs offer a closer analogy with the freer

international exhibitions. Aspects of this approach can be seen in the work of a number of architects whose oeuvre included the design of furniture.

This Scandinavian synthesis of modernism found at least partial expression in furniture designed by Swedish architect Gunnar Asplund (1885–1940), but is perhaps better associated with the molded plywood and laminated birch chair designs of a younger Finnish architect named Alvar Aalto (1898–1976). Aalto's furniture was featured in an international exhibition in Paris in 1937, at a solo exhibition at the Museum of Modern Art in 1938, and at the 1939 New York World's Fair for which he designed the Finnish pavilion. His armchairs (fig. 9.57), still manufactured by Artek, the company he established in Helsinki in 1935, were inspired by the light tubular metal furniture designed by Marcel Breuer at the Bauhaus (see fig. 9.28, page 186). While committed to the use of industrial processes, Aalto preferred wood to tubular metal, and experimented with laminated birch (although bentwood chairs made of beech were also manufactured in Germany by Thönet). Aalto favored the use of native birch, an abundant natural resource in Finland, and adapted the technology of laminated wooden skis to the structural requirements of a variety of chair designs (including those based upon the cantilever principle) strong enough to

9.57 Alvar Aalto, Paaimio armchair, laminated birch and plywood, manufactured by Huonekalu-ja Rakennustyötendas, Turku, Finland, 26 x 23 ¾ x 34 ⅞ in (166 x 60.3 x 88.6 cm), 1931. Alvar Aalto Museum, Finland.

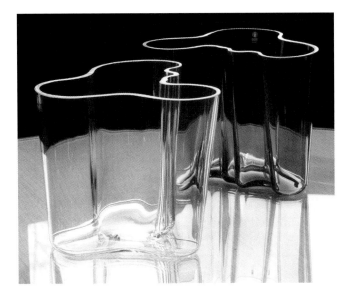

9.58 Alvar Aalto, Savoy vase, mold-blown glass, 5 ½ in (14 cm) high, manufactured by Karhula-Ittala, Finland, 1936. Alvar Aalto Museum, Finland.

and more irregular abstract forms of Surrealism. Aalto was able to explore such connections further in the design of glassware that also suggests analogies to the suggestive forms of Automatic Surrealism, particularly the sculptures of Belgian-born sculptor Jean Arp. This can be seen in Aalto's so-called Savoy vase of *c.*1936 (fig. 9.58), with its amoeba-like forms and attempt to incorporate and activate negative space. Such esthetic considerations were also adapted to furniture by other Scandinavian designers, whose works will be examined in the context of postwar design in Part IV. Aalto's well-reasoned approach may be appreciated from the following excerpt from a speech he delivered to the Swedish Arts and Crafts Society in 1935. The expansion of the rational basis for design to include psychological considerations further distinguishes Aalto's understanding of modern design from earlier and contemporary approaches to prefabrication and standardization in which industrial design was often viewed as a vehicle for solving social problems and tied to an ideology of collective rather than individual expression:

> In other words, we can say that one of the ways to arrive at a more and more humanely built environment is to expand the concept *rational*. We should rationally analyze more of the requirements con-nected with the object than we have to date ... A series of requirements that can be made of almost every object and that up to now has been given scant con-sideration surely belongs in the sphere of another sci-ence-psychology, As soon as we include psychological requirements, or, let us say, when we can do so, then we will have already expanded the rational method to an extent that, to a greater degree than previously, has the potential of excluding inhuman results. (Wrede, *The Architecture of E.G. Asplund*, p. 156)

In Sweden the use of laminated woods and organic forms was pioneered in the 1930s by Bruno Mathsson (1907–88), who throughout his career manufactured orig-inal furniture designs in a family workshop. His 1934 armchair (fig. 9.59) consists of a broad curving seat with webbing rather than upholstery whose sculptural contour conforms to Mathsson's measurements and studies for ideal sitting positions for the human body for a variety of tasks, including simply "lounging." The legs of the chair repeat and balance the gently curving shape of the com-bined seat and back, while the arms provide support for the back. In basing his designs primarily upon standards of comfort derived from the careful study of people in the

9.59 Bruno Mathsson, armchair, beech and birch plywood, hemp upholstery, 32 ¾ x 19 ¼ x 29 ⅛ in (83 x 49 x 74 cm), manufactured by Karl Mathsson, Vämamo, Sweden, 1934.

9.60 Kaare Klint, mahogany sideboard, 37 ⁹⁄₁₆ x 59 ¹³⁄₁₆ x 24 ¹⁄₂ in (95.4 x 152 x 62 cm), manufactured by Rudolf Rasmussens Snedkerier, Denmark, 1930. Danske Kunstindustrimuseu, Copenhagen.

performance of a variety of activities, Mathsson was able to integrate elements of both utility and economy on the one hand and a broader range of human considerations affecting design.

Denmark also contributed to the development of Scandinavian modern design both before and after World War II. Silversmith Georg Jensen (1866–1935) established an international reputation for original high quality hand-crafted designs for cutlery and tableware, and was represented at the Paris International Exhibition of 1925. At the same time, however, the interests of some artists in a more democratic approach resulted in a shift to industrial methods and designs for simpler, less expensive, and more standardized goods, exemplified in the work of Kaare Klint (1888–1954). In addition to reducing or even eliminating carved ornament while retaining the beauty of natural wood surfaces, Klint also based his furniture designs upon studies undertaken in the Furniture Department of the Royal Danish Academy of Arts, which he helped to found and where he served as an instructor. The dimensions of Klint's sideboard (fig. 9.60) were based upon average sizes for dishes, cups, saucers, and other dining room furnishings in relation to efficient storage. The research suggests Klint's intention to produce designs to meet the perceived needs of simple working-class households rather than for wealthy individual consumers. Klint's assessment of average needs was not, however, limited to efficiency or the anonymous production envisioned by Le Corbusier's concept of the "machine for living in;" rather, his principle of efficiency extended to the design of folding and stacking chairs constructed from standardized components and lightweight webbing to replace traditional upholstery, and also preserved the interest in traditional materials such as wood and an appreciation for hand-rubbed surfaces and simple finishes.

Scandinavian furniture and houseware design demonstrated the ability to address both the relationship between design, technology, and social responsibility as well as the connection between design and individual expression that emerged internationally in the more favorable economic circumstances following the end of World War I. In addition to a favorable critical reception in Paris and New York in the late 1930s, Aalto's bent-plywood furniture was marketed in Britain, though clients tended to be architects designing interiors for offices and public spaces rather than individuals seeking to furnish their own domestic interiors.

Chapter 10

Art, Design, and Industry in the United States

10.11 Reuben Haley, *Ruba Rombic* vase, glass, molded, blown, and acid-etched, 16 ½ x 8 ⅞ x 8 ⅞ in (42 x 22.5 x 22.5 cm), 1928–30. Consolidated Lamp and Glass Company, Pittsburgh. Toledo Museum of Art.

In the United States, craft-based industries tended to remain conservative in terms of design until the mid-1920s, unaffected by the self-consciously esthetic approaches of art moderne designers in France and elsewhere in Europe. On the recommendation of then Secretary of Commerce, Herbert Hoover, the United States declined to participate in the 1925 Exposition Internationale des Arts Décoratifs et Industriels Modernes in Paris because, in his opinion, designers were unable to comply with the criteria of submitting products that were modern and original. The United States did, however, dispatch a large delegation to the exhibition, headed by the President of the American Association of Museums, Charles Richards, whose charge included organizing a traveling exhibition of works selected in Paris. This traveling exhibition, and others sponsored by institutions such

10.1 Gottlieb Eliel Saarinen, side chair, fir with black and ocher paint, red horse-hair upholstery, 37 ⅝ x 17 x 19 in (95.6 x 43.2 x 48.5 cm), 1929–30, upholstery fabric by Loja Saarinen. Collection of Cranbrook Academy of Art Museum.

10.2 Sidney Waugh, *Gazelle* bowl, cut glass with engraving, 7 ¼ x 6 ½ in (18.4 x 16.5 cm), 1935, Corning Glass Works, New York. Toledo Museum of Art.

as the Metropolitan Museum of Art, New York, stimulated public and commercial interest in newer designs, aimed mostly at a sophisticated audience. By the later 1920s ensembles of interior furnishings by Jean Dunand and other French designers of luxury goods could be seen in the windows of New York department stores such as Lord and Taylor, and American retailers began to recognize the commercial advantages of supporting contemporary designs in a wide range of consumer goods. Museums promoted modern styles along broadly educational lines, emphasizing the integration of art into the lives of the middle class and the ability of the decorative arts to raise the level of public taste and contribute to cultural progress. In addition magazines such as *Vogue* and *Vanity Fair* used photography and illustration to cultivate an idealized and exclusive image of modern life associated with fashion, sport, travel, and other leisure activities.

The Metropolitan Museum of Art was one of eight venues for the traveling exhibition from the 1925 Paris exhibition, and it continued to sponsor a series of annual exhibitions devoted to modern decorative arts throughout

the 1920s, a project initiated after World War I. In such exhibitions a variety of new forms and new materials emerge. These include the wooden (fir) chairs with flared backs accentuated by vertical strips designed by Danish-born architect Gottlieb Eliel Saarinen (1873–1950, fig. 10.1), as well as the etched crystal glass bowls designed by Massachusetts-born sculptor Sidney Waugh (1904–1963) for the Steuben Glass company (fig. 10.2). Steuben Glass soon became the "designer" branch of the Corning Glass Company in Corning, New York. Saarinen was named director of an artists' community founded in 1923 by newspaper publisher George Booth in Bloomfield Hills, Michigan, which later became the Cranbrook Academy of Art and focused upon design education. Saarinen's wife, Loja (1879–1968), was also trained as an artist in Finland and initiated the hand-weaving workshop at Cranbrook. Other American companies produced artists' designs for rugs and embroideries. Marguerite Zorach (1887–1968) studied painting in Paris but returned to the United States, producing contemporary designs for rugs reminiscent of Fauve painting and Poiret's *Atelier Martine*. Zorach designed a rug woven from wool and jute for the Crawford Shops in New York, dating to 1936. Entitled *Jungle*, the rug makes use of muted red-orange, gray, and brown hues arranged in a densely-packed composition that achieves remarkable unity through consistent tone and abstract organic shapes (fig. 10.3).

Following the 1925 Paris exhibition the Gorham Silver Company of Providence, Rhode Island hired Danish-born and German-trained silversmith Erik Magnussen (1884–1961) to design modern silver. An example of his work for Gorham is the 1928 Manhattan tea and coffee service. This service features traditional tapered cylindrical forms overlaid with gold and silver "facets" arranged asymmetrically to suggest a Cubist-inspired esthetic associated with the modern, urban environment (fig. 10.4, compare figs. 8.29 and 8.30, pages 160–1). This new vocabulary is also the basis for the great set-back profiles and sculpted decorative motifs of the skyscrapers of the interwar era in the United States. Indeed, the term Skyscraper Style is sometimes used to refer to the expressive buildings and furnishings of the era, whether in William van Alen's Chrysler Building or German-born Paul Frankl's series of Skyscraper bookcases (fig. 10.5).

10.3 Marguerite Zorach, *Jungle*, handhooked rug, wool, jute, 42 x 60 in (106.7 x 152 cm), 1936. Museum of Modern Art, New York.

10.4 Erik Magnussen, Manhattan coffee and tea service, burnished silver with gold and oxidized gray panels, coffee pot: 9 ½ in (24 cm) high, Gorham Silver Company, 1927. Collection of Charles H. Carpenter, Jr.

10.5 Paul Frankl, "Skyscraper" bookcase, birch, lacquer, 84 x 39 x 14 in (213 x 99 x 37 cm), 1926. Private collection.

10.6 Raymond Hood, in collaboration with Henry V. K. Henderson, *Business Executive's Office* room setting designed for "The Architect and the Industrial Arts: An Exhibition of Contemporary American Design", 1929. The Metropolitan Museum of Art, New York.

10.7 Ruth Reeves, *Electric*, hand-printed cotton, 74 ⅛ x 42 ⅛ in (188 x 107 cm), 1930. Sloane Company. Collection of the estate of Ruth Reeves.

Architects such as Raymond Hood (1881–1934), who designed the Empire State Building in Manhattan, played a leading role in creating furniture and interiors celebrating modern industrial materials and angular geometric decoration. It is seen, for instance, in his Business Executive's Office designed for an exhibition held at the Metropolitan Museum early in 1929 (fig. 10.6).

American artist Ruth Reeves (1892–1966), who had studied painting with Fernand Léger in Paris, designed textiles that featured the new vocabulary of Cubist-inspired forms. Her "Electric" design (fig. 10.7), manufactured by the Sloane Carpet Company from 1928 to 1930, uses zig-zag overlapping shapes to convey the speed and man-made power of electric energy, while Kneeland Green (1892–1956) used stenciled typography of varied sizes to create dense printed patterns such as *Cheerio* in 1927 for fabrics and wall coverings (fig. 10.8). Such admiration for the excitement and beauty of new forms and an accelerated pace of life generated by technology and the metropolis are seen as well in the paintings of American artists such as Joseph Stella (1877–1946) and John Marin (1870–1953). Stella's series of works devoted to the Brooklyn Bridge, or Marin's watercolor interpretations of tall buildings in downtown Manhattan from the 1920s, are

examples of the fascination with man-made rather than natural beauty. The works of these artists demonstrate a reverence for the exhilarating and heroic character of the modern metropolis. The aural equivalent of this sensibility is found in the emergence of jazz in urban centers along the Mississippi River such as Kansas City and Chicago, and also in the Harlem section of New York City. Textile designers also explored new processes and materials. British-born Henriette Reiss (1889–1992) produced textiles using the technique of screen-printing, as seen in her *Rhythm Series* pattern of 1928 (fig. 10.9). Photographer Edward Steichen (1879–1973) and designer Charles B. Falls (1874–1960) also created detailed and complex, syncopated patterns for printed textiles on silk using photographs of ordinary domestic objects such as sugar cubes, matchbooks, thread, and needles (fig. 10.10). In both of these examples, designs are applied directly or transferred (in the case of photographic images) to thin, porous

10.8 Kneeland L. Green, *Americana Print: Cheerio* textile, printed silk, 24 ⅜ x 38 ½ in (62 x 98 cm), 1927, manufactured by Stehli Silks Corporation, New York. Metropolitan Museum of Art, New York.

10.10 Charles B. Falls, *Americana Print: Pegs* textile, printed silk, 29 ¼ x 38 ½ in (74.3 x 97.2 cm), 1927, manufactured by Stehli Silks Corporation, New York. Metropolitan Museum of Art, New York.

10.9 Henriette Reiss, *Rhythm Series*, textile, screen-printed on cotton, 51 ⅛ x 50 ⅛ in (131 x 128.6 cm), 1928. Goldstein Gallery, University of Minnesota.

screens of tightly woven silk. After the non-image areas of the design are blocked out, fabric is then placed beneath the screens, through which ink is pressed using a squeegee. The ink only passes through the design and is resisted elsewhere, and the screen may be reused for printing in more than one color.

In addition to the role played by museum exhibitions and upscale department stores, modern design reached a broader and more diverse public through illustrations and advertisements in mass-circulation magazines and in public entertainment through the constructed interior sets of the popular cinema. In the later 1920s, modern decorative motifs, derived from Cubism and Futurism, began to appear in less expensive products, as the market for new designs associated with the "image" of an idealized and modern lifestyle emerging on screen and in advertisements expanded beyond wealthy buyers. Until the stock-market crash in late 1929, industrial production was fueling an economic boom and lower-income households were able to imitate their wealthier countrymen and women by buying inexpensively manufactured personal

10.11 Reuben Haley, *Ruba Rombic* vase, glass, molded, blown, and acid-etched, 16 ½ x 8 ⅞ x 8 ⅞ in (42 x 22.5 x 22.5 cm), 1928–30. Consolidated Lamp and Glass Company, Pittsburgh. Toledo Museum of Art.

and domestic products. Examples include Pittsburgh-born Reuben Haley's (1872–1933) *Ruba Rombic* line of sculptural and facetted frosted glass vases, which was designed for the Consolidated Glass Company in the Pennsylvania town of Coraopolis, near Pittsburgh (1928–30, fig. 10.11) and manufactured from 1928 until 1930.

Industrial Design and Fordism

Despite the efforts of museums such as the Metropolitan Museum of Art to encourage the production and consumption of modern domestic products for the home, it is not surprising that large-scale industries for the mechanized mass production of consumer goods and appliances were reluctant to embrace design as a conscious element

in their product development and marketing until the later 1920s. Great advances in techniques of mass production, pioneered in the automobile industry by Henry Ford's concentration upon the production of a single and virtually unchanging Model T and extending to the manufacture of household appliances in the 1920s, were admired almost without reservation in capitalist as well as socialist circles and governments of Europe as a model for the successful mechanization of industry. The social benefits offered by the machine in the democratization of culture and widespread improvement in the general standard of living were also widely acknowledged. The Ford Company opened an automobile factory in Germany in 1924, and by 1929 the United States was responsible for more than eighty percent of automobile production worldwide. American industrialization was seen as the basis for prosperity and economic recovery, especially, as noted above, in Germany as well as in Soviet Russia. Praise for business, the machine, and the assembly line had overtly religious overtones: skyscrapers were called "cathedrals of commerce," and Calvin Coolidge commented: "The factory is a temple—the worker worships there."

The success of the Model T and other products of moving assembly line production stemmed from managing costs through more efficient machinery, standardized, interchangeable parts and the application of techniques of scientific management to labor. This represented a commitment to a combination of increasing both the speed of assembly as well as the precision and uniformity of manufactured parts. The revolutionary success of the Ford Motor Company took place within a decade, and until 1927, when its production halted, more than fifteen million Model T Fords had rolled off the assembly line, virtually identical in their black lacquer finish and carriage-based body form. Sometimes dubbed "Fordism," this approach to industrial design was summarized by Henry Ford himself, with echoes of Adam Smith's encomium to the division of labor in a pin manufactory (see page 32): "the way to make automobiles is to make one automobile like another automobile, to make them all alike, to make them come from the factory all alike, just like one pin is like another when it comes from a pin factory."

Clearly little development in design occurred within such a framework for production—in fact, its success seemed to be based upon the suppression of market

10.12 Chevrolet "Superior", 1923.

differentiation through design and the concentration of all effort upon the reduction of cost and the acceleration of worker productivity in the plant. Capital investment in equipment and rationalization of the role of work mitigated against variation in product; and, as pointed out by several observers, this combination of factors led to reductions in the cost of the Model T during the course of its production. In 1916 the Model T sold for $360 dollars, less than one-half its cost in 1910, and well below the cost of other domestic automobile manufacturers; in 1919 the cost for each model was $265! Without real competition in the marketplace Fordism was a tremendous success and an inspiration for the economic promise of mechanized mass production. To help offset the pressures of the assembly line and the unrest caused by accelerated production schedules and the repetitive routine of the assembly line, Ford introduced a profit-sharing plan labeled the "five dollar day" for workers in 1914, who in time were able, via credit-purchase, to realize the dream of owning their own Model T, initiating a process of turning workers into mass consumers.

But as more Americans became owners of second cars and as the automobile became integrated into the leisure as well as work activities of the public, comfort, luxury, and styling became desirable to more consumers and increasingly influenced the decision to purchase new vehicles. General Motors, formed in 1918 from the consolidation of a number of individual manufacturers under the leadership of its new president, Alfred Sloan, was responsive to these new consumer trends through stronger ties to its retail dealers. In time their strategy was adopted by Ford, who could not fail to notice that market saturation had slowed new car purchases and that used car sales were beginning to outstrip demand for new cars (after all, older Fords were virtually identical with more recent models). General Motors began to distinguish their vehicles through the introduction of variety in color, made possible by new enamel paints that dried almost as quickly as the traditional black lacquer. The company also introduced a series of minor styling changes and buyer options. These are first seen in the 1923 Chevrolet Superior, whose contour appears more unified and compact than that of Ford's Model T (fig. 10.12). General Motors also invested more heavily in advertising as a means to stimulate sales, a strategy whose important ramifications will be more thoroughly discussed below.

In 1927 Henry Ford succumbed to pressure to modify his stance on uniformity and standardization, introducing a new Model A together with a massive advertising campaign (virtually the first in the company's history) and the completion of a vast new production plant at the River Rouge near Dearborn, Michigan. In 1927 General Motors hired Harley Earl to head an Art and Color Section within the corporation, based upon Earl's success in redesigning the 1927 Cadillac Lasalle, a less expensive variation of the company's traditional luxury sedan. Earl came to GM as a designer of custom automobiles, in which lower profiles and a more unified approach to body design, found in expensive European automobiles such as the Hispano-Suiza, were substituted for the traditional high chassis and collection of unrelated elements such as bumpers, wheel covers, and headlights of more standardized American cars (fig. 10.13). One of Earl's contributions as a designer for the automobile industry was that the new elements he introduced rarely required significant engineering changes or substantial capital investment in new machinery. Providing choice and variety in the automobile market

10.13 Cadillac Lasalle Model 303, designed by Harley Earl, 1927.

10.14 Karl Emanuel Martin (Kem) Weber (attributed), *Zephyr* Electric Clock, brass, bakelite, 3 ¼ x 8 x 3 ⅛ in (8.3 x 20.3 x 8 cm), *c.* 1934. Lawson Time Inc. (Pasadena, California). Metropolitan Museum of Art, New York

without significantly raising production costs constituted a manufacturing strategy that maximized the profitable relationship between novelty and consumer appeal, as well as acknowledging the role of advertising in generating demand. The economic climate of the later 1920s made manufacturers recognize that uniformity and standardization in industrially manufactured goods were not sufficient to continue to guarantee success, but rather that the need for change was a necessity for generating continued profits and growth. Significantly, the Art and Color Section of General Motors was renamed the Styling Division in 1937: the new name appears to reflect the corporation's acknowledgment of the need for frequent model changes, as well as their understanding of design change as being superficial or cosmetic, in effect a branch of advertising. As noted above, the Ford Motor Company promoted its new Model A Ford in 1927 with an advertising campaign, marking a major change in the corporation's business strategy. One of the labels of this new strategy (see fig. 7.9, page 134) involving advertising and design was "planned obsolescence" (some authors use the phrases "artificial obsolescence" or "progressive obsolescence"). Obsolescence referred to the annual or seasonal introduction of new colors, patterns, or forms that made existing products appear outmoded and encouraged consumers to purchase the latest, most "modern" item. It helped to control the risks of introducing substantively new products and of keeping an eclectic variety of products in continual production.

Although criticized at times as a form of consumer manipulation, the planned obsolescence operated on what

Roland Marchand has called the new "consumer ethic," a recognition that consumption fueled production, putting people back to work in a period of high unemployment and restoring buyer confidence. Although product styling was sometimes adopted tentatively, the potential profit encouraged many companies to think of design as an integral part of the overall manufacturing process, and to turn to advertisers and retailers to suggest new or modified products.

In many ways the automobile industry was cautious in its approach to industrial design, despite Alfred Sloan's commitment to styling and Earl's growing importance in General Motors. In other industries, designers were hired on a contract basis rather than as full-time employees to stimulate sales. The phenomenon of the "consultant industrial designer" is significant in American manufacturing in the 1930s. It indicates that aside from the "styling" departments created by the automobile industry in the later 1920s, corporations were ill-equipped to stimulate demand through design or respond to surveys of consumer preference. Rather, they thought more in terms of product "engineering" than design, focusing upon what Jeffrey Meikle describes as the "functional arrangement of a product's mechanical parts" instead of a variety of factors that might create consumer appeal. Moreover, the concept of a "consultant industrial designer" implied greater autonomy and a freedom to experiment with solutions to the various demands of a particular brief, from a number of different perspectives, to balance commercial success with esthetic ideals and social responsibility.

Case Studies in American Industrial Design

Kem Weber (1889–1963) opened an industrial design office in Los Angeles in the early 1930s. Weber was born in Germany and had worked in Berlin under designer Bruno Paul. He traveled to the United States in 1913 and remained there after the start of World War I. As a consultant for industry, Weber designed an electric clock with digital (rather than traditional analog) readout (fig. 10.14), manufactured by the Lawson Company of Alhambra, California in 1934. Made of copper and aluminum, the rectangular form of the clock is swept back at the left edge in a curve rather than at a ninety degree angle to produce a smooth or streamlined look suggestive of frictionless movement rather than the angularity and staccato rhythms of setback Skyscraper forms. Historians have noted the use of such forms in the buildings and project designs of German architect Erich Mendelsohn (1887–1953), whose work was also admired by Frank Lloyd Wright. Such forms may also be seen in the lower stories of the 1932 Philadelphia Saving Fund Society Building designed by the firm of Howe and Lescaze.

A number of early industrial designers were artists who had worked directly in advertising or were successful in fields such as stage and set design for the theater. Often recommended to manufacturers by advertising agencies, industrial designers occupied an often precarious middle ground between advertising's concerns for consumer appeal and planned obsolescence, broadly humanistic concerns with progress through improved performance and social responsibility, a desire to work closely in relationship to engineering in the organization of a product's working parts, and individual creative expression. Industrial design offices often employed large staffs, and in addition to redesigning products were responsible for package design, labels, advertising, and merchandising. And although the success of the profession in the 1930s was often based upon the value and marketability of individual names such as Raymond Loewy (1893–1986), whose portrait appeared on the cover of a 1942 issue of *Time* magazine, industrial design office practice usually involved the contributions of many individuals working together as a team according to a division of labor. In some ways the team-based approach of industrial design offices approximated the existing conditions and complexities of the manufacturing industry rather than the studio of the

10.15 Advertisement for gas range, Geo. D. Roper Corporation, Rockford, Illinois, from *Good Housekeeping*, August 1923.

creative fine artist or the academic confines of the classroom, where isolation often produced compelling ideologies but few mass-produced goods.

Studies of the work of American industrial designers in the 1930s reveal the dynamic interrelationships between esthetic, commercial, social, and production considerations. For example, Norman Bel Geddes (1893–1958) was hired by the Standard Gas Equipment Corporation in 1933 to redesign its kitchen ranges in the hope of creating consumer demand. Market research revealed that ease of cleaning was the primary consideration of housewives in their decision to purchase a new range. Geddes's response to market research was to use large rectangular panels of enamel-coated sheet metal (including a panel to fit over the burners) rather than cast iron to create a more enclosed and unified, essentially box-like form, eliminating open areas that collected dust as

10.17 Walter Dorwin Teague, "Bantam Special" camera, metal and enamel, 3 ½ x 4 x 1 ¼ (9 x 10 x 4.4 cm), 1936. Eastman Kodak Company, Rochester, New York. Metropolitan Museum of Art, New York.

10.16 Norman Bel Geddes, sheet metal stove, approximately 36 x 37 x 25 ¼ in (91.4 x 94 x 65.4 cm), 1933. Standard Gas Equipment Company. Wolfsonian Florida International University.

well as the clutter of decorative handles and other hardware (fig. 10.15). In order to reduce damage in shipping as a result of replacing cast iron with the lighter and thinner sheet metal, Geddes attached the panels to a sturdy tubular metal frame at the corners. The new model presented a more integrated, unified housing, while advertising identified smooth surfaces and simple forms with improved hygiene as well as reduced housework. Many of these characteristics are also found in a 1935 stove manufactured for the Magic Chef Corporation (fig. 10.16), whose thin, tubular steel frame is left partially exposed. Bel Geddes' industrially re-designed stove demonstrated the commercial advantages of pressed metal production technology, with structural changes for strength, integrated esthetic form, and responsiveness to market research.

This approach, balancing new housing with mechanical or structural change resulting in improved performance, appears to have been the ideal toward which many of the consultant industrial designers directed their efforts, that is, to a point somewhere beyond mere "styling" or

10.18 Raymond Loewy, "Coldspot Super Six" refrigerator, porcelain on steel and aluminum, 58 ³⁄₁₆ x 30 x 26 in (147.8 x 76 x 66 cm), Sears, Roebuck and Company, Chicago, 1935.

A Simpler and Different Electric Refrigerator

The Creation of General Electric

GE Refrigerator

HERE is a new development in electric refrigerators for the home that every person interested in a refrigerator will want to see —the creation of General Electric.

It marks an entirely new conception of electric refrigeration. It marks an entirely *new* type of icing unit—a type unlike any other you have ever seen.

The entire mechanism of the General Electric Icing Unit is housed on top of the cabinet in one hermetically sealed casing. (Note illustration.) That is *all* the mechanism—none below the box. None in the basement. There are no pipes, no drains, no attachments.

All bulky machinery is eliminated

—virtually all servicing. Operating automatically, you need never touch it—never oil it. Current consumption is reduced to a minimum.

The result of fifteen years of intensive research

This new-day refrigerator embodies the best thought of the leading electrical research organization of the world.

It has reduced electric refrigeration to a point of *simplicity* which makes it almost as easy to operate as an electric fan—and almost as portable. You may place it anywhere—move it anywhere. Just plug it into any electric outlet and it starts.

The General Electric Refrigerator —designed to accommodate this revolutionary icing unit—has distinct advantages. It can be installed anywhere. It maintains a most uniform temperature. It needs no attention. It is unusually quiet. It is always clean because the circulation of air through the coils drives dust away—preventing it from settling.

You will want to see this refrigerator. But, meanwhile, send for booklet No. 7-G which tells all about it, including the various sizes which are available.

Electric Refrigeration Department of General Electric Company
Hanna Building, Cleveland, Ohio

GENERAL ELECTRIC

In using advertisements see page 6   113

10.19 Advertisement for electric refrigerator, General Electric Company, Cleveland, Ohio, from *Good Housekeeping*.

cosmetic change. It also helped to create some semblance of a partnership between designer and engineer. Another example is Raymond Loewy's design for British manufacturer Sigmund Gestetner's duplicating machine of 1929. Gestetner came to Loewy in New York for assistance in improving the appearance of his duplicating machine. Loewy's new design provided a housing that concealed many of the machine's working parts. Whether by intention or happy accident, the new shell reduced cost by making the nickel-plating of exposed mechanical parts unnecessary and improved performance by reducing the amount of space between parts where dust tended to accumulate.

Walter Dorwin Teague (1883–1960) worked as an artist for an advertising agency in New York before designing products for industrial production. Many of his designs were informed by a desire for simplicity and unity

as well as a belief in the ability of design to improve the quality of life by promoting an awareness of taste and discrimination. He re-designed several cameras for the Kodak Corporation, including the entire line of Brownie models, introducing smooth plastic housing with vertical ribs to each model in the line, as well as the 35 millimeter Bantam Special or "bullet" model of 1936 (fig. 10.17). The Kodak Bantam enclosed the lens into a unified housing with rounded sides and thin, horizontal metal ribs. Teague explained that the ribs functioned to reduce the cracking of the black lacquer finish of the casing: thus ribbing was as much an element of design engineering as of modern styling, and the design process involved demonstrated Teague's desire for a balance between novelty and functional improvement.

In some designs small improvements were made annually after a major innovation was introduced. For instance, Loewy's 1935 Coldspot refrigerator for Sears Corporation (fig. 10.18), as well as an earlier 1933 refrigerator designed for General Electric by Henry Dreyfuss, both integrated the condenser element into the body of the design. This created a unified shell or housing, unlike earlier models in which the unit appeared on top of the refrigerator (fig. 10.19). As Jeffrey Meikle has explained, Loewy added refinements each year to the Sears Coldspot, virtually eliminating protruding elements and accentuating vertical elements through the introduction of ribs both above and below the large refrigerator door. Such changes conformed to advertising strategy and made each year's model "new." The Coldspot broke records for sales, even though the economy was steadily approaching pre-Depression manufacturing levels by 1937. The title of Loewy's autobiography, *Never Leave Well Enough Alone*, characterizes his approach to design change and his understanding of its relationship to marketing and advertising.

Another area of American interwar industrial design covers the broad topic of streamlining in the transportation industry. During the 1920s tests by engineers demonstrated that teardrop-shaped forms reduced wind resistance, enabling both faster speeds as well as improved fuel consumption for land-based transportation. Integrating the results of this research into production technology proved elusive but several prototypes were developed. Hungarian designer Paul Jaray built a teardrop-shaped automobile as early as 1922, and in Britain A. E. Palmer designed a car in 1930 with a rear-engine permitting lower

10.20 Airflow Imperial Coupe, manufactured by Chrysler Corporation, 1934. Photograph: *Automobile Quarterly* magazine.

10.21 Gordon Buehrig, Cord Model 810 Westchester Sedan, manufactured by Auburn Automobile Company, 1936. Auburn-Duesenberg Museum, Auburn, Indiana.

ground clearance that also incorporated the new streamlined form. While the teardrop may have promised efficiency for production automobiles on the basis of research, the American automobile industry was hesitant to adopt such a radical retooling of its factory equipment. Norman Bel Geddes's prototype for a streamlined automobile (1932) was never put into production, and a later streamlined three-wheel model based upon the teardrop shape and known as the Dymaxion was only produced as a prototype by inventor Buckminster Fuller. The Dymaxion achieved notoriety in the media and at the Century of Progress World's Fair in Chicago in 1933, but was never mass-produced.

Geddes did serve as a consultant to the Chrysler Corporation for the 1934 Airflow, which adapted a more unified approach to the construction of the grill, hood, and windshield to traditional front-engine production technol-ogy with flat sides (fig. 10.20). The advertising campaign for the Chrysler Airflow generated excitement and numerous orders, but negative publicity about flaws in the first units to reach the market doomed the car, and in any case the changes it introduced had little to do either with fuel efficiency or speed. The Cord 810 was another example of the adaptation of streamlining to automobile design in terms of styling rather than performance (fig. 10.21). Designed by Gordon Buehrig in 1936, the Cord was a high-end luxury vehicle that featured a wrap-around grill with horizontal chrome ribbing, headlights that were hidden into the wheel covers, and a body whose front and sides were constructed to look as if they were molded into a single unit.

Outside the United States less superficial approaches to streamlining were adopted. In Germany, for instance, an inexpensive "peoples' car" or Volkswagen was manufactured beginning in 1937 with a middle-class market in

10.22 Ferdinand Porsche, Volkswagen, *c.* 1937.

10.23 Burlington Zephyr, Budd Manufacturing company, 1934. Museum of Science and Industry, Chicago.

mind (fig. 10.22). Designed by Ferdinand Porsche, the Volkswagen featured an air-cooled rear engine found in earlier streamlined prototypes and a simple, unified sloping body form. The design provided economical fuel consumption, adequate passenger and storage space, and was influenced by the results of wind-tunnel testing. The Volkswagen was not mass-produced until after World War II, but remained in production with few changes well into the 1970s, and enjoyed renewed popularity in the United States during the 1960s in part as a reaction against the marketing strategies of the large American automobile manufacturers). Like the "Peoples Radio", the Volkswagen demonstrates that the National Socialist Party adopted at least some of the technological and collective implications of modern industrial design emerging in Europe in the 1930s.

The American railway industry also adopted streamlining for locomotive design. Threatened with increasing competition from the automobile industry and the beginnings of commercial aviation, railways had seen a steady decline in passengers and profits since the 1920s. Early examples of streamlined passenger trains were shown in the second year of the 1933 Century of Progress World's Fair in Chicago. They employed lighter construction materials such as corrugated steel (rather than heavier steel of a uniform thickness) combined with diesel engines to improve fuel efficiency. Broad curved front ends and reduced space between cars emphasized speed, as seen in the Budd Manufacturing Company's Burlington Zephyr for the Burlington Railway Company in 1934 (fig. 10.23).

The combination of product improvement with commercial viability found in industrial design of the 1930s also characterizes the design practice of Henry Dreyfuss (1904–1972). Dreyfuss shared with other industrial designers of the period a belief that successful and more or less "final" solutions to design problems for many products were possible. He defined a product's "survival" form as being simple and having a satisfying esthetic that fulfilled its humanistic, production, and commercial requirements. This theory allowed for changes while retaining a memorable feature or form that created product identity. The Type 300 combined handset for the Bell Telephone Corporation, designed in 1937, is one of Dreyfuss's best-known projects. The combined handset had replaced earlier upright models with separate speakers and microphones in the later 1920s. Not subject to market pressures and competition, the design could be developed

10.24 Henry Dreyfuss, "Type 300",
handset, Bell Telephone Corporation,
1937. Photograph: Bell Laboratories.

on the basis of ease of use, stability, cleaning, and durability (fig. 10.24). When Dreyfuss learned that he would be unable consult with engineers when preparing a new telephone design for AT&T, he refused to participate in the competition. After the company rejected proposals from other designers, Dreyfuss was given the commission for the new phone. The Type 300 was more cohesive than its predecessors, and appears to adapt a number of basic features from a combined handset phone designed by Jean Heiberg for the L. M. Ericsson Company of Stockholm, Sweden in 1930. After World War II, Dreyfuss made several small improvements to his design, switching from metal to plastic, and placing the numbers outside rather than inside the dialing mechanism for legibility. Perhaps the most important improvement to the postwar phone was the design of the receiver, whose lightness and flattened form made it possible for the user to cradle it between ear and shoulder, freeing the hands to perform other tasks while talking on the phone.

More traditionally craft-based industries, such as furniture and ceramics, also hired contract or in-house designers to develop new products for industrial manufacture during the 1930s based upon smooth forms and restrained decoration. The career of Gilbert Rohde (1894–1944) offers an early example of industrial design in the American furniture industry. Rohde designed modern displays and furnished rooms for the 1933 World's Fair in Chicago, but is perhaps best-known as the design consultant for the Herman Miller Furniture Company of Zeeland, Michigan from 1932 until his death in 1944. Miller furniture sold primarily through department stores such as Macy's in New York and John Wanamaker in

Early catalog featured modular desk system.

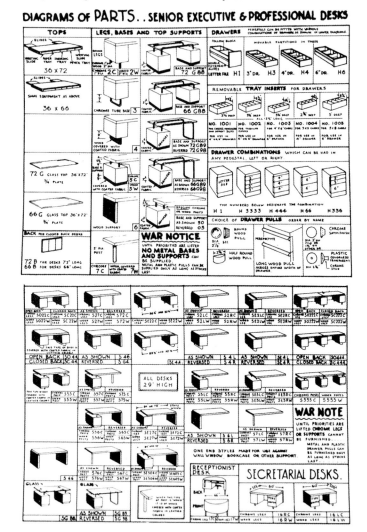

10.25 Diagram for modular desk units based upon designs of Gilbert Rohde, Herman Miller Corporation, Zeeland, Michigan, c. 1935.

10.26 Frederick Hurten Rhead, *Fiestaware* earthenware, variable dimensions, Laughlin China Company (West Virginia), 1936. The Globus Collection.

Philadelphia, and on a contract basis to architects in the design of interiors for office and other public buildings. During the years he spent as consultant to Miller, Rohde developed a series of furniture designs using more industrial methods of production based upon sectional or modular rectangular units for seating, storage, and shelving and a restrained use of decoration (fig. 10.25), broadly influenced by the social and economic ideologies of Constructivism and the Dessau Bauhaus. D. J. DePree, the President of Herman Miller who hired Rohde, responded to the notion of a relationship between modern design and the promotion of ethical and egalitarian values of economy and efficiency, especially relevant as a response to the social unrest and the hardship of the Depression.

One popular domestic application for European-influenced practicality was in production ceramics, seen in the line of table service known as Fiestaware, designed in 1936 by British-born ceramicist Frederick Hurten Rhead (1880–1942) for the Laughlin China Company in West Virginia, where he worked as artistic director during that time. Fiestaware (fig. 10.26) eschewed traditional connections with handicraft through the elimination of painted or printed patterns, sculptural contours, and relief decoration in favor of plain circular shapes with slightly raised concentric ribbing. Fiestaware's uniformity invoked the standardization of industrial manufacturing, but such anonymity was offset by a wide variety of brightly-colored and highly durable glazes developed by Rhead.

Rhead's designs retained some traditional elements such as the handles or feet for serving dishes, but also on occasion introduced novel designs, as with the "cutaway" pitcher the handle of which is unified into its circular shape. Such non-traditional approaches to ceramic design for utilitarian dinnerware also emerge in the work of American Russel Wright (1904–1976), whose career as an industrial designer included but was not limited to ceramics (J. J. DePree considered him as a designer for Herman Miller Furniture Company in 1944, following the death of Gilbert Rohde). Wright's American Modern dinnerware was designed in 1937 but not manufactured until 1939 by

10.27 Russel Wright, *American Modern* dinnerware, variable dimensions, 1937. Steubenvile Pottery (Ohio), manufacture beginning in 1939. Collection of John C. Waddell. Metropolitan Museum of Art, New York

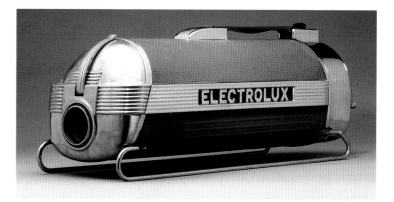

10.29 Lurelle Guild, Electrolux model 30 vacuum cleaner, chrome-plated steel, vinyl, rubber, 8 ½ x 23 x 7 ¼ in (21.6 x 58.4 x 19.7 cm), 1937. Electrolux Corporation, Dover, Delaware. Collection of John Waddell. Metropolitan Museum of Art, New York.

10.28 Russel Wright, spherical vase, spun aluminum, 5 x 6 ⅞ in (12.7 x 17.5 cm), 1932. Private collection.

the Steubenville (Ohio) Pottery Company (fig. 10.27). It featured asymmetric, organic shapes for pitchers and dishes at a time when such ovoid forms were also being introduced for the manufacture of metals and plastics used in the production of automobiles and in appliance housings. The commercial success of American Modern demonstrated the impact that "modern" designs could make upon sales, as well as the growing role of so-called "consultant" or contract designers.

Wright also was a pioneer in exploring new uses for aluminum, including modern designs for traditional household products. His pitcher of 1932 (fig. 10.28) uses the method of "spun" aluminum to create a smooth and swelling tube-like cylindrical form with no decoration. Another product using the strong and lightweight aluminum in connection with modern forms is the Electolux Model 30 vacuum cleaner designed by Lurelle Guild (1898–1985) beginning in 1930 (fig. 10.29). Guild, like a number of other industrial designers, worked first as an illustrator, and his interior designs were featured in the magazine *House and Garden*. The vacuum cleaner moves along the carpet on chrome-plated steel skids, presumably the motivation for the form and molded ribbing of its front end, strikingly similar to streamlined locomotives. Electrolux vacuum cleaners were manufactured in the United States in Dover, Delaware, though the company's origins were in Sweden before World War I.

10.30 Aerial view of 1939 New York World's Fair, 1939–1940.

The 1939 New York World's Fair

The 1939 New York World's Fair centered upon the theme of "Building the World of Tomorrow." Walter Dorwin Teague was on the planning board for the fair, and Norman Bel Geddes was hired by the General Motors Corporation to design the company's popular *Futurama* exhibit. For both of these men, the World's Fair provided an opportunity to extend the range of their industrial design practice beyond contracts for products and appliances and to realize, if only ephemerally and sometimes in miniature, a unified conception for a future in which design contributed directly to the overall quality of life.

The vision was embodied in the centralized design of the fair, where several multicolored avenues converged in a circular space that contained the fair's symbolic Trylon and Perisphere. Both the avenues to one side of the circle and the area to the other side were organized thematically for various activities such as transportation, international exhibits, and amusement and entertainment. Democracity, a miniature world of tomorrow, was contained within the large globe-shaped Perisphere, and connected with the other symbol, the tall pyramidal Trylon by a walkway (fig. 10.30). Democracity was characterized by a single "Streamlined" style of architecture with round-edged buildings. Like the fairgrounds themselves, Democracity was separated by function into "zones" for business in which tall towers dominated, for industry, and for living where communities of houses permitted a closer relationship to the natural environment. In Geddes's Futurama exhibit traffic flow in the modern metropolis (*c*.1960) was managed by multilane highways and banked exit ramps, as well as by a radio-controlled system that monitored speed and distance between vehicles; the exhibit stressed the importance of highways, and paralleled the lobbying efforts of automobile and tire manufacturers and oil companies to expand the nation's road system and further stimulate the purchase of new cars—conspicuously absent were mass-transit systems (other than buses) and pedestrian traffic in the city was kept separate from vehicular traffic by elevated platforms. Like the utopian vision of Le Corbusier's Voisin plan from the mid-1920s, a single style

10.32 Morris Lapidus, storefront for Hoffritz Cutlery store, New York, 1939.

10.31 Norman Bel Geddes, *City of 1960, Futurama* exhibit, General Motors Pavilion, New York's World's Fair, 1939–40. Theatre Arts Collection, University of Texas, Austin.

prevailed in Democracity as well as in GM's Futurama that defined collective rather than heterogeneous needs, taking advantage of the efficiency and logic of modern technology and materials to erase differences, contradictions, conflicts, and irritants (fig. 10.31).

Corporate exhibitions commodified the vision of the planners through the display and demonstration of products and appliances, translating the clean, optimistic vision of Democracity and the Futurama into a present rather than distant reality, often with an emphasis upon the relationship of technology to increased leisure time. Exhibits documented the steady and sure progress of "science," the attainment of frictionless speed in the transportation industry, for instance, and tested how machines reduced toil and increased comfort and the expansion of free time. In one exhibit for the Westinghouse Corporation, designed by Gilbert Rohde (see page 218), "Mrs. Drudge" washed dishes by hand while her counterpart, "Mrs. Modern," loaded an automatic dishwashing machine. Still in the wake of the Depression, aware of the hardship caused by economic dislocation, and fearful of mounting tension and conflict in Europe (already present in the exclusion of Nazi Germany from participation and the inability of a number of European nations to participate), the products and demonstrations of the fair exhibits provided some kind of tangible "proof" of improvement and sufficient cause for optimism, in addition to the fantastic and utopian visions of science fiction.

Modern critics of the 1939 New York World's Fair have commented that its planners conditioned the experience of visitors, aiming through dramatic devices such as lighting and perspective to elicit a sequence of particular responses leading to a climax that gave substance to tomorrow's world today. Such devices were the stock and trade of architects and interior designers such as Morris Lapidus (1902–2001) who was a successful storefront designer during the interwar period. Lapidus employed techniques such as mirrors to create the effect of spaciousness and curving windows leading window-shoppers toward the entrance. He installed bright signs and bright lighting to create contrast or what he called a "moth" principle, intended to induce potential customers to enter a place of business. Such devices may be seen, for instance, in Lapidus's 1939 storefront for Hoffritz for Cutlery in Manhattan (fig. 10.32). The mingling of utopian ideology and consumer engineering was characteristic of the 1939 World's Fair, representing the strategies of advertising agencies and the balancing of competing, even contradictory priorities that characterized the profession of industrial design in American life during the interwar period.

Planners and promoters expressed optimism that the provocative exhibits of the World of Tomorrow would last five years, but even with publicity in newsreels and other media, the exhibits closed before the end of 1940. Like much popular entertainment, the 1939 World's Fair caused great excitement initially but failed to sustain interest beyond the fleeting impact of glitter and a sense of escape from harsher realities. While some of the organizers felt the fair offered solutions and even proof of reduced hardship, alienation, and conflict, its longevity depended upon ticket sales from a public who saw the fair as a short-lived collection of novelties with little meaning beyond the immediacy and excitement of their initial impact. As an experience based upon techniques derived from the advertising industry, it was, in a sense, a victim of the planned obsolescence that helped to shape it—without continued novelty and progressive change, the World of Tomorrow too quickly became yesterday's news. Interestingly, the idea of a more limited but nonetheless "progressive" fair resurfaced during the 1950s with the traveling "Motorama" showcases sponsored by General Motors.

The United States and International Modernism

During the 1930s the Museum of Modern Art in New York (founded in 1929) helped to define and to embrace a view of industrial design that incorporated elements of Constructivism, the Dessau Bauhaus and the theories of Le Corbusier. MoMA had little interest in the commercial realities and compromises at work in the emerging profession of industrial design in the United States. Instead, its approach to modern design leaned toward a more restrained functional architecture (referred to as the International Style and featured in a well-publicized exhibition in 1932), rejecting decoration and the widespread adoption of streamlining and obsolescence. In 1934 MoMA housed an exhibition entitled *Machine Art*, curated by architect Philip Johnson. This exhibition acknowledged the contributions of the Dessau Bauhaus and promoted a more collective, anonymous approach to design for the modern world along the lines suggested by architects like Le Corbusier. The exhibition organizers argued for a universal machine esthetic related to geometry, use, new materials, industrial rather than "craft" production, and the rejection of ornament. In their view, ornament was unnecessary to the functional requirements of the new architecture; not being necessary, decoration was extravagant, even irresponsible in the context of widespread unemployment and hardship during the Depression.

Machine Art exhibited a wide range of domestic, industrial, and even laboratory equipment to demonstrate, along Corbusian lines, the inevitability and austere beauty of particular modern forms, including machine parts like ball-bearings, tools and medical instruments, kitchen utensils, and tubular steel furniture. In promoting the relationship between geometric purity and the methods of industrial production, the *Machine Art* exhibition presented a reductive and somewhat limited interpretation of modern design and the activities of the "artist-engineer." It only partially addressed the problem of declining industrial production and consumption of domestic goods and furnishings beyond the narrow range of examples included by the organizers. Only gradually did an expanded International Style of industrial design, known generally as "good design," gain broader acceptance after the end of World War II, incorporating standards reminiscent of reform in their balance of individual expression, restraint, and practicality. The genesis of this approach to industrial design will be a focus of Part IV.

Advertising, Art, and the Selling of Modern Design in the United States

The history of modern design in the United States in the interwar period cannot be written without discussing the importance of advertising in the formation of a "culture of consumption." The overwhelming achievements of materials technology and mechanized mass production could not be sustained without exciting desire and channeling it through the sale of products. Before the advent of television, the tools of advertising included illustration,

10.33 Advertisement for Dodge Brothers "Senior Line", *Vogue*, 1923.

10.34 Earl Horter, advertisement for Steinway piano with reproduction of *Rhapsody in Blue*, watercolor and graphite on board, 21 ⁷/₁₆ x 27 in (54.5 x 68.6 cm). Private Collection, 1927.

photography, layout, and typography for effective, provocative visual communication. These elements and their context in the interwar period in the United States are examined below.

Museum initiatives supporting modern decorative arts and a closer connection between fine and applied art dovetailed with the strategies of advertising agencies to build and strengthen the link between products and the hedonistic pursuits of confident and energetic participants in the modern scene. In the 1920s, advertisements were decidedly upscale, promising charisma and success in exchange for the purchase of a wide variety of products ranging from toothpaste to toasters. An example is a 1923 advertisement from *Vogue* for a Dodge Brothers automobile (fig. 10.33), whose copy mentions the speed of the vehicle as well as the enthusiastic response of hunters, golfers, and polo players for the car: "Wielders of the polo mallet, hunters of the moose, hard hitters from the tee— are enthusiastic about this car. For them its virility and boundless eagerness to go have irresistible appeal."

Advertisers helped to define an emerging "good life," grounded in leisure and experienced by an elite group of people engaged in an active and social life with whom an increasingly diverse audience could identify. The triumphs and conflicts of this group formed the subjects of popular fiction in mass circulation magazines such as *True Story* and *Ladies Home Journal*, and also included color illustrations to augment the frequently serialized stories. Companies and the advertising agencies they hired to promote their products turned to artists–illustrators to provide suitable images for products in magazines and even on large billboards that lined the boulevards and highways of a more mobile society. Fueled by the success of persuasive posters in public relations campaigns to enlist recruits and sell war bonds after the United States' entry into World War I, advertising agencies saw illustration as a vehicle to shape the consumer values shared by an expanding and increasingly heterogeneous mass market.

Some companies promoted the use of art in advertising, part of an initiative to familiarize a broader audience with modern art and link companies with public improvement and education. These ads had little to do with products but rather with establishing a paternalistic role for companies in support of values of quality, integrity, and culture. An example is an advertisement from 1927 by Philadelphia artist and illustrator Earl Horter, whose Futurist-inspired painting entitled *Rhapsody in Blue* was reproduced in an advertisement for the renowned piano manufacturer Steinway (fig. 10.34). Advertising executive Elmo Calkins (1868–1968) supported such an approach to advertising, and employed artists such as Horter to demonstrate that an advertising "art" was in the public interest and enhanced the reputation of business.

Many advertising executives believed, however, that the purpose of advertisements was to sell products, and that references to individual artists or to works of art focused attention upon the ad as an "object" rather than as the vehicle for promoting a product. Art directors and consultants from the advertising industry recognized the importance of images in selling products, but also felt it was necessary, more often than not, to present familiar and recognizable images that could be easily grasped by the public rather than abstract ones. Companies turned to illustrators to accomplish this task, creating the idealized types with whom buyers readily identified and connected with products. The blurring between illustration and advertising was felt as a constraint by some artists. On one hand it provided a steady and lucrative market for their work, while on the other it could lead to stale repetition of formulaic representations at the expense of the individual expression that often had formed the basis of their education and training at universities and academies. In general the advertising profession equated effective techniques of persuasion with naturalism rather than with more modern abstract styles (see, for instance, figs . 8.20 and 8.21. page 154).

In the early part of the century Charles Dana Gibson's (1867–1954) "Gibson Girl" provided an ideal for the modern active woman in numerous magazine covers. As early as 1907, Joseph Leyendecker (1874–1951) created the "Arrow Collar Man" in a series of popular ads that drastically reduced the amount of text often used for magazine ads (fig. 10.35). Leyendecker's chiseled, confident ideal may have been removed from the lives of white-collar working men, but any threat to the reader's self-esteem created by the image offered at the same time its solution.

10.35 Joseph Leyendecker, 'Arrow Shirt' advertisement, 1920s.

Buying an Arrow shirt collar reduced the fear of not fitting into the uncertainties presented to the ordinary man by a modern urban and industrial culture experienced directly as well as indirectly through an emerging mass media of magazines increasingly dominated by advertising. Another popular advertising illustration was McClelland Barclay's "Fisher Body Girl," appearing in advertisements for this manufacturer of automobile chasis to General Motors brands such as Cadillac, Buick, Oldsmobile, and Pontiac (fig. 10.36). This slender and well-dressed figure was usually found in the company of men in connection with cars, as well as on the covers of the *Saturday Evening Post* engaged in a variety of leisure pastimes.

In the mid-1930s photography began to compete and gradually to eclipse illustration for advertising and for popular fiction. Illustration persisted, however, for magazine and book covers. Although advertisements formed part of

10.36 McClelland Barclay, "Fisher Body" advertisement, *American Magazine*, 1928.

10.37 Norman Rockwell, cover, *Saturday Evening Post*, 1933.

his extensive oeuvre, Norman Rockwell (1894–1978) enjoyed a long relationship with the *Saturday Evening Post*. Rockwell's color illustrations for the *Post* lent themselves to narrative interpretation. They presented a variety of familiar themes drawn from common middle-class experience, frequently related to seasonal activities and holidays. Rockwell was familiar with the conventions of narrative art in the western tradition, relying upon pyramidal composition to provide focus or climax as well as to guide the viewer. Frequently his covers and posters seem to suggest continuity with the sense of community and comfort provided by family and neighborhood, an antidote to the impersonal modernity of factory and city. The use of reassuring common experiences and techniques of naturalistic illustration to communicate those values were the hallmarks of Rockwell's cover images. A *Post* cover from November, 1933 (fig. 10.37) illustrates a young mother spanking her child on a chair which is a simple design based upon a Neoclassical model, and less frequent in Rockwell's

illustrations than carved and more heavily upholstered furniture inspired by earlier eighteenth-century examples. Notwithstanding the political incorrectness of suggesting any form of physical abuse or threat in our own day, the story is clearly and simply told. The child has used a hammer to destroy a piece of fine decorative china, and the mother has responded with a traditional form of punishment. Her response, however, is not the result of an emotional outburst or of continuity with standard and inherited child-rearing practice. While the mother raises her hand, she holds a psychology book that has guided her actions. In fact, the "read" response is precisely the same as the inherited one, and modern psychology has recommended a solution with which we are already familiar anyway. The illustration makes the reader feel more comfortable with some of the discomforting information that threatens our confidence in dealing with everyday existence.

As Michele Bogart has suggested, Rockwell may have been ambivalent about his own contributions despite the

10.38 Norman Rockwell, *Freedom from Want*, oil painting, 1943. The Norman Rockwell Museum at Stockbridge, Massachusetts.

success and celebrity he attained and his own attempts to experiment with more expressionistic approaches to painting were rejected by his editors at the *Post*. It may also be helpful to view his illustrations in the context of mass images that seek at once to reflect as well as to shape common experience in periods of great social and political change. Rockwell's poster illustrating a festive family meal is one of four from a series entitled *The Four Freedoms*, in this case *Freedom from Want* (fig. 10.38). The composition suggests references to countless images of the *Last Supper* that lend formality, even solemnity to the otherwise ordinary meal. Rockwell executed the series in

1942, in the midst of World War II, amid government-imposed rationing and shortages in support of the war effort. Like advertising illustrations connecting products with the good life, Rockwell's images steered away from troubling associations, and like advertising his illustrations indulge in escapism and fantasy as elements in the definition of mass culture. Minorities, for instance, find little place within Rockwell's oeuvre, and popular appeal seemed to preclude representing blacks or commenting on contemporary social problems.

Other examples of contemporary public art seemed to address more directly the hardship of many Americans during the Depression. The murals painted for the federally-sponsored Work Progress Administration (WPA) presented artists with an opportunity both to work, and to work in a traditionally accessible naturalistic style. Thomas Hart Benton (1889–1975), for instance, was responsible for several murals in post offices and other public buildings during the 1930s. Benton used swelling shapes and sweeping curvilinear lines to invest his figures with energy and movement, often lending an heroic character to the depiction of ordinary everyday activities of traditional work and recreation during a time of high unemployment in the hope of building national unity and optimism (fig. 10.39). Beyond Rockwell's appealing illustration and Benton's message of solidarity stood other artists whose realism moved in a wider variety of directions. The less narrative and more introspective realism of

10.39 Thomas Hart Benton, *Arts of the West*, tempera, 7 ft 10 in x 13 ft 5 in (239 x 409 cm). The New Britain Museum of American Art, New Britain, Connecticut.

artists like Ben Shahn (1898–1969) and Edward Hopper (1882–1967) reveal an experience of alienation and loneliness in the modern world. Their work represents viewpoints on contemporary private life and is occasionally critical of both business and government. Only rarely, however, did their paintings reach the mass audience that read or subscribed to the *Saturday Evening Post* during the interwar period. After the war, progressive art editors such as William Golden and Cipe Pineles invited Shahn and other contemporary American artists to contribute illustrations for stories in journals such as *Seventeen* and in print advertisements for CBS radio and television.

Photography and Graphic Design

While illustration continued to find a place on the covers of weeklies such as the *Saturday Evening Post*, the launching of *Life* magazine in 1936 and *Time* in 1937 provides evidence of a gradual shift toward photography as the most compelling medium disseminating news, entertainment, and advertising. The term "photojournalism" refers to this shift in the print media. Even earlier in the 1930s a number of art directors turned increasingly to photographic reproduction for its sense of objective "truth," immediacy, and visual impact. Advertisers were attracted to the medium for the same reasons, as well as by the ability of commercial photographers to both simulate as well as to manipulate narrative situations in order to make products irresistible. Instead of relying upon copy to sell products or report events, art directors and the advertising industry relied upon photographs to reach an expanding readership.

The painter and commercial photographer Charles Sheeler (1883–1965) was commissioned to produce a series of photographs of the Ford Motors River Rouge facility that coincided with the introduction of the Model A (see page 211), intended to communicate the inspiring grandeur and efficiency of the machine-dominated environment (fig. 10.40). Historians have noted that in these photographs, as well as in a series of paintings by Charles Sheeler of the Rouge plant reproduced in magazines such as *Fortune*, the human presence is often entirely absent or overwhelmed by the power of machinery. This in turn reflects the view that the progress guaranteed by mechanization, for better or worse, diminishes the importance of the individual worker, a telling indication of a conflicting relationship between man and machine as well as between labor and management in the factory system. Indeed the success of Ford's moving assembly line was due to the replacement of skilled by *un*skilled labor, with increasing emphasis upon the performance of single tasks in required sequences measured against the clock and under the watchful eye of factory foremen. But while the focus of Sheeler's Rouge photographs from the later 1920s was upon the power and productivity of machines, the strategies of large manufacturing corporations, including Ford, were moving increasingly toward consumption and the need to stimulate buying through promotion and advertising. As noted above, the alienating effects of the assembly line and the general mechanization of the workplace were balanced by the consumption in which workers now participated. The power of Sheeler's River Rouge photographs lies in the combination of their documentary authority with their subtle role in communicating the interests of large corporations.

In addition to product advertisements (which often accounted for fifty percent of their content), mass-circulation magazines also carried regular features on contemporary fashion, literature, travel, and entertainment. Photography played a key role in the presentation of such material, in particular the studio portraits by Edward Steichen, Charles Sheeler, and other contemporary photographers. Through photography the pages of *Vogue, Vanity Fair, Fortune, Harper's Bazaar*, and other monthly periodicals increasingly blurred the lines between advertising and art. With the hiring of European-trained artists to oversee art direction, monthly magazines began to acquire a more self-consciously modern, integrated presentation of photography, text, and titles in the later 1920s. At *Vogue* and *Vanity Fair*, art director Dr. Mehemed Fehmy Agha (1896–1978) adapted some of the distinctive asymmetrical experiments of the "New Typography" to cover design and page layout. Agha was born in the Ukraine of Turkish parents and was working as art director for German *Vogue* when he was asked by *Vogue's* publisher, Condé Nast, to be the magazine's American art director in 1929. Nast hoped that Agha would bring a "new look" to American *Vogue*, a feeling for modernity seen at the 1925 *Exposition des Arts Décoratifs et Industriels Modernes* in Paris

10.40 Charles Sheeler, *Stamping Press*, photograph, Ford Plant at River Rouge, Michigan, 1927. Library of Congress.

but generally absent in the pages of American mass-circulation magazines. Agha's art direction reveals a concern with the overall expressive arrangement of every element, often across a two-page spread, utilizing contrasts of shape and tone to create striking rhythms and dramatic effects. The strong contrast and dramatic lighting employed by well-known photographers such as Edward Steichen were integral features of art direction in the pages of *Vogue* and *Vanity Fair*. The new look of such layouts can be seen in a two-page spread from a 1936 issue of *Vogue*, featuring Steichen photographs of the latest fashions for that spring season (fig. 10.41). *Vogue's* content throughout this period focused upon fashion and leisure activities of international

celebrities including royalty, film stars, writers, musicians, and artists. Technically and creatively demanding as an art director, Agha brought to this lifestyle the sensation of change, excitement, and the drama of the unexpected in its visual presentation. Agha's association for Nast publications lasted until 1943. In the 1930s, *Vogue* competitor *Harper's Bazaar* hired Alexey Brodovitch (1898–1971) as art director. Brodovitch worked as a stage designer at the Ballet Russe in Paris prior to coming to the United States, and continued to oversee art direction at *Harper's Bazaar* well into the 1950s.

In his covers for *Vanity Fair*, Agha used simplified abstract forms together with text in subtle ways to convey meaning for content that included contemporary political and social issues. *Vanity Fair* introduced color photography and illustration in the early 1930s. An example is a 1933 cover designed by Cipe Pineles, using the technique of collage to portray two figures against a dark background that includes a mass of red ink (fig. 10.42). The figures, one bloated and smoking a cigar, the other thin and rumpled, are cut from newsprint from the stock market pages of the business section. The tall hat and goatee of the thin figure strongly resembles Uncle Sam, whose profile appears frequently on the covers of *Vanity Fair* throughout this period. Pineles's focus upon compositional unity

10.42 M. F. Agha, cover for *Vogue*, Cipe Pineles, artist, 1933.

among the elements of page design possessed both clarity and conciseness, and was initially compelling as well as sufficiently subtle to sustain visual and symbolic meaning.

The methods of expressively orchestrating text and image as abstract elements on a magazine page or cover describes the activity of graphic design as practiced by Agha or contemporary Russian art director Alexei Brodovitch at *Harper's Bazaar* and increasingly acknowledged in the printing industry. Using photography and adapting the experimental strategies of the "New Typography," interwar graphic designers set high technical and esthetic standards for their publications. Characteristics such as the reinforcement of diagonal movement across the page, off-center layout, asymmetrical composition, unframed photographs that "bleed" to the edges of the page or blend completely with the white paper, and the juxtaposition of images helped to create visual interest in layouts and advertisements throughout the 1930s. Unlike van Doesburg, graphic designers such as Agha and Brodovitch were neither publishers nor political activists. Their approach to visual communication was essentially esthetic, and involved a recognition that attracting readers' attention demanded creative originality rather than cliché. They applied their awareness of modern art and the "New Typography" to serve the needs of the publishers who employed them, engaging the reader in a new awareness, appreciation, and identification with modern life that focused increasingly upon consumption as a vehicle for self-realization.

American artist Lester Beall (1903–69) also employed characteristics of the "New Typography" and modern abstract art in a series of government-sponsored public service posters promoting the use of electricity through the Rural Electrification Administration in the 1930s. Beall's approach is seen in a poster illustrating a light bulb connected to a home by a series of white lines against a background divided into bands of highly saturated red and blue colors (fig. 10.43). The sense of contrast is strong and the imagery is striking for its simple and direct communication. Using flat shapes and schematic drawing to convey a message with minimal use of text, Beall's work anticipates the simplified elements of information graphics and corporate identity that took shape during and after World War II.

Through illustration, photography, and graphic design, mass magazines and their advertising created a

10.43 Lester Beall, "Light/Rural Electrification" administration, poster, silkscreen, 40 x 30 in (101.6 x 76 cm), 1937. Metropolitan Museum of Art, New York.

visual culture for the modern age in the United States. Advertising was a necessary corollary to sustaining the growth of an industrially-based capitalist economy through focusing upon consumption. The advertising profession gained recognition and respectability through its connection with elevating public taste through art and reinforcing shared beliefs and values, and linking these public-minded interests to products. Sales, whether of magazine subscriptions or of the products advertised on their pages, came to depend upon seductive images and asymmetrical layouts to attract attention and create distinction. In this way the "New Typography" found an outlet in the competitive commercial context of interwar America, in which the "new" and the "fashionable" were interchangeable, and where consumption was linked to status and self-improvement. Whether in illustrations or photographs, representations played a significant role in advertising and graphic design. As explained by Roland Marchand,

> Pictures surpassed copy not only in their ability to intensify emotion but also in their capacity to say several things at the same time. Visual imagery effectively reached the less literate portions of the population. It also conveyed dense messages. By setting up harmonics of atmosphere and imagery that resonated at a variety of levels, visual images also obscured problems of internal contradictions or irrational association. Such harmonics were exactly what gave style products their added value beyond pragmatic utility. Evocative pictures upped the consumption ante by inducing the customer to obtain the fullest satisfaction by "buying the ad" along with the product.

Industrial Design and Austerity

Alvar Aalto (see page 202) designed the Finnish Pavilion for the 1939 New York World's Fair, and in that same year the Museum of Modern Art sponsored an exhibition of Scandinavian design including a selection of Aalto's own furniture. MoMA reacted in the 1930s against the commercial motivations that influenced American industrial design, and advocated standards based upon "suitability to purpose, material, and process of manufacture." Such standards were implied in the 1934 *Machine Art* exhibition (see page 223) and were embodied in the household products chosen for a series of traveling exhibits entitled *Useful Objects under Ten Dollars*.

In 1940 MoMA sponsored a competition entitled *Organic Design in Home Furnishings*. By "organic" the exhibition's curator, Eliot F. Noyes (1910–1977), an architect who later was responsible for formulating a design policy for the IBM corporation (see Part IV), meant molded forms that were manufactured using industrial processes and materials such as laminated woods. Flexibility was also a consideration, and demanded "units" or "modules" for furniture and storage pieces that might be easily constructed, expanded, and configured in a variety of ways. Department stores agreed to display the winning designs and expressed a commitment to find manufacturers to produce and market them.

One of the winning designs from the competition was a molded plywood chair upholstered in foam rubber covered with fabric, entered by Eero Saarinen (1910–1961) and Charles Eames (1907–1978), both of whom trained as architects (fig. 10.44). Saarinen was the son of the Finnish architect and president of the Cranbrook Academy of Art, Gottlieb Eliel Saarinen, and his wife, Loja (see page 206), and Eames had remained at Cranbrook following a fellowship there as instructor and head of a new department in industrial design. The originality of the Saarinen/Eames collaboration lay in the more contoured three-dimensional molding of the plywood, easily seen in comparison with the plywood seat and back of Aalto's armchair for the Paimio Tuberculosis Sanitarium from 1931 (see fig. 9.57, page 202). In other respects the industrial materials and processes as applied to furniture and an overall impression of lightness (the wooden legs were originally planned to be made from a thinner aluminum) recall basic aspects of Scandinavian modern design of the 1930s (see pages 201–4).

Eames also designed unit furniture for the Red Lion Company in the early 1940s, consisting of mahogany-veneered cabinets with sliding doors and tables utilizing

10.44 Eero Saarinen and Charles Eames, armchair, molded plywood and foam upholstery with fabric, 1940. MOMA Organic Design for Home Furnishings Exhibition, New York.

10.45 Eero Saarinen and Charles Eames, storage cabinets, Honduras mahogany veneer, 18 or 36 in (45.7 or 91.4 cm), 22 x 18 in (56 x 45.7 cm), Red Lion Furniture Company, Reading, Pennsylvania 1942.

10.46 Jens Risom, chair, birch and plastic webbing, 30 $\frac{5}{16}$ x 17 $\frac{1}{2}$ x 20 $\frac{1}{4}$ in (77 x 44.5 x 51.4 cm), manufactured Hans G. Knoll Furniture, 1942. Musée des Arts Décoratifs de Montreal.

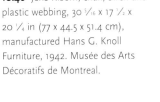

standardized dimensions and equipped with simple pullers and handles (fig. 10.45). A series of tables with dowel-like legs were also designed to support these units in a variety of combinations or to serve as benches.

Organic Design in Home Furnishings hoped to demonstrate the ability of design to meet the practical needs of modern living using technology and modern methods of manufacture and to replace the "weary" forms, materials, and methods of production in much traditional furniture. After the bombing of Pearl Harbor by the Japanese, and United States entry into World War II in December 1941, the emphasis upon usefulness was further seen as a proper response to shortages, restrictions, and the retooling of industries to meet the demand for goods and materials to outfit and support the war effort. In this climate the German émigré Hans Knoll (1914–1955) manufactured and marketed the furniture of Danish-born and Scandinavian-trained designer Jens Risom (b.1916) for the company he had founded (Knoll Associates) in 1938. Risom's 1942 wood chair with cloth webbing (fig. 10.46) was originally manufactured using the synthetic material nylon purchased from US Army surplus and was constructed from a small number of standardized and undecorated parts.

In Europe, particularly in Britain, civilian austerity within the context of patriotism in the war with Germany also provided conditions in which a utilitarian version of modern design found acceptance with the aid of government sponsorship. British designer Gordon Russell (1892–1980) was responsible for the design of "utility" furniture under the auspices of the British Board of Trade in the early 1940s. Designs imbodied standards to insure economy in the use of government-controlled raw materials such as timber and shortages in skilled labor as well.

10.47 Advisory Committee on Utility Furniture, mahogany table, 30 in (76.2 cm) high, *c.* 1945, England. Geffrye Museum, London.

10.49 Hans Coray, Landi chair, molded, heat-treated, and stained aluminum, 1945, manufactured by Blattmann Metallwarenfabrik AG, Switzerland.

10.48 Ernest Race, BA3 chair, stove, enameled cast aluminum and cotton-velour upholstery, 28 ¾ x 17 ½ x 16 ¼ in (73 x 44.5 x 41.3 cm), manufactured by Race Furniture Ltd. England, 1945. Carnegie Museum of Art, Pittsburgh.

Utility dining room furniture (fig. 10.47) dates to 1945 and met the standards of economy and solid construction required of British manufacturers in the 1940s. Rather than experimenting with new materials or even industrial methods of production, this table uses traditional woods and construction. Modern furniture during this time was aimed to meet the needs of newlyweds setting up households and victims of bombing who had lost their possessions. The standards for the austere utilitarian furniture of the 1940s was motivated in part by the same paternalistic interest in influencing and elevating public taste as earlier standards of the nineteenth century, and also recalled strongly the honesty and socialist leanings seen in some manifestations of the Arts and Crafts Movement (see page 111–12). They were imposed, however, in the national interest of conserving resources, rather than through the advocacy of new materials and production technologies. More inventive is the "BA" aluminum chair designed by Ernst Race in 1945 amid government control of supplies of wood (fig. 10.48). Light in appearance, the aluminum legs required little bracing and were produced using methods of mold casting. Other aluminum furniture of the period includes the Landi chair (fig. 10.49), designed by Hans

Coray (1906–1991) for the Swiss National Exhibition held in 1939. The perforated one-piece molded shell again takes advantage of the lightness and strength of the material, as well as permitting drainage for the chair's intended outdoor use.

Graphic Design During World War II

While more conventionally representational posters using a naturalistic narrative style of illustration continued to be produced to support the war effort, a number of graphic designers began using the more direct and economical means of simplified text and visual image to serve a variety of public service purposes during World War II. French designer Jean Carlu (1900–1989) visited the United States in 1940 as an employee of the French Information Service and remained during the Nazi occupation of France. While in America he designed his "Production" poster for the Office of Emergency Management using a clever combination of typography and image for the lower case "o" that serves also as a hex nut, turned by a wrench tightly gripped by a powerful, gloved hand (fig. 10.50). Herbert Matter (1907–1984) was

a Swiss-born designer who emigrated to the United States. Matter designed posters for the Container Corporation of America, whose spare copy and juxtaposed photographs and diagrams emphasized the role played by cardboard packaging in conserving the use of metal as part of the war effort (fig. 10.51). Graphic designers during World War II not only created posters for recruitment, public service, and influencing public opinion, but also designed training manuals in which effective and efficient communication of information was seen as essential. German-born Will Burtin (1908–1972) organized the presentation of visual and textual information in the design of instructions for operating guns. His approach was neither as artist nor propagandist, but rather as analyst, devising the clearest method for combining words and images for the purposes of instruction. Burtin took in consideration eye

10.50 Jean Carlu, *America's Answer: Production*, lithograph, 29 ⅞ x 39 ⅝ in (76 x 100.6 cm), United States Government Printing Office, Washington, D. C., 1941. Museum of Modern Art, New York.

10.51 Herbert Matter, poster for Container Corporation of America, 1943. American Art Museum, Smithsonian Institution, Washington, D.C.

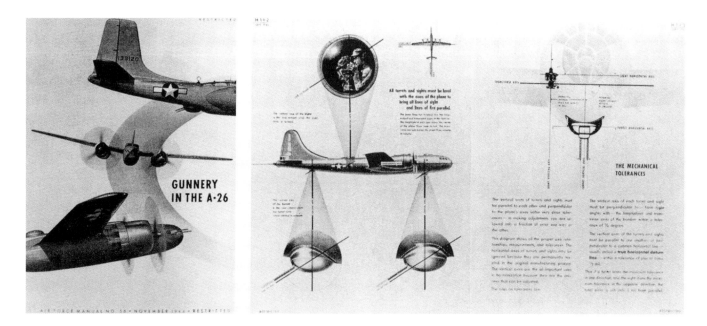

10.52 Will Burtin, training manual for A-26 Gunnery, United States Armed Forces, 1944.

movement, hierarchy, and flow of information across two-page spreads (fig. 10.52). The design solution flowed from the requirements of the brief, and while not inevitable as the outcome of those requirements, the task of the designer was certainly related to that of the engineer rather than the artist or advertiser. According to Richard Hollis, Burtin's training manual helped to reduce the training time for gunners from twelve and six weeks.

Conclusion

No single theme or even pair of interrelated concepts emerges from the material covered in the three chapters contained in Part III. While original and expressive approaches to craft production and decoration persisted during the period under consideration, it was the concept and practice of *industrial* design that took root and underwent considerable development in a variety of social, political, and economic conditions stemming in turn from the events and aftermath of World War I both in Europe and in the United States. Industrial design embraced mechanized mass production, new materials, and a more expansive understanding of the designer's role that included ease of construction, hygiene, and the use of standardized

and interchangeable parts. Under the broad banner of Constructivism, industrial design emerged as a theoretical attitude appropriate to a new, universal, egalitarian state in which artists directed their energies to meeting the perceived, minimum needs of a mass society. Alternatively, in the United States the industrial design profession was often seen and promoted as a commercial strategy to stimulate consumer interest in a wide range of products and furnishings through the integration of planned obsolescence.

In the formulation of their ideas and the products and prototypes that resulted from them, industrial designers struggled to reconcile the collective model of their new enterprise with the legacy of individuality, self-expression, and the craft process that they inherited from the earlier modernism of the pre-war era. Some designers welcomed and incorporated new principles of abstract and elementary geometric form that expressed a universal esthetic. Others embraced uniformity and the rejection of decoration as an inevitable expression of social equality in a new world order. Still others saw the new skills and machine-age vocabulary of form as enabling a new and satisfying versatility for the designer exercising creative ability in a wide variety of media and materials. In Scandinavia, industrial design within the craft-based traditions of furniture, glassware, and ceramics appeared to synthesize the democratic social ideology of the machine age with a more natural and organic esthetic derived from molded materials and the consideration of ergonomics. In the United States, the principles of mechanized mass production had achieved undreamed-of levels of productivity, but business leaders had to contend with the problems of sustaining industrial growth and addressing the specter of labor unrest as sales leveled amid market saturation in the later 1920s. The advertising profession offered capitalist enterprise a solution to the anxieties of over-production, and their focus upon consumer engineering helped to lay the groundwork for the profession of industrial design in the United States. No view of the period would be complete without recognizing the continued inventiveness of artists and artisans experimenting directly with materials and processes, expanding the range of their possible application with great freedom and boldness. Such experiments might lend themselves to mechanized mass production, but might just as easily involve considerable handwork and target a narrower market.

To a certain degree these varied activities on both sides of the Atlantic and on both sides of the political spectrum remain united in their relationship to differing cultural attitudes in the aftermath of World War I. On one hand conservatism in France following the war led to an interest in the return to traditional craft models of production and an emphasis upon reasserting the international reputation for luxury and individual artistic expression. Fears of social unrest amid the destruction of property and deprivations of the war sparked the polemic stance of Le Corbusier, who argued for the necessity of pre-fabricated building materials for housing and the mass-production of "anonymously" designed utilitarian household goods and furnishings. Such objects embodied permanent standards of beauty and were beyond the whims and indulgences of individual expression. In Germany collective approaches to design were tied to efforts to alleviate economic distress in the aftermath of defeat and hardship, leading to

experimentation with alternative solutions to the relationship between design, new materials technology, and industrial production, often with government support; related efforts also took place in Russia and to a degree in Holland along more utopian lines.

The United States enjoyed industrial growth uninterrupted by the disasters of a war fought on its own soil or by the failure of confidence it could produce. As a result, production and consumption, symbolized by the success of the Ford Model T, grew, together with increasingly sophisticated marketing and advertising strategies, including the assimilation of original designs for goods and furnishings by European émigrés and American artists who were familiar with contemporary trends in decoration, as well as the use of illustration, photography, and sophisticated approaches to graphic design in mass-circulation magazines promoting "modern" lifestyles and products. Amid the crisis in consumer confidence of the 1930's marketing strategies such as planned obsolescence were employed as a model for a modern industrial design to stimulate consumption. The culmination of these efforts was the 1939 New York World's Fair and its vision of a single clean, rational, streamlined "world of tomorrow" offering a steady flow of new products and gadgets that demonstrated the relationship between new technology and the improvement of the quality of life for all.

Some observers believed that the novelty and obsolescence in American industrial design fueled false desires rather than addressing genuine need. In its exhibitions and competitions, the Museum of Modern Art asserted a more narrow, and European-influenced interpretation of modern design, focusing upon the application of technology to stricter standards of efficiency, economy, and utility for manufactured products. After World War II and amid economic recovery, a relaxation of this austere interpretation of modern design permitted an expansion that included a greater degree of individual expression and commercial considerations. Such a synthesis, under the name of "Good Design," will occupy much of our attention in Part IV.

PART IV

Humanism and Luxury: International Modernism and Mass Culture After World War II 1945-1960

Introduction

Industrial design initiatives took root internationally amid strong economic recovery and reconstruction following the end of World War II. The role assumed by the United States in this expansion was paramount, both in terms of its own elastic market for manufactured goods as well as the national interest in stimulating the industrial production of European countries through initiatives such as the Marshall Plan (1948–52). Such initiatives fostered capitalist enterprise in response to Soviet expansion into eastern Europe amid the emergence of Cold War tensions. Out of these particular economic and political conditions arose a broader constituency for the vision and products of modern design. This constituency included large multinational corporations such as IBM and CBS and the conscious development of their prominent visual identity and image programs, as well as efforts to link modern industrial design with economic, social, and cultural progress through exhibitions, merchandising, and magazine publication. Unlike the European interwar movements, which had advocated the use of mechanical mass production directed, in theory at least, toward the needs of the working class, the audience for postwar industrial design was presumed to be increasingly discriminating and sophisticated—advocates for a "new humanism" that harmoniously balanced individualism with the self-imposed responsibility of citizens toward the wider community. And while products of postwar modern industrial design sought to embody shared standards, at the marketing of products frequently called attention to the "aura" or cult of objects associated with "star" designers, rather than with anonymity or earlier theories such as Le Corbusier's "mechanical selection."

At times there was a didactic, even polemic tone accompanying the promotion of much industrial design in the early postwar years. Advocates embraced familiar paternalistic themes of improving and educating the public to appreciate the esthetic, social, and practical advantages of modern design. Occasionally criticism was leveled against a narrow and monolithic view of the commercialism of mass media and progressive obsolescence, both equated with the absence of responsible standards and the exploitation of the consumer. Standards for postwar design combined new materials such as plastic, fiberglass, and plywood with production technologies such as molding to create furniture and furnishings that implied comfort, technological innovation, and individual self-expression. This is seen most clearly in the relationship between furniture and abstract sculpture associated with the movements of Automatic Surrealism and Constructivism.

Expanding beyond earlier design concerns with economy and efficiency in relation to minimum working-class needs, industrial designers and advocates in the postwar period often characterized their approach more broadly as "fitness to purpose." This term embraced ergonomics and anthropometry, defined as the science of designing for the ease and comfort of human use. Research of this kind was part of an attempt to place the profession of industrial design within an empirical, "problem-solving" context. Such views served to distinguish the designer from the mere "product stylist" whose intentions were subverted by fashion and commercialism. Housing was also an area in which such attitudes toward modern design emerged. Architects and interior designers concentrated upon accommodating new and efficient patterns of family life through simple construction, central heating, open plans, large expanses of glass, and avoiding decorative moldings and other features of more traditional construction methods. Indeed the tenets or standards of modern international industrial design were promoted as being in the public interest and distinct from the relativism implied by fashion. Shared standards and limits to the expression of individual will, whether in product design, graphic design, or in political or moral attitudes, were viewed as bulwarks against manipulation by advertisers or demagogues, especially in an age of mass communication and amid lingering fears of totalitarianism. Indeed, mass media, whether as a vehicle for marketing products or for disseminating political views, permitted an unprecedented expansion of the ability of corporations and governments to influence public opinion. The example of the pervasive power of totalitarian propaganda prior to and during World War II suggested that responsible standards were an important matter that went well beyond the issue of mere "taste" to embrace the role of design in strengthening shared cultural values and democratic ideals.

11.33 Poul Henningson, hanging lamp, opal glass and brass, diameter 19 ⅝ in (50 cm), Louis Poulsen and Company, Copenhagen, 1926.

The expanding international industrial design, often promoted as "good design," was effectively marketed through exhibitions such as the Milan Triennale, individual competitive awards, journals and publications such as *Domus* and *Design Quarterly*, and organizations like the Council of Industrial Design (COID) in Britain and their counterparts in Japan and Scandinavia. Also important were the continuing efforts of the Museum of Modern Art in New York to raise awareness and increase the level of public discrimination through its exhibitions and competitions.

As mentioned above, large and diverse corporations with global interests were also among the strongest advocates and clients for postwar industrial design: their headquarters, office interiors, products, organization, and promotional materials both expressed and contributed to the shaping of shared values of efficiency, rationalism, progress, dependability, responsibility, and public education. A design policy, or "house style," not only created product identity but also reinforced conformity and loyalty among employees.

Yet for many consumers, the "good design" model was not seen as a universal set of standards shaping or contributing to general cultural awareness and progress. Rather its products and promotion were simply one among many possibilities for individual fulfillment in an age of awakening affluence and leisure, a matter of "both ... and" rather than "either ... or." Perhaps seeking to escape the shortages and government-imposed restrictions on materials and manufacturing during the war, the American middle-class in particular responded enthusiastically to novelty, fantasy, and instant gratification. Such attractions went considerably beyond the boundaries of the "new humanism" and its standards, which included the esthetics of abstract art, technological development, cultural education, and ergonomics. In terms of products, this response is perhaps best exemplified in the popularity of the Detroit-manufactured automobiles of the 1950s and the role of electronic media such as television in stimulating desire through obsolescence and the identification of materialism with freedom, luxury, power, and social mobility. Models for defining and stimulating mass taste included the Hollywood film industry (enhanced through the widespread use of Technicolor) and popular magazines, whose images and advertisements offered the promise of emulation through consumption and vicarious thrills for a generation of youthful consumers. Eventually such images were appropriated by the Pop Art movement in the United States, Britain, and elsewhere in Europe. The allure of mass culture for artists ranged from its bold esthetics to a recognition of the role of mass media in generating ideal images of beauty and fulfillment traditionally supplied by the fine arts.

The advent of postwar suburban housing and communities was another part of the particular kind of idealism embodied in mass design, sometimes referred to as the American Dream. Many Americans moved from inner-city neighborhoods to newly created suburbs, where the availability of land for development and affordability of automobiles helped to dictate patterns of consumption. Inexpensive gasoline prices, made possible by American-based corporate control of Middle East oil fields and refineries, made commuting affordable and reasonably comfortable. At the same time mass-produced methods of construction for detached housing, initiated in communities such as Levittown, New York, offered alternatives to apartment living and featured conveniences such as automatic washers, dryers, and modern kitchen appliances. For many Americans, individual home ownership brought with it the promise of leisure, green space, independence, security, and the freedom of personal mobility.

Progressive obsolescence and eclecticism in mass culture were criticized during and after World War II from a number of perspectives. Some commentators complained about consumers' lack of discrimination and questioned the morality of conspicuous consumption in encouraging conformity to manufactured ideals of beauty and health. Others viewed mass culture as a form of social control reinforcing traditional family and gender roles of the white middle class, offering commodified (fetishized) substitutes for individual expression. Still others dismissed popular culture as "kitsch," debased mass-produced imitations of authentic culture standing at the lowest common denominator of taste, that is, of pure physical sensation renewed and manipulated by a commercial culture industry. In this view culture is synonymous with leisure and entertainment rather than with more abiding values that contribute to well-being, enlightenment, self-realization, and active participation in a responsible democracy.

Eventually the monolithic view of mass culture derided by social critics and educators crumbled, insufficiently narrow to embrace a strain of vitality, popular expression, subversion, and irrationality found in comic books, film noir, tailfins, and rock 'n' roll. At the same time, proponents of rational standards and research in design were less able to justify and defend the inflated claims for design as a vehicle for meaningful social progress and enlightenment. The dualism that characterized the opposition between "good" design and mass taste also appears as particular to the decade immediately following World War II. Today, and ostensibly by the later 1950s, both types of cultural artifact emerge as expressions of capitalist expansion. Both may also be seen as characteristic of the subtle and leveling shift from production to consumption in all areas of economic life. These manifestations of postwar design required variety and innovation to stimulate demand and fuel production; aspects of modernism required purging of their interwar associations with radical social reform or earlier more threatening associations with working-class revolution.

In sum, despite an acknowledged critical dichotomy between the new humanism and mass taste, both strains of postwar industrial design co-existed, and both came to express for their constituencies an association with democratic expression directed against the threat of Communism and Collectivism. Whether conditioned by a new and broader set of criteria for a discriminating international audience or giving inventive form to popular images of power, dissent, freedom, and luxury for the American middle-class, industrial design thrived in the prosperity of the postwar period amid unprecedented increases in production and with escalating levels of commodity consumption.

Chapter 11

International Modernism: From Theory to Practice

11.81 Sori Yamagi, Butterfly stool, plywood and metal, 15 ¹¹⁄₁₆ x 16 ⁹⁄₁₆ x 12 ¹⁄₁₆ in
(40 x 42 x 31 cm), manufactured by Tendo Mokko, Tendo, 1956.
Philadelphia Museum of Art.

Although shortages, rationing, and austerity continued to inform the practice of design in the years immediately following the end of World War II, especially in Britain, economic recovery, optimism, and consumer confidence were stimulated by the example of the United States and by the staging of national and international exhibitions such as the Milan Triennales and the Festival of Britain (1951), the latter commemorating the centennial of the Great Exhibition. The brighter European and American economic outlook permitted the marketing and transformation of largely theoretical attitudes toward modern design into more practical realities on an international scale. In the United States, a number of modern design

initiatives undertaken in the years immediately following the end of World War II were based upon adapting new materials and technologies to domestic consumption and efficiency, and some continue to be produced today. In 1947 Earl Tupper (1907–1983) began to market Tupperware, a line of flexible plastic storage and serving containers with self-sealing airtight lids to prevent spilling and preserve freshness (fig. 11.1). Tupperware utilized smooth, simple, often stackable forms and standardized sizes that permitted interchangeability for lids. After being sold as conventional store-bought items, Tupperware was available after 1951 exclusively through catalogues available from neighborhood vendors who demonstrated the products in the home. Such merchandising emphasized an identity between buyer and user rather than the less personal connection between buyer and salesperson, and avoided comparisons and competition with related shelf products. It also reduced consumer resistance to industrial materials being used in the home to replace products traditionally associated with craft such as ceramic storage items. Tupper's commercial success dated to the 1950s, but was based upon his invention of a new pliable plastic called Poly-T in 1942, manufactured by DuPont and other chemical companies as part of the war effort. This interest in harnessing wartime technologies and high-volume industrial production to improve domestic life through new, practical products played a large role in shaping positive attitudes toward modern design in the decade following the end of World War II. It also helps to explain the leading role assumed by large corporations in promoting modern design, as it enabled them to sustain production during peacetime.

Other household domestic products were also developed through modern industrial design after the war. A series of Bubble hanging lamps were designed by George Nelson Associates beginning in 1952 and manufactured by the Michigan-based Howard Miller Clock Company. The lamps were constructed from steel wire attached to rings (rather than welded) and sprayed with a plastic to create translucent shells in a variety of rounded shapes (fig. 11.2). The originality of non-traditional shapes for lighting and industrial production suggests creative approaches to technology applied to modern lifestyles. In articles for the journal *Industrial Design*, Nelson cited instances of the vitality of the industrial design profession in comparison with traditional forms and methods of production that were less relevant to modern life and too sedate for the emerging dynamic world of international business.

Consultant designer Henry Dreyfuss (see page 251) continued to emphasize practicality as a determinant in product housings for a variety of manufactured goods. In addition to introducing lightweight plastic and other user-friendly features to his combined handset for Bell Telephone in 1946 (see pages 217–8 and fig. 10.24), another well-known, "classic" postwar example of his industrial design is the round, wall-mounted thermostat designed for the Honeywell Corporation (fig. 11.3). Honeywell dominated the market for thermostats to

11.1 Earl Tupper, cereal bowls and seals, polyolefin, 6 1/2 in (16.5 cm) in diameter, manufactured by Tupper, *c.* 1949. Philadelphia Museum of Art.

11.2 George Nelson & Associates, "Bubble" hanging lamps, steel wire and sprayed plastic shell, height of largest lamp 33 in (84 cm), manufactured by Howard Miller Clock Company, Zeeland, Michigan, from 1952. Philadelphia Museum of Art.

regulate temperature in homes and offices, but the idea of a round control was attractive to the company from a marketing standpoint as it would differentiate the company's product immediately from its competitors. Although company records indicate some interest in a round model from the early 1940s, the new model did not appear until 1953. Adapting the thermostat mechanisms to a round

11.3 Advertisement for Honeywell round thermostat, plastic and painted aluminum housing, Henry Dreyfuss, 3 in (7.6 cm) diameter, manufactured by Honeywell Corporation, 1953, advertised in *Saturday Evening Post*, and *Life*.

housing necessitated significant invention, credited to the company engineer Carl Kronmiller. Kronmiller developed a spring coil to replace the conventional glass-enclosed mercury-filled thermometer that was difficult to manufacture in a curved form. While the costs of development were considerable, the final manufactured product was less expensive than earlier models. Dreyfuss liked the idea of the round control from the standpoint of mounting, that is, rectangular models almost always looked crooked when mounted on the wall. A further refinement Dreyfuss developed was a concentric metal plate that fitted easily around the clear plastic readout and control, and he was also responsible for suggesting that the concentric plate be manufactured in a variety of colors to match the wall. Dreyfuss's name was frequently mentioned in advertising campaigns, but the development process of this product began before he was hired and required considerable

collaborative effort. Inexpensive, efficient, inconspicuous, and attractive in its simple and concentric forms, the Honeywell Round demonstrated the advantages of postwar industrial design and companies often promoted the integral and creative role of the industrial designer.

American designers were also eager to demonstrate the advantages of modern materials and methods of production in creating furniture to contribute to a modern, efficient, and comfortable standard of living that accompanied the postwar boom in housing. The market for their efforts also included the interior design of corporate and professional office space. As in the interwar period, original designs were manufactured and effectively promoted by the Herman Miller Company of Zeeland, Michigan (see page 294 and figs. 11.4, 11.5, and 11.6). Following the untimely death of Gilbert Rohde in 1944, Miller president D. J. De Pree hired the architect and writer George Nelson

(1908–1986) as chief designer for the company. In turn, Nelson seized the opportunity and encouraged De Pree to manufacture and market the furniture of other designers, including Charles Eames. Trained as an architect at Washington University in St. Louis, Eames was hired as an artist-in-residence and instructor at the Cranbrook Academy of Art in Bloomfield Hills, Michigan from 1938 until 1941. His design for a molded fiberglass chair, a collaboration with Eero Saarinen, son of Cranbrook's director Eliel Saarinen and his wife, Loja, won first prize at the Museum of Modern Art-sponsored competition for "Organic Design for the Home" in 1940 (see page 232 and fig. 10.44). While working for the United States Navy, Eames experimented with plywood molding processes in the development of lightweight and flexible splints to treat wounded soldiers. At the end of the war he adapted this technology to the molding of forms for seating. Unlike earlier plywood molding techniques used, for instance, by Aalto, Eames's approach to molding was three-dimensional—what Peter Dormer has called "vessel and valley" forms as a reference to their more organic, sculptural character. In 1946 Eames designed a molded plywood chair with separate seat and back supported by a thin, welded tubular steel frame and mounted with rubber shocks, eventually manufactured by Herman Miller.

Eames continued to experiment with molded fiberglass for furniture in the later 1940s, and his simple, unupholstered dining armchair of 1950, also mounted on a tubular metal frame, won another international competition sponsored by the Museum of Modern Art for "Low-Cost Furniture." In 1954 an armless, stacking version of the fiberglass chair was introduced by Miller, and became immensely successful for seating in schools and other institutions by virtue of its light weight and ability to be easily stored and moved. Like Tupper's Poly-T plastic, fiberglass was used as a lightweight and inexpensive material extensively during World War II, and was developed for use in the home and office afterward, demonstrating the connections between industrial materials technology and modern design, and meeting domestic needs on the civilian front.

Mechanized production and industrial technology were not only the agents of improved efficiency but also of a new sense of individual fulfillment, expressed through an emerging esthetic of biomorphic sculptural forms. Eames, for instance, also explored the organicism of molded plywood in his well-known lounge chair and footstool, designed for Herman Miller beginning in 1956 (fig. 11.4). This chair was constructed of three separate pieces of molded plywood, was upholstered in leather, and was supported by a five-legged metal pedestal base. The

11.4 Charles Eames, lounge chair and ottoman, chair: 33 x 33 ¼ x 32 in (84 x 86 x 81 cm), ottoman 24 ¼ x 17 x 21 ¼ in (63 x 43 x 54 cm), laminated rosewood, aluminum, and leather upholstery, manufactured by Herman Miller Company, Zeeland, Micchigan, 1956. Philadelphia Museum of Art.

248

Eames lounge chair relates to individual comfort, abstract sculptural form, and expense beyond the earlier "low-cost" furniture, indicating motivations extending beyond efficiency. Fueled by optimism stemming from faith in wartime technology, modern designers in the first postwar decade more expansively defined the relationship between their products and the quality of modern life, allowing for

the self-expression of the designer and the comfort of the owner. It is not surprising that the context for postwar modern design was also shaped by manufacturers and marketing executives. In addition to a continuous supply of new designs with advantages to the consumer in terms of comfort, lightness, efficiency, or beauty, marketing strategies focused upon the individual designer, who lent uniqueness to serially-manufactured goods. Herman Miller, for instance, also manufactured abstract sculptural designs by Japanese-American artist Isamu Noguchi (1904–1988), such as his glass table, which is supported by an ebonized wood base consisting of two irregular forms, again suggestive of Automatic Surrealism (fig. 11.5). Although elements of the egalitarian social ideology of the first machine age remained after World War II, it was the transformation of that ideology that often best exemplifies the International Modernism of the period, producing a benevolent "marriage of commerce and culture."

Another area of integration between industrial design and furniture manufacturing was modularity, seen for instance in storage and shelving, which had appeared earlier in Eliot Noyes' vision of "organic design" for the Museum of Modern Art exhibition of 1940–1 (see page 232). Eero Saarinen and Charles Eames designed a series

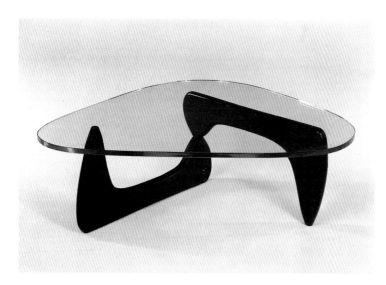

11.5 Isamo Noguchi, coffee table, glass and ebonized birch, 15 ⅛ x 50 x 36 in (40 x 127 x 91 cm), manufactured by Herman Miller Company, Zeeland, Michigan, c. 1947. Private collection.

11.6 Charles Eames, Eames Storage Unit (ESU), painted plywood and steel, 1950, manufactured by Herman Miller Company, Zeeland, Michigan.

11.7 Skidmore, Owings, Merrill, Lever House, Manhattan, 1951–52.

in the postwar period, for instance the Lever House office building on Park Avenue in Manhattan, designed by Skidmore, Owings, and Merrill in 1952 (fig. 11.7).

The refinement of Eames's lounge chair and subsequent office chair designs in cast aluminum was also incorporated into furniture designs manufactured by German émigré Hans Knoll, who established the company known as the Knoll Corporation in 1943. Knoll's wife and partner, Florence Schust Knoll (b.1917), studied at the Cranbrook Academy in Bloomfield Hills, Michigan, and did much to establish the company's association with industrial design. Knoll manufactured the furniture prototypes of architect and former director of the Bauhaus, Mies van der Rohe (see above, page 188), for instance, his steel and upholstered leather Barcelona chair designed for the German Pavilion at the 1929 international exhibition held in Spain. The company also produced designs by Cranbrook faculty and students such as the Italian-born sculptor Harry Bertoia (1915–1978). Bertoia's Diamond chair made of welded steel (fig. 11.8) was manufactured by Knoll from 1952 and features the molded "vessel and valley" forms also seen in plywood and plastic designs for chairs by Saarinen and Eames (see page 247). Bertoia had worked

of modular units for domestic interiors for the Red Lion Company in Pennsylvania, which were constructed of plywood with dowel-like legs and sliding doors for cabinets (see fig. 10.45). Eames's small shelving units, known as the ESU system for Miller (fig. 11.6), used light steel bracing for strength and support, as well as rectangular molded plywood sliding doors with embossed circular designs to create variations in texture. Moreover, Miller designs and other modular shelving units approximated in three dimensions the asymmetrical balance of paintings by Mondrian and the principles of de Stijl, as described earlier with van Doesburg's invitation to create "walk-in paintings" (see page 168). They also bring to mind the abstract rectilinear character of steel and glass architecture

11.8 Harry Bertoia, Diamond chair, steel wire and upholstery, 30 1/2 x 33 1/4 x 28 in (77.5 x 86 x 71 cm), manufactured by Knoll Associates, New York, 1952.

11.9 Eero Saarinen, TWA International Airport, Long Island, New York, 1958–62.

with Eames on molded plywood designs in California. The chair's form approximates an abstract approach to the wingspan of a bird in flight, enhanced through the open and elastic web-like treatment of the welded steel wires.

Eero Saarinen (see page 206) designed a modern furniture group using pedestals as support for Knoll, manufactured in 1956. Like Bertoia, Saarinen was interested in exploring the organic possibilities of modern industrial materials, in this case molded fiberglass, with chairs and tables supported by a painted aluminum base providing support as well as visual balance and harmony (fig. 11.9). Graphic designer Herbert Matter used the inventive pedestal support for the Saarinen chair, labeled the Tulip chair, as the basis for surprise in a well-known advertisement on two successive pages for the Knoll Corporation (see fig. 11.11).

The growing taste for modern industrial materials treated with expressive individuality also helped to renew public appreciation for the original designs of American architect Frank Lloyd Wright in the 1950s, thanks at least in part to articles written by George Nelson and published in the journal *Architectural Digest*. From 1943 to 1959 Wright designed New York's spiraling Guggenheim Museum using reinforced concrete to create a series of sweeping interior ramps. Other related architectural designs featuring the sculptural possibilities of reinforced concrete included Eero Saarinen's John F. Kennedy International Airport in Long Island, New York, built between 1958 and 1962

(fig. 11.9). The possibilities of new production technologies for metals and other materials continue to provide sculptural flexibility in architecture, for instance, in Frank Gehry's Guggenheim Museum in Bilbao, Spain (1997).

A more restrained sculptural esthetic is seen in the interior design of passenger airplanes, in particular Walter Teague's design for the Boeing 707 aircraft of 1955–6 (fig. 11.10). Like Henry Dreyfuss, Teague established his career as a consultant industrial designer in the interwar period and was committed to a consideration of human factors and an understanding of manufacturing processes in products such as the 1934 Kodak Bantam camera (see fig. 10.17). Teague's airline interior demonstrates preference for recessed indirect lighting, curving molded plastic surfaces without projections or decoration, and maximum use of space; all of which suggested a combination of safety and had a calming psychological effect, tested through the construction of a full-scale interior model to gauge passenger reaction prior to manufacturing. Teague remained a vigorous spokesman for research and broadly-based standards in design, articulated in books and in articles published in the journal *Industrial Design*.

The use of molded surfaces, concave moldings around windows, and recessed indirect interior lighting in commercial airliners remain legacies of Teague's approach to

11.10 Walter Teague, full-scale model for interior, Boeing 707, *Interior* (magazine), 1955–56.

industrial design. More recently headphones and personal movie screens provide added means of more comfortably occupying the traveler during longer flights as well as during delays. The same cannot be said of the industry's efforts to maximize profits by increasing the number of seats in coach class. It is interesting to note that when American Airlines began to advertise more leg room in coach class in the year 2000, the company based its claim on the measurement between the bolts that secure each row of seats to the floor of the aircraft known as "pitch." American had increased this measurement to 33 inches (83.8 cm) from the industry standard of 31 inches (78.7 cm). By comparison, in his 1960 book *The Measure of Man*, Henry Dreyfuss estimated the minimum pitch measurement for airline seating at between 34 and 35 inches (86 and 89 cm).

Promoting Postwar Design: Art Direction and the New Advertising

In 1944 the Museum of Modern Art organized a solo exhibition of Charles Eames's furniture designs. In 1946 the Detroit Institute of Arts also featured Eames's work as well as that of other designers. These exhibitions displayed the characteristics of organicism and flexibility as well as new materials and technologies directed toward redefining the practical and esthetic character of modern offices and domestic living spaces. Modern designs provided the setting for Hollywood films such as *The Man in the Grey Flannel Suit* (1956), and were visible in manufacturer showrooms and in department store windows in major cities across the United States. Features on the new designs appeared in journals such as *Art and Architecture*, *Industrial Design*, and *Architectural Digest*, whose readers included the architects and interior designers who served as consultants for corporate, professional, and individual clients.

Advertisements for new furniture and product designs were part of a tendency known as the "new advertising" that often favored the use of photography over illustration and simple copy over narrative. The Swiss-born photographer and graphic designer Herbert Matter (1907–1984) began his career before World War II (see page 235), and stayed in the United States following a visit in 1936. Matter directed print advertising for the Knoll Corporation from the later 1940s through the mid-1960s. He used photography both for visual accuracy and as an element in the overall esthetic composition of the

11.11 Herbert Matter, advertisement for Knoll Tulip Chair, 1956.

advertisement that communicated an essential characteristic of the product. His 1956 advertisement for the Saarinen Tulip chair (fig. 11.11) was originally produced for a brochure in succeeding right-hand pages. The sequence involves the element of surprise, as the chair, draped in plain wrapping paper for the first page, is removed to reveal a seated model occupying it in the second. Aside from the company name at the bottom there is no accompanying text extolling the virtues of the chair. Only the combination of a casually-dressed model and the contrast between her black-and-white attire and the more softly modeled forms of the chair itself, with its unusual (for the time) pedestal base, engage the viewer's attention. The

11.12 Paul Rand, advertisement for Coronet Brandy, 1947.

techniques that could be combined to create a layout from which a flat printing plate could be produced. Newer agencies such as Doyle Dane Bernbach, founded in 1949, helped to introduce the more visually-arresting approach to advertising, also seen in the work of Paul Rand (1901–1996), whose own extensive work in advertising is sometimes overshadowed by his consultant work for corporations (see page 291). Rand worked for the Weintraub Agency in New York, the same office where William Bernbach worked as a copy-editor before beginning his own practice. Rand's *Thoughts on Design* (1947) is a short but well-illustrated essay on the "new advertising," which discusses the enduring value of symbols, humor, and surprise to convey messages about products through a variety of pictorial means available to the designer. Intuition and experiment play a major role in the sensibility of the designer, and freshness of vision is both creative for the artist and persuasive, even educational, for the viewer. Rand's quotations from philosopher and educator John Dewey (1859–1952) and his invocation of "the integration of the beautiful and useful" to describe advertising and other forms of visual communication, suggest a link with standards and reform, the latter directed against the traditional visual and narrative conventions of advertising illustration:

> Visual statements such as illustrations which do not involve esthetic judgment and which are merely literal descriptions can be neither intellectually stimulating nor visually distinctive.... The visual statement, on the other hand, which seeks to express the essence of an idea, and which is based on function, fantasy, and analytic judgment, is likely to be not only unique but meaningful and memorable as well.

Rand's 1946 copy-less magazine advertisement for Coronet Brandy (fig. 11.12) features a collage of cocktail glasses being effortlessly juggled by a waiter whose head is shaped like that of a brandy snifter. Rand explains that the dotted background suggests the effervescence of soda water used for mixed drinks. As an added element of surprise, Rand's flat cut-out shapes are contrasted with a photograph of a flower pinned to the waiter's lapel. Rand's approach to visual communication stressed creative solutions to the presentation of products in which the artist's originality and viewer's interest in surprise, symbol, and humor were compatible and satisfying to the client.

elements of surprise and contrast in the photographs work together to communicate a modern esthetic and associate Knoll products with that sensibility, involving comfort and bold innovation. Even the model's direct confrontation of the viewer plays a part in the surprise of the advertisement. The New York based Art Directors Club featured examples of such advertising in yearly publications (*Annual of Advertising and Editorial Art and Design*) and also established awards in a variety of categories.

The new advertising owed much of its power to the combined impact and persuasiveness of word and image, creating interdependence that actively engaged the viewer. Visual metaphors and puns informed the approach, as did figurative typography. The more widespread use of photographic printing processes (rather than letterpress) stimulated experiment and the free use of a variety of

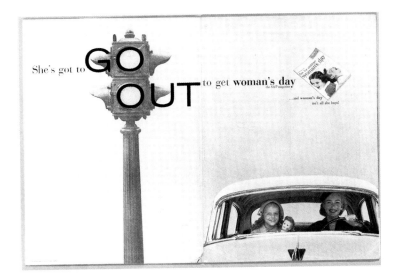

11.13 Gene Federico, advertisement for *Women's Day* magazine, double-page spread in *New Yorker* magazine, 1953.

Figurative typography is seen to great effect in a series of double-page spreads for the magazine *Women's Day* designed by Gene Frederico (b. 1918) and appearing in *New Yorker* (1951–4). Frederico used routine errands as the basis for arresting advertisements that communicated the potential buying power of post-war era housewives. The ads appealed both to would-be subsribers as well as to advertisers (fig. 11.13). At the left the sans serif "o" letters of "go" and "out" double as the lamps of a traffic signal. The signal faces the viewer as well as the well-dressed mother and daughter in an automobile directory across the page, creating an identity between female reader, idealized model, and an active and satisfying lifestyle based upon consumption. Again, simplicity, strong tonal contrast, and the unified, imaginative conception of photography and typography characterise the ad. The image was one of several double-page spreads for *New Yorker* set dramatically against gray or black backgrounds, whose repeated stylistic elements and format become familiar and identifiable from issue to issue.

The element of surprise, relationships with tendencies in contemporary fine art, and expressive use of typography also characterize much progressive postwar graphic design for book covers and record album covers. Alvin Lustig (1915–1955) harnessed these vehicles to create a number of original designs using a wide variety of techniques for covers published by New Directions Books in

New York. Lustig employed a wide range of formal means, including photography, color, texture, and typography to convey a visual equivalent to content. An album cover for the music of the Italian eighteenth-century composer Antonio Vivaldi (fig. 11.14) has evenly spaced letters arranged above and below a horizontal ground line, suggesting both the rhythm as well as the notes of the music. The triangular shapes of the sans serif lettering are echoed in the background pattern as well. Whether using montage or abstraction, Lustig's book jackets, magazine covers, and album covers, like Rand's advertisements, are suggestive rather than literal or illustrative in their approach to conveying the relationship of form (and typography) to meaning. The application of a wide range of creative, open-ended solutions to design problems or challenges helps to define the individual character of postwar graphic design in a context that permitted artistic freedom. In a published essay from 1954, Lustig characterized the "artistic" nature of the graphic designer:

The role of the designer and his most important "must" is to remain free, as free as he possibly can, from the prejudices and the ruts which affect so many

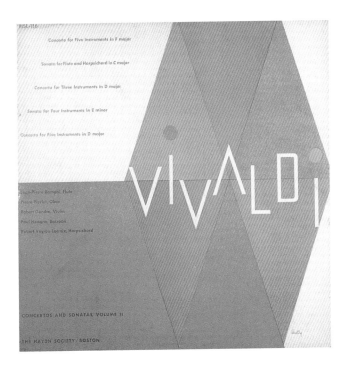

11.14 Alvin Lustig, record jacket cover, "Vivaldi", 1951. Rochester Institute of Technology, Archives and Special Collections, New York.

others in the field of design. He must be constantly on guard, cleansing his mind of the tendency to relax into a routing format, ready to experiment, play, change, and alter forms. If he lacks the inherent ability, the insight, the intuitive selection of what is right for his time, he will not go far and will eventually be forced to enter another field. If he is equipped with these essential characteristics, he will lead the way to new and more effective approaches to design in all its forms.

Some of the same characteristics were also apparent in the art-directed magazines that circulated widely in American households in the years after World War II. Dr. M. F. Agha (see page 229) remained as art director for *Vogue*, *Vanity Fair*, and other Condé Nast publications during most of the war years. He was responsible for the modern and integrated approach to the layout of feature articles on fashion, travel, health, and other activities characterizing modern living aimed at a discriminating readership. Agha's approach to art direction stressed experiment and intuition in design decisions regarding typography, photography, illustration, margins, color, and composition. Such an approach demanded large staffs of copywriters and assistants, freelance photographers and illustrators, and also took advantage of the most up-to-date techniques for color reproduction and hi-quality printing. Fashion or "Style" magazines were large in format (*Vogue* and its rival *Harper's Bazaar* measured 9 ¾ x 12 ¼ inches (25 x 32 cm)) and replete with color. Their covers used striking compositions of photography and inventive uses of typography, while feature articles on fabrics or hair styling also used photography and color to advantage in expressing the richness and vitality of modern lifestyles.

Such qualities are also found in new or revamped publications that appeared during and after the war, such as *Seventeen*, *Glamour*, and *Charm*. Cipe Pineles (1910–1991) served as art director for *Seventeen* and *Charm*, after working under Agha's direction at *Vogue* during the 1930s. Pineles, editor-in-chief Helen Valentine, and promotion editor Estelle Ellis were unique as a team of women in the male-dominated publishing industry, and Pineles became the first woman named as a member of the Art Directors Club in New York. *Seventeen* acknowledged the particular tastes and interests (and buying power) of young women in the United States as distinct from their adult parents,

11.15 Cipe Pineles, feature layout for *Seventeen*, 1950.

and was specifically geared, through the choice of models and the editorial pages, to both reflecting and shaping their experience. Fiction articles were illustrated in full color by artists such as Ben Shahn (see page 228), who was often given wide latitude in interpretation for his images. An often-repeated story involving creative freedom and related by Pineles involves an illustration assignment for a short story:

It (the story) concerned a 14-year-old boy, a keen tennis player, who is ashamed of his mother because she is very pregnant, and he is determined to keep this fact from his friends. To do this he keeps them from using the family tennis court, which up to the time of the pregnancy had been the center of social activity. I gave Ben a two-week deadline. He could do anything he pleased, in any shape and under any number of colors. There was only one restriction. The hero and his friends must be clearly recognizable as youngsters in their teens. Three days later the finished job came in and it was plenty clear. There was no hero. There were no friends to be seen. Instead, stretching across two pages in a long, thin picture, was the most deserted, clearest, biggest tennis court in a brilliant color, marked with the sharpest, neatest, traditional white lines. It was a breathtaking beautiful shock of a painting to go with that story.

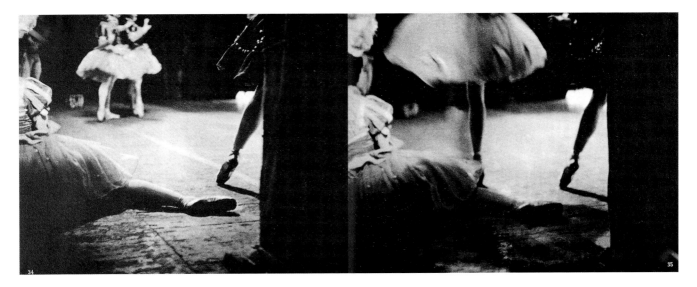

11.16 Alexey Brodovitch, (photographs), and Edward Denby (text), *Ballet*, New York, J. J. Augustin, 1945

Layout for *Seventeen* was generally asymmetrical but less varied than at *Vogue* or *Vanity Fair* under Agha. Photographs rarely employed bleeding and were usually arranged with parallel vertical edges. Typographically there was more experimentation, both in the sizes used for titles and in occasional integration of drawing for emphasis or visual puns. An example of the latter is a feature that appeared in a 1951 issue of *Seventeen* on rainwear, where a sequence of models was juxtaposed with the black vertical lines of musical staves symbolizing rain (fig. 11.15).

Other magazines rivaled the innovations and technical excellence achieved by Condé Nast publications. *Esquire*, under the art direction of Henry Wolf (*b.*1925) beginning in 1953, and *McCalls*, under Otto Storch (*b.*1913), both provided numerous examples of expressive possibilities for layout using the integration of photography, illustration, color, and typography. The careful and expressive sequencing of images combined with text and titles emerged as well in *Ballet* (1945), a volume of black-and-white photographs by Alexey Brodovitch (fig. 11.16). Brodovitch (see page 230) used the blurred and bled images of dancers, often caught off-guard and cut by the edge of the page reminiscent of the paintings of Edgar Degas. The horizontal format, double-page spreads, use of white space for the text portions, and horizontal format convey the unique drama and excitement of the stage, taking full consideration of the range of graphic means at the designer's

disposal. The striking esthetic effect of Brodovitch's photojournalism continues to appear in the work of many of his protégés and collaborators. Richard Avedon (*b.*1923), whose photographic portraits often appear today in the pages of the *New Yorker* magazine worked with Brodovitch at *Harper's Bazaar*, where he served as art director until 1958. Avedon produced the black silhouette image for a

11.17 Feature layout for *Harper's Bazaar*, 1951. Art director: Alexey Brodovitch, photographer: Richard Avedon.

11.18 Bradbury Thompson, spread from *Westvaco Inspirations*, 1958. Courtesy of MeadWestvaco Corporation.

feature on beauty in a 1950/51 issue of *Harper's Bazaar* (fig. 11.17). The photograph emphasizes rhythmic contour and strong contrast, while its placement on the page and relation to the text further enhances the active role of negative space.

Creative freedom in a wide variety of techniques related to printing appears in issues of *Westvaco Inspirations*, a trade journal for the printing industry published by the Westvaco Corporation, formerly the West Virginia Paper Company. The art director for *Westvaco Inspirations* was Bradbury Thompson (*b*.1911), who also served in the same capacity for the mass-circulation fashion magazine *Mademoiselle*. Each issue of *Westvaco Inspirations* contained two-page spreads filled with imaginative compositions combining lettering, text, illustration, and photography to advertise the potential of modern print advertising. A spread from a 1958 issue illustrates the idea of "dance" with text elements, lettering, and high-contrast black-and-white photographs of dancers encouraging the

viewer to turn the page clockwise. The poses and angles of the limbs of the figures create signposts for the reader and help to activate the design (fig. 11.18).

Utilizing an increasingly broad array of techniques derived from modern art, elements of the "New Typography," and creative latitude, advertising designers and magazine art directors brought visual excitement and intellectual sophistication to the presentation of products and to features focused upon the character of modern living as revealed in travel, fashion, entertainment, and cuisine. The combination of creative freedom and experimentation with the effective visual communication of ideas provided an "ethos" that defined a progressive role for graphic design. That role echoed themes similar to those of design reform, namely raising the level of public awareness of design and harmonizing individual freedom and expression with responsibility in expanding and refining the means of graphic communication. The glamorous world of *Harper's Bazaar*, *Vogue*, or *Esquire* may not have corresponded to the social reality of these magazines' broad readership. And yet the thrill of imagining oneself in the company of celebrities or dressed in haute couture fashion, conveyed in provocative graphic presentation, was pleasurable on many levels, and constituted a significant form of consumption, not necessarily of products, but of the reality of vicarious experience. The enjoyment of that experience continues into our own time, where digital means of reproduction and manipulation make the designer's means even more provocative and engaging, and the reality of images more compelling.

Graphic Design and Technical Information

During World War II, German-born graphic designer Will Burtin (see page 235) used the elements of graphic presentation to produce training manuals to teach airforce crewmen to understand and operate complex aerial guns. After the war the clear visual presentation of technical information became the focus of Burtin's long and distinguished career. His assignments covered a wide range of activities, from art direction for *Fortune* magazine (1945–49) to design consultant for the Upjohn pharmaceutical company, and his work also included the design of three-dimensional exhibits. Guiding Burtin's varied projects was an abiding conviction that the increasingly complex and specialized scientific information upon which technological progress depended could be clearly and effectively communicated to a broader public through the means available to the graphic designer. Translating information into effective graphic design was a creative act of problem-solving as well as a form of public service. Burtin's success was testimony to his great powers of analysis and organization, as he searched for the underlying structure of complex processes. As art director both for Upjohn and its house journal, *Scope*, as well as for *Fortune*, Burtin frequently juxtaposed images that included diverse media, drawing with photography, color with black-and-white, precise line drawing with spontaneous brushwork. Such juxtapositions, with roots in Dada and Surrealist photomontage and collage in the interwar period, stimulated a creative, imaginative reading of medical research developments for an audience less familiar with particular technical knowledge of the field (fig. 11.19).

11.19 Will Burtin, cover design, *Fortune* magazine, June, 1946. Rochester Institute of Technology, Archives and Special Collections, New York.

Burtin's projects for Upjohn were not limited to the printed page. He also explored information design in three dimensions, designing a 24-foot (7.3-meter) working model of a human cell for Upjohn in 1958 (fig. 11.20). A tour-de-force that included lights and circuits to show movement and arouse interest in the wonders of science, Burtin's work in this area extended the boundaries of graphic presentation to include dramatic, interactive displays. He demonstrated that the term "design" can be applied not only to products but to "information" as well, in relation to the broad promotion of corporate interests. In 1971, for instance, Charles Eames and his wife, Ray, designed a series of informational exhibits for the IBM Corporation (see fig. 11.90, page 293). Postwar designers such as Burtin and the Eameses saw themselves as contributing, through information design, to the shaping of a shared belief and

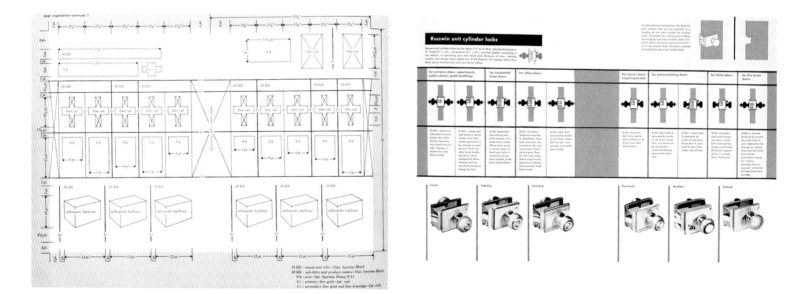

11.20 Will Burtin, Upjohn Cell Exhibit, plastic model, 24 ft (7.3m) in diameter, 1958. Upjohn Pharmaceutical Company.

specializing in visual systems to communicate information for products primarily serving the building industry and parts manufacturers. In books such as *Catalog System Progress*, published in 1950, Sutnar and his collaborator K. Lönberg-Holm created standards for the graphic presentation of technical information based upon reduced use of text and visual clarity (fig. 11.21). The authors cited signage for the transportation industry, such as road signs on highways, as examples of the necessity and importance of clarity and recognition as guiding principles of information graphics. They explained further in the introduction to their book that

> To many people, standards mean only uniformity and restriction, something negative and static. Opposed to this concept of the word is one which may be illustrated by a commonly used expression, like *living standards*. This may suggest variation, as among the living standards of different parts of the world, or progress, as from the time of the earliest American settlers to the present. In short, the word has potentials for implying something dynamic, not static—something which is always changing, advancing.

public confidence in broad cultural progress through technology within the framework of corporate capitalism.

Burtin occasionally used the services of the Czechoslovakian designer Ladislav Sutnar (1897–1976) for the presentation of charts and other quantitative information. Living in the United States from 1940, Sutnar worked for Sweet's Catalog Service, a company

Sutnar brought the same clarity and order to the creation of unified graphic standards for Carr's self-service

11.21 Ladislav Sutnar, page from Lonberg-Holm, K. and Sutnar Ladislav, *Catalog design progress*, Sweet's Catalog Service (Division of F. W. Dodge Corporation), New York, 1950.

department stores in New Jersey (1956–7), and a system of easily recognized symbols for the Bell Telephone Company. Both projects are examples of the adoption of visual systems for identifying products and communicating a sense of organization through visual order and consistency. Such work made Sutnar a pioneer in the development of "house styles" for many large businesses in the postwar era.

Whether through advertising, art direction for fashion magazines, or information design, designers such as Burtin, Brodovitch, Agha, Rand, Sutnar, and Lustig expanded the vocabulary and techniques of graphic design in a variety of contexts in the decade following the end of World War II. These ranged from product advertisements to magazine covers and layouts, to trademarks and house styles, technical manuals, and the design of information for exhibits and displays. Design projects used high-quality color reproduction of illustrations and photographs, and solutions proceeded with technical freedom made possible through reduced reliance upon metal type. Large corporations and publishers helped to provide designers with a wealth of varied opportunities to develop original solutions to the challenges not only of selling products, but also of building public support for the promise of research and technology to a postwar audience.

Scandinavia and Britain

Scandinavian designers also contributed directly and indirectly to the expansion of postwar modern design, in the industrial production of domestic and institutional furniture as well as in the manufacture of glassware, ceramics, lighting, and metal. Scandinavian designs consistently won prizes at the postwar triennial exhibitions held in Milan, Italy, and were manufactured by or influenced the production of furniture companies such as Herman Miller and Knoll. The Scandinavian reputation for new materials and production technologies, and the consideration of factors of comfort and fitness to purpose, combined with a respect for individual expression and the appreciation of natural materials cultivated first in the 1930s, characterize the broader criteria of an international modernism successfully marketed for domestic furnishings after World War II.

In the 1950s Finnish designer Alvar Aalto designed a stool featuring curved, fan-shaped legs constructed of laminated plies of birch, creating an almost seamless transition

from support to weight (fig. 11.22). Aalto compared the fan-shaped leg to a column and capital: it could be used interchangeably as a basic component in the construction of a variety of tables and stools, and, like the orders of Classical architecture, its form also clearly expressed its function. Like Aalto's earlier stools with bent plywood legs bolted to the bottom of the circular seat, the fan-legged stool could be stacked and easily stored, emphasizing the economical use of space characteristic of efficient modern living, permitting both comfort and beauty without lavishness or waste. The continued influence of craft in the career of Aalto is seen in the persistence of materials such as brick or tile, explored for their effects of color and texture in the exterior and interior of buildings such as the Baker House dormitory at the Massachusetts Institute of Technology, built between 1949 and 1953 (fig. 11.23). The interiors feature exposed plumbing and maximize efficient storage utilizing the space beneath beds as well as built-in closets and cabinets (all designed by Aalto and manufactured by Artek), while the plan creates rooms of varied irregular shapes. The combination of variety and standardization preserves a balance between individual and social considerations in design. It is not surprising that Aalto eulogized Henri van de Velde (see pages 96–7) after his death in 1957 with words of praise for the individual artistic and human qualities of his oeuvre.

11.22 Alvar Aalto, "X" stool, birch plywood, 17 ¹¹/₁₆ in (45 cm) high, manufactured by Huonekalutehdas Korhonen for Artek International Contract Furnishings Inc., New York 1954.

Equally committed to industrial methods of production using lightweight materials and metals was the Danish designer Poul Kjaerholm (1929–1980). Kjaerholm was trained as a traditional furniture-maker, and his chair designs continued to use natural materials such as leather, cane, and wicker combined with steel construction. His steel and wicker chair (fig. 11.24) has a startlingly simple design based upon the balance of the opposing curves for the seat and one-piece footed legs, joined by clamps. Manufactured by the E. Kold Christensen Company of Copenhagen from 1956–57, the chair combines an economical use of materials, industrial methods of production, as well as an emphasis upon factors of comfort and esthetic refinement. Danish designer Hans Wegner (b.1914) was also traditional in his approach to furniture. His so-called Peacock armchair of 1949 (fig. 11.25) is based upon the anonymous English eighteenth-century Windsor chair. The chair accentuates the broad curves, fan-like slats and natural expansion and contraction of legs and armrests while eschewing hand-carved decoration.

11.23 Alvar Aalto, student's room, Baker House, campus of the Massachusetts Institute of Technology, Cambridge, Massachusetts, 1946–48.

11.24 Poul Kjaerholm, chair, steel and wicker, 28 in (71 cm high), manufactured by E. Kold Christensen (Copenhagen), 1955. Danske Kunstindustrimuseum, Copenhagen.

11.25 Hans J. Wegner, Peacock armchair, ash and teak, 41 in (102.5 cm) high, manufactured by Johannes Hansen, Copenhagen, 1947. Philadelphia Museum of Art.

The furniture of Danish designer Arne Jacobsen (1902–1971) illustrates the more individual and esthetic character of Scandinavian design especially in the post-World War II period. Jacobsen's Egg chair of 1957 (fig. 11.26) was constructed of molded fiberglass, upholstered in foam rubber, covered in leather (as well as in a variety of other fabrics), and supported by a stainless steel pedestal base. The Egg chair and accompanying ottoman were designed for the Scandinavian Airlines System (SAS) hotel and terminal in Copenhagen. Jacobsen also

served as the architect for this complex, and designed its full range of furnishings from carpeting to cutlery. The organic forms of the Egg chair, in their deep cavities and wing-like projections, go considerably beyond considerations of ergonomics and the psychology of comfort and recall the abstract sculpture of Henry Moore or Jean Arp. They demonstrate the sculptural possibilities of modern industrial materials such as fiberglass as a basis for individual expression. Jacobsen's designs are an intersection of technology and art rather than technology as a vehicle

11.26 Arne Jacobsen, Egg chair, fiberglass and chromed steel with leather-covered foam rubber upholstery, 41 ⅞ in (106.4 cm) high, 1957. Fritz Hansen, Allerød, Denmark.

11.27 Finn Juhl, armchair,
teak and leather upholstery,
32 in (81 cm), 1951,
manufactured by Baker, 1951.
Philadelphia Museum of Art.

for social reform and the achievement of universal collective standards based primarily upon utility. A similar exploration of organic forms for furniture can also be seen in the designs of Finn Juhl (*b*.1912). In 1951 Juhl designed a chair constructed of teak wood with seat and back in upholstered leather (fig. 11.27). The simple constructive elements for legs and seat support are slightly swollen and avoid the tube-like uniformity of metal. Also, the backrest not only has a comfortable contoured form but also resembles the biomorphic shapes of Automatic Surrealism, as seen, for instance, in the contemporary paintings of artists such as Joan Miró (fig. 11.28).

In addition to furniture, the Scandinavian approach to industrial design included other products with strong craft traditions behind them, such as glassware, ceramics, textiles, and metalwork. The glassware of Alvar Aalto has already been mentioned (see fig. 9.58). Finnish designer Tapio Wirkkala (*b*.1915) also explored organic shapes in smooth blown glassware, wood, and ceramics. Wirkkala's Kantterelli vase was manufactured by the Finnish company Iittala beginning in 1947 (fig. 11.29). The form of the vase evolves from a simple pinched cylinder into an asymmetrical and irregular petal-like opening at the top, with delicate etched lines echoing the form.

A similar emphasis upon craft and the exploration of materials can be seen in the metalwork of Danish designer Henning Koppel (1918–1981). Koppel's designs in silver were exclusive products manufactured by Georg Jensen.

11.28 Joan Miró, *Women in the Night*, oil, goache, aquarelle, pastel on canvas, 13 x 25 ¼ in (33 x 64 cm). Henie-Onstad Foundation, Norway, 1946.

11.29 Tapio Wirkkala, "Kanterelli" vase, clear, blown glass, 9 in (22.4 cm) high, Finland, 1947. Metropolitan Museum of Art, New York.

11.30 Henning Koppel, wine pitcher, silver, 13 ⅞ in (34 cm) high, manufactured by Georg Jenson Sølvsmedie, Copenhagen, Denmark, 1948. Musée des Arts Decoratifs de Montreal.

His silver pitcher (fig. 11.30) suggests the smooth surfaces and abstract sculptural character of Jensen's designs, particularly in the treatment of the curved handle whose form seems to connect organically with the pitcher's base and lip.

In Scandinavian glassware and ceramics, a more practical expression in the postwar period continues with the work of Finnish designer Kaj Franck (b.1911), whose Kilta earthenware table service was manufactured by the Arabic Company in Helsinki beginning in 1952 (fig. 11.31). This tableware exhibits a preference for slightly tapered cylindrical forms in bright colors with undecorated surfaces. Handles and knobs are equally simple and unobtrusive, and the consistency of these elements surpasses in its purity and unified expression the equally utilitarian Fiestaware (see fig. 10.26) whose pieces retain molded and scalloped handles and bases. Danish designer Gertrude Vasegaard (b.1913) combined simple forms with heavier materials and slightly textured surfaces to effect a compromise between the demands of serial production and the appeal of natural finishes. Examples recall handmade

11.31 Kaj Franck, Kilta table service, glazed earthenware, diameter of largest plate 9 ⅛ in (23 cm), manufactured by Wärtsilä Arabia Company, Helsinki, Finland, 1952.

vessels, as seen in her porcelain tea service of 1957 for Bing and Grøndahl of Copenhagen (fig. 11.32).

In lighting, the hanging lamps of Poul Henningsen (1894–1967), manufactured by the Louis Poulsen Company in Copenhagen as early as 1926 (they were exhibited at the 1925 Exposition Internationale des Arts Décoratifs et Industriels Modernes in Paris), combine simple curved geometric forms in concentric and inverted arrangements to evenly diffuse interior light (fig. 11.33). After World War II, Henningson expanded the vocabulary of elementary geometric components so characteristic of interwar modernism into the more intricate and sculptural designs, such as the Artichoke hanging lamp of 1951 (fig. 11.34). The transformation is characteristic of an increasing freedom and esthetic dimension in Scandinavian design, seen as part of an ideology stressing comfortable living in relation to a cold climate, long distances between major cities, and consequently large amounts of time spent indoors.

At the same time, flexibility remained a principle of Scandinavian design. For instance, when George Nelson

11.34 Poul Henningson, Artichoke lamp, copper, 27 ⅛ in (69 cm) high, 33 ⅛ in (84 cm) in diameter, Louis Poulsen and Company, Copenhagen, 1958.

praised the virtues of Scandinavian design in urban housing, he also cited the efficiency of design planning for open, multipurpose apartments filled with modular furniture. According to Nelson such efficiency was complimented by the provision of social services for childcare and emphasis upon how a sense of community reduced the need for individual families to own large homes to satisfy every need.

The qualities of comfort combined with fitness-to-purpose may also be seen in Scandinavian industrial design,

11.35 Saab 92 automobile, Svenska Aeroplan Aktiebolaget Company, Linköping, Sweden, 1950.

11.36 George Cawardine, Anglepoise lamp, lacquered metal and bakelite, 35 7/16 in (90 cm) high, manufactured by Herbert Terry and Sons, Redditch, England, 1932. National Museum of Science and Industry, London.

particularly in the Saab 92 automobile manufactured in 1950 by Svenska Aeroplan Aktiebolaget Company in Linköping, Sweden. As a consultant to the airline company that produced the original model, Swedish industrial designer Sixton Sasen (1912–1967) contributed to the 1956 Saab 93 (fig. 11.35). With swept-back hood and angled headlights, the Saab is streamlined and strongly unified in appearance, less geometric in form than the German Volkswagen. Perhaps owing to the aviation orientation of the company that produced it, the gauges and controls on the Saab 92 and Saab 93 were placed to ensure easy recognition and operation. As a result of meeting practical needs and integrating an aerodynamic approach to the form of the body, these early models underwent few changes, remaining in production for almost thirty years.

The influence of Scandinavia, as well as a more gradual shift in modern industrial design from standardized and low-cost solutions toward more individual interpretations of modernism, also may be seen in Britain following World War II. Between the wars, British industrial designers often followed a utilitarian and practical approach, seen, for instance, in the well-known Anglepoise desk lamp designed by George Carwardine (1887–1948) in 1932 (fig. 11.36). The exposure of the lamp's mechanical parts suggests a relation to technical equipment rather than

domestic furnishings. Following the war, lingering austerity stemming from material shortages and rationing (not lifted until 1952) favored the continuation of an economical approach at the expense of esthetic considerations. The British interpretation of modern design also incorporated the heritage of craft traditions and natural materials to give products a distinctively national identity in the hope of competing in the export market. At the same time government-sponsored design initiatives such as the Design Research Group emphasized research to encourage manufacturers to hire industrial designers, while department stores such as Heals sold simple furniture designs inspired by Scandinavian (chiefly Danish) models, with construction focusing upon ease of assembly, lightness, and undecorated wooden components. Government regulation required that furniture designs be approved before they could be manufactured on the basis of economy and a sense of discrimination based along utilitarian

11.37 Photograph of British Interior with "Utility" furniture, c. 1942.

11.38 Ernst Race, Antelope chair, enameled steel and painted plywood, 31 ⅛ in (79 cm), manufactured by Race Furniture, England, 1951. Victoria and Albert Museum, London.

guidelines, as seen in a photograph of a domestic interior from 1951 (fig. 11.37) and a chair (see fig. 10.47, page 234). Such guidelines formed the basis of the 1946 exhibition entitled *Britain Can Make It*, but were relaxed to admit more creative design solutions for the 1951 Festival of Britain, for instance Ernst Race's (1913–1963) Antelope chair featuring the use of metal wire (fig. 11.38). The Festival of Britain marked the 100th anniversary of the Great Exhibition (see figs 1.44 and 1.45, pages 51–3).

In British postwar interiors, walls were generally white rather than papered, and upholstery fabric emphasized textural variety with muted earth tones rather than bright colors. A broad range of new surface designs were developed for the Festival of Britain, with patterns for curtains and ceramics often featuring delicate line drawing in an abbreviated, often child-like style and a variety of abstract organic shapes and representational motifs. Examples include Viennese-born Marianne Mahler's

(1911–1983) Bird and Bowl design from 1951, printed on the synthetic fabric rayon and manufactured by David Whitehead Ltd. (fig. 11.39). Another source of inspiration for abstract textile patterns was the microscopic world of molecular structures, revealed in the woven fabric entitled "Surrey" designed by Mariann Straub (1909–1994) for Warner & Sons, Ltd. in 1951 (fig. 11.40). Whether through textile design, materials technology in home furnishings, or in marketing for the pharmaceutical industry, many initiatives in design internationally dealt with the humanization of science. Such efforts, at the Festival of Britain and elsewhere, are related in their promotion of community

11.39 Marianne Mahler, *Bird and Bowl* pattern, roller-printed rayon 18 in (46 cm), manufactured by David Whitehead Ltd., 1951.

11.40 Marianne Straub, "Surrey", wool and cotton tapestry, red, gold, and cream, Warner and Sons Ltd., for the Festival Pattern Group Scheme and used for curtains in the Regatta Restaurant, the Royal Festival Hall, London.

11.41 Sir Terence Conran, *Chequers* range, molded earthenware with printed and sponged decoration, for W. R. Midwinter Ltd., Burslem.

and understanding in a complex world of technical and specialized knowledge and information.

Industrial materials and methods of production were also applied to contemporary ceramics and interior furnishings from the early 1950s. Sir Terence Conran (b.1931) designed earthenware dinnerware in square and rectangular forms with rounded edges, decorated with a hand-drawn checkerboard background filled with colored swatches and irregular patterns of lines, dots, and dashes (fig. 11.41). In many ways such examples are similar to the playful patterns seen in textile design from the same period (see fig. 11.39). The 1950s also saw the introduction of new resins used as an alternative to ceramics for table service. A. H. Woodfull (b.1912) together with John Vale and Roy Midwinter designed a tea set in 1956 called Midwinter Modern (fig. 11.42). Marketed as "break-resistant"

tableware, the white tea set was made of Melamine, a form of hard industrial plastic. Midwinter Modern featured round-edged rectangular plates and sloping edges for the creamer and sugar bowl, emphasizing smooth but irregular organic forms. In the United States, Russel Wright designed several comparable sets of dinnerware using

11.42 John Vale and Roy Midwinter, "Midwinter" Modern tea set, Melamine, cup 3 in (7.6 cm) high, plate diameter 6 1/4 in (16 m) diameter, sugar bowl 3 in (7.6 cm) high, manufactured by Midwinter Modern Line, 1956.

11.43 Anonymous, adjustable desk lamps, painted aluminum and brass, average 20 in (51 cm), c. 1955, various manufacturers (Oswald Hollman Ltd., Beckenham, Troughton & Young Ltd.), London.

plastics and intended for informal, festive home entertaining, with instructions for how to arrange plates and utensils for serving published by Wright in his 1950 book *Guide to Easier Living*. This period also saw the introduction of metal in a variety of lighting fixtures, from desk lamps to standing lamps resembling microphone stands. Bulbs were enclosed in a variety of conical forms and the lamps were generally made of thin steel rods and painted aluminum, marketed for their adjustable height and direction (fig. 11.43). Esthetically they possess the thin, wiry forms favored for their lightness and harmony in built-in furniture, reduced upholstery, and more open interior spaces.

In London, maximizing available space led to new approaches to efficient housing, with more open plans and modern construction techniques using steel girders, permitting larger expanses of windows, and combined living and dining areas. Such design solutions stressed informal living geared to families and accommodating home entertainment in the form of stereo systems and television sets as well as wall units and other built-in furniture to create open and flexible floor space. This efficient, economical and utilitarian approach was shaped by shared egalitarian values and parallels the introduction of government-sponsored socialized services for medicine and welfare for the unemployed. More or less official views of design promoted a clear understanding of the distinction between *needs* and *wants* and an acceptance of the realities and restrictions of urban population density. Later in the decade such values and the standards upon which they were based came under attack. The result was a renewed emphasis on one hand upon the importance of research and ergonomics in product development and on the other hand skepticism toward practicality and utility as the self-evident and abiding determinants of design. Yet despite growing fascination with American popular culture in Britain, and a search for alternatives to practical standards, the premises of economy and efficiency continued to inspire such successful products as the 1959 Mini automobile, designed for the British Motor Corporation by Alec Issigonis in 1959. This efficient and space-saving vehicle was the British counterpart to the earlier Fiat 600 in Italy for inexpensive personal transportation (fig. 11.44).

Also in Britain the legacy of craft and values associated with the dialogue between artisan and materials found expression in the oeuvre of Bernard Leach (1887–1979).

11.44 Alec Issigonis, Morris Mini, Morris Motor Company, Birmingham, 1959.

11.45 Bernard Leach, bowl, stoneware, diameter 6 in (15 cm). Victoria and Albert Museum, London.

Italy

The conscious development of an international market and national image for Italian design was a phenomenon of the postwar era, even though mechanized mass production was introduced by a small number of Italian manufacturing companies in the interwar period. Perhaps the most potent symbol of industrial design in post-Fascist Italy was the Vespa motor scooter, designed in 1946 by Corradino d'Ascanio (1891–1981) for the Piaggio Corporation (fig. 11.46). The Vespa was an efficient, practical, and inexpensive mode of personal transportation, but the emphasis upon streamlined housing, the enclosure of mechanical parts, and the cutaway profile of the seat introduced a graceful, sculptural element to the design, giving visible expression to an identification between freedom, democracy, and mobility in the Italian postwar *riconstruzione*. Other standardized industrially manufactured products, for instance the tiny Fiat 600 of 1955 designed by Dante Giacosa, were more aligned with utilitarian and practical considerations in both economical production and performance, providing affordable four-wheel transportation and contributing to the tremendous domestic increase in automobile sales, estimated at 400 percent between 1950 and 1961 (fig. 11.47).

Following the American industrial design model of the 1930s, and strongly supported by the Marshall Plan,

Leach was active at least from the end of World War I, when he returned from Japan after having studied pottery with a well-known Japanese ceramic master. Leach practiced the technique of *raku* ceramics, fired at lower temperatures and molded rather than thrown on a wheel. His designs, such as a stoneware vase from 1957 (fig. 11.45), preserve and extend the vitality of handicraft traditions as they were practiced in Japan and became a part of the Aesthetic and related movements in Europe and the United States in the later nineteenth century. Leach also designed teapots and other wares for serial production as an alternative to newer industrial materials. Unrelated to earlier movements of reform or utopian ideology, the persistence of craft continued in Britain and elsewhere as a viable aspect of the history of modern design.

11.46 Coradino d'Ascanio, Vespa Motorscooter, Piaggio Corporation, 1946.

11.48 Marcello Nizzoli, Lexikon 80 typewriter, enameled metal housing, manufactured by Olivetti ING., 1948.

11.47 Dante Giacosa, Fiat 600, Fiat Motor Company, 1955.

11.49 Camillo Olivetti, MI typewriter, Olivetti ING., metal, 14 ¹⁵/₁₆ in (38 cm) high, *c.* 1911.

Italian companies adopting mechanized mass production technology generally relied upon consultants to provide new designs, often for the export market. With a steady and inexpensive supply of labor, guaranteed by weak labor unions and government subsidies to industry, Italian manufacturers could justify the added cost of incorporating a modern approach to design by expanding the international market for their products. The value of those products was in turn enhanced by an association with individual designers who left their unique mark upon manufactured goods. The Olivetti Corporation, for instance, relied upon painter and architect Marcello Nizzoli (1887–1969). Although hired in the later 1930s by Adriano Olivetti, son of the company's founder, Nizzoli assumed a more significant role in product design after World War II. An early example was the Lexikon 80

typewriter of 1948 (fig. 11.48), distinguished by its fluid, organic housing and integrated curved panel covering the mechanism, creating a sense of abstract sculptural form in comparison with the angular, black, standardized models manufactured earlier by Olivetti (fig. 11.49).

Such originality provided an esthetic dimension for any number of ordinary standardized utilitarian products,

for instance, Gio Ponti's (1891–1979) asymmetrically balanced commode and flared pedestal sink designed for Ideal Standard in 1953/4 (figs. 11.50 and 11.51). An esthetic direction can also be seen in products ranging from metal door handles to espresso coffee machines, characterized by graceful curvilinear forms, attention to smooth, reflective surfaces, and a harmonious interrelation of parts (fig. 11.52).

The independence and esthetic contribution of the consultant designer was an acknowledged feature in Italian industrial manufacturing for corporations such as Olivetti after World War II. The designer was an integral member of a process that included marketing and engineering. The dialogue among participants was often distinguished by a sense of drama and conflict rather than hierarchical directive. As described by Sybil Kircherer in her study of the Olivetti Corporation, the strategy resulted in creativity and a dynamic internal as well as external company identity.

Ponti's bathroom fixtures illustrated above received recognition at the 1957 Milan Triennale. These exhibitions, organized as early as the 1920s, were responsible for increasing the visibility of Italian design in an

11.50 Gio Ponti, sink, porcelain, 31 ½ in (80 cm) high, manufactured by Ideal Standard, Milan, 1953–4.

11.51 Gio Ponti, commode, porcelain, 15 in (38 cm) high, manufactured by Ideal Standard, Milan, 1953–4.

11.52 Gio Ponti, coffee machine, for La Pavoni, 1947.

international setting. Italian products were featured alongside those of Scandinavian, German, American and British designers, aimed at the sophisticated, high-end market and often exhibited in response to a theme, such as the "Form of the Useful" (1951). The Triennale competition awarded prizes (known as the "golden compass") for the integration of esthetic and practical elements in the design of products for industrial production. The reputation of Italian design in an international context was also promoted in the journal *Domus*, particularly under the editorship of Ernesto Rogers (1909–1969) and Gio Ponti, which likewise stressed the human and creative element in modern industrial design as well as its practical and social benefits.

The Turinese manufacturer Cassina adopted mass production technology for furniture in the years immediately after World War II. In the 1950s the firm emerged as an industrial leader, integrating the use of modern materials such as plywood and tubular steel with the tapered, organic forms featured in other products, and allowing freedom for individual designers to explore esthetic possibilities of new techniques. In many ways the experiments of Italian designers parallel the interests of designers such as Charles and Ray Eames in molded industrial materials. Marco Zanuso (*b*.1916) experimented with the use of foam rubber to replace conventional upholstery in the design of his Lady chair for the Arflex Company in 1951 (a division of the Pirelli Corporation, otherwise known for rubber tire manufacturing). The chair is composed of broad, regular curving forms supported by metal legs, and also received an award at the Milan Triennale of that year (fig. 11.53).

Equally inventive during the decade following the end of World War II were examples of lighting developed in Italy. Simple and flexible, designs such as the 1949 Tubino by Achille (*b*.1918) and Pier Giacomo Castiglioni (1913–1968) and manufactured by Arredoluce, eschewed conventional fabric shades and pedestal bases in favor of plastics, light metal, and thin tubing to conceal electric wiring (fig. 11.54). The simplicity of the Castiglionis' designs derives from the brothers' stated subordination of the fixture itself to the "effects of light it produces." Yet the remaining form, however negligible, retains an undeniable abstract esthetic character, akin to a delicate line drawing or to automatic writing.

The flexible plastics used for a number of Italian lighting designs in the 1950s also appear in domestic kitchenwares

11.53 Marco Zanuso, Lady armchair, wood, metal, and elastic webbing, with fabric-covered foam-rubber upholstery, 32 ¼ in (82 cm), manufactured by Arflex, Milan, 1951.

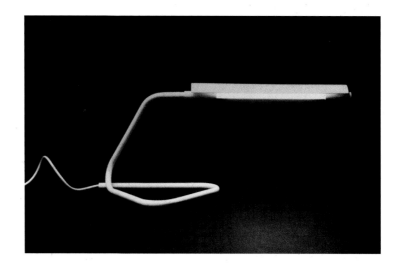

11.54 Achille and Pier Giacomo Castiglioni, Tubino desk lamp, enameled metal and aluminum, 11 ¹¹⁄₁₆ in (28 cm) high, manufactured by Arredoluce, 1949.

11.55 Gio Ponti, "Superleggera" chair, tinted ash and cane, 32 in (81.3 cm) high, manufactured by Figli di Amedeo Cassina, Milan, 26⅗ in (65 cm) 1957. Philadelphia Museum of Art.

11.56 Franco Albini and Franca Helg, Margherita armchair, rattan and upholstery, 39 ⅛ in (99.4 cm) high, manufactured by Vittoria Bonacina, 1950/1951.

pioneered by the Kartell Company, whose in-house designer, Gino Colombini (b.1915) developed an array of containers and simple kitchen machines with tapered forms that not only fulfilled functional requirements but also introduced a colorful and playful element into design. Bright colors and bold advertising combined to reduce the association of cooking and cleaning with demeaning labor and made it instead part of a "modern" lifestyle linked to ease and a carefree atmosphere.

In addition to the role of the individual artist in the design and marketing of Italian postwar industrial products, another humanizing factor in the success of Italian design was the persistence and continued transformation of traditional artesanal production. A case in point is Gio Ponti's Superleggera chair of 1957 (fig. 11.55), which is a modern interpretation of a nineteenth-century wood and rush-seat design, emphasizing the light, tapered forms seen in plywood and metal, but implying the relationship between such qualities and the national heritage. A number of design historians have pointed out that the Italian furniture industry did not abandon entirely its craft roots, despite the shift to industrial materials and other modern production technologies. It still maintained small workshops, primarily because they were capable of shorter production runs and were less reliant upon costly capital investment. These factors led to a combination of innovation and variety together with standardization that included a receptivity to craft, seen in the Superleggera as well as in the Margherita armchair designed by Franco Albini (1905–1977) and Franca Helg. The latter was manufactured by the Bonacina company in 1950, using traditional cane as well as a bentwood frame, in a design emphasizing the relationships of abstract curved and oval shapes (fig. 11.56). The craft element in Italian design surfaced as well in the growing reputation of leather goods and fashion in the postwar period, again allied with "name" designers to lend distinction to products and accessories. While Fendi and Ferragamo are perhaps best associated internationally with this industry today, these designers inherited a postwar tradition initiated by Gucci leather accessories (named for Guccio Gucci, 1881–1953, fig. 11.57).

Finally, while the Fiat models 500 and 600 dominated the domestic market for automobiles, accounting for ninety percent of sales in 1961, Italian car manufacturers also addressed the international high-end market with

11.57 Gucci leather handbag, *c.* 1955–60.

more streamlined, sculptural models, where the legacy of custom coach-building and individuality expressed in graceful sculptural form continued. A well-known example is the 1946 Cisitalia sports car designed by Sergio Pininfarina (fig. 11.58), while models for industrial production included the more restrained Alfa Romeo Spider from the mid-1950s.

In parallel with American and Scandinavian industrial designers, Italy helped to define the "new humanism" of

11.58 Sergio Pininfarina, Cisitalia Coupé, sports car, 1946.

the postwar era, embracing mechanized mass production and new materials technology while establishing a forceful role for the artist–designer within industry in the creation of useful, elegant products and an acknowledged esthetic and individual element. Through periodicals and the Milan Triennale exhibitions, Italian industrial design achieved both visibility and national identity within an international market. Together with the United States and other European countries, Italian postwar design shared standards of fitness to purpose, modern materials technology, individual esthetic expression along the lines of abstract organic sculpture, and a modern reinterpretation of enduring objects and craft traditions.

Germany

Design also played a large role in the economic reconstruction of West Germany following World War II. A number of examples of German industrially manufactured products demonstrate a kinship with the humanizing tendencies expressed through organic forms molded from modern materials, but more typically German industrial design is associated with objective standards based upon the systematic investigation of materials and processes. This is due in part to the influence exerted by the newly founded Hochschule für Gestaltung at Ulm (1953–68) and to the manufacturing role of a small number of large German corporations such as Braun (Frankfurt). Such corporate and educational institutions tended to limit the role of individual expression and embraced a belief in research-based design solutions linked to performance and practicality for an international market. These efforts were aided by the establishment of a German Design Council in 1949 and by the investment of the United States through the Marshall Plan to stimulate industrial production, economic recovery, and the restoration of consumer confidence.

Shortly after the war, Germany put into mass production the inexpensive and standardized Volkswagen Beetle designed by Ferdinand Porsche in 1937 as a "People's Car" and manufactured along Fordist lines to meet basic personal and family transportation needs primarily for the national market. As in Italy, however, automobile manufacturing also extended to an international luxury market. Companies such as Daimler-Benz, Porsche, and BMW

11.59 501 limousine, manufactured by BMW, AG Bayerische Motorenwerke Aktiengesellschaft, Munich, 1951.

were more receptive to combining fluid streamlined body housing with precision and a tradition of customized coach-building to produce high-performance vehicles in a higher price range, for instance the rear-engine streamlined 1952 Porsche 356 or the stately 1951 BMW 501 limousine model (fig. 11.59). An equally sculptural approach to product housing may also be seen in the stainless steel VE6 electric food slicing machine dated to 1959 and manufactured by the Bizerba-Waagen-Verkaufsgesellschaft of Balingen (fig. 11.60).

11.60 VE6 electric food slicer, Bizerba-Waagen-Verkaufsgesellschaft, Balingen, 1959.

Precision and functional simplicity were factors in the international success of electrical appliances in postwar Germany, associated foremost with the Braun Corporation of Frankfurt, founded in 1921 and rebuilt in 1945. The company established a connection with the newly-founded Hochschule für Gestaltung at Ulm (1953) through Fritz Eichler (*b*.1911), a member of the Board of Directors. Max Bill (*b*.1908), the Hochschule's first director, was a graduate of the Bauhaus and sought to revive an approach to industrial design that emphasized studio practice and social responsibility in the design of prototypes for simple, practical, and efficiently-produced furniture and objects of everyday use. Bill advocated practical considerations (both in production and use) in industrial design on theoretical rather than on strict formalist principles, emphasizing the improvement of living standards rather than esthetic experiment and expression that might be exploited commercially; in many ways Bill's approach to industrial design shared many elements not only with the Dessau Bauhaus but also with the practical standards and suppression of individuality for products and furnishings recommended by Hermann Muthesius under the auspices of the Deutscher Werkbund and seen in the work of Peter Behrens for the AEG (see page 203 and fig. 9.58). Both Swiss-educated Hans Gugelot (1920–65) and Dieter Rams (*b*.1932), who worked as consultant designers for Braun, also served as faculty members at Ulm, creating a unified product identity for the corporation in response particularly to miniaturization, for instance with the use of transistors in electronics equipment, a technology that had emerged in the early 1940s. The SK4 radio-phonograph was designed by Max Braun, Rams, and Gugelot in 1956, and nicknamed "Snow White's Coffin" (fig. 11.61). The SK4 is a long rectangular box with hinged transparent plastic cover, housing controls, speaker grille, and other moving parts (tone-arm and turntable). All visible parts are reduced to circular or rectangular forms placed against smooth and flat surfaces. The arrangement of parts is controlled by a rectangular grid system for simple organization. The esthetic purity and systematic approach to Braun design retain a relationship with geometric abstraction in the fine arts, seen for instance in Josef Albers' series of paintings entitled *Homage to the Square*, or to Max Bill's own black granite sculptures (fig. 11.62). Just as such minimalist approaches to fine art seem to demand a sophisticated and educated audience, so Braun products and

11.63 Gerd Alfred Müller, "Kitchen Machine", polystyrol housing, 10 ¼ x 15 x 9 ½ in (26 x 38 x 24 cm), manufactured by Braun AG Taunus, West Germany, 1957.

11.61 Max Braun, Dieter Rams, and Hans Gugelot, SK4 radio-phonograph, Braun, 1956.

design policy were not directed toward a mass market but rather to a discriminating public with a more conscious awareness of abstract esthetics and a belief in the connection between efficiency and simple, undecorated forms.

Braun products emphasized enduring forms and determinants for design based upon considerations of production technology and fitness-to-purpose rather than upon commercial manipulation and obsolescence. In addition, products such as the Kitchen Machine of 1958 (fig. 11.63) possessed a sense of restraint, precision, and laboratory-like efficiency expressed through polished surfaces, qualities mentioned above in relation to contemporary abstract fine art and seen as well in the cool impersonality of buildings such as Mies van der Rohe's Seagram Building of 1954–8. The design of Braun products was not the inevitable outcome of a functional approach to industrial design, but a combination of factors that included architectural and social theory, as well as a conscious and sophisticated esthetic organization of forms.

11.62 Max Bill, *Unit of Three Equal Elements*, granite, 30 x 44 x 44 in (76 x 112 x 112 cm), 1965, Storm King Art Center, Mountainville, New York.

The International Typographic Style (Die Neue Grafik)

Also connected with Germany as well as Switzerland in the postwar period was the development of standards for graphic design and typography often referred to as the International Typographic Style or *Die Neue Grafik*. This approach to graphic communication for book design, posters, advertising, trademarks, and other business and organizational needs was promoted in journals such as *Graphis* and *Die Neue Grafik*, and formed the basis for the education of graphic designers at the Hochschule für Gestaltung at Ulm and the Kunstgewerbeschule in Basle. This combination of theoretical ideas, exploration of the visual components of graphic expression, and the use of those components for effective communication in an international context gave the movement a reputation for high standards and social responsibility in design. The hegemony of the International Typographic Style as the "voice" of modern graphic design was promoted in museum exhibitions and books, and was contemporary with a similar faith in the modern esthetic and practical advantages of the tectonic steel-and-glass architecture of the "International Style." This approach to architecture dominated large public and corporate building projects in the decades after World War II, and was equally praised at the time for its beauty, efficiency, and responsible use of modern methods of construction.

Max Bill, who lived and worked in Switzerland during and after World War II before accepting the directorship at the Hochschule für Gestaltung at Ulm, contributed to the development of the International Typographic Style. Along with several Swiss and other European artists and designers, Bill developed and worked within a framework of formal and ideological principles for graphic communication. These designers consciously moved away from illustration and were sparing in their use of both photography and color. Their shared interest was to communicate ideas universally and effectively with simple, reductive means. At the foundation of their approach were an acknowledgement of the increasing complexity, fragmentation, and interdependence of knowledge, and a mistrust of the growing sophistication of the mechanical reproduction of images used to manipulate the public in mass advertising.

Bill's posters show a mastery of the "New Typography," gained during the years he spent as a student at the Dessau Bauhaus from 1927 to 1929. A 1940 poster for a Christmas exhibition and sale at the Applied Arts Museum (Kunstgewerbemuseum) in Zurich uses star-shapes to organize information hierarchically as well as provide unity and an eye-catching symbol constructed from triangles with strong contrast of figure and ground.

In addition, Bill used the early twentieth-century sans serif typeface known as Akzidenz Grotesk (see page 191) throughout, as well as only lower-case letters. One of the main features of the objective and scientific approach taken by German and Swiss practitioners of the International Typographic style was the use of a grid system to govern layouts, so that all individual elements were subordinated to the grid, thereby maintaining unity. The grid created modules as units of measurement to establish relationships for the emphasis and meaning of text. Another exhibition poster for modern art from the collection of Peggy Guggenheim, on show in Zurich in 1951, reveals the horizontal and vertical arrangement of text in an asymmetrical composition. The use of white space, vertical text, sans serif typography, and hierarchy of information based upon type sizes and placement constitute the basic elements of the International Typographical Style and demonstrate continuity with Jan Tschichold's "New Typography" (see page 193).

Visual symbols also played an important role in the International Typographic movement. Armin Hofmann (b.1920) and Anton Stankowski (b.1906) are only two among a group of artists who used simple shapes together with sans serif typography to convey complex or mundane information with striking clarity and elegance. Hofmann was responsible for extensive series of posters for museums and other arts organizations in Switzerland, and used typography and simple two-dimensional shapes to convey the essence of a subject with utmost economy. Such work reveals how much may be accomplished with the most rudimentary elements of basic black-and-white abstract shapes. Another example is a 1958 poster for the upcoming season of performances at the State Theater in Basle (fig. 11.64). Here parallel, perpendicular, and angled lines, in combination with the brief phrase "Are you a subscriber?" provide a wide range of associations to the stage, from the raised arms of a conductor, to musical notes, dancers, sweeping movements, and stage props.

While Hofmann's theater poster brings to mind a playful and esthetic treatment of Otto Neurath's ISOTYPE diagrams (see page 201), Anton Stankowski demonstrated in a remarkable series of posters how simple abstract form was capable of communicating complex processes. This is seen, for instance, in the poster illustrating the chemical transfer of heat using series of broken undulating lines that change color from cool

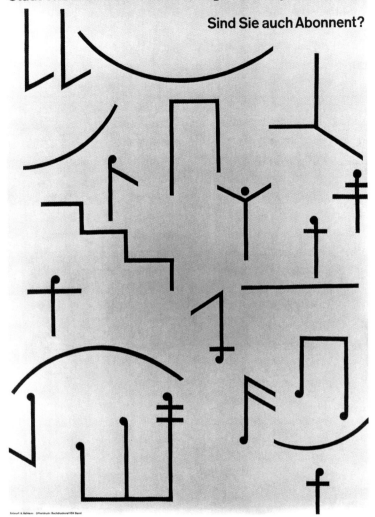

Stadt Theater Basel   Saison-Beginn 19. September 1958

Sind Sie auch Abonnent?

11.64 Armin Hoffmann, State Theater in Basle, poster, 35.4 x 50 in (90 x 128 cm), lithograph, 1958.

11.65 Anton Stankowski, page from a calendar for Viessmann.

blue to warm red as they cross a barrier indicated by a heavy black vertical line (fig. 11.65). Stankowski's exploration of simple abstract form in relation to the design of information recalls the earlier and more intuitive research of Kandinsky to determine a systematic psychology of color while teaching in Russia in the early 1920s (see page 174). Both artists shared an interest in research and experiment as part of the design process, as well as an inclination to see abstract form as being universal in nature.

A more dynamic approach to abstract shape was taken by Max Huber (*b*.1919), who also worked in Switzerland. Huber was less constrained by the flatness of the page or poster, and used perspective and an elastic approach to line to communicate speed, as in a well-known poster for the Monza motor race in Italy in 1956 (fig. 11.66). Huber's dynamic treatment of space has a long history in Constructivist graphic design of the interwar period. It recalls similar experiments by Moholy-Nagy in a poster from around 1926 for pneumatic tires (fig. 11.67) as well as the spatial ambiguities inherent in the Proun exercises produced by El Lissitsky (see fig. 9.12, page 174). An experimental approach within the parameters of the International Typographic Style also characterizes the work of Josef Muller-Brockmann (*b*.1914). His 1960 poster entitled *Less Noise* (fig. 11.68) uses a sharply focused photographic image of a figure whose forearms create a vise-like grip on a pained face viewed from below. The cropped

11.66 Max Huber, *Monza Motor Race*, offset printing, 39.4 x 55 in (100 x 140 cm), 1948. Kunstgewerbemuseum, Zurich.

image and heavy black areas further create a sense of claustrophobic space, and even the direction of the letters adds to the feeling of tension. Here the photographic image and typography communicate like symbolic shapes in an abstract composition to convey a meaning, not unlike the *Beat the Whites with the Red Wedge* poster of El Lissitsky from 1919 (see fig. 9.12, page 174). Indeed, Lissitsky's poster was illustrated in Müller-Brockmann's 1971 book *A History of Visual Communication*.

The grid system and basic sans serif families of type were also well-suited to the consistent presentation of information and products for corporations. The repeated use of a "family" of graphic elements such as typography, trademarks, and elements in a layout insured a uniform template that could be expanded while retaining subordination to overall standards found in all types of corporate graphics. These could be disseminated in house-style manuals to insure the maintenance of standards and identity. An example is Stankowski's public graphics for the city of Berlin, all of which incorporated a thin horizontal line divided by a vertical line to symbolize the division of the city into East and West by a wall from 1948 until 1989. The interest of multinational corporations in visual systems for products and publications during the postwar period created broad interest in the International Typographic Style.

Examples of the International Typographic Style appeared in journals and were the subject of museum exhibitions in Europe and in the United States at the Museum of Modern Art. Many practitioners held teaching positions that enabled them to publish guides and exercises intended to encourage students to develop formal sensibility to design. Armin Hofmann, for instance, taught at the Applied Arts School in Basle and held faculty positions at the School of the Philadelphia Museum of Art (now known as the University of the Arts) and at Yale University. Also in the United States, the Massachusetts Institute of Technology created a graphic design program that worked to create a visual system for the institute that could be applied to a variety of academic and public

11.67 László Moholy-Nagy, sketch for a poster for pneumatic tires, montage with photographic and graphic elemoents, Weimar, *c.* 1926. Verlag der Kunst, Mainz.

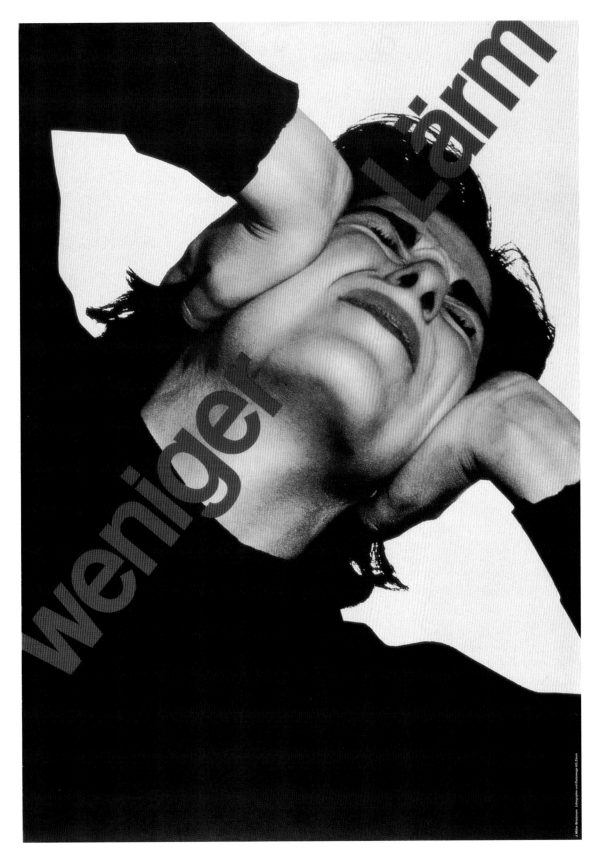

11.68 Josef Müller-Brockmann, campaign poster *Less Noise*, offset printing, 35.4 x 50 in (90 x 128 cm). Kunstgewerbemuseum, Zurich.

11.69 Rudolph de Harak, *Techniques of Executive Control*, book cover, 1964. McGraw Hill Publishers, New York.

from the interwar period as "breakthroughs," all leading to "the present" in which system and the economy of means prevail. Gerstner illustrated numerous trademarks and reductive imagery, as well as photography of products. In one sequence of images he contrasted advertisements in which women's high-heeled shoes were photographed from the profile and bird's eye views for Lord & Taylor (1949) with an I. Miller advertisement in which a women's leg is photographed wearing the shoe (1956) with the following caption, indicating the strong distinction that was drawn at times between the International Typographic Style and more illustrative techniques of the advertising industry:

> One way of advertising shoes is to show a picture of them. Another is to make the picture promise the fulfillment of a wish: If you buy my shoes you will have beautiful legs (the shoe itself seems to have become a minor consideration). It is all rather like a fairy story and nobody troubles to check the truthfulness of such promises.

Postwar designers in Switzerland and Germany favored monotone sans serif typefaces for their simplicity and uniform stroke weights. Until the 1950s designers such as Max Bill were comfortable using the early twentieth-century typeface Akzidenz Grotesk (see page 191). Swiss designer Adrien Frutiger (*b*.1928) developed the Univers

relations information and materials and which embodied the characteristics of the International Typographic Style. Rudolph de Harak (*b*.1924), a self-taught designer familiar with the movement and working in New York, developed a series of more than 350 book jackets for the McGraw Hill Company that used a common sans serif typeface and employed a mathematical grid for layout (fig. 11.69).

In 1959 Swiss designer Karl Gerstner (*b*.1930) published a tri-lingual history of modern graphic design entitled *Die Neue Graphik—The New Graphic Art—Le Nouvel Art Graphique*. This book presented the history of graphic design as the linear development toward clarity and simplicity as guidelines for the presentation of information to suit the needs of advertising and technical information. Gerstner illustrated canonical examples of chromolithographic posters from the later nineteenth and early twentieth centuries as "beginnings," and the more systematic use of asymmetric layout and vertical typography

ABCDEFGHIJKL
MNOPQRSTUVW
XYZ   abcdefghijk
lmnopqrstuvwxyz
.,-;:!? 123456789

11.70 Adrian Frautiger, Univers typeface, 1950, Debegny Peignot Foundry, Paris, 1957.

283

typeface in 1957 for the French foundry Deberny Peignot (fig. 11.70). In addition to numerous variations of weight and width that were made available when it was introduced, Univers letter forms have slight variations in stroke width as compared with interwar sans serif faces, for example, in the slight tapering of the bowls of lower case "p" or "g" as they near the vertical strokes, or in the narrowing of the "o" at the top and bottom. Frutiger thought these changes made the face more versatile and better suited than monotone sans serifs to reading as well as display. In response, the Berthold Foundry in Berlin began working on a revision to its Akzidenz Grotesk font with a number of the same variations from monotone stroke widths. Originally named Neue Haas Grotesk, the name was changed to Helvetica, the Latin name for Switzerland (fig. 11.71). The development of postwar sans serif typefaces for use in International Typographic Style graphic design reveal the painstaking consideration of letter forms in terms of small variations in stroke and space, in relation to printing techniques, effects upon different kinds of paper, and different kinds of printing jobs. The research into the means of expression in a given medium brings to mind Josef Albers' Homage to the Square series of paintings, where laboratory-like experimentation with color combinations reveal distinctions and variations in the formal perception of spatial relationships on a two-dimensional surface (fig. 11.72). Not all graphic designers in Europe subscribed to the exclusive use of sans serif

11.72 Josef Albers, *Homage to the Square*, oil on wood fibreboard, 23 ⅛ in (59 cm) square, 1961. National Gallery of Modern Art, Rome.

ABCDEFGHIJKLMN OPQRSTUVWXYZ? abcdefghijklm nopqrstuvwxyz! 1234567890

11.71 Helvetica typeface, Berthold Foundry, Germany. Line drawing by John Langdon.

typography as did the practitioners of the International Typographic Style. Jan Tschichold (see page 192) became disillusioned with the dogmatism of his own "New Typography," and his work after World War II shows a respect for tradition for both typography and layout in book printing. Tschichold's rejection of universal criteria for graphic design is seen in the format he designed for Penguin Books in Britain. This series employs borders, occasional decoration, symmetrical layouts, and the use of more traditional Roman faces (see fig. 9.53, page 199). Respect for traditional typography is also seen in the new serif faces invented by graphic designer Hermann Zapf (b.1918). A self-taught calligrapher and art director for the Stempel type foundry in Frankfurt-am-Main, Germany, Zapf was strongly influenced by the example of Rudolf Koch (see page 192). Zapf developed several influential serif typefaces in the postwar period, including Palatino in 1950 (fig. 11.73). He was also responsible for the *Manuale Typographicum*, a compendium of material for typographers with a great understanding of both tradition and new principles of design. Palatino was designed for letterpress printing and was intended to maintain its legibility for printing type on inexpensive

ABCDEFGHIJKLMN
OPQRSTUVWXYZ?
abcdefghijklm
nopqrstuvwxyz!
1234567890

11.73 Hermann Zapf, Palatino typeface, 1958. Line drawing by John Langdon.

ABCDEFGHIJKLMN
OPQRSTUVWXYZ?
abcdefghijklm
nopqrstuvwxyz!
1234567890

11.74 Hermann Zapf, Optima typeface, 1952–58. Line drawing by John Langdon.

papers. Its letter forms show a smooth and controlled transition from thick to thin strokes, a characteristic that also identifies Optima (fig. 11.74), which Zapf developed between 1952 and 1958. Optima appears to lie somewhere between serif and sans serif typefaces. It possesses the boldness and close spacing of the latter and yet preserves some transition between thick and thin strokes of Roman letter forms. Some historians of typography praise Zapf for combining the best features of both traditions in the design of Optima.

Means and Ends

The connection between the International Typographic Style, museum exhibitions, and the education of graphic designers in universities and other schools invites comparison with contemporary fine art, revealing similarities as well as differences. On the one hand there is continuity between the shared elements of form among abstract artists and graphic designers, on the other hand there are also important distinctions. Graphic designers used typography, images, and symbols as related means to clearly convey information. Advocates and practitioners of the International Typographic Style saw their work as inherently creative, objective, and socially responsible. Such work embodied a sense of restraint as well as reform, removed from the excesses of commercial art direction at one end and the indulgence of individual expression for a more exclusive audience at the other.

On a more theoretical level, the International Typographic Style is often mentioned in relation to semiotics, defined as the study or science of signs. Emerging first in the field of linguistics, semiotics holds that the meaning of language is the outcome of a process that involves both the "signifier" or means of communication (letters, words, images) and the "signified," that is, the way in which those means of communication are understood. Words, as well as images, do not have fixed meanings in relation to the objects or ideas they represent. Rather, meaning is constructed or mediated socially in an active rather than passive process that involves both intention as well as reception. Such an approach meant that, in the absence of objective communication, graphic designers needed to focus great attention upon both acknowledging the possible range of meaning in the signs they constructed and establishing the context through which such signs might be most clearly, even universally understood. Word and image, composition, and hierarchy of information constituted the elements of a responsible approach to graphic communication within the framework of semiotics.

In 1955 Max Bill resigned as director of the Hochschule für Gestaltung, and Argentinean-born Tomás Maldonado (b.1922) was appointed as his successor. Maldonado moved the curriculum of the school away from the experimentation with materials and visual practice toward a stronger involvement with social theory, reducing the way in which materialism reinforces the existing power structure and social inequality in industrialized and urbanized capitalist societies. Along these lines, he argued for an approach to design education that emphasized social consciousness and responsibility. Inevitably such an approach led away both from integrating commercial as well as expressive considerations into the design process, and his views were further to the political left than the more reformist position and ideology of the German and Swiss community of designers practicing the International Typographic Style. Difficulty in gaining unilateral support among faculty for his political attitudes toward the future of design and the education of designers led to tension at Ulm. Combined with financial problems that forced consolidation with a nearby vocational school, the Hochshule für Gestaltung closed in 1968.

Maldonado's interest in environmental design, however, was echoed by other contemporary theorists who were equally concerned with more radical possibilities of linking design with broader mandates for social change and individual responsibility. These views strayed farther from the more product-and-process-oriented mainstream of international modern industrial design into the realm of social and political activism. In fine art as well, contemporary artists such as Joseph Beuys were less concerned with making objects (objects-as-commodities) than with reaching their audiences and provoking response alternatively through performance and demonstration, suggesting the possibility for a relevant public role for the arts outside the gallery or museum.

The primacy of environmental rather than commercial or humanistic concerns also informed the theory and practice of other, more radical design practitioners and critics, including American architect and designer Buckminster Fuller (1895–1983) as well as Austrian-born architect Richard Neutra (1892–1970). In the 1940s Fuller, inspired by the development of lightweight building materials, devised a technique for constructing "geodesic" domes using triangular components. Fuller advocated the new construction principle as a response to concerns about the efficient use of resources in a global society. Despite their relationship to the domestication of technology, Fuller's ideas were often couched in utopian terms, and the degree of pre-fabrication and uniformity implied a collective approach that was not popular in an age of

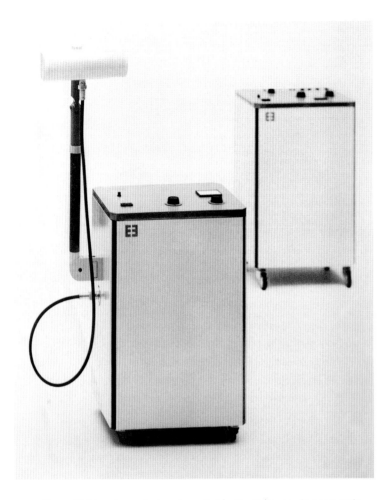

11.75 Tomas Maldonado, medical equipment, Erbe Co., Tubingen, Germany, 1961

the emphasis upon studio work while concentrating upon redefining the role of design and the designer in a global context that was critical of materialism and commercialism. As a practicing designer, Maldonado served as a consultant to the Erbe medical equipment company in Tübingen, Germany in the early 1960s. His product housings emphasize geometric forms, simple manufacturing techniques, smooth surfaces to promote hygiene, and subordination to the impersonal architecture and furnishings of the laboratory (fig. 11.75).

Articulate and forthright in his condemnation of the underlying conformity inherent in capitalism and its dependence upon consumption and advertising, Maldonado criticized the "new humanism" of postwar industrial design in the context of broad global considerations including hunger, disease, and pollution, as well as

11.76 Sori Yamagi, record player and radio, wood, plastic, and metal, 16 ⅛ x 19 ¹¹⁄₁₆ x 12 ³⁄₁₆ in (41 x 50 x 31 cm), manufactured by Nihon-Columbia, Tokyo, 1952. Yanagi Product Design Institute, Tokyo.

Japan

Attitudes toward industrial design in postwar Japan were strongly influenced by government economic policy as actively promoted through the awarding of prizes such as the G-Mark and regulated by agencies that set and reinforced standards for quality and recognition in the international export market beginning in the mid-1950s. The process began with the investment in mechanized mass production of automobiles, trucks, and other durable products for reconstruction and rebuilding the economy following Japan's defeat in World War II and the period of American occupation that ended in 1952. Yet for much of this early postwar period the phrase "made in Japan" connoted cheap toys and knock-off electronic products of often inferior quality, manufactured to the specifications of foreign buyers and merchandisers interested in marketing goods for the mass public without the reputation or quality of the original items they imitated.

With government support a number of Japanese manufacturers began to make a conscious, pragmatic effort to enter the export market for the more sophisticated products of good design, focusing particularly upon electronic communications, motor scooters and motorcycles, and cameras, and even touching later upon fashion and furniture. Through sponsored prizes for original products of industrial design, Japanese manufacturers were

advertising and expanded materialism. Fuller's hopes for sponsorship of his building plans failed to materialize, perhaps as they were too far removed from the suburban ideal that was taking shape in Levittowns and other communities throughout the United States. Nevertheless, Fuller's message of social responsibility and the conservation of natural resources helped to make him something of a "cult" figure in the later 1960s in a more volatile political and social climate.

Neutra's response to postwar design was a book entitled *Survival Through Design*, published in 1954, an indictment of the commercial values inherent in postwar popular culture and a search for standards based upon basic human needs in a global setting. In his writing Neutra proposed the indivisibility of the man-made and natural creation, and hoped that this thought should inform the future of architecture. He advocated stringent performance standards for industrially manufactured building materials, and the application of his ideas would have required a level of regulation and control not possible in the expanding economic framework of developed capitalism.

11.77 Sony Radio, Tokyo Telecommunications Engineering Corporation, plastic housing, 4 ⅛ x 2 ½ x 1 in (11 x 16.4 x 2.5 cm), 1957.

encouraged to hire designers, and were also discouraged from pirating the original designs of other countries. Government initiatives brought American industrial designer Raymond Loewy to Japan, who was hired to redesign the packaging and graphic design for a popular brand of cigarettes, following the success of "Lucky Strike" packaging and the Japanese translation of his autobiography in 1953, and sent Japanese corporate leaders to the United States for exposure to the role of design in industry. The role of government agencies in the success of Japanese industrial design emerges as a distinctive feature of the country's postwar development. The Ministry of International Trade and Industry (MITI), Japan External Trade Organization (JETRO), the Good Design Selection System (responsible for the G-Mark), the Design Promotion Organization, and the Japan Design House, are only the most well-known of the agencies responsible for establishing standards for export products, developing markets for Japanese goods, promoting design through conferences, competitions, and as an element within corporate organization, and helping to sustain a system for design education. The results of this approach have been to transcend a particular look or identity for Japanese products, by demonstrating a willingness to absorb and build upon shared characteristics of practicality, individualism, human factors, indigenous craft traditions, as well as continual innovation in the design of modern industrial products with a broad international market appeal.

Sori Yamagi's (b.1915) radio-phonograph for Nihon-Columbia Corporation of Tokyo in 1952 is an example of a modern practical approach to product design in comparison with the more self-conscious esthetic considerations in similar Braun products (fig. 11.76). The possibility for compact and even portable design for electronic products was pioneered by Akio Moriti, founder of the Tokyo Telecommunications Engineering Company that later became known as Sony. Moriti purchased the technology for the use of transistors from the American corporation Western Bell Laboratories in 1953, initiating its development for the domestic market in the production of small, portable radios, and acquiring a reputation for miniaturization in the manufacture of consumer electronics products (fig. 11.77). In the later 1950s miniaturization found expression in portable television sets, and the concept was applied

to the Sony Walkman personal tape player of the 1970s. Such miniaturization was easily seen both as a convenience in defining more mobile lifestyles as well as contributing to flexibility and space-saving approaches to interior design, all elements subsumed under the term organic design as conceived by Eliot Noyes (see below page 291) and later known broadly as good design.

In addition to the emerging reputation for the application of technology to the domestic market, Japanese companies Nikon and Canon successfully competed with German counterparts such as Hasselblad and Leica in the market for high-quality professional photographic equipment through refinements in design that appealed to the educated user. Nikon's 1957 SP3 single reflex camera (fig. 11.78) featured a wider horizontal viewing window than comparable models such as the Leica M3 of

11.78 Nikon Camera, metal, 3 ³⁄₁₆ x 5 ⅝ x 1 ⅝ in (8 x 14.3 x 4 cm), Nikon Inc., 1957.

11.79 Ernst Leitz Gmbtt, M3 Leica camera, injection mold aluminum, brass, 1954, Wetslar, Germany.

11.80 Zenichi Mano, National Radio, plastic, 7 x 14 x 5 ½ in (18 x 35.6 x 14 cm), manufactured by Matushita Electrical Industrial Company, Osaka, 1953.

shapes subdivided into units based upon wooden shutters and screens derived from Japanese architecture such as the Palace at Kyoto (fig. 11.80). Other references to Japanese architecture can be seen in the "Butterfly" stool designed by Sori Yamagi for the Tendo Mokko company in 1956 and constructed of two identical curved molded plywood pieces easily assembled by a metal rod (fig. 11.81). The plywood technology was developed first in connection with industrial and wartime production for containers and aircraft requiring exact measurements and specification, but later was used extensively in furniture primarily for public buildings. Yamagi's stool has been compared to the roofline of Japanese buildings, but the abstract contour also recalls examples of modern abstract sculpture.

Nakashima and Nature

The beauty of natural materials, sensitive craftsmanship, original designs, and simple construction also characterizes the furniture of designer George Nakashima (1905–1990). Nakashima was born in the United States but worked in Japan for an architectural firm after completing studies in architecture at M.I.T. After World War II (during which he spent a year in an internment camp for Japanese-Americans), Nakashima established a workshop for making his own furniture in New Hope, Pennsylvania (1946). Designs such as the Conoid Bench with Back from 1961 (fig. 11.82) display an interest in preserving the irregular beauty of natural forms often combined with slightly irregular and uneven dowel-like supports or rails for chair backs. Nakashima's oeuvre relies upon a balance of modern and traditional approaches to furniture design. Although a small number of early designs for chairs were manufactured by Knoll, Nakashima preferred workshop production and direct contact between craftsmen, materials, and processes.

Japan: A Summary

Unified standards, large corporate initiative, international marketing, and the encouragement of innovation in Japanese design appear as the successful embodiment of Werkbund ideology in the postwar period. Moreover, for Japanese corporations there seems to be less of a

1954 (fig. 11.79), demonstrating careful understanding of the design requirements for the highly technical and specialized equipment of experienced professional photographers. The continuing success of this approach has been demonstrated in more recent years by its extension, via increased automation, to 35 millimeter camera technology for a larger segment of the general public.

Critics have also noted the continuity between the practicality and esthetic simplicity in Japanese postwar industrial design and indigenous traditions of Japanese architecture and interior design. Zenichi Mano's (b.1916) 1953 National Radio for the Matushita company of Osaka featured an asymmetrical composition of rectangular

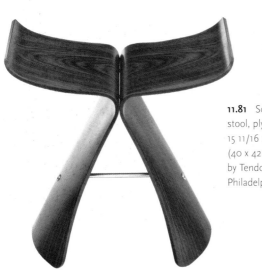

11.81 Sori Yanagi, "Butterfly" stool, plywood and metal, 15 11/16 x 16 9/16 x 12 3/16 in (40 x 42 x 31 cm), manufactured by Tendo Mokko, Tendo, 1956. Philadelphia Museum of Art.

11.82 George Nakashima, Conoid Bench with Back, walnut, hickory, 31 x 113 x 40 in (79 x 287 x 102 cm), 1961. Nakashima Studios.

dichotomy between standards, with their implication of socially responsible progress, and commercialism, where obsolescence is associated pejoratively with conspicuous consumption and the exploitation of the mass market. The policies initiated through MITI and other design organizations in Japan were successful in revitalizing the Japanese economy, raising the income level and standard of living at home, and establishing a reputation for quality and technological and esthetic innovation abroad. At the same time the products of Japanese industrial design made personal electronic products virtually a necessary counterpart to individual fulfillment, from transistor radios in the 1950s to pocket calculators and the Walkman in the 1960s and 1970s, Karoake in the 1980s, and compact disc players (Discman) in the 1990s. Such a blurring between commercialism, innovation, and progress in design is a phenomenon we will encounter internationally in the 1960s. Its emergence in Japanese design is prescient: it appears to signify a sometimes subtle but significant shift in economic policy from production to consumption, with the latter creating its own justification, requiring both new markets and intensified advertising through the mass media.

Design and Corporate Culture

A conscious connection between corporations and industries and the promotion of education and cultural awareness through information design may be seen in the work of designers like Will Burtin (see page 235), as well as in advertising campaigns undertaken by the Columbia Broadcast System (CBS) under creative director William Golden (1911–1959) and the Container Corporation of America under its president Walter Paepke (1896–1960). These executives sponsored fine artists and designers to develop posters and advertisements for company products and services as well as for more general advertisements that simply link the corporation to creative activities perceived by many to be an expression of democratic principles. Golden was responsible for a massive campaign to attract attention and sponsors to CBS with a series of creative advertisements to demonstrate the power of radio and the newer medium of television to reach diverse audiences. In an advertisement intended for a trade periodical, Golden based his image upon a drawing by artist Nathan Polsky that depicts small white ghost-like figures floating from left to right against a black background. Brief copy appears to the lower right, while a heavier title reads "The air is full customers," referring to the medium of radio (fig. 11.83). A designer in his own right, Golden also developed the "eye" trademark for CBS.

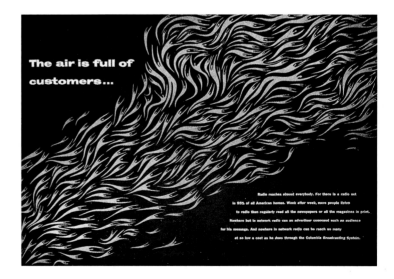

11.83 Print advertisement, Columbia Broadcast System, artist: N. Polsky, art director: William Golden, 1950, thirtieth annual *Art Directors' Annual.*

Walter Paepke was another businessman who promoted the educational value of modern design through his large Chicago-based company, the Container Corporation of America (CCA). Paepke also sponsored a series of advertisements by modern artists including French painter Fernand Léger, helped to support the creation of the New Bauhaus in Chicago under the direction of László Moholy-Nagy, and established the Design Conference in Aspen, Colorado beginning in 1951, where he owned a vacation home. Paepke saw the corporation as a participant in public education, identifying culture with high intellectual and creative pursuits, products of an enlightened democracy. As explained by James Sloan Allen, Paepke's interests were parallel to the efforts of University of Chicago president Robert Hutchins to establish educational standards based upon "great books" that contribute to the education of the individual in a democratic society. Like design reform in earlier periods, the view of culture promoted by CCA was paternalistic, reflecting the interests and biases of an educated and powerful class, and removed from the complex social and economic realities of the postwar period. Nevertheless, such endeavors and projects suggest the cultural climate in which postwar design developed, in which multinational corporations were aligned with education, standards, and the promotion of shared cultural values.

11.84 Geismar and Chermayoff, Exhibition Design, 1958. United States Pavilion, Brussels, Belgium.

Trademarks and Beyond

Paul Rand, in his 1947 book *Thoughts on Design*, noted an almost "magical power" exerted by letter forms. This "aura" surrounding letters found expression in the postwar period, especially in the proliferation of memorable trademarks for corporations and organizations operating on a multinational scale. The role of letters as a leitmotif of mid-twentieth-century industrial culture emerged in the United States Pavilion for the World's Fair held in Brussels in 1957 (fig. 11.84), designed by graphic artists Tom Giesmar (b.1931) and Ivan Chermayoff (b.1932). By that year, corporate trademarks using striking combinations of bold type were already commonplace in advertising and display.

In the postwar period many large multinational corporations saw the advantages of consistent policies toward design. Recalling the precepts of the Werkbund (see pages 99–100), standards of "good design" translated easily into corporate culture, subordinating the individual to the group whose shared ethos was guided by dependability and consistent performance. Corporations such as Olivetti in Italy, Braun in West Germany, Lufthansa Airlines in Holland, and Sony in Japan all drew upon consultant or in-house industrial designers to create identity programs, implemented with the support of top levels of management. The increasingly international nature of business in many hi-tech industries such as pharmaceuticals, oil, transportation, and communications relied upon letters rather than lengthier company names for intelligibility and recognition in a global market. The economic climate of aggressive growth through takeovers and mergers often created interest in maintaining corporate identity and the services of professional designers. Their activities ranged from the development of logos, liveries, and product lines to the effective establishment and reinforcement of corporate organizational standards and ethos. Product design and trademark development only form part of corporate identity. Many corporations rely upon packaging, architecture, signage, advertising, and exhibition design in the creation of their image, particularly if their business is in soft drinks, energy transmission, or oil and gasoline products rather than on a line of consumer domestic wares such as coffee-makers, toasters, or cassette players.

The corporate image of the Olivetti Corporation, as seen in showrooms throughout Italy in the later 1940s,

11.85 Paul Rand, trademark, IBM Corporation, 1956. Line drawing by John Langdon.

prompted IBM president Thomas Watson, Jr. to pursue a unified and effective corporate identity program. To direct this program Watson hired Eliot F. Noyes (1910–1977), an architect who previously was curator of industrial design at the Museum of Modern Art. IBM may serve as a paradigm of sorts for the corporate promotion of design under capitalism. IBM identity was not only related to the coherent design of products and promotional materials directed toward clients and investors, but also toward reinforcing community and exclusivity among employees, that is, in establishing visible signs and a framework for a corporate culture. Such a team-based approach had advantages in providing guidelines or standards not only for design but also for dress and behavior and their effect upon internal and external perception. Some observers noted the downside to the new corporate culture. As observed by sociologist David Riesman in his book *The Lonely Crowd* (1950), and seen earlier in the strategies of the advertising industry after World War I, a corporate "image" could have an alienating effect upon individuals, who felt that they had to "fit in" with the group in order to be successful. In Riesman's view, such corporate behaviour was part of a shift from "inner-directed" to "other-directed"

values that he saw emerging as the dominant form of conformity particularly in American society.

The IBM logo was designed by Paul Rand (see page 252), one of several specialists hired by Noyes (fig. 11.85). Like many global corporations, the success of the IBM logo depends upon simple recognition and the substitution of letters for longer, often complicated names. Rand used a square-serif display face known as City Medium, produced in Germany in 1930. Serif letters are less usual in corporate logos, but in this case contribute to strong figure-ground contrast through close spacing, creation of squared negative spaces between letters for added unity, and to the stability of the design. Similar use of serif faces in the later 1940s and early 1950s are found in the trademarks by Swiss designer Herbert Matterfor the New Haven Railway in 1954 and for the Knoll Corporation around 1950 (fig. 11.86). These examples also create unified images out of letter forms, and the letters of the Knoll trademark consist of connecting thin lines of uniform thickness ending in square shapes. The relation of trademarks to products or services of a company is seen in Rand's re-design of the Westinghouse "W," where circular serifs and lines construct the letter and symbolize electrical circuitry (fig. 11.87). More common in logo design, however, is sans serif typography, seen, for instance, in Rand's design for the American Broadcast Corporation in 1965 (fig. 11.88). This trademark uses a variant of the Futura typeface with its "bowl a" rather than Roman lower case "a," resulting in an identity among the shapes of the three initial letters.

Subsequently Rand retained the basic elements of his IBM logo, but expanded its treatment through repetition and color variation on packaging, introducing horizontal

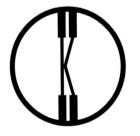

11.86 Herbert Matter, trademark "K" for Knoll Corporation, 1950. Line drawing by John Langdon.

11.87 Paul Rand, trademark for Westinghouse Corporation, 1960.

11.88 Paul Rand, trademark for ABC, 1964.

stripes that run through the heavy letter forms, and even playfully substituting an eye and a bee in place of the "I" and "B" letters. This last variation is indeed a testimony to the power of letters that he noted in *Thoughts on Design*. Noyes was responsible for the product design of typewriters for IBM. An electric typewriter from 1958 (fig. 11.89) does not possess the organic sculptural contour of Nizzoli's designs for Olivetti, but a sleek, cutaway form houses the mechanical parts from the late 1950s onward, and was retained in a number of designs in subsequent years to distinguish the IBM product line.

Noyes' success at IBM was based in part upon his close working relationship with company president Watson. Both men agreed that design could be a tool for greater cooperation among the various IBM divisions as well as communicating both internally and externally a coherent and consistent approach to design and corporate structure. Noyes' efforts were an extension of the belief in the ability of design to shape shared attitudes and values. He believed that standards in design should be based upon the adaptation of modern technology and considerations of fitness to purpose in which decoration and superficial change played little or no responsible part. Noyes worked as a young architect for Walter Gropius and Marcel Breuer after graduating from Harvard University and, as

mentioned above, was curator for industrial design at the Museum of Modern Art in New York. It is not surprising that given this familiarity with European-based interwar modernism, he extended to the multinational corporation the responsibility for setting high standards of efficiency and taste in design. Corporate identity gained visibility and respect for the design profession.

Another outcome of Noyes' contract with IBM was the hiring of Charles Eames as a consultant designer of exhibits and films for the corporation. Eames' work for IBM focused upon communicating technological and economic progress through images, in exhibits for the IBM Pavilion at the 1964 New York World's Fair and in the three-dimensional timeline for "A Computer Perspective" exhibit held in the IBM corporate headquarters in New York in 1971 (fig. 11.90). Eames' exhibits, like those of Will Burtin's for the Upjohn Pharmaceutical Company (see fig. 11.20, page 258), express the postwar belief in the integration of business, government, and technology to impact upon living standards globally. It also provides evidence of the continuation of the tradition of versatility among modern industrial designers, who viewed their varied efforts as means toward serving human needs rather than as directed solely toward creating products for a market. Such a view emphasizes a broad, humanistic understanding of the profession.

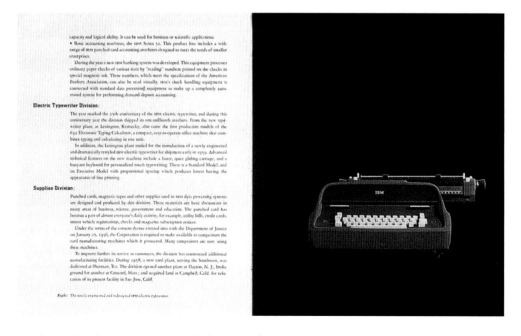

11.89 Paul Rand, IBM annual report, with photograph of IBM electric typewriter, designed by Eliot Noyes, 1958.

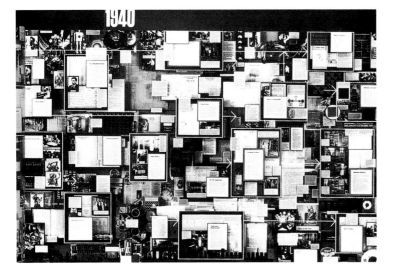

11.90 Charles Eames, panel from *A Computer Perspective* (History Wall or Timeline), one of six 8 ft (2.4 m) panels, 1971. Exhibit Design, IBM Corporate Exhibit Center, New York.

In addition to his special consultant relationship with IBM, Noyes also worked for Mobil, Westinghouse, and other large, multinational corporations. His career documents the attempt to use design to form the basis of a consistent and responsible corporate image, even when technical and organizational considerations in such large businesses made uniformity and conformity difficult to achieve. His successes, featured in articles for *Industrial Design*, were based upon cooperation with executives whose authority helped to gain agreement and compliance with centralizing policies. The International Typographic Style provided the basis for the visual systems developed for many international companies. Otl Aicher (1922–91) was a faculty member at the Hochschule für Gestaltung at Ulm who developed corporate identity and advertising for the Dutch airline Lufthansa in the early 1960s with specifications that included grid layout, typography, and symbols.

Other examples of the development of conscious policies toward design in a global market include the Philips Corporation of Eindhoven, The Netherlands. Recognizing competition and global markets for a variety of products ranging from light bulbs to stereos, televisions, and medical equipment in the postwar period, Philips' management developed a consistent design policy and integrated design into the corporate decision-making process. For Philips this did not result in a recognizable "look" for products as with Braun, but rather in a process of training and communication across a number of product divisions and brand names that had grown autonomously. While recognized as Philips for consumer electronics in Europe, in the United States Philips products continue to be known by brand-names such as Norelco, Sylvania, and Philco. There is no effort to create uniformity across products, but design is used to reinforce considerations of ergonomics, fitness-to-purpose, as well as target audience in the development of products.

Good design within the global corporation has been a marketing and organizational strategy emphasizing consistency, recognition, and technical standards in a world made more accessible through communications and mechanized mass production. It was not, however, the only corporate approach to design. Particularly in the United States, brand differentiation among products manufactured by a single company was another effective corporate strategy, giving the impression of variety and choice under the control of tight policies governing the parameters of change. Such strategies, involving massive advertising campaigns, were effective in limiting competition from smaller companies, and will be explored below in the section on mass culture.

Chapter 12

Design and Mass Appeal: A Culture in Consumption

12.6 Advertisement for Cadillac Eldorado, from *Life*, 1957.

Standards of "good design," as described in Chapter 11, were embraced by private institutions such as the Museum of Modern Art in New York, and provided the framework for discourse at schools like the Hochschule für Gestaltung at Ulm. "Good design" formed the basis of policy and identity for corporations such as IBM and Braun, and was supported by government-sponsored agencies in countries like Britain, Japan, and Italy. "Good design" was marketed through international journals, books, and exhibitions, and informed the practices of contract industrial designers whose furniture and product prototypes were manufactured by Herman Miller or became part of the product line for companies like Olivetti. Through such efforts, as well as the United States' investment and incentives for peacetime economic reconstruction and growth in Europe, the products and accompanying ethos of progress through design

reached a broader audience than ever before. "Good design" was the visible expression of a clear and socially responsible approach to change motivated by technological progress and a shared commitment to improving the quality of life internationally under the embrace of capitalist free enterprise.

But in the early 1950s in the United States, the middle class and a growing segment of an industrial working class reaping the benefits of increased production and higher wages entered the expanding and elastic market for residential housing, home furnishings, and other industrially manufactured products. The attitudes and expectations of this large and diverse consumer audience both incorporated and transcended the standards and paternalism of museums, identity systems, and a new humanism embracing social responsibility, esthetic awareness, fitness-to-purpose, and comfort. New, broader needs were shaped not only by economic stability and postwar optimism but also by the unprecedented role assumed by mass media in relation to the expansion of consumption and the shaping of values. The term mass culture may be used to describe the common features of the American market especially after World War II. This term refers not simply to products that reached this broad market, but also to the attitudes of consumers in relation to the mass media.

The apparent indifference of the mass market to the standards of "good design" may be seen in the success of a wide variety of postwar products ranging from automobiles to kitchen appliances, portable electronics to furniture. In all of these examples there was a tremendous receptivity to the phenomenon of progressive obsolescence, that is, the calculated efforts of manufacturers to generate demand with a seemingly unending supply of "new" products. Obsolescence had the effect of making current products seem "old," conditioning the buying public to continual cycles of consumption and frequent replacement. In addition, while modern materials and methods of production were used, products made frequent references to the past, to the present, as well as to the future, replacing principles such as "fitness to purpose" with greater freedom of choice integrating expendability and a broad eclecticism. Indeed the phenomena of newness, an accelerated pace of change, and continual replacement tended to erode in some degree the very notion of fixed standards and the authority they imply. After all, standards suggest permanence and durability for products, while obsolescence and novelty imply a perpetual state of "becoming," of desire, where consumption itself becomes a way of life. British design historian and critic Reyner Banham (1922–1988) aptly described this phenomenon as a "throwaway culture."

Despite the commercial potential of novelty and obsolescence, the implementation of frequent product change entailed great economic risks: the retooling required for changes in the manufacturing process as well as the increased investment in the complex process of design translated either into higher, less competitive prices or lower profit margins for companies and their investors. Thus the successful implementation of obsolescence required corporations to manage risks of higher investment costs by limiting the role of design to superficial elements of product housing rather than integrating design

with engineering, ergonomics, or other research-based considerations. Moreover, the success of this strategy also depended upon marketing the products of industrial design through a variety of media ranging from popular magazines and radio to the cinema and emerging medium of television. In many ways these media often employed similar strategies for the mass production of entertainment. An example is the form of serial programming, utilizing the same familiar characters facing new conflicts or crises each week, or stereotypical Hollywood film heroes following the same plot line in an array of different settings. In these cases originality was limited to particular elements of the creative process in order to generate ever "new" products for consumers to watch or to buy while minimizing the efficient expenditure of capital resources and investment. Also, popular design and entertainment were even more interrelated, since advertisement was sold to corporate sponsors of products and services on the basis of delivering an audience for the purposes of marketing.

Most historians believe that the success of product obsolescence for the mass market could not have taken place without the stimulation of advertising and added incentives such as term and credit buying. Whether through illustration, photography, or the emerging medium of television, advertisements linked products to the achievement of status, beauty, and social acceptance. On the basis of polls and other consumer studies, advertisers often targeted housewives and children, who played a large role in buying patterns in a majority of middle-class families. Such techniques extended Veblen's theory of conspicuous consumption to an age of industrial production and mass consumption. Manufacturing and new strategies for design, marketing, and advertising combined to create forms and associations that appealed to a diverse audience linked by a belief that consumption and materialism were the means to individual fulfillment. Such a seductive combination of forces was hard to resist. Strip malls, discount stores, promotions, and expanded distribution further reduced resistance to shopping for the products of mass culture. While the phenomenon of national brands may be traced to the early twentieth century, the postwar era accelerated the substitution of the national for the local and regional through chain stores, hotels, and restaurants such as Korvettes, Holiday Inn, and Colonel Sanders Kentucky Fried Chicken or

McDonalds restaurants. The result was an emerging shared, homogeneous culture of consumption that extended to many areas of American life.

Detroit: Transportation as Symbol

The Detroit-manufactured automobile illustrates the attitudes and practices governing the production and consumption of mass design. The manufacture of new automobiles for the civilian market had ceased in 1942 as automobile makers contributed to meeting the material needs of the war effort. Although demand for new cars was strong in the years following the end of World War II and the resumption of manufacturing for the domestic market, there were signs of market saturation and a slowed rate of growth in automobile purchases in the early 1950s. Postwar automobiles resembled their pre-war counterparts, and the differentiating role of design was limited by the interest in meeting demand by increasing productivity and keeping the costs of capital investment at a minimum.

Stimulating sales through annual styling changes was not a new idea in the automobile industry, and it re-emerged with renewed vitality in the early 1950s. At General Motors, president Alfred Sloan renewed his plan for greater differentiation and more noticeable annual styling changes, minimizing costs through standardized parts for the chassis and other mechanical elements that could be shared among the company's numerous product lines. It was Sloan's dream to create a vehicle "for every purse," defining a series of gradations from efficiency to luxury in terms of visible differences in styling. Encompassing the ends as well as the broad middle of the market, General Motors effectively helped to equate car buying with social as well as personal mobility and to stimulate more frequent automobile purchases while remaining competitive with smaller manufacturers of both luxury and economy cars.

Harley Earl (see page 211), chief of General Motors' Styling Department since its inception in 1927 as the Art and Color Section, benefited from a close relationship with Sloan, and was able to carry out the president's corporate vision with great imagination. Earl preferred longer and lower bodies for GM cars and accentuated these characteristics by adding decoration in the form of chrome

12.1 Harley Earl, Buick Y-Job convertible coupé, 1937. General Motors Corporation. Sloan Museum, Flint, Michigan.

accents, wraparound bumpers, and introducing the tailfin. Earlier pre-war prototypes, such as the 1937 two-door Buick Y-Job (fig. 12.1), announced Earl's approach, and Sloan's embrace of planned obsolescence created the kind of sponsorship that gave designers greater freedom within the corporation, provided the results could be measured in increased sales and profits.

To approach the ideal of a longer and lower body, Earl favored flowing curvilinear forms and an integration of hoods, fenders, trunks, windshields, and roofs. As explained by Stephen Bayley, designers working for Earl made prototypes in clay rather than wood or metal to achieve more unified and modeled sculptural forms; in production, longer widths of steel, available as early as 1934, reduced the gap between prototype and

12.2 Harley Earl, Cadillac Eldorado coupé, 1953. Cadillac Museum, Hachenburg, Germany.

12.4 Buick Roadmaster, advertisement, General Motors Corporation, Detroit, Michigan, 1954. *Better Homes and Gardens,* August 1954.

manufactured product. Earl introduced the tailfin first in the 1948 Cadillac, General Motors' high-end luxury car, and persisted with the feature despite an initial lukewarm reception by other company executives. The fins were a form of overt product symbolism, the result of Earl's fascination with the twin-body Lockheed P-38 Fighter plane and its dual tailfins for increased stability (figs. 12.2 and 12.3). In Earl's estimation, the tailfin was a "visible receipt" for the consumer's dollar. Its widespread success in the 1953 Cadillac encouraged Earl to include the feature in General Motors' lower-end models, where it appeared in the 1955 Chevrolet, thus making available to average customers a realm of product association previously available only to wealthier buyers. The identification was encouraged through advertising, for instance, linking the potential buyer of the 1954 Buick Roadmaster with success and status (fig. 12.4). Interest in the tailfin and other features accentuating longer and lower bodies, for instance Buick's small bullet-shaped chrome "portholes,"

12.3 P-38 fighter plane, inspiration for tailfins.

wraparound bumpers, or curved windshields, were often derived from GM's futuristic "dream cars." Dream cars were fantastic non-production models featured in traveling shows known as *Motoramas* or in dealer showrooms, related as well to a subculture of do-it-yourself car-buffs throughout the period who crafted customized versions of standard production vehicles (fig. 12.5). The *Motorama* has sometimes been described as a traveling world's fair, encouraging the kinds of associations between buying and social mobility and self-realization.

The broad marketing strategy and financing of annual model changes across different brand names such as Oldsmobile, Pontiac, Buick, Chevrolet, and Cadillac, favored large companies such as General Motors and led to their increasing control of the market. In addition to their focus upon brand differentiation through styling, the large automobile manufacturers possessed the resources for advertising and other forms of marketing, such as the *Motorama*. Independent manufacturers like Hudson, Packard, Nash, and Kaiser either ceased production or became divisions of new conglomerates, gradually losing their identity. These smaller companies were unable to compete with or differentiate themselves from the larger companies and their comprehensive advertising, sales, and marketing programs. Thus, despite the apparent variety and choice available to the consumer in terms of brands and models, American automobile manufacturing also became more homogeneous, controlled by a small number of large manufacturers with less room in the mass market for individual entrepreneurship. These large companies did not pursue a unified corporate image or identity but rather were successful in promoting "brand" identification with particular groups of consumers. Such a strategy seemed better suited to progressive obsolescence through annual model changes and the introduction of new brands or sub-brands, for instance, the "compact cars" of the later 1950s such as the Chevrolet Corvair .

The 1955 Chevrolet introduced not only the tailfin to the low-end of its product line, but also the powerful, high-compression V-8 engine. For the average-income buyer, features such as styling, horsepower, air-conditioning, motorized convertible-tops, all added a sense of individual expression and exhilaration to the experience of personal mobility. The continuing appeal of these associations was celebrated nostalgically in the 1973 film *American Graffiti*

12.5 *Motorama*, General Motors, 1954.

or the 1988 film *Rainmaker*, long after fuel prices, fears of gasoline shortages, pollution, and foreign competition had taken their toll on the United States' "love affair" with the automobile. Advertisements for the American automobile of the later 1950s often combined references in the copy to practical advantages of roominess or advanced engineering with images that identified automobile ownership with luxurious living. These generally featured attractive, well-dressed couples returning home from an evening out or arriving in style at an upscale hotel (fig. 12.6). Indeed, such product symbolism must be what Karl Gerstner had in mind in his endorsement of straight product photography rather than emotional promises in advertising (see page 282).

Contemporary cinema also featured the appeal of varied activities associated with personal mobility. Examples include the family outing of *Mr. Hobbs Takes a Vacation* (1962), the carefree spontaneity of *Two for the Road* (1967), or a reckless, self-destructive element in *Rebel Without a Cause* (1957). The automobile also formed a part of the lyrics and pace of emerging rock 'n' roll music, for instance, Chuck Berry's "No Particular Place to Go:"

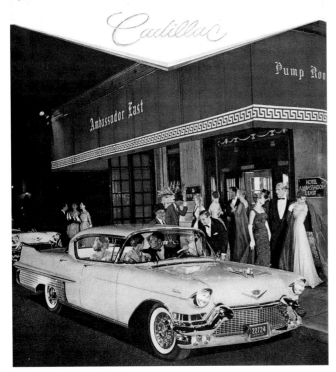

There Are Some Secrets a Man Can't Keep ...

12.6 Advertisement for Cadillac Eldorado, from *Life*, 1957.

Riding along in my automobile
My baby beside me at the wheel
I stole a kiss at the turn of a mile
My curiosity running wild
Cruisin' and playin' the radio
With no particular place to go.

The development of the powerful V-8 engine for regular production vehicles also took advantage of the inexpensive fuel prices in the United States, a result of favorable business agreements between American-based oil companies and refineries located in the Middle East. By the early 1970s the oil-producing nations would assert their independence from foreign oil companies, raise the price of fuel, and redefine the basis for automobile design as established by General Motors in the period under discussion. But until that time, a large segment of the consuming public in the United States enjoyed the associations of styling, the anticipation of new annual models, and the varied appeal of the open road.

General Motors was perhaps the largest but certainly was not the only manufacturer to adopt styling and obsolescence in industrial design. The Ford Corporation introduced the Thunderbird sports car in 1954, a small two-seater appealing to the prospective buyer's personal indulgence rather than practical considerations of family space or comfort. The design, somewhat rectangular, seemed a restrained version of the more sculptural examples of Italian luxury coach-building (see page 275), but the Thunderbird was priced to appeal to a wider market of buyers who wished to indulge more overtly in the excitement of the open road. In 1952 Chrysler Corporation promoted Virgil Exner, a former associate both of Harley Earl at General Motors and of Raymond Loewy, to vice-president in charge of styling. Exner's designs for Chrysler emphasized longer and lower profiles, but minimized the rounded panels and swollen forms of General Motors cars in favor of more angular, tapered forms. In the industry this was known as the forward look, thought to be modeled upon the saber-nosed body and swept-back wings of jet fighter planes that appeared in the early 1950s. The effect was enhanced through decorative features such as overarching "eyebrows" above headlights, sweeping chrome strips reaching from front to rear and echoing the contour of the body, low and sloping rooflines, and tremendous tailfins with a pronounced upward sweep emphasizing length (fig. 12.7).

12.7 Virgil Exner, Plymouth coupé, 1957, Chrysler Corporation.

Critics of Styling

By the later 1950s there was a tendency to criticize tailfins and other automobile styling features both as superfluous and tasteless. Raymond Loewy, for instance, who served as design consultant to the automobile manufacturer Studebaker, took aim at the American automobile industry in a speech of 1955, comparing that year's new designs to "gaudy merchandise" and "jukeboxes on wheels:" even the author of *Never Leave Well Enough Alone*, who well understood the need to demonstrate the commercial advantages of design in industrial manufacturing, was offended by the degree to which outer form had departed from a more substantive relation to its mechanical basis, or to broader considerations of performance and the ideal of beauty embodied in the characteristics of a streamlined modernism. Loewy's own designs for Studebaker were original and aerodynamic, pioneering the sloping roofline later introduced by former associate Virgil Exner for the 1957 Plymouth (fig. 12.8). But the Studebaker lacked the symbolic jet-age references of its General Motors, Ford, and Chrysler counterparts. In the end its appeal was more limited and it proved commercially unsuccessful.

For critics of the postwar American automobile industry, the manufacturer was often viewed as the manipulator of desire in the consumer: the manufacturer is seen as active and the consumer as passive, with the latter cast in the role of unwitting victim. Yet a look at the period shows that not all of the large auto makers' styling initiatives were successful, and that efforts to "manipulate" the public often demonstrated naïveté and resulted in disaster (as easily observed in the high number of short-lived network television series produced each autumn). In other words, the phenomenon of mass design was and remains an unpredictable, risky investment demanding nuanced scrutiny rather than the polemic and dismissive treatment that its critics often preferred.

One of the most widely known industry miscalculations of the mass market was Ford's introduction of the 1958 Edsel, a project that failed to attract consumer interest despite a heavy investment in styling and promotion. The Edsel debacle reveals the complexity of predicting or manipulating the market for products intended to have mass appeal. As a result, two viewpoints toward mass culture emerge. On one hand, mass design may be seen as a form of exploitation manipulated as it were from above

12.8 Raymond Loewy, Studebaker, 1957.

and masking the desire for corporate profit and power under the banner of freedom of choice and the democratization of luxury, heavily dependent upon advertising and product symbolism. On the other hand, we may see the phenomenon as being in touch with the everyday experience of ordinary folk, a popular expression of the desire for individuality for a diverse audience. In this view mass culture fulfills a basic desire to gratify material appetites, or to assert independence and even to resist both the efforts of corporations and advertisers alike. The elements of resistance, escape, self-expression, and difference within this popular culture emerges through products, fashion, and also through the medium of popular music, particularly rock 'n' roll with its roots in Afro-American culture and its rebellious challenge to conventional behavior and authority. Some of these latter attitudes linking popular music to grass roots expression may be seen in the career of rock musician and songwriter Bruce Springsteen. When Springsteen accepted the Oscar for Original Score at the 1993 Academy Awards for a song written for the film *Philadelphia* (March 1994; the movie dealt with AIDS and discrimination against its victims) he accepted the award saying: "You do your best and hope that it pulls out the best in your audience, and some piece of it spills over into the real world and peoples' everyday lives and allows us to recognize each other through our veil of differences." Thus popular culture reveals a paradox, for its expressions may be viewed both as a form of resistance to conformity on the one hand and as acceptance of the ephemeral criteria of mass appeal on the other. In either case, however, the status of the commodity and the capitalist system that creates and distributes it remains paramount, for even resistance most often takes the form of consumption rather than threatening social or political action.

Author Thomas Hine noted that when United States Vice-President Richard Nixon met visiting Soviet Premier Nikita Kruschev in 1959 during a well-publicized meeting of the leaders of the global superpowers during the Cold War, the Vice-President proudly showed the Soviet leader an American washing machine as proof of the high standard of living enjoyed by American families. Nixon identified, in effect, materialism with the achievement of democratic ideals. While Americans might have feared the progress of the Soviets in space and weapons technology in the wake of the successful 1957 launch of the *Sputnik* satellite, there was little doubt that in the area of consumption and consumer choice the United States occupied a position of strength and confidence. Despite differences in regard to the issues of standards, proponents of "good design" and the products of mass culture in the later 1950s could both promote their approaches to design in terms that equated technology and material prosperity with fulfillment and the achievement of democratic ideals under capitalism.

Resorts and Luxury

Together with the Detroit-manufactured automobile and the development of the new suburban tract home, popular design in postwar America was also defined by the resort hotel, first built in Miami Beach, Florida and later in Las Vegas, Nevada. Miami's Fontainebleau, built in 1954 and named for the eighteenth-century royal château outside of Paris, was one of several Florida beachfront hotels designed by Morris Lapidus. Trained as an architect in New York, Lapidus had spent much of his career prior to the war as a successful designer of retail storefronts and interiors (see page 222 and fig. 10.32). Postwar affluence expanded the market for travel and leisure, providing Lapidus with the opportunity to design on a larger and more lavish scale, and to indulge the popular imagination for drama, escape, fantasy, and luxury gleaned from both the past as well as from the future. Lapidus's resort hotels often displayed a preference for sweeping curves and recurves, for instance in the opposition of entranceway and facade at the Fontainebleau (fig. 12.9). Curving hallways rather than the repetitive rhythm of doorways and hall-lights created a sense of anticipation for the guest. Mezzanines, grand staircases, suspended ceilings with circular holes for chandeliers, and support beams hidden beneath sheathings of wood and textured materials were closer in experience to movie sets than to waiting and gathering areas. In art historical terms Lapidus's designs tended toward the openness and grandeur of the Italian Baroque, and seemed to reduce the barrier separating Hollywood from the experience of Americans escaping for a week of vacation at the beach. Many of Lapidus's ideas derived from the expressive possibilities of shaping

12.9 Morris Lapidus, garden façade, Fontainebleau Hotel, Miami Beach, Florida, 1954.

12.10 Morris Lapidus, coffee shop, Fontainebleau Hotel, Miami Beach, Florida, 1954.

Raymond Loewy's *Never Leave Well Enough Alone*, Lapidus entitled his own 1996 autobiography *Too Much is Never Enough*. The variety of Lapidus's conceptions, intended to satisfy his clients and appeal to the aspirations and fantasies of the hotel's clientele, characterized a "both ... and" rather than "either ... or" attitude toward design. It was this broad eclecticism that was often criticized at the time for its commercialism and lack of discrimination between architecture and amusement parks, but later Lapidus began to gain critical acceptance and even praise for his imagination and sense of playfulness and fun. Such acceptance was acknowledged amid a growing realization that perhaps "good design" had failed to shape the values of society at large for the better. However indulgent or escapist, Lapidus's ideal of luxury gave to the many a glimpse of what had been the entitlement of the few, if only for a week or even a weekend. And if not experienced directly, the version of luxury embodied in the Fontainebleau and elsewhere was experienced vicariously in film, on television, and in the features and advertisements of magazines such as *Holiday*.

It is hardly surprising that one of Lapidus's sources of inspiration for luxury interiors was France. Following a trip to France in the mid-1950s Lapidus commissioned dozens of copies of oil paintings after masterpieces in the Louvre, and even the name Eden Roc was inspired by a resort at Cap d'Antibes on the French Riviera. Indeed the postwar period witnessed the resurgence of the association of France with the most cultivated tastes, particularly

modern reinforced concrete. He admired the experimental architecture of German architect Erich Mendelsohn (1887–1953) and the organic forms and recesses of Surrealist art. Yet his hotels also featured decoration drawn from eighteenth-century French furniture and Italian Renaissance architecture, as in the Coffee Shop at the Fontainebleau from 1954 and the "Mona Lisa" room at the Eden Roc, also in Miami Beach and built in 1956 (figs. 12.10 and 12.11). It is no surprise that, paraphrasing

12.11 Morris Lapidus, "Mona Lisa" room, Eden Roc Hotel, Miami Beach, Florida, 1956.

the aura of the designer. But in general evening wear and daywear represented the first reaction against the austerity and severity of the war years. Called "the New Look" by the editor of *Harper's Bazaar* in 1947, postwar high fashion called attention, through ample use of fabric and contrasts between thin waistlines and full skirts and bodices, to an ideal of fullness and sensuality in the female form. Dior compared his creations to flowers, with stem-like waists and flowing, petal-like skirts (fig. 12.13). The hourglass was another apt metaphor for many postwar New Look fashions.

The sensory excitement of Lapidus's Miami Beach resort hotels, extended even further by neon lights and the lure of the gaming tables and slot machines in resort areas such as Las Vegas, Nevada, was captured by Tom Wolfe

12.12 Hubert Givenchy with model, photograph in *New Yorker*.

12.13 Christian Dior, black velvet and satin evening gown, 1953.

in regard to French high fashion and especially with the emergence of French designers such as Christian Dior (1905–1957), Pierre Balmain (1914–1982), and Hubert de Givenchy (*b*.1927, fig. 12.12), or designers working in France like Cristóbal Balenciaga (1895–1972). These couturiers maintained a reputation for elegance and the highest levels of craft and individual creativity seen earlier in French fashion, furniture, and the decorative arts from the period before and after World War I. Although exclusive, it came to the attention of a wider international audience through the medium of cinema, as well as via photography in the context of art-directed magazines such as *Vogue* and *Harper's Bazaar* (see page 255 and fig. 11.17). The mass media created a cult of celebrity around movie stars, whose images provided models of ideal beauty. An example is film star Audrey Hepburn, known for her devotion to the designs of Givenchy. The haute-couture fashions of this period were varied and individuality was essential to

12.14 Richard Hamilton, *Just what is it that makes today's homes so different, so appealing?*, collage, 10 ½ x 9 ¾ in (27 x 25 cm), 1956. Kunsthalle, Tübingen.

(b.1931) in articles published first in *Esquire* in the early 1960s and in book form as *The Kandy-Kolored Tangerine-Flake Streamline Baby* in 1963. Wolfe likened the glitz and provocative sexuality of the Las Vegas strip to an image of paradise as a garden of delights for the senses above which humanity rarely rises. Such an invocation recalls the common human themes in the work of sixteenth-century Flemish painter Pieter Bruegel (1525/9–1569). Indeed, modern popular culture offered almost unlimited delights for the senses, amplified through technology, available vicariously through the cinema and magazine, or in reality through the resort. These included movies in Technicolor for the eyes, stereo sound for the ears, processed foods for the palette, just to name a few.

Even earlier than Tom Wolfe in the United States, Reyner Banham was questioning the elitism and paternalistic overtones of "good design" in a series of articles written for newspapers and periodicals in Britain. Banham recognized mass culture's combination of fantasy, escapism, and healthy expression of the popular will in a consumer culture dominated by large multinational industrial corporations rather than individual producers. Such attitudes also help to account for the emergence of Pop Art both in Britain and in the United States, in part as a reaction to the elitism and esoteric tendencies of avant-garde art. When Richard Hamilton (b.1922) and Eduardo Paolozzi (b.1924) created collage images such as Hamilton's *Just what is it that makes today's homes so different, so appealing?* (fig. 12.14), lifting photographs and illustrations directly out of American popular mass circulation magazines, the images were less an indictment of materialism and commercialism than a celebration of the pleasures of the senses, a time-honored theme of the fine arts in earlier eras when the arts were indeed more approachable.

Housing: Suburbia, Domesticity, and Conformity

Automobile styling in the United States was also contemporary with the transformation of the housing construction industry and the emerging patterns of life in large suburban developments. New approaches to home building were a response to a severe housing shortage for returning veterans coupled with slow growth in housing starts during the Depression. The elastic markets for housing and automobiles after the war were not unrelated. Indeed the growth of new suburban communities, constructed on inexpensive tracts of land located further from commuter rail lines, increased the dependence upon the automobile for commuting to the workplace. They also account for the commercial success of new shopping centers and later of malls, designed to bring dozens of businesses together in an area built with abundant space for vehicular parking. In fact, both industries supported and even lobbied successfully for government-funded highway projects to help guarantee the success of their enterprise. Also contributing to the success of the suburban development was the ease of obtaining federally-sponsored low-interest mortgage loans from agencies such as the Veterans Administration (VA) and the Federal Housing Administration (FHA), encouraging young couples and families to purchase new homes.

Builder William Levitt pioneered mass-production techniques in the housing industry after World War II in "Levittown" communities located in suburban New York, New Jersey, and Pennsylvania. Using pre-assembled parts and teams of specialized workers, each assigned to repeating a particular task in a rationalized approach to the building process, Levitt became the "Henry Ford" of the housing industry. His methods enabled the construction of houses in less than six weeks on inexpensively purchased land beyond the limits of urban centers, in communities with as many as 17,000 new houses. Levitt's homes were build on concrete slabs rather than on foundations with basements, and his construction process quickly became the industry standard due to the affordability of the units, which began as low as $7900. In addition, buyers could purchase homes with as little as a one-dollar down payment and federally-guaranteed mortgages that minimized the builder's risk.

Postwar housing in the United States differed significantly from its European counterparts. Whereas dense, efficient, and uniform housing after World War II was normal in communities outside most large European cities, in the United States new building materials and mass production techniques reinforced traditional associations between property, status, and independence. Individual home ownership implied stability and permanence, linked in the popular imagination to self-sufficiency and levels of comfort formerly available only to wealthier Americans. In lowering the economic threshold for ownership, the home became a realizable part of the American dream for a larger proportion of the working and middle classes, and was a clear measure of improvement in comparison with the apartments and row-houses in which many new homeowners had grown up. Within this appealing ideological framework it is not surprising that while the construction of early postwar suburban homes entailed new standardized methods of construction as well as new prefabricated materials such as drywall (as opposed to plaster), the design of these same homes recalled modest and traditional rather than contemporary housing types. Among the most common was the so-called "Cape Cod" style, rectangular in shape with pitched roof sloping toward the front (fig. 12.15). Buyers were also attracted to the new homes by a number of practical considerations. Kitchens, for instance, featured picture windows to allow parents to watch their children play in the yard, and attached garages that kept automobiles off the street and allowed entry directly into the home. The attraction of individual home ownership and the added convenience of appliances such as washing machines and even television sets, often included in the selling price, seemed to outweigh the drawbacks of a conformity often noted by critics. Author Lewis Mumford (1895–1990) was one such critic, who saw few advantages to the postwar suburb in comparison with its more idyllic, village-like predecessors, and predicted negative consequences should the trend continue:

The ultimate outcome of the suburb's alienation from the city became visible only in the twentieth century, with the extension of the democratic ideal through the instrumentalities of manifolding and mass production. In the mass movement into suburban areas a new kind of community was produced, which caricatured both the historic city and the archetypal suburban refuge: a multitude of uniform, unidentifiable houses, lined up inflexibly, at uniform distances, on uniform roads, in a treeless communal waste, inhabited by people of the same class, the same income, the same tasteless pre-fabricated foods, from the same freezers, conforming in every outward and inward respect to a common mold, manufactured in the central metropolis. Thus the ultimate effect of the suburban escape in our time is ironically, a low-grade uniform environment from which escape is impossible. What has happened to the suburban exodus in the United States now threatens, through the same mechanical instrumentalities, to take place, at an equally accelerating rate, everywhere else.

12.15 Levittown model home, *New York Times* advertisement, 1950.

The identification of home ownership with the lifestyle of the average family was also mirrored in the emerging television industry. Television families, such as the Nelsons of Ozzie and Harriet or the Cleavers of Leave it to Beaver, owned homes in suburban communities. Notable exceptions were the childless Cramdens of The Honeymooners, who suffered the frustrations of noise and lack of privacy found in urban apartment houses, or the family of nightclub entertainer Danny Thomas. Mr. Thomas's career required that his own precocious children live in a spacious Manhattan apartment dominated by adults rather than by other children.

I remember a story from my grade-school reader written in the mid-1950s. In this illustrated story the child of a young family who recently moved into a new subdivision is troubled by an inability to distinguish his own home from the others on his block. The problem is solved when each family creates its own weather vane to add character and individual identity to otherwise bland and uniform surroundings. The housing industry also offered solutions to the practical as well as social desire for differentiation in the market. Attracting new buyers from the city to the suburb or encouraging suburbanites to "trade up" during the 1950s led to an expansion of the range of housing types, featuring much inventiveness in introducing variations available for consumers to express preferences and "customize" their purchase. In addition to the standard "Cape Cod" home, builders began to include a wider variety of traditional types such as Colonial or Tudor, as well as modern Ranch models. The last included large expanses of windows and low single-story designs, or a "split level" with half-stories to either side of a central entrance (fig. 12.16). Informal family rooms and eat-in kitchens became ways to expand living space and move beyond basic housing needs toward comfort and entertainment, visible signs of success judged in comparison to one's neighbor, encouraging conformity to an ever-escalating level of consumption.

The reduction of standardization in interior design and decoration resulted from the new industrial materials whose potential for variation was exploited by manufacturers. Examples include Formica, a hard plastic surface available in a variety of patterns for use in kitchen surfaces to replace enameled metal or stainless steel, and Linoleum, a softer surface used for flooring in kitchens and recreation rooms. The more colorful and textured

12.16 Feature on prefabricated homes from *Better Homes and Gardens*, August 1954.

effects of Formica and Linoleum, as well as Naughahyde upholstery, made the kitchen less of a "laboratory" or workplace than a room for leisure and relaxation. The reduction of toil implied in this new interpretation of the kitchen was to a great degree supported by advertising, in which appliances such as dishwashers as well as household cleaning products were viewed as improvements bringing new quantities of freedom and leisure. Fashionably dressed housewives were generally pictured along with the dishwasher or new dinette, marveling at the ease of loading the new appliance, admiring the sparkling cleanliness of the glassware, or enjoying time spent with family members (fig. 12.17). Comfort found expression less in the plywood and pedestal-based Eames

12.17 Advertisement, refrigerator, manufactured by Frigidaire Corporation, Dayton, Ohio, *Good Housekeeping*, 1954.

12.18 Advertisement, Stratolounger lounge chair with Naugahyde vinyl upholstery, manufactured by U. S. Naugahyde, illustrated in *Good Housekeeping*.

lounge than in the more massive and heavily upholstered reclining chair known as the La-Z-boy or variations such as the Barcalounger and Stratolounger (fig. 12.18). Elements of the La-Z-boy derived from cushioned railway cars. Advertisements focused upon the variety of available fabrics and upholstery styles from which the buyer could choose, as well as upon the relaxed (mostly male) occupant resting after a long day at the office. The world of children's leisure was filled with a never-ending array of ephemeral fads and toys, from spinning tops to butterfly yo-yos, hoola-hoops and frisbees, creating a market that is today augmented with videogames and their captivating virtual reality, all requiring the considerable contributions of a new generation of designers.

New domestic uses were also identified and successfully marketed for aluminum in the 1950s in an industry effort to maintain wartime production levels. The Alcoa

Aluminum Company advertised creative uses of aluminum in mass-circulation magazines as part of a forecasting program using the word "imagineering." One of the more popular products to emerge in the early 1950s was sets of anodized aluminum tumblers in rainbow colors manufactured as Heller Hostess ware (fig. 12.19). Lightweight and certainly unbreakable, aluminum drinking cups were easily dented, especially around the lip, and their uniform weight created a high center of gravity that made them tip over easily when filled. Despite such shortcomings, the festive colors, novelty, and associations with the informality and pleasure of picnics and barbecues helped to make aluminum tumblers commercially successful. Such products might be contrasted with the use of heavier stainless steel in Scandinavian dinnerware of the same period, characterized by a plain metallic finish and used for serving rather than eating or drinking (fig. 12.20). Another example of "imagineering" in the 1950s was the

12.19 Tumblers, anodized aluminum, Heller Hostess ware, 5 ⅛ x 2 ⅞ in (13 x 7.3 cm), 1946–c. 1955.

12.21 Folding chair, aluminum and nylon webbing, 31 ¾ x 22 ⅛ in (81 x 56 cm), 1964.

12.20 Sigurd Persson, vegetable dish, stainless steel, 8 ⁷⁄₁₆ in (21.4 cm) in length, manufactured by Silver & Stål, 1953. Philadelphia Museum of Art.

folding aluminum chair, made of lightweight tubular aluminum (first developed for seating in the aircraft industry) and plastic webbing (fig. 12.21). There was nothing durable or particularly ergonomic about this anonymous outdoor chair. Unstable if placed on uneven ground and irreparable when the plastic webbing was torn or detached from the rivets that held it to the frame, the portable chairs were and remain the kind of expendable, replaceable, everyday product characteristic of mass culture.

The increased availability and popularity of packaged and processed foods is another component of mass culture, a further instance of the equation of leisure with progress. Instead of baking from scratch, cake mixes included pre-measured ingredients to enable housewives to perform "miracles" in the kitchen. Not surprisingly, such products were endorsed by the matronly Bette Crocker to preserve the comforting sense of pride in being

12.22 Advertisement for Bette Crocker, products manufactured by General Mills Corporation, from *Better Homes and Gardens*.

a traditional homemaker (fig. 12.22). This combination of new goods with reassuring values of home and family is a characteristic often found in the products of mass culture. Both the desire for increased leisure and ease along with the satisfaction of being a responsible homemaker are addressed. The phenomenon of packaged foods exemplifies a shift from the commodity itself to the motivation for its purchase, that is, from production to consumption. Packaging, from toothpaste to dishwashing liquids, was often bright and festive, with lettering in different colors and in different alignments, a decorative accent to bathroom or kitchen. Other products meant to reduce toil included Jiffy popcorn, where the fry pan itself was disposable after being used on top of the stove, and synthetic fabrics such as Dacron Permapress, which required no ironing.

The Elusive Promise of Mass Culture

While advertising outlined the applications of newly-found leisure in a variety of products and appliances, such leisure was at times problematic for the American housewife. Dissatisfaction with the suburban lifestyle and the ways in which it defined fulfillment found expression in Betty Friedan's *The Feminine Mystique* (1963), an outgrowth of the author's experience as a mother and housewife in the 1950s. Following the end of World War II, hundreds of thousands of women were displaced from jobs by the return of soldiers, and found little opportunity to resume or begin careers. Mass media, in the form of women's magazines such as *Ladies Home Journal*, *McCalls*, and *Redbook*, as well as most network television housewives, encouraged women to focus their energies upon the home, defining their role primarily as consumers while husbands went off to work. Friedan's experience demonstrated that the patterns of postwar suburban living and the ideals of beauty, comfort, luxury, and well-being advertised in magazines and on television did not always provide options for women outside a range of activities confined for the most part to home and family. It is no wonder that surveys conducted at the time indicated less satisfaction with suburban life among women in comparison with men.

In addition to the sense of conformity described above, exclusivity was also an issue of the postwar suburban housing boom, and presented a different reality to the one imagined through the mass media and advertising. Conspicuously absent from these new suburban neighborhoods and their television counterparts were Afro-Americans and other minorities. Historians of the period such as Kenneth Jackson have noted that in addition to the uniformity implied by standardization, suburban housing communities tended to create economic as well as racial homogeneity. This occurred particularly through zoning laws that inhibited industrial building and prevented construction of housing for lower-income families, as well as overt policies by builders that denied access to black buyers. At the same time increasing numbers of black families were migrating from the rural south to the urban and industrial north, in search of higher-paying jobs or a new beginning after serving in the armed forces during the war.

Beyond High and Low Art: Revisiting the Critique of Mass Culture

Throughout the first decade of the postwar period a number of writers and critics condemned virtually every manifestation of the emerging mass culture and mass media on political, moral, and esthetic grounds. Most criticism of popular culture was based upon the views of an educated and sophisticated elite seeking to universalize a set of criteria that itself preserved and extended a design discourse inherited from the very beginnings of industrialization and class conflict. Much criticism adopted a polemic tone and dismissive treatment of its target. In the immediate postwar years, commercially motivated mass culture and mass media were criticized for a lack of social

responsibility. In part this was a response both to the exaggerated claims of early advertising as well as to the control of media and propaganda by Fascist regimes during the 1930s and 1940s. Common to both charges was the belief that the essentially passive "masses" could be easily manipulated with false promises. The tone of criticism of this kind can be sensed from the following remarks of Robert Hutchins in 1940, president of the University of Chicago:

> In order to believe in democracy we must believe that there is a difference between truth and falsity, good and bad, right and wrong, and that truth, goodness, and right are objective standards even though they cannot be experimentally verified.... Political organization must be tested by conformity to ideals. Its basis is moral. Its end is the good for man.... These are the principles which we must defend if we are to defend democracy.
>
> Are we prepared to defend these principles? Of course not. For forty years and more our intellectual leaders have been telling us they are not true. They have been telling us in fact that nothing is true which cannot be subject to experimental verification. In the whole realm of social thought there can, therefore, be nothing but opinion. Since there is nothing but opinion, everybody is entitled to his own opinion.... If everything is a matter of opinion, force becomes the only way of settling differences of opinion. And, of course, if success is the test of rightness, right is on the side of the heavier battalions.

The warning against manipulation also appears in a 1957 book by Vance Packard entitled *The Hidden Persuaders*. The book dealt with sophisticated psychological techniques and motivational analysis by market researchers as well as advertising used to sell products to unaware consumers. Packard's analysis emphasized the role of insecurity in the promotion of consumption, for instance, in the need for men to feel "masculine" being met by cigarettes or after-shave lotions in a society where conformity dictated the patterns and frustrations of everyday life. Packard quoted extensively from the heads of advertising agencies and marketing consultants, and used the terms "motivational research" (abbreviated as MR in the book) and "depth analysis" as labels for the persuasive techniques of selling derived from psychological surveys of consumers. Packard concluded that what motivates people to buy is not need but rather a desire to feel better about themselves. He was alarmed that such techniques of persuasion were being used not only for consumer goods but also in the political arena, and feared the consequences. Basic to Packard's rhetoric is the manipulation of the irresistible unconscious urges of the public by advertisers and those employed by them as consultants. *The Hidden Persuaders* saw advertising techniques as dehumanizing, suggesting that such techniques might be used to program our actions and thoughts:

> What the probers are looking for, of course, are the *whys* of our behavior, so that they can more effectively manipulate our habits and choices in their favor. This had led them to probe why we are afraid of banks; why we love those big fat cars; why housewives typically fall into a hypnoidal trance when they get into a supermarket; why men are drawn into auto showrooms by convertibles but end up buying sedans; why junior loves cereal that pops, snaps, and crackles.
>
> We move from the genial world of James Thurber into the chilling world of George Orwell and his Big Brother, however, as we explore some of the extreme attempts at probing and manipulating now going on.

Other critics also took aim at the housing industry, echoing familiar concerns about the public interest and improving the level of public taste. In 1946 George Nelson published a book advocating modern designs over traditional ones and describing the modern suburban "Cape Cod" house as a sham reflection of its prototype, unsuited to the esthetic and social conditions of contemporary life. As mentioned above, Lewis Mumford decried the uniformity of the suburban tract and the consequent decline of the quality of city life as resources were poured into roads rather than into the upkeep of urban residential neighborhoods, and as traffic congestion appeared to compromise the virtues of suburban living.

The criticism of mass culture was equally severe in European Marxist circles. Here issues of taste were combined with bitter disappointment and disillusionment at the subversion of techniques of mass production and mass communication first to Fascist regimes in the interwar period and then to capitalist enterprise and the fetishization of commodities rather than to the attainment of more enlightened socialist egalitarian ends. Part of the historical critique of capitalism in general focuses upon the need for large corporations to reap a return on their investment by guaranteeing a market for products of mechanized mass production through seductive advertising and marketing techniques. The result is a combination of design change and mass advertising that magnifies the symbolism of the product in a process often referred to as commodification or reification. While recognizing the much larger scale of mechanized mass production in the mid-twentieth century, the process nevertheless recalls the role of commodities as criticized by design reformers in Victorian England or social critics in turn-of-the-century America. The German critic Theodor Adorno, for instance, used the term "culture industry" to refer to the methods of mass media and the capitalist control of the means of production that underwrote the system of entertainment and related industries. By equating culture with leisure there was a tendency to devalue and corrupt the entire enterprise of design under capitalism. In this view one sees consumption as the reward of compliance within a system so pervasive as to eradicate even awareness of its power to compromise and subvert the freedom of the individual. Such a situation offers no alternative aside from revolution or the pursuit of an alternative lifestyle akin perhaps to the Arts and Crafts communities of the late nineteenth century and their rejection of industrial society.

More recently the views of Adorno and other critics have been seen as being based upon a narrow and dismissive understanding of mass culture, one which presupposes a monolithic cultural homogeneity. Students of mass culture argue persuasively that in addition to the manipulative and dehumanizing associations described by critics, the phenomenon has a richness and complexity that earlier authors were unwilling to admit. As a result the facile dualism of many critics appears less tenable than was once believed.

The appreciation of mass culture is based upon a number of considerations, including a better understanding of the system of production, distribution, and consumption of cultural products, as well as a recognition of the various ways in which an audience responds to those products. Rather than a passive role for the consumer, students of mass culture suggest that the audience participates or is active in its response to the products of design—thus the product not only is created for an audience, but is also in effect created by its audience, and expresses that audience's preferences and values. One example of the rich and varied reaction to American popular culture was demonstrated during the later 1960s when it was embraced by German youth as a form of protest against government and corporate regulation of education and politics. Other observers have described the "sociability" of mass culture, that is, the way in which it appeals to a broad audience and communicates a variety of meanings.

The Marxist critique of popular culture has lost little of its ability to illuminate the underlying structures and mechanisms at work in our daily lives as citizens and consumers in a capitalist world, even if its political motivations have lost some of their credibility and if angry and revolutionary motivations tended to exaggerate their authors' polemic tone. In the end it is perhaps worthwhile to keep in mind the range of responses to popular culture and the dynamic relationship between the "culture industry" and an expanding, diverse new audience. The middle class found an array of outlets for consuming products, reacting to billboards and advertising images in weekly magazines, listening to the radio, going to the cinema, and watching television at home. As noted by author Clive James, popular culture represented a "step up" for the working and middle classes, though perhaps not a step toward the culture envisioned by the advocates of "good design."

Curiously, while the proponents of "good design" defended their activities on the basis of noble aims that included the education of the masses, the fine arts generally retreated from pursuing a relation to the general public. Instead, the emerging New York art world sought a more rarefied atmosphere in which creativity was unfettered either by commercialism, the mass market, or the international standards of "good design" and its ideology of shared cultural values and social responsibility. The influential American art critic Clement Greenberg neatly divided the post World War II art world into three groups. There were the avant-garde, advocates of high art who were the guardians of individualism and originality in the arts, seeking abstraction as a field of interest. A second group consisted of practitioners of middlebrow art, who interpreted aspects of high art in more useful goods but undermined and compromised their esthetic purity and independence. Finally there was low (mass) art, described simply as "kitsch," catering to the uneducated masses with the appeal of the traditional and debased borrowings from more authentic forms of expression. Such distinctions began to erode in the 1960s with the growing influence of Pop Art and the development of more pluralistic approaches to the study of culture.

Conclusion

The postwar period witnessed the expansion of industrial design involving the application of wartime technology to domestic products, fueled by the United States' investment in the reconstruction of western European and Japanese peacetime economies through industrial manufacturing. There was a broadening of the understanding of the industrial design profession to include ergonomics and a wider range of problem-solving skills pertaining to product development. The emergence of mass communication also served to market and to affect the design of products to an ever-increasing audience through obsolescence and product symbolism. In the context of Cold War tensions in the later 1950s, consumption, technology, and materialism, whether motivated by social mobility or by social responsibility, became increasingly identified with democracy and freedom. The result was a blurring of the distinction that critics had drawn between commercial styling and the more humanistic approach once understood as "good design." Such critical awareness tended to provide justification for an appreciation and understanding of mass culture, while at the same time raised some doubts about the benevolent association between modern design and social and economic progress. An appreciation of the immediate postwar era includes thinking less in terms of a dichotomy between high and low art than in terms of a "continuum" in which commercial, esthetic, reformist, scientific, and technological considerations operated in varied measure.

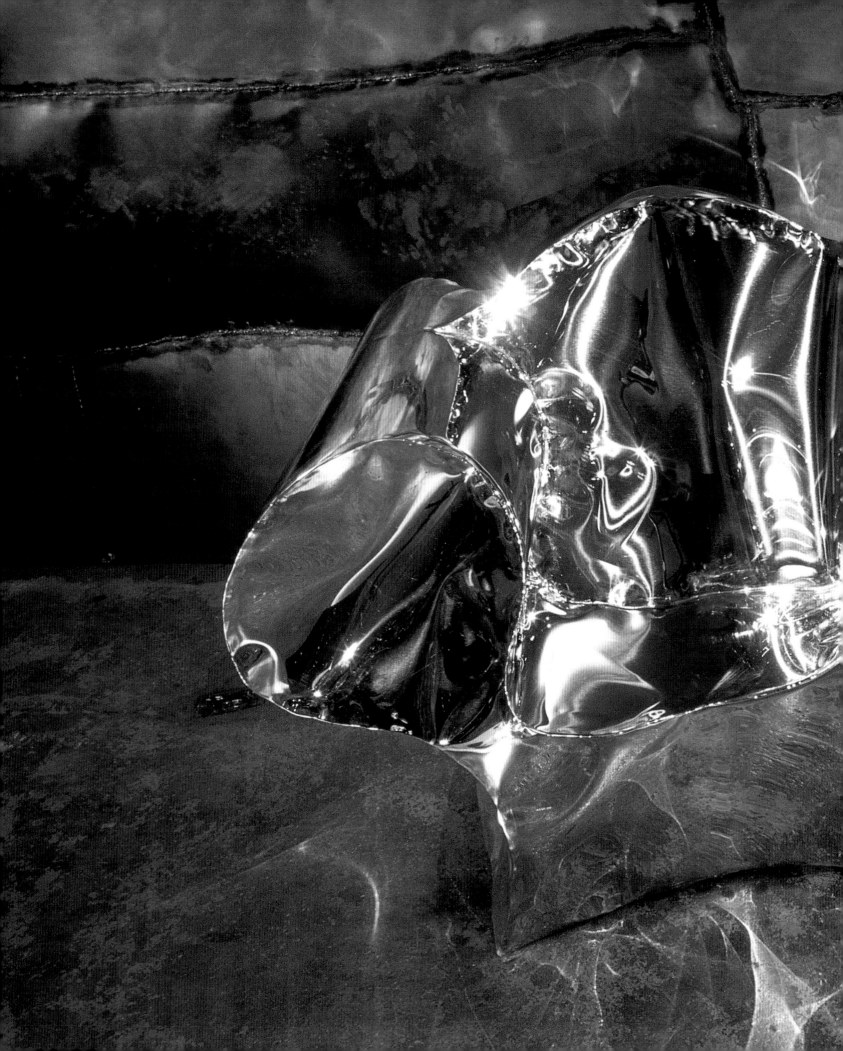

PART V

Progress, Protest, and Pluralism:
1960–2000

Introduction

Fulfilling the promise of the partnership between technology and design in the postwar period has proven to be a challenging, often elusive goal, as the social, moral, economic, and political tensions that characterized the somewhat turbulent 1960s continue to be felt at the beginning of a new century and millennium. Food processors, microwave ovens, cellular phones, compact disks, and personal computers are only among the most obvious examples of technologies affecting the contemporary world of products, extending the range of our powers and redefining the relationship between work and leisure in the industrially developed nations of the world. Personal computers and the Internet have not only stimulated the marketing and merchandising of these and countless other products, but also have accelerated the emphasis upon the design of information and communications technology. The growth of the Internet is a clear indication of an emerging *post*-industrial age in which information, intellectual property, and a wide range of human services are increasingly the sources of economic power, and where manufacturing often takes place in the less developed nations of the world. The expansion of markets for commodities has been further stimulated by the deregulation and privatization of communications industries, by the growth and sophistication of credit buying, by computerized techniques of product development and manufacturing, and by advertising, telemarketing and electronic- or e-commerce. Meanwhile, the breakup of the Soviet Union in 1989 and the emerging independence of former Eastern Bloc countries have further extended the hegemony of market-based capitalist economies and their dependence upon expanding the production and consumption of commodities both domestically and internationally.

And yet this ever-increasing flood of new products and electronic communication appears at times to make us the victims as well as the beneficiaries of both technology and the information age, defining us perhaps too narrowly as little more than machines for programmed consumption, reducing the exercise of freedom to the choice between endless varieties of products. At the same time, concerns with environmental as well as for social responsibility on a broader global scale undermine at least some of the confidence in the future we are designing. Awareness of these contradictions and uncertainties, of the combination of hopes as well as fears for the future of design, form the basis for this final part of our study.

Chapter 13

New Materials, New Products

13.1 Robin Day, polyprop stacking chair, polypropylene and steel, 29 in (74 cm) high, manufactured by Hille, 1964.

Materials technology continued to stimulate a number of original product designs in the 1960s, reinforcing the ideology of "good design" as it emerged in the first postwar decade. Certainly a significant part of this growth revolved around developments in synthetic plastics materials and production processes. British industrial designer Robin Day (b.1915) used a new flexible plastic known as polypropylene to compete with fiberglass in the design of seating. Day's 1963 Polyprop chair (fig. 13.1), manufactured by Hille, shares much in common with the Eames' and Saarinen's earlier examples of molded chairs (see page 232 and fig. 10.44), but offered refinements in ease

of assembly and a variety of thin steel supporting structures. Day's designs for Hille were successfully marketed internationally, while British designer and entrepreneur Sir Terence Conran expanded his contract furniture and fabric design business by opening a number of retail outlets in London under the name Habitat, beginning in 1964. Conran's Habitat stores expanded the marketing for modern design beyond the scope of contract commissions from architects, corporations, and sophisticated clientele who constituted much of the audience in the immediate postwar decade. Habitat obtained rights to manufacture and distribute contemporary designs from Italy and

13.2 Counter display, Habitat store, London, *c.* 1965.

Plastics and Their Progeny

Also beginning in the 1960s the process of injection-molding combined with stronger polymers further extended possibilities for furniture design using plastic. Joe Columbo's (1930–1971) side chair of 1965, manufactured by the Italian company Kartell beginning in 1968, was designed as a molded seat and back to which plastic legs could be inserted. (fig. 13.3). Less organic than most of its predecessors, Columbo's plastic side chair was a unified design where legs, seat, and back were parallel or perpendicular to each other as well as to the walls, floors, and ceilings of the rooms they occupied. A single injection-molded form was Scandinavian designer Verner Panton's (*b.*1926) stacking chair, designed in 1960 and manufactured by Herman Miller beginning in 1967 (fig. 13.4).

Scandinavia and also offered simple and practical mass-produced furniture imitating period styles, as well as craft items produced for export, such as traditional Japanese cookware and utensils.

The advertising and merchandising components of Habitat, featuring displays modeled on interiors filled with home furnishing products and accessories, also were beginning to blur the lines that had distinguished "good design" from mass-marketed commodities during the 1950s (fig. 13.2). Inevitably the array of goods, changing displays, and variations of new but similar products, stimulated the link between products and self-realization aimed at increasingly affluent and upwardly-mobile consumers. The products and merchandising strategies of Habitat were geared to commodity consumption as an end in itself rather than to the more broadly humanistic or paternalistic motivations of industrial designers and manufacturers in the immediate postwar years, obscuring the distinction between design and fashion, between needs and wants. In print media and on television, a similar blurring was taking place between journalism and advertising.

13.3 Joe Columbo, stacking chair, nylon and polypropylene (injection-mold plastic), 28 in (71 cm) high, manufactured by Kartell, 1965. Photograph: Kartell USA, Easley, South Carolina.

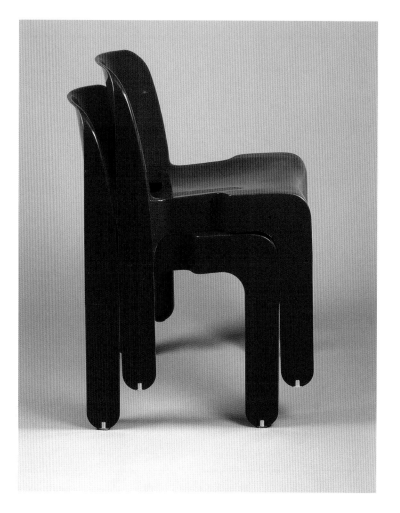

13.4 Verner Panton, stacking chair, fiberglass-reinforced polyester, 32 ¼ in (83.2 cm) high, manufactured by Herman Miller, 1960. Philadelphia Museum of Art.

13.5 Charles and Ray Eames, Tandem sling multiple seating (five-seat unit), aluminum, black steel bars, padded vinyl, 33 ¾ x 117 ¼ x 28 in (86 x 298 x 71 cm), manufactured by Herman Miller Company, 1962.

Unlike Columbo's side chair, Panton's unified design preserves an organic, sculptural quality reminiscent of the 1950s, while the thin, concave base was designed to provide stability as well as to take advantage of the material's lightness by permitting interlocking. Both designs eliminated the need for steel, wooden, or aluminum supporting structures.

Not every original design from the 1960s was inspired by the possibilities of newly developed materials or processes. Aluminum emerged in the interwar period as a constructive material for lightweight industrial furniture in aircraft as well as for outdoor use commercially, and was used after the war as well for the cone-shaped pedestals in Saarinen's Tulip furniture for Knoll in the mid-1950s (see page 251 and fig. 11.11). Knoll also replaced steel with aluminum in manufacturing Mies van der Rohe's Barcelona, a chair designed first for an exhibition in 1929 and re-released after World War II. In 1962 Charles Eames used aluminum construction for his Tandem Sling, manufactured by Herman Miller for seating that continues to be used in airport terminal gate areas (fig. 13.5). The design of the Tandem Sling responded to a variety of requirements. Easily assembled in flexible units from a small number of parts, with seats made from nylon (like plastic, another synthetic polymer) contoured

13.9 Enzo Mari, Pogo Pogo vase, ABS plastic, 11 ³⁄₁₆ in (28.4cm), 1969, manufactured by Danese, Milan.

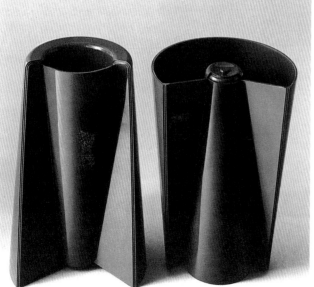

13.10 Achile and Pier Giacomo Castiglioni, Taccia table lamp, aluminum and glass, 21 in (53.3 cm), manufactured by Flos (Brescia, Italy), 1966. Philadelphia Museum of Art, gift of Atelier International Ltd.

323

possibilities of alternative arrangements of its "components" as well as the ability to create in effect a kind of sculptural room divider or screen.

An esthetic approach to plastic domestic goods might also be found in brightly colored containers and other wares, such as the vase designed by Enzo Mari (*b.*1932) for the Italian Company Danese in 1969 (fig. 13.9). Smooth and elegantly tapered, the design is also playful in its reversibility, crediting the designer's imagination as well as demonstrating the esthetic possibilities of new materials, in this case hard and durable ABS plastic. Similar esthetic qualities apply to the Taccia table lamp manufactured by Flos and designed by Achille and Pier Giacomo Castiglioni in 1966 (fig. 13.10). Here the bulb is contained within a short, cylindrical base wrapped in a black plastic sleeve resembling a fluted column. Resting on this base is an asymmetrical white plastic parabola directing light upward and outward. Again, the smooth shapes and compact design recall the purity of hard-edged abstraction, as well as a hint of its cool precision. In the 1960s, industrial designers played an important part in strengthening Italy's international reputation for original and sophisticated products, supplying new designs and name recognition for furniture, machines, lighting, and household products manufactured by numerous companies such as Venini (glass), Kartell (plastic), Pirelli (rubber), Flos (lighting), and Gavina (furniture).

Product Housing

Housings, of course, constitute a broad category in industrial design, but generally refer to the shells enclosing mechanical products ranging from domestic appliances to office and laboratory machines and audiovisual equipment. During the 1960s, the bulbous and sculptural forms of many appliances and office machines in metal housings were generally replaced by more compact, rectangular shapes in both metal and plastic, while transistor and other electronics technologies also tended to produce small, portable products with simple unobtrusive forms.

A lead comparison might be between Marcello Nizzoli's 1948 Lexikon 80 typewriter for Olivetti (fig. 11.48), and the tapered rectangular Praxis 48 electric typewriter (fig. 13.11) designed for Olivetti in 1964 by Hans Klier and Ettore Sottsass, Jr. (*b.*1917). Sottsass, who later questioned some of the social implications of the designer's role in the corporation, worked as a consultant to Olivetti to provide visual unity in the design of its Elea 9003 office computer. A further state of refinement and simple, compact form can be seen in the rectangular bright red manual portable typewriter known as the Valentine, manufactured by Olivetti beginning in 1969 and housed in a smooth plastic sleeve (fig. 13.12).

Miniaturization was a determining factor in the design of housings for a number of products such as

13.11 Hans Klier and Ettore Sottsass, Jr., Praxis 48 electric typewriter, plastic housing, manufactured by C. Olivetti, Milan, 1964.

13.12 Ettore Sottsass, Jr., and Perry King, Valentine portable typewriter and case, ABS plastic housing, 13 ¼ x 12 in (34 x 30 cm), 1969, manufactured by C. Olivetti, Milan.

13.13 Portable television, metal housing, 8 ½ in (21.6 cm) wide, manufactured by the Sony Corporation, Tokyo, 1959.

televisions, tape-recorders, and cameras. Sony pioneered the design of portable televisions using transistors as early as 1959, employing a thin metal casing around the irregular and slightly tapered picture tube, a carrying handle, and a steel track to support a visor that reduced glare (fig. 13.13). A similar design, with housing constructed of plastic, was introduced in 1962 in Italy by Brionvega, designed by Richard Sapper (b.1932) and Marco Zanuso (see page 348), also emphasizing lightness and portability. These designs contrasted with more conventional, cabinet-like housings (often including hinged doors to hide the screen) constructed of wood in a variety of traditional furniture styles. Perhaps the most widely accepted compromise between the wooden cabinet and portable approaches to housing was the Sony Trinitron color television which appeared in 1965. The Trinitron was rectangular in form, adaptable to a variety of shelves or moving stands, and had a wood-grained plastic laminate surface that harmonized more readily with traditional furniture in the domestic

13.14 Trinitron television, metal housing with wood-grained finish, manufactured by the Sony Corporation, Tokyo, from 1965.

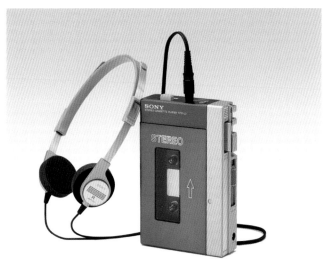

13.15 Walkman portable cassette player, anodized aluminum housing, 5 ¼ in (13.3 cm) high, manufactured by the Sony Corporation, Tokyo, 1978.

13.16 Hans Gugelot and Reinhold Hocker, Carousel slide projector machine, 15 in (38 cm) square, manufactured by Eastman Kodak Company, Rochester, New York, 1964.

13.17 Gino Valle, Cifra 3, table clock, plastic case, 7 ¹/₆ x 3 ¹/₄ in (18 x 9.5 cm), manufactured by Solari & C., Udine, Italy, 1966.

13.18 Visotronic DN 50 table-top clock and alarm with electronic digital readout, manufactured by Braun AG, Kronberg, Germany, 1979.

interior (fig. 13.14). Further miniaturization of the speakers, picture tube, and the use of remote-control operation have led to even more compact and minimal designs, characterized by ever-thinner rectangular integrated housings, for instance, in flat-screen televisions (see fig. 16.24).

Another example of miniaturization was in sound recording, where cassettes replaced reels for the consumer market resulting in greater ease-of-use in the 1970s. Hand-held mini-cassette recorders were introduced in Japan in the mid-1960s, while Sony's portable cassette player, known as the Walkman, was introduced in 1978 (fig. 13.15). In addition to miniaturization, cassettes eliminated the need for the operator to manually thread reel-to-reel tapes. The new compact forms in product housing were often the result of integrating miniaturized technology, or of simply rethinking performance, as in the audio tape cassette or in the design of slide projection equipment. In 1963 Swiss designer Hans Gugelot, who also worked as a contract designer for the Braun Corporation (see page 276), contributed to the development of a new and more automated approach to projecting slides for the Kodak Corporation. The new design used a rotating carousel that dropped slides consecutively in front of the lens using a remote-control device. The Carousel projector,

constructed of high-quality plastic, reduced the projector to a rectangular box surmounted by a short cylinder (carousel) containing the slides (fig. 13.16). The 1960s also saw the increased use of digital rather than analog clocks, whose numerical read-out implied greater precision and accuracy (fig. 13.17) and might display the digits of the Arabic number sequence using an electronic read-out consisting of just seven dashes (fig. 13.18). In lighting, the

13.19 Michael Lax, Lytegem table lamp, zinc, brass, and aluminum, 15 in (38 cm) high when extended, manufactured by Lightolier, 1965.

development of high-intensity bulbs spawned a generation of minimal designs for table lamps, including Michael Lax's metal Lytegem table lamp of 1965 for Lightolier, which featured a collapsible, antenna-like arm, making the lamp into little more than a 6-inch tall paperweight when not in use (fig. 13.19). Lightolier also developed systems featuring modular cylinder-shaped housings for lights, attached to ceiling tracks permitting lateral and rotational flexibility and reducing the need for table or floor lamps. Track lighting is compact, but still rather substantial in comparison with the more recent types of illumination using halogen lamps. Halogen technology for lighting has further reduced the size while increasing the intensity (as well as the heat) of illumination, and has created a variety of esthetic possibilities as well. The almost weightless appearance of

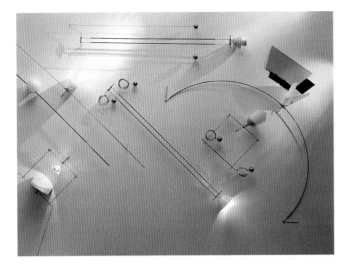

13.20 Ingo Maurer, YaYaHo lighting system, glass, ceramic, metal, and plastic, 19 ½ x 118 ⅛ in (49.5 x 300 cm), manufactured by Design M Ingo Maurer, Munich, Germany, 1981–84.

13.21 T-2000 tennis racquet, aluminum, nylon, and other materials, 26 ⅞ in (68 cm) long, manufactured by Wilson Sporting Goods Company, 1967.

halogen bulbs suspended from barely visible wires is seen, for instance, in Ingo Maurer's YoYaHo lighting system from the early 1980s (fig. 13.20), exploring three-dimensional space like illuminated hanging wire mobile sculptures.

Sports, Equipment, and Progress

While it is not possible to include all areas of consumer products that emerge or are transformed by new materials and technologies, sports equipment is one area that might be considered in terms of technology in product design during the last thirty or forty years. This is not simply because new materials may be linked to better performance, but also because small changes following the initial development of a product provide new possibilities for expanded obsolescence, blurring any possible or meaningful distinction between progress and fashion. A case study might be the tennis racquet industry, where metal racquets began to compete with traditionally crafted wood-framed racquets in the mid-1960s, with the T-2000 model aluminum racquet first introduced by the Wilson Sporting Goods Company in the United States in 1967 (fig. 13.21).

The acceptance of the new racquets, first among younger audiences, was stimulated through endorsements by younger tennis professionals such as Jimmy Connors, and the increased exposure of professional tennis programming on television (Wilson had used endorsements prior to the advent of television for its top of the line Jack Kramer model—this model was still on sale long after Jack Kramer retired from active tennis in the early 1950s, an almost unthinkable circumstance with today's marketing emphasis upon currency and the most recent star athletes). A resulting tennis "boom," beginning in the later 1960s, produced a series of equipment improvements, such as racquets with larger heads, followed by the replacement of steel racquets consecutively by aluminum, graphite, lightweight ceramic materials, and more recently the even lighter titanium. It becomes difficult to separate the development of new technologies from their relation to the tennis "stars" who market particular brands or whose personalities, both on and off the court, are linked to the product and by extension to the consumer. Once again, the complex nature of design during in the 1960s makes it increasingly difficult to distinguish between progress, performance, and commercialism, or more simply between improvement and novelty.

Visual Identity, Information, and Art Direction

Rational graphics and corporate identity programs, as described in the postwar era in Part IV, gained prominence in the 1960s. Paul Rand (see page 252), who was hired by Eliot Noyes to design the logo for IBM (1956), continued to develop a number of clear, bold logos for multinational corporations, including the Westinghouse Corporation (1960, see fig. 11.87, page 291), and the American Broadcast Company (ABC, 1965, see fig. 11.88, page 291). The New York-based firms of Chermayoff and Geismar as

Mobil

13.22 Tom Geismar of Chermayeff and Geismar Associates, Mobil oil trademark, 1964. Line drawing by John Langdon.

13.23 Saul Bass and Associates, AT&T Trademark, line drawing, 1969.

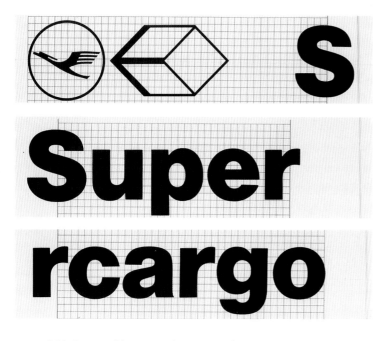

13.24 Otl Aicher, in collaboration with Tomas Gonda, Fritz Querengasser and Nick Roericht (Ulm Development Group), Lufthansa's Boeing Fleet Department of Visual Communication, 1962.

well as Saul Bass & Associates were also responsible for creating consistent and recognizable corporate identity systems, including Mobil Oil Corporation (1964, fig. 13.22), American Telephone and Telegraph Corporation (AT&T, 1969, fig. 13.23), and the Chase Manhattan Bank, all employing easily-recognized symbols and bold sans serif typography. In Europe, a group of faculty at the Hochschule für Gestaltung at Ulm, including Otl Aicher, developed the visual identity program for Lufthansa German Airlines Corporation (1962), based upon a unifying grid system and used for an entire range of labeling, scheduling, and advertising information (fig. 13.24).

Strategies for developing visual systems for agencies and corporations take into consideration the characteristics of the audience to be served, for instance, in terms of age and nationality. Banks use common elements of layout for identity in series of brochures promoting their range of services. The National Park Service, in the U.S. whose audience includes visitors of all ages and nationalities, uses a related approach involving careful analysis of multiple areas of content and their combination in unified ways for each of its parks and monuments. The National Park Service identity system, developed from 1977 by a team of consultants including Massimo Vignelli (*b*.1931), Vincent Gleason, and Dennis McLaughlin, consisted of a "Unigrid" system for the design of charts and brochures to provide consistent information on the nation's federally-maintained sites. The system included bold white-on-black sans serif typography for bordered titles, photography, simple maps, short text, charts, symbols identifying services for parking, camping, restrooms and other services, and diagrams (fig. 13.25). Armed with their series of fold-out brochures, travelers can be assured of basic information that reduces the anxiety of navigating the park and facilitates the process of selecting and enjoying those areas one wants to visit. Recognizing the international attraction of such sites as the Grand Canyon and the Liberty Bell, the printed guides were translated into Japanese, German, French, and Spanish with the text treated as an "interchangeable part."

Massimo Vignelli's career has encompassed a wide range of activities including the design of furniture and products, but the firm Vignelli & Associates, with offices in New York and Milan, has been responsible for visual systems that include brand recognition (American Airlines, 1967, Bloomingdales Department Store, 1972),

13.25 Massimo Vignelli and staff, Unigrid system for National Park Service brochures, from 1977.

13.26 Yoshiro Yamashita, pictograms for Eighteenth Olympic Games, Tokyo, 1962.

information graphics (the New York Metropolitan Subway System, 1966), and creative freedom (Knoll International from 1966, where he succeeded Herbert Matter, see page 291). The solution to each client's brief requires an understanding of the market, the flexibility of a basic visual system in adapting to differing formats and future needs, and the careful manipulation and composition of a full range of technical graphic means including photography, drawings, diagrams, and typography.

Complex identity systems emphasize the rational, problem-solving side of graphic design in the 1960s and beyond, with roots in the "New Typography" and contributions in the design of information associated with the

International Typographic Style and pioneers such as Otto Neurath and Ladislav Sutnar (see page 258). Such efforts often call attention to the role of the graphic design profession in simplifying the complex and bewildering nature of modern information through the understanding of visual symbols and organization as well as addressing universal requirements for information in a multinational setting, whether for business or transportation. Graphic identity for the Olympic Games provides examples of visual systems designed for an international audience for clarity and attracting excitement for the location and for the events themselves. The use of reductive symbols based upon abstract shapes to convey universal messages was successfully employed in a series of pictograms for the 1964 Tokyo Olympic Games, designed by Yoshiro Yamashita (fig. 13.26). Like logos, these pictograms also use a simple series of related shapes to signify the parts of the human body and the field or equipment connected with a particular sport. Again in an international context, such an approach became common on packaging to

13.27 Roger Cook and Don Shanosky, Signage Symbol System for United States Department of Transportation, printed poster, 29 ¾ x 21 ½ in (76 x 55 cm), 1974–76. Private collection.

encourage careful handling or later for graphics developed for airports, for instance the series of pictograms designed by Cook and Shanosky in 1975 for the United States Department of Transportation (fig. 13.27). Similar reductionism in the transportation industry is seen in the cardboard tags used to mark luggage in airports, which are color-coded and display three-letter abbreviations for the world's airports in a bold sans serif typeface that can easily be read by baggage handlers. Increasing globalization in a number of industries also encourages the use of abstraction in information graphics, for instance for the operation of tape-decks and CD players without the need for written instructions for commands such as "forward" or "fast forward."

13.28 Herb Lubalin (with Tom Carnase, letterer), proposed journal logo, 1965.

13.29 Herb Lubalin (Sudler, Hennessey & Lubalin), journal advertisement.

13.30 Herb Lubalin, typeface for *Avant Garde*, available for commercial use after 1970.

13.31 Milton Glaser, paperback book covers for *Shakespeare Plays*, original drawings in pen, ink, and watercolor. New American Library.

In addition to the generally rational methods used for information graphics and corporate identity systems, modern graphic design also encompasses more open-ended and often personal approaches to the fields of typography and art direction. The expressive use of typography in relation to the meaning of words or phrases is seen in the work of American Herb Lubalin (1918–1981). Although Lubalin designed several eccentric typefaces combining elements from serif and sans serif families of type, his transformations of the letters of words to convey ideas demonstrate a fascination with the possibilities of type. Examples include the phrase "Mother and Child" (fig. 13.28, intended as the title and cover for a journal) with the ampersand doubling as a pictogram of a fetus inside the "O," or the illusion of torn paper breaking apart the word "cough" to suggest irritation and roughness in an advertisement for a pharmaceutical company (fig. 13.29). Lubalin also served as art director for several journals that permitted great freedom in typography, photography, illustration, and layout, including *Avant Garde*, for which he also invented a sans serif typeface combining regular and italic forms for close spacing and a unified image (fig. 13.29). Whereas a biography of Eric Gill (see page 198) bears the title *The Man Who Loved Letters*, Lubalin's future biographer might be tempted to entitle his or her work *The Man Who Loved Words*. Taking liberties with letters in order to provide interpretation of their meaning without obscuring verbal recognition required intuition

and experiment along with discipline and analysis. Both sensibilities are complimentary aspects of the graphic design profession.

Milton Glaser (*b.*1929) also exemplified the more intuitive aspects of graphic design during the 1960s and beyond. His oeuvre owes much to testing the limits of traditional representational illustration through the use of a variety of techniques and media as well as reductive and subjective approaches to drawing. Results are seen in posters, book jackets, as well as in books of poetry and children's book illustration. A series of book covers for paperback editions of the plays and poetry of Shakespeare (fig. 13.31) is unified through the use of ample white space, heavy black borders and delicate wash drawings featuring a central character or grouping from each play. Abbreviating both technique and narrative promotes an active response from the viewer, and distinguishes the series from competitive editions.

Suggestion and active response also characterize Glaser's children's illustrations, for instance the series that accompanies author George Mendoza's *A Fish in the Sky*, published in 1971. An example (fig. 13.32) juxtaposes the image of a covered bridge with a goblet emitting smoke ("an old covered bridge crossing the still-deeps is not just a bridge under the dark, it's the murmuring of mist men gathered for a smoke and a glass of fog...") connected through flattened space and strong figure-ground contrast for areas of yellow fog and orange sky.

13.32 Milton Glaser, illustration from Mendoza, George, *A Fish in the Sky*, watercolor, Doubleday Inc. 1971.

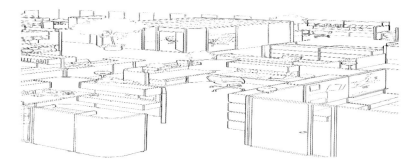

13.33 Robert Propst and George Nelson, Action Office, Herman Miller, 1964.

Laminated Materials

In addition to plastics, plywood and plastic laminates were also common materials for industrially designed furniture. In 1964 Robert Propst (b.1921) and George Nelson (see page 265) introduced the Action Office system for modular office furniture, manufactured by Herman Miller (fig. 13.33). Available in a combination of surfaces including hygienic white laminated plastic, the Action Office system was meant to be adaptable to large areas of open floor space, with the possibility of flexible configuration for group clusters or individual offices. Dimensions were the result of determining average space needs and proximity between elements of individual components for the efficient and optimum performance of office-related tasks. Another advocate for the importance of measurement and research as determinants in the design process to contribute to safety and reduce fatigue or injury was Henry Dreyfuss (see pages 217–8), who published his *The Measure of Man: Human Factors in Design* in 1960 (fig. 13.34).

The plastic laminated surfaces available for the Action Office system provided a smooth and durable work surface that could be easily cleaned. The appeal of this material also led to its popularity for table and cabinet surfaces in the kitchen, manufactured and widely marketed by the Formica Company. Originally developed as a form of plastic insulation and a coating for machine gears, the application of Formica as a laminate for furniture grew after World War II. The development of a variety of colors and patterns for Formica, like that of vinyl tile flooring, belongs more to the history of mass design and will be treated accordingly below (see page 338).

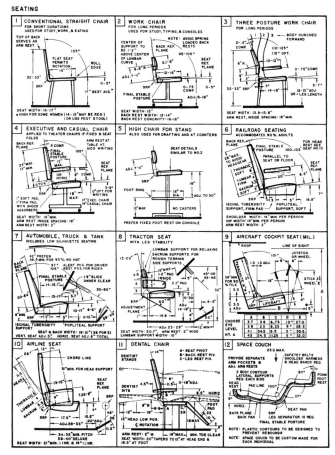

13.34 Henry Dreyfuss, illustration from *The Measure of Man: Human Factors in Design* 1960.

13.35 Reiko (Murai) Tanabe, stool, teak plywood, 14 ³/₁₆ x 17 ¹¹/₁₆ x 17 ¹/₁₆ in (36 x 45 x 43 cm), manufactured by Tendo Mokko, Tendo Company Ltd., 1960.

Laminated plywood was also used for a variety of furniture designs in the 1960s. Alvar Aalto's stools and tables featuring fan-shaped legs were designed in 1954 (see fig. 11.22, page 259), but predict the more restrained approach to molded forms in the 1960s. A good example from Japan is Reiko Tanabe's teak plywood stool designed for Tendo Mokko in 1960 (fig. 13.35). The self-contained form is designed for efficient construction with three identical molded components that are glued together.

Nature and Craft

In addition to new industrial materials and processes, the preservation and development of craft traditions continued to humanize design in the 1960s through the use of natural woods in furniture as well as natural fibers for fabrics, curtains, rugs, and table-coverings. Occasionally, synthetic materials such as polyester were introduced, for instance, with stretch upholstery, or to explore new textures or combinations of textures, as in Swiss textile designer Suzanne Huguenin's Nylon Homespun fabric manufactured by Knoll beginning in 1958 (fig. 13.36). Sheila Hicks's (*b.*1934) Badagara fabric, dating to 1966, is woven from cotton in horizontal bands of irregular diameter, one of several designs manufactured and commissioned by the Indian government to stimulate local craft production in developing nations (fig. 13.37). In Britain, potter Bernard Leach promoted an Arts and Crafts revival movement, encouraging designers' direct involvement with materials along psychological and esthetic lines (see page 269). Borrowings from indigenous and non-western traditions also occurred in popular culture, with tie-dyed designs on cotton T-shirts and tops, at first done in one's own washbasin and later available off-the-rack. Whether an exploration of unmined sources for esthetic effect or part of a tendency to see in non-western traditions and motifs an alternative to or integration with industrial technology, handicraft emerged as an aspect of both avant-garde as well as popular culture. Craft fairs often accompanied folk music festivals, and self-sufficiency, organic foods, and the use of natural rather than synthetic materials were choices that directed the daily patterns of life toward nature rather than to the man-made culture of industrial civilization. The association of craft with nature is also seen in the furniture of George Nakashima, whose

13.36 Suzanne Huguenin, Nylon Homespun fabric, nylon, 50 in (127 cm) wide, manufactured by Knoll International, New York.

designs for chairs and other elements of the domestic interior were discussed in Part IV (see page 288). Nakashima's approach to craft emphasized the workman's partnership with materials as related to Zen Buddhist philosophy and the linking of animate and inanimate nature.

Scandinavia remained in the forefront of the promotion of a variety of esthetic as well as utilitarian directions in textile design, and served as an inspiration to designers in the United States, particularly at the Cranbrook Academy in Bloomfield Hills, Michigan. In many cases woven and printed fabric designs were manufactured by Knoll and Herman Miller, as well as by Scandinavian companies such as Marimekko. Finnish designer Maija Isola's (*b.*1927) bold printed cotton Melooni fabric, manufactured in Finland by Printex (which also introduced the Marimekko name) dates to 1963 and is reminiscent of the post-painterly abstract canvases of Ellsworth Kelly, Frank

13.37 Sheila Hicks, Badagara fabric, cotton, 120 in (305 cm) wide, made by Commonwealth Trust, Calcutta, India, 1966, and still made today.

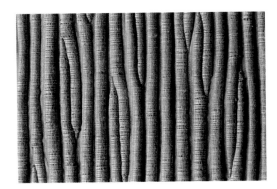

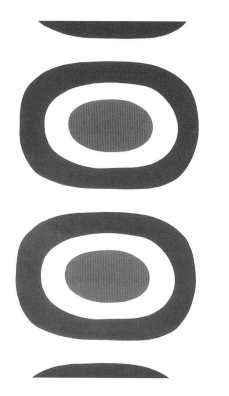

13.38 Maija Isola, Melooni fabric, screen-printed, 54 in (137 cm) wide, manufactured by Printex, Helsinki, for Marimekko Oy.

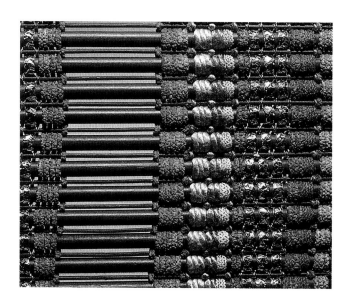

13.39 Dorothy Liebes, fabric, orlon and metallics, 50 in (127 cm) wide, manufactured by Dorothy Liebes Design. American Craft Museum, New York.

13.40 Jack Lenor Larson, Magnum Golden fabric, wool, nylon, acrylic, and Mylar, 55 ½ x 53 ½ in (141 x 136 cm), 1970, manufactured by Jack Lenor Larsen Incorporated, New York. Metropolitan Museum of Art, New York.

Stella, or Kenneth Noland (fig. 13.38). Simple woven patterns in cotton and wool continued to be produced by Scandinavian manufacturers as well as by the American-based Dansk Corporation beginning in the later 1950s.

The appreciation of abstract form in shapes and textures produced by experimentation with materials and processes also served to sustain an alliance between fine art and craft, strengthened through museum and other international exhibitions, journals, and in education, including the foundation of the American Craft Museum in Manhattan in 1956. Combinations of materials in textile design appear in the work of many designers, including a number of remarkable women such as Dorothy Liebes (1899–1972), Sheila Hicks (see page 333) and Anni Albers (1899–1994), wife of the painter and Bauhaus teacher Josef Albers. During the 1950s Liebes made window blinds using a combination of fabrics to bind together wooden slats. In the 1960s she created fabrics for mass

13.41 Wharton Esherick, music stand, cherry, 43 x 19 ½ x 16 in (109 x 49.5 x 41 cm), 1962. Metropolitan Museum of Art, New York.

13.42 Ludovico de Santillana and Tobia Scarpa, Battuto bowl, blown glass, 6 in (15 cm) high, 1960, manufactured by Venini, Murano, Italy.

production using a variety of media, including synthetics such as Orlon and foil-like metal (fig. 13.39). Another American textiles designer and manufacturer was Jack Lenor Larson (*b.*1927), whose Magnum fabric of 1970 is woven from a combination of cotton, vinyl, nylon, and polyester (fig. 13.40). Original forms involving craft rather than industrial production were designed by Philadelphia area furniture-maker Wharton Esherick (1887–1970), whose music stand accentuates the abstract beauty of an arched curve (fig. 13.41). Slight irregularities and asymmetry inform some of the work of Italian glass designer Ludovico de Santillana (*b.*1935) as seen in his Battuto bowl of 1960 (fig. 13.42), manufactured by the Venini glass company, founded in Murano, Italy, in 1925.

Chapter 14

Dimensions of Mass Culture

14.1 Advertisement for built-in kitchen appliances, Frigidaire Company, Dayton, Ohio. *Better Homes and Gardens*, March 1962.

Obsolescence remained a guiding principle in industrial design for the mass market, but during the 1960s many products relinquished flamboyance and playful novelty in favor of greater standardization and conformity. Appliances like washing machines, refrigerators, electric toasters, and clothes dryers abandoned earlier bulbous, or even streamlined housings for rectangular forms and sharp rather than rounded edges—an esthetic change related at least in part to new developments in sheet metal fabrication as well as marketing. As a result, appliances could more easily assume the character of being built-in, part of a unified and space-saving ensemble for the laundry or kitchen (fig. 14.1). Color and accessories offered variety and choice but added little to production cost; at the same time they minimized the role of the industrial designer in terms of styling and invention.

Perhaps even more noticeable in this regard was the homogeneity in the Detroit automobile industry in the 1960s. The vitality and variety provided by chrome detailing, flame-like tailfins and other symbolic features in the 1950s were toned down, replaced by more rectangular body designs and less variation among models and makes, for instance, the 1964 Buick *Le Sabre* Sedan (fig. 14.2). Again color options and interior accessories (such as

14.2 Buick *Le Sabre* Sedan, 1962, General Motors Corporation.

A family-pleaser—with a price to match—It's a dependable, perky new-sized car that can do big things for your family pride. Easy to look at, ride in—and own. You couldn't ask for anything handier to have around home (or away from it!) than this one—

THE NEW

Chevy II

That Chevy II sedan you see below has plenty of room for family of six—bag and baggage. And there's a full line of models to pick from, including a convertible, hardtop a wagons. Every one is built with sturdiness that reduces s maintenance. Major front-end sections, including fender for easy fixin' in case of repairs. And, whether you pick th or spunky 6 (there's a choice in most models), you can kind of diehard dependability that runs in the Chevrol Combine that with the custard-smooth comfort of the Che (new Mono-Plate rear springs at work here) and you've g a car that blends liveliness and luxury at a low, low price. Just check your dealer and see.

Chevy II 300 4-Door Sedan

14.3 Advertisement for Chevrolet Compact automobiles, General Motors Corporation. *Better Homes and Gardens*, March 1962. Ford Falcon, 1963.

for American families and featured more restrained styling and an emphasis upon practicality (fig. 14.3).

More organic and tapered than many contemporary American automobiles of the 1960s, Raymond Loewy's design for the upscale 1963 Studebaker Avanti (fig. 14.4) received much critical acclaim for its sculpted contour, but did not find a niche in a luxury market dominated by the more familiar General Motors Cadillac and Ford Lincoln . Despite the name-value of Loewy as a noted "personality" in industrial design, and the efforts to compete with lower-priced compact models by the introduction of its Lark model, the Studebaker Corporation finally went the way of Hudson, Kaiser, Packard, and others in 1964. As a result, even fewer North American competitors remained for the "Big Three" automobile giants: Chrysler, General Motors, and Ford.

At the 1964 New York World's Fair, the major automobile manufacturers and other large corporations dominated the fairgrounds. Their pavilions featured moving dioramas dramatizing progress in civilization through technology, linked to the improvement of the human condition and the stated themes of "achievements in an expanding universe," "peace through understanding," and "it's a small world." The showpiece of the fair, designed by Gilmore Clarke and Peter Muller-Munk, was the Unisphere, a steel-framed globe with the continents in relief, encircled by steel wires like the familiar representation of an atom with encircling electrons (fig. 14.5). In exhibitions, corporations engaged in forms of mass education and the promotion of pro-technology values:

"bucket" seats and instrument consoles) still allowed consumers to customize or individualize their purchases, but the form-giving aspect of design was more constrained by the consideration of cost and the fear of repeating failures such as the 1958 Ford Edsel (see page 300). The decade also produced a series of new compact cars such as the Ford Falcon, Plymouth Valiant, Chevrolet Corvair and Chevy II, which were marketed primarily as "second" cars

14.4 Raymond Loewy, Studebaker Avanti, 1964.

14.5 Peter Muller-Munk and Gilmore Clarke, Unisphere, steel. New York World's Fair, 1964.

14.6 General Electric Corporation Pavilion, New York World's Fair, 1964.

General Electronic's space-age pavilion, for instance, featured moving theatres viewing the history and future of electricity and power generation (fig. 14.6). The 1964 New York World's Fair was contemporary with the first manned space missions and continuing Cold War tensions with the Soviet Union, as well as with corporate support of cultural programming on television as a form of public service. An early example of the latter was *General Electric Theatre*, appearing first in 1954 and hosted by actor (and future governor of California and president of the United States) Ronald Reagan. Mobil Oil Corporation's *Masterpiece Theatre* premiered in 1971 through the Public

Broadcasting System (PBS). Such sponsorship increased with the growth of multinational corporations, who sought to minimize or offset possible areas of conflict between company self-interest and the greater public good.

Mass Design and the Home

Technology also inspired many new products aimed primarily at expanding and fulfilling the wants and needs of the mainstream mass market. Such efforts were particularly evident in the growing area of domestic furnishings and interior design. At the 1964 New York World's Fair, the Formica Company, owned from 1957 by the giant chemical corporation American Cyanamid, created a series of model kitchens for a World's Fair House, including designs by Raymond Loewy. Formica, a form of hard plastic laminate attached to plywood backing for tables and countertops, was manufactured in an ever-increasing array of colors and patterns suitable to every taste, including simulated natural and traditional materials such as

14.7 Advertisement for masonite wall paneling, Masonite Corporation, Chicago, Illinois. *Better Homes and Gardens*, January 1962.

wood, marble, and other types of stone. Its success was contemporary with a similar expansion of varied textures and patterns for vinyl flooring suitable for game rooms, kitchens, and enclosed patios. Moreover, products such as vinyl flooring, Formica, and plywood paneling appeared in popular magazine advertisements and continued to be featured in articles as pre-fabricated "do-it-yourself" products, manufactured in sizes to conform to the standardized dimensions of new housing construction for ease of installation, maintenance, and remodeling projects (fig. 14.7).

Today, such products continue to fuel the growing home-improvement and do-it-yourself markets, contributing to the nationwide success of large outlets such as Home Depot and other more specialized suppliers. Wall coverings, paneling, cabinets, ceramic and lapidary tiles, and window blinds, are only a sample of the myriad products involved in home remodeling and decorating that offer variety and a steady stream of new variations to stimulate consumer interest in home as well as self-improvement. As in the past, such products continue to be advertised in magazines such as *Better Homes and Gardens*, mail-order catalogues, and through the Internet. Expanded notions of comfort, convenience, privacy, and self-fulfillment, new materials and techniques of application that narrow the gap between professional and amateur, and the satisfaction of participating in the process of selection and installation combine and continue to make home improvement an integral component of middle-class home-owning. Moreover, former negative associations between synthetic products and kitsch tend not to apply so strictly to such products: increasingly industrially manufactured marble can simulate the natural varieties without obvious difference, undermining both the esthetic and social distinctions between "real" and "fake."

The advertising for many of these products during the 1960s, almost exclusively featuring women either marveling at their new products or appropriately dressed to play hostess, now seems naïve in its appeal to traditional gender stereotypes; indeed, the rejection of traditional role models was also a phenomenon of the 1960s, emerging, for instance, in Betty Friedan's 1963 book *The Feminine Mystique* (see page 310) and later in the women's liberation movement. During the 1960s women debated and protested sexual discrimination and sought alternatives to the gender stereotypes socialized through education and the media. Certainly the marketing of home products may

be seen as a subtle form of social control, tied to familiar associations with women's roles in the nuclear family and fulfillment within rather than outside of the home.

And yet at the same time the playful, democratic, and creative element in mainstream consumer culture was also being recognized, especially toward the end of the decade in books such as Robert Venturi, Denise Scott Brown, and Steven Izenour's *Learning from Las Vegas* (based upon travels and teaching beginning in 1966, published in book form in 1972). These authors, in addition to coining the phrase "less is a bore," embraced the existing man-made, eclectic, and blatantly commercial architecture of billboards, neon signs, glitz, and historical references as evidenced in the carnival-like atmosphere of the Las Vegas strip and its casinos. Limiting and perhaps repressive in some ways, home-improvement products such as Formica, vinyl flooring and tile, and plywood paneling also provided a creative outlet and promised self-realization for many middle-class homeowners, and represented a popular form of the democratization of leisure in postwar America.

Marxist critics have long pointed out that the increasing comfort and estheticism associated with the domestic interior amounts to self-deception rather than liberation. In this view privacy and comfort do little more than hide an often empty, insecure, and unsettling existence, reinforcing social control and conformity by big business, all outgrowths of a capitalist system increasingly closed off to avenues for self-realization other than consumption and materialism. Even the family is not immune from contempt, since the hegemony of the nuclear family is a twentieth-century phenomenon that creates a separation between work and leisure, of private and public, which is itself artificial and normative only within advanced capitalism. The advent of electronic media such as television and film only erodes the ability of the public to discern the capitalist agenda at work in these increasingly seductive forms of communication and advertising. But while consumption certainly has its dangers and excesses, it has not precluded the emergence of alternative approaches and strategies for design, including considerations of social and environmental responsibility. Indeed, many recent discussions of mass culture focus upon an inherent variety of response and reception, stressing an active rather than passive role for the consumer and a rethinking of the dynamics of production and consumption. Responses to popular culture cannot always be programmed, as noted by Venturi, Scott Brown, and Izenour in *Learning from Las Vegas*: "You can like billboards without approving of strip mining in Appalachia." Whether in the late nineteenth century or in the later twentieth century, and whether as a response to early or advanced industrialism, the appreciation for and creative use of materials and processes by designers, craftspeople, and ordinary renters or homeowners remains a tribute to the inventiveness of both producers and consumers. Without their complex, multi-layered character, such design forms could not exert their mass appeal. Some of these alternative readings and interpretations of the phenomenon of mass culture are considered below.

Mass Design: The Fringes

Stimulated by the mass media of television, radio, and film, European countries, and in particular Britain, first absorbed and then contributed to and even dominated the expanding youth market for commodities and music. The economic growth and resulting affluence of the later 1950s and 1960s in Europe produced challenges to traditional class boundaries as well as to social norms of behavior, which in turn found expression in clothing, dance, film, and music emphasizing freedom and self-fulfillment. Such tendencies, particularly among youth, tested the limits of inherited values and constraints. Occasionally they brought condemnation and even censorship, but such initial tension was often followed by tolerance and wider imitation, acceptance, and commercial exploitation. Subgroups formed on the fringes of a generalized youth movement directed toward greater permissiveness and self-expression. As argued by British Historian, Arthur Marwick, an increasingly diversified youth culture was joined by other marginal groups in the 1960s, including racial minorities, women, and homosexuals, each with a strong desire for recognition. Rebellions against inhibitions and prohibitions during this period ranged from skirt-lengths and marijuana-use to abortion, the death penalty, freedom of speech, racial discrimination, the voting age, and foreign policy—for instance the United States' participation in the Vietnam war. The co-existence of several fringe or sub-cultures was a characteristic of the 1960s, not only as applied to popular culture and

14.8 Ford Mustang, 1965.

connected through the mass media, but also to the fine arts, where the splintering of the avant-garde and the emergence of galleries on the American West Coast were easily contrasted with the pervasiveness of abstract art and the dominance of the New York art world during most of the 1950s.

New attitudes and behaviors were easily commercially exploited or commodified as fashion products and accessories, and thus entered the world of design in relation to commodity consumption. Even in the increasingly conservative and homogenous United States automobile industry there were some popular successes, for instance the Ford Mustang (fig. 14.8), first manufactured toward the end of 1964 and appealing to an expanding youth-oriented audience with features such as tapered concave cutaway door panels derived from earlier sports cars such as the Chevrolet Corvette. The legendary appeal of the Pontiac GTO, introduced in 1964, was based more upon a powerful V-8 engine than its conventional rectangular body, and the exhilaration of pushing the speed limit was much celebrated in popular youth culture, for instance in the rock music hit "Little GTO," recorded by Ronnie and the Daytonas in 1964. The song was a top forty hit in the U.S., complete with simulated motor sounds:

> Little GTO, you're really lookin' fine
> Three deuces and a four-speed and a 389
> Listen to her tachin' up now, listen to her why-ee-eye-ine
> C'mon and turn it on, wind it up, blow it out GTO.

Other examples of the youth-oriented popular culture in the period came from the world of fashion and emerged

14.9 Mary Quant (centre) and models presenting the "Viva Viva" line, Milan, 1967.

early on in England. British designer and entrepreneur Mary Quant (*b*.1934) designed and sold clothing aimed at young buyers, based upon simple, even traditional pinafore patterns but featuring higher hemlines, bold colors, and a series of fashion accessories ranging from dark fishnet stockings and knee-length leather boots, creating a look associated with an active, energetic, and hedonistic lifestyle (fig. 14.9). Quant is credited with inventing the miniskirt and with helping to launch the careers of international models such as Twiggy in the mid-1960s who exemplified the new "look", as well as with influencing the trend toward more youthful approaches to fashion even among Parisian haute couture designers.

In music, the early recordings of the Liverpool-based band The Beatles demonstrate a complete assimilation and mastery of 1950s forms of rock 'n' roll music from the United States. The band's performance skills and gifts for original songwriting achieved an unprecedented degree of

international success and in part through the marketing efforts of the group's manager, Brian Epstein (1934–1967). The Beatles' mop-like hairstyles and modish clothing, and the use of live concerts were significant elements in the marketing of their music through an appeal to lifestyle and cultivation of celebrity. By the mid-1960s, youth-oriented and American-inspired popular culture had not only become an international phenomenon, it had expanded beyond its youthful audience, as popular weekly television variety programs such as the prime-time Sunday evening *Ed Sullivan Show* began to feature rock 'n' roll groups as part of their regular entertainment features, broadcast from New York and targeting mainstream audiences more than the daily Philadelphia-based *American Bandstand*. In addition to the wave of British rock 'n' roll groups, the mid-1960s also witnessed the skyrocketing success of Detroit-based (Motown) black singing groups to a national audience extending far beyond racial barriers, including the Temptations, among others, the Supremes, and the Four Tops. The acceptance of Soul music to a broad national audience via the mass media contrasted with the racial tension and outbreaks of violence in American industrial cities and with the emergence of black separatist movements, reacting impatiently to the slow pace of economic and social improvements for minorities, and questioning the ideology of integration in relation to issues of black identity.

Pop and Protest

The broad and varied role of popular rock music in the 1960s can hardly be overestimated, and emerges as a paradigm for the widespread interpenetration and relaxation of boundaries between traditional and underground behaviors, mainstream and fringe, pop and avant-garde. From general permissiveness and self-expression among youth and those older groups wishing to identify with a more open lifestyle, to non-conformism and rebelliousness by some subculture groups or advocacy for drugs by others, this most accessible medium of rock music involved an active, inclusive role for the audience. In short, the 1960s' maxim "do your own thing" did not mean the same to everyone.

Social conservatism, conformity, the dangers of technology, violence, capital punishment, and government

14.10 Andy Warhol, Big Electric Chair, silkscreen enamel and acrylic on canvas, 54 x 73 ⅛ in (137 x 186 cm), 1967. The Menil Collection, Houston.

foreign policy were all targets of the expanding Pop Art movement in the early 1960s. Andy Warhol's series of stark, black-and-white silkscreen images taken from press photographs of suicide victims, fatal car accidents, and the electric chair chamber in a prison provide a grim commentary on violence in the United States, where the grainy quality of the image and its repetition also demonstrates a combination of sensationalism with the often numbing effect of mass media (fig. 14.10). That such images still had an edge in the early 1960s was demonstrated at the 1964 New York World's Fair when city officials whitewashed Warhol's monumental mural of the thirteen most-wanted criminals in America, commissioned for the façade of the New York State pavilion. Strategies employed by Pop artists used the familiar forms of photography and other techniques of mass-produced imagery, and, like their counterparts in the rock music industry, may be seen in part as an attempt to expand the political base of a new, vernacular art. Expanding beyond the gallery and the commercial associations between art objects and brand-name celebrity of artists was also the motivation behind Happenings, Performance Art, Earth Art, and other efforts of artists to engage in creative activities on the margins of consumer culture while attempting to mobilize a more broadly-based audience.

Amid growing racial tensions in large U.S. cities such as Los Angeles and Detroit, concern over escalation of the United States' involvement in the Vietnam war, worker

strikes and student protests both in Europe and the United States, the political aspirations of Pop artists and rock musicians appeared as part of a wider struggle to engage the mass media and public opinion.

Graphics and the Underground

In addition to rock music and happenings, protest movements created a number of distinctive cultural forms in the field of graphic design. The massive demonstrations and disruptive confrontations between police and students on college campuses over issues of free speech and United States' involvement in Vietnam were media events whose tactics possessed elements of performance and provocation related to the extremes of art world happenings and the rock music concerts, a world where guitars were occasionally smashed and American flags burned, culminating in the 1969 gathering at Woodstock in upper-state New York and the currency of the term counterculture. Posters were a part of popular protest in the later 1960s, accompanying the public sit-ins, demonstrations, and concerts on pedestrian-friendly university campuses throughout the United States and Europe. The poster forms were adopted as well for album covers for rock music groups (larger and more "poster-like" than today's compact disk packaging). Many poster designs eschewed precise,

14.11 Wes Wilson, concert poster. Fillmore West, 1967.

14.12 Waldemar Swierzy, poster for Jimi Hendrix, 1974.

hard-edged letterforms in favor of a more calligraphic and elastic typography often derived from l'Art Nouveau and blurring distinctions between text, illustration, and decoration. An example is Robert Wesley (Wes) Wilson's (*b.*1937) poster for the Otis Rush/Grateful Dead/Canned Heat concert held at San Francisco's Fillmore Auditorium in 1967 (fig. 14.11). Illustration and expressive decoration merge as well in the 1974 poster depicting rock star Jimi Hendrix by Polish illustrator Waldemar Swierzy (*b.*1931), where nervous lines vibrate about the clothing and hair of the monumental portrait (fig. 14.12). As noted by Philip Meggs, posters constituted a significant popular art form in Poland after World War II and the establishment of communist rule. Jerzy Janiszewski's logo for the

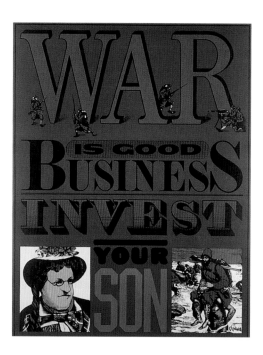

14.13 Jerzy Janiszweski, Solidarity logo, *c.* 1980.

14.14 Seymour Chwast, *Graphic Statement about War*, 1967.

14.15 Peter Blake and Janna Haworth, *Sergeant Pepper's Lonely Hearts Club Band*, album cover, 1967.

Solidarity labor union (*c.*1980, fig. 14.13) evokes in its sweeping and uneven strokes and drips the destructive and disruptive nature of public graffiti.

The incorporation of earlier styles of typography and self-conscious use of primitive, unsophisticated approaches to illustration (including graffiti) also emerges in the work of illustrator Seymour Chwast (*b.*1931), who shared a studio with Milton Glaser and a number of other New York illustrators through the 1950s and 1960s and published examples of new approaches to graphic design in the *Push Pin Almanac.* Chwast's re-use of different styles of Victorian typography, and his incorporation of stock images for a mother and soldier in a Vietnam-era anti-war statement (fig. 14.14), suggests a product from a basement printing press rather than a professional studio, linking the poster to the expression of unofficial, underground, resistant viewpoints. Such an approach was used for the cover of the Beatles' 1967 album *Sergeant Pepper's Lonely Hearts Club Band*, by Peter Blake and Janna Haworth (with photographer Michael Cooper), where elements of juxtaposition between past and present, reminiscent of Dada and Surrealist collage, provide a visual analogue to references to psychedelic drugs contained in the lyrics for a number of the tracks for the album (fig. 14.15).

Anti-Design in Italy

Protest was also a direction in design acknowledged in the *Italy: The New Domestic Landscape* exhibition held at the Museum of Modern Art in New York in 1972. In 1968 student protestors and workers staged demonstrations in Milan, disrupting the Fourteenth Milan Triennale and forcing an early closing of this major international showcase for industrial design in the postwar period. Protests, strikes, and sit-ins were prevalent in many Italian cities during that year: on university campuses student demonstrators rebelled against authoritarian administrations and biased admissions policies, and in factories workers organized for better wages as a response to frustrated expectations for higher standards of living. In solidarity with students and workers, a number of Italian industrial designers began to view their role in the creation of sophisticated domestic objects as part of a repressive collaboration between government and corporate management that reinforced class distinction and fueled

commodity consumption for the wealthy. In sympathy with the unrest on campuses and in factories (at Fiat and Pirelli, for instance), designers looked to alternative strategies that might initiate a redefinition of the relation of design to society.

Design curator Emilio Ambasz organized the 1972 MoMA exhibition. It included both new and familiar examples of postwar modern Italian design in furniture, lighting, and machine housings featuring molded plastics and abstract sculptural forms, as well as a section devoted to modular and flexible designs for seating and storage (see figs. 13.3, 13.9, 13.10, and 13.17). An additional category, however, featured "objects selected for their socio-cultural implications," which Ambasz defined in the following way:

> The second ... attitude is motivated by a profound concern for the designer's role in a society that fosters consumption as one means of inducing individual happiness, thereby insuring social stability. Torn by the dilemma of having been trained as creators of objects, and yet being incapable of controlling either the significance or the ultimate uses of these objects, they find themselves unable to reconcile the conflicts between their social concerns and their professional practices. They have thus developed a rhetorical mode to cope with these contradictions. Convinced that there can be no renovation of design until structural changes have occurred in society, but not attempting to bring these about themselves, they do not invent substantially new forms; instead they engage in rhetorical operation of redesigning conventional objects with new, ironic, and sometimes self-deprecatory sociocultural and aesthetic references.

In addition to individual designers represented in this section of the exhibition, a number of design groups were included, such as Archizoom and Superstudio, both founded in the later 1960s and devoted to experimental ideas in architecture and design, and seen as being outside the usual relationship between individual "star" industrial designers and the corporation.

Ambasz's definition of experimental industrial design in the 1972 MoMA exhibition was tentative, but references to American popular culture were certainly an important element in the selection of objects for this category. Paolo Lomazzi, Donato D'Urbino, and Jonathan De

14.16 Lomazzi, D'Urbino, and De Pas, Joe chair, polyurethane foam covered with leather, 65 ¼ in (167cm) wide, manufactured by Poltronova (Pistoia, Italy), 1970.

14.17 Archizoom, Elettro Rosa model bed from series "Rosa Imperiale", designed by Archizoom, 1967.

Pas's Joe chair (1970/71), made of polyurethane foam covered in leather in the shape of a (left-handed) baseball mitt (fig. 14.16), eschewed the sophisticated abstraction of much contemporary Italian design and referenced images of everyday banal consumer culture associated with post-war American affluence. According to Andrea Branzi (b.1939), a founding member of Archizoom, one of the intentions of such objects was to invert the message of popular culture, to create a design situation in which "consumption coincides with opposition." Blatantly anti-functional and garish furniture, with exaggerated elements drawn from luxurious Art Deco or American popular culture such as the model "dream" beds and interiors designed by Archizoom (fig. 14.17), demonstrated a sense of the designer's liberation in moving outside of the accepted parameters for sophisticated contemporary industrial design. It is not difficult to see parallels for such

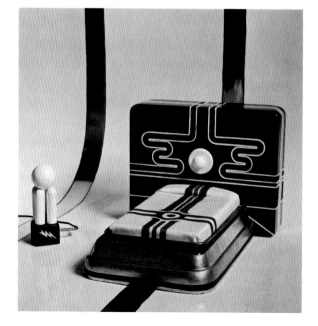

14.18 Claes Oldenburg, Bedroom Ensemble, Replica 1, installation, 303 x 512 x 845 in (770 x 1300 x 2146 cm), 1969. (Original installation 1963, Whitney Museum of American Art, New Yok.)

subversive, political interpretations of the banal object in the fine arts. For instance Claes Oldenburg also produced installations or environments of everyday objects and furniture, a strategy employed in the contemporary art world to move outside the white walls of conventional New York galleries and to more actively engage the spectator. Such projects included his *Bedroom Ensemble* (1963), which featured diagonal rather than square furnishings such as beds and dressing tables, constructed of wood and covered in lively, clashing surface patterns of manufactured Formica, not unlike a walk-in Pop Art painting assembled by Tom Wesselman (figs. 14.18 and 14.19). Again, the acceptance of popular culture and open-mindedness to heterogeneity, playfulness, and multiple readings of cultural expressions provide the basis for a new kind of artistic freedom involving greater participation on the part of the spectator. At the same time the approach embraced the products of mass culture, and thus stood outside of the abstract conventions of modern design, now seen as increasingly exclusive and dogmatic.

Even where a dialogue with abstract sculpture is invoked, its meaning is subverted. An example of such a strategy is Gaetano Pesce's (*b.*1939) Donna chair, designed

14.19 Tom Wesselman, *Still Life Number 36*, oil and collage on canvas, four panels, 120 x 192 ¼ in (305 x 488 cm), 1964. Whitney Museum of American Art, New York.

It is worthwhile recognizing that the works characterized by Ambasz as "socio-cultural" in intent were often more experimental than practical. Some examples included theoretical tracts and drawings accompanying, for instance, a series of "counter design" environments commissioned for the 1972 MoMA exhibition, such as Ettore Sottsass, Jr.'s entry (fig. 14.21). The brief for the visionary environments by Sottsass and others calls to mind the guidelines for contributors to the 1925 Exposition des Arts Décoratifs et Industriels Modernes, who also were encouraged to submit designs to express "new modes of living" through design; indeed it was this brief that produced Le Corbusier's model apartment for the Pavilion de l'Esprit Nouveau.

Counter-design activities were not intended primarily for consumption: generally designers wished to liberate themselves from a repressive system in which they felt

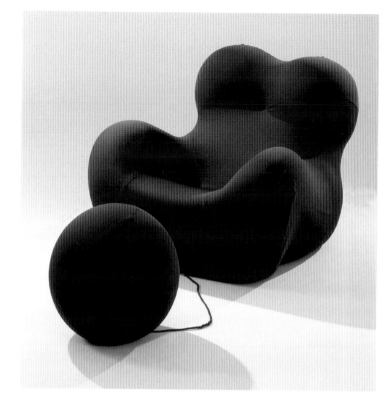

14.20 Gaetano Pesce, Donna chair, cold foam-molded polyurethane foam and nylon jersey fabric, 32 ¼ x 46 x 54 in (82 x 117 x 137 cm), 1970-73, manufactured by Cassina and Busnelli, Como, Italy.

in 1969 and manufactured between 1970 and 1973 by Cassina & Busnelli (fig. 14.20). The Donna chair, constructed of polyurethane foam covered with nylon jersey, brings to mind earlier postwar chairs with female names by Italian designers, most notably Marco Zanuso's 1951 Lady chair (see fig. 11.53, page 273). Its concave and convex forms are suggestive of the female form as evoked in Neolithic fertility figures as well as in the contemporary sculpture of Henry Moore. Yet the round ottoman attached to the chair with a cord creates alternative meanings, alluding to issues relating to the women's liberation movement, undermining the sensual reading. As Pesce wrote:

> In this design I have expressed my idea of women. A woman is always confined, a prisoner of herself against her will. For this reason I wanted to give this chair the shape of a woman with a ball chained to her foot to use the traditional image of a prisoner.

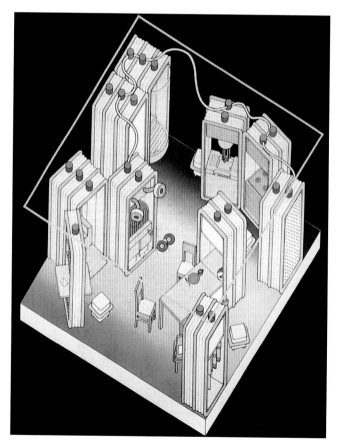

14.21 Ettore Sottsass, Jr., Modular Environment, manufactured by Kartell, Boffi, Ideal-Standard, for "The New Domestic Landscape" exhibition at the Museum of Modern Art, 1972.

their role circumscribed and used their research to provoke and undermine the practices of consumers and manufacturers alike. Some, such as Enzo Mari, were more interested in language than in products, and viewed inactivity itself as a political stance; Mari produced a polemic essay rather than a physical environment for MoMA's 1972 exhibition. While embracing popular culture as subversion and advocating radical political change, the activities of this "counter-design" rarely extended beyond the boundaries of exhibition spaces, catalogues, and journals; the relation of "counter-design" to workers' strikes and student protests was distant, and rarely included sharing the real-life dangers and confrontation on the front lines, although the boycott and demonstrations at the 1968 Triennale in Milan suggests that the militant spirit of the later 1960s in Italy did indeed have design practice as a target.

Radical Reform: Technology, Safety, and the Environment

The 1960s also marked the resurgence of several alternative strategies aimed at redirecting the practice of the corporate-based industrial design community along the lines of public and environmental responsibility, often spurred by adopting a global perspective that added urgency to the rhetoric of reform. Calls for reform ranged from consumer safety to considerations of a wider variety of technologies to improve living conditions in the Third World to futuristic, utopian visions based upon a more efficient use of the world's limited natural resources. The search for new principles or standards of design sometimes questioned the faith in industrial technology as well as unbridled individualism as manipulated by the commercial interests of free market capitalism. In some ways the voices of reform were not always in harmony with the hedonism that informed many expressions of the counter-culture, though both movements shared a strong sense of mission and idealism.

Criticism of design issued both from within and from outside the design community, often with the interest of a public mobilized by articulate spokespeople and activists, advocating for the rights of consumers and minorities. The impact of grass-roots movements remains part of our understanding of the 1960s, part of a perceived ability of ordinary citizens to "change the system" through strikes, sit-ins, rallies, boycotts, and the engagement of the cameras and microphones of the mass media. Although social activism was indeed a theme that engaged artists and designers, other design activities of the period recall in some ways earlier efforts to establish standards and practices to balance corporate profits and individual expression with social and environmental responsibility.

Unlike earlier efforts of reform, criticism directed at industrial design did not take the form of a single, unified theme or objective, nor did it originate with the endorsements or proclamations of organizations, museums, or government committees. In general reform efforts resulted from an ideological confrontation between the optimism and affluence of the postwar "American Dream" and "European Economic Miracle" and the realities of lingering inequities and unfulfilled promise.

One form of industrial design criticism targeted a number of large corporations on behalf of the consumers whose interests the corporation was supposed to be serving. A pioneer in this effort was Ralph Nader (b.1934), whose 1965 book *Unsafe at Any Speed: the designed-in dangers of the American automobile* attacked the General Motors Corporation for neglecting significant safety issues in the design of the aluminum rear-engine compact Corvair, introduced by Chrevolet in 1960. According to Nader, GM had ignored evidence that this type of rear-engine vehicle had a tendency to spin out of control under certain road conditions, even though warnings of this and other design flaws during model's development were brought to the attention of company management. The implication of Nader's book was that GM spent significant sums for styling to boost sales, while ignoring safety, product reliability, and public welfare. *Unsafe at Any Speed*, and the subsequent Senate investigation of GM efforts to silence Nader by conducting surveillance in the hope of uncovering damaging information concerning his character and background, made this lawyer and author a champion for the rights of individuals to question corporate practice and to assert their power as private citizens through the mass media, boycotts, organized protest, and litigation. Nader extended his investigations of corporate business practice to include chemical food preservatives in popular American products such as hot dogs; in this and other cases the evidence was convincing and the result was to undermine consumer and public confidence in

14.22 Honda Motor Company, Hamamatsu, Honda Civic automobile, 147 ¹³⁄₁₆ x 59 ¹⁄₄ x 52 ¹⁄₈ in (375 x 150.5 x 132 cm), American Honda Motor Company Inc., Torrance, California.

corporate responsibility. Eventually such efforts led litigation for more informative product labeling as a measure of consumer education and protection, as well as other regulatory requirements.

While Nader did not bring an end to the "big three" automakers' emphasis upon styling, his efforts did ignite a wave of consumer awareness and the initiation of legislation to monitor automobile safety. Another response to corporate self-interest in the American automobile industry was a steady rise in the sales of imported cars less subject to the marketing practices of annual model changes by large American manufacturers. Rather than comply with the American strategy of progressive obsolescence, buyers could exercise freedom of choice by choosing not to buy an American car. Perhaps the best-known alternative of this sort was the small rear-engine air-cooled Volkswagen Beetle, designed in 1937 but not manufactured continuously in Germany until after the end of World War II (see page 275). Sales of the Beetle increased during the 1960s mostly through popularity with younger buyers, while individual owners sometimes customized its standardized form through hand-painted designs rather than factory options and accessories.

The appeal of smaller, standardized vehicles received yet another, and stronger boost after 1973 when the oil-producing nations of the Middle East established a cartel (the Organization of the Petroleum Exporting Countries or OPEC) that fixed oil prices and eliminated concessions to multinational oil companies for inexpensive oil prices in the United States. Within a year of the formation of OPEC, fuel prices in the United States rose from below fifty cents per gallon to over one dollar. Both in person and through television, the sight of filling stations with gas lines and the resulting public fear of shortages and dwindling natural reserves for oil also spelled disaster for the major auto manufacturers, locked into large-engine vehicles and unconcerned with fuel efficiency and conservation.

As American automakers began to consider issues of fuel consumption in their designs, foreign manufacturers became increasingly competitive. Perhaps the biggest winner in the automobile market was the Japanese manufacturer Honda, whose 1975 Civic met consumer expectations in a new era of fuel economy (fig. 14.22). The rival Japanese Nissan Motor Company Ltd. (under the brand name Datsun), as well as Toyota, also provided several economical alternatives to gas guzzling Detroit models, earning a foothold in the large North American market that has not been relinquished.

Amid skepticism toward corporate ideology linking design, technology, and progress, new alternative voices for reform sounded the battle cry for social responsibility, often with an added sense of urgency based upon the environmental costs of technology, consumption, and waste. The anger directed at industrial design in the 1960s may be felt in the preface of a book written at the end of the era, Victor Papanek's *Design for the Real World*, published in 1971:

> There are professions more harmful than industrial design, but only a very few of them. And possibly only one profession is phonier. Advertising design, in persuading people to buy things they don't need, with money they don't have, in order to impress others who don't care, is probably the phoniest field in existence today. Industrial design, by concocting the tawdry idiocies hawked by advertisers, comes a close second... By designing criminally unsafe automobiles that kill or maim nearly one million people around the world each year, by creating whole new species of permanent garbage to clutter up the landscape, and by choosing materials and processes that pollute the air we breathe, designers have become a dangerous breed. And the skills needed in these activities are taught carefully to young people.

The Austrian-born and British-educated Papanek (1926–1998) was an outspoken critic of styling and obsolescence in industrial design, advocating an approach that took account of limited natural resources and the satisfaction of needs as opposed to wants. Like R. Buckminster Fuller, who supplied the preface to *Design for the Real World*, Papanek was both utopian as well as apocalyptic: both designers envisioned a world in which governments and large organizations benevolently directed design projects for housing and products in the broad public interest for safety and the efficient use of resources, and warned of the global effects of unlimited production in terms of pollution and other environmental hazards. He also lamented the lost opportunities for designers to play a more active role in meeting basic needs in developing countries. Papanek considered design as an inclusive and multi-faceted problem-solving activity that addresses considerations of materials, processes, and use in relation to issues of social and political responsibility. The gravity, the relevance, of his hope for design emerges again in this passage from *Design for the Real World*:

Isn't it too bad that so little design, so few products are really relevant to the needs of mankind? Watching the children of Biafra dying in living color while sipping a frost-beaded martini can be kicks for lots of people, but only until *their* town starts burning down. To an engaged designer, this way of life, this lack of design, is not acceptable.

Papanek attempted to restore a sense of urgency to design as an activity integral to the survival of the planet in environmental as well as in social terms. Although less universal in his approach to the activity of design, Papanek's urgency reminds one of Le Corbusier's provocative question at the conclusion of *Towards a New Architecture:* "Architecture or Revolution?" Both authors believed in the ability of design to alter the conditions of life. Papanek provided numerous examples of socially- and environmentally-directed projects that explored the problem-solving context of his approach to design. As an example he cited an anonymously-designed low-cost stove constructed of re-used automobile license plates for families in underprivileged societies, as well as a design he developed with John Hennessey for a cooling unit to keep food products fresh without the need for electricity (fig. 14.23). In addition to his own designs, Papanek directed student projects at a number of universities. In no sense

14.23 Victor Papanek and James Hennessey, drawing and prototype for cooling unit for perishable foods, using no electricity.

was Papanek anti-technological; rather he argued for responsible technology, known also as appropriate technology, where local materials, energy sources, and other considerations may argue for simpler rather than "hi-tech" solutions to design problems—solutions that enable people to help themselves rather than reinforce dependence upon massive external technological investment and the consequences of such investment.

The career of visionary designer R. Buckminster Fuller stretched over five decades, beginning with prototypes for a mass-produced Dymaxion house and the three-wheel streamlined Dymaxion automobile displayed at the 1933 "Century of Progress" World's Fair in Chicago (see page 216). Fuller believed that conservation of energy and materials were industrial design imperatives in the twentieth century. His lightweight geodesic domes, developed after World War II as a strategy to meet tremendous housing shortages, were fabricated from triangular units that could be made from a variety of materials; they could be used as a framework to support panels, windows, or even hang fabric to provide portable shelter. Like many of Fuller's projects, geodesic domes had limited commercial viability (see page 285); his design and promotional efforts had a utopian and visionary quality stemming from a belief in the ability of applied technology to solve global problems irrespective of markets and considerations of social and cultural difference. The apotheosis of

14.24 Buckminster Fuller, Geodesic dome for United States Pavilion, Montreal, Canada, 1967.

the geodesic dome was its use for the United States Pavilion at the 1967 World Fair in Montreal, Canada (fig. 14.24).

Despite the collectivist implications of his vision, Fuller's public appearances (lectures often lasting for hours on university campuses as well as television and news magazine interviews) attracted the interest of many youth counter-culture groups, who embraced communal living as an alternative to either suburb or city. Fuller represents a point of connection between the romanticism associated with youth counter-culture movements of the later 1960s and the radical reform views of industrial designers wishing to redirect technology away from materialism toward the elimination of human suffering. Both

movements were motivated by idealism, but in fact the universal implications of Fuller's utopia were quite removed from the unbridled sensory indulgence of the hippie counterculture of the 1970s. And yet both were in their own ways "anti-establishment," part of a broad spectrum of subcultures with a belief in an alternative vision for a future society.

More mainstream solutions to social problems involving the application of minimum collective needs might be seen in the low-cost, high density housing projects and urban planning initiatives undertaken in the later 1950s and 1960s in a number of American cities. There is widespread agreement that these massive, universalist efforts at urban "redevelopment," underwritten by local, state, and federal governments, were well-intentioned failures. Within two decades of their construction high-density housing projects were deteriorating as physical structures and were failing as well to build a sense of community and shared responsibility. British historian David Harvey commented that the demolition of the 1955 Pruitt-Igoe development in St. Louis in 1972 signifies the demise of the belief that a rational approach to modern design could help promote social or racial equality. As Jane Jacobs noted in her 1961 book *The Death and Life of Great American Cities*, housing standards based upon universal esthetic principles or social determinism do not seem to be able to effectively address the challenges of creating safe and self-supporting communities. As a result, design solutions must take into account a variety of factors that include the perspectives of the population being served, the psychological effects of environment, and zoning considerations that affect the nurturing of community.

Chapter 15

Politics, Pluralism, and Postmodernism

15.4 Frank Gehry, Easy Edges rocking chair, cardboard, made by Jack Brogan, 42 in (107 cm) long, 1971–72. Private collection.

The 1960s did not spark social or political revolution as foreshadowed in campus riots in the United States and in Europe or the disruption of the 1968 Democratic Party National Convention in Chicago. As argued, however, by Arthur Marwick, British historian and author, the challenge of new viewpoints stemming from minority groups, whether women, blacks, gays, or students, produced more open-minded attitudes toward difference and the protection of individual rights.

In the U.S. Federal enforcement of the 1964 Civil Rights Act and widely broadcast demonstrations such as the 1963 March on Washington served to bring issues of racial equality to national attention. Also, Government initiative created the Environmental Protection Agency (EPA) in 1970 and the passage of laws aimed at reducing highway deaths through seatbelt laws and mandatory

manufacturer recalls on defective parts and systems eventually resulted from Ralph Nader's spirited challenge to unquestioned faith in corporate power. For almost twenty years, the oil crisis of the early 1970s and concerns for fuel efficiency and automobile safety produced lower speed limits (55 mph) on most of the nation's highways. Other legislation permitted abortion (Roe vs. Wade, 1973), required the reading of rights to individuals placed under arrest (Miranda vs. Arizona, 1966), and made divorces easier to obtain. On campuses, quota systems for the admission of minorities were abolished and the percentage of students able to attend colleges and universities began to rise through need-based and merit-based scholarships and loans. And finally in 1976, though long-overdue for many Americans, broad-based pressure helped to bring an end to the drawn-out war in

Vietnam, which had caused so much protest and anger both within the United States and directed toward the United States from its neighbors.

The 1960s also signaled the critical recognition of several co-existing cultural expressions in the areas of art and design, a situation sometimes referred to as Pluralism, in which no single approach to modernity dominated, and where the exchange value of all commodities overshadowed former distinctions between "good," mass, and popular design. The situation accommodated, and even encouraged diversity, but only within an acknowledged common culture of consumption. Perhaps late twentieth-century Pluralism may be understood simply as the commercialization of diversity: the margins do not exist without a dominant mainstream, but the mainstream also demands the margins to nurture new markets. Thomas Crow has cogently summarized the situation: "The avant-garde is the research and development branch of the culture industry."

Capital investment in business following the break-up of the Soviet Union, and trade negotiations between the United States and the Peoples Republic of China, reveals that economic expansion consistently dominates politics in international relations, with human rights serving as a bargaining chip to insure the political consent of congress on behalf of their broad-based constituencies. Scarcely more than a century ago, William Morris joined the Socialist League in protest over the British government's support of Turkish interests in the Balkans, despite evidence of atrocities by Turkish soldiers against Bulgarian citizens. For dissenters such as Morris, Britain's support was based upon economic self-interest rather than upon humanitarian concerns. Today, in general, the press and the public it represents readily accept that the United States' foreign policy is governed by a convenient dovetailing between the concern for human rights and the exploration of new markets for goods and services. If in the end the interests of human rights are served through such compromise it is rarely due to the pressure exerted by fringe activism. This process tends to minimize differences between existing mainstream political parties, who continue to link, often uncritically, technology with economic growth and progress.

Within this framework acknowledging the hegemony of capitalism and equating progress with consumption and economic expansion, a variety of perspectives on modern design co-exist, often symbiotically. This generally healthy heterogeneity reduces the dichotomy between a "cultural" modernism based upon standards and social responsibility, and an "economic" modernism governed by free enterprise and addressing the mass market that lent to the first two centuries of modern design history a particular kind of heroism, urgency, and vision. In the present context of inclusiveness and relativity, notions of reform, alienation, resistance, and subversion have relinquished a measure of their power to define what has been a vital aspect of the history of modern design.

Toward the end of the 1970s the pop-culture challenge to modern architecture and "good design" was becoming more widespread. At the same time this movement continued to relinquish the subversive political overtones it had in Italy and elsewhere in the later 1960s, and acquired an international high-end commercial cachet. In Italy, particularly in Milan, organizations espousing new directions were initiated in the later 1970s. Alchymia (1976) and Memphis (1981), for instance, included contributions of not only Italian but also Japanese and North and South American designers. The activities of Memphis and other groups or individuals designing ambiguous but less threatening interpretations of popular culture are often described as being postmodern, a term now commonly used among critics and historians, and even filtering into more general usage.

For design, postmodernism encompasses projects and forms that signal an end to the polemic between esthetically- or socially-directed design and commercially-motivated design that emerged as a strain of modernism in the early nineteenth century and that dominated design theory for much of the two decades following World War II. It may also be described even more broadly as an attitude through which various tendencies of modernism in design are deprived of their oppositional status or pretensions. Theoretically, postmodernism shares with mass culture a user-oriented approach to design that emphasizes multiple interpretations and meanings and often embraces the ephemeral rather than the permanent characteristics of the design enterprise, exemplified by connections with the improvisational, open-ended nature of performance art and the inclusiveness of popular art forms.

Design and Postmodernism

The term postmodernism is also often found in conjunction with others such as post-industrialism and late capitalism, all referring to a culture in which consumption is the common subtext, emerging first in the early years of postwar affluence in the United States and spreading to Europe and other developed nations. Late capitalism signifies investment directed toward increasingly segmented (rather than collective) audiences, and a readiness of businesses to design, manufacture, and market products with increasing speed, responsiveness, and sophistication in a highly competitive environment, stimulated even further by an accelerated interactivity between design, manufacturing, and marketing through the use of digital technology. As an example, British design historian Nigel Whitely cites the success of the Swatch wristwatches first in Britain and then internationally in the 1980s, the result of inexpensive plastic materials and mass production, and an especially fashion-oriented approach to wristwatches to complement clothing styles (fig. 15.1). The ephemeral, almost disposable Swatch (the name combines the words "switch" and "watch"), manufactured by the Swiss company Eta beginning in 1983, targeted a young audience less likely to be influenced by the emotional attachments sometimes associated with personal objects and heirlooms.

Post-industrialism is another broad and useful contemporary term signaling that the heroic age of industrial mass production has been superceded by an increased emphasis upon the research, service, and communications sectors of economies and expanded creative efforts in fields such as product semantics rather than more traditional "form-making" associated with industrial design. In some traditional manufacturing industries, capital investment in

15.1 Wristwatch, plastic housing, approximately 9 in (23 cm) in length, manufactured by Eta, Switzerland, c. 1980–85. Photograph: Swatch Company.

robotics reduces the need for unskilled, assembly-line labor; even in high-tech companies, selective use of sophisticated mechanized equipment still requires elements of specialized craftsmanship to maintain quality and expand markets. In some ways an extension of human factors into the realm of communication rather than physical interaction, the area of product semantics deals with the interface of machines with human beings to break down barriers for understanding, use, and sales. Examples include the development of the mouse for desktop computers (see below, page 374), tracking devices for laptop computers, color-coding and other simplifications for the wiring of electronic connections for home stereo equipment, or diagrams accompanying personal computers and printers that permit virtually effortless set-up and operation. Emphasis upon the user also extends to accelerating product change through the introduction of small differences in similar products to create consumer choice and faster rates of obsolescence. An instance of the blurring between technology, progress, and consumption is described below with reference to the telephone (see pages 368–9), while the use of computers to generate patterns for machine-knit sweaters provides another instance of an acceleration of the interface between design and manufacturing.

Recent theory often refers to contemporary design as being "soft," a term implying a number of related concepts, including the designer's manipulation of virtual rather than real materials and forms via computer imaging in a more dynamic, interactive, and collaborative process, and emphasizing process rather than product. Nevertheless, "soft" design, linked as well to *soft*ware and the digital age is often a metaphor for an esthetic sensibility that combines nostalgia for science fiction, past and present, near and far, in an exciting, fast-paced, seamless (if fragmented) image characteristic of contemporary culture in the information age.

Postmodern Products

Postmodern design emerged in organizations such as Memphis, made up of industrial designers "liberated" from their contracts with particular companies, with the freedom to pursue directions beyond the parameters of "good design." Postmodernism, or Pluralism, also was the

15.2 Ettore Sottsass, Jr., Tartar table, reconstituted veneer, lacquer, and plastic laminate, 30 x 75 ¼ x 32 ¼ in (76 x 192 x 82 cm), manufactured by Memphis, 1985.

15.3 Stanley Tigerman, *Tête-à-Tête* double easy-chair, Formica and colorcore, 1983.

overriding theme of the exhibition entitled *Design Now: Industry or Art* held in the German Architecture Museum in Frankfurt in 1989.

Ettore Sottsass, Jr., who worked under contract to Olivetti in the 1960s in the design of office machines and personal typewriters (see figs. 13.11 and 13.12), independently designed prototypes for furniture in the 1980s using industrial materials such as plywood and plastic laminates in bright colors and patterns. These examples made references to Hollywood-style historical set design, celebrating the sensory excitement of billboard advertising and rock music (Memphis is the home of rock icon Elvis Presley, immortalized in Warhol's silkscreen images and in the furnishings of the singer's own Graceland mansion). An example is Sottsass's 1981 Tartar table (fig. 15.2), whose laminated surfaces and juxtapositions of patterns recall Oldenburg's *Bedroom Ensemble* installation of 1963 or Wesselman's *Still Life Number 36* mural (see figs. 14.18 and 14.19). Memphis organized group exhibitions in Milan, and the Formica Corporation invited members of the group to design furniture using its new ColorCore product, a solid variation of the material that could be molded and cut, producing results such as Stanley Tigerman's *Tête à Tête* chairs of 1983 (fig. 15.3). Tigerman's abstract design bears some resemblance to architect/designer Frank O. Gehry's more experimental

15.4 Frank Gehry, Easy Edges rocking chair, cardboard, made by Jack Brogan, 42 in (107 cm) long, 1971–72. Private collection.

15.5 Robert Venturi, Chippendale chair, bent laminated yew and plastic laminate, 37 ⅛ x 25 ½ x 23 ¼ in (95 x 65 x 59 cm), manufactured by Knoll International, New York, 1978–84. Philadelphia Museum of Art.

15.6 Philippe Starck, "Tippy Jackson" table, painted tubular steel and sheet metal, 28 in (71 cm), manufactured by Driade, 1985.

Easy Edges rocking chair made from laminated cardboard a decade earlier (fig. 15.4). High-end commercial interest in the new Pluralism is seen in Robert Venturi's series of chairs manufactured by Knoll. Venturi's Chippendale chair of 1984 appears to mock important tenets of modern industrial design, first in imitating an eighteenth-century style, second in using an industrial material to imitate an original design in a natural material (here made even more obvious through painting), and third by flaunting decoration rather than eliminating it or treating it as subservient to function. Indeed Venturi, who encouraged architects to think of themselves as "jesters," chose the chair as a focus, since it has been a paradigm of the very standards toward which contemporary designers direct their irony and through which they champion the "complexity and contradiction" of postmodernism (fig. 15.5).

French architect and designer Philippe Starck (b.1949) emerged in the mid-1980s with original furniture for sophisticated clients such as fashion designer Pierre Cardin and French Prime Minister François Mitterand. He is in this regard the heir to the luxury French Art Deco tradition of Émile-Jacques Ruhlmann, but using assembled industrial materials, employing simple, often abstract geometric shapes with elegant solutions to support systems and collapsibility for storage, as in his metal "Tippy Jackson" table of 1985 (fig. 15.6). The fashion connection is also a resonant one, for earlier in Part III we illustrated a bathroom by Armand-Albert Rateau for the apartment of Jean Lanvin, who also supported original and exclusive furniture and interior designs (see fig. 8.7).

The chair has remained a focus for postmodern explorations of new esthetic experience. Abstract shapes and flexible arrangements utilizing upholstery emerge in the work of German designer Holger Scheel and were featured in the *Design Today* exhibition of 1989, for instance, his La Matrice easy chair (fig. 15.7). Another direction

15.7 Holger Scheel, "La Matrice" easy chair, wooden frame, high gloss paint, corded upholstery, silk covers, 142 x 100 x 85 in (361 x 254 x 216 cm), manufactured by Schurr, 1981.

15.8 Shiro Kuramoto, "How High the Moon" armchair, nickel-plated steel, 28 ¼ x 37 ⅜ x 32 in (72 x 95 x 81 cm), 1986, manufactured by Vitra, Switzerland. Metropolitan Museum of Art, New York.

In domestic wares, the Italian manufacturer Alessi has been active in promoting original design in silver. American architect Michael Graves (b.1934) designed the moderne-inspired tea and coffee service that featured polished-ribbed surfaces, ebony feet, ivory handles, and non-functional blue knobs (fig. 15.9), while Austrian Hans Hollein's (b.1934) coffee and tea service (fig. 15.10) recalls the geometric simplicity of Jean Puiforcat (fig. 8.19, page 153), here recalling the form of an aircraft carrier. Both designs appear in a section of the *Design Now* exhibition entitled "Micro-architecture," a reference to the resurgence of decoration and popular symbolism in many postmodern buildings.

While the political activism of Memphis participants was subdued in comparison with earlier counter-design activities of the later 1960s, other contemporary designers continue to employ elements of popular culture to raise political and environmental awareness. One direction for this activity has been the re-use of materials, seen for instance in Ron Arad's (b.1951) Rover chair of 1981, constructed from used automobile seats attached to a tubular metal frame. More complex in construction is Arad's asymmetrical "Big Easy Volume 2" sofa of 1988. This

utilizing industrial materials is Japanese designer Shiro Kuramoto's "How High the Moon" chair (1986, fig. 15.8), manufactured in Switzerland by Vitra. Perhaps surprisingly, the metal mesh construction is both strong enough for support and flexible enough for comfortable sitting. Yet "How High the Moon" does not seem to have been designed with sitting as its main or sole intention, as the lightness and transparency of its material, together with the precision of its curves and joints, exert an especially strong esthetic appeal.

15.9 Michael Graves, tea and coffee service (prototype), silver, lacquered aluminum, mock ivory and Bakelite, tray 3 ½ x 16 in (9 x 41 cm), manufactured by Officina Alessi, 1980–83. Metropolitan Museum of Art, New York.

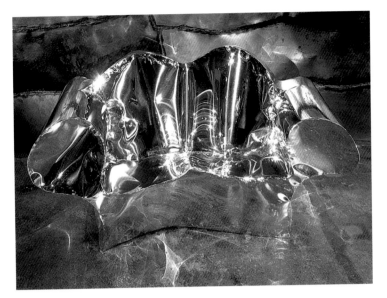

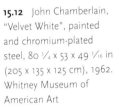

15.11 Ron Arad, "Big Easy Volume 2" sofa, stainless steel and steel, 34 ¼ in (87 cm) high, made by One Off, London, 1988.

15.12 John Chamberlain, "Velvet White", painted and chromium-plated steel, 80 ¼ x 53 x 49 ¹⁄₁₆ in (205 x 135 x 125 cm), 1962. Whitney Museum of American Art

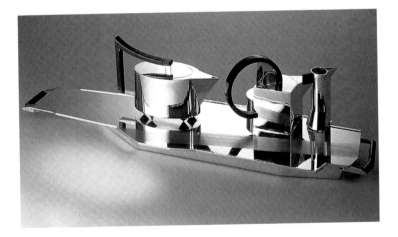

15.10 Hans Hollein, five-piece coffee and tea service, silver, tray 1 ¼ x 36 x 12 in (4.5 x 92.4 x 31 cm), manufactured by Alessi.

piece consists of sheets of industrial steel cut, shaped, and painstakingly welded to conform to the contours of a traditionally-carved wooden seat and form of a heavily upholstered and well-worn sofa, bringing to the mind of the informed viewer the crushed metal sculpture of John Chamberlain, such as *Velvet White* (figs. 15.11 and 15.12), dating to 1962 and made from the wreckage common in automobile graveyards. Both examples focus attention upon the esthetic qualities of an industrial material in an

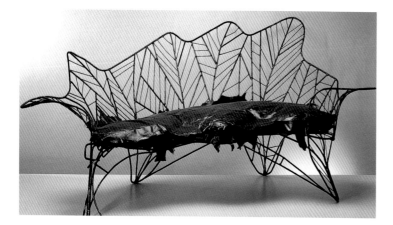

15.13 Bohuslav Horak, "Autumn leaf" sofa, steel, aluminum, leather, 76 x 36 x 28 in 9190 x 90 x 70 cm), 1988.

untraditional form or setting. Nuances of decay appear in other examples of furniture with environmental or ecological overtones, indicative of new meanings of discarded or decomposing objects. An example is Czech designer Bohuslav Horak's 1988 "Autumn Leaf" sofa (fig. 15.13). Such objects demonstrate ambiguities of intention and interpretation. Clearly this kind of furniture is not intended for mass production. Often the results seem contrived and undermine any possible desire to reach beyond a sophisticated audience entirely prepared to view such objects esthetically or as a form of socio-political commentary. And yet there remains an effort, in making references to banal materials and everyday experience, to stimulate reflection in the viewer and to question some of the conventional associations of commodity consumption and materialism.

Despite museum exhibitions, commissions from companies such as Alessi or Formica to individual designers and groups such as Memphis, and the emergence of small galleries and boutiques that promote interest in the self-conscious complexities that lend meaning to contemporary experiments in furniture, the majority of furniture and other domestic products in the broad mass market owe little to the clever ironies of much postmodernism. While there may be reasons to think that the forms of many postmodern designers may yet reach a wider market, the belief that postmodernism's eclectic sources encourage a healthy tolerance for diversity in society is not without its critics. Uncertainty regarding the movement's inclusiveness or exclusiveness is ongoing, and in addition the whole issue of tolerance and liberation remains a

matter of debate: Robert Hughes, in *Culture of Complaint: The Fraying of America* (1993) found little cause for optimism, seeing instead a Balkanization of subcultures in the products of a culture obsessed with the delineation of difference rather than with commonality or quality. Marxist critics continue to lament the lack of forms of art and design that nurture the seeds of resistance, and the growing gap between developed nations and the Third World strengthens, for some critics, the need for a more thorough sense of social responsibility in design on a global scale. Cultural and technological disparity remains an undercurrent in envisioning the role of design in the future: efforts to lobby for the need for Internet access throughout the schools and households of the United States are typical of the ideology of progress, yet ignore the fact that a majority of the population in many underdeveloped countries lack a basic telephone service and call into question the meaning or reality of the term "global village."

Postmodernism and Resistance

Another challenging aspect of postmodern culture surfaces in the behaviors, dress, and accessories associated with the punk movement beginning in the later 1970s and early 1980s. Aggressive, destructive, and uninhibited, the expressions of punk culture in music, poetry, and the visual arts simultaneously attacked mainstream culture with practices such graffiti, and used highly commercialized products such cosmetics and hair dyes to achieve exaggerated and provocative effects in personal appearance. In graphic design, punk culture found expression in the work of many artists, among them British-born Neville Brody (*b.*1957). Brody experimented with original lettering and trademarks that seemed to parody the uniformity and consistency of corporate graphics, as in the 1985 logo for a London hat company (fig. 15.14). His typefaces were used in magazines such as *The Face*, and were developed to convey moods and attitudes beyond the range of fonts available from foundries. Brody's Industria (1984) is a bold sans serif typeface with a combination of blunt rectangular positive and negative shapes and knife-edged terminations for a number of letters (fig. 15.15). Despite its strong geometric, consistent character, letters such as the lower case "g" stand out as being unusual (it looks more

15.14 Neville Brody, logo for Hat company, 1985.

15.17 Neville Brody, record jacket for Cabaret Voltaire, 1980.

15.15 Neville Brody, Industria typeface, designed for *The Face*, 1984.

15.16 Neville Brody, Contents logo, *The Face*, no. 49, May *c.* 1980.

like a symbol of some kind than a traditional letter) and were used by Brody in expressive titles for the journal (fig. 15.16). In addition to typography and lettering, Brody used record jackets and music posters as vehicles for evoking an emotional response in the viewer, accomplished through photographs, photocopies, typography, and video-generated images. He intended to relate his covers and posters in some way to the content of the music, rather than to follow the mainstream music industry's tendency to emphasize the celebrity of rock stars through photography. To this end he employed images suggested or even provided by the musicians, and cultivated an array of techniques that avoided easy recognition or a consistent style. For a 1980 poster for the rock group Cabaret Voltaire (fig. 15.17), Brody juxtaposed a blurred image of a running man with a jet airplane against a blue background with black-and-white textured strips as lateral borders and within the central image. Photomontage, as well as the group's name (the Cabaret Voltaire, in Zurich, was a nightclub and meeting place for Dada artists and performers beginning in 1916) recalls the juxtaposed and manipulated images of

15.18 Advertisement for Philips' Tracer electric shaver, manufactured by Philips Corporation, Eindhoven, the Netherlands.

15.19 R. Crumb, "Keep on Truckin", c. 1970.

Dada posters and covers (see page 195) and the early influence of Dada on Brody's work. Yet the "CV" logo for the group is reminiscent of a corporate trademark and avoids a sense of direct borrowing from the past. In a similar fashion, Brody's imagery and comments about his work reveal the contradictory nature of the early 1980s in Britain. There is a desire to break away from the contemporary commodity culture that threatens freedom of expression, and yet the recognition that living within that culture forces compromises and acknowledges the limited and ephemeral ways in which artistic freedom functions:

> On every cover I have done for Cabaret Voltaire, the dominant theme is decay through process, the loss of human identity that results from communication being transmitted through machines that condition,

not serve, human interaction. Decay through process is also about repetition, and the loss of quality that you suffer when information is abstracted from its human origin....

Punk was about individual expression, and more than anything, it was a reaction against authority. It couldn't really describe itself as "independent" unless the authority was completely circumvented—which, for a very short time, it was. But as soon as the whole phenomenon was categorised as "the independent scene," this insured that it would become exactly its opposite.

The punk phenomenon belongs within the framework of postmodernism, complex in its relationship to popular culture, subverting but hardly rejecting the multiple signs and meanings of our commodity-minded world. An example of adapting the counterculture aspects of the punk movement to advertising for products usually characterized by brand standardization was the Philips Tracer electric shaver, also sold in a variety of colors and targeting a youthful market (fig. 15.18).

To the punk phenomenon in graphic design might be added illustrations for underground comic books by a number of artists including Robert Crumb (b.1943). Many images, such as Crumb's "Keep on Truckin'" (c.1971) with its striding foreshortened foot, reached a broad popular audience via bumper stickers and decals. Their origins, however, were in the very private and often scurrilous world of offbeat comic books, from where they migrated to record jackets and beyond (fig. 15.19).

Chapter 16

Design in Context: An Act of Balance

16.1 Poang chair, layer-glued beech with cotton cover 26 ¾ x 32 ⅝ x 39 ⅜ in (68 x 83 x 100 cm), manufactured by IKEA, 1999 catalogue.

Somewhere between universal standards based upon taste, safety, human factors, or environmental impact, and a democratic embrace of the seemingly insatiable desire for individual fulfillment through commodity consumption, there may lie a middle-ground that sustains hope for the future of design, a balance between the permanent and the ephemeral, between nature and the consumer-dominated culture that has emerged during the past 200 years. The shape of that future will indeed depend upon the manner in which a number of competing attitudes and approaches to the field continue to develop and also upon the degree to which such attitudes may be reconciled. These approaches have been discussed in relation to the broad history of modern design as described in each of the major parts of the present study. They include the roles of technology and production, consumption and commercialism, craft and esthetics, and social and global responsibility. Each is increasingly interwoven with the others in a synthesis that may yet remain vital, dynamic, and enriching.

lighting

7. TUNNA table lamp
brings a rustic yet elegant
feeling to your home with
its shapely, black steel
base. Shown with **ÅR
shade**, 14"(36cm).
H11⅞"(30cm). 3-way
switch. Max 100W.
RA.   **$22.95**

**8. VALLÅT reading floor
lamp** makes reading
easier on your eyes by
supporting directional
light on an adjustable
arm. Black steel. Shown
with **ÅR reading shade**,
8"(20cm). Height adjusts
from 50¾" to 57⅛"
(128–145cm). 3-way
switch. Max 100W.
RA.   **$38.95**

9. Transform a room just
by changing the shades.
Choose yellow, eggshell,
blue, green or rust.
ÅR shades
14"(36cm) $9ea.
18"(45cm) $12ea.
Reading shades in blue
or eggshell only.
8"(20cm) $4ea.

TUNNA/ÅR table lamp
$22⁹⁵

91

16.2 Vallat standing reading lamp, black steel, 50 ⅛ in (128 cm), adjustable height, manufactured by IKEA, 1999 catalogue.

Consumption

There is little doubt that for the past half-century consumption has dominated the practice of design; since the 1960s and the emergence of Pop Art and Pop-inspired industrial design it has played a large role in the theory of design as well, deconstructing a binary opposition that had existed between art and commodities. Meanwhile broad international economic growth throughout much of the 1990s contributed to the belief that consumption is indeed self-justifying, fueling still further growth by creating jobs and stimulating the research and development of new products, services, and marketing tools on an increasingly global scale. Whether threatening or liberating, consumption is the pervasive element motivating and affecting design as we enter the third millennium.

The future of consumer- or marketing-led design continues to present virtually limitless possibilities, and even the high-minded maxims of international modernism,

such as "fitness to purpose" (see page 240) are increasingly subsumed under its banner. Habitat stores (see page 318, fig. 13.2), or more recently the international success of the IKEA Corporation of Sweden, originally founded in 1943, have successfully expanded and marketed a warehouse approach to Scandinavian and international modernism in many large European cities as well as (since 1985) in affluent American suburbs. IKEA stores are presently found in more than twenty-five countries globally. Large color catalogues of merchandise, off-the-shelf availability, flat, carry-home packaging, as well as do-it-yourself assembly instructions and tools for fastening bolts all contribute to the appeal of IKEA, together with the affordability of products ranging from furniture and lighting to fabrics, household, and kitchen wares. IKEA offers a large variety of molded plywood furniture and modular units for shelving and using veneers attached to inexpensively-manufactured pressed board, and many products are based upon the interwar and postwar furniture designed by Aalto or Klint (fig. 16.1). Other individual examples and ensembles include upholstered chairs and sofas, American Colonial designs, as well as craft-inspired furnishings in woven rattan or inexpensive cast metals with textured finishes (fig. 16.2). Furniture designed especially for children is heavily marketed at IKEA, as are desks and shelving for the apartments of young professionals and university-age students. In the catalogue and on the showroom floor prices appear in bold sans serif typography, and despite the odd-sounding names given to "families" of items (at least to American ears), nowhere is the IKEA name linked to a specific country of origin. The overriding character of the merchandise and the shopping experience is *ease*, that is, ease of packing, shipping, transporting, assembling (some might argue this point, but one is saving the cost of assembly by doing it oneself), affording, and perhaps most importantly, ease of replacing. Obsolescence is here taken for granted in an industry whose products usually take longer to make and are at least generally intended to last longer as well. It is also easy for families with small children to shop at IKEA, as stores provide are monitored playrooms permitting parents to shop without distraction.

At the higher end of the market for modern industrially manufactured furniture, the smooth surfaces and precise geometric shapes associated with the International Style continue to surface in new examples of esthetic purity in design. Sir Norman Foster's (*b*.1935) Nomos desk

16.3 Sir Norman Foster, adjustable desk, "Nomos Office System", glass and chromium-plated steel, 25–28 in (64–72 cm), adjustable height, manufactured by Tecno, United Kingdom, 1986.

with aluminum legs and circular pod-like feet and supports for the glass surface (1987, fig. 16.3) uses modern industrial materials to suggest the perfection and precision of a hi-tech environment and the weightlessness of a space module making a lunar landing.

Environmental awareness has also become linked to consumption, for instance in the expanding industry of products promoting healthy living and ethically conscious shopping. Nigel Whitely has noted, for instance, the way in which Body Shop stores equate the purchase of their cosmetics with the protection of animal rights in carrying out product testing and the environment. Body Shop promotional materials assert that: "our future planning will be based upon achieving a balance between the need to limit the environmental impact of our business whilst not compromising our long term commercial viability." Ethical consuming suggests an awareness of the broader consequences of consumption, but many critics remain unsatisfied, arguing that Body Shop products use mostly synthetic, non-renewable substances, and that the appropriate response to environmental concerns posed by the cosmetics industry lies in curbing consumption, not in making people feel better about the products they buy.

Another area in which consumption and social responsibility are linked is the health food industry. In this growing sector of the food products industry, manufacturers borrow increasingly from the methods used to market

convenience products. While labels and advertising copy point to more natural ingredients and processes, and logos and emblems suggest a closer relationship between such products and nature, many products are themselves geared to easy-preparation with pre-measured and pre-packaged ingredients. Natural foods are available in a vast array of flavorings and producers offer an increasing number of snack foods such as nacho-chips, organic pretzels, cereals, and flavored whole-grain crackers (fig. 16.4). They conflate convenience not simply with better nutrition but with generally healthier and more natural living through advertising.

The celebration of playfulness and complexity, much-cited in postmodern theory as the basis for irony and subversion, has also become part of accepted practice in industrial design for large corporations. Companies such as Philips maintain divisions responsible for developing product ideas independently from engineering or cost considerations, as a means of encouraging creativity and flexibility in the design process. An example of such pure "concept design" is the brightly-colored Beethoven radio developed by Philips in 1983 (fig. 16.5). These products are in some ways the progeny of the dream cars modeled in the styling sections of General Motors in the early 1950s under the direction of Harley Earl (see page 211). Indeed, such an approach may yet penetrate the mainstream, at

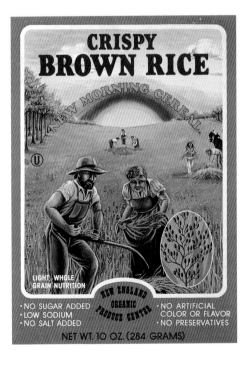

16.4 "Crispy Brown Rice" cereal packaging, cardboard, 8 x 10 in (20 x 25 cm), manufactured by New England Organic Produce Center, c. 1988.

16.5 Philips, Beethoven radio product concept, 1983.

least if household and other consumer goods are any indication of future trends. As recently as 1999, for instance, Michael Graves (see fig. 15.9) designed a series of kitchen products manufactured in lightweight aluminum and plastics rather than silver or stainless steel, and sold at Target franchise discount stores in the United States. Illustrations of these toasters and tea kettles appeared in the bargain-oriented Sunday newspaper supplements (fig. 16.6). The advertisement reads: "finding the fun in functional."

As to the automobile industry in the 1990s, industrial design focused upon the high end of the market, less to inventive body styling than to the interior where comfort, quality sound, and individualized climate control are the focus. Peter Finch observes that the anxiety caused by traffic has contributed to this concentration upon making the automobile a refuge and escape from overcrowded streets, traffic lights, and noise, and the restrictions they place upon our freedom, enabling wealthy car owners to separate themselves from the frustrations of road congestion. The copy of an advertisement for a 1999 Lexus ES 300, for example, imagined the vehicle itself sporting an "attitude"

and speaking to a red traffic light, in defiant refusal to acknowledge the constraints of the road: "Okay, fine. I'll just wait here. You think I care? I'll just wait here in my oh-so-comfortable car and stare you down. Until I get you to change your tiny, red mind."

Although recognizable by insignia and "family" resemblances, only minor differences distinguish many of the vehicles at the high end of the luxury automobile market, which includes the Japanese Lexus, Infiniti, and Acura, the German BMW and Mercedes Benz, and the British Jaguar and Rolls Royce.

Obsolescence remains the cornerstone of consumer-led design, involving the stimulation of desire through novelty on one hand and the effective management of production costs on the other. Manufacturing similar products while projecting individual appeal are thus the goals. These ideals have become successful strategies for a number of corporations, perhaps most notably in the marketing of GAP clothing to a youth-oriented market attracted to an image of informal, fun-loving, and relaxed behavior easily recognized by fabrics such as khaki and cotton for pants and T-shirts. Here advertising helps to seamlessly merge standardized products with carefree, youthful behavior and rapid change with an enduring image.

GAP clothing continues to use color as a major component for the exercise of individual consumer preference, and this very basic strategy for introducing variety remains effective for merchandising. Recently the Heinz Corporation introduced its tomato ketchup in green rather than red (changing colors but not taste), combined with labeling for the original product that read "not green." The company reported more than a five percent increase in sales and a larger share of the market.

Outside of GAP and its competitors, the business of fashion remains heavily dependent upon a more provocative novelty and strong ties to advertising in directing the consumer to associate clothing with alternative lifestyles, often exemplified by celebrity "supermodels" who serve as ideal paradigms for a particular look. Fabien Baron (b.1959) has, since the early 1990s, been a successful art director for several fashion magazines, including *Harper's Bazaar*, *Interview*, and Italian *Vogue*. He has been responsible for a lean, simple approach to page layout in these journals, incorporating large areas of white space and dramatic black-and-white photography as well as combining different sizes of a single typeface on the page. In these

finding the fun
in functional

The highly acclaimed work of Michael Graves has restored a sense of humanity to modern architecture, which in turn makes him one of the most recognized architects of our time. Notable for his ability to craft inventive items for the home, Michael has designed products for companies such as Alessi, FAO Schwarz, Disney and Steuben.

The Michael Graves Design™ collection is an inspired balance of form and function. At once it is sensible and sublime, practical and whimsical, utilitarian and aesthetically pleasing. Michael Graves creates useful objects which not only carry their own weight, but simultaneously lift our spirits.

Michael Graves

Denver Central Library

16.6 Michael Graves, toaster, aluminum and plastic, advertisement for Target Stores, 1999.

practices he continues an esthetic approach to layout pioneered by Alexey Brodovitch and M. F. Agha (see page 229). But Baron is perhaps best known for using a provocative eroticism to sell clothing and fashion accessories such as fragrances, engaging the imagination of male and female spectators by appealing to sexual fantasies and permissiveness, sometimes involving violence and sadomasochism, as in advertisements for a new line of sportswear by Kikit (fig. 16.7). More mainstream variations, for instance with Ralph Lauren fragrances, include black-and-white images of waif-like models in intimate rather than public surroundings, engaging the spectator's participation in completing a story usually involving the theme of seduction and the aura of mystery, secrecy, or danger (fig. 16.8). It is difficult to decide if Baron's so-called "look" derives from the clothes, or if the clothes are created by the "look." Marketing and design go hand in hand, and in either case everyone appears to benefit: the designer, the journal in which advertisements appear, and the reputation of the art director.

The Kikit campaign featuring overt images of sexual aggression and gun play riled conservative and feminist groups alike. Baron dismisses the criticism: "The media and the critics try to see all the little things and miss the big picture. Don't tell me that the ad promotes violence. Legal guns and illegal drugs promote violence."

16.7 Fabien Baron, advertisement for Kikit fashion design, appearing in Vogue, c. 1995.

16.8 Advertisement for Ralph Lauren fragrances, New Yorker, 1999.

In the fashion industry advertising, merchandising, celebrity, television and cinema, middle-class affluence, and the ability of manufacturers to respond quickly to trends and forecasts due to accelerated communications and the role of computer-assisted design (CAD), all transpire to stimulate production and consumption of clothing and clothing accessories. In addition to the broad economic impact of the fashion industry, dress also has attracted the attention of art historians and cultural critics within the pluralistic framework of postmodernism. As a significant element within consumer culture, women's apparel reveals a mixture of conformity and resistance that characterizes the postmodern approach to popular culture, moving considerably beyond the usual theoretical framework of emulation. As targets of the advertising industry in the emerging culture of consumption of the later nineteenth and early twentieth centuries, the active as well as passive roles of women as consumers raise awareness of dress and female identity in our society. The cultural meanings of dress, however, need not be applied only to women's clothing. The popularity not only of tight-fitting clothes but also of clothes that appear to be "outgrown" (pants that do not reach to the ankle or jerseys that do not reach to the waist), for instance, beginning in the 1980s, is a phenomenon that appears both in men's and women's fashion. According to design historian Lee Wright, such clothing suggests a variety of often contradictory meanings. "Outgrown" clothing may call attention to particular parts of the body with strong sexual overtones. It may make the body appear larger and more powerful than normal (like the "Incredible Hulk" cartoon character), or at the same time imprison the body, as a child who uncomfortably wears clothes that are not just tight but simply too small.

And finally, we should keep in mind the marketing efforts that deliver products to the consumer and the expanding role of credit buying whether in malls, catalogue shopping by telephone, or via the Internet as e-commerce and its virtual shopping carts, rebates, and other incentives to consumption. Sophisticated store merchandising uses the analysis of the habits of shoppers to place particular products where they are more likely to attract attention and sales. Industry expos and conventions bring individual consumers and store buyers into contact with recently manufactured merchandise or prototypes of future products. All of these efforts attest to the stimulation of consumption in ever creative ways, breaking down any lingering resistance to shopping in terms of store hours or even the necessity of stores themselves. The notion of a permanent, omnipresent spectacle comes to mind, no longer confined to material space but extending into the uncharted realms of cyberspace with the click of a mouse.

Reform and Social Responsibility

Mistrust of consumer-led design and commercialism in design has a long history, stretching back at least as far as Pugin and reformers such as Henry Cole in the mid-nineteenth century. Fears of declining esthetic or moral standards, of conspicuous consumption, or the democratization of consumption as a threat to an established social order and cohesive cultural values, of commodity consumption as a form of unwitting political consent and conformism, are all part of this history. Yet universal standards governing esthetic or practical aspects of product design have rarely been either successful or popular outside of certain contexts such as information graphics and the imposed manufacturing restrictions in Britain during and immediately after World War II; even in the nineteenth century the paternalism of Pugin and Cole appeared elitist and reactionary to writers like Charles Dickens. Today the postwar warnings of manipulation by authors such as Vance Packard seem alarmist, and even the bare mention of standards begs the question of "whose standards?" and is construed as a needless impediment to self-fulfillment in an age preoccupied with diversity and difference, an age that either overlooks or accepts for the most part the relation between advertising and conformism, between mass consumption, insecurity, and manipulation.

Still, one wonders whether we are indeed at the threshold of self-realization. One case in point is the telephone. Before 1984 when the United States government broke up the American Telephone and Telegraph Corporation (AT&T) into smaller companies, telephones were relatively standardized products available only through a small number of outlets operated by subsidiary Bell Telephone. A standard desk or table handset unit was designed by Henry Dreyfuss in 1937 (see pages 217–8 and fig. 10.24) and redesigned in 1946. New models, such as

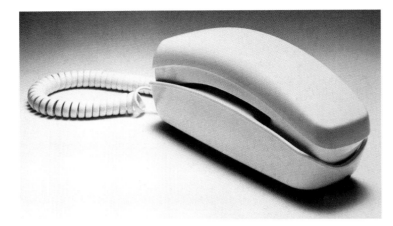

16.9 Henry Dreyfuss Associates, "Trimline" telephone, plastic housing, 8 ⁷⁄₁₆ in (21 cm) in length, manufactured by Western Electric for Bell telephone company, New York, 1965. Philadelphia Museum of Art.

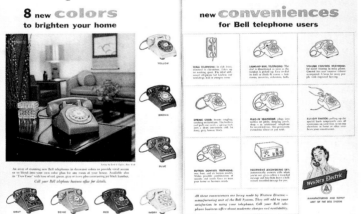

16.10 Advertisement for Bell Telephone Company telephones. *Better Homes and Gardens*, November 1954.

16.11 Advertisement for telephones at Best Buy stores. *Philadelphia Inquirer*, 2000.

the compact "Trimline" of 1965 (fig. 16.9) appeared, and features such as touch-tone rather than rotary dialing were added beginning in the 1970s. Color also provided an element for individual consumer choice. Since industry deregulation telephones have been sold in a variety of hardware, electronics, and discount stores, and are available in ever-increasing variations of shape, color, and weight. They are constructed of different materials, ring with different tones, and have more recently become cordless and portable, spurring yet more variations and possibilities for consumers, including prices so low as to make

some models suitable as giveaway and promotional items (fig. 16.10). Like so many contemporary products, phones have become lifestyle accessories, styled to suit our age and help us achieve the image of who we'd like to be. And yet one wonders whether the result of deregulation has been an advantage to consumers: how many types of telephone are "too many" (fig. 16.11)? Does telephone communication require so many choices? Is phone shopping an area of the market that demands such dizzying possibilities for self-expression? Is this indeed an instance of real choice, or has the reduced durability of materials and components combined with variety made it instead another vehicle for planned obsolescence in an increasingly "throwaway" culture, where discarding old phones, and buying new ones rather than repairing them, is more often than not the case, as elsewhere in the electronics industry? Is there not a part of ourselves that actually longs for standards to assist us in making choices so that we may use our time in ways other than comparison shopping for items that last less than six months? What in the end is liberating, and what inhibits freedom? There are, it seems, legitimate issues to be addressed by considering the meaning of choice: consumers seem to accept the idea of standards in matters of product safety, and for the compatibility of components in communications and utilities industries, for instance in matters of computer cable connectors, operating systems, sizes of outlets, fuses, plugs, plumbing and gas pipe fittings just to name a few areas where regulation persists. Whether government or industry regulated, however, standards may be viewed as promoting a shared language of product semantics reinforcing basic guidelines for use and dependability in the market. Thus standards might indeed serve, together with diversity, as partners in promoting tolerance and understanding for the consuming public: it is not so much that consumption is dangerous or that it obscures values, but that it seems worthwhile to reserve a place for alternatives within a system of capitalist free enterprise for alternative approaches to design that offer perhaps less choice, but for generally acceptable reasons. Graphic design also plays a role in the area of standards, developing appropriate labels for hazardous materials or recognizable symbols to designate inappropriate reading or viewing materials for children.

While regulation and standards affect fewer types of products, social responsibility continues to impact design through attention to the needs of special populations such as those with disabilities through research, determining for instance new forms and materials in the design of many everyday products and transportation systems. Government and foundation sponsorship helps to address special needs through design, while occasionally such markets also attract private, for-profit investment. One of the best-known organizations of this kind is Ergonomi Design Gruppen, established in Bomma, Sweden in 1979 as a collective of smaller groups, whose aim is to design solutions for special needs while at the same time

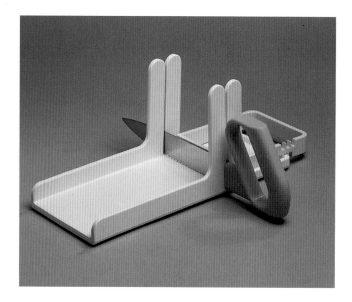

16.12 Maria Benktzon and Sven-Eric Juhlin, Ergonomi Design Gruppen, knife and cutting frame, plastic and steel, 13 ¼ in (35 cm), 1974, manufactured by Gustavsberg AB, Gustavsberg, Sweden. Statens Konstmuseer, Stockholm.

appealing to broader markets as well through attention to esthetics and commercial possibilities. The designers working for collectives such as Ergonomi conduct studies, for instance, to determine the strength needed for holding and gripping of objects and test the design of products like knives or cutlery to see which forms are best suited to their purpose, primarily but not exclusively from the standpoint of disabled users. Successful designs of this type include the Knife and Cutting Frame designed in 1974 by Maria Benktzon and Sven-Eric Juhlin, made of Propene plastic and stainless steel and manufactured in Sweden by Gustavsberg (fig. 16.12). This design, based upon the principle of a mitre box, not only accomplished the specific purpose for which it was intended by safely guiding the knife and protecting the user, but also attracted wider popularity through its simple and clear statement of function and practicality. Marketed even more widely beyond an audience with special needs are the soft, rubber-handled kitchen utensils manufactured by the Oxo corporation and designed to be easy to hold and grip (fig. 16.13). Oxo products exemplify the criteria of "Universal Design," embraced by a number of institutes and organizations and addressing the broad design needs of the disabled, the ageing, and children. Supported by corporations and foundations, Universal Design groups study and develop solutions to problems ranging from transportation, parks

16.13 "Good Grips" peeler, rubber and stainless steel, 6in (15 cm) in length, manufactured by Oxo, England, 2000.

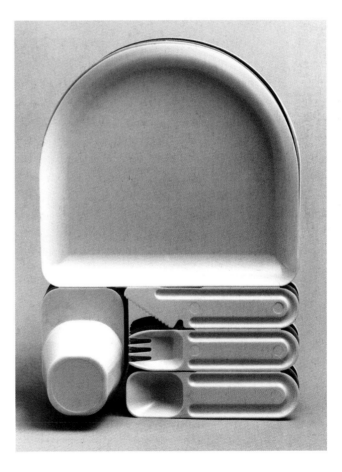

manufacturers and the conservation of natural resources, to more radical efforts that make environmental impact the overriding consideration in the design process and promote the reduction in consumption and materialism as the only responsible directions for a future industrial design. A measure of changing attitudes and green awareness in design is the 1977 disposable plastic picnic ware by Jean-Paul Vitrac (b.1944) for Diam (fig. 16.14). What might have seemed a good example of efficiently manufactured, easily-stored, and easy-to-use eating utensils in the 1970s now appears at least in part as wasteful and environmentally hazardous; while much green ideology tends to be dualistic and even apocalyptic, it stands in the tradition of reform advocating for shared standards based upon considerations beyond the perspective of the individual and toward the interrelationship between people and the environment we often take for granted. Jonathon Porritt outlines this view:

and playgrounds, housing, and kitchens. Universal Design is defined as "the design of products and environments to be usable by all people, to the greatest extent possible, without the need for adaptation or specialized design," and their principles include equitable use, flexibility in use, simple and intuitive use, perceptible information, tolerance for error, low physical effort, and size and space for approach and use.

Another area outside the usual framework of market-led product design mechanisms is addressing the needs of developing nations. Papanek considered this area in the 1970s in developing ideas about appropriate technology, advocating an approach that included working within existing conditions, using local materials, revitalizing vernacular traditions, and involving the local population rather than only adopting paternalistic or hi-tech solutions. Penny Sparke has described such a varied, "multi-level" approach to addressing design needs in India, ranging from industrial technology for an international market to investing in the promotion of local craft production, to seeking efficient solutions to everyday problems by introducing low-cost products like plastic pails and monsoon shoes using industrial materials.

Social responsibility in design has also found an outlet in environmental awareness and reform. Often known as Green Design, environmentally-conscious approaches to design range from the use of recyclable materials by

16.14 Jean-Paul Vitrac, disposable picnic set, polystyrene, 11 in (28 cm) in length, 1977, manufactured by Diam. Philadelphia Museum of Art, gift of Janet Kerr.

To "see green" is to see all nations and all people, however divided or different they may appear to be, as members of one interdependent human family, linked by their responsibility to each other and to the care and maintenance of our planet....

And:

From our side of the divide it's clear that all nations are pursuing an unsustainable path. Every time we opt for the "conventional" solution, we merely create new problems, new threats. Every time we count on some new technological miracle, we merely put off the day of reckoning. Sheer common sense suggests alternative remedies, yet vested economic interests and traditional political responses ensure that the necessary steps are never taken. The old system endures, dominated by competition between various groups struggling for power so as to be able to promote the interest of a particular class, clique, or ideology.

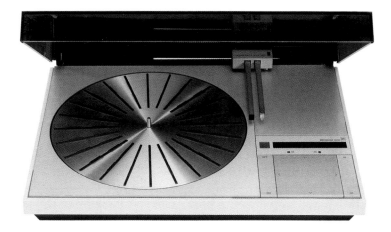

16.15 Jacob Jensen, "Beogram 4000" turntable, wood, aluminum and stainless steel housing, 18 ⅞ in (48 cm) wide, 1972, manufactured by Bang & Olufsen A/S, Struer.

Production Technology: Meanings of Miniaturization

New technologies during the past three decades continue to make miniaturization a significant consideration in industrial design. Integrated circuits, for instance, using silicon chips for industrial or domestic electronic equipment reduce the size requirements for many products, from portable hand-held calculators and telephones to home audio systems. Examples include thin components for stereo equipment such as the "Beogram 4000" turntable designed by Jacob Jensen for the Bang & Olufsen Company of Denmark in 1972 (fig. 16.15), and the Finnish-manufactured Nokia portable cellular telephone (2000, fig. 16.16). Lightweight and compact, such products employ minimal and unified housings and a harmonious relationship among parts. Miniaturization in electronic products places constraints upon the industrial designer and leads to a certain conformity among several manufacturers, though there is considerable creativity in devising solutions to reducing clutter, hiding dials and buttons, and achieving a high degree of geometric esthetic purity, as with the Beogram 4000 turntable. In this example the tone arm can be activated without lifting the cover by lightly touching the side of the unit, a feature that creates a smooth and uninterrupted external surface. The expense of portable and home electronic products often stems

16.16 Cellular phone, 4 in (10 cm), manufactured by Nokia, Finland, 2000.

more from the cost of research, capital equipment for mechanically manufactured components, and the expense of consultant designers rather than from the materials themselves. Despite mechanization in manufacturing, labor is often still required for assembly. Increasingly this manual labor is carried out wherever it can be purchased cheaply, often in China, Indonesia, and in areas of Latin America. In many sectors of the fashion industry similar circumstances prevail. For clothing manufacturing, consumer activism operates to police the regulation of the ages of workers' ages, hours, and factory conditions, backed by the fear of press exposure and the threat of boycott.

For sound, digital technology, in which audio information is transmitted as electrical impulses and recorded as a sequence or code of binary numbers, is used to produce the small, circular 5-in (12.7-cm) compact disc and CD players. These devices have replaced both long-playing records and cassette tapes and players for recording and listening to music. The small CDs are resistant to wear and damage, and the devices that play them are compact, available for installation in computers, automobiles, and as part of integrated home stereo systems. Divided into discreet "tracks," the listener can program a CD in a sequence of selections without lifting a tone arm or pressing "rewind" or "fast-forward" buttons. CD players are also easily activated through remote control devices. Maintaining them is easier than caring for cassette players or turntables, requiring less cleaning or attention to mechanical parts. Housing is generally compatible with the other rectangular box-like components of a home stereo system, and often permits the user to access several CDs at once (fig. 16.17). Their miniature size has also produced an endless variety of individual and expandable storage units for the home, from variations on traditional bookshelves to anthropomorphic wire sculptures that house dozens of CDs.

Digital technology also paved the way for the advent of personal computers, including desktop, laptop, and palm-held units. Pioneered by the Intel Company in 1971, the processing of digital information on microchips reduced the mechanical and space requirements of earlier computers. Since the mid-1980s personal computers eclipsed and now generally have replaced typewriters for business, research, and home use. They have also expanded the possibilities of information processing and organization to include databases, charts, and spreadsheets.

16.17 Stereo system with compact-disc player, Philips, 2002.

Industrial design for cellular phones and computers, as well as portable cellular and wireless telephones, may be studied from a number of viewpoints. Designers develop the most efficient, lightweight, and compact plastic or aluminum housing given the space requirements of the various integrated circuits, speakers, microphones, keys, and screens. They consider human factors involving the final form and location of speakers, buttons, and keys, both in terms of how easy they are to operate and how well they communicate their function to the user. An example of an ergonomic approach to computer design is an alternative keyboard for personal computers, designed using curves to conform to the more natural position of the wrists of operators to reduce fatigue as well as prevent injury and nerve damage. Designers also determine possible novelties in color, form, and even texture that might attract consumer attention in a competitive market. Even in housing for computers and cellular phones, the combination of miniaturized equipment and commercial considerations rarely results in stable "type" forms. Computer hard drive components may be horizontal and located beneath the monitor, or vertical and more commonly placed on the floor or held in place by metal straps, creating more work space on the surface of a table or desk. A recent example of such variety is the Apple Macintosh iMac desktop computer (1998), which has a translucent housing, more rounded, sculptural form, and choices of pastel colors (fig. 16.18). For cellular phones, manufacturers advertise interchangeable plastic plates to personalize the product, featuring a wide variety of patterns, colors, and simulated textures (fig. 16.19).

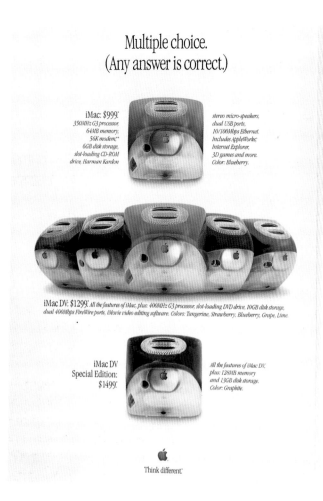

16.18 Advertisement for IMAC desktop computer, manufactured by Macintosh Corporation, 1998.

16.19 Interchangeable plastic faceplates for cellular telephones.

Design also may be considered in relation to product semantics or the intersection of technology and the user, particularly in the field of personal computing. In order to harness both the speed and potential creativity offered by microprocessing, designers connect the operating systems of personal computers to familiar experiences in order to break down the barriers between new products and less venturesome consumers. Here, two of the more recognizable examples are the mouse and the Apple operating system. Rather than learning to execute a series of commands for the keyboard in order to operate software for word processing and other tasks, the mouse integrates habitual tactile and demonstrative actions like pointing and arranging objects on a "desktop," creating a friendly virtual environment in which the user may function more confidently.

A new frontier with implications for miniaturization is nanotechnology, involving the manipulation and restructuring of particles of matter at the level of nanometers, far smaller than the micrometers currently used in computer circuitry. While nanotechnology is unlikely to soon displace microprocessing in the design of electronic devices like computers, its impact in organic chemistry has already been substantial. In this regard, graphic designers play a role in giving visual form to the presentation of research on the subject, for instance, in articles that appear in journals like *Nature* (fig. 16.20). In this capacity they contribute to an enterprise that engaged the talents of postwar designers like Will Burtin (see page 235).

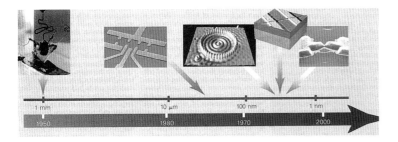

16.20 Illustration and timeline for the shrinkage of electronic components including nanotube technology, from *Nature*, July 1998.

Design and Softness

In recent years some writers and theorists have moved toward a very broad and inclusive definition of design emphasizing information rather than materials or products, and embracing software development and computer programming. As mentioned above (see page 355), the term "soft" refers to the ways in which designers are able to modify ideas quickly in a virtual environment so that solutions are rarely final and exist more naturally in a state of flux. It also encompasses the design of information as instructions for the development of "*soft*ware" and applications in a wide range of other fields. This breadth is seen, for instance, in a definition of design articulated by computer scientist Herbert Simon:

> Everyone designs who devises courses of action aimed at changing existing situations into preferred ones. The intellectual activity that produces materials artifacts is no different fundamentally from the one that prescribes remedies for a sick patient or the one that devises a new sales plan for a company or a social welfare policy for a state. Design, so construed, is the core of all professional training: it is the principal mark that distinguishes the professions from the sciences.

Digital technology affects a number of different fields, such as information systems, computer science and engineering, as well as industrial design. Simon's emphasis upon the intellectual rather than physical or esthetic activity in design embraces a range of diverse disciplines. In this view both the computer and the notion of information become the new common denominators of design activity.

Within the history of modern design, however, there is nothing entirely new or revolutionary in attempting to move the definition of design "beyond the object" or beyond the role of the individual creator. Certainly in the interwar period, Alexander Rodchenko and László Moholy-Nagy pursued a versatile range of activities and interests that extended beyond traditional or marketable objects (see page 184). Will Burtin as well as Charles and Ray Eames also pursued less product-oriented approaches to design during the 1960s and early 1970s. After World War II, these versatile designers created exhibits and interactive installations that sought to humanize the complexities of technical information for a general audience.

At the Hochschule für Gestaltung at Ulm, Tomás Maldonado advocated a curriculum for design that balanced the shaping of materials with the study of social and political theory focusing upon strategies for the relation between capitalism and the industrial design profession (see page 284). Victor Papanek was also less interested in designing products than in promoting responsible design thinking. Each of these examples contains elements of "softness" before the digital age. Information may indeed be a common denominator characterizing the design of our time, but it did not emerge *ex nihilo*. Moving "beyond the object" has been a recurrent theme in design since the advent of the Industrial Revolution, both as the extension of the division of labor and mechanized mass production as well as in the reaction against industrial technology.

In our present "post-industrial" age of electronic information and imagery, the term "soft" includes not only the digital manipulation of virtual images so prominent in many areas of design, but also refers to the complex task of creating information systems or instructions (software) to accommodate the nature of manipulation itself. In this way the boundaries between design and information science have become more fluid, and collaboration in academic and industry settings suggests that the relationship between technology and the existing training and practice of modern design is indeed changing. As machines become more sophisticated, a greater understanding of human psychology and thought makes traditional boundaries permeable, not just boundaries between machines and craft production, but also boundaries between machines and the creative process itself.

Graphic Design in a Digital Age

Digital technology has had a major impact upon the practice of graphic design. As the varied methods of graphic designers extend into the virtual space of the computer monitor, the experience of the user shifts from turning pages or unfolding pamphlets to clicking links triggering animations and revealing multiple windows filled with information that is seen, read, and heard, often simultaneously. The result is thus more interactive than traditional print media. The technologies that make such explorations possible provide designers with flexibility beyond that of photomechanical processes for producing typography and manipulating images both in speed and in the range of experiment open to the designer. Graphic processing and manipulation with the computer opens up opportunities for designers that unite photography, filmmaking, and more traditional graphic design and illustration. While the term "digital media" is sometimes used to refer to such activities, the degree of overlap in education and in practice makes discipline-based thinking appear narrow and out of touch with the graphic design industry. Such media convergence is at the root of the Media Lab developed at the Massachusetts Institute of Technology beginning in 1984, that continues to explore interrelationships and interactivity in the digital realm. At the same time, the new tools that equip the designer with converging and overlapping means for communicating information require an ability to balance versatility with the specialized nature of sophisticated technology and these remain challenges for universities and professionals alike.

Using computers to generate digital type and manipulate digital images for graphic presentation began in 1984 with the operating system and user interface developed by the Apple Corporation for its Macintosh computers. The translation of type and images into electronic code on a low-resolution computer screen was not entirely new. But creating and controlling those impulses with a computer mouse on a virtual desktop with pull-down windows rather than programming them with instructions on a keyboard was unique at that time to the Apple Corporation. This graphic interface used terms like "cut and paste" for functions familiar to graphic designers and amateurs alike. Amateurs used the new interface to democratize the printing and graphic design industries through desktop publishing. Manipulating fonts with a

16.21 April Greiman, poster, 1986.

range of effects with the click of a mouse became commonplace, and office assistants could produce and edit reports and other communications with logos, borders, and images, generating a wide variety of materials formerly produced by professional printers and graphic designers. In completing these tasks, amateur designers borrowed from among thousands of symbols and popular graphics or "clip art" stored on five-inch compact disks.

The Macintosh also appealed to a small group of enthusiastic professional graphic designers, not as a "tool" to replace existing camera-ready design or printed output, but as a distinct form of communication offering new

Emperor

OAKLAND

Emigre

16.22 Zuzana Licko, title.

Template Gothic:
AaBbCcDd
EeFfGgHhIiJjKkLlM
mNnOoPpQqRrSsTt
UuVvWwXxYyZz
(1234567890)

16.23 Barry Deck, Template Gothic typeface, Émigré.

forms of expression. The office of Los Angeles designer April Greiman (*b*.1948) was receptive to Macintosh-based techniques from the mid-1980s, while Dutch-born Rudy VanderLans (*b*.1955) launched the first issue of the annual journal *Emigre* in San Francisco in 1984. In later issues of the journal VanderLans worked with Czechoslovakian-born Zuzana Licko (*b*.1961) and other designers. *Emigre* published work by international artists in a variety of media, and explored new territories in graphic design including the Macintosh as well as other desktop technologies like xerography. Early computer-generated digital images and text appeared primitive in comparison with letterpress or photomechanical typography. Its most recognizable aspect during this time was the distinctive effect of enlarged letters that revealed origins in coordinates based upon square pixels, resulting in "jaggy" transitions from vertical to horizontal elements of letter forms rather than smooth, curved ones. Another early use of digital output was through patterns and textures, generated both as "tools" by programs such as *MacDraw* or by digitized photographs that produced simplified, abstracted images. All three digital techniques are seen in a Greiman poster from 1986 (fig. 16.21).

Typography underwent tremendous expansion as a result of digitization, with the invention of new typefaces and experimentation with a seemingly endless array of effects. Zusana Licko, for instance, created modular typefaces on the Macintosh for *Emigre*, taking into account the "jaggy" corners of letter forms that resulted from the low-resolution capabilities of the computer, but with the freedom of an inexpensive alternative to costly equipment for typesetting (fig. 16.22). These typefaces, like "Emperor," employ modularity where possible to construct forms economically from a limited number of elements, similar to the strategy used by Herbert Bayer for his "universal alphabet" (see page 187, fig. 9.29). New software and higher resolution eliminated the "jaggy" edges of earlier digital typefaces and led to variety of new fonts that were published in *Emigre* in the 1990s, like Barry Deck's "Template Gothic" (fig. 16.23). This typeface breaks down the traditional distinctions between sans serif and serif, mechanical and calligraphic, impersonal and expressive. Licko's sentiments were democratic and alternative in nature, as revealed in the following remarks:

For centuries the design of typefaces has existed as an exclusive discipline reserved for specialists; today the personal computer provides the opportunity to create customized alphabets with an increased potential for personalization and expression. The design and manufacture of fonts can now be integrated into a single medium allowing for a more interactive design approach.... Digital technology has advanced the state of graphic art by a quantum leap into the future, thereby turning designers back to the most primitive of graphic ideas. Integrating design and production, the computer has reintroduced craft as a source of inspiration.

16.24 Flat-screen television, manufactured by Sharp Corporation, advertisement. *New Yorker*, September, 2001.

Licko's analogy between computer and craft seems not to refer to the manual drawing of fonts or the cutting of punches, but to the digital designer's versatility rather than specialization. In addition, the excitement of experiment recalls the explosion of display types in the early nineteenth century. Just as the uses of typography expanded beyond the limited market for expensive printed books during that time, desktop publishing represented the late-twentieth century incarnation of this phenomenon, in which more individualized expression for projects such as invitations, catalogues, or even student term papers became desirable. In addition to Emigre, new digital fonts now appear in a wider variety of publications such as U&lc.

Developments in technology during the 1990s made the computer the industry and educational standard for the graphic design profession. Students entering the field began to generate projects using software packages such as QuarkXpress and Adobe Photoshop, and universities replaced drafting tables and light tables (the latter used to cut and paste images and type for photographic reproduction) with computer work stations, scanners, and high-resolution printers. Hand-drawn calligraphy gave way to computer-generated typography on the Macintosh operating system, many of whose features were incorporated in the Windows system (first released in 1983 but more comparable in Windows95) developed by the Microsoft Corporation for IBM and IBM-compatible personal computers. Students began to carry packages of floppy disks in addition to (or rather than) toolboxes filled with Exacto knives and felt-tipped markers, while administrators looked to the computer industry to help underwrite the tremendous cost of software licensing and workstations as a form of research and marketing. Higher resolution monitors and printers, and an expanding desktop toolbox allowed designers to achieve exacting standards on a par with the most technically advanced art-directed magazines, including a wide range of colors and subtle tonal effects, and seamless manipulations of images and complex layering. Computer-generated images blur boundaries between animation and photography and create imagined worlds with a tremendous capacity to persuade the viewer, often in connection with advertising. An example is a 2001 advertisement for Sharp Electronics (*New Yorker*) that connects the high-quality resolution of a flat-screen television with the immediacy of the viewer's experience (fig. 16.24). With the rapid expansion of product and service marketing via the World Wide Web, web page design emerged as a new virtual space not only for hi-tech layering, but for movement, time, and extensive multimedia communication beyond the limitations of the static two-dimensional surface of a page, poster, or cover.

Computer-generated graphic design began almost as an "underground" movement by young artists experimenting outside mainstream professional channels with novel but unsophisticated, amateur production techniques utilizing the Macintosh computer. Within a decade the field developed into the ultimate high-end technology of professional multimedia communication, with limitless possibilities both for the manipulation of images by

LOCAL WILDLIFE

"About 200,000 women work five days a week for Uncle Sam. They come from every corner of the nation. And no matter how long they remain here, few of them ever really live here."

"Let it not be assumed that this is a major deterrent for the Washington wolf, before whom is spread a field alabaster with white lambs generously interlarded with black sheep. Yet the fine art of subtle, sophisticated flirtation, with skill, poise and aplomb ... seems extinct here. Those in residence are boors: the transients are in a hurry. ... Not all wolves are single. We will not divulge names, or tell how they cover up. ... Not all wolves, of course, are Senators or such with official immunity."

From "Washington Confidential," by Jack Lait and Lee Mortimer (1951)

Sex and This City

Even without the harsh glare of scandal, Washington's sexual dynamic has always had a uniquely predatory cast. By Andrew Sullivan

Like countless other Washingtonians, I came to the capital city as an intern. The place is full of them. Each June and September, a new wave lands ashore, just as fresh and vigorous as the last one. If you catch the G2 bus in the morning as it wends its way from the dorm rooms and group houses toward downtown or if you hop on the Metro toward Union Station and Capitol Hill, you will see them in droves: dozens of former high-school presidents, khakis everywhere, red ties and sensible red dresses, hair still wet from a rushed shower.

They are one of the things that make Washington different. Most cities have a variety of neighborhoods, old people, young people and every age in between. But D.C. has a uniquely strange demography, skewed toward young interns in their 20's and elder patrons in their 50's and 60's. The dynamic between them is so old and so cherished that, like any of the city's famous monuments, it eventually just blends into the background. Except, that is, when something goes wrong. Famously, Bill Clinton and Monica Lewinsky. Ominously, Gary Condit and Chandra Levy.

And both of these roles — intern and pol — can be lonely ones. Almost all politicians have spouses and children, but they leave them hundreds or thousands of miles behind and work long, stressful hours in a city that isn't their home. And many interns, in a city completely new to them, with few old friends and many new faces, easily lose their bearings. They aren't here long. Many internships, like Chandra Levy's, are designed to last only a few months: long enough to fall in love or make an impression but not long enough to settle into their surroundings, to build a network of close friends who look out for one another.

Sex is often the result. Yes, I know it sounds strange to think of D.C., Wonk Central, as a place throbbing with libidinal promise. That's supposed to be Miami or Los Angeles or New York. Washington politicians are obliged by ritual to be pillars of family values, upholding moral duty. Nary a one admits to being a libertine. But take a walk through the marble corridors of the Hill, and you find something a little different. The place can crackle with

Andrew Sullivan is a contributing writer for the magazine. He writes daily for www.andrewsullivan.com.

Photograph by Jessica Craig-Martin

16.25 Page layout, *New York Times Magazine*, July, 2001. Photograph: Jessica Craig Martin.

designers (and interactive capabilities for users), the seduction of consumers, and endless upgrades by software developers and personal computer manufacturers which accelerate new purchases.

Computer preparation of type and layout now dominate the printing industry, although most printing continues to be done on offset presses from photographic plates rather than directly from the computer to the press. During the past decade daily newspapers have begun to rival weekly magazines in color reproduction of photographs and advertisements, and daily rather than only Sunday editions use color for the comics pages. Art direction in many magazines reveals sophisticated approaches to layout for feature stories with integrated pictures, illustrations, titles and text to interest the reader. Before the

attack on the World Trade Center and the Pentagon in September, 2001 focused the attention of the United States on its own security, the dominant story of the summer news dealt with the extra-marital affairs of Washington's lawmakers. The *New York Times Magazine* featured an article on the subject with the title "Sex and This City," bringing to mind a popular television show with a similar name (fig. 16.25) in one of a regular series of features devoted to current news topics. A centered title at the top gives only the date in arabic numerals (a repeated element in the series), while below, a cropped and off-center photograph shows a man's hand reaching across the thigh of a young seated woman wearing a short skirt (but toward the reader). The photograph cuts into the text column at the right of the page. The asymmetrical layout, irregular column width, and secondary title below with the word "Sex," all create visual and emotional interest. Art direction for fashion magazines remains more dramatic and immediate, geared to strong contrast and stronger emotional appeal, as in the work of Fabien Baron discussed above (see pages 366–7 and fig. 16.7).

Materials Technology

New synthetic materials and new uses for older industrial materials remain further areas of technological development affecting industrial design. Sporting goods manufacturers continue to introduce strong but lightweight materials like titanium for bicycles and tennis racquets, while graphite is now used commonly for the shafts of golf clubs. The aluminum industry continues to experiment with uses of its product to stimulate sales. For instance, the Emeco company, manufacturers of a lightweight aluminum chair for the United States Air Force in 1944, commissioned French designer Philippe Starcke to design a contemporary version of the product in 2000. This marketing strategy contributed to nostalgic interest in the inventive designs for aluminum housewares during the interwar period while at the same time capitalizing upon Starck's international celebrity as a furniture designer. Clothing is another area in which new fabrics stimulate new products. An example is the iridescent fabric woven from metallic yarns developed by Japanese designer Reiko Sudo (b.1953) for the Numo Manufacturing Corporation in 1991 (fig. 16.26).

16.27 Werner Aisslinger, "Soft Chaise
Longue", aluminum and Technogel,
manufactured by Zanotta, Italy, 1998.
Metropolitan Museum of Art,
New York.

16.26 Reiko Sudo, "Rusted Silver Washer" fabric,
cotton, polyester and aluminum lamé, 259 x 41 in
(658 x 104 cm), 1991, manufactured by Numo
Corporation, 1991.

16.28 Anonymous, patio lounge
chair, steel and rubber webbing.

In addition to new fabrics for clothing, new forms of plastic are integrated with traditional furniture forms, for instance in Werner Aisslinger's (b.1964) Soft Chaise Longue dating to 1999 and manufactured in Italy by Zanotta (fig. 16.27). The lounge chair is made of steel and aluminum and covered in a thin material called TechnoGel that is also used to more comfortably cover bicycle seats and some hospital beds without the usual thickness associated with coil springs or foam pads. Beyond these and other examples of hi-tech products linked to individual artist-designers, international exhibitions, and museum collections, other domestic uses for industrial materials emerge in anonymous yet extremely popular furniture available at discount stores, and advertised in weekend newspaper flyers. One example of such an item is the adjustable folding aluminum lounge chair constructed of a lightweight steel frame wrapped in hollow rubber tubing resembling a colored version of an uninflated bicycle tire tube. The folding mechanism locks in different positions for sitting or carrying (fig. 16.28), The wide range of bright colors that fade with time and sunlight, the rust that accumulates in the folding mechanisms, and the weight of the steel, hardly endear these chairs to their owners. And yet their expendability and cost make them appropriate for taking to the beach or leaving on the patio as a form of ubiquitous late twentieth-century industrial furniture that is attuned to the leisure activities of mainstream America.

Craft: The Persistence of Process

While electronic imagery and the ability of software extend the possibilities of image manipulation and projection, it has often not been possible, nor even desirable, to eliminate skills in drawing, model-building, draping and tailoring, and a host of other more traditional techniques common in most design professions. Increasingly computer interface also permits a great deal of experimentation, emphasizing the playfulness inherent in process rather than a shortcut to a pre-determined result. Experimentation, tinkering, intuition, often exist in the very nature of the craft process, and even in front of the computer screen. It was fear of the elimination of this aspect of process that aroused the indignation of Ruskin and Morris more than a century ago.

16.29 Sally Bowen Prange, "Barnacle Teapot", 6 x 11 x 6 ½ in (15 x 28 x 16 cm), stoneware, silicon carbide.

Craft remains a vehicle for esthetic exploration and individual expression, with a growing number of opportunities for exhibition in museums and galleries. Despite a market limited at times by high costs and criticism of the commercial exploitation of star names, craft continues to chart new territory for expression and materials exploration, often without the theoretical demands and historical familiarity placed upon the audience for contemporary fine art. Craft also often includes the contributions of women, who are less represented in many areas of industrial design. In ceramics, for instance, Sally Bowen Prange's (b.1927) stoneware "Barnacle Teapot" experiments with a Variety of textures to simulate the effects of time and sea water upon human-made products, both wearing them away while at the same time transforming them into new, almost animate creations (fig. 16.29). While Prange's teapot remains within a tradition of utilitarian products, weaver Olga de Amaral (b.1937) focuses more on exploring esthetic effects of new combinations of materials, as in her Alquimia XIII hanging of 1984, woven from cotton, linen, rice, paper, gesso, paint, and gold leaf (fig. 16.30). In this work strands of thread hover in front of rectangles of linen painted tarnished silver at the bottom and gold as they eye

16.30 Olga de Amaral, Alquimia XIII, wall hanging, cotton, linen, rice paper, gesso, paint, gold leaf, 71 x 29 ½ in (180 x 75 cm), 1984. Metropolitan Museum of Art, New York.

16.31 Martin Rakotoaramanana, weaving, silk, 70⅛ x 108⅜ in, 1999. Metropolitan Museum of Art, New York.

moves upward. The texture and color of the materials suggest a mysterious transformation or purification. Modern weavings also provide continuity with local traditions throughout the world, preserving and extending the varied role of craft in non-western and pre-industrial societies. One example is a 1999 weaving from Madagascar by Martin Rakotoarimanana (*b.*1963, fig. 16.31). The weaving consists of vertical strips of brightly colored symbols creating a strong sense of pattern and great complexity.

Furniture-makers continue to explore original approaches working with both natural as well as industrially manufactured woods. An example of the latter is Michael Gilmartin's Ayos 2000 armchair (fig. 16.32) using thick, specially manufactured laminated plywood for identical bent forms that serve as legs, arms, and support for back and seat.

The desire for freedom of expression, the enjoyment of working with materials, the excitement of discovering the richness of effect, all combine to continually renew the possibilities of satisfaction in the craft process, and deserve to be included in any present or future understanding of design. Craft exhibitions range from the local to the national and international, and provide a venue for direct sales to the public or purchase prizes from major museums. The range of media at most craft exhibitions is broad and is organized as a combination of folk and guild traditions. Categories include, for instance, baskets and handmade fibers, as well as glass, furniture, leather, and ceramics. In most cases, however, work is highly

16.32 Michael Gilmartin, Ayos 2000 armchair, laminated plywood, 32 x 26 in (81 x 66 cm). Gilmartin Studios, Atlanta, Georgia.

16.33 Frank Gehry, Fish Lamp, steel, wood, Colorcore Formica plastic laminate, and electric lights, manufactured by New City Editions, 1983–84.

individual rather than utilitarian, and original rather than making references to historical styles. Statements by the artists include references to keeping alive self-sufficient pre-industrial patterns of life, and using craft to humanize the impersonal character of contemporary existence dominated by technology.

Contradicting traditional associations of craft with natural materials is Frank Gehry's 1983/4 fish lamp (fig. 16.33). Based upon the organic and asymmetrical shape of a fish or serpent, Gehry created rich effects of light and color using the synthetic material Formica Colorcore to suggest skin or scales attached to a wire armature. The intricate assembly and novel effects of light recall the tradition of esthetic approaches to craft, while the use of Colorcore outside of interior surfaces and furniture is

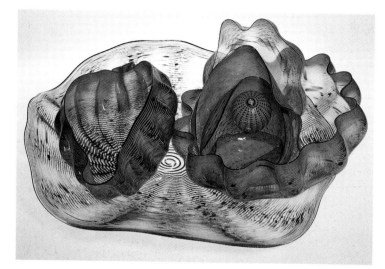

16.34 Dale Chihuly, White Sea Form set with black lip wraps,
14 × 25 × 20 in (36 × 63.5 × 51 cm), 1990. Victoria and Albert Museum.

reminiscent of the strategies of Pop artists in making sculptures from non-traditional materials.

In the medium of glass, the work of Dale Chihuly (*b*.1941) is celebrated both for its inventiveness and virtuosity. The blown-glass *Sea Form* is but one of numerous examples of his work, featuring a variety of organic forms, textures, and patterns (fig. 16.34). In the case of Chihuly, large commissions and the celebrity deriving from being featured in mass magazines and on television have led to

a separation between design and execution, with the majority of glass blowing now being carried out by assistants under Chihuly's supervision.

Conclusion: Creativity, Responsibility, and Resilience

Design's strength lies in its breadth, its interaction with so many sources of inspiration and areas of consideration: through technology designers are in constant contact with new materials and processes that stimulate ideas for original products or transformations in existing products; through production designers work with manufacturers, investors, and must take account of markets, costs, and sales; as artists designers are able to integrate an interest in esthetics as well as self-expression and experimentation; from consumers designers work to incorporate human factors, user-friendly and appealing forms, stimulating a wide range of possible meanings and interpretations. Design can be team-based and anonymous or individual and heroic, ephemeral and self-indulgent or universal and relatively unchanging, negligent, amoral, or socially and globally conscious. Through this dynamic range of possibilities designers remain actively engaged with the world in all its excitement, complexity, and ambiguity. Its history helps us to unite what design has been with what it might be, in continued responsiveness to production, consumption, society, and the environment, all of which stimulate, condition, and sustain its efforts.

History of Modern Design Timeline

Seventeenth century

1650–1700 Mortlake Tapestry manufactory in England, founded by James I, 1619 • French Academy for painting est. Rome, 1656 • Charles LeBrun opens Royal Tapestry manufactory, Gobelins, 1666 • Trade Fair in Holland, 1689.

Eighteenth century

1701–1750 André Charles Boulle, cabinet-maker (1642–1732) • Meissen Porcelain manufactory founded, 1710 • glass manufacture at Murano, near Venice, Italy, 1736 • Vincennes Porcelain manufactory founded, 1738.

1751–1775 Chippendale *Director* published, 1754 • Foundation of Royal Academy of Fine Art in England, 1765 • Robert Adam "Lansdowne House", 1765 • Wedgwood manufactory est. Etruria, 1769.

1776–1800 "Modern" typefaces developed by printing family of Didot, Paris, and Bodoni in Parma, Italy • Caslon and Baskerville active as printers in Britain • Watt invents rotary steam engine • copper cylinder printing for calico fabric, 1783 • Vincennes Porcelain Manufactory founded 1783 • Sheraton *Drawing Book*, 1791–4 • Senefelder invents lithography, 1798.

Nineteenth century

1801–25 Ébénistes Weisweiler and Riesener active in Paris, 1807 • Pleyl founds manufactory for pianofortes, 1807 • Schinkel cast-iron chair, c. 1810 • *Hope Household Furniture and Decoration*, 1807 • Ackermann's *Repository of the Arts* published, from c. 1813 • coil spring upholstery, Vienna, c. 1818.

1826–50 Bentwood chairs manufactured by Michael Thonet • papier maché used for furniture and for printing formes for mechanical presses • illustrated children's books published by Henry Cole • Academy of Design, New York, est. 1826 • specimen books by Thorowgood and Figgins, c. 1830 • beginnings of chromolithography, 1830s • Charles Knight's *Penny Magazine*, from 1832 • Paris Industry Fair, 1834 • block printed wallpaper manufactured widely • National Gallery in London opened, 1838 • Simeon North develops firearm manufacturing with interchangeable parts, 1840 • Pugin and Barry design Houses of Parliament c. 1840 • Richard Redgrave Wellspring vase, 1847 • first sewing machine patented in New York by Howe (NYC) 1846, improved by Singer 1851 • block-printed wallpaper manufactured widely.

1851–75 Ruskin *Stones of Venice* 1851-3 • Wm. Perkin develops first aniline (chemical) dyes, 1856 • Morris and Company from 1858 • London Great Exhibition (Crystal Palace), 1851 and catalogue • Owen Jones' *Grammar of Ornament* 1856 • Victoria & Albert Museum, London, opened as Museum of Ornamental Art • Thomas Nast illustrations for *Harper's Weekly* from 1858 • first extraction of alumi-num; cork linoleum invented, 1860 • Dresser's *Art of Decorative Design*, 1862 • World Exhibition, London 1862 • Paris World's Fair, 1855 and 1867 • chromo-lithography widely used • Charles Worth in Paris from c. 1860, haute couture • Union Central des art decoratifs et industriels established, France, 1864 • E. Remington begins to manufacture typewriters, 1873.

1876–1900 Herter Brothers active from c. 1875 • children's illustrations by Caldecott and Greenaway from c. 1875 • Tiffany founds company for interior decoration, 1879 • Edison and Swan invent first practical electric lights, 1880 • Sears catalogue, 1881 • Eastman perfects Kodak Box Camera, 1888 • Meier-Grafe's "La Maison Moderne" (Paris) • Toulouse-Lautrec music hall posters c. 1890 • Gallé glass, Cheret posters, Mucha posters, Will Bradley, Kelmscott Press, 1890 • Eastman invents coated photographic paper • Private Press Movement, 1890 • Roycrofter Craft Community founded near Buffalo, US, 1893 • Beardsley drawings for Oscar Wilde's *Salome* (1894) • Gillette invents and manufactures Safety Razor, 1895 • S. Bing opens "Art Nouveau" showrooms, Paris 1895 • *Die Jugend* and *Simplicissimus* begin publication in Munich from 1896 • Stickley founds "Craftsman Workshops" near Syracuse, US, 1900 • Moravian Tile Works c. 1900 • Mackintosh designs shown at World's Fair in Vienna, 1900 (and Turin, 1902).

Twentieth century

1901–10 Societe des Artistes Decorateurs est. 1901 • Wiener Werkstatte founded 1903 • Fauve Exhibition, Paris 1905 • Deutscher Werkbund founded, 1907 • AEG hires Peter Behrens as design consultant, 1907 • Howard Pyle illustrations for journals and books • first daily comic strip, 1907 • First Cubist exhibition, 1907 • Frank Lloyd Wright Robie House, Chicago 1907 • Applied Arts Exhibition, Munich 1908 • *Futurist Manifesto* published, 1909 • Palais Stocklet, Brussels, 1911–15.

1911–20 Salon d'automne, 1911 • Maison Cubiste 1912 • mass production of Model T Ford begins at Highland park plant MI, US, 1913 • Werkbund Exhibition, Cologne, 1914 • Christine Frederick's *Principles of Household Management*, 1915 • moderne furniture by Ruhlmann, Süe et Mare, etc. from c. 1915 • De Stijl journal begins, 1917 • Manifesto of Purism in France, 1918 • Bauhaus founded in Weimar, Germany, 1919 • Constructivism emerges at schools and in exhibitions in Russia, 1919 • Hald designs glass for Orrefors (Sweden), from c. 1919 • Svenska Slodforeningen founded in Sweden c. 1920.

1921–30   Kandinsky and Klee hired at Bauhaus, c. 1922 • Milan Triennale, 1923 • Herman Miller Furniture (Michigan) Company founded, 1923 • Le Corbusier's *Vers une Architecture*, 1923 • Bauhaus Exhibition, Weimar, 1923 • Vkutemas (Higher State Technical Workshops) est. USSR, c. 1924–5 • Bauhaus moves to Dessau • Tschiscold *The New Typography* 1927 • General Motors Art and Color Section founded, 1927 • Union des Artistes Modernes (UAM) est. France, 1929• Ford introduces Model A, 1927 • Tubular steel chair manufactured, Germany (Thonet), 1928 • Frankfurt Kitchen, 1925–30, Wiessenhof Siedlung, 1928 • Ford builds plant in Germany • Museum of Modern Art founded, New York, 1929 • Weissenhof Seidlung, 1928 • *Fortune* magazine est. 1930.

1931–40   Molded plywood furniture, e.g. Aalto for Paimio Sanatorium, Finland 1932 • "Landi" aluminum chair, 1933 • Kandinsky and Klee flee Germany, Bauhaus closed, 1933 • *S.S. Normandie* launched, 1933 • Raymond Loewy designs locomotives and other projects for Pennsylvania Railroad • Loewy Coldspot refrigerator for Sears, 1935 • polyethylene developed, synthetic fabric nylon patented by W. Carothers (Dupont), used for stockings, 1936 • Dreyfuss telephone headset for Western Electric, 1937 • *Life* magazine launched, 1937, ballpoint pen invented by Biro, 1938.

1941–50   First magnetic recording tape, 1942 • Organic Design for the Home at MoMA, 1940 • Utility clothing and furniture in Britain, 1941 • Dacron synthetic fabric invented, 1941 • Tupperware patented and expands marketing, 1945 • Vespa motorscooter for Piaggo, 1946 • Design Research Unit (DRU) in Britain • first jet airplanes tested • Dior pioneers "New Look" for fashion, 1947 • Bell Laboratories invent transistor, 1947 • Le Corbusier "Unite d'Habitation",

low-cost housing apartment building, Marseilles, 1947 • Marcelo Nizzoli Lexikon 80 typewriter for Olivetti, 1948 • Porsche 356, 1948 • "Low Cost Furniture" exhibition at MoMA • Hermann Zapf Palatino typeface, 1950 • Sixton Sasson Saab 92, 1950 • first Sony tape recorder.

1951–60   Color television introduced, US 1951 • Bertoia Wire chair, 1952 • Lever House built by Skidmore, Owings, Merrill, New York, 1952 • Cadillac with tailfins, 1953 • Chevrolet Corvette, Ford Thunderbird: sportscars, US, 1953–4 • Adrian Frutiger Univers typeface, 1954 • Lapidus Fontainebleu Hotel, Miami Beach, US, 1954 • Hochschule für Gestaltung opens, Ulm, Germany 1955 • Paul Rand logo for IBM, 1956 • Saarinen plastic Womb Chair, 1957 • Eames molded plywood reclining chair, 1957 • first all-transistor radio by Sony, Braun radio-phonograph (Snow White's Coffin) • Hermann Zapf Helvetica typeface, 1957 • Chrysler "Forward Look", c. 1957 • Guggenhim Museum built by Frank Lloyd Wright, 1957–8 • Dupont patents "Lycra" synthetic fabric, 1958 • Optima, 1958 • stereo recordings introduced, 1958 • Morris Mini (Alec Issagonis), 1959 • first all-transistor television by Sony, 1959 • Eero Saarinen TWA Terminal, New York, 1958–62.

1961–70   Audio cassette invented, 1962 • Loewy, Studebaker "Avanti", 1962 • injection mold plastics used for Joe Columbo side chair for Kartell, 1964 • Eames Tandem Sling aluminum seating for Herman Miller, 1964 • portable calculator using integrated circuitry developed (Sharp Corporation), Japan, 1964 • Robert Propst Action Office for Herman Miller, 1964 • ABC and Mobil logos • Sir Terence Conran's Habitat store, London 1964 • Wes Wesley posters for Filmore Auditorium • graphics for Tokyo Olympic Games, 1964 • Ford "Mustang", 1965 • Mary Quant miniskirt • R. Matta "Malitte" seating system for Gavina, 1966 • "Sacco" chair • "Pop Art" Exhibition, New York • Venturi's *Complexity and Contradiction in Architecture*, 1966 • Bang and Olufsen "Beosystem" stereo system, 1967 • steel and aluminum frame tennis racquets, from 1967 • Superstudio and Archizoom

groups founded, Italy, 1968–9 • Hochschule für Gestaltung at Ulm, closed, 1969.

1971–80   Intel Corporation founded (microprocessor) • Table–top microwave oven, 1971 • launching of Honda Civic and Accord in US • Papanek, *Design for the Real World*, 1971 • Vitrac disposable plastic picnic set, 1971 • Robert Venturi et al, Learning from Las Vegas, 1972 • Cuisinart food processor, 1973 • Knife with Cutting Frame, Ergonommi Grupen, Sweden, 1974 • laser printers invented, 1975 • ink-jet printers invented, 1976 • Sony Walkman, 1978 • Ergonommi Group founded in Sweden, 1979 • Frank Gehry Little Beaver chair, 1980 • Solidarity logo, 1980 • floppy disk introduced, 1980.

1981–90   IBM inaugurates Personal Computer (PC), 1981 • Memphis Design Group formed, Milan, 1981 • journal *Emigré* begins publication 1982 • Formica introduces "colorcore" product 1982 • Sony and Philips introduce compact disk players, 1982 • modern coffee and tea service designs commissioned in silver for Alessi Corporation, Italy, 1983 • Venturi plywood laminated chairs for Knoll International, 1983 • Frank Gehry, fish Lamp, 1983–4 • Neville Brody typeface "Face 2", 1984 • improvements to silicon microchip, 1984 • CD ROM invented, 1984 • Apple Macintosh graphic interface for personal computer, 1984 • Microsoft unveils "Windows" Operating System for personal computers, 1985 • Norman Foster "Nomos": office furniture, 1985 • Musée d'Orsay opens in former train station, Paris, 1986 • Design Museum opens, London, 1989 • prototypes for software "Photoshop" tested by Adobe Systems, 1989 • Dale Chihuly, White Seaform Set, 1990.

1991–2002 Rick Poynor *Typography Now: The Next Wave*, 1991 • Reiko Sudo, polyester and aluminum fabric, 1991 • Werner Aisslinger Soft Chaise, Technogle, 1998 • iMac desktop computer c. 1998 • Nokia digital cellular phone with interchangeable faceplates c. 1998 • Michael Graves, Whistling Tea Kettle and other products for Target, 1998 • Martin Rakotoaramanana, weaving, 1999 • Sharp Flat–screen television, 1999 • OXO good grips kitchen tools, 2000.

Bibiliography

General

Albus, Volker, Kraus, Reyer, and Woodham, Jonathan M., *Icons of Design: the 20th century*, Munich and New York, Prestel, 2000

Appadurai, Arjun, ed., *The social life of things. Commodities in cultural perspective*, Cambridge, Melbourne, and New York, Cambridge University Press, 1986

Auslander, Leora, *Taste and Power: Furnishing Modern France*, Berkeley and Los Angeles, University of California Press, 1996

Aynsley, Jeremy, *A Century of Graphic Design, Graphic Pioneers of the 20th Century*, Hauppage NY, Barron's, 2001

Aynsley, Jeremy, *Graphic Design in Germany 1890–1945*, Berkeley and Los Angeles, University of California Press, 2000

Banham, Reyner., *The Architecture of the Well-Tempered Environment*, London, The Architectural Press, 1969

Barthes, Roland, *Mythologies*, Selected and translated Annette Lavers, New York, Hill and Wang, 1972 (first published 1957)

Baudrillard, Jean, *The Consumer Society: Myths and Structures*, London, Sage Publications, 1998 (first published 1970)

Baudrillard, Jean, *The System of Objects*, trans. James Benedict, London and New York, Verso, 1996 (first published 1968)

Bayley, Stephen. *In Good Shape: Style in Industrial Products. 1900–1960*, New York, Van Nostrand Reinhold, 1979

Benton, T., Benton, C. eds. *Architecture and Design: 1890–1939, An International Anthology of Original Articles*, New York, Whitney Library of Design, Watson-Guptill Publications, 1975

Bierut, Michael, Helfand, Jessica, Heller, Steven, and Poynor, Rick, eds., *Looking Closer 3: Classic Writings on Graphic Design*, New York, Allworth Press, 1999

Blum Dilys E., *The Fine Art of Textile: the Collections of the Philadelphia Museum of Art*, Philadelphia, Philadelphia Museum of Art, 1997

Brunhammer, Yvonne and Tise, Suzanne. *The decorative arts in France, 1900–1942: la Société des artistes décorateurs*, New York : Rizzoli, 1990

Buchanan, Richard, and Margolin, Victor, *Design: explorations in design studies*, Chicago, University of Chicago Press, 1995

Byars, Mel, *The Design Encyclopedia*, New York, John Wiley & Sons, 1994

Coatts, Margot, ed., *Pioneers of Modern Craft*, Manchester and New York, Manchester University Press and St. Martin's Press, 1997

de Marly, Diana. *The History of Haute Couture, 1850–1950*, London, Batsford, 1980

Dormer, Peter. *Design Since 1945*, New York and London, Thames and Hudson, 1993

Fenichell, Stephen, *Plastic: the making of a synthetic century*, New York, HarperBusiness, 1997

Fiell, Charlotte and Peter, *Design of the 20th century*, Cologne, Taschen, 2000

Fleming, John, and Honour, Hugh, *The Penguin Dictionary of Decorative Arts*, London, Viking, new edition, 1989

Forty, Adrian, *Objects of Desire: Design and Society Since 1750*, London, Thames and Hudson, 1986

Frank, Isabelle, ed., *The Theory of Decorative Art. An Anthology of European and American Writings 1750–1940.* New Haven and London, Yale University Press, 2000

Garner, Philippe. *Twentieth-Century Furniture*, New York, Van Nostrand Reinhold, 1980

Garner, Phillipe, *The Contemporary Decorative Arts from 1940 to the present*, New York, Facts on File, 1980

Giedion, S. *Mechanization Takes Command: A Contribution to Anonymous History*, New York, Oxford University Press, 1948

Gombrich, E.H. *The Sense of Order. A Study of the Psychology of Decorative Art.* The Wrightsman Lectures, Ithaca, Cornell Press, 1979

Greenhalgh, Paul, ed. *Quotations and Sources on Design and the Decorative Arts*, Manchester and New York, Manchester University Press, 1993

Hayden, Dolores, *The Grand Domestic Revolution: A History of Feminist Design for American Homes, Neighborhood, and Cities*, Cambridge MA and London, MIT Press, 1981

Heller, Steven and Ballance, Georgette, eds., *Graphic Design History*, New York, Allworth Press, 2001

Heller, Steven and Pettit, Elinor, *Graphic Design Timeline: A Century of Design Milestones*, New York, Allworth Press, 2000

Heskett, John, *Industrial Design*, New York and Toronto, Oxford University Press, 1980

Hiesinger, Kathryn B. and Marcus, George H., *Landmarks of Twentieth Century Design. An Illustrated Handbook*, New York, Abbeville Press, 1993

Hiesinger, Kathryn B., and Fischer, Felice, *Japanese Design: A Survey Since 1950*, Philadelphia Museum of Art, 1994

Hiesinger, Kathryn B., and Marcus, George H., eds., *Design Since 1945*, Philadelphia, Philadelphia Museum of Art, 1983

Hounshell, David A., *From the American System to Mass Production 1800–1932: the development of manufacturing technology in the United States*, Baltimore, Johns Hopkins University Press, 1984

Jervis, Simon, *The Facts on File Dictionary of Design and Designers*, New York, Facts on File, 1984 (also published by Penguin Books, Harmondsworth, 1984)

Julier, Guy, *The Encyclopedia of Twentieth-Century Design and Designers*, New York, Thames and Hudson, 1993

Kirkham, Pat, ed., *Women Designers in the USA 1900–2000: Diversity and Difference*, New Haven, Yale University Press, 2000

Lawson, Alexander, *Anatomy of A Typeface*, Boston, David R. Godine, 1990

Lucie-Smith, Edward. *Furniture: A Concise History*, New York, Oxford University Press, 1979

Margolin, Victor and Buchanan, Richard, eds., *The Idea of Design: A Design Issues Reader*, Cambridge, MA and London, MIT Press, 1995

Margolin, Victor, ed., *Design Discourse. History-Theory-Criticism*, Chicago, University Press, 1989

Martin, Richard, ed. *The St. James Fashion Encyclopedia: A Survey of Style from 1945 to the Present*, Detroit, Visible

Ink Press, 1996

McCracken, Penny, *Women Artists and Designers since 1800: An Annotated Bibliography*, two volumes, New York, G. K. Hall & Company, 1998

McFadden, David Revere, general ed., *Scandinavian Modern Design 1880–1980*, New York, Harry N. Abrams, 1982

Meggs, Philip B., *A History of Graphic Design*, 2nd edition, NY, Van Nostrand Reinhold, 1992 (first edition 1983)

Meikle, Jeffrey, *American Plastic: a Cultural History*, New Brunswick, NJ, Rutgers University Press, 1995

Naremore, James, and Patrick Brantlinger, eds., *Modernity and Mass Culture*, Bloomington, Indiana University Press, 1991

Nichols, Sarah, et al., *Aluminum by Design*, Pittsburgh, Carnegie Museum of Art, 2000

Pevsner, Nikolaus, *Pioneers of Modern Design*, Harmondsworth, Penguin, 1960

Phillips, Lisa. *The American Century: Art and Culture 1950–2000*, New York, Whitney Museum of American Art and W. W. Norton and Company, 1999

Remington, R. Roger, and Hodik, Barbara J., *Nine Pioneers in American Graphic Design*, Cambridge, MA, The MIT Press, 1989

Russell, Douglas, *Costume History and Style*, Englewood Cliffs, Prentice Hall, 1983

Sabin, Roger, *Comics, Commix, and Graphic Novels*, London, Phaidon, 2001 (first published 1997)

Snodin, Michael, and Styles, John, eds. *Design and the Decorative Arts. Britain 1500–1900*, London, V&A Publications, 2001

Sparke, Penny, *Design in Italy: 1870 to the Present*, New York, Abbeville, 1988

Sparke, Penny. *An Introduction to Design and Culture in the Twentieth Century*, New York, Harper and Row (Icon Editions), 1986 (paperback)

Trench, Lucy, ed., *Materials and Techniques in the Decorative Arts. An Illustrated Dictionary*, Chicago, University of Chicago Press, 2000

Twyman, Michael, *Printing 1770–1970. An illustrated history of its development and uses in England*, London, Eyre & Spottiswoode, 1970

Von Vegesack, Alexander, Peter Dunes, and Mathias Schwartz-Clauss, eds. *100 Masterpieces of Furniture from the Vitra Design Museum Collection*, Weil am Rhein, Vitra Design Museum, 1996

Woodham, Jonathan M., *Twentieth Century Design*, Oxford and New York, Oxford University Press, 1997

Part I

Anderson, Patricia, *The Printed Image and the Transformation of Popular Culture 1790–1860*, Oxford, Clarendon Press, 1991

Atterbury, Paul, and Wainwright, Clive, eds., *Pugin: a Gothic Passion*, New Haven, Yale University Press, 1994

Atterbury, Paul, ed., *A. W. N. Pugin: Master of Gothic revival*, New Haven, Yale University Press, 1995

Bell, Quentin, *The Schools of Design*, London, Routledge and Kegan Paul, 1963

Bloom, Jonathan M., *Paper Before Print: The History and*

Impact of Paper in the Islamic World, New Haven and London, Yale University Press, 2001

Bodini, Giambattista, *Manuale tipografico del cavaliere Giambattista Bodoni, Parma, Presso la vedova, 1818* London, Holland Press, 1960

Braudel, Fernand, *Civilization and Capitalism 15th–18th centuries*, three volumes, trans. Sian Reynolds, New York, Harper & Row, 1979

Brewer, John, and Porter, Roy, *Consumption and the World of Goods*, London and New York, Routledge, 1993

Chippendale, Thomas, *The gentlemen and cabinet-maker's director*, New York, Dover, 1966

Crow, Thomas E. , *Painters and Public Life in Eighteenth-Century Paris*, New Haven and London, Yale University Press, 1985

Diderot encyclopedia: the complete illustrations 1762–1777, five volumes, New York, Harry N. Abrams, 1978

Eriksen, Svend and de Bellaigue, Geoffrey, *Sèvres Porcelain: Vincennes and Sèvres 1740–1800*, London and Boston, Faber and Faber, 1987

Gilbert, Christopher, *The Life and Work of Thomas Chippendale*, two volumes, London, Studio Vista, 1978

Good, Edwin M. *Giraffes, Black Dragons, and other Pianos. A Technological History from Cristofori to the Modern Concert Grand*, Stanford, University Press, 1982

Goodison, Nicholas. *Ormolu: The Work of Matthew Boulton*, London, Phaidon, 1974

Gray, Nicolete, *Nineteenth Century Ornamented Typefaces*, Berkeley and Los Angeles, University of California Press, 1976 (first published 1938)

Harris, Eileen, *The Genius of Robert Adam: his interiors*, New Haven, Yale University Press, 2001

Hilton, Tim, *John Ruskin*, 2 volumes, New Haven, Yale University Press, 1995–2000

Hope, Thomas. *Household Furniture and Interior Decoration*, classic style book of the Regency Period, New York, Dover Books, 1971 (first published 1807)

Johnson, Paul, *The Birth of the Modern: world society 1815–1830*, New York, HarperCollins, 1991

Jones, Owen, *The Grammar of Ornament*, New York, Dover Publications, 1991, (first published 1856)

Joubert, Fabienne, Fefébure, Amaury, Bertrand, Pascal-François, *Histoire de la tapisserie en Europe, du Moyen Âge à nos jours*, Paris, Flammarion, 1995

Lewis, Michael J. *The Gothic Revival*, New York, Thames and Hudson, 2002

Lucie Smith, Edward. *The Story of Craft. The Craftsman's Role in Society*, New York, Phaidon, 1981

Marchands Merciers of Eighteenth-Century Paris, London, Victoria and Albert Museum in association with the J. Paul Getty Museum, 1996

McKendrick, Neil, Brewer, John, and Plumb, J.H. *The Birth of a Consumer Society. The Commercialization of Eighteenth-Century England*, Bloomington, Indiana University Press, 1985

McLean, Ruari, *Victorian Book Design and Colour Printing*, New York, Oxford University Press, 1963

Morley, John, *Regency Design, 1790–1840: Gardens, Buildings, Interiors, Furniture*, New York, Harry N. Abrams, 1993

Pradère, Alexandre, *French Furniture Makers: The Art of the Ébéniste from Louis XIV to the Revolution*, trans. Perran Wood, Malibu (CA), The J. Paul Getty Museum, 1989

Ribeiro, Aileen, *Dress in Eighteenth-Century Europe 1715–1789*, New York, Holmes & Meier, 1985

Ribeiro, Aileen, *Ingres in fashion: representations of dress and appearance in Ingres's images of women*, New Haven, Yale University Press, 1999

Richards, Thomas, *The Commodity Culture of Victorian England: advertising and spectacle 1851–1914*, Stanford, Stanford University Press, 1990

Rothstein, Natalie, *Silk Designs of the Eighteenth Century: in the collection of the Victoria and Albert Museum, London, with a Complete Catalogue*, London, Thames and Hudson, 1990

Sargentson, Carolyn, *Merchants and Luxury Markets. The Marchands Merciers of Eighteenth-Century Paris*, London, Victoria and Albert Museum in association with the J. Paul Getty Museum, 1996

The Crystal Palace Exhibition Illustrated catalogue, London 1851: an unabridged republication of the Art-journal special issue, New York, Dover Publications, 1970

Tinterow, Gary, and Conisbee, Philip, eds., *Portraits by Ingres. Image of an Epoch*, New York, Metropolitan Museum of Art, 1999

Updike, Daniel Berkeley, *Printing Types. Their History, Forms, and Use*, Cambridge, Massachusetts, Harvard University Press, 1962, two volumes (first published 1922)

Weigert, Roger-Armand, *French Tapestry*, trans. Donald and Monique King, London, Faber and Faber, 1962

Part II

American Art Pottery. Cooper-Hewitt Museum, Seattle and London, University of Washington Press, 1987

Anscombe, Isabelle and Charlotte Gere, *Arts and Crafts in Britain and America*, NY, Rizzoli, 1978

Arwas, Victor et al., *Alphonse Mucha. The Spirit of Art Nouveau*, Virginia, Art Services International, 1998

Bembace, Anthony, *Will H. Bradley: his work, a bibliographic guide*, New Castle, DE, Oak Knoll Press, 1995

Benzi, Fabio, ed., *Il liberty in Italia*, Milan, F. Molta, 2001 (catalogue for an exhibition at the Chiostro del Bramante, Rome)

Bolger Burke, Doreen et al., *In Pursuit of Beauty. Americans and the Aesthetic Movement*, New York, Rizzolli, 1986 (catalogue for exhibition of same name at Metropolitan Museum of Art, October–January 1986–87

Broido, Lucy, *The Posters of Jules Cheret: 46 full-color plates and an illustrated catalogue raisonné*, New York, Dover Publications, 1980

Buddensieg, Tilmann, et al., *Industriekultur: Peter Behrens and the AEG, 1907–1914*, translated Iain Boyd Whyte, Cambridge, MIT Press, 1984 (first published 1979)

Campbell, Joan. *The German Werkbund. The Politics of Reform in the Applied Arts*, Princeton, University Press, 1978

Cave, Roderick, *The Private Press*, 2nd edition, New York and London, R. R. Bowker Co., 1983

Clark, Kenneth, ed. *John Ruskin: Selected Writings*, London, Penguin Books, 1991, first published 1964

Crawford, Alan, *C.R. Ashbee. Architect, Designer, and Romantic Socialist*, New Haven and London, 1985

Csenkey, Éva, and , Steinert, Ágota, eds., *Hungarian Ceramics from the Zsolnay Manufactory 1853–2001*, New Haven, Yale University Press, 2002

Cumming, Elizabeth, and Kaplan, Wendy. *The Arts and Crafts Movement*, London, Thames and Hudson, 1991

De Marly, Diana, *Worth: Father of Haute Couture*, New York, Holmes & Meier, 1990

Denvir, Bernard, *Toulouse-Lautrec*, London, Thames and Hudson, 1991

Dresser, Christopher, *Principles of Victorian Decorative Design, with 184 illustrations*, New York, Dover Publications, 1995

Dresser, Christopher, *Traditional Arts and Crafts of Japan*, New York, Dover, 1994 (originally published 1882)

Duncan, Alastair, *Art Nouveau*, New York, Thames and Hudson, 1994

Durant, Stuart, *Christopher Dresser*, London, Academy Editions, 1993

Eastlake, Charles L., *Hints on Household Taste. The Classic Handbook of Victorian Interior Decoration*, New York, Dover, 1969 (originally published 1868)

Engen, Rodney K., *Kate Greenaway*, New York, Harmony Books, 1976

Engen, Rodney K., *Randolph Caldecott. Lord of the Nursery*, London, Oresko Books, 1976

Escritt, Stephen, *Art Nouveau*, London, Phaidon, 2000

Fahr-Becker, Gabriele, *Art Nouveau*, Cologne, Konemann, 1997

Fiell, Charlotte and Peter, eds., *1900–1910 Decorative Art: a Sourcebook*, Cologne, Taschen, 2000

Franklin, Colin, *The Private Presses*, London, Studio Vista, 1969

Freeman, Dr. Larry, *Louis Prang: Color Lithographer. Giant of a Man*, Watkins Glen, New York, Century House Inc. 1971

Gagnier, Regina, *Idylls of the Marketplace: Oscar Wilde and the Victorian Public*, Stanford, Stanford University Press, 1986

Gere, Charlotte, *The House Beautiful: Oscar Wilde and the Aesthetic interior*, London, Lund Humphries in association with the Geffrye Museum, London, 2000

Gere, Charlotte and Whiteway, Michael, *Nineteenth Century Design from Pugin to Mackintosh*, New York, Harry N. Abrams, 1994 (first published in Britain 1993)

Greenhalgh, Paul, ed., *Art Nouveau 1890–1914*, New York, Harry N. Abrams, 2000

Groom, Gloria, *Beyond the Easel: Decorative Painting by Bonnard, Vuillard, Denis, and Roussel 1890–1930*, New Haven and London, Yale University Press, 2001

Halén, Widar, *Christopher Dresser*, Oxford, Phaidon, 1990

Hárs, Éva, *Zsolnay Kerámica*, Pécs (Budapest), Felelos Kiadó, 1998

Heinz, Thomas A., *Frank Lloyd Wright Interiors and Furniture*, London, Academy Editions, 1994

Heskett, John. *German Design 1870–1918*, New York, Taplinger, 1986

Hiesinger, Kathryn Bloom, ed. *Art Nouveau in Munich: Masters of Jugendstil from the Stadtmuseum, Munich and other Public and Private Collections*, Philadelphia Museum of Art in association with Prestel Verlag, 1988

Howe, Katherine S. et al., *Herter Brothers: furniture and interiors for a gilded age*, New York, Harry N. Abrams, 1994

Kanigel, Robert, *One best way: Frederick Winslow Taylor and the enigma of efficiency*, New York, Viking Press, 1997

Kaplan, Wendy, ed., *Charles Rennie Mackintosh*, New York, Abbeville Press, 1996

Kaplan, Wendy, *The Art That is Life: The Arts and Crafts Movement in America, 1875–1920*, Boston, Little, Brown, 1987

Kardon, Janet, ed., *The Ideal Home 1900–1920*, New York, Harry N. Abrams and the American Craft Museum, 1993

Kramer, Stella. *The English Craft Guilds*, New York, 1967

Macleod, Dianne Sachko, *Art and the Victorian middle class: Money and the making of Cultural Identity*, Cambridge, University Press, 1996

Marzio, Peter, *Chromolithography 1840–1900. The Democratic Art. Pictures for a 19th-Century America*, Boston, David R. Godine, 1979

Miller, Michael B., *The Bon Marche: Bourgeois Culture and the Department Store, 1869–1920*, Princeton, University Press, 1981

Muthesius, Hermann, *Das englische Haus*, 3 vol., (Berlin, 1904), trans. J. Seligman, London, 1979

Naylor, Gillian. *The Arts and Crafts Movement*, Cambridge, MIT Press, 1980 (originally published 1971)

Nye, David E., *Image Worlds: Corporate Identities at General Electric, 1890–1930*, Cambridge, MIT Press, 1985

Parry, Linda, ed., *William Morris*, New York, Harry N. Abrams, 1996

Peck, Amelia, *Candace Wheeler: the art and enterprise of American Design 1875–1900*, New Haven, Yale University Press, 2001

Peterson, Wm. S. *The Kelmscott Press. A History of William

Morris's Typographical Adventure, Berkeley, University of California Press, 1991

Pevsner, Nikolaus, *Studies in Art, Architecture and Design. Victorian and After*, Princeton, University Press, 1968

Pitz, Henry C., *Howard Pyle. Writer, Illustrator, Founder of the Brandywine School*, New York, Clarkson N. Potter, 1975

Reed, Cleota, *Henry Chapman Mercer and the Moravian Pottery and Tile Works*, Philadelphia, University of Pennsylvania Press, 1996

Schwartz, Frederic J., *The Werkbund: Design Theory and Mass Culture before the First World War*, New Haven and London, Yale University Press, 1996

Schweiger, Werner. *Wiener Werkstätte, Design in Vienna 1903–1932*, New York, Abbeville Press, 1984

Sembach, Klaus-Jurgen, *Henry van de Velde*, trans. Michael Robinson, New York, Rizzoli, 1989

Silverman, Debora L., *Art Nouveau in Fin-de-Siecle France: Politics Psychology, and Style*, Berkeley, Los Angeles, and London, University of California Press, 1989

Soros, Susan Weber, ed., *E. W. Godwin. Aesthetic Movement Architect and Designer*, New Haven and London, Yale University Press and the Bard Graduate Center for Studies in the Decorative Arts, New York, 1999

Stickley, Gustav, *Craftsman Homes: Architecture and Furnishings of the American Arts and Crafts Movement*, New York, Dover Publications, 1979

Stickley, Gustav, *The 1912 and 1915 Gustav Stickley Furniture Catalogs*, New York, Dover Publications, 1991

Szabadi, Judit, *Art Nouveau in Hungary*, Budapest, Corvina, 1989

Via, Marie, and Searl, Marjorie, eds., *Head, Heart and Hand: Elbert Hubbard and the Roycrofters*, Rochester, University of Rochester Press, 1994

Weisberg, Gabriel, and Menon, Elizabeth K., *Art Nouveau: A research guide for Design Reform in France, Belgium, England, and the United States*, New York and London, Garland Publishing, 1998

Whiteway, Michael, *Christopher Dresser: 1834–1904*, Milan, Skira, 2001

Williams, R.H. *Dream Worlds: Mass Consumption in Late-Nineteenth Century France*, Berkeley, 1982

Wilmer, Clive, ed., *William Morris: News from Nowhere and Other Writings*, London, Penguin Books, 1993

Part III

Aav, Marianne and Stritzler-Levine, Nina, eds., *Finnish modern design: Utopian Ideals. Everyday realities, 1930–1997*, New Haven, Yale University Press (and the Bard Graduate center for Studies in the Decorative Arts), 1998

Arwas, Victor, *Art Deco*, New York, Abradale Press, 2000 (revised and expanded edition of Abrams 1980)

Banham, Reyner. *Theory and Design in the First Machine Age*, Cambridge, MIT Press, Second Edition, 1960

Bogart, Michele H., *Advertising, Artists, and the Borders of Art*, Chicago and London, University of Chicago Press, 1995

Camard, Florence. *Ruhlmann. Master of Art Deco*, translated David Macey, New York, Harry N. Abrams, 1984 (published in French 1983)

Cohen, Arthur A., *Herbert Bayer: The Complete Work*, Cambridge and London, MIT Press, 1984

Cohen, Arthur A., *Sonia Delaunay*, New York, Harry N. Abrams, 1975 (reprinted 1988)

Compton, Susan, *Russian Avant-Garde Book 1917–34*, Cambridge MA, MIT Press, 1993 (first published 1992)

DeperoFuturista: Rome-Paris-New York 1915–132 and more (exhibition held at the Wolfsonian Museum in Miami Florida, March 11–July 26, 1999), Skira, Milan, 1999

Drucker, Joanna, *The Visible Word. Experimental Typography and Modern Art, 1909–1923*, Chicago and London, University of Chicago Press, 1994

Duncan, Alastair, *Art Deco Furniture: the French designers*, New York, Thames and Hudson, 1992

Duncan, Alastair, *American Art Deco*, New York, Harry N. Abrams, 1986

Duncan, Alastair, *Art Deco*, New York and London, Thames and Hudson, 1988

Duncan, Alastair, *The Encyclopedia of Art Deco*, New York, Knickerbocker Press, 1998

Eidelberg, Martin, Brohan, Torsten, eds., *Glass of the Avant-Garde. The Torsten Brohan Collection from the Museo Nacional de Artes Decorativas, Madrid*, Munich, London, and New York, Prestel Verlag, 2001

El Lissitsky 1890–1941: architect, painter, photographer, typographer, Eindhoven, Municipal Van Abbemuseum, 1990

Ericsson, Anne-Marie et al., *The Brilliance of Swedish Glass, 1918–1939: an alliance of art and industry*, New Haven, Yale University Press for the Bard Graduate Center for Studies in the Decorative Arts, 1996

Fiell, Charlotte and Peter, eds., *20s Decorative Art: a sourcebook*, Cologne, Taschen, 2000

Fiell, Charlotte and Peter, eds., *30s and 40s Decorative Art: a sourcebook*, Cologne, Taschen, 2000

Fox, Richard Wightman, and Lears, T. J. Jackson, eds. *The Culture of Consumption: Critical Essays in American History 1880–1980*, New York, Pantheon Books, 1983

Garafola, Lynn. *Diaghilev's Ballets Russes*, New York and Oxford, Oxford University Press, 1989

Garner, Philippe, *Eileen Gray: design and architecture 1878–1976*, Köln, Benedikt Tashcen Verlag, 1993

Gronberg, Tag, *Designs on Modernity: exhibiting the city in 1920s Paris*, Manchester and New York, University of Manchester Press, 1998

Gunta Stölzl: Meisterin am Bauhaus Dessau. Textilientwürfe un freie Arbeiten 1915–1983, Dessau, Verlag Gerd Hatje, 1997

Hillier, Bevis. *Art Deco of the 20s and 30s*, London, Studio Vista, 1968

Jaffé, Hans Ludwig C., *De Stijl 1917–1931: The Dutch Contribution to Modern Art*, Cambridge, Belknap Press and Harvard University Press, 1986, first published 1956

Johnson, J. Stewart, *American Modern. 1925–1940 – Design for a New Age*, Harry N. Abrams and the American Federation of the Arts, 2000

Johnson, Philip, *Machine Art*, New York, The Museum of Modern Art and W. W. Norton & Co., 1934

Kardon, Janet, ed., *Craft in the Machine Age 1920–1945*, New York, Harry N. Abrams and the American Craft Museum, 1995

Le Corbusier, *Towards a New Architecture*, London, Architectural Press, 1974

Ling, Peter. *America and the automobile: technology, reform and social change 1893–1923*, Manchester (UK), University Press, 1990

Lodder, Christina, *Russian Constructivism*, London and New Haven, Yale University Press, 1983

Mackrell, Alice, *Paul Poiret*, New York, Holmes & Meier, 1990

Marchand, Roland, *Advertising the American Dream: Making Way for Modernity 1920–1940*, Berkeley, University of California Press, 1985

Marcilhac, Felix, *Dunand*, New York, Harry N. Abrams, 1991

McLean, Ruari, *Jan Tschichold: Typographer*, Boston, David R. Godine, 1975

Meikle, Jeffrey L. *Twentieth Century Limited: Industrial Design in America, 1925–1939*, Philadelphia, Temple University Press, 1979 (revised 2001)

Naylor, Gillian, *The Bauhaus reassessed: sources and design theory*, New York, E. P. Dutton, 1985

Overy, Paul, *De Stijl*, London, Thames and Hudson, 1991

Peto, James, and Loveday, Donna, eds. *Modern Britain*

1929–1939, (Exhibition 20 January–6 June 1999 at the Design Museum, London), London, Design Museum, 1999

Poggi, Christine, *In Defiance of Painting: Cubism, Futurism, and the Invention of Collage*, New Haven, Yale University Press, 1992

Pommer, Richard, and Otto, Christian F. *Weissenhof 1927 and the Modern Movement in Architecture*, Chicago and London, University of Chicago Press, 1991

Porter, Glenn, *Raymond Loewy: Designs for a Consumer Culture*, Wilmington DE, Hagley Museum and Library, 2002

Pozharskaya, Militsa and Volodina, Tatiana, *The Art of the Ballets Russes: The Russian Seasons in Paris 1908–1929*, New York, Abbeville Press, 1990

Smith, Terry, *Making the Modern. Industry, Art, and Design in America*, Chicago and London, University of Chicago Press, 1993

Spencer, Herbert. *Pioneers of Modern Typography*, New York, Hastings House, 1970 (first published 1969)

The Great Utopia. The Russian and Soviet Avant-Garde, 1915–1932, New York, the Guggenheim Museum, 1992

Troy, Nancy J. *Modernism and the Decorative Arts in France. Art Nouveau to Le Corbusier*, New Haven and London, Yale, 1991

Troy, Nancy, *The De Stijl Environment*, Cambridge, the MIT Press, 1983

Tschichold, Jan, *the New Typography: A Handbook for Modern Designers*, translated Ruari McLean, Berkeley and Los Angeles, University of California Press, 1995

Weltge, Sigrid Wortmann, *Women's Work. Textile Art from the Bauhaus*, San Francisco, Chronicle Books, 1993, also published by Thames and Hudson, 1993

Whitford, Frank. *Bauhaus*, London, Thames and Hudson, 1984

Wilk, Christopher, *Marcel Breuer, furniture and interiors*, New York, Metropolitan Museum of Art, 1981

Wingler, Hans M., *The Bauhaus: Weimar, Dessau, Berlin, Chicago*, translated Wolfgang Jabs and Basil Gilbert, Cambridge, MA, MIT Press, 1969

Wrede, Stuart, *The Architecture of Erik Gunnar Asplund*, Cambridge, MA, MIT Press, 1980

Part IV

Abercrombie, Stanley, *George Nelson: The Design of Modern Design*, Cambridge and London, MIT Press, 1995

Albrecht, Donald et al., *Russel Wright: creating American lifestyle*, New York, Harry N. Abrams (in conjunction with the Cooper-Hewitt National Design Museum), 2001

Allen, James Sloan. *The Romance of Commerce and Culture. Capitalism, Modernism, and the Chicago-Aspen Crusade for Cultural Reform*, Boulder, Colorado, University Press of Colorado, 2001

Austerity to Affluence: British Art and Design 1945–1962, London, Merrell Holberton, 1997

Bayley, Stephen. *Sony. An Exhibition in the boilerhouse at the Victoria and Albert Museum*, London, 1982 (The Conran Foundation)

Blake, John and Avril, *The Practical Idealists. Twenty-five years of designing for industry*, London, Lund Humphries, 1969

Caplan, Ralph, *The Design of Herman Miller*, New York, Whitney Library of Design, 1976

Dreyfuss, Henry. *The Measure of Man: Human Factors in Design*, Revised and Expanded 2nd Edition, New York, Whitney Library of Design, 1960

Erlhoff, Michael, ed., *Designed in Germany Since 1949*, Munich, Prestel-Verlag, 1990

Fiell, Charlotte and Peter, eds., *50s decorative art: a sourcebook*, Cologne, Taschen, 2000

Fleck, Glen, ed., *A Computer Perspective: by the office of Charles and Ray Eames*, Cambridge, Harvard University, 1973

Flinchum, Russell, *Henry Dreyfuss, industrial designer: the man in the brown suit*, New York, Cooper Hewitt National Design Museum and Rizzoli, 1997

Fuller, R.B. *Utopia or Oblivion: the Prospects for Humanity*, New York, Overlook Press, 1969.

Gans, Herbert, *The Levittowners: Ways of Life and Politics in a New Suburban Community*, New York, Pantheon Books, 1967

George Nakashima and the Modernist Movement, Steven Beyer, curator, Doylestown PA, James A. Michener Museum, 2001

Gerstner, Karl, *Die neue Graphic. The new graphic art. Le nouvel art graphique*, Switzerland, Arthur Niggli Ltd., 1959

Greenberg, Clement, *Art and Culture: Critical Essays*, Boston, Beacon Press, 1961

Halberstam, David, *The Fifties*, New York, Villard Books, 1993

Heskett, John, *Philips. A Study of the Corporate Management of Design*, London, Trefoil Publications, 1989

Hine, Thomas, *Populuxe*, New York, Knopf, 1986

Hofmann, Armin, *Graphic Design Manual: Principles and Practice*, New York, Reinhold, 1965

Jackson, Kenneth T., *Crabgrass Frontier. The Suburbanization of the United States*, New York and Oxford, Oxford University Press, 1985

Jackson, Lesley, *The New Look – Design of the Fifties*, New York, Thames and Hudson, 1991

Jacobs, Jane, *The Death and Life of Great American Cities*, New York, Random House, 1961

Kicherer, Sibylle, *Olivetti: a study of the corporate management of design*, New York, Rizzoli, 1990

Lapidus, Morris, *Too Much is Never Enough*, New York, Rizzoli, 1996

Larson, Jack Lenor, *Jack Lenor Larson: A Weaver's Memoir*, New York, Harry N. Abrams, 1998

Lindinger, Herbert, ed. *Ulm design: the morality of objects*, translated David Britt, Cambridge MA, MIT Press, 1991

Lonberg-Holm, K., and Sutnar, Ladislav, *Catalog design progress*, New York, Sweet's Catalog Service (Division of F. W. Dodge Corporation), 1950

Maldonado, Tomás, *Design, Nature, and Revolution. Toward a Critical Ecology*, trans. Mario Domandi. New York, Evanston, San Francisco, and London, Harper and Row, 1972 (first published, 1970)

Massey, Anne. *Modernism and mass culture in Britain 1945–1959*, Manchester and New York, Manchester University Press, 1995

Mumford, Lewis, *The City in History: Its Origins, Its Transformations, and Its Prospects*, San Diego, New York and London, Harcourt Brace Jovanovich, 1961

Neutra, Richard. *Survival Through Design*, New York, Oxford, 1954

Olins, Wally, *The Corporate Personality: An Inquiry into the Nature of Corporate Identity*, New York, Mayflower Books, 1978

Packard, V., *The Hidden Persuaders*, Harmondsworth, New York, David McKay, 1957

Rand, Paul, *Thoughts on Design*, New York, Reinhold, 1970 (first published 1947)

Reed, Peter, *Alvar Aalto. Between Humanism and Materialism*, New York, The Museum of Modern Art, 1998

Riesman, David, with Nathan Glazer and Reuel Denney, *The Lonely Crowd: A Study of the Changing American Character*, New Haven and London, Yale University Press, 2001, first abridged edition 1961, first published 1950

Rouland, Steven and Linda, *Knoll Furniture 1938–1960*, Atglen PA, Schiffer Publishing, 1999

Scotford, Martha, *Cipe Pineles: A Life of Design*, New York, W. W. Norton & Company, 1999

Sparke, Penny, ed. *Reyner Banham: Design by Choice*, London, Academy Editions, 1981

The Work of Charles and Ray Eames: A Legacy of Invention, New York, Harry N. Abrams, 1997

Wichmann, Hans, ed. *Armin Hofmann: His Work, Quest and Philosophy*, trans. D. Q. Stephenson, Basel and Boston, Birkhäuser Verlag, 1989

Wolfe, Tom, *The kandy-colored tangerine flake streamline baby*, New York, Bantam Books, 1999 (published earlier by Farrar, Strauss, & Giroux, 1965)

Part V

Ambasz, Emilio, *Italy: The New Domestic Landscape. Achievements and Problems of Italian Design*, New York, The Museum of Modern Art, New York, in Collaboration with Centro Di, Florence, 1972

Ash, Juliet, and Wilson, Elizabeth, eds. *Chic Thrills. A Fashion Reader*, Berkeley and Los Angeles, University of California Press, 1993

Bell, Daniel, *The Coming of Post-Industrial Society: An Adventure in Social Forecasting*, New York, Basic Books, 1999 (first published 1973)

Brand, Stewart, *The Media Lab: Inventing the future at MIT*, New York, Viking, 1987

Brownlee, David, DeLong, David G., and Hiesinger, Kathryn B., *Out of the Ordinary. Robert Venturi, Denise Scott Brown and Associates. Architecture, Urbanism, Design*, Philadelphia, Philadelphia Museum of Art, 2001

Collins, Michael, and Papadakis, Andreas, *Post-Modern Design*, New York, Rizzoli, 1989

Crow, Thomas, "Modernism and Mass Culture in the Visual Arts", Buchloh, H. D., Guilbaut, Serge, and Solkin, David, eds., *Modernism and Modernity: the Vancouver conference papers*, Halifax, N. S., The Press of the Nova Scotia College of Art and Design, 1983, 215–264

Crow, Thomas. *The Rise of the Sixties: American and European Art in the Era of Dissent*, New York, Harry N. Abrams, 1996

De la Haye, Amy, and Wilson, Elizabeth, eds. *Defining Dress. Dress as object, meaning, and identity*, Manchester, Manchester University Press, 1999

Docker, John, *Postmodernism and Popular Culture. A Cultural History*, Cambridge, Cambridge University Press, 1994

Dormer, Peter, ed., *The culture of craft: status and future*, Manchester and New York, Manchester University Press and St. Martin's Press, 1997

Fiell, Charlotte and Peter, eds., *Designing the 21st century = Design des 21: Jahrhunderts = Le design du 21e siècle*, Cologne, Taschen, 2001

Fiell, Charlotte and Peter, eds., *60s decorative art: a sourcebook*, Cologne, Taschen, 2000

Fiell, Charlotte and Peter, eds., *70s decorative art: a sourcebook*, Cologne, Taschen, 2000

Fischer, Volker, ed., *Design Now: Industry or Art?*, Munich, Prestel Verlag, 1989

Garner, Philippe, *Sixties Design*, Cologne, Taschen, 1996

Greiman, April, *Hybrid Imagery. The fusion of technology and graphic design*, New York, Watson Guptill, 1990

Harper, Laurel, *Radical Graphics Radicals*, San Francisco, Chronicle Books, 1999

Höger, Hans, *Ettore Sottsass, jun. Designer. Artist. Architect*, Tubingen and Berlin, Wasmuth, 1993

Hughes, Robert, *Culture of Complaint: The Fraying of America*, Oxford, Oxford University Press, 1993

Huyssen, Andreas. *After the Great Divide: Modernism, Mass Culture, Postmodernism*, Bloomington, 1985

Jackson, Lesley, *Robin and Lucienne Day: pioneers of modern design*, New York, Princeton, Architectural Press, 2001

Jackson, Lesley, *The Sixties: decade of design revolution*, London, Phaidon, 1998

Jameson, Frederic, *Postmodernism, or the cultural logic of late capitalism*, Durham NC, Duke University Press, 1991

Julier, Guy, *The Culture of Design*, London, Sage Publications, 2000

Kaplan, E. Ann, ed., *Postmodernism and its Discontents. Theories, Practices*, London and New York, Verso, 1988

Lupton, Ellen, *Skin: Surface, substance, and design*, New York, Princeton Architectural Press, 2002

Marwick, Arthur, *The Sixties: cultural revolution in Britain, France, Italy, and the United States c. 1958 – c. 1974*, Oxford and New York, Oxford University Press, 1998

Miller, Daniel. *Material Culture and Mass Consumption*, Oxford, Blackwell, 1987

Nader, Ralph, *Unsafe at any speed: the designed-in dangers of the American automobile*, New York, Grossman, 1965

Palmer, Jerry, and Dodson, Mo, *Design and Aesthetics: A Reader*, London, Routledge, 1996

Papanek, Victor. *Design for the Real World: Making to Measure*, London, Thames and Hudson, 1972

Polhemus, Ted, *Streetstyle: from sidewalk to catwalk*, London, Thames and Hudson, 1994

Popalski, Peter, *The R. Crumb coffee table art book*, Boston, Little Brown, 1997

Porritt, Jonathon, *Seeing Green: the politics of ecology explained*, Oxford and New York, B. Blackwell, 1985 (c.1984)

Poynor, Rick, and Booth-Clibborn, Edward, eds., *Typography Now: the next wave*, London, Internos Books, 1991

Radice, Dorothy. *Memphis: Research, Experiences, Results, Failures and Successes of New Design*, New York, Rizzoli, 1984

Snyder, Gertrude, and Peckolik, Alan, *Herb Lubalin: Art Director, Graphic Designer and Typographer*, New York, American Showcase, Inc., 1985

Thackara, John, ed. *Design After Modernism: Beyond the Object*, New York, Thames and Hudson, 1988

VanderLans, Rudy, Licko, Zuzana with Gray, Mary E., *Émigré (The Book): Graphic Design into the Digital Realm*, New York, Van Nostrand Reinhold, 1993

Venturi, Robert, Brown, Denise Scott, and Izenour, Steven, *Learning from Las Vegas*, Cambridge, MA and London, MIT Press, revised edition 1998 (first published 1972)

Venturi, Robert, *Complexity and Contradiction in Architecture*, New York, The Museum of Modern Art, 1977 (first published 1966)

von Vegesack , Alexander and Remmele, Mathias, eds., *Vernor Panton: the collected works*, Weil am Rhein, Vitra Design Museum, 2000

Whiteley, Nigel, *Pop Design: Modernism to Mod*, London, The Design Council, 1987

Whitely, Nigel, *Design for Society*, London, Reaktion Books, 1993

Wozencroft, Jon, *The Graphic Language of Neville Brody*, New York, Rizzoli, 1988

Suggestions for Further Reading

The following sources have been useful in compiling material for the *History of Modern Design*, and provide a starting point for further investigation of topics treated in the text. Students may also browse the selected bibliography beginning on page 387.

For primary source material, see Greenhalgh, *Quotations and Sources on Design and the Decorative Arts* (1993), Benton and Benton, eds. *Architecture and Design 1890–1939: An International Anthology of Original Articles* (1975), and Frank, *The Theory of Decorative Art. An Anthology of European and American Writings 1750–1940* (2000). Design dictionaries with useful entries include Honour and Fleming, *Penguin Dictionary of Decorative Arts* (revised edition 1989), Byars, *The Design Encyclopedia* (1994) and Julier, *The Encyclopedia of Twentieth-Century Design and Designers* (1993).

Definitions and approaches to the study of modern design appear in a number of recent studies, including Heskett, *Industrial Design* (1980), Sparke, *Introduction to Design and Culture in the Twentieth Century* (1986), Forty, *Objects of Desire: Design and Society since 1750* (1986), and Woodham, *Twentieth Century Design* (1997). See also Buchanan's review in *Journal of Design History*, Vol. 11, no. 3, 1998, 259–263).

Introduction and Part I: Demand, Supply, and Design, 1700–1850

For State-owned manufactures see Heskett, *Industrial Design* (1980), while the role of guilds, specialization, and the typology of furniture in the eighteenth century appear in Lucie-Smith, *The Story of Craft: The Craftsman, Role in Society* (1981). On the Gobelins manufactory within the context of the history of tapestry in Europe, see Weigert, *French Tapestry* (1962). The illustrations from Diderot, *Encyclopedia* have been published in facsimile as *Diderot encyclopedia: the complete illustrations 1762–1777* (1978). On the marchand merciers see Sargentson, *Merchants and Luxury Markets. The Marchands Merciers of Eighteenth-Century Paris* (1996). For materials and techniques see Trench, *Materials and Techniques in the Decorative Arts. An Illustrated Dictionary* (2000). On the Sèvres manufactory, see Eriksen and G de Bellaigue, *Vincennes and Sèvres 1740–1800* (1987), and on Ébénistes, see Pradère, *French Furniture Makers: The Art of the Ébéniste from Louis XIV to the Revolution* (1989). For revolutionary and post-revolutionary furniture, the best source is Ledoux-Lebard, *Les Ébénistes du XIXe Siecle 1795–1889* (1965).

Meggs' *History of Graphic Design* (1983, 1992) remains a solid and well-illustrated survey of its subject. Updike, *Printing Types. Their History, Forms, and Use* (1962, first pub. 1927) still provides useful analyses of individual printers, typefaces, and a wealth of examples for further study.

For England, see McKendrick, Brewer and Plumb, *The Birth of a Consumer Society: The Commercialization of Eighteenth-Century England* (1985). Students will also benefit from Forty, *Objects of Desire: Design and Society Since 1750* (1986), with case studies on the interrelation of marketing, design, and production.

For Chippendale, see his *Gentlemen and Cabinet Maker's Director* (1966) as well as Gilbert, *The Life and Work of Thomas Chippendale* (two volumes, 1978). The furniture and interiors of Robert Adam are the subject of Harris, *Furniture of Robert Adam* (1963) and *The Genius of Robert Adam: his interiors* (2001). For pre-revolutionary fashion, see Ribeiro, *Dress in Eighteenth-Century Europe 1715–1789* (1985).

For the United States, Hounshell, *From the American System to Mass Production 1800–1932: the development of manufacturing technology in the United States* (1984) is indispensable for an understanding of the methods and circumstances of manufacturing. Heskett (1980) also devotes a chapter to "The 'American system' and mass-production".

For the history of printing technology see Twyman, *An illustrated history of its development and uses in England* (1970), while the standard work on Victorian typography remains Gray, *Nineteenth Century Ornamented Typefaces* (1976, first published 1938). A good source for fashion plates is Holland, *Hand-Colored Fashion Plates 1770-1899* (1955), and for wallpaper see Greysmith, *Wallpaper* (1976).

For the career and oeuvre of Augustus Pugin see *Pugin: a Gothic Passion* (1994) (containing the essay by Belcher referred to in the text), and *A. W. N. Pugin: Master of Gothic revival* (1995). The general topic of Gothic Revival is now treated by Lewis, *The Gothic Revival*, (2002). For popular images and reform is Anderson, *The Printed Image and the Transformation of Popular Culture 1790–1860* (1991). I'm not aware of a monographic study devoted to Sir Henry Cole, but the Great Exhibition of 1851 is the subject of Richards' *The Commodity Culture of Victorian England: advertising and spectacle* (1991). Also the *Crystal Palace Exhibition Illustrated catalogue* has been issued as a reprint (1970), as has Owen Jones, *The Grammar of Ornament* (1966). Examples of Richard Redgrave's paintings form part of the Sheepshank collection in the Cole Wing of the Victoria & Albert Museum, and the collection and its relation to reform are discussed in an excellent study by Macleod, *Art and the Victorian middle class: Money and the making of Cultural Identity* (1996) For Charles Dickens's *Hard Times* in relation to design reform see Gombrich, *sense of Order. A Study of the Psychology Decorative Art* (1979). *A Study of the Psychology of Decorative Art* (1979). On illustration and book printing, including the activities of Henry Cole as a publisher of children's literature, see McLean, *Victorian Book Design* (1963), while once again Twyman (1970) or Meggs (1992) are reliable for the development of chromolithography.

The two standard books on his oeuvre and career are Keller, *The Art and Politics of Thomas Nast* (1968) and Paine, *Thomas Nast, his period and his pictures* (1904). For Louis Prang see Freeman, *Louis Prang: Color Lithographer. Giant of a Man* (1971) and Marzio *Chromolithography 1840-1900. The Democratic Art. Pictures for a 19th-Century America* (1979).

Braudel, *Civilization and Capital 15th– 18th Centuries* (1979), quoted in the conclusion to Part I, is a lengthy three-volume study, but vol. 2 (*The Wheels of Commerce*) provides insights for the emerging commercial and social circumstances in which the activity of design takes place in Europe through the eighteenth century.

Part II: Arts, Crafts, and Machines (1850–1914)

For Christopher Dresser, see Durant, *Christopher Dresser* (1993) and Halén, *Christopher Dresser* (1990). Also two of Dresser's own studies have also been reprinted, *Principles of Victorian Decorative Design* (1995) and *Traditional Arts and Crafts of Japan* (1994). For the Aesthetic Movement in Britain, see Gere and Whiteway, *Nineteenth Century Design from Pugin to Mackintosh* (1994) and Gere, *The House Beautiful: Oscar Wilde and the Aesthetic Interior* (2000). The most recent and comprehensive study for the centers of the Aesthetic Movement and Art Nouveau is Greenhalgh, ed., *Art Nouveau 1890–1914* (2000).

For Godwin, see Soros, ed., *E. W. Godwin. Aesthetic Movement Architect and Designer* (1999). For Japanese influence see Wichmann, *Japonisme. Japanese influence on Western art since 1858* (1981) and sections of Gombrich (1979) and Gere (2000).

For Lafarge and Tiffany see Burke, *In Pursuit of Beauty. Americans and the Aesthetic Movement* (1986). For Herter Brothers, see Howe, *Herter Brothers: furniture and interiors for a gilded age* (1994). The political, economic, and social context for women's domestic roles against the background of the rise of industrial capitalism is the subject of Hayden, *The Grand Domestic Revolution: A History of Feminist Design for American Homes, Neighborhood, and Cities* (1981). For women in the decorative arts see Kirkham (ed.), *Women Designers in the USA, 1900–2000: Diversity and Difference* (2000).

On Charles Frederick Worth, see Saunders, *The age of Worth: couturier to the Empress Eugénie* (1955) and de Marly, *Worth: Father of haute couture* (1990). For the department store see Miller, *The Bon Marché: Bourgeois Culture and the Department Store, 1869–1920* (1981).

On the origins, politics, and social interpretation of Art Nouveau in France, see Silverman, *Art Nouveau in Fin-de-Siècle France: Politics Psychology, and Style* (1989). For general surveys that include France see Fahr-Becker, *Art Nouveau* (1997), Escritt, *Art nouveau* (2000), and Greenhalgh, (ed.) *Art Nouveau 1890–1914* (2000) mentioned above.

Posters are treated in Greenhalgh (ed.) *Art Nouveau 1890–1914* (2000). For Jules Cheret see Broido, *The Posters of Jules Cheret: 46 full-color plates and an illustrated catalogue raisonné* (1980). On Toulouse-Lautrec, see Denvir, *Toulouse-Lautrec* (1991), and for Alphonse Mucha, see Arwas et al., *Alphonse Mucha. The Spirit of Art Nouveau* (1998). On the career of Will Bradley see Meggs (1992) Fahr-Becker (1997), and Hornung, *Will Bradley: His Graphic Art, A Collection of his Posters, Illustrations, Typographic Designs & Decorations* (1974).

On Charles Rennie Mackintosh, see Kaplan, ed., *Charles Rennie Mackintosh* (1996). For Austria and the Wiener Werkstätte see Schweiger, *Wiener Werkstätte, Design in Vienna 1903–1932* (1984). The career of Henry van de Velde is the subject of Sembach, *Henry van de Velde* (1989). For Jugendstil in Munich the standard treatment is Hiesinger (ed.), *Art Nouveau in Munich: Masters of Jugendstil from the Stadtmuseum, Munich and other Public and Private Collections* (1988).

Sections on Art Nouveau in Scandinavia and Italy also are contained in the Art Nouveau surveys. Art Nouveau ceramics in Hungary are the subject of Csenkey and Steinert (eds.), *Hungarian Ceramics from the Zsolnay Manufactory 1853–2001* (2002), while glass from Eastern Europe in the early twentieth century is the focus of Eidelberg and Brohan, *Glass of the Avant-Garde. The Torsten Brohan Collection from the Museo Nacional de Artes Decorativas* (2001).

For the Arts and Crafts Movement in England, see Naylor, *The Arts and Crafts Movement* (1980) and Anscombe and Gere, *Arts and Crafts in Britain and America* (1978). See also Kaplan, *The Art That is Life: The Arts and Crafts Movement in America, 1875-1920* (1987), Kardon (ed.), *The Ideal Home 1900-1920* (1993) and Parry (ed.), *William Morris* (1996). A number of Gustav Stickley publications are reprinted by Dover Publications (for example, *The Illustrated Mission Furniture Catalog 1912–13*, Linoff, ed, 1991), while Elbert Hubbard's Roycroft community is the subject of Via and Searl (eds.), *Head, Heart and Hand: Elbert Hubbard and the Roycrofters* (1994). For Henry Chapman Mercer see Reed, *Henry Chapman Mercer and the Moravian Pottery and Tile Works* (1996). William Morris's Kelmscott printing venture is the subject of Peterson, *The Kelmscott Press. A History of William Morris, Typographical Adventure* (1991), while other contributors to the Private Press movement are treated by Updike (*Printing Types*, volume 2, first published 1927), Twyman (1970), Franklin, *The Private Presses* (1969), Cave, *The Private Presses* (1983), and Lawson, *Anatomy of a Typeface* (1990). For printing technology (monotype, linotype, half-tone) see Meggs (1992) and Twyman (1970). For Randolph Caldecott and Kate Greenaway, see. Engen, *Randolph Caldecott. Lord of the Nursery* (1976), and *Kate Greenaway* (1976).

Frank Lloyd Wright's contributions to design are discussed by Heskett (1980) as well as in Crawford, *C.R. Ashbee. Architect, Designer, and Romantic Socialist* (1985). For Wright interiors, see. Heinz, *Frank Lloyd Wright Interiors and Furniture* (1994). Again, Greenhalgh (ed.) *Art Nouveau* (2000) offers a section devoted to Chicago that includes Wright but also mentions a wider range of Chicago designers. Mechanized production in the automobile industry is treated by Ling in *America and the Automobile: technology, reform and social change 1893-1923* (1990), Hounshell (1984, and Smith, *Making the Modern: Industry, Art, and Design in America* (1993). Frederick W. Taylor and scientific management has been the subject of several studies, most recently Kanigel, *One Best Way: Frederick Winslow Taylor and the enigma of efficiency* (1997). See also Taylor's own *Principles of Scientific Management* (1911). Other works on industrial capitalism include Nye, *Image Worlds: Corporate Identities at General Electric, 1890–1930* (1985).

For Germany a good source is Heskett, *German Design 1870–1918* (1986), as well as Buddensieg, *Industriekultur: Peter Behrens and the AEG, 1907–1914* (1984, first published 1979). The history of the German Werkbund is treated by Campbell, *The German Werkbund. The Politics of Reform in the Applied Arts* (1978) and more recently by Schwartz, *The Werkbund: Design Theory and Mass Culture before the First World War* (1996).

Part III: After the Great War (1918–1944): Art, Industry, and Utopias

Tuchman, *The Guns of August* (1962) provides an introduction to the events precipitating the First World War and the disparity between ideology, rhetoric, and the realities of warfare in the new century. More comprehensive is Fussell, *The Great War and Modern Memory* (1975). The reactions of avant-garde artists to World War I are the subject of a chapter in Hughes, *The Shock of the New* (1982) and in a more recent study by Silver, *Esprit de Corps: the art of the Parisian avant-garde and the First World War, 1914–1925* (1989). Silverman, *Reconstructing Europe After the Great War* (1982), presents an economic view of the aftermath of World War I.

On Paris and Art Moderne, see foremost Troy, *Modernism and the Decorative Arts in France. Art Nouveau to Le Corbusier* (1991). The standard introduction to Art Moderne (Deco) is Hillier, *Art Deco of the 20s and 30s* (1968) and since its publication many well-illustrated and handsomely-produced coffee-table-style books on Art Moderne have also appeared, such as Arwas, *Art Deco* (1980 and rev. 2000). A brief but informative guide to the style is Duncan, *Art Deco* (1988) in paperback.

On the Ballets Russes see Garafola, *Diaghilev, Ballets Russes* (1989), as well as Pozharskaya and Volodina, *The Art of the Ballets Russes: The Russian Seasons in Paris 1908-1929* (1990). Matisse's "Notes of a Painter" is translated and discussed in Benjamin, *Matisse, "Notes of a painter": criticism, theory, and context, 1891–1908* (1987), while the relation of Cubism to popular newspapers and other mass-manufactured commodities is explored, albeit briefly, in Crow, "Modernism and Mass Culture in the Visual Arts", in *Modernism and Modernity: the Vancouver conference papers* (1983). More recently Poggi, *In Defiance of Panting: Cubism. Futurism, and the Invention of Collage* (1992) treats this subject in greater detail. Poiret's patronage of modern art and the reception of the style after the outbreak of World War I is explored in Silver, *Esprit de Corps: the art of the Parisian avant-garde and the First World War, 1914–1925* (1989). The work of A. M. Cassandre is illustrated in Mouron, *A. M. Cassandre* (1985).

For the 1925 Paris Exposition, see Brunhammer and Tise, *The decorative arts in France, 1900–1942: la Société des artistes décorateurs* (1990), Troy (1991) and Gronberg, *Designs on Modernity: exhibiting the city in 1920s Paris* (1998). For Le Corbusier, see also Troy (1991).

For the decorative arts in Futurism, see Hulten, *Futurismo & Futurismi = Futurism & Futurisms* (1986). On avant-garde typography see Drucker, *The Visible Word. Experimental Typography and Modern Art, 1909-1923* (1994). For Sonia (Terk) Delaunay, see Cohen, *Sonia Delaunay* (1975, 1988).

For the U. A. M. see Barré-Despond, *Union des artistes modernes* (1986). Eileen Gray is the subject of Garner, *Eileen Gray: design and architecture 1878–1976* (1993). The fundamental reassessment of the modern movement and the 'first machine age' is Banham, *Theory and Design in the First Machine Age* (1960). For de Stijl, see Overy, *De Stijl* (1991) as well as Troy, *The De Stijl Environment* (1983), and Jaffé, *De Stijl 1917–1931: The Dutch Contribution to Modern Art* (1986, first published 1956). On Weissenhof, the standard survey is Pommer and Otto, *Weissenhof 1927 and the Modern Movement in Architecture* (1991).

For Constructivism see Lodder, *Russian Constructivism* (1983) and *The Great Utopia. The Russian and Soviet Avant-Garde, 1915-1932* (1992). For graphic design see Compton, *Russian Avant-Garde Books 1917-34* (1993). For Rodchenko see Kahn-Magomedov, *Rodchenko. the Complete Work* (1986) and for El Lissitsky, see *El Lissitsky 1890–1941. architect, painter, photographer, typographer* (1990).

For an overview of the Bauhaus, see Whitford, *Bauhaus* (1984). The early years are covered in Franciscono, *Walter Gropius and the Creation of the Bauhaus: the ideals and artistic theories of its founding years* (1971), while Naylor offers an assessment of shifting and competing ideologies at the school in *The Bauhaus reassessed: sources and design theory* (1985). A good source for documents and illustrations is Wingler, *The Bauhaus: Weimar, Dessau, Berlin, Chicago* (1969), while the history of the textile workshop is the subject of Weltge, *Women, Work. Textile Art from the Bauhaus* (1993).

For German graphic design not directly related to the Bauhaus, see Aynsley, *Graphic Design in Germany 1890–1945* (2000). For Jan Tschichold see McLean, *Jan Tschichold: Typographer* (1975), and Tschichold's own *The New Typography: A Handbook for Modern Designers* (1995). Also useful is Spencer, *Pioneers of modern typography* (1970). On the Frankfurt Kitchen see Heskett (1980) and Woodham, *Twentieth Century Design* (1997).

For British design in the interwar period, see Peto and Loveday, eds., *Modern Britain 1929–1939* (1999). Typography is treated by Twyman (1970) and Frank Pick is the subject of a chapter in Forty (1986) and an article by Pevsner, *Studies in Art, Architecture and Design. Victorian and After* (1968). For Scandinavia, see Beer, *Scandinavian Design* (1971) and McFadden, (ed.) *Scandinavian Modern Design 1880–1980* (1982). For Alvar Aalto, see Reed, *Alvar Aalto: Between Humanism and Materialism* (1998).

For American design in the interwar period, see Duncan, *American Art Deco* (1986), Kardon (ed.), *Craft in the Machine Age 1920-1945* (1995), Johnson, *American Modern. 1925–1940 – Design for a New Age* (2000), and Meikle's illuminating, *Twentieth Century Limited: Industrial Design in America, 1925–1939* (1979, 2001). On graphic design see Remington and Hodik, *Nine Pioneers in American Graphic Design* (1989), and on advertising and illustration, Bogart, *Advertising, Artists, and the Borders of Art* (1995), Marchand, *Advertising the American Dream: Making Way for Modernity 1920–1940* (1985) and Fox and Lears, eds., *The Culture of Consumption: Critical Essays in American History 1880–1980* (1983). Industrial technology, labor, art, advertising, public relations, and corporate strategies are combined in a study by Smith (1993). The history of the Herman Miller Corporation is the subject of Caplan, *The Design of Herman Miller* (1976), and an introduction and several entries on austerity in design during World War II are found in Hiesinger and Marcus, *Landmarks of Twentieth Century Design. An Illustrated Handbook* (1993).

Part IV: Humanism and Luxury: International Modernism and Mass Culture after World War II

On "good design" see Hiesinger and Marcus, *Design Since 1945* (1983) and by the same authors' *Landmarks of Twentieth*

Century Design: An Illustrated Handbook (1993). Also helpful are Dormer, *Design Since 1945* (1993), Eidelberg, *Design 1935–1965: What Modern Was: Selections from the Liliane and David M. Stewart Collection* (1991), Bayley, *In Good Shape: Style in Industrial Products. 1900–1960* (1979), and the same author and others, *Twentieth Century Style & Design* (1986). On individual designers and manufacturers see Flinchum, *Henry Dreyfuss, industrial designer: the man in the brown suit* (1997), *The Work of Charles and Ray Eames: A Legacy of Invention* (1997), Albrecht, *Russel Wright: creating American lifestyle* (2001), Caplan, *The Design of Herman Miller* (1976), Rouland, *Knoll Furniture 1938-1960,* (1999), Heskett, *A Study of the Corporate Management of Design* (1989), Bayley, *Sony. An Exhibition in the boilerhouse at the Victoria & Albert Museum* (1982), and Abercrombie, *George Nelson: The Design of Modern Design* (1995).

For graphic design, including scientific illustration in this era, see Remington and Hodik (1989) and relevant pages in Meggs (1992). Also useful is Rand, *Thoughts on Design* (1970, first published 1947), and a recent study of Cipe Pineles (*Cipe Pineles: A Life of Design*) by Scotford (1999). The promotion of modern design is treated in, *The Romance of Commerce and Culture. Capitalism, Modernism, and the Chicago-Aspen Crusade for Cultural Reform* (2001).

For Scandinavian design see Hiesinger and Marcus (1982 and 1993), Beer, *Scandinavian Design* (1971) McFadden, *Scandinavian Modern Design 1880–1980* (1980), and Reed, *Alvar Aalto. Between Humanism and Materialism,* 1998*).* For Britain, see *Austerity to Affluence: British Art & Design 1945–1962* (1997) and Massey, *Modernism and mass culture in Britain 1945–1959* (1995). For Italy see Sparke, *Design in Italy: 1870 to the Present* (1988). For Germany see Erloff, ed., *Designed in Germany Since 1949* (1990). On the design school at Ulm, see Woodham (1997) and Lindinger, *Ulm design: the morality of objects* (1991). For the views of Tomás Maldonado see his *Design, Nature, and Revolution. Toward a Critical Ecology* (1970).

On the International Typographic Style, see Meggs (1992) as well as Wichmann (ed.), *Armin Hofmann: His Work, Quest and Philosophy* (1989) and books and manuals by the practitioners themselves, e.g. Armin Hofmann, *Graphic Design Manual: Principles and Practice* (1965), Karl Gerstner, *The New Graphic Art. Le nouvel art graphique* (1959), and Josef Muller-Brockmann, *A History of Visual Communications. From the Dawn of Barter in the Ancient World to the Visualized Conception of Today* (1971). While graphic design comprises only a very small part of the literature on semiotics, students may consult the introduction and conclusion in Drucker (1994), and the article by Gui Bonsiepe reprinted in Beirut, Helfand et al. (eds.), *Looking Closer 3: Classic Writings on Graphic Design* (1999). For Buckminster Fuller, see his *Utopia or Oblivion: the Prospects for Humanity* (1969) and for Richard Neutra, see his *Survival Through Design* (1954). For postwar Japan see Hiesinger and Fischer, *Japanese Design: A Survey Since 1950* (1994), and for Nakashima, see *George Nakashima and the Modernist Movement* (2001).

Design and corporate policy are the subject of Olins, *The Corporate Personality: An Inquiry into the Nature of Corporate Identity* (1978) and Blake, *The Practical Idealists. Twenty-five years of designing for industry* (1969). See also Dormer, *Design Since 1945* (1993) and Woodham (1997) with additional bibliography. Studies of design for individual corporations (Sony, Phililps, Herman Miller) are cited above, and articles by Eliot Noyes and others in the journal *Industrial Design*.

For mass culture in the post war era, see Halberstam, *The Fifties* (1993), and Riesman, *The Lonely Crowd: A Study of the Changing American Character* (first published 1950), See also Hine, *Populuxe* (1986), and articles by Reyner Banham, in Sparke, *Reyner Banham: Design by Choice* (1981). Banham's significance as a critic is summarized by Sparke (1986) and analyzed more recently by Whitely, *Reyner Banham: Historian of the Immediate Future* (2002). Also useful are Bigsby, ed., *Superculture. American Popular Culture and Europe* (1975) and Docker, *Postmodernism and Popular Culture. A Cultural History* (1994). Invectives against mass culture include Vance Packard, *The Hidden Persuaders* (1957), while the criticism of mass art and design is carefully presented by Nöel Carroll, *A Philosophy of Mass Art*, (1998). On postwar housing see Jackson, *Crabgrass Frontier: The Suburbanization of the United States* (1985), and for Harley Earl see Bayley, *Harley Earl* (1990). For the role of aluminum in the post-war era, see Nichols (et al.), *Aluminum by Design* (2000), and for plastic see Fenichell, *Plastic: the making of a synthetic century* (1997) and Meikle, *American Plastic: a cultural history* (1995).

On Morris Lapidus, see the architect's autobiography, *Too Much is Never Enough*, New York, Rizzoli, 1996. For fashion design see de la Haye and Wilson (eds.), *Defining Dress. Dress as object, meaning, and identity* (1999) and Ash and Wilson (eds.) *Chic Thrills: A Fashion Reader* (1993). Fashion designers are listed in a number of encyclopedias and surveys including Martin, *Fashion Encyclopedia: A Survey of Style from 1945 to the Present* (1996) and *The Fashion Book* (1998).

Part V: Progress, Protest, and Pluralism: 1960-2000

Hiesinger and Marcus (1983) remains a reliable source for "good design" in the nineteen-sixties and nineteen-seventies. Dormer (1993) and Hiesinger and Fischer (1994) also provide an overview, along with Garner, *Sixties Design* (1996) and Jackson, *The Sixties: decade of design revolution* (1998), all illustrating a variety of materials and processes. Studies of manufacturers Herman Miller (Caplan, 1976) and Knoll (1981) also provide examples of technologically and aesthetically-oriented furniture design. For plastics in Italy, see Sparke (1988) and Fenichell (1997) cited above. See also Miller, *Modern Design 1890-1990 in the Metropolitan Museum of Art* (1990), and for aluminum sports equipment and other products of the nineteen sixties and beyond, see Nichols (2000).

For graphic design see Meggs (1992) and Erlhoff (1990). On individual graphic designers see *Vignelli – Design* (1981), Snyder and Peckolik, *Herb Lubalin: Art Director, Graphic Designer and Typographer* (1985), and *Milton Glaser – Graphic Design* (1983). On craft see the examples illustrated in Hiesinger and Marcus (1983), and Coatts (ed.), *Pioneers of Modern Craft* (1997)

The literature on ergonomics and anthropometrics is extensive and often specialized, of interest both to historians as well as practitioners. See, for instance, Henry Dreyfuss, *The Measure of Man: Human Factors in Design* (revised edition 1960), as well as in an excellent study of design for the bathroom involving a variety of research considerations in Kira, *The Bathroom* (1976). Students might also consult essays on the practice of design from a number of different perspectives in Buchanan and Margolin, eds., *Design: explorations in design studies* (1995).

The critical appreciation of design for mass culture is found in Venturi, Brown, and Izenour, *Leaving Las Vegas* (1998, first published 1972) and is considered as well in Docker (1994).

On the theme of protest through art see Crow, *The Rise of the Sixties: American and European Art in the Era of Dissent* (1996), while a broad social and political study of the decade is Marwick, *The Sixties: cultural revolution in Britain, France, Italy, and the United States c. 1958 – c. 1974* (1998). For oppositional tendencies in Italian design in the 1960s see Sparke (1988) and Ambasz, *Italy: The New Domestic Landscape. Achievements and Problems of Italian Design* (1972).

On Ralph Nader see his *Unsafe at any speed: the designed-in dangers of the American automobile* (1965) as well as Whiteside, *The Investigation of Ralph Nader. General Motors vs. One Determined Man* (1972). Papanek, *Design for the Real World: Making to Measure* (1972) remains worthwhile reading, and Papanek's views are also the starting point for Whiteley, *Design for Society* (1993).

The broad issues of Pluralism, Late Capitalism, and Post-industrialism that form the basis for the presentation of Postmodernism in this book are treated in numerous studies in a variety of disciplines that include but are not limited to art and design history. The consumer underpinnings of Postmodern design are characterized clearly by Whitely (1993). Consumption is the subject of Douglas and Isherwood, *The World of Goods: Towards and Anthropology of Consumption* (1979, 1996), Miller, *Material Culture and Mass Consumption* (1987), and Appadurai ed., *The social life of things. Commodities in cultural perspective* (1986). The wider meanings of consumption also form the basis of studies by the French scholars Baudrillard, *The System of Objects* (1968, 1996) and Barthes, *Mythologies* (1957, 1972). On Post-industrialism see Bell, *The Coming of Post-Industrial Society: An Adventure in Social Forecasting* (1999, first published 1973).

For an introduction to postmodernism see Jameson, *Postmodernism, or the cultural logic of late capitalism* (1991). For Postmodern perspectives on design see Thackara (ed.), *Design After Modernism: Beyond the Object* (1988), and Margolin (ed.), *Design Discourse. History-Theory-Criticism* (1989) and by the same author in collaboration with Buchanan, *The Idea of Design: A Design Issues Reader* (1995). Recent materials technology in relation to products is the focus of Lupton, *Skin: Surface, substance, and design* (2002), and the essay on "outgrown" fashions referred to in the text by Lee Wright appears in Ash and Wilson (eds., 1993). For other more product-oriented surveys of postmodern design, see B.Radice, *Memphis: Research, Experiences, Results, Failures and Successes of New Design* (1984), Collins and Papadakis, *Post-Modern Design* (1989), and Fischer (ed.), *Design Now: Industry or Art?* (1989). A recent glimpse into design in the new millennium, focusing upon furniture and high-tech gadgets, is provided by Fiell, *Designing the 21st century = Design des 21: Jahrhunderts = Le design du 21e siècle* (2001).

On graphic design in relation to the "Punk" scene, see Wozencroft, *The Graphic Language of Neville Brody* (1988). On Robert Crumb see Popalski, *The R. Crumb coffee table art book* (1997) and on comics more generally Sabin, *Comics, commix & graphic novels* (2001, first published 1996). For social and environmental responsibility in design see Whiteley (1993) and Porritt, *Seeing Green: the politics of ecology explained* (1985). For graphic design in the computer age, see VanderLans et al., *Emigre (The Book): Graphic Design into the Digital Realm* (1993) and Poynor and Booth-Clibborn, eds., *Typography now: the next wave*, (1994, first published 1991). Landmarks in the history of the graphic design profession are documented in bullet-point fashion by Heller and Pettit, *Graphic Design Timeline: A Century of Design Milestones* (2000).

Sources for Quotations: **PART I** Josiah Wedgwood, (Papers E25-18167, nd, probably September 15, 1767), in Robin Reilly, Josiah Wedgwood 1730-1795, London, Macmillan, 1992, 42; Jane Austen, *Mansfield Park*, ed James Kinsley, Oxford, University Press, 1998, 384; Adam Smith, *An Inquiry into the Nature and Causes of the Wealth of Nations*, Laurence Dickey, ed., Indianapolis and Cambridge, Hackett Publishing Company, 1993, 4; Thomas Carlyle, Past and Present, ed Richard B. Attick, New York, New York University Press, 1998, 7. Reprinted with permission of New York University Press; A. Welby Pugin, *The True Principles of Pointed or Christian Architecture*, reprint of 1st edition (1841), London, Academy Editions/New York, St. Martin's Press, 1973, 1; Charles Dickens, Hard Times, 2nd edition, Ford, George, and Sylvère Monod, New York and London, W. W. Norton and Company, 1990, 11; Owen Jones, *The Grammar of Ornament*, London, Bernard Quaritch, 1868, 5 and 6; Charles L. Eastlake, *Hints on Household Taste. The Classic Handbook of Victorian Interior Decoration*, New York, Dover, 1969, 114 (originally published 1868); Fernand Braudel, *Civilization and Capitalism 15th – 18th centuries, volume 2: The Wheels of Commerce*, trans. Sian Reynolds, New York, Harper & Row, 1979, 482. **PART II** Oscar Wilde, "The Critic as Artist", The Artist as Critic: Critical Writings of Oscar Wilde, ed. Richard Ellman, New York, Random House, 1968, 398; Christopher Dresser, Principles of Victorian Decorative Design, with 184 illustrations, New York, Dover Publications, 1995, 17, footnote; Christopher Dresser, *Traditional Arts and Crafts of Japan*, New York, Dover, 1994, 180, (originally published 1882 under the title Japan: Its Architecture, Art and Art Manufactures)'; C. R. Mackintosh, Letter, in Werner Schweiger, Wiener Werkstätte, Design in Vienna 1903-1932, New York, Abbeville Press, 1984, pages 26-27. The letter was probably addressed to Fritz Waerndorfer, a wealthy patron of the Wiener Werkstätte, dating to March 17, 1903, and is a German translation from the English, probably by Waerndorfer for Hoffmann; Kathryn Bloom Hiesinger, ed. Art Nouveau in Munich: Masters of Jugendstil from the Stadtmuseum, Munich and other Public and Private Collections, exhibition cat. (Philadelphia Museum of Art in assocation with Prestel Verlag, 1988, 95, from a drawing by Bruno Paul for Simplicissimus; John Ruskin, The Stones of Venice, vol. II, chapter VI, § 16 (Kenneth Clark, ed. John Ruskin: *Selected Writings*, London, Penguin Books, 1991, first published 1964, 282-3; John Ruskin, *The Seven Lamps of Architecture*, V, § 24, (Clark, Kenneth, ed. John Ruskin: *Selected Writings*, London, Penguin Books, 1991, first published 1964, 236); John Ruskin, The Stones of Venice, vol. II, chapter VI, § 15, italics added (Kenneth Clark, ed. John Ruskin: *Selected Writings*, London, Penguin Books, 1991, first published 1964, 282); John Ruskin, *The Seven Lamps of Architecture, V, § 24*, (Clark, Kenneth, ed. John Ruskin: Selected Writings, London, Penguin Books, 1991, first published 1964, 235-236);William Morris, "The Lesser Arts" ("The Decorative Arts"), lecture given to the Trades Guild of Learning, 1877, reprinted in *Hopes and Fears for Art*, London 1882 (Wilmer, Clive, ed., William Morris: *News from Nowhere and Other Writings*, London, Penguin Books, 1993, 233-4); William Morris, evidence given to the Royal Commission on Technical Instruction (1882), reprinted in Naylor, Gillian, ed., William Morris by himself: Designs and Writings, Boston, Little, Brown and Company, 1988, page 212; William Morris, "How I Became a Socialist", published in Justice, 16 July 1894 (Wilmer, Clive, ed., William Morris: News from Nowhere and Other Writings, London, Penguin Books, 1993, 379); William Morris, "The Lesser Arts" ("The Decorative Arts"), lecture given to the Trades Guild of Learning, 1877, reprinted in Hopes and Fears for Art, London 1882 (Wilmer, Clive, ed., William Morris: News from Nowhere and Other Writings, London, Penguin Books, 1993, 250); William Morris, "Some Hints on Pattern-Designing", lecture given at the Workingmen's College, London, 1881, (Wilmer, Clive, ed., William Morris: News from Nowhere and Other Writings, London, Penguin Books, 1993, 270); William Morris, News From Nowhere or An Epoch of Rest, being some chapters from a Utopian Romance, serialized in the Commonweal, 11 January to 4 October 1890, published in book form and revised, Boston 1890 and London, 1891 (Wilmer, Clive, ed., William Morris: *News from Nowhere and Other Writings*, London, Penguin Books, 1993, 122-123); (Arthur Mackmurdo), from Gillian Naylor, *The Arts and Crafts Movement*, Cambridge, MIT Press, 1980 (originally published 1971), 116; (William Lethaby), from Gillian Naylor. The Arts and Crafts Movement, Cambridge, MIT Press, 1980 (originally published 1971), 181; (Charles Ashbee), from Gillian Naylor, *The Arts and Crafts Movement*, Cambridge, MIT Press, 1980 (originally published 1971), 167; Frank Lloyd Wright, "The Art and Craft of the Machine", 1901, in Bruce Brooks Pfeiffer, Frank Lloyd Wright Collected Writings, vol. 1 1894-1930, New York, Rizzoli in association with the Frank Lloyd Wright Foundation, 1992, 64; Hermann Muthesius, *The English House*, Sharp, Dennis, ed. trans. Janet Seligman, London, Crosby, Lockwood, Staples, 1979, 52; Robert Kanigel, *The Best Way: Frederick Winslow Taylor and the Enigma of Efficiency*, New York, Viking, 1997, 214. **PART III** Henri Matisse, "Notes of a Painter", in Roger Benjamin, Matisse's "Notes of a painter": criticism, theory, and context, 1891-1908, Ann Arbor, MI, UMI Research Press, 1987, page 208. (original in French, pp. 741-742, also reproduced in its entirety in *Benjamin; René Gimpel, Diary of an Art Dealer*, trans. John Rosenberg, New York, Farrar, Strauss and Giroux, 1966. page 138; Filippo Marinetti, "Futurist Manifesto", 1909, in Umbro Apollonis, ed. Futurist *Manifestos (The Documents of 20th Century Art)*, New York, Viking, 1973, pages 21-22, or R. W. Flint, ed., Let's Murder the Moonshine: Selected Writings F. T. Marineeti, trans. R. W. Flint and Arthur A. Coppotelli, Los Angeles, Sun & Moon Classics, 1991; Amedee Ozenfant, and C-E Jeanneret., "Le Purisme" (translation), in Robert L Herbert, ed. Modern Artists on Art: Ten Unabridged Essays, Englewood Cliffs, NJ, Prentice Hall, 1964, page 64; Penny Sparke. *An Introduction to Design and Culture in the Twentieth Century*, New York, Harper and Row (Icon Editions), 1986 (paperback), page 46; Reyner Banham. Theory and Design in the First Machine Age, Cambridge, MIT Press, Second Edition, 1980 (first published 1960), 321; From De Stijl, vol. 2, no. 1, November 1918, translated in Paul Overy, De Stijl, London and New York, Thames & Hudson, 1991, 47; from De Stijl, vol. 2, no. 1, November 1918, pages 102-103; translated in Nancy Troy, *The De Stijl Environment*, Cambridge, the MIT Press, 1983, page 22; Piet Mondrian, "Neo Plasticism: The General Principle of Plastic Equivalency", published in French by the Galerie de L'Effort Moderne, Paris, 1920, in Harry Holtzman and Martin S. James, eds. and translators, *The New Art – the New Life: the Collected Writings of Piet Mondrian*, Boston, G. K. Hall & Company, 1986, Reprinted by permission of the Gale Group, 139-140; Piet Mondrian, "The New Plastic in Painting", published in De Stijl, 1917, in Harry Holtzman and Martin S. James, eds. and translators *The New Art – the New Life: the Collected Writings of Piet Mondrian*, Boston, G. K. Hall & Company, 1986, 50, Reprinted by permission of the Gale Gro; Piet Mondrian, "The Realization of Neo-Plasticism in the Distant Future and in Architecture Today", published in De Stijl, 1922, in Harry Holtzman and Martin S. James, eds. and translators The New Art – the New Life: the Collected Writings of Piet Mondrian, Boston, G. K. Hall & Company, 1986, 167, from. Reprinted by permission of the Gale Group; Nancy Troy, *The De Stijl Environment*, Cambridge, the MIT Press, 1983, page 133; Gillian Naylor, *The Bauhaus reassessed: sources and design theory*, New York, E. P. Dutton, 1985, 97; Manifesto of the Bauhaus, April 1919, Hans Wingler, Bauhaus, Cambridge and London, MIT Press, 1996, 31. Reprinted with permission of Hans Wingler, Bauhaus, and the MIT Press; Gillian Naylor, The Bauhaus reassessed: sources and design theory, New York, E. P. Dutton, 1985, 99; Herbert Spencer. Pioneers of modern typography, New York, Hastings House, 1970 (first published 1969), 4; Gunnar Asplund, "Rationalism and Man", speech delivered May 1935 at a meeting of the Swedish Arts and Crafts Society, in Stuart Wrede, *The Architecture of Erik Gunnar Asplund*, Cambridge, MA, MIT Press, 1980, 153. (see also Schildt, Göran, ed. Sketches, trans. Stuart Wrede, Cambridge MA, MIT Press, 1978; Henry Ford, as told to John Anderson (attorney), 1903, reprinted in Nevins, Allan, with the collaboration of Frank Ernest Hill, Ford. *The Times, the Man, the Company*, vol. 1, New York, Scribners, 1954, 276; Roland Marchand, *Advertising the American Dream: Making Way for Modernity 1920-1940*, Berkeley, University of California Press, 1985, 154. **PART IV** Paul Rand, *Thoughts on Design*, New York, Reinhold, 1970 (first published 1947), 36; Alvin Lustig, in The Collected Writings of Alvin Lustig, ed. Holland R Melson., New York, Thistle Press, 1958, 73; Cipe Pineles, from a speech given to the AIGA (1958), in Martha Scotford, Cipe Pineles: A Life of Design, New York, W. W. Norton & Company, 1999, 66; K. Lonberg-Holm, and Ladislav Sutnar, Catalog design progress, New York, Sweet's Catalog Service (Division of F. W. Dodge Corporation), 1950, Introduction (unpaged); Karl Gerstner, *Die neue Graphic. The new graphic art.* Le nouvel art graphique, Switzerland, Arthur Niggli Ltd., 1959, 148; Chuck Berry, No Particular Place to Go, released 1964 by Chess Records. By permission from ARC Music Corporation, New York; Bruce Springsteen, Academy Awards Presentation, March 21, 1994, from Atlanta Journal and Constitution, March 22, 1994, Section D, 6; Lewis Mumford, excerpt from *The City in History: Its Origins, its Transformations, and its Prospects*, San Diego, New York and London, Harcourt Brace Jovanovich, 1961 and renewed 1989 by Lewis Mumford, 486. By permission of Harcourt, Inc.; Robert Hutchins, in Mortimer Adler, Reforming Education: the schooling of a people and their education beyond schooling, Boulder CO, Westview Press, 1977, 24-25 {Allen, James Sloan. *The Romance of Commerce and Culture. Capitalism, Modernism, and the Chicago-Aspen Crusade for Cultural Reform*, Chicago and London, University of Chicago Press, 1983, 96 w/ footnote.}; Vance Packard, *The Hidden Persuaders*, Harmondsworth, Penguin, 1960, or New York, David McKay, 1957, 45. **PART V** Ronny and the Daytonas, GTO, 1964, originally recorded for the Mala label, written by John Wilkin. By permission of Buck-Wilkin Music, Nashville, Tennessee; Emilio Ambasz, Italy: The New Domestic Landscape. Achievements and Problems of Italian Design, New York, The Museum of Modern Art, New York, in Collaboration with Centro Di, Florence, 19-20; Victor Papanek. *Design for the Real World: Human Ecology and Social Change*, New York, Random House (Pantheon Books), 1971, xxi;Victor Papanek. *Design for the Real World: Human Ecology and Social Change*, New York, Random House (Pantheon Books), 1971, 51; Neville Brody, in Jon Wozencroft, *The Graphic Language of Neville Brody*, New York, Rizzoli, 1988, 60; Quoted from the "Values" link on the Body Shop website: http://thebodyshop.com (2000) "our future planning will be based upon achieving a balance between the need to limit the environmental impact of our business whilst not compromising our long term commercial viability"; Jonathon Porritt, *Seeing Green: the politics of ecology explained*, Oxford (UK) and New York, B. Blackwell, 1985 (c.1984), xiii, and 15; Herbert Simon, "The Science of Design: Creating the Artificial", The Sources of the Artificial, Cambridge. MIT Press, 1969, 54; Rudy VanderLans and Zuzana, Licko with Mary E. Gray, *Émigré (The Book): Graphic Design into the Digital Realm*, New York, Van Nostrand Reinhold, 1993, 23.

Picture credits

1.1 RMN-Jean/Schormans
1.2 Stapleton Collection
1.3 Waddesdon, The Rothschild Collection (The National Trust) Photo: Hugo Meartens
1.4, 1.6 Trustees of the Wallace Collection
1.5 The Jules Bache Collection, 1949 (49.7.117) Photograph © 2003 The Metropolitan Museum of Art
1.7 Bridgeman Art Library
2.1, 2.2 Images by courtesy of the Wedgwood Museum Trust, Barlaston, Staffordshire, England
2.3 Gift of Grame Lorimer and Sarah Moss Lorimer in memory of George Horace Lorimer. Photo: Graydon Wood, 1996
2.4, 2.5 Private Collection
2.7 Photo: Graydon Wood, 1989
2.8 © Christie's Images Ltd.
3.5 © Christie's Images Ltd.
3.6 Gift of George Lowther, 1906
3.7 Private Collection
3.8 © Photothèque des musées de la ville de Paris/Cliché: Habouzit
3.9 RMN-M.Beck-Coppola
3.11 Stapleton Collection
3.15 Courtesy Alfred Dunhill Museum & Archive, London
3.18 Photo: Laurent-Sully James
4.1 © Sonia Halliday Photographs
4.12, 4.16, 4.17, 4.18 Private Collection
5.1, Private Collection
5.2 Courtesy Haslam & Whiteway Ltd.
5.3 Courtesy Fine Art Society PLC
5.4 Gift of Charles Lang Freer F1904.61
5.6 Image © The Art Institute of Chicago
5.7 Bridgeman Art Library
5.9 Gift of Susan Dwight Bliss, 1930. Photo: David Allison, © 1986 The Metropolitan Museum of Art
5.10 Gift of Hugh J. Grant, 1974. Photo: © 1998 The Metropolitan Museum of Art
5.12 Gift of Charles W. Gould
5.13 Photography by Hedrich Blessing, courtesy of the Chicago Department of Cultural Affairs, copyright 2003, All rights reserved.
5.14 Gift of George Wood Furness. Photo: Graydon Wood, 1995
5.15 Gift from the Estate of Mrs. James J. Goodwin
5.16 Stapleton Collection
5.19 Bridgeman Art Library - Arkhangelsk Cathedral Museum, Moscow
5.22 RMN K.Ignatiadis
5.23 Courtesy Sotheby's, Monaco
5.24 RMN-Jean Schormans
5.26 RMN-M.Beck-Coppola
5.28 ©Paul M.R. Maeyaert
5.30, 5.32, 5.33, 5.34, 5.45 Christie's Images Ltd.
5.36 © ADAGP, Paris and DACS London 2003
5.37 © Photothèque des musées de la ville de Paris/Cliché: Ladet/Briant
5.38 © Glasgow School of Art
5.39 Museum Purchase: Roy A. Hunt Fund, Gift of the Hunt Foundation and Patrons Art Fund, 85.20

5.40 © Hunterian Art Gallery, University of Glasgow, Mackintosh Collection
5.41, 5.42 Sotheby's Picture Library
5.43 Museum Purchase, Lita Annenberg Hazen Charitable Trust Gift, 1986. (1986.146)/Photo by Mark Darley
5.49 © ADAGP, Paris and DACS, London 2003
5.50 ©Beauvais, Musée de L'Oise - Photos-Contact
5.53 Purchased with the Fiske Kimball Fund, 1991. Photo: Graydon Wood/© DACS 2003
5.54 Photo: Wolfgang Pulfer/© DACS 2003
5.55, 5.56 Museum of Art and Design, Helsinki
5.57 Private Collection
5.59, 5.60 Zsolnay Museum, Pécs
5.62 Photo: Bruce White
5.63 Philippe Garner
6.5 © Stapleton Collection
6.8 Gift of Adele R. Levy, 1958
6.9, 6.12, 6.14 Private Collection
6.10 Purchase, Friends of Twentieth Century Decorative Arts Gift, 1979. Photo: ©1980 The Metropolitan Museum of Art
6.17 Gift of Dr. and Mrs. Matthew Newman
6.20 Photo: Ognan Borissov
6.21 Given by Mr. and Mrs. Julius Zieget
6.23 Private Collection
6.24 ©Wayne Andrews/Esto
6.25 © ARS, NY and DACS, London 2003
6.26 Sullivania Collection, Ryerson & Burnham Archives. Courtesy the Art Institute of Chicago. All Rights Reserved
7.1 Münchener Stadtmuseum/Foto: P.Fliegauf/© DACS 2003
7.2 RIBA/© DACS 2003
7.3 Bildarchiv Foto Marburg/© DACS 2003
7.4 Sotheby's Picture Library/© DACS 2003
7.5 © DACS 2003
7.7 Neue Sammlung, Munich/© DACS 2003
7.8, 7.9 From the Collections of Henry Ford Museum and Greenfield Village

Page 141l Roger-Viollet, Paris/© ADAGP, Paris and DACS London 2003
Page 141r Imperial War Museum
8.1, 8.22, 8.31 Christie's Images Ltd.
8.3 Courtauld Institute/© ADAGP, Paris and DACS London 2003
8.4 Private Collection
8.5 Philippe Garner/© ADAGP, Paris and DACS, London 2003
8.6 Purchase, Edgar Kaufmann, Jr. 1973, and Bequest of Collis P. Huntington, by exchange, 1973. Photo: Mark Darley ©1989 The Metropolitan Museum of Art
8.8, ©Stapleton Collection/ADAGP, Paris and DACS, London 2003
8.9 Purchase, Edward C. Moore, Jr. Gift, 1923. Photo: Mark Darley ©1989 The Metropolitan Museum of Art/©ADAGP, Paris and DACS, London 2003
8.10 RMN-H. Lewandowski/© ADAGP, Paris and DACS, London 2003

8.11 Gift of Mademoiselle Florence Marinot, 1967
8.12 Sotheby's Picture Library/© ADAGP, Paris and DACS London 2003
8.13, 8.16, 8.23 © ADAGP, Paris and DACS London 2003
8.14 ©Stapleton Collection
8.15 Image © The Art Institute of Chicago/© ADAGP, Paris and DACS London 2003
8.17 © ADAGP, Paris and DACS London 2003
8.18 Gift of Frederick R. Koch, 94.242
8.19 Decorative Arts Department Deaccession Funds, the Putnam Dana McMillan Fund, and gift of the Decorative Arts Council in honor of Dr. Michael Conforti, Chief Curator and Bell Memorial Curator/© ADAGP, Paris and DACS London 2003
8.20, 8.21 ©Mouron. Cassandre. All rights reserved. License Number 2003-28-05-03
8.25 © FLC/ADAGP, Paris and DACS, London 2003
8.26 Private Collection/© DACS 2003
8.27, 8.28 Private Collection/© DACS 2003
8.29 © Tate, London 2002
8.30 A.E. Gallatin Collection. Photo: Graydon Wood, 1992/© ADAGP, Paris and DACS London 2003
8.33, 8.34, 8.35 Vitra Museum
9.1, 9.2, 9.16, 9.17 © DACS 2003
9.3 Christie's Images Ltd.
9.4, 9.6, 9.9 Frank den Oudsten Associates
9.5 Gemeentemuseum den Haag
9.7 Frank den Oudsten Associates/© DACS 2003
9.10 SCR Photo Library/© DACS 2003
9.12, 9.13 © DACS 2003
9.14, 9.15, 9.18, 9.19, 9.21, 9.23, 9.41 David King Collection, London/DACS 2003
9.20 Private Collection/© DACS 2003
9.39, 9.40 Private Collection
9.22 Novosti (London)
9.25 ©VG Bild-Kunst, Bonn
9.26, 9.27 Staatliche Bildstelle, Berlin
9.28, 9.34 Bauhaus -Archiv, Berlin
9.29, 9.44 © DACS 2003
9.30 ©VG Bild-Kunst, Bonn/© DACS 2003
9.31 The Cynthia Hazen Polsky Fund, 1989. Photo: Mark Darley ©1989 The Metropolitan Museum of Art
9.32 Purchase, Theodore R. Gamble Jr. Gift, in honor of his mother Mrs. Theodore Robert Gamble, 1980. Photo: ©1981 The Metropolitan Museum of Art/© DACS 2003
9.33 Image © The Art Institute of Chicago/© DACS 2003
9.42 © DACS 2003
9.43 Stiftung Archiv der Akademie der Künste/© DACS 2003
9.49, 9.55 London Transport Museum
9.53 Pelican Books
9.54 © Peter Kent, London
9.56 Orrefors Glass Museum/© DACS 2003
9.60 © Ole Woldbye
10.2 Gift of William E. Levis, 1936.36
10.6 Photo: © The Metropolitan Museum of Art
10.8 John C. Waddell Collection, Promised Gift of John C. Waddell to The Metropolitan Museum of Art. Photo:

1.1 RMN-Jean/Schormans
1.2 Stapleton Collection
1.3 Waddesdon, The Rothschild Collection (The National Trust) Photo: Hugo Meartens
1.4, 1.6 Trustees of the Wallace Collection
1.5 The Jules Bache Collection, 1949 (49.7.117) Photograph © 2003 The Metropolitan Museum of Art
1.7 Bridgeman Art Library
2.1, 2.2 Images by courtesy of the Wedgwood Museum Trust, Barlaston, Staffordshire, England
2.3 Gift of Grame Lorimer and Sarah Moss Lorimer in memory of George Horace Lorimer. Photo: Graydon Wood, 1996
2.4, 2.5 Private Collection
2.7 Photo: Graydon Wood, 1989
2.8 © Christie's Images Ltd.
3.5 © Christie's Images Ltd.
3.6 Gift of George Lowther, 1906
3.7 Private Collection
3.8 © Photothèque des musées de la ville de Paris/Cliché: Habouzit
3.9 RMN-M.Beck-Coppola
3.11 Stapleton Collection
3.15 Courtesy Alfred Dunhill Museum & Archive, London
3.18 Photo: Laurent-Sully James
4.1 © Sonia Halliday Photographs
4.12, 4.16, 4.17, 4.18 Private Collection
5.1, Private Collection
5.2 Courtesy Haslam & Whiteway Ltd.
5.3 Courtesy Fine Art Society PLC
5.4 Gift of Charles Lang Freer F1904.61
5.6 Image © The Art Institute of Chicago
5.7 Bridgeman Art Library
5.9 Gift of Susan Dwight Bliss, 1930. Photo: David Allison, © 1986 The Metropolitan Museum of Art
5.10 Gift of Hugh J. Grant, 1974. Photo: © 1998 The Metropolitan Museum of Art
5.12 Gift of Charles W. Gould
5.13 Photography by Hedrich Blessing, courtesy of the Chicago Department of Cultural Affairs, copyright 2003, All rights reserved.
5.14 Gift of George Wood Furness. Photo: Graydon Wood, 1995
5.15 Gift from the Estate of Mrs. James J. Goodwin
5.16 Stapleton Collection
5.19 Bridgeman Art Library - Arkhangelsk Cathedral Museum, Moscow
5.22 RMN K.Ignatiadis
5.23 Courtesy Sotheby's, Monaco
5.24 RMN-Jean Schormans
5.26 RMN-M.Beck-Coppola
5.28 ©Paul M.R. Maeyaert
5.30, 5.32, 5.33, 5.34, 5.45 Christie's Images Ltd.
5.36 © ADAGP, Paris and DACS London 2003
5.37 © Photothèque des musées de la ville de Paris/Cliché: Ladet/Briant
5.38 © Glasgow School of Art
5.39 Museum Purchase: Roy A. Hunt Fund, Gift of the Hunt Foundation and Patrons Art Fund, 85.20
5.40 © Hunterian Art Gallery, University of Glasgow,

Mackintosh Collection
5.41, 5.42 Sotheby's Picture Library
5.43 Museum Purchase, Lita Annenberg Hazen Charitable Trust Gift, 1986. (1986.146)/Photo by Mark Darley
5.49 © ADAGP, Paris and DACS, London 2003
5.50 ©Beauvais, Musée de L'Oise - Photos-Contact
5.53 Purchased with the Fiske Kimball Fund, 1991. Photo: Graydon Wood/© DACS 2003
5.54 Photo: Wolfgang Pulfer/© DACS 2003
5.55, 5.56 Museum of Art and Design, Helsinki
5.57 Private Collection
5.59, 5.60 Zsolnay Museum, Pécs
5.62 Photo: Bruce White
5.63 Philippe Garner
6.5 © Stapleton Collection
6.8 Gift of Adele R. Levy, 1958
6.9, 6.12, 6.14 Private Collection
6.10 Purchase, Friends of Twentieth Century Decorative Arts Gift, 1979. Photo: ©1980 The Metropolitan Museum of Art
6.17 Gift of Dr. and Mrs. Matthew Newman
6.20 Photo: Ognan Borissov
6.21 Given by Mr. and Mrs. Julius Zieget
6.23 Private Collection
6.24 ©Wayne Andrews/Esto
6.25 © ARS, NY and DACS, London 2003
6.26 Sullivania Collection, Ryerson & Burnham Archives. Courtesy the Art Institute of Chicago. All Rights Reserved
7.1 Münchener Stadtmuseum/Foto: P.Fliegauf/© DACS 2003
7.2 RIBA/© DACS 2003
7.3 Bildarchiv Foto Marburg/© DACS 2003
7.4 Sotheby's Picture Library/© DACS 2003
7.5 © DACS 2003
7.7 Neue Sammlung, Munich/© DACS 2003
7.8, 7.9 From the Collections of Henry Ford Museum and Greenfield Village

Page 141l Roger-Viollet, Paris/© ADAGP, Paris and DACS London 2003
Page 141r Imperial War Museum
8.1, 8.22, 8.31 Christie's Images Ltd.
8.3 Courtauld Institute/© ADAGP, Paris and DACS London 2003
8.4 Private Collection
8.5 Philippe Garner/© ADAGP, Paris and DACS, London 2003
8.6 Purchase, Edgar Kaufmann, Jr. 1973, and Bequest of Collis P. Huntington, by exchange, 1973. Photo: Mark Darley ©1989 The Metropolitan Museum of Art
8.8, ©Stapleton Collection/ADAGP, Paris and DACS, London 2003
8.9 Purchase, Edward C. Moore, Jr. Gift, 1923. Photo: Mark Darley ©1989 The Metropolitan Museum of Art/©ADAGP, Paris and DACS, London 2003
8.10 RMN-H. Lewandowski/© ADAGP, Paris and DACS, London 2003
8.11 Gift of Mademoiselle Florence Marinot, 1967
8.12 Sotheby's Picture Library/© ADAGP, Paris and DACS

London 2003
8.13, 8.16, 8.23 © ADAGP, Paris and DACS London 2003
8.14 ©Stapleton Collection
8.15 Image © The Art Institute of Chicago/© ADAGP, Paris and DACS London 2003
8.17 © ADAGP, Paris and DACS London 2003
8.18 Gift of Frederick R. Koch, 94.242
8.19 Decorative Arts Department Deaccession Funds, the Putnam Dana McMillan Fund, and gift of the Decorative Arts Council in honor of Dr. Michael Conforti, Chief Curator and Bell Memorial Curator/© ADAGP, Paris and DACS London 2003
8.20, 8.21 ©Mouron. Cassandre. All rights reserved. License Number 2003-28-05-03
8.25 © FLC/ADAGP, Paris and DACS, London 2003
8.26 Private Collection/© DACS 2003
8.27, 8.28 Private Collection/© DACS 2003
8.29 © Tate, London 2002
8.30 A.E. Gallatin Collection. Photo: Graydon Wood, 1992/© ADAGP, Paris and DACS London 2003
8.33, 8.34, 8.35 Vitra Museum
9.1, 9.2, 9.16, 9.17 © DACS 2003
9.3 Christie's Images Ltd.
9.4, 9.6, 9.9 Frank den Oudsten Associates
9.5 Gemeentemuseum den Haag
9.7 Frank den Oudsten Associates/© DACS 2003
9.10 SCR Photo Library/© DACS 2003
9.12, 9.13 © DACS 2003
9.14, 9.15, 9.18, 9.19, 9.21, 9.23, 9.41 David King Collection, London/DACS 2003
9.20 Private Collection/© DACS 2003
9.39, 9.40 Private Collection
9.22 Novosti (London)
9.25 ©VG Bild-Kunst, Bonn
9.26, 9.27 Staatliche Bildstelle, Berlin
9.28, 9.34 Bauhaus -Archiv, Berlin
9.29, 9.44 © DACS 2003
9.30 ©VG Bild-Kunst, Bonn/© DACS 2003
9.31 The Cynthia Hazen Polsky Fund, 1989. Photo: Mark Darley ©1989 The Metropolitan Museum of Art
9.32 Purchase, Theodore R. Gamble Jr. Gift, in honor of his mother Mrs. Theodore Robert Gamble, 1980. Photo: ©1981 The Metropolitan Museum of Art/© DACS 2003
9.33 Image © The Art Institute of Chicago/© DACS 2003
9.42 © DACS 2003
9.43 Stiftung Archiv der Akademie der Künste/© DACS 2003
9.49, 9.55 London Transport Museum
9.53 Pelican Books
9.54 © Peter Kent, London
9.56 Orrefors Glass Museum/© DACS 2003
9.60 © Ole Woldbye
10.2 Gift of William E. Levis, 1936.36
10.6 Photo: © The Metropolitan Museum of Art
10.8 John C. Waddell Collection, Promised Gift of John C. Waddell to The Metropolitan Museum of Art. Photo: ©2000 The Metropolitan Museum of Art
10.10 Gift of Stehli Silk Corporation, 1927. Photo: ©1983 The Metropolitan Museum of Art
10.11 Purchased with funds from the Libbey Endowment, Gift of Edward Drummond Libbey, 1993.60
10.12 N. Wright/National Motor Museum
10.13 Hulton Getty
10.14 Gift of David A. Hanks, 1986. Photo: ©2000 The Metropolitan Museum of Art
10.16 Photo: Author
10.17 John C. Waddell Collection, Gift of John C. Waddell to The Metropolitan Museum of Art 2002. Photo: ©2000 The Metropolitan Museum of Art
10.18 AKG London

Index